KARL MARX
FREDERICK ENGELS
COLLECTED WORKS
VOLUME
25

KARL MARX
FREDERICK ENGELS

COLLECTED
WORKS

LAWRENCE & WISHART
LONDON

KARL MARX
FREDERICK‧ENGELS

Volume
25

FREDERICK ENGELS:
ANTI-DÜHRING
DIALECTICS OF NATURE

1987
LAWRENCE & WISHART
LONDON

This volume has been prepared jointly by Lawrence & Wishart Ltd., London, International Publishers Co. Inc., New York, and Progress Publishers, Moscow, in collaboration with the Institute of Marxism-Leninism, Moscow.

Editorial commissions:
GREAT BRITAIN: Eric Hobsbawm, John Hoffman, Nicholas Jacobs, Monty Johnstone, Martin Milligan, Jeff Skelley, Ernst Wangermann.
USA: Louis Diskin, Philip S. Foner, James E. Jackson, Leonard B. Levenson, Betty Smith, Dirk J. Struik, William W. Weinstone.
USSR: for Progress Publishers—A. K. Avelichev, N. P. Karmanova, V. N. Sedikh, M. K. Shcheglova; for the Institute of Marxism-Leninism— P. N. Fedoseyev, L. I. Golman, A. I. Malysh, M. P. Mchedlov, V. N. Pospelova, A. G. Yegorov.

ISBN 0 85315 446 5

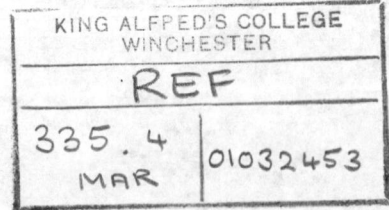
Printed in the Union of Soviet Socialist Republics

Contents

DIALECTICS OF NATURE

FROM THE PREPARATORY MATERIALS

APPENDICES

NOTES AND INDEXES

ILLUSTRATIONS

TRANSLATORS:

EMILE BURNS: *Anti-Dühring.*
Herr Eugen Dühring's Revolution
in Science
CLEMENS DUTT: *Dialectics of Nature*

Preface

Volume 25 of the *Collected Works* of Marx and Engels contains two of Engels' most celebrated works, *Anti-Dühring* and *Dialectics of Nature.*

In *Anti-Dühring,* one of his most popular and widely known writings, Engels not only expounded the fundamental propositions of Marxism, but made substantial progress in the development of revolutionary theory. Lenin wrote that *Anti-Dühring* analyses the "highly important problems in the domain of philosophy, natural science and the social sciences" (V. I. Lenin, *Collected Works,* Vol. 2, p. 25). *Anti-Dühring* made a substantial contribution to the ideological victory of Marxism over reformism and the various trends of utopian socialism.

Anti-Dühring became Marxist science's answer to the demands of a new stage in the development of the international working-class movement, which owed its inception to the heroic struggle of the Parisian Communards in 1871. The experience of the Paris Commune showed that a proletarian revolution could not succeed without a mass working-class party based on the principles of scientific communism. It was for this reason that in the 1870s the task of forming such parties in various countries became paramount. As the international working-class movement gained impetus and the influence of scientific socialism grew among the progressive part of the proletariat, attacks on Marxism were stepped up by its ideological opponents, the representatives of anarchism, reformism and petty-bourgeois utopian socialism.

Moreover, the rapid growth of the working-class movement and the authority of the Social Democratic parties that were being founded and becoming the main opposition to ruling classes, were attracting into the ranks of these parties members of the other classes, especially those from the petty-bourgeoisie. This led to the spread in the working-class movement of unscientific views hostile to Marxism which diverted the proletariat from the true goals of its economic and political struggle.

These phenomena were inherent in the whole working-class movement, but by the mid-1870s they became most clearly manifest in Germany, where the exacerbation of the class struggle facilitated the rapid growth of political consciousness and organisation on the part of the proletariat and its conversion into a significant political force. It was to Germany that the centre of the European working-class movement shifted after the defeat of the Paris Commune. Germany was the first country where, in 1869, at a congress in Eisenach, a mass working-class party was founded based on the ideological and organisational principles of Marxism. In the first half of the 1870s, among German workers who were active members of the socialist movement, there was a growing tendency towards the unification of the Social Democratic Workers' Party (the Eisenachers) with the General German Workers' Union (the Lassalleans). In 1875, at a congress in Gotha, both organisations were combined into a single party, the Eisenachers accepting an ideological compromise with the opportunist views of the Lassalleans. Marx and Engels regarded the concessions by the Eisenachers as a serious mistake fraught with grave consequences (see Marx's *Critique of the Gotha Programme* and Engels' letter to Bebel of March 18-28, 1875, present edition, vols. 24 and 45).

The apprehensions of Marx and Engels were justified. After the unity congress in Gotha, the theoretical level of German Social Democracy fell significantly, when the views of Dr. Eugen Dühring, lecturer at Berlin University, became widespread among some Party members including its leaders. He became popular because of his speeches in defence of the oppressed masses and his struggle against the reactionary professors of that institution. Dühring's views were an eclectic mixture of various vulgar materialist, idealist, positivist, vulgar economic and pseudo-socialist views. As distinct from former opponents of Marxism, who had denounced mainly its political principles, Dühring attacked all the component parts of Marxism and claimed to have created a new all-embracing system of philosophy, political economy and socialism, openly opposing his views to the revolutionary proletarian world outlook.

The spread of Dühring's views among members of the Social Democratic Party of Germany was a real threat to this major contingent of the international working-class movement and to its theoretical foundations. Engels therefore considered it his duty to defend and publicise the principles of Marxism within the German Social Democratic movement. In two years (1876-78), he wrote a major work that was first printed in *Vorwärts,* the newspaper of the Social Democratic Party of Germany, and was brought out as a separate book in 1878 under the title *Herrn Eugen Dührings Umwälzung der Wissenschaft (Herr Eugen Dühring's Revolution in Science*—known in English as *Anti-Dühring),* in which Engels subjected Dühring's views to devastating criticism. Alongside his criticism of Dühring Engels expounded his own views on the problems that had at the time scientific and practical significance. His criticism of Dühring, to quote Engels himself, was turned into a positive exposition "of the dialectical method and of the communist world outlook" (this volume, p. 8).

Anti-Dühring not only disclosed and defended the basic postulates of Marxism, it also elaborated a number of fundamental new problems of revolutionary theory. It provided the first ever comprehensive presentation of Marxism as an integral, indivisible science. Engels' work met the objective need of the working-class movement for a true social science, namely Marxism.

Later, in the Preface to the second edition of *The Housing Question,* Engels explained why he personally had been obliged to take the initiative in the ideological struggle with Dühring: "As a consequence of the division of labour that existed between Marx and myself, it fell to me to present our opinions in the periodical press, and, therefore, particularly in the fight against opposing views, in order that Marx should have time for the elaboration of his great basic work [*Capital.—Ed.*]. Because of this, I had to expound our views in the majority of cases in polemical form, counterposing them to other views" (see present edition, Vol. 26).

Marx also took a direct part in the writing of *Anti-Dühring.* Engels consulted him when planning the work; Marx also helped to collect the necessary material, wrote a critical outline of Dühring's views on the history of economic doctrines, which was used as the basis for Chapter X of Part II of *Anti-Dühring* (pp. 211-43) and, finally, read and approved the whole manuscript. *Anti-Dühring* was thus the result of creative collaboration by Marx and Engels, reflecting their joint views and giving a generalised account of the main propositions of Marxism.

Engels' book could only have arisen out of the theoretical foundations created by the development of Marxism from the moment of its emergence in the mid-1840s up to the mid-1870s. Engels made masterly use of the method, jointly created by him and Marx, of materialistic dialectics. He drew on a vast store of knowledge from philosophy, political economy, history, and on his own researches into natural science and the art of war. *Anti-Dühring* draws on the experience acquired by Marx and Engels in many years of ideological struggle. The book is notable for its polemical skill, which Marx and Engels had constantly perfected ever since their early appearances in print. In *Anti-Dühring,* Engels used and popularised not only Volume I of *Capital* and *A Contribution to the Critique of Political Economy,* but the ideas of Marx that were contained in his economic manuscripts, above all in those of 1857-1858 and 1861-1863 (see present edition, vols. 28-34), and also separate propositions from Marx's at the time still unpublished *Critique of the Gotha Programme.* All these ideas were repeatedly discussed by Marx and Engels both in private and in their correspondence.

In the Introduction to *Anti-Dühring,* Engels outlines in brief the development of the theoretical prerequisites of scientific socialism. While giving full recognition to the merits of Saint-Simon, Fourier and Owen, he stresses that their "socialism is the expression of absolute truth, reason and justice and has only to be discovered to conquer all the world by virtue of its own power" (p. 20). As distinct from the utopians, Marxism put socialism on a realistic footing, demonstrating its close connection with the economic development of society and the class struggle. "Now," writes Engels, "idealism was driven from its last refuge, the philosophy of history ... and a method found of explaining man's 'knowing' by his 'being', instead of, as heretofore, his 'being' by his 'knowing'" (pp. 26-27). In this work Engels for the first time made a conclusion that Marx's two great discoveries, the materialist understanding of history and the theory of surplus-value, laid the theoretical foundations of scientific socialism (p. 27).

In Part I of *Anti-Dühring,* the philosophical teaching of Marxism is systematically expounded. A strictly materialist approach to the solution of the fundamental problem of philosophy runs through the whole of Engels' exposition. In the controversy with Dühring, he formulates and substantiates the most important thesis of material-ism, namely, that the "unity of the world consists in its materiality"

(p. 41). Elaborating the dialectic teaching on the indivisibility of matter and motion, Engels shows that the infinitely multiform phenomena of nature are only various forms of the motion and development of matter. Thinking is a reflection of the material world. "To me," writes Engels, "there could be no question of building the laws of dialectics into nature, but of discovering them in it and evolving them from it" (pp. 12-13). Engels formulates here the classic definition of the interrelationship between matter and motion: *"Motion is the mode of existence of matter"* (p. 55). In this work, the materialistic interpretation of space and time as fundamental forms of all being is developed (see pp. 48-49).

Engels gives a detailed account of dialectics and explains its fundamental difference from the metaphysical mode of thinking. "To the metaphysician, things and their mental reflexes, ideas, are isolated, are to be considered one after the other and apart from each other, are objects of investigation fixed, rigid, given once for all" (p. 22). The dialectical method, however, takes things and their thought reflections in mutual connection, in movement, in emergence and disappearance.

Engels examines in detail the law of the unity and struggle of opposites, the transformation of quantitative changes into qualitative, and the law of negation of the negation. Referring to Marx's *Capital*, he quotes, in particular, examples from the field of economic relations in which it is stated that the quantitative change transforms the quality of things and, in the same way, the qualitative transformation of things changes their quantity (see p. 117). Stressing the fundamental significance of the law of negation of the negation, Engels shows that as distinct from the usual understanding of negation as simple elimination, dialectical negation is an essential factor in the emergence of a new quality, a universal form of the development process. The law of negation of the negation, writes Engels, is "an extremely general—and for this reason extremely far-reaching and important—law of development of nature, history, and thought" (p. 131).

After giving a definition of dialectics as "the science of the general laws of motion and development of nature, human society and thought" (ibid.), Engels also discloses the content of its categories: necessity and chance, essence and appearance, causality and interaction. He explains the interrelation between formal and dialectical logic and works out the basic laws of the second; he discloses the chief problems of the Marxist theory of cognition, including the interrelationship between absolute and relative truth. Criticising Dühring's subjective voluntaristic views, Engels shows

the actual correlation between freedom and necessity; and by
clarifying the dialectic interrelation of these two categories he
shows that freedom is based on the understanding of necessity, on
cognition and use of the objective laws of nature and society.
"Freedom of the will..." writes Engels, "means nothing but the
capacity to make decisions with knowledge of the subject" (p. 105).

Proving the necessity for the dialectic-materialist method, Engels
writes in *Anti-Dühring* that its application and the verification of
the theory by practice make it possible to solve the most complex
problems of the natural and social sciences.

The economics section of *Anti-Dühring* draws on the achievements of Marx's political economy. Engels substantiates in detail
the scientific understanding of the subject of political economy,
points to the difference between political economy in the wide as
well as the narrow sense, and shows the historical character of the
laws and categories of this science (see pp. 135-40). He also
expounds ideas developed by Marx in the Economic Manuscripts of
1857-1858 about the dialectics of production, exchange and
distribution, laying emphasis on the primacy of production. Engels
singles out in particular the Marxist understanding of value, capital
and surplus-value.

Anti-Dühring was a further stage in the development of the
political economy of Marxism, above all in the economic substantiation of the theory of scientific communism. Engels indicates that
Marx's explanation of the nature of capitalist exploitation and the
creation of the theory of surplus-value is the central point of
scientific socialism.

In *Anti-Dühring*, Engels notes new phenomena in the economics
of the capitalist society which were to develop widely later, in the
era of monopoly capitalism: the growth of joint-stock companies,
the transfer of a number of branches of the national economy into
the hands of the bourgeois state. Moreover, Engels stresses that
these tendencies are not changing the exploitatory essence of the
bourgeois mode of production, nor are they weakening the
contradictions of the capitalist society but, on the contrary, are
exacerbating them: "But the transformation, either into joint-stock
companies, or into state ownership, does not do away with the
capitalistic nature of the productive forces... The modern state, no
matter what its form, is essentially a capitalist machine, the state of
the capitalists, the ideal personification of the total national capital...
The workers remain wage-workers—proletarians. The capitalist
relation is not done away with. It is rather brought to a head...
State ownership of the productive forces is not the solution of the

conflict, but concealed within it are the technical conditions that form the elements of that solution" (pp. 265-66).

Drawing on the study of trends in the development of capitalism, Engels puts forward in *Anti-Dühring* a scientifically grounded conception of the economic basis of the future communist society, formulates a number of its laws, drawing special attention to the planned nature of its development, and discloses the essence and machinery of the mutual interaction of production and distribution: "Distribution..." writes Engels, "will be regulated by the interests of production, and ... production is most encouraged by a mode of distribution which allows *all* members of society to develop, maintain and exercise their capacities with maximum universality" (p. 186). He speaks of the necessity for a rational distribution of productive forces and predicts certain features which must be inherent in labour under communism.

In Part III of his work, Engels gives an expanded exposition of the history and theory of scientific communism and indicates the qualitatively new stage achieved by Marxist thought in comparison with its predecessors (see pp. 244-54).

In *Anti-Dühring*, Engels develops the Marxist postulate that scientific communism is the theoretical expression of the pro-letarian movement and, using the results of Marx's research into the antagonisms prevalent in capitalist society, he discloses the proposition, finally formulated in Volume I of *Capital,* on the inevi-tability of the collapse of capitalism and the victory of the socialist revolution. Drawing on the materialist interpretation of history, Engels shows that the basic contradiction of capitalism lies in the contradiction between the social character of produc-tion and the private form of appropriation. It manifests itself as an opposition between the organisation of production at each separate enterprise and the anarchy of production in all society, as an antagonism between the proletariat and the bourgeoisie. It finds its solution in the proletarian revolution. The proletariat takes over power and converts the means of production into public property.

Engels examined the main features of the future communist society. As distinct from the representatives of critical utopian socialism, who constructed "the elements of a new society out of their own heads, because within the old society the elements of the new were not as yet generally apparent" (p. 253), he showed how, in the framework of the capitalist mode of production, conditions ripen for a transition to the new social system.

Discussing the transition from capitalism to communism, Engels stresses that when the means of production are in the hands of the socialist society and new relations of production are established that exclude the exploitation of man by man, anarchy in production will be replaced by its planned organisation in society as a whole. The growth of productive forces will be accelerated, and this will lead, once the higher phase of communism has been attained, to the complete disappearance of the negative consequences of the division of labour for the development of the individual. Labour will be changed from a heavy burden into the first demand of life (see pp. 269-70, 279-80). The antithesis between mental and physical labour and between town and country will disappear (see pp. 282-84). Class distinctions will be abolished and the state will die out: the government of persons will be replaced by the administration of things, and by conduct of processes of production (see pp. 267-68). Education will be combined with labour (see p. 306). Religion will disappear (see p. 302). People will become the real and conscious masters of nature and society. "The extraneous objective forces that have hitherto governed history pass under the control of man himself. Only from that time will man himself, with full consciousness, make his own history... It is the humanity's leap from the kingdom of necessity to the kingdom of freedom" (p. 270).

Engels' work resulted in the total theoretical refutation of Dühring's views and the loss of their influence over the German Social Democrats. Engels irrefutably demonstrated that Dühring, with his claim to having created a system of his own superior to all the socialist theories, including Marxism, was merely a typical representative of that "bumptious pseudo-science" which "is forcing its way to the front everywhere and is drowning everything with its resounding—sublime nonsense" (p. 7). *Anti-Dühring* facilitated the adoption of Marxism by many representatives of the international working-class movement. Thanks to this book, eminent members of the German and international working-class movement, on their own admission, accepted Marxism as a whole world outlook that embraced philosophy, political economy and socialism, and as the strategy and tactics of the proletariat's class struggle. The international working-class movement acquired a true encyclopaedia of Marxist knowledge on which many generations of socialists of all countries were raised. As Lenin put it, *Anti-Dühring* became a "handbook for every class-conscious worker" (V. I. Lenin, *Collected Works*, Vol. 19, p. 24).

Several years before beginning work on *Anti-Dühring*, Engels began writing a major work entitled *Dialectics of Nature*. From 1873 to 1876, he collected a considerable amount of material and wrote an Introduction to the planned work. Engels continued, in fact, to be preoccupied with these problems while working on *Anti-Dühring* (1876-78), in which he, in particular, drew on his drafts for *Dialectics of Nature*. However, the main chapters and articles, and also some fragments of *Dialectics of Nature*, were written after the publication of *Anti-Dühring*, from 1878 to 1882. Work on *Dialectics of Nature* remained unfinished since, after Marx's death, Engels shouldered the responsibility for the leadership of the international working-class movement, and the preparation for the press of volumes II and III of *Capital*, which were still in manuscript form. *Dialectics of Nature* gathered dust in the archives of the German Social Democratic Party for nearly half a century and was first published in the USSR in 1925. Although this work was unfinished and certain of its component parts are preparatory drafts and disjointed notes, it is in fact a complete whole, united by its general basic ideas and overall plan.

When creating a complete world outlook, Marx and Engels not only critically revised the achievements of their predecessors in philosophy, political economy and socialist and communist teachings, but they inevitably had to arrive at the necessity for also generalising in philosophical terms the main achievements of contemporary natural science, to disclose the dialectical character of the development of nature and thereby show the universality of the basic laws of materialist dialectics. In the Preface to the second edition of *Anti-Dühring*, Engels wrote: "Marx and I were pretty well the only people to rescue conscious dialectics from German idealist philosophy and apply it in the materialist conception of nature and history. But a knowledge of mathematics and natural science is essential to a conception of nature which is dialectical and at the same time materialist" (p. 11).

The deep interest shown by Marx and Engels in natural science and the development of technology was neither haphazard nor temporary, and it evinced itself very early. Their range of interests in natural science was very wide; they followed closely all outstanding discoveries in biology, anatomy, physiology, astronomy, physics, chemistry and other sciences. Furthermore, each had his own special interests. Marx was much preoccupied with mathematics and applied natural science, and also with the history of engineering and agrochemistry, which was to a considerable extent determined by his researches into political economy. Engels was more familiar with the achievements of physics and biology, and he devoted much attention to the problems of theoretical natural science.

Since Marx was wholly absorbed in his main work, *Capital*, it was Engels who undertook the solution of the latest theoretical tasks raised by the whole course of development of the natural sciences. Practical opportunities for this appeared after Engels retired from the Manchester firm and moved to London. However, as it was necessary to work out a strategy for the working class, given the new historical conditions created by the Franco-Prussian War of 1870-71 and the Paris Commune, and because of his involvement in the International, Engels was only able to devote himself to theoretical work from 1873.

The task that Engels set himself in working on *Dialectics of Nature* (as on Part I of *Anti-Dühring*), was formulated in the Preface to the second edition of *Anti-Dühring*: "My recapitulation of mathematics and the natural sciences was undertaken in order to convince myself also in detail—of what in general I was not in doubt—that in nature, amid the welter of innumerable changes, the same dialectical laws of motion force their way through as those which in history govern the apparent fortuitousness of events" (p. 11).

In *Dialectics of Nature*, Engels drew on a mass of material concerning the history of natural science to demonstrate that the need for the development of productive forces had stimulated progress in engineering and science, especially natural science, particularly those aspects of it which in one way or another were connected with the demands of practice, of production itself.

There were three great landmarks in the development of natural science in the last century: the discovery in 1838-39 by M. J. Schleiden and T. Schwann of an integral cell theory of living organisms; the discovery and substantiation in 1842-47 of the law of the conservation of energy by R. Mayer, J. P. Joule, W. R. Grove, L. A. Colding and H. Helmholtz; and the appearance of Darwin's theory of the evolution of organic life. In a letter to Engels dated December 19, 1860, Marx stressed that Darwin's *On the Origin of Species by Means of Natural Selection* is the book which "in the field of natural history, provides the basis for our views" (see present edition, Vol. 41, p. 232).

The philosophical significance of these natural science discoveries was that they proved in highly concentrated form the dialectical character of natural processes. However, as Engels showed in *Dialectics of Nature*, a contradiction clearly emerged in the second half of the 19th century between the dialectical character of the new natural science material and the metaphysical method prevalent among the absolute majority of natural scientists. "The bulk of natural scientists are still held fast in the old metaphysical categories and helpless when these modern facts ... have to be rationally explained and brought into relation with one another" (p. 486).

This tendency made itself felt most distinctly among the representatives of vulgar materialism and positivism. In spite of serious differences, vulgar materialism and positivism converged to a considerable extent over the solution to the problem of the mutual relationship between philosophy and natural science. The representatives of vulgar materialism in Germany—K. Vogt, L. Büchner and J. Moleschott—found themselves brought closer to A. Comte, the founder of positivism, by the general tendency to reject philosophy and dialectics as speculative "drivel", useless to positive science.

Engels' service is that for the first time in the history of Marxism, in *Dialectics of Nature,* he comprehensively investigated the problem of the mutual relationship between philosophy and natural science, establishing their inseverable connection and constant mutual action. He showed that "the metaphysical conception has become impossible in natural science owing to the very development of the latter" and that "dialectics divested of mysticism becomes an absolute necessity for natural science" (pp. 313, 486). He presented the natural scientists with the task of consciously mastering the method of dialectic materialism.

Engels disclosed the content of materialist dialectics as a science dealing with universal connections, with the most general laws of all motion, with the laws of the development of nature, society and human thought. As in *Anti-Dühring,* he distinguished between the objective dialectics of the real world and its reflection—the subjective dialectics of thought. As in *Anti-Dühring,* he defined the basic laws of dialectics. He indicated that "the dialectical laws are real laws of development of nature, and therefore are valid also for theoretical natural science" (p. 357).

In *Dialectics of Nature,* Engels elaborates in detail on such problems and categories of dialectics as causality and interaction, necessity and chance, the classification of forms of judgment, the correlation of induction and deduction, and the role of hypothesis as a form of the development of natural science (see, for example, pp. 356-61, 505-08, 520, etc.).

Engels develops the basic propositions of dialectic materialism concerning matter and motion, space and time. In *Dialectics of Nature,* he works out a classification of the forms of motion of matter and a corresponding classification of the sciences. Engels wrote: "*Classification of the sciences,* each of which analyses a single form of motion, or a series of forms of motion that belong together and pass into one another, is therefore the classification, the arrangement, of these forms of motion themselves according to their inherent sequence, and herein lies its importance" (p. 528).

Outlining the development of the different sciences— mathematics, mechanics, physics, chemistry and biology, Engels singles out in mathematics the problem of the apparent *a priori* forms of mathematical abstractions (see pp. 323, 327, 333, etc.), in astronomy—the problem of the origin and development of the solar system (see pp. 510, 546-49), in physics—the doctrine of the transformation of energy (see p. 505), in chemistry—the problem of atomic structure (see pp. 358-59, 530-31, etc.), in biology—the problem of the origin and essence of life (see. pp. 329, 334-35, etc.), cell theory (see pp. 326, 328-29, etc.) and Darwinism (see pp. 452-54, 478, etc.). Engels' approach to the analysis of the fundamental problems of the separate sciences is a model of the dialectic-materialist principle of research into the mutual relations of philosophy and natural science. An analysis of the concrete sciences enriches Marxist philosophy which, in its turn, creates a methodological foundation for the given branch of knowledge.

In an essay *The Part Played by Labour in the Transition from Ape to Man*, Engels elaborated a labour theory of anthropogenesis and sociogenesis. He pointed out the decisive role of labour and the manufacture of tools both in the formation of man and in the emergence of human society. Drawing on the current facts of natural science and, in particular, on Darwin's discoveries, he showed how from the ape-like ancestor, as a result of a prolonged historical process, a qualitatively distinct thinking and creating being was formed—man.

Engels analyses various aspects of the problem of the interaction between man and nature. As distinct from the majority of 19th-century natural scientists and philosophers, who usually despised research into the influence of the practical and labour activity on the development of human thought, he wrote: "It is precisely the *alteration of nature by men*, not solely nature as such, which is the most essential and immediate basis of human thought, and it is in the measure that man has learned to change nature that his intelligence has increased" (p. 511).

Engels criticised the views of the scientists who, trading on Darwin's name, tried to reduce "the whole manifold wealth of historical development, and complexity" to a "meagre and one-sided phrase 'struggle for existence'" (p. 584). "The interaction of bodies in non-living nature," he wrote in a fragment "The Struggle for Life", "includes both harmony and collisions, that of living bodies conscious and unconscious co-operation as well as conscious and unconscious struggle. Hence, even in regard to nature, it is not permissible one-sidedly to inscribe only 'struggle' on one's banners" (ibid.). He spoke out even more firmly against the vulgarising attempts to treat in a like spirit the history of society. He showed how more substantial was the dialectic-materialist approach to the analysis of the processes of the development of human society, drawing on the fundamental propositions of the materialist conception of history: "The conception of history as a series of class struggles is already much richer in content and deeper than merely reducing it to weakly distinguished phases of the struggle for existence" (p. 585).

Engels devoted much attention to examining the role of theoretical thought in understanding the world. He showed that the theoretical thought of each era has had various forms and different content, that "the science of thought is ... a historical science, the science of the historical development of human thought" (pp. 338-39). Engels also wrote about the fate of dialectics in the history of philosophy: about the birth of dialectical ideas among the ancient Greek thinkers and about the development of Hegelian dialectical philosophy. He pointed to the historical significance of Hegel's dialectics as one of the theoretical sources of Marxist philosophy. However, in calling the Hegelian system "a comprehensive compendium of dialectics", Engels pointed out that it developed "from an utterly erroneous point of departure" (p. 342). In *Dialectics of Nature*, he shows that only dialectics reworked in materialist terms could become a component part of Marxist philosophy.

Engels constantly emphasised the role of materialist dialectics as the sole method that gave the clue to an understanding of the laws of the development of nature and society. He said that "dialectics cannot be despised with impunity" (p. 354), and that it is the sole method of thought appropriate in the highest degree to the current stage of development of natural science (see pp. 493-94). Bestowing high praise on D. I. Mendeleyev's creation of the periodic system of chemical elements, Engels writes: "By means of the—unconscious—application of Hegel's law of the transformation of quantity into quality, Mendeleyev achieved a scientific feat which it is not too bold to put on a par with that of Leverrier in calculating the orbit of the until then unknown planet Neptune" (p. 361). Engels shows that progressive philosophy not only serves as a theoretical and methodological basis for the natural science of its time, but also partly anticipates the development of specific fields of science and predicts future discoveries. Engels himself in *Dialectics of Nature* was able to anticipate several of the later discoveries by science.

In *Dialectics of Nature*, Engels examines the laws of scientific progress and its prospects. He affirms that scientific progress tends to increase man's chances of taking into consideration all the more remote consequences of his practical activity for the natural and social environment. All the existing modes of production had in view only the nearest, most immediate effects of labour and could not fully regulate its consequences. "This regulation," writes Engels, "however, requires something more than mere knowledge. It requires a complete revolution in our hitherto existing mode of production, and simultaneously a revolution in our whole contemporary social order" (p. 462).

In *Dialectics of Nature*, Engels wages an implacable war on various anti-scientific tendencies among the representatives of natural science—against vulgar materialism, metaphysics, idealism and agnosticism, against one-sided empiricism and mechanism, spiritualism and the influences of religious ideology. In an article "Natural Science in the Spirit World", he shows that contempt for dialectical thinking is fraught with the most baleful consequences for science: "The empirical contempt for dialectics is punished by some of the most sober empiricists being led into the most barren of all superstitions, into modern spiritualism" (p. 354). Engels firmly opposed any ideas that did not correspond to the latest achievements of the science of that time and decelerated further research. Thus, in *Dialectics of Nature*, he attacks the hypothesis of R. Clausius, W. Thomson and J. Loschmidt on the so-called "death of the universe through lack of heat".

Needless to say, during the past decades of the spectacular and revolutionary development of natural science, the factual material drawn on by Engels and also certain propositions put forward by him have inevitably dated. However, the general methodology and the general conception of *Dialectics of Nature* have retained and will continue to retain their abiding significance.

Even in its incomplete form, this work by Engels impresses with the wealth and depth of its theoretical content. *Dialectics of Nature* is an important stage in the development of dialectical materialism. In it, Engels substantially developed materialist dialectics and marked out the road to the solution of the main problems of the natural science of his time.

* * *

The present volume reproduces for the first time in English the rough draft of the Introduction to *Anti-Dühring*, published in the language of the original by the Institute of Marxism-Leninism of the CC CPSU in the volume: *Marx/Engels Gesamtausgabe*. Friedrich Engels, *Herrn Eugen Dührings Umwälzung der Wissenschaft/Dialektik der Natur*. Sonderausgabe, Moscow-Leningrad, 1935, pp. 396-400.

Dialectics of Nature is being published in accordance with the thematic arrangement of the material as adopted in the following publications: K. Marx and F. Engels, *Works,* Second Russian Edition, Vol. 20, Moscow, 1961 and Marx/Engels, *Werke,* Vol. 20, Berlin, 1962. In the present publication of *Dialectics of Nature,* corrections made in the preparation of Volume 26, *Marx/Engels Gesamtausgabe* (MEGA), Berlin [1985] have been taken into consideration.

The end of *Dialectics of Nature* is followed by Engels' list of titles and tables of contents of the folders (see p. 588 and Note 130).

The subsection "From Engels' Preparatory Writings for *Anti-Dühring*" does not contain the items which Engels himself used for *Dialectics of Nature*. They are included in the text of *Dialectics of Nature*. Among the other supplements, the volume contains Engels' manuscript, "Infantry Tactics, Derived from Material Causes. 1700-1870", and "Additions to the Text of *Anti-Dühring* Made by Engels in the Pamphlet *Socialism Utopian and Scientific*".

In addition to the notes, name index and the indices of quoted and mentioned literature and periodicals, there is an index of contents of the folders of *Dialectics of Nature* and a chronological list of chapters and fragments of *Dialectics of Nature*. As compared with previous editions, considerable additions have been made to the notes, especially to the dating of certain fragments of *Dialectics of Nature*. Compared with the Russian edition and *Werke,* the index of quoted and mentioned literature has been substantially augmented.

The page numbers of works quoted, and also editorial headings and inserts are given in square brackets. Words written in English in the original are given in small caps. Quotations from Greek and French authors are given in English with an indication of their original language in the footnotes. Latin quotations are published in the text in the language of the original with a translation given in the footnotes.

The volume was compiled, the text prepared and notes written by Tatyana Chikileva (*Anti-Dühring*) and Yuri Vasin (*Dialectics of Nature*). The editor of the volume was Valentina Smirnova. The preface was written by Tatyana Chikileva, Valentina Smirnova and Yuri Vasin. The name index, the indices of quoted and mentioned literature and of periodicals were prepared by Tatyana Chikileva and Yuri Vasin (Institute of Marxism-Leninism of the CC CPSU).

The translations were made by Emile Burns and Clemens Dutt (Lawrence & Wishart) and edited by Natalia Karmanova, Margarita Lopukhina, Mzia Pitskhelauri, Andrei Skvarsky (Progress Publishers) and Georgi Bagaturia, scientific editor (Institute of Marxism-Leninism of the CC CPSU).

The Volume was prepared for the press by the editors Nadezhda Rudenko and Yelena Vorotnikova (Progress Publishers).

Frederick Engels

ANTI-DÜHRING

HERR EUGEN DÜHRING'S REVOLUTION IN SCIENCE [1]

Written in September 1876-June 1878

Published in *Vorwärts* from January 3, 1877 to July 7, 1878

First published as a separate book in Leipzig in 1878

Published according to the text of the 1894 edition

Herrn Eugen Dühring's

Umwälzung der Wissenschaft

Von

Friedrich Engels

Dritte, durchgesehene und vermehrte Auflage

Stuttgart

Verlag von J. H. W. Dietz

1894

Title page of the third edition of Engels' *Anti-Dühring*

PREFACES TO THE THREE EDITIONS

I

The following work is by no means the fruit of any "inner urge". On the contrary.

When three years ago Herr Dühring, as an adept and at the same time a reformer of socialism, suddenly issued his challenge to his age,[a] friends in Germany repeatedly urged on me their desire that I should subject this new socialist theory to a critical examination in the central organ of the Social Democratic Party, at that time the *Volksstaat*. They thought this absolutely necessary if the occasion for sectarian divisions and confusions were not once again to arise within the Party, which was still so young and had but just achieved definite unity.[2] They were in a better position than I was to judge the situation in Germany, and I was therefore duty bound to accept their view. Moreover, it became apparent that the new convert was being welcomed by a section of the socialist press with a warmth which it is true was only extended to Herr Dühring's good will, but which at the same time also indicated that in this section of the Party press there existed the good will, precisely on account of Herr Dühring's good will, to take also, without examination, Herr Dühring's doctrine into the bargain.[3] There were, besides, people who were already preparing to spread this doctrine in a popularised form among the workers.[4] And finally Herr Dühring and his little sect were using all the arts of advertisement and intrigue to force the *Volksstaat* to take a definite stand in relation to the new doctrine which had come forward with such mighty pretensions.[5]

---

[a] Ironic paraphrase of a famous dictum from F. Schiller's *Don Carlos*, Act 1, Scene 9.— *Ed.*

Nevertheless it was a year before I could make up my mind to neglect other work and get my teeth into this sour apple. It was the kind of apple that, once bitten into, had to be completely devoured; and it was not only very sour, but also very large. The new socialist theory was presented as the ultimate practical fruit of a new philosophical system. It was therefore necessary to examine it in the context of this system, and in doing so to examine the system itself; it was necessary to follow Herr Dühring into that vast territory in which he dealt with all things under the sun and with some others as well. That was the origin of a series of articles which appeared in the Leipzig *Vorwärts,* the successor of the *Volksstaat,* from the beginning of 1877 onwards and are here presented as a connected whole.

It was thus the nature of the object itself which forced the criticism to go into such detail as is entirely out of proportion to the scientific content of this object, that is to say, of Dühring's writings. But there are also two other considerations which may excuse this length of treatment. On the one hand it gave me, in connection with the very diverse subjects to be touched on here, the opportunity of setting forth in a positive form my views on controversial issues which are today of quite general scientific or practical interest. This has been done in every single chapter, and although this work cannot in any way aim at presenting another system as an alternative to Herr Dühring's "system", yet it is to be hoped that the reader will not fail to observe the connection inherent in the various views which I have advanced. I have already had proof enough that in this respect my work has not been entirely fruitless.

On the other hand, the "system-creating" Herr Dühring is by no means an isolated phenomenon in contemporary Germany. For some time now in Germany systems of cosmogony, of philosophy of nature in general, of politics, of economics, etc., have been springing up by the dozen overnight, like mushrooms. The most insignificant *doctor philosophiae* and even a student will not go in for anything less than a complete "system". Just as in the modern state it is presumed that every citizen is competent to pass judgment on all the issues on which he is called to vote; and just as in economics it is assumed that every consumer is a connoisseur of all the commodities which he has occasion to buy for his maintenance—so similar assumptions are now to be made in science. Freedom of science is taken to mean that people write on every subject which they have not studied, and put this forward as the only strictly scientific method. Herr Dühring, however, is one

F. Engels. Portrait. 1888

of the most characteristic types of this bumptious pseudo-science which in Germany nowadays is forcing its way to the front everywhere and is drowning everything with its resounding—sublime nonsense. Sublime nonsense in poetry, in philosophy, in politics, in economics, in historiography, sublime nonsense in the lecture-room and on the platform, sublime nonsense everywhere; sublime nonsense which lays claim to a superiority and depth of thought distinguishing it from the simple, commonplace nonsense of other nations; sublime nonsense, the most characteristic mass product of Germany's intellectual industry—cheap but bad—just like other German-made goods, only that unfortunately it was not exhibited along with them at Philadelphia.[6] Even German socialism has lately, particularly since Herr Dühring's good example, gone in for a considerable amount of sublime nonsense, producing various persons who give themselves airs about "science", of which they "really never learnt a word".[7] This is an infantile disease which marks, and is inseparable from, the incipient conversion of the German student to Social Democracy, but which our workers with their remarkably healthy nature will undoubtedly overcome.

It was not my fault that I had to follow Herr Dühring into realms where at best I can only claim to be a dilettante. In such cases I have for the most part limited myself to putting forward the correct, undisputed facts in opposition to my adversary's false or distorted assertions. This applies to jurisprudence and in some instances also to natural science. In other cases it has been a question of general views connected with the theory of natural science—that is, a field where even the professional natural scientist is compelled to pass beyond his own speciality and encroach on neighbouring territory—territory on which he is, therefore, as Herr Virchow has admitted, just as much a "semi-initiate"[a] as any one of us. I hope that in respect of minor inexactitudes and clumsiness of expression, I shall be granted the same indulgence as is shown to one another in this domain.

Just as I was completing this preface I received a publishers' notice, composed by Herr Dühring, of a new "authoritative" work of Herr Dühring's: *Neue Grundgesetze zur rationellen Physik und Chemie*. Conscious as I am of the inadequacy of my knowledge of physics and chemistry, I nevertheless believe that I know my Herr Dühring, and therefore, without having seen the work itself, think that I am entitled to say in advance that the laws of physics and chemistry put forward in it will be worthy to take their place, by

---

[a] R. Virchow, *Die Freiheit der Wissenschaft im modernen Staat*, p. 13.—*Ed.*

their erroneousness or platitudinousness, among the laws of
economics, world schematism, etc., which were discovered earlier
by Herr Dühring and are examined in this book of mine; and also
that the rhigometer, or instrument constructed by Herr Dühring
for measuring extremely low temperatures, will serve as a measure
not of temperatures either high or low, but simply and solely of
the ignorant arrogance of Herr Dühring.

London, June 11, 1878

II

I had not expected that a new edition of this book would have
to be published. The subject matter of its criticism is now
practically forgotten; the work itself was not only available to many
thousands of readers in the form of a series of articles published
in the Leipzig *Vorwärts* in 1877 and 1878, but also appeared in its
entirety as a separate book, of which a large edition was printed.
How then can anyone still be interested in what I had to say about
Herr Dühring years ago?

I think that I owe this in the first place to the fact that this
book, as in general almost all my works that were still current at
the time, was prohibited within the German Empire immediately
after the Anti-Socialist Law[8] was promulgated. To anyone whose
brain has not been ossified by the hereditary bureaucratic
prejudices of the countries of the Holy Alliance,[9] the effect of this
measure must have been self-evident: a doubled and trebled sale
of the prohibited books, and the exposure of the impotence of the
gentlemen in Berlin who issue prohibitions and are unable to
enforce them. Indeed the kindness of the Imperial Government
has brought me more new editions of my minor works than I
could really cope with; I have had no time to make a proper
revision of the text, and in most cases have been obliged simply to
allow it to be reprinted as it stood.

But there was also another factor. The "system" of Herr
Dühring which is criticised in this book ranges over a very wide
theoretical domain; and I was compelled to follow him wherever
he went and to oppose my conceptions to his. As a result, my
negative criticism became positive; the polemic was transformed
into a more or less connected exposition of the dialectical method
and of the communist world outlook championed by Marx and
myself—an exposition covering a fairly comprehensive range of
subjects. After its first presentation to the world in Marx's *Misère*

de la philosophie[a] and in the *Communist Manifesto,*[b] this mode of
outlook of ours, having passed through an incubation period of
fully twenty years before the publication of *Capital,*[c] has been
more and more rapidly extending its influence among ever
widening circles, and now finds recognition and support far
beyond the boundaries of Europe, in every country which contains
on the one hand proletarians and on the other undaunted
scientific theoreticians. It seems therefore that there is a public
whose interest in the subject is great enough for them to take into
the bargain the polemic against the Dühring tenets merely for the
sake of the positive conceptions developed alongside this polemic,
in spite of the fact that the latter has now largely lost its point.

I must note in passing that inasmuch as the mode of outlook
expounded in this book was founded and developed in far greater
measure by Marx, and only to an insignificant degree by myself, it
was self-understood between us that this exposition of mine should
not be issued without his knowledge. I read the whole manuscript
to him before it was printed, and the tenth chapter of the part on
economics ("From *Kritische Geschichte*")[d] was written by Marx[10]
but unfortunately had to be shortened somewhat by me for purely
external reasons. As a matter of fact, we had always been
accustomed to help each other out in special subjects.

With the exception of one chapter,[e] the present new edition is
an unaltered reprint of the former edition. For one thing, I had
no time for a thoroughgoing revision, although there was much in
the presentation that I should have liked to alter. Besides I am
under the obligation to prepare for the press the manuscripts
which Marx has left, and this is much more important than
anything else. Then again, my conscience rebels against making
any alterations. The book is a polemic, and I think that I owe it to
my adversary not to improve anything in my work when he is
unable to improve his. I could only claim the right to make a
rejoinder to Herr Dühring's reply. But I have not read, and will
not read, unless there is some special reason to do so, what Herr
Dühring has written concerning my attack[11]; in point of theory I
have finished with him. Besides, I must observe the rules of
decency in literary warfare all the more strictly in his regard,
because of the despicable injustice that has since been done to him

---

[a] *The Poverty of Philosophy.* See present edition, Vol. 6.— *Ed.*
[b] See present edition, Vol. 6.— *Ed.*
[c] Ibid., Vol. 35.— *Ed.*
[d] See this volume, pp. 211-43.— *Ed.*
[e] Ibid., pp. 254-71.— *Ed.*

by the University of Berlin. It is true that the University has not gone unpunished. A university which so abases itself as to deprive Herr Dühring, in circumstances which are well known, of his academic freedom [12] must not be surprised to find Herr Schweninger forced on it in circumstances which are equally well known.

The only chapter in which I have allowed myself some additional elucidation is the second of Part III, "Theoretical". This chapter deals simply and solely with the exposition of a pivotal point in the mode of outlook for which I stand, and my adversary cannot therefore complain if I attempt to state it in a more popular form and to make it more coherent. And there was in fact an extraneous reason for doing this. I had revised three chapters of the book (the first chapter of the Introduction and the first and second of Part III) for my friend Lafargue with a view to their translation into French [13] and publication as a separate pamphlet [a]; and after the French edition [b] had served as the basis for Italian [c] and Polish [d] editions, a German edition was issued by me under the title: *Die Entwicklung des Sozialismus von der Utopie zur Wissenschaft.* This ran through three editions within a few months, and also appeared in Russian [14] and Danish [e] translations. In all these editions it was only the chapter in question which had been amplified, and it would have been pedantic, in the new edition of the original work, to have tied myself down to its original text instead of the later text which had become known internationally.

Whatever else I should have liked to alter relates in the main to two points. First, to the history of primitive society, the key to which was provided by Morgan only in 1877. [f] But as I have since then had the opportunity, in my work: *Der Ursprung der Familie, des Privateigenthums und des Staats* (Zurich, 1884) [g] to work up the material which in the meantime had become available to me, a reference to this later work meets the case.

The second point concerns the section dealing with theoretical

---

[a] Published in English under the title: *Socialism Utopian and Scientific.* See present edition, Vol. 24.— *Ed.*

[b] *Socialisme utopique et socialisme scientifique.— Ed.*

[c] *Il socialismo utopico e il socialismo scientifico.— Ed.*

[d] *Socyjalizm utopijny a naukowy.— Ed.*

[e] *Socialismens Udvikling fra Utopi til Videnskab.— Ed.*

[f] Engels refers to Morgan's main work *Ancient Society or Researches in the lines of human progress from savagery, through barbarism to civilisation.— Ed.*

[g] See present edition, Vol. 26.— *Ed.*

natural science. There is much that is clumsy in my exposition and much of it could be expressed today in a clearer and more definite form. I have not allowed myself the right to improve this section, and for that very reason am under an obligation to criticise myself here instead.

Marx and I were pretty well the only people to rescue conscious dialectics from German idealist philosophy and apply it in the materialist conception of nature and history. But a knowledge of mathematics and natural science is essential to a conception of nature which is dialectical and at the same time materialist. Marx was well versed in mathematics, but we could keep up with natural science only piecemeal, intermittently and sporadically. For this reason, when I retired from business and transferred my home to London,[15] thus enabling myself to give the necessary time to it, I went through as complete as possible a "moulting", as Liebig calls it,[16] in mathematics and the natural sciences, and spent the best part of eight years on it. I was right in the middle of this "moulting" process when it happened that I had to occupy myself with Herr Dühring's so-called natural philosophy. It was therefore only too natural that in dealing with this subject I was sometimes unable to find the correct technical expression, and in general moved with considerable clumsiness in the field of theoretical natural science. On the other hand, my lack of assurance in this field, which I had not yet overcome, made me cautious, and I cannot be charged with real blunders in relation to the facts known at that time or with incorrect presentation of recognised theories. In this connection there was only one unrecognised genius of a mathematician [a] who complained in a letter to Marx [17] that I had made a wanton attack upon the honour of $\sqrt{-1}$.[b]

It goes without saying that my recapitulation of mathematics and the natural sciences was undertaken in order to convince myself also in detail—of what in general I was not in doubt—that in nature, ·amid the welter of innumerable changes, the same dialectical laws of motion force their way through as those which in history govern the apparent fortuitousness of events; the same laws which similarly form the thread running through the history of the development of human thought and gradually rise to consciousness in thinking man; the laws which Hegel first developed in all-embracing but mystic form, and which we made it one of our aims to strip of this mystic form and to bring clearly

---

[a] H. W. Fabian.— Ed.
[b] See this volume, p. 112.— Ed.

before the mind in their complete simplicity and universality. It goes without saying that the old philosophy of nature—in spite of its real value and the many fruitful seeds it contained*—was unable to satisfy us. As is more fully brought out in this book, natural philosophy, particularly in the Hegelian form, erred because it did not concede to nature any development in time, any "succession", but only "co-existence". This was on the one hand grounded in the Hegelian system itself, which ascribed historical evolution only to the "spirit", but on the other hand was also due to the whole state of the natural sciences in that period. In this Hegel fell far behind Kant, whose nebular theory had already indicated the origin of the solar system,[c] and whose discovery of the retardation of the earth's rotation by the tides also had proclaimed the doom of that system.[d] And finally, to me there could be no question of

---

* It is much easier, along with the unthinking mob à la Karl Vogt, to assail the old philosophy of nature than to appreciate its historical significance. It contains a great deal of nonsense and fantasy but not more than the unphilosophical theories of the empirical natural scientists contemporary with that philosophy, and that there was also in it much that was sensible and rational began to be perceived after the theory of evolution became widespread. Haeckel was therefore fully justified in recognising the merits of Treviranus and Oken.[a] In his primordial slime and primordial vesicle Oken put forward as a biological postulate what was in fact subsequently discovered as protoplasm and cell. As far as Hegel is specifically concerned, he is in many respects head and shoulders above his empiricist contemporaries, who thought that they had explained all unexplained phenomena when they had endowed them with some force or power—the force of gravity, the power of buoyancy, the power of electrical contact, etc.—or where this would not do, with some unknown substance: the substance of light, of heat, of electricity, etc. The imaginary substances have now been pretty well discarded, but the power humbug against which Hegel fought still pops up gaily, for example, as late as 1869 in Helmholtz's Innsbruck lecture (Helmholtz, *Populäre Vorlesungen,* Issue II, 1871, p. 190).[b] In contrast to the deification of Newton which was handed down from the French of the eighteenth century, and the English heaping of honours and wealth on Newton, Hegel brought out the fact that Kepler, whom Germany allowed to starve, was the real founder of the modern mechanics of the celestial bodies, and that the Newtonian law of gravitation was already contained in all three of Kepler's laws, in the third law even explicitly. What Hegel proves by a few simple equations in his *Naturphilosophie,* § 270 and Addenda (Hegel's *Werke,* 1842, Vol. 7, pp. 98 and 113 to 115), appears again as the outcome of the most recent mathematical mechanics in Gustav Kirchhoff's *Vorlesungen über mathematische Physik,* 2nd ed., Leipzig, 1877, p. 10, and in essentially the same simple mathematical form as had first been developed by Hegel. The natural philosophers stand in the same relation to consciously dialectical natural science as the utopians to modern communism.

---

[a] E. Haeckel, *Natürliche Schöpfungsgeschichte,* pp. 83-88.— *Ed.*
[b] See this volume, pp. 372-74.— *Ed.*
[c] Ibid., p. 24.— *Ed.*
[d] Ibid., pp. 392-96.— *Ed.*

building the laws of dialectics into nature, but of discovering them in it and evolving them from it.

But to do this systematically and in each separate department, is a gigantic task. Not only is the domain to be mastered almost boundless; natural science in this entire domain is itself undergoing such a mighty process of being revolutionised that even people who can devote the whole of their spare time to it can hardly keep pace. Since Karl Marx's death, however, my time has been requisitioned for more urgent duties, and I have therefore been compelled to lay aside my work.[a] For the present I must content myself with the indications given in this book, and must wait to find some later opportunity to put together and publish the results which I have arrived at, perhaps in conjunction with the extremely important mathematical manuscripts left by Marx.[18]

Yet the advance of theoretical natural science may possibly make my work to a great extent or even altogether superfluous. For the revolution which is being forced on theoretical natural science by the mere need to set in order the purely empirical discoveries, great masses of which have been piled up, is of such a kind that it must bring the dialectical character of natural processes more and more to the consciousness even of those empiricists who are most opposed to it. The old rigid antagonisms, the sharp, impassable dividing lines are more and more disappearing. Since even the last "true" gases have been liquefied, and since it has been proved that a body can be brought into a condition in which the liquid and the gaseous forms are indistinguishable, the aggregate states have lost the last relics of their former absolute character.[19] With the thesis of the kinetic theory of gases, that in perfect gases at equal temperatures the squares of the speeds with which the individual gas molecules move are in inverse ratio to their molecular weights, heat also takes its place directly among the forms of motion which can be immediately measured as such. Whereas only ten years ago the great basic law of motion, then recently discovered, was as yet conceived merely as a law of the *conservation* of energy, as the mere expression of the indestructibility and uncreatability of motion, that is, merely in its quantitative aspect, this narrow, negative conception is being more and more supplanted by the positive idea of the *transformation* of energy, in which for the first time the qualitative content of the process comes into its own, and the last vestige of an extramundane creator is obliterated. That the quantity of motion (so-called energy) remains unaltered when it is

---

[a] I.e., on *Dialectics of Nature*. See Note 130.— *Ed.*

transformed from kinetic energy (so-called mechanical force) into electricity, heat, potential energy, etc., and vice versa, no longer needs to be preached as something new; it serves as the already secured basis for the now much more pregnant investigation into the very process of transformation, the great basic process, knowledge of which comprises all knowledge of nature. And since biology has been pursued in the light of the theory of evolution, one rigid boundary line of classification after another has been swept away in the domain of organic nature. The almost unclassifiable intermediate links are growing daily more numerous, closer investigation throws organisms out of one class into another, and distinguishing characteristics which almost became articles of faith are losing their absolute validity; we now have mammals that lay eggs, and, if the report is confirmed, also birds that walk on all fours. Years ago Virchow was compelled, following on the discovery of the cell, to dissolve the unity of the individual animal being into a federation of cell-states—thus acting more progressively rather than scientifically and dialectically [20]—and now the conception of animal (therefore also human) individuality is becoming far more complex owing to the discovery of the white blood corpuscles which creep about amoeba-like within the bodies of the higher animals. It is however precisely the polar antagonisms put forward as irreconcilable and insoluble, the forcibly fixed lines of demarcation and class distinctions, which have given modern theoretical natural science its restricted, metaphysical character. The recognition that these antagonisms and distinctions, though to be found in nature, are only of relative validity, and that on the other hand their imagined rigidity and absolute validity have been introduced into nature only by our reflective minds—this recognition is the kernel of the dialectical conception of nature. It is possible to arrive at this recognition because the accumulating facts of natural science compel us to do so; but one arrives at it more easily if one approaches the dialectical character of these facts equipped with an understanding of the laws of dialectical thought. In any case natural science has now advanced so far that it can no longer escape dialectical generalisation. However it will make this process easier for itself if it does not lose sight of the fact that the results in which its experiences are summarised are concepts, that the art of working with concepts is not inborn and also is not given with ordinary everyday consciousness, but requires real thought, and that this thought similarly has a long empirical history, not more and not less than empirical natural science. Only by learning to assimilate the results of the development of philosophy during the past two and a half thousand years will it rid itself on the one hand of any natural philosophy standing apart from it, outside it and above it, and on the other hand also of its own limited method of thought, which is its inheritance from English empiricism.

London, September 23, 1885

III

The following new edition is a reprint of the former, except for a few very unimportant stylistic changes. It is only in one chapter—the tenth of Part II: "From *Kritische Geschichte*" [a] that I have allowed myself to make substantial additions, on the following grounds.

As already stated in the preface to the second edition, this chapter was in all essentials the work of Marx. I was forced to make considerable cuts in Marx's manuscript, which in its first wording had been intended as an article for a journal; and I had to cut precisely those parts of it in which the critique of Dühring's propositions was overshadowed by Marx's own revelations from the history of economics. But this is just the section of the manuscript which is even today of the greatest and most permanent interest. I consider myself under an obligation to give in as full and faithful a form as possible the passages in which Marx assigns to people like Petty, North, Locke and Hume their appropriate place in the genesis of classical political economy; and even more his explanation of Quesnay's economic *Tableau,* which has remained an insoluble riddle of the sphinx to all modern political economy. On the other hand, wherever the thread of the argument makes this possible, I have omitted passages which refer exclusively to Herr Dühring's writings.

For the rest I may well be perfectly satisfied with the degree to which, since the previous edition of this book was issued, the views maintained in it have penetrated into the social consciousness of scientific circles and of the working class in every civilised country of the world.

London, May 23, 1894

F. *Engels*

---

[a] See this volume, pp. 211-43.— *Ed.*

INTRODUCTION

I. GENERAL

Modern socialism is, in its essence, the direct product of the recognition, on the one hand, of the class antagonisms existing in the society of today between proprietors and non-proprietors, between capitalists and wage-workers; on the other hand, of the anarchy existing in production. But, in its theoretical form, modern socialism originally appears ostensibly as a more logical extension of the principles laid down by the great French philosophers of the eighteenth century. Like every new theory, modern socialism had, at first, to connect itself with the intellectual stock-in-trade ready to its hand, however deeply its roots lay in economic facts.

The great men, who in France prepared men's minds for the coming revolution, were themselves extreme revolutionists. They recognised no external authority of any kind whatever. Religion, natural science, society, political institutions—everything was subjected to the most unsparing criticism; everything must justify its existence before the judgment-seat of reason or give up existence. Reason became the sole measure of everything. It was the time when, as Hegel says, the world stood upon its head [a]; first in the sense that the human head, and the principles arrived at by its thought, claimed to be the basis of all human action and association; but by and by, also, in the wider sense that the reality which was in contradiction to these principles had, in fact, to be turned upside down. Every form of society and government then existing, every old traditional notion was flung into the lumber-

---

[a] G. W. F. Hegel, *Vorlesungen über die Philosophie der Geschichte. In: Werke*, Bd. 9, pp. 535-36; see this volume, pp. 630-31.— *Ed.*

Vorwärts

Central-Organ der Sozialdemokratie Deutschlands.

Nr. 1.   Mittwoch, 3. Januar.   **1877.**

Die feindlichen Brüder.

Herrn Eugen Dühring's Umwälzung der Philosophie.

Von Friedrich Engels.

I.

Parlamentarischer Tugendspiegel.
(Schluß.)

First article of *Anti-Dühring* published in the newspaper *Vorwärts* on January 3, 1877

room as irrational; the world had hitherto allowed itself to be led solely by prejudices; everything in the past deserved only pity and contempt. Now, for the first time, appeared the light of day, henceforth superstition, injustice, privilege, oppression, were to be superseded by eternal truth, eternal Right, equality based on nature and the inalienable rights of man.

We know today that this kingdom of reason was nothing more than the idealised kingdom of the bourgeoisie; that this eternal Right found its realisation in bourgeois justice; that this equality reduced itself to bourgeois equality before the law; that bourgeois property was proclaimed as one of the essential rights of man; and that the government of reason, the Contrat Social of Rousseau,[21] came into being, and only could come into being, as a democratic bourgeois republic. The great thinkers of the eighteenth century could, no more than their predecessors, go beyond the limits imposed upon them by their epoch.

But, side by side with the antagonism of the feudal nobility and the burghers, was the general antagonism of exploiters and exploited, of rich idlers and poor workers. It was this very circumstance that made it possible for the representatives of the bourgeoisie to put themselves forward as representing not one special class, but the whole of suffering humanity. Still further. From its origin the bourgeoisie was saddled with its antithesis: capitalists cannot exist without wage-workers, and, in the same proportion as the mediaeval burgher of the guild developed into the modern bourgeois, the guild journeyman and the day-labourer, outside the guilds, developed into the proletarian. And although, upon the whole, the bourgeoisie, in their struggle with the nobility, could claim to represent at the same time the interests of the different working classes of that period, yet in every great bourgeois movement there were independent outbursts of that class which was the forerunner, more or less developed, of the modern proletariat. For example, at the time of the German Reformation and the Peasant War, Thomas Münzer; in the great English Revolution, the Levellers[22]; in the great French Revolution, Babeuf. There were theoretical enunciations corresponding with these revolutionary uprisings of a class not yet developed; in the sixteenth and seventeenth centuries utopian pictures of ideal social conditions[23]; in the eighteenth, actual communistic theories (Morelly and Mably). The demand for equality was no longer limited to political rights; it was extended also to the social conditions of individuals. It was not simply class privileges that were to be abolished, but class distinctions themselves. A communism, ascetic, Spartan, was the first form of the new teaching. Then came the three great utopians: Saint-Simon, to whom the middle-class movement, side by side with the proletarian, still had a certain significance; Fourier, and Owen, who in the country where capitalist production was most developed, and under the influence of the antagonisms begotten of this, worked out his proposals for the removal of class distinctions systematically and in direct relation to French materialism.

One thing is common to all three. Not one of them appears as a representative of the interests of that proletariat which historical development had, in the meantime, produced. Like the French philosophers, they do not claim to emancipate a particular class, but all humanity. Like them, they wish to bring in the kingdom of reason and eternal justice, but this kingdom, as they see it, is as far as heaven from earth, from that of the French philosophers.

For the bourgeois world, based upon the principles of these philosophers, is quite as irrational and unjust, and, therefore, finds its way to the dust-hole quite as readily as feudalism and all the earlier stages of society. If pure reason and justice have not, hitherto, ruled the world, this has been the case only because men have not rightly understood them. What was wanted was the individual man of genius, who has now arisen and who understands the truth. That he has now arisen, that the truth has now been clearly understood, is not an inevitable event, following of necessity in the chain of historical development, but a mere happy accident. He might just as well have been born 500 years earlier, and might then have spared humanity 500 years of error, strife, and suffering.

This mode of outlook is essentially that of all English and French and of the first German socialists, including Weitling. Socialism is the expression of absolute truth, reason and justice and has only to be discovered to conquer all the world by virtue of its own power. And as absolute truth is independent of time, space, and of the historical development of man, it is a mere accident when and where it is discovered. With all this, absolute truth, reason, and justice are different with the founder of each different school. And as each one's special kind of absolute truth, reason, and justice is again conditioned by his subjective understanding, his conditions of existence, the measure of his knowledge and his intellectual training, there is no other ending possible in this conflict of absolute truths than that they shall be mutually exclusive one of the other. Hence, from this nothing could come but a kind of eclectic, average socialism, which, as a matter of fact, has up to the present time dominated the minds of most of the socialist workers in France and England. Hence, a mish-mash allowing of the most manifold shades of opinion; a mish-mash of less striking critical statements, economic theories, pictures of future society by the founders of different sects; a mish-mash which is the more easily brewed the more the definite sharp edges of the individual constituents are rubbed down in the stream of debate, like rounded pebbles in a brook.

To make a science of socialism, it had first to be placed upon a real basis.

In the meantime, along with and after the French philosophy of the eighteenth century had arisen the new German philosophy, culminating in Hegel. Its greatest merit was the taking up again of dialectics as the highest form of reasoning. The old Greek philosophers were all born natural dialecticians, and Aristotle, the most encyclopaedic intellect of them, had already analysed the most essential forms of dialectic thought. The newer philosophy, on the other hand, although in it also dialectics had brilliant exponents (e.g., Descartes and Spinoza), had, especially through English influence, become more and more rigidly fixed in the so-called metaphysical mode of reasoning, by which also the French of the eighteenth century were almost wholly dominated, at all events in their special philosophical work. Outside philosophy in the restricted sense, the French nevertheless produced masterpieces of dialectic. We need only call to mind Diderot's *Le neveu de Rameau*[24] and Rousseau's *Discours sur l'origine et les fondemens de l'inégalité parmi les hommes.* We give here, in brief, the essential character of these two modes of thought. We shall have to return to them later in greater detail.

When we consider and reflect upon nature at large or the history of mankind or our own intellectual activity, at first we see the picture of an endless entanglement of relations and reactions in which nothing remains what, where and as it was, but everything moves, changes, comes into being and passes away. This primitive, naive but intrinsically correct conception of the world is that of ancient Greek philosophy, and was first clearly formulated by Heraclitus: everything is and is not, for everything is *fluid,* is constantly changing, constantly coming into being and passing away.

But this conception, correctly as it expresses the general character of the picture of appearances as a whole, does not suffice to explain the details of which this picture is made up, and so long as we do not understand these, we have not a clear idea of the whole picture. In order to understand these details we must detach them from their natural or historical connection and examine each one separately, its nature, special causes, effects, etc. This is, primarily, the task of natural science and historical research: branches of science which the Greeks of classical times, on very good grounds, relegated to a subordinate position, because they had first of all to collect the material. The beginnings of the exact natural sciences were first worked out by the Greeks of the Alexandrian period,[25] and later on, in the Middle Ages, by the Arabs. Real natural science dates from the second half of the fifteenth century, and thence onward it has advanced with constantly increasing rapidity. The analysis of nature into its individual parts, the grouping of the different natural processes and objects in definite classes, the study of the internal anatomy of organic bodies in their manifold forms—these were the fundamental conditions of the gigantic strides in our knowledge of nature that have been made during the last four hundred years. But this method of work has also left us as legacy the habit of observing natural objects and processes in isolation, apart from their connection with the vast whole; of observing them in repose, not in motion; as constants, not as essentially variables; in their death, not in their life. And when this way of looking at things was transferred by Bacon and Locke from natural science to philosophy, it begot the narrow, metaphysical mode of thought peculiar to the preceding centuries.

To the metaphysician, things and their mental reflexes, ideas, are isolated, are to be considered one after the other and apart from each other, are objects of investigation fixed, rigid, given once for all. He thinks in absolutely irreconcilable antitheses. "His communication is 'yea, yea; nay, nay'; for whatsoever is more than these cometh of evil."[a] For him a thing either exists or does not exist; a thing cannot at the same time be itself and something else. Positive and negative absolutely exclude one another; cause and effect stand in a rigid antithesis one to the other.

At first sight this mode of thinking seems to us very luminous, because it is that of so-called sound common sense. Only sound common sense, respectable fellow that he is, in the homely realm of his own four walls, has very wonderful adventures directly he ventures out into the wide world of research. And the metaphysical mode of thought, justifiable and even necessary as it is in a

---

a Matthew 5:37.—*Ed.*

number of domains whose extent varies according to the nature of the particular object of investigation, sooner or later reaches a limit, beyond which it becomes one-sided, restricted, abstract, lost in insoluble contradictions. In the contemplation of individual things, it forgets the connection between them; in the contemplation of their existence, it forgets the beginning and end of that existence; of their repose, it forgets their motion. It cannot see the wood for the trees.

For everyday purposes we know and can say, e.g., whether an animal is alive or not. But, upon closer inquiry, we find that this is, in many cases, a very complex question, as the jurists know very well. They have cudgelled their brains in vain to discover a rational limit beyond which the killing of the child in its mother's womb is murder. It is just as impossible to determine absolutely the moment of death, for physiology proves that death is not an instantaneous momentary phenomenon, but a very protracted process.

In like manner, every organic being is every moment the same and not the same; every moment it assimilates matter supplied from without, and gets rid of other matter; every moment some cells of its body die and others build themselves anew; in a longer or shorter time the matter of its body is completely renewed, and is replaced by other atoms of matter, so that every organic being is always itself, and yet something other than itself.

Further, we find upon closer investigation that the two poles of an antithesis, positive and negative, e.g., are as inseparable as they are opposed, and that despite all their opposition, they mutually interpenetrate. And we find, in like manner, that cause and effect are conceptions which only hold good in their application to individual cases; but as soon as we consider the individual cases in their general connection with the universe as a whole, they run into each other, and they become confounded when we contemplate that universal action and reaction in which causes and effects are eternally changing places, so that what is effect here and now will be cause there and then, and vice versa.

None of these processes and modes of thought enters into the framework of metaphysical reasoning. Dialectics, on the other hand, comprehends things and their representations, ideas, in their essential connection, concatenation, motion, origin, and ending. Such processes as those mentioned above are, therefore, so many corroborations of its own method of procedure.

Nature is the proof of dialectics, and it must be said for modern science that it has furnished this proof with very rich materials increasing daily, and thus has shown that, in the last resort, nature works dialectically and not metaphysically. But the naturalists who have learned to think dialectically are few and far between, and this conflict of the results of discovery with preconceived modes of thinking explains the endless confusion now reigning in theoretical natural science, the despair of teachers as well as learners, of authors and readers alike.

An exact representation of the universe, of its evolution, of the development of mankind, and of the reflection of this evolution in the minds of men, can therefore only be obtained by the methods of dialectics with its constant regard to the innumerable actions and reactions of life and death, of progressive or retrogressive changes. And in this spirit the new German philosophy has worked. Kant began his career by resolving the stable solar system of Newton and its eternal duration, after the famous initial impulse had once been given, into the result of a historic process, the formation of the sun and all the planets out of a rotating nebulous mass.[a] From this he at the same time drew the conclusion that, given this origin of the solar system, its future death followed of necessity. His theory half a century later was established mathematically by Laplace, and half a century after that the spectroscope proved the existence in space of such incandescent masses of gas in various stages of condensation.[26]

This new German philosophy culminated in the Hegelian system. In this system—and herein is its great merit—for the first time the whole world, natural, historical, intellectual, is represented as a process, i.e., as in constant motion, change, transformation, development; and the attempt is made to trace out the internal connection that makes a continuous whole of all this movement and development. From this point of view the history of mankind no longer appeared as a wild whirl of senseless deeds of violence, all equally condemnable at the judgment-seat of mature philosophic reason and which are best forgotten as quickly as possible, but as the process of evolution of man himself. It was now the task of the intellect to follow the gradual march of this process through all its devious ways, and to trace out the inner law running through all its apparently accidental phenomena.

That Hegel did not solve the problem is here immaterial. His epoch-making merit was that he propounded the problem. This

---

[a] I. Kant, *Allgemeine Naturgeschichte und Theorie des Himmels, oder Versuch von der Verfassung und dem mechanischen Ursprunge des ganzen Weltgebäudes, nach Newton'schen Grundsätzen abgehandelt.*—Ed.

problem is one that no single individual will ever be able to solve. Although Hegel was—with Saint-Simon—the most encyclopaedic mind of his time, yet he was limited, first, by the necessarily limited extent of his own knowledge and, second, by the limited extent and depth of the knowledge and conceptions of his age. To these limits a third must be added. Hegel was an idealist. To him the thoughts within his brain were not the more or less abstract pictures of actual things and processes, but, conversely, things and their evolution were only the realised pictures of the "Idea", existing somewhere from eternity before the world was. This way of thinking turned everything upside down, and completely reversed the actual connection of things in the world. Correctly and ingeniously as many individual groups of facts were grasped by Hegel, yet, for the reasons just given, there is much that is botched, artificial, laboured, in a word, wrong in point of detail. The Hegelian system, in itself, was a colossal miscarriage—but it was also the last of its kind. It was suffering, in fact, from an internal and incurable contradiction. Upon the one hand, its essential proposition was the conception that human history is a process of evolution, which, by its very nature, cannot find its intellectual final term in the discovery of any so-called absolute truth. But, on the other hand, it laid claim to being the very essence of this absolute truth. A system of natural and historical knowledge, embracing everything, and final for all time, is a contradiction to the fundamental laws of dialectic reasoning. This law, indeed, by no means excludes, but, on the contrary, includes the idea that the systematic knowledge of the external universe can make giant strides from age to age.

The perception of the fundamental contradiction in German idealism led necessarily back to materialism, but, *nota bene,* not to the simply metaphysical, exclusively mechanical materialism of the eighteenth century. In contrast to the naively revolutionary, simple rejection of all previous history, modern materialism sees in the latter the process of evolution of humanity, it being its task to discover the laws of motion thereof. With the French of the eighteenth century, and with Hegel, the conception obtained of nature as a whole, moving in narrow circles, and forever immutable, with its eternal celestial bodies, as Newton, and unalterable organic species, as Linnaeus, taught. Modern materialism embraces the more recent discoveries of natural science, according to which nature also has its history in time, the celestial bodies, like the organic species that, under favourable conditions, people them, being born and perishing. And even if nature, as a whole, must still be said to move in recurrent cycles, these cycles assume infinitely larger dimensions. In both cases modern materialism is essentially dialectic, and no longer needs any philosophy standing above the other sciences. As soon as each special science is bound to make clear its position in the great totality of things and of our knowledge of things, a special science dealing with this totality is superfluous. That which still survives, independently, of all earlier philosophy is the science of thought and its laws—formal logic and dialectics. Everything else is subsumed in the positive science of nature and history.

Whilst, however, the revolution in the conception of nature could only be made in proportion to the corresponding positive materials furnished by research, already much earlier certain historical facts had occurred which led to a decisive change in the conception of history. In 1831, the first working-class rising took place in Lyons; between 1838 and 1842, the first national working-class movement, that of the English Chartists, reached its height. The class struggle between proletariat and bourgeoisie came to the front in the history of the most advanced countries in Europe, in proportion to the development, upon the one hand, of modern industry [*grosse Industrie*], upon the other, of the newly-acquired political supremacy of the bourgeoisie. Facts more and more strenuously gave the lie to the teachings of bourgeois economy as to the identity of the interests of capital and labour, as to the universal harmony and universal prosperity that would be the consequence of unbridled competition. All these things could no longer be ignored, any more than the French and English socialism, which was their theoretical, though very imperfect, expression. But the old idealist conception of history, which was not yet dislodged, knew nothing of class struggles based upon economic interests, knew nothing of economic interests; production and all economic relations appeared in it only as incidental, subordinate elements in the "history of civilisation".

The new facts made imperative a new examination of all past history. Then it was seen that *all* past history was the history of class struggles[27]; that these warring classes of society are always the products of the modes of production and of exchange—in a word, of the *economic* conditions of their time; that the economic structure of society always furnishes the real basis, starting from which we can alone work out the ultimate explanation of the whole superstructure of juridical and political institutions as well as of the religious, philosophical, and other ideas of a given historical period. But now idealism was driven from its last refuge, the philosophy of history; now a materialistic treatment of history was propounded, and a method found of explaining man's "knowing" by his "being", instead of, as heretofore, his "being" by his "knowing".

But the socialism of earlier days was as incompatible with this materialistic conception as the conception of nature of the French materialists was with dialectics and modern natural science. The socialism of earlier days certainly criticised the existing capitalistic mode of production and its consequences. But it could not explain them, and, therefore, could not get the mastery of them. It could only simply reject them as bad. But for this it was necessary (1) to present the capitalistic method of production in its historical connection and its inevitableness during a particular historical period, and therefore, also, to present its inevitable downfall; and (2) to lay bare its essential character, which was still a secret, as its critics had hitherto attacked its evil consequences rather than the process of the thing itself. This was done by the discovery of *surplus-value*. It was shown that the appropriation of unpaid labour is the basis of the capitalist mode of production and of the exploitation of the worker that occurs under it; that even if the capitalist buys the labour-power of his labourer at its full value as a commodity on the market, he yet extracts more value from it than he paid for; and that in the ultimate analysis this surplus-value forms those sums of value from which are heaped up the constantly increasing masses of capital in the hands of the possessing classes. The genesis of capitalist production and the production of capital were both explained.

These two great discoveries, the materialistic conception of history and the revelation of the secret of capitalistic production through surplus-value, we owe to *Marx*. With these discoveries socialism became a science. The next thing was to work out all its details and relations.

This, approximately, was how things stood in the fields of theoretical socialism and extinct philosophy, when Herr Eugen Dühring, not without considerable din, sprang on to the stage and announced that he had accomplished a complete revolution in philosophy, political economy and socialism.

Let us see what Herr Dühring promises us and how he fulfills his promises.

II. WHAT HERR DÜHRING PROMISES

The writings of Herr Dühring with which we are here primarily concerned are his *Kursus der Philosophie,*[a] his *Kursus der National- und Sozialökonomie,*[b] and his *Kritische Geschichte der Nationalökonomie und des Sozialismus.*[28] The first-named work is the one which particularly claims our attention here.

On the very first page Herr Dühring introduces himself as

"the man who *claims to represent* this power" (philosophy) "in his age and for its immediately foreseeable development"[c] [D. Ph. 1].

He thus proclaims himself to be the only true philosopher of today and of the "foreseeable" future. Whoever departs from him departs from truth. Many people, even before Herr Dühring, have *thought* something of this kind about themselves, but—except for Richard Wagner—he is probably the first who has calmly blurted it out. And the truth to which he refers is

"a final and ultimate truth" [2].

Herr Dühring's philosophy is

"the *natural* system or the *philosophy of reality...* In it reality is so conceived as to *exclude any tendency* to a visionary and subjectively limited conception of the world" [13].

This philosophy is therefore of such a nature that it lifts Herr Dühring above the limits he himself can hardly deny of his personal, subjective limitations. And this is in fact necessary if he is to be in a position to lay down final and ultimate truths, although so far we do not see how this miracle should come to pass.

This "natural system of knowledge which in itself is of value to the mind" [508] has, "without the slightest detraction from the profundity of thought, *securely established* the basic forms of being" [556-57]. From its "really critical standpoint" [404] it provides "the elements of a philosophy which is real and therefore directed to the reality of nature and of life, a philosophy which cannot allow the validity of any merely apparent horizon, but *in its powerfully revolutionising movement unfolds all earths and heavens of outer and inner nature*" [430]. It is a "new mode of thought" [543], and its results are "from the ground up original conclusions and views ... system-creating ideas [525] ... established truths" [527]. In it we have before us "a

---

[a] *Cursus der Philosophie als streng wissenschaftlicher Weltanschauung und Lebensgestaltung.—Ed.*

[b] *Cursus der National- und Socialökonomie einschliesslich der Hauptpunkte der Finanzpolitik.—Ed.*

[c] In all the quotations from Dühring's works italics by Engels.— *Ed.*

work which must find its strength in concentrated initiative" [38]—whatever that may mean; an "investigation *going to the roots* [200] ... a *deep-rooted* science [219] ... a *strictly scientific* conception of things and men [387] ... an *all-round penetrating* work of thought [D. C. III] ... a *creative* evolving of premises and conclusions controllable by thought [6] ... the *absolutely fundamental*" [150].

In the economic and political sphere he gives us not only

"historical and systematically comprehensive works" [532], of which the historical ones are, to boot, notable for "*my* historical depiction *in the grand style*" [D. K. G. 556], while those dealing with political economy have brought about "creative turns" [462],

but he even finishes with a fully worked-out socialist plan of his own for the society of the future, a plan which is the

"practical fruit of a *clear* theory *going to the ultimate roots of things*" [D. C. 555-56]

and, like the Dühring philosophy, is consequently infallible and offers the only way to salvation; for

"*only in that* socialist structure which *I* have sketched *in my Cursus der National- und Socialökonomie* can a true Own take the place of ownership which is merely apparent and transitory or even based on violence" [D. Ph. 242]. And the future has to follow these directions.

This bouquet of glorifications of Herr Dühring by Herr Dühring could easily be enlarged tenfold. It may already have created some doubt in the mind of the reader as to whether it is really a philosopher with whom he is dealing, or a—but we must beg the reader to reserve judgment until he has got to know the above-mentioned "deep-rootedness" at closer quarters. We have given the above anthology only for the purpose of showing that we have before us not any ordinary philosopher and socialist, who merely expresses his ideas and leaves it to the future to judge their worth, but quite an extraordinary creature, who claims to be not less infallible than the Pope, and whose doctrine is the only way to salvation and simply must be accepted by anyone who does not want to fall into the most abominable heresy. What we are here confronted with is certainly not one of those works in which all socialist literature, recently also German, has abounded—works in which people of various calibres, in the most straightforward way in the world, try to clear up in their minds problems for the solution of which they may be more or less short of material; works in which, whatever their scientific and literary shortcomings, the socialist good will is always deserving of recognition. On the contrary, Herr Dühring offers us principles which he declares are final and ultimate truths and therefore any views conflicting with these are false from the outset; he is in possession not only of the exclusive truth but also of the sole strictly scientific method of investigation, in contrast with which all others are unscientific. Either he is right—and in this case we have before us the greatest genius of all time, the first superhuman, because infallible, man. Or he is wrong, and in that case, whatever our judgment may be, benevolent consideration shown for any good intentions he may possibly have had would nevertheless be the most deadly insult to Herr Dühring.

When a man is in possession of the final and ultimate truth and of the only strictly scientific method, it is only natural that he should have a certain contempt for the rest of erring and unscientific humanity. We must therefore not be surprised that Herr Dühring should speak of his predecessors with extreme disdain, and that there are only a few great men, thus styled by way of exception by himself, who find mercy at the bar of his "deep-rootedness".

Let us hear first what he has to say about the philosophers:

"*Leibniz,* devoid of any nobler sentiments ... that best of all court-philosophisers" [D. Ph. 346].

Kant is still just about tolerated; but after him everything got into a muddle [197]:

there followed the "wild ravings and equally childish and windy stupidities of the immediately succeeding epigoni, namely, a *Fichte* and a *Schelling* [227] ... monstrous caricatures of ignorant natural philosophising [56] ... the post-Kantian monstrosities" and "the delirious fantasies" [449] crowned by "a *Hegel*" [197]. The last-named used a "Hegel jargon" [D. K. G. 491] and spread the "Hegel pestilence" [D. Ph. 486] by means of his "moreover even in form unscientific demeanour" and his "crudities" [D. K. G. 235].

The natural scientists fare no better, but as only Darwin is cited by name we must confine ourselves to him:

"Darwinian semi-poetry and dexterity in metamorphosis, with their coarsely sentient narrowness of comprehension and blunted power of differentiation [D. Ph. 142] ... In our view what is specific to Darwinism, from which of course the Lamarckian formulations must be excluded, is *a piece of brutality directed against humanity*" [117].

But the socialists come off worst of all. With the exception at any rate of Louis Blanc—the most insignificant of them all—they are all and sundry sinners and fall short of the reputation which they should have before (or behind) Herr Dühring. And not only in regard to truth and scientific method—no, also in regard to their character. Except for Babeuf and a few Communards of 1871 none of them are "men" [D. K. G. 239]. The three utopians are called "social alchemists" [237]. As to them, a certain indulgence is shown to Saint-Simon, in so far as he is merely charged with "exaltation of mind" [252], and there is a compassionate suggestion that he suffered from religious mania. With Fourier, however, Herr Dühring completely loses patience. For Fourier

"revealed every element of insanity ... ideas which one would normally have most expected to find in madhouses [276] ... the wildest dreams ... products of delirium..." [283]. "The unspeakably silly Fourier" [222], this "infantile mind" [284], this "idiot" [286], is withal not even a socialist; his phalanstery [29] is absolutely not a piece of rational socialism, but "a caricature constructed on the pattern of everyday commerce" [283].

And finally:

"Anyone who does not find those effusions" (of Fourier's, concerning Newton) "... sufficient to convince himself that in Fourier's name and in the whole of Fourierism it is only the first syllable" (fou—crazy) "that has any truth in it, should himself be classed under some category of idiots" [286].

Finally, Robert Owen

"had feeble and paltry ideas [295] ... his reasoning, so crude in ethics [296] ... a few commonplaces which degenerated into perversions ... nonsensical and crude way of looking at things [297] ... the course of Owen's ideas is hardly worth subjecting to more serious criticism [298] ... his vanity" [299-300]—and so on.

With extreme wit Herr Dühring characterises the utopians by reference to their names, as follows: Saint-Simon—saint (holy), Fourier—fou (crazy), Enfantin—enfant (childish) [303]; he only needs to add: Owen—o woe! and a very important period in the history of socialism has in four words been roundly condemned; and anyone who has any doubts about it "should himself be classed under some category of idiots".

As for Dühring's opinion of the later socialists, we shall, for the sake of brevity, cite him only on Lassalle and Marx:

Lassalle: "Pedantic, hair-splitting efforts to popularise ... rampant scholasticism ... a monstrous hash of general theories and paltry trash [509] ... Hegel-superstition, senseless and formless ... a horrifying example [511] ... peculiarly limited [513] ... pompous display of the most paltry trifles [514] ... our Jewish hero [515] ... pamphleteer [519] ... common [520] ... inherent instability in his view of life and of the world" [529].

Marx: "Narrowness of conception ... his works and achievements in and by themselves, that is, regarded from a purely theoretical standpoint, are without any permanent significance in our domain" (the critical history of socialism), "and in the general history of intellectual tendencies they are to be cited at most as symptoms of the influence of one branch of modern sectarian scholastics [D. K. G. 495] ... impotence of the faculties of concentration and systematisation ... deformity of thought and style, undignified affectation of language ... anglicised vanity ... duping [497] ... barren conceptions which in fact are only bastards of historical and logical fantasy ... deceptive twisting [498] ... personal vanity [499] ... vile mannerisms ... snotty ... buffoonery pretending to be witty ... Chinese erudition [506] ... philosophical and scientific backwardness" [507].

And so on, and so forth—for this is only a small superficially culled bouquet out of the Dühring rose garden. It must be understood that, at the moment, we are not in the least concerned whether these amiable expressions of abuse—which, if he had any education, should forbid Herr Dühring from finding *anything* vile and snotty—are also final and ultimate truths. And—for the moment—we will guard against voicing any doubt as to their deep-rootedness, as we might otherwise be prohibited even from trying to find the category of idiots to which we belong. We only thought it was our duty to give, on the one hand, an example of what Herr Dühring calls

"the select language of the considerate and, in the real sense of the word, moderate mode of expression" [D. Ph. 260],

and on the other hand, to make it clear that to Herr Dühring the worthlessness of his predecessors is a no less established fact than his own infallibility. Whereupon we sink to the ground in deepest reverence before the mightiest genius of all time—if that is how things really stand.

Part I

PHILOSOPHY

III. CLASSIFICATION. APRIORISM

Philosophy, according to Herr Dühring, is the development of the highest form of consciousness of the world and of life [D. Ph. 2], and in a wider sense embraces the *principles* of all knowledge and volition. Wherever a series of cognitions or stimuli or a group of forms of being come to be examined by human consciousness, the *principles* underlying these manifestations of necessity become an object of philosophy. These principles are the simple, or until now assumed to be simple, constituents of manifold knowledge and volition [8]. Like the chemical composition of bodies, the general constitution of things can be reduced to basic forms and basic elements. These ultimate constituents or principles, once they have been discovered, are valid not only for what is immediately known and accessible, but also for the world which is unknown and inaccessible to us. Philosophical principles consequently provide the final supplement required by the sciences in order to become a uniform system by which nature and human life can be explained [9]. Apart from the fundamental forms of all existence, philosophy has only two specific subjects of investigation—nature and the world of man [14]. Accordingly, our material arranges itself *quite naturally* into three groups, namely, the general scheme of the universe, the science of the principles of nature, and finally the science of mankind. This succession at the same time contains *an inner logical sequence*, for the formal principles which are valid for all being take precedence, and the realms of the objects to which they are *to be applied* then follow in the degree of their subordination [15].

So far Herr Dühring, and almost entirely word for word.

What he is dealing with are therefore *principles*, formal tenets derived from *thought* and not from the external world, which are to be applied to nature and the realm of man, and to which therefore nature and man have to conform. But whence does thought obtain these principles? From itself? No, for Herr Dühring himself says: the realm of pure thought is limited to logical schemata and mathematical forms [42] (the latter, moreover, as we shall see, is wrong). Logical schemata can only relate to *forms of thought*; but what we are dealing with here is solely forms of *being,* of the external world, and these forms can never be created and derived by thought out of itself, but only from the external world. But with this the whole relationship is inverted: the principles are not the starting-point of the investigation, but its final result; they are not applied to nature and human history, but abstracted from them; it is not nature and the realm of man which conform to these principles, but the principles are only valid in so far as they are in conformity with nature and history. That is the only materialist conception of the matter, and Herr Dühring's contrary conception is idealistic, makes things stand completely on their heads, and fashions the real world out of ideas, out of schemata, schemes or categories existing somewhere before the world, from eternity—just like *a Hegel.*

In fact, let us compare Hegel's *Encyclopaedia*[30] and all its delirious fantasies with Herr Dühring's final and ultimate truths. With Herr Dühring we have in the first place general world schematism, which Hegel calls *Logic.* Then with both of them we have the application of these schemata or logical categories to nature: the philosophy of nature; and finally their application to the realm of man, which Hegel calls the philosophy of mind. The "inner logical sequence" of the Dühring succession therefore leads us "quite naturally" [D. Ph. 15] back to Hegel's *Encyclopaedia,* from which it has been taken with a loyalty which would move that wandering Jew of the Hegelian school, Professor Michelet of Berlin, to tears.[31]

That is what comes of accepting "consciousness", "thought", quite naturalistically, as something given, something opposed from the outset to being, to nature. If that were so, it must seem extremely strange that consciousness and nature, thinking and being, the laws of thought and the laws of nature, should correspond so closely. But if the further question is raised what thought and consciousness really are and where they come from, it becomes apparent that they are products of the human brain and that man himself is a product of nature, which has developed in and along with its environment; hence it is self-evident that the products of the human brain, being in the last analysis also products of nature, do not contradict the rest of nature's interconnections but are in correspondence with them.[32]

But Herr Dühring cannot permit himself such a simple treatment of the subject. He thinks not only in the name of humanity—in itself no small achievement—but in the name of the conscious and reasoning beings on all celestial bodies.

Indeed, it would be "a degradation of the basic forms of consciousness and knowledge to attempt to rule out or even to put under suspicion their sovereign validity and their unconditional claim to truth, by applying the epithet 'human' to them" [2].

Hence, in order that no suspicion may arise that on some celestial body or other twice two makes five [30-31], Herr Dühring dare not designate thought as being human, and so he has to sever it from the only real foundation on which we find it, namely, man and nature; and with that he tumbles hopelessly into an ideology[33] which reveals him as the epigone of the "epigone" Hegel [197]. By the way, we shall often meet Herr Dühring again on other celestial bodies.

It goes without saying that no materialist doctrine can be founded on such an ideological basis. Later on we shall see that Herr Dühring is forced more than once to endow nature surreptitiously with conscious activity, with what in plain language is called God.

However, our philosopher of reality had also other motives for shifting the basis of all reality from the real world to the world of thought. The science of this general world schematism, of these formal principles of being, is precisely the foundation of Herr Dühring's philosophy. If we deduce world schematism not from our minds, but only *through* our minds from the real world, if we deduce principles of being from what is, we need no philosophy for this purpose, but positive knowledge of the world and of what happens in it; and what this yields is also not philosophy, but positive science. In that case, however, Herr Dühring's whole volume would be nothing but love's labour lost.

Further: if no philosophy as such is any longer required, then also there is no more need of any system, not even of any natural system of philosophy. The perception that all the processes of nature are systematically connected drives science on to prove this systematic connection throughout, both in general and in particular. But an adequate, exhaustive scientific exposition of this interconnection, the formation of an exact mental image of the world system in which we live, is impossible for us, and will always remain impossible. If at any time in the development of mankind such a final, conclusive system of the interconnections within the world—physical as well as mental and historical—were brought about, this would mean that human knowledge had reached its limit, and, from the moment when society had been brought into accord with that system, further historical development would be cut short—which would be an absurd idea, sheer nonsense. Mankind therefore finds itself faced with a contradiction: on the one hand, it has to gain an exhaustive knowledge of the world system in all its interrelations; and on the other hand, because of the nature both of men and of the world system, this task can never be completely fulfilled. But this contradiction lies not only in the nature of the two factors—the world, and man—it is also the main lever of all intellectual advance, and finds its solution continuously, day by day, in the endless progressive development of humanity, just as for example mathematical problems find their solution in an infinite series or continued fractions. Each mental image of the world system is and remains in actual fact limited, objectively by the historical conditions and subjectively by the physical and mental constitution of its originator. But Herr Dühring explains in advance that his mode of reasoning is such that it excludes any tendency to a subjectively limited conception of the world. We saw above that he was omnipresent—on all possible celestial bodies. We now see that he is also omniscient. He has solved the ultimate problems of science and thus nailed boards across the future of all science.

As with the basic forms of being, so also with the whole of pure mathematics: Herr Dühring thinks that he can produce it *a priori*, that is, without making use of the experience offered us by the external world, can construct it in his head.

In pure mathematics the mind deals "with its own free creations and imaginations" [D. Ph. 43]; the concepts of number and figure are "the adequate object of that pure science which it can create of itself" [42], and hence it has a "validity which is independent of *particular* experience and of the real content of the world" [43].

That pure mathematics has a validity which is independent of the *particular* experience of each individual is, for that matter, correct, and this is true of all established facts in every science, and indeed of all facts whatsoever. The magnetic poles, the fact that water is composed of hydrogen and oxygen, the fact that Hegel is dead and Herr Dühring alive, hold good independently of my own experience or that of any other individual, and even independently of Herr Dühring's experience, when he begins to sleep the sleep of the just. But it is not at all true that in pure mathematics the mind deals only with its own creations and imaginations. The concepts of number and figure have not been derived from any source other than the world of reality. The ten fingers on which men learnt to count, that is, to perform the first arithmetical operation, are anything but a free creation of the mind. Counting requires not only objects that can be counted, but also the ability to exclude all properties of the objects considered except their number—and this ability is the product of a long historical development based on experience. Like the idea of number, so the idea of figure is borrowed exclusively from the external world, and does not arise in the mind out of pure thought. There must have been things which had shape and whose shapes were compared before anyone could arrive at the idea of figure. Pure mathematics deals with the space forms and quantity relations of the real world—that is, with material which is very real indeed. The fact that this material appears in an extremely abstract form can only superficially conceal its origin from the external world. But in order to make it possible to investigate these forms and relations in their pure state, it is necessary to separate them entirely from their content, to put the content aside as irrelevant; thus we get points without dimensions, lines without breadth and thickness, a and b and x and y, constants and variables; and only at the very end do we reach the free creations and imaginations of the mind itself, that is to say, imaginary magnitudes. Even the apparent derivation of mathematical magnitudes from each other does not prove their *a priori* origin, but only their rational connection. Before one came upon the idea of deducing the *form* of a cylinder from the rotation of a rectangle about one of its sides, a number of real rectangles and cylinders, however imperfect in form, must have been examined. Like all other sciences, mathematics arose out of the *needs* of men: from the measurement of land and the content of vessels, from the computation of time and from mechanics. But, as in every department of thought, at a certain stage of development the laws, which were abstracted from the real world, become divorced from the real world, and are set up against it as something independent, as·laws coming from outside, to which the world has to conform. That is how things happened in society and in the state, and in this way, and not otherwise, *pure* mathematics was subsequently *applied* to the world, although it is borrowed from this same world and represents only one part of its forms of interconnection—and it is only *just because of this* that it can be applied at all.

But just as Herr Dühring imagines that, out of the axioms of mathematics,

"which also in accordance with pure logic neither require nor are capable of substantiation" [34],

he can deduce the whole of pure mathematics without any kind of empirical admixture, and then apply it to the world, so he likewise imagines that he can, in the first place, produce out of his head the basic forms of being, the simple elements of all knowledge, the axioms of philosophy, deduce from these the whole of philosophy or world schematism, and then, by sovereign decree, impose this constitution of his on nature and humanity. Unfortunately nature is not at all, and humanity only to an infinitesimal degree, composed of the Manteuffelite Prussians of 1850.[34]

Mathematical axioms are expressions of the scantiest thought-content, which mathematics is obliged to borrow from logic. They can be reduced to two:

1) The whole is greater than its part. This statement is pure tautology, as the quantitatively conceived idea "part" is from the outset definitely related to the idea "whole", and in fact in such a way that "part" simply means that the quantitative "whole" consists of several quantitative "parts". In stating this explicitly, the so-called axiom does not take us a step further. This tautology can even in a way *be proved* by saying: a whole is that which consists of several parts; a part is that of which several make a whole; hence the part is less than the whole—in which the inanity of repetition brings out even more clearly the inanity of content.

2) If two quantities are equal to a third, they are equal to each other. This statement, as Hegel has already shown, is a conclusion, the correctness of which is vouched for by logic,[a] and which is therefore proved, although outside of pure mathematics. The remaining axioms relating to equality and inequality are merely logical extensions of this conclusion.

These meagre principles do not cut much ice, either in mathematics or anywhere else. In order to get any further, we are obliged to bring in real relations, relations and space forms which are taken from real bodies. The ideas of lines, planes, angles, polygons, cubes, spheres, etc., are all taken from reality, and it requires a pretty good portion of naive ideology to believe the mathematicians that the first line came into existence through the movement of a point in space, the first plane through the movement of a line, the first solid through the movement of a plane, and so on. Even language rebels against such a conception. A mathematical figure of three dimensions is called a solid body, *corpus solidum,* hence, in Latin, even a tangible object; it therefore has a name derived from sturdy reality and by no means from the free imagination of the mind.

But why all this prolixity? After Herr Dühring, on pages 42 and 43,[35] has enthusiastically sung the independence of pure mathematics

---

[a] G. W. F. Hegel, *Encyklopädie der philosophischen Wissenschaften im Grundrisse*, § 188; also *Wissenschaft der Logik*, Book 3, Section I, Chapter 3, "d. Vierte Figur", and Section III, Chapter 2, "3. Der Lehrsatz".— *Ed.*

from the world of experience, its apriority, its preoccupation with the mind's own free creations and imaginations, he says on page 63:

> "It is, of course, easily overlooked that those mathematical elements (number, magnitude, time, space and geometric motion) are *ideal only in their form*, ... *absolute magnitudes* are therefore something completely *empirical*, no matter to what species they belong", ... but "mathematical schemata are capable of characterisation which is adequate even though *divorced* from experience."

The last statement is more or less true of *every* abstraction, but does not by any means prove that it is not abstracted from reality. In world schematism pure mathematics arose out of pure thought—in the philosophy of nature it is something completely empirical, taken from the external world and then divorced from it. Which are we to believe?

IV. WORLD SCHEMATISM

> "All-embracing being is *one*. In its self-sufficiency it has nothing alongside it or over it. To associate a second being with it would be to make it something that it is not, namely, a part or constituent of a more comprehensive whole. Due to the fact that we extend our *unified* thought like a framework, nothing that should be comprised in this thought-*unity* can retain a duality within itself. Nor, again, can anything escape this thought-unity... The essence of all thought consists in bringing together the elements of consciousness into a unity [D. Ph. 16] ... It is the point of unity of the synthesis where the *indivisible idea of the world* came into being and the universe, as the name itself implies, is apprehended as something in which everything is united into *unity*" [17].

Thus far Herr Dühring. This is the first application of the mathematical method:

> "Every question is to be decided *axiomatically* in accordance with simple basic forms, as if we were dealing with the simple ... principles of mathematics" [224].

"All-embracing being is one." If tautology, the simple repetition in the predicate of what is already expressed in the subject—if that makes an axiom, then we have here one of the purest water. Herr Dühring tells us in the subject that being embraces everything, and in the predicate he intrepidly declares that in that case there is nothing outside it. What colossal "system-creating thought" [525]!

This is indeed system-creating! Within the space of the next six lines Herr Dühring has transformed the *oneness* of being, by means of our unified thought, into its *unity*. As the essence of all thought consists in bringing things together into a unity, so being, as soon as it is conceived, is conceived as unified, and the idea of the world as indivisible; and because *conceived* being, the *idea of the world*, is unified, therefore real being, the real world, is also an indivisible unity. And with that "there is no longer any room for things beyond, once the mind has learnt to conceive being in its homogeneous universality" [D. Ph. 523].

That is a campaign which puts Austerlitz and Jena, Königgrätz and Sedan completely in the shade.[36] In a few sentences, hardly a page after we have mobilised the first axiom, we have already done away with, cast overboard, destroyed, everything beyond the world—God and the heavenly hosts, heaven, hell and purgatory, along with the immortality of the soul.

How do we get from the oneness of being to its unity? By the very fact of conceiving it. In so far as we spread our unified thought around being like a frame, its oneness becomes a unity in thought, a thought-unity; for the essence of *all* thought consists in bringing together the elements of consciousness into a unity.

This last statement is simply untrue. In the first place, thought consists just as much in the taking apart of objects of consciousness into their elements as in the putting together of related elements into a unity. Without analysis, no synthesis. Secondly, without making blunders thought can bring together into a unity only those elements of consciousness in which or in whose real prototypes this unity already *existed before.* If I include a shoe-brush in the unity mammals, this does not help it to get mammary glands. The unity of being, or rather, the question whether its conception as a unity is justified, is therefore precisely what was to be proved; and when Herr Dühring assures us that he conceives being as a unity and not as twofold, he tells us nothing more than his own unauthoritative opinion.

If we try to state his process of thought in unalloyed form, we get the following: I begin with being. I therefore think what being is. The thought of being is a unified thought. But thinking and being must be in agreement, they are in conformity with each other, they "coincide". Therefore being is a unity also in reality. Therefore there cannot be anything "beyond". If Herr Dühring had spoken without disguise in this way, instead of treating us to the above oracular passages, his ideology would have been clearly visible. To attempt to prove the reality of any product of thought by the identity of thinking and being was indeed one of the most absurd delirious fantasies of—a Hegel.

Even if his whole method of proof had been correct, Herr Dühring would still not have won an inch of ground from the spiritualists. The latter would reply briefly: to us, too, the universe *is* simple; the division into this world and the world beyond exists only for our specifically earthly, original-sin standpoint; in and for itself, that is, in God, all being is a unity. And they would accompany Herr Dühring to his other beloved celestial bodies and show him one or several on which there had been no original sin, where therefore no opposition exists between this world and the beyond, and where the unity of the universe is a dogma of faith.

The most comical part of the business is that Herr Dühring, in order to prove the non-existence of God from the idea of being, uses the ontological proof for the existence of God. This runs: when we think of God, we conceive him as the sum total of all perfections. But the sum total of all perfections includes above all existence, since. a non-existent being is necessarily imperfect. We must therefore include existence among the perfections of God. Hence God must exist. Herr Dühring reasons in exactly the same way: when we think of *being*, we conceive it as *one* idea. Whatever is comprised in *one* idea is a unity. Being would not correspond to the idea of being if it were not a unity. Consequently it must be a unity. Consequently there is no God, and so on.

When we speak of *being,* and *purely* of being, unity can only consist in that all the objects to which we are referring—*are*, exist. They are comprised in the unity of this being, and in no other unity, and the general dictum that they all *are* not only cannot give them any additional qualities, whether common or not, but provisionally excludes all such qualities from consideration. For as soon as we depart even a millimetre from the simple basic fact that being is common to all these things, the *differences* between these things begin to emerge—and whether these differences consist in the circumstance that some are white and others black, that some are animate and others inanimate, that some may be of this world and others of the world beyond, cannot be decided by us from the fact that mere existence is in equal manner ascribed to them all.

The unity of the world does not consist in its being, although its being is a precondition of its unity, as it must certainly first *be* before it can be *one*. Being, indeed, is always an open question beyond the point where our sphere of observation ends. The real unity of the world consists in its materiality, and this is proved not by a few juggled phrases, but by a long and wearisome development of philosophy and natural science.

To return to the text. The *being* which Herr Dühring is telling us about is

"not that pure, self-equal being which lacks all special determinants, and in fact represents only the counterpart of the idea of *nothing* or of the absence of idea" [D. Ph. 22].

But we shall see very soon that Herr Dühring's universe really starts with a being which lacks all inner differentiation, all motion and change, and is therefore in fact only a counterpart of the idea of nothing, and therefore really nothing. Only out of this *being-nothing* develops the present differentiated, changing state of the universe, which represents a development, a *becoming*; and it is only after we have grasped this that we are able, even within this perpetual change, to

"maintain the conception of universal being in a self-equal state" [D. Ph. 23].

We have now, therefore, the idea of being on a higher plane, where it includes within itself both inertness and change, being and becoming. Having reached this point, we find that

"genus and species, or the general and the particular, are the simplest means of differentiation, without which the constitution of things cannot be understood" [24].

But these are means of differentiation of *qualities*; and after these have been dealt with, we proceed:

"in opposition to genus stands the concept of magnitude, as of a homogeneity in which no further differences of species exist" [26];

and so from *quality* we pass to *quantity*, and this is always "*measurable*" [26].

Let us now compare this "sharp division of the general effect-schemata" [D.C. 6] and its "really critical standpoint" [D. Ph. 404] with the crudities, wild ravings and delirious fantasies of a Hegel.[a] We find that Hegel's logic starts from *being*—as with Herr Dühring; that being turns out to be *nothing*, just as with Herr Dühring; that from this being-nothing there is a transition to *becoming* the result of which is determinate being [Dasein], i.e., a higher, fuller form of being [Sein]—just the same as with Herr Dühring. Determinate being leads on to *quality*, and quality on to *quantity*—just the same as with Herr Dühring. And so that no essential feature may be missing, Herr Dühring tells us on another occasion:

"From the realm of non-sensation a transition is made to that of sensation, in spite of all quantitative gradations, only through a *qualitative leap*, of which we ... can say that it is infinitely different from the mere gradation of one and the same property" [142].

This is precisely the Hegelian nodal line of measure relations, in which, at certain definite nodal points, the purely quantitative

---

[a] See this volume, p. 30.—*Ed.*

increase or decrease gives rise to a *qualitative leap*; for example, in
the case of heated or cooled water, where boiling-point and
freezing-point are the nodes at which—under normal pressure—
the leap to a new state of aggregation takes place, and where
consequently quantity is transformed into quality.

Our investigation has likewise tried to reach down to the roots,
and it finds the roots of the deep-rooted basic schemata of Herr
Dühring to be—the "delirious fantasies" of a Hegel, the
categories of Hegelian *Logic*, Part I, the Doctrine of Being,[a] in
strictly old-Hegelian "succession" and with hardly any attempt to
cloak the plagiarism!

And not content with pilfering from his worst-slandered
predecessor the latter's whole scheme of being, Herr Dühring,
after himself giving the above-quoted example of the leaplike
change from quantity into quality, says of Marx without the
slightest perturbation:

"How ridiculous, for example, is the reference" (made by Marx) "to the Hegelian
confused, hazy notion that *quantity is transformed into quality*!" [D. K. G. 498].

Confused, hazy notion! Who has been transformed here? And
who is ridiculous here, Herr Dühring?

All these pretty little things are therefore not only not
"axiomatically decided", as prescribed, but are merely imported
from outside, that is to say, from Hegel's *Logic*. And in fact in
such a form that in the whole chapter there is not even the
semblance of any internal coherence unless borrowed from Hegel,
and the whole question finally trickles out in a meaningless
subtilising about space and time, inertness and change.

From being Hegel passes to essence, to dialectics. Here he deals
with the determinations of reflection, their internal *antagonisms*
and contradictions, as for example, positive and negative; he then
comes to *causality* or the relation of cause and effect and ends with
necessity. Not otherwise Herr Dühring. What Hegel calls the
doctrine of essence Herr Dühring translates into "logical properties of being" [D. Ph. 29]. These, however, consist above all in the
"antagonism of forces" [31], in *opposites*. Contradiction, however,
Herr Dühring absolutely denies; we will return to this point later.
Then he passes over to *causality*, and from this to *necessity*. So that
when Herr Dühring says of himself:

"We, who do not philosophise *out of a cage*" [41],

---

[a] G. W. F. Hegel, *Wissenschaft der Logik.—Ed.*

he apparently means that he philosophises *in* a cage, namely, the cage of the Hegelian schematism of categories.

V. PHILOSOPHY OF NATURE. TIME AND SPACE

We now come to *philosophy of nature.* Here again Herr Dühring has every cause for dissatisfaction with his predecessors.

Natural philosophy "sank so low that it became an arid, spurious doggerel founded on ignorance", and "fell to the prostituted philosophistics of a Schelling and his like, rigging themselves out in the priesthood of the Absolute and hoodwinking the public". Fatigue has saved us from these "deformities"; but up to now it has only given place to "instability"; "and as far as the public at large is concerned, it is well known that the disappearance of a great charlatan is often only the opportunity for a lesser but commercially more experienced successor to put out again, under another signboard, the products of his predecessor". Natural scientists themselves feel little "inclination to make excursions into the realm of world-encompassing ideas", and consequently jump to "wild and hasty conclusions" in the theoretical sphere [D. Ph. 56-57].

The need for deliverance is therefore urgent, and by a stroke of good luck Herr Dühring is at hand.

In order properly to appreciate the revelations which now follow on the development of the world in time and its limitations in space, we must turn back again to certain passages in "world schematism" [15].

Infinity—which Hegel calls *bad* infinity [a]—is attributed to being, also in accordance with Hegel (*Encyclopaedia*, § 93), and then this infinity is investigated.

"The clearest form of an infinity which can be conceived *without contradiction* is the unlimited accumulation of numbers in a numerical series [18] ... As we can add yet another unit to any number, without ever exhausting the possibility of further numbers, so also to every state of being a further state succeeds, and infinity consists in the unlimited begetting of these states. This *exactly conceived* infinity has consequently only one single basic form with one single direction. For although it is immaterial to our thought whether or not it conceives an opposite direction in the accumulation of states, this retrogressing infinity is nevertheless only a rashly constructed thought-image. Indeed, since this infinity would have to be traversed in reality in the *reverse* direction, it would in each of its states have an infinite succession of numbers behind itself. But this would involve the impermissible contradiction of a counted infinite numerical series, and so it is contrary to reason to postulate any second direction in infinity" [19].

The first conclusion drawn from this conception of infinity is that the chain of causes and effects in the world must at some time have had a beginning:

---

[a] G. W. F. Hegel, *Encyklopädie der philosophischen Wissenschaften im Grundrisse,* § 94.— *Ed.*

"an infinite number of causes which assumedly already have lined up next to one another is inconceivable, just because it presupposes that the uncountable has been counted" [37].

And thus a *final cause* is proved.
The second conclusion is

"the law of definite number: the accumulation of identities of any actual species of independent things is only conceivable as forming a definite number". Not only must the number of celestial bodies existing at any point of time be in itself definite, but so must also the total number of all, even the tiniest independent particles of matter existing in the world. This latter requisite is the real reason why no composition can be conceived without atoms. All actual division has always a definite limit, and must have it if the contradiction of the counted uncountable is to be avoided. For the same reason, not only must the number of the earth's revolutions round the sun up to the present time be a definite number, even though it cannot be stated, but all periodical processes of nature must have had some beginning, and all differentiation, all the multifariousness of nature which appears in succession must have its roots in one *self-equal state.* This state may, without involving a contradiction, have existed from eternity; but even this idea would be excluded if time in itself were composed of real parts and were not, on the contrary, merely arbitrarily divided up by our minds owing to the variety of conceivable possibilities. The case is quite different with the real, and in itself distinguished content of time; this real filling of time with distinguishable facts and the forms of being of this sphere belong, precisely because of their distinguishability, to the realm of the countable [64-65]. If we imagine a state in which no change occurs and which in its self-equality provides no differences of succession whatever, the more specialised idea of time transforms itself into the more general idea of being. What the accumulation of empty duration would mean is quite unimaginable [70].

Thus far Herr Dühring, and he is not a little edified by the significance of these revelations. At first he hopes that they will "at least not be regarded as paltry truths" [64]; but later we find:

"Recall to your mind *the extremely simple* methods by which *we* helped forward the concepts of infinity and their critique to a *hitherto unknown import* ... the elements of the universal conception of space and time, which have been given such *simple* form by the sharpening and deepening now effected" [427-28].

We helped forward! The deepening and sharpening now effected! Who are "we", and when is this "now"? Who is deepening and sharpening?

"Thesis: The world has a beginning in time, and with regard to space is also limited.—Proof: For if it is assumed that the world has no beginning in time, then an eternity must have elapsed up to every given point of time, and consequently an infinite series of successive states of things must have passed away in the world. The infinity of a series, however, consists precisely in this, that it can never be completed by means of a successive synthesis. Hence an infinite elapsed series of worlds is impossible, and consequently a beginning of the world is a necessary condition of its existence. And this was the first thing to be proved.—With regard to the second, if the opposite is again assumed, then the world must be an infinite given total of co-existent things. Now we cannot conceive the dimensions of a quantum, which is not given within certain limits of an intuition, in any other way than by means of the synthesis of its parts, and can conceive the total of such a quantum only by means of a completed synthesis, or by the repeated addition of a unit to itself. Accordingly, to conceive the world, which fills all spaces, as a whole, the successive synthesis of the parts of an infinite world would have to be looked upon as completed; that is, an infinite time would have to be regarded as elapsed in the enumeration of all co-existing things. This is impossible. For this reason an infinite aggregate of actual things cannot be regarded as a given whole nor, therefore, as given *at the same time.* Hence it follows that the world is not infinite, as regards extension in space, but enclosed in limits. And this was the second thing" (to be proved).

These sentences are copied word for word from a well-known book which first appeared in 1781 and is called: *Kritik der reinen Vernunft* by *Immanuel Kant,* where all and sundry can read them, in the first part, Second Division, Book II, Chapter II, Section II: The First Antinomy of Pure Reason. So that Herr Dühring's fame rests solely on his having tacked on the *name*—Law of Definite Number—to an idea expressed by Kant, and on having made the discovery that there was once a time when as yet there was no time, though there was a world. As regards all the rest, that is, anything in Herr Dühring's exegesis which has some meaning, "We"—is Immanuel Kant, and the "now" is only ninety-five years ago. Certainly "extremely simple"! Remarkable "hitherto unknown import"!

Kant, however, does not at all claim that the above propositions are established by his proof. On the contrary; on the opposite page he states and proves the reverse: that the world has no beginning in time and no end in space; and it is precisely in this that he finds the antinomy, the insoluble contradiction, that the one is just as demonstrable as the other. People of smaller calibre might perhaps feel a little doubt here on account of "a Kant" having found an insoluble difficulty. But not so our valiant fabricator of "from the ground up original conclusions and views" [D. Ph. 525]; he indefatigably copies down as much of Kant's antinomy as suits his purpose, and throws the rest aside.

The problem itself has a very simple solution. Eternity in time, infinity in space, signify from the start, and in the simple meaning of the words, that there is no end in *any* direction, neither forwards nor backwards, upwards or downwards, to the right or to the left. This infinity is something quite different from that of an infinite series, for the latter always starts from one, with a first term. The inapplicability of this idea of series to our object becomes clear directly we apply it to space. The infinite series, transferred to the sphere of space, is a line drawn from a definite point in a definite direction to infinity. Is the infinity of space expressed in this even in the remotest way? On the contrary, the idea of spatial dimensions involves six lines drawn from this one point in three opposite directions, and consequently we would have six of these dimensions. Kant saw this so clearly that he transferred his numerical series only indirectly, in a roundabout way, to the space relations of the world. Herr Dühring, on the other hand, compels us to accept six dimensions in space, and immediately afterwards can find no words to express his indignation at the mathematical mysticism of Gauss, who would not rest content with the usual three dimensions of space[37] [See D. Ph. 67-68].

As applied to time, the line or series of units infinite in both directions has a certain figurative meaning. But if we think of time as a series counted from *one* forward, or as a line starting from a *definite point,* we imply in advance that time has a beginning: we put forward as a premise precisely what we are to prove. We give the infinity of time a one-sided, halved character; but a one-sided, halved infinity is also a contradiction in itself, the exact opposite of an "infinity conceived without contradiction". We can only get past this contradiction if we assume that the *one* from which we begin to count the series, the point from which we proceed to measure the line is any *one* in the series, that it is any one of the points in the line, and that it is a matter of indifference to the line or to the series where we place this *one* or this point.

But what of the contradiction of "the counted infinite numerical series"? We shall be in a position to examine this more closely as soon as Herr Dühring has performed for us the clever trick of *counting it.* When he has completed the task of counting from $-\infty$ (minus infinity) to 0 let him come again. It is certainly obvious that, at whatever point he begins to count, he will leave behind him an infinite series and, with it, the task which he is to fulfil. Let him just reverse his own infinite series $1 + 2 + 3 + 4 \ldots$ and try to count from the infinite end back to 1; it would obviously only be attempted by a man who has not the faintest understanding of what the problem is. And again: if Herr Dühring states that the infinite series of elapsed time has been counted, he is thereby stating that time has a beginning; for otherwise he would not have been able to start "counting" at all. Once again, therefore, he puts into the argument, as a premise, the thing that he has to prove.

The idea of an infinite series which has been counted, in other words, the world-encompassing Dühringian law of definite number, is therefore a *contradictio in adjecto*,[a] contains within itself a contradiction, and in fact an *absurd* contradiction.

It is clear that an infinity which has an end but no beginning is neither more nor less infinite than that which has a beginning but no end. The slightest dialectical insight should have told Herr Dühring that beginning and end necessarily belong together, like the north pole and the south pole, and that if the end is left out, the beginning just becomes the end—the *one* end which the series has; and vice versa. The whole deception would be impossible but for the mathematical usage of working with infinite series. Because in mathematics it is necessary to start from definite, finite terms in order to reach the indefinite, the infinite, all mathematical series, positive or negative, must start from 1, or they cannot be used for calculation. The abstract requirement of a mathematician is, however, far from being a compulsory law for the world of reality.

For that matter, Herr Dühring will never succeed in conceiving real infinity without contradiction. Infinity *is* a contradiction, and is full of contradictions. From the outset it is a contradiction that an infinity is composed of nothing but finites, and yet this is the case. The limitedness of the material world leads no less to contradictions than its unlimitedness, and every attempt to get over these contradictions leads, as we have seen, to new and worse contradictions. It is just *because* infinity is a contradiction that it is an infinite process, unrolling endlessly in time and in space. The removal of the contradiction would be the end of infinity. Hegel saw this quite correctly, and for that reason treated with well-merited contempt the gentlemen who subtilised over this contradiction.

Let us pass on. So time had a beginning. What was there before this beginning? The universe, which was then in a self-equal, unchanging state. And as in this state no changes succeed one another, the more specialised idea of time transforms itself into the more general idea of *being*. In the first place, we are here not in the least concerned with what ideas change in Herr Dühring's head. The subject at issue is not the *idea of time*, but *real* time, which Herr Dühring cannot rid himself of so cheaply. In the second place, however much the idea of time may convert itself into the more general idea of being, this does not take us one step further. For the basic forms of all being are space and time, and

---

[a] Contradiction in definition.— *Ed.*

being out of time is just as gross an absurdity as being out of space. The Hegelian "being past away non-temporally"[a] and the neo-Schellingian "unpremeditatable being"[b] are rational ideas compared with this being out of time. And for this reason Herr Dühring sets to work very cautiously; actually it is of course time, but of such a kind as cannot really be called time; time, indeed, in itself does not consist of real parts, and is only divided up at will by our mind—only an actual filling of time with distinguishable facts is susceptible of being counted—what the accumulation of empty duration means is quite unimaginable. What this accumulation is supposed to mean is here beside the point; the question is, whether the world, in the state here assumed, has duration, passes through a duration in time. We have long known that we can get nothing by measuring such a duration without content just as we can get nothing by measuring without aim or purpose in empty space; and Hegel, just because of the weariness of such an effort, calls such an infinity *bad.* According to Herr Dühring time exists only through change; change in and through time does not exist. Just because time is different from change, is independent of it, it is possible to measure it by change, for measuring always requires something different from the thing to be measured. And time in which no recognisable changes occur is very far removed from *not* being time; it is rather *pure* time, unaffected by any foreign admixtures, that is, real time, time *as such.* In fact, if we want to grasp the idea of time in all its purity, divorced from all alien and extraneous admixtures, we are compelled to put aside, as not being relevant here, all the various events which occur simultaneously or one after another in time, and in this way to form the idea of a time in which nothing happens. In doing this, therefore, we have not let the concept of time be submerged in the general idea of being, but have thereby for the first time arrived at the pure concept of time.

But all these contradictions and impossibilities are only mere child's play compared with the confusion into which Herr Dühring falls with his self-equal initial state of the world. If the world had ever been in a state in which no change whatever was taking place, how could it pass from this state to alteration? The absolutely unchanging, especially when it has been in this state from eternity, cannot possibly get out of such a state by itself and pass over into

[a] G. W. F. Hegel, *Wissenschaft der Logik,* Book 2: "Das Wesen". In: *Werke,* Bd. 4, p. 3.— *Ed.*

[b] F. Engels, *Schelling and Revelation.* See present edition, Vol. 2, p. 220.— *Ed.*

a state of motion and change. An initial impulse must therefore have come from outside, from outside the universe, an impulse which set it in motion. But as everyone knows, the "initial impulse" is only another expression for God. God and the beyond, which in his world schematism Herr Dühring pretended to have so beautifully dismantled, are both introduced again by him here, sharpened and deepened, into natural philosophy.

Further, Herr Dühring says:

"Where magnitude is attributed to a constant element of being, it will remain unchanged in its determinateness. This holds good ... of matter and mechanical force" [D. Ph. 26].

The first sentence, it may be noted in passing, is a precious example of Herr Dühring's axiomatic-tautological grandiloquence: where magnitude does not change, it remains the same. Therefore the amount of mechanical force which exists in the world remains the same for all eternity. We will overlook the fact that, in so far as this is correct, Descartes already knew and said it in philosophy nearly three hundred years ago[a]; that in natural science the theory of the conservation of energy has held sway for the last twenty years; and that Herr Dühring, in limiting it to *mechanical* force, does not in any way improve on it. But where was the mechanical force at the time of the unchanging state? Herr Dühring obstinately refuses to give us any answer to this question.

Where, Herr Dühring, was the eternally self-equal mechanical force at that time, and what did it put in motion? The reply:

"The original state of the universe, or to put it more plainly, of an unchanging existence of matter which comprised no accumulation of changes in time, is a question which can be spurned only by a mind that sees the acme of wisdom in the self-mutilation of its own generative power" [78-79].

Therefore: either you accept without examination my unchanging original state, or I, Eugen Dühring, the possessor of creative power, will certify you as intellectual eunuchs. That may, of course, deter a good many people. But we, who have already seen some examples of Herr Dühring's generative power, can permit ourselves to leave this genteel abuse unanswered for the moment, and ask once again: But Herr Dühring, if you please, what about that mechanical force?

Herr Dühring at once grows embarrassed.

In actual fact, he stammers, "the absolute identity of that initial extreme state does not in itself provide any principle of transition. But we must remember that at

---

[a] This proposition was the most fully developed in R. Des-Cartes, *Principia Philosophiae*, Pars secunda, XXXVI.— *Ed.*

bottom the position is similar with every new link, however small, in the chain of existence with which we are familiar. So that whoever wants to raise difficulties in the fundamental case now under consideration must take care that he does not allow himself to pass them by on less obvious occasions. Moreover, there exists the possibility of interposing successively graduated intermediate stages, and also a bridge of continuity by which it is possible to move backwards and reach the extinction of the process of change. It is true that from a purely conceptual standpoint this continuity does not help us pass the main difficulty, but to us it is the basic form of all regularity and of every known form of transition in general, so that we are entitled to use it also as a medium between that first equilibrium and the disturbance of it. But if we had conceived the so to speak" (!) "motionless equilibrium on the model of the ideas which are accepted without any particular objection" (!) "in our present-day mechanics, there would be no way of explaining how matter could have reached the process of change." Apart from the mechanics of masses there is, however, we are told, also a transformation of mass movement into the movement of extremely small particles, but as to how this takes place—"for this up to the present we have no general principle at our disposal and consequently should not be surprised if these processes take place somewhat *in the dark*" [79-80, 81].

That is all Herr Dühring has to say. And in fact, we would have to see the acme of wisdom not only in the "self-mutilation of our generative power" [79], but also in blind, implicit faith, if we allowed ourselves to be put off with these really pitiable rank subterfuges and circumlocutions. Herr Dühring admits that absolute identity cannot of itself effect the transition to change. Nor is there any means whereby absolute equilibrium can of itself pass into motion. What is there, then? Three lame, false arguments.

Firstly: it is just as difficult to show the transition from each link, however small, in the chain of existence with which we are familiar, to the next one.—Herr Dühring seems to think his readers are infants. The establishment of individual transitions and connections between the tiniest links in the chain of existence is precisely the content of natural science, and when there is a hitch at some point in its work no one, not even Herr Dühring, thinks of explaining prior motion as having arisen out of nothing, but always only as a transfer, transformation or transmission of some previous motion. But here the issue is admittedly one of accepting motion as having arisen out of immobility, that is, *out of nothing*.

In the second place, we have the "bridge of continuity". From a purely conceptual standpoint, this, to be sure, does not help us over the difficulty, but all the same we are entitled to *use* it as a medium between immobility and motion. Unfortunately the continuity of immobility consists in *not* moving; how therefore it is to produce motion remains more mysterious than ever. And however infinitely small the parts into which Herr Dühring minces his transition from complete non-motion to universal motion, and however long the duration he assigns to it, we have not got a ten-thousandth part of a millimetre further. Without an act of creation we can never get from nothing to something, even if the something were as small as a mathematical differential. The bridge of continuity is therefore not even an asses' bridge [a]; it is passable only for Herr Dühring.

Thirdly: so long as present-day mechanics holds good—and this science, according to Herr Dühring, is one of the most essential levers for the formation of thought—it cannot be explained at all how it is possible to pass from immobility to motion. But the mechanical theory of heat shows us that the movement of masses under certain conditions changes into molecular movement (although here too one motion originates from another motion, but never from immobility); and this, Herr Dühring shyly suggests, may possibly furnish a bridge between the strictly static (in equilibrium) and dynamic (in motion). But these processes take place "somewhat in the dark". And it is in the dark that Herr Dühring leaves us sitting.

This is the point we have reached with all his deepening and sharpening—that we have perpetually gone deeper into ever sharper nonsense, and finally land up where of necessity we had to land up—"in the dark". But this does not abash Herr Dühring much. Right on the next page he has the effrontery to declare that he has

"been able to provide a real content for the idea of self-equal stability directly from the behaviour of matter *and the mechanical forces*" [D. Ph. 82].

And this man describes other people as "charlatans"!

Fortunately, in spite of all this helpless wandering and confusion "in the dark", we are left with one consolation, and this is certainly edifying to the soul:

"The mathematics of the inhabitants of other celestial bodies can rest on no other axioms than our own!" [69].

---

[a] In the original a play on words: *Eselsbrücke* (asses' bridge) means in German also an unauthorised aid in study used by dull-headed or lazy students; a crib or pony.— *Ed.*

VI. PHILOSOPHY OF NATURE. COSMOGONY, PHYSICS, CHEMISTRY

Passing on, we come now to the theories concerning the manner in which the present world came into existence.

A state of universal dispersion of matter, we are told, was the point of departure of the Ionic philosophers, but later, particularly from the time of Kant, the assumption of a primordial nebula played a new role, gravitation and the radiation of heat having been instrumental in the gradual formation of separate solid celestial bodies. The contemporary mechanical theory of heat makes it possible to deduce the earlier states of the universe in a far more definite form. However, "the state of gaseous dispersion can be a starting-point for serious deductions only when it is possible to characterise beforehand more definitely the mechanical system existing in it. Otherwise not only does the idea in fact remain extremely nebulous, but also the original nebula, as the deductions progress, really becomes ever thicker and more impenetrable; ... meanwhile it all still remains in the vagueness and formlessness of an idea of diffusion that cannot be more closely determined", and so "this gaseous universe" provides us with "only an extremely airy conception" [D. Ph. 85-87].

The Kantian theory of the origin of all existing celestial bodies from rotating nebular masses was the greatest advance made by astronomy since Copernicus. For the first time the conception that nature had no history in time began to be shaken. Until then the celestial bodies were believed to have been always, from the very beginning, in the same states and always to have followed the same courses; and even though individual organisms on the various celestial bodies died out, nevertheless genera and species were held to be immutable. It is true that nature was obviously in constant motion, but this motion appeared as an incessant repetition of the same processes. Kant made the first breach in this conception, which corresponded exactly to the metaphysical mode of thought, and he did it in such a scientific way that most of the proofs furnished by him still hold good today. At the same time, the Kantian theory is still, strictly considered, only a hypothesis. But the Copernican world system, too, is still no more than this,[38] and since the spectroscopic proof of the existence of such red-hot gaseous masses in the starry heavens, proof that brooks no contradiction, the scientific opposition to Kant's theory has been silenced. Even Herr Dühring cannot complete his construction of the world without such a nebular stage, but takes his revenge for this by demanding to be shown the mechanical system existing in this nebular stage, and because no one can show him this, he applies all kinds of depreciatory epithets to this nebular stage of the universe. Contemporary science unfortunately cannot describe this system to Herr Dühring's satisfaction. Just as little is it able to answer many other questions. To the question: Why do toads have no tails?—up to now it has only been able to answer: Because they have lost them. But should anyone get excited over that and say that this is to leave the whole question in the vagueness and formlessness of an idea of loss which cannot be determined more closely, and that it is an extremely airy conception, such an application of morality to natural science does not take us one step further. Such expressions of dislike and bad temper can be used always and everywhere, and just for that reason they should never be used anywhere. After all, who is stopping Herr Dühring from himself discovering the mechanical system of the primordial nebula?

Fortunately we now learn that

the Kantian nebular mass "is far from coinciding with a completely identical state of the world medium, or, to put it another way, with the self-equal state of matter" [D. Ph. 87].

It was really fortunate for Kant that he was able to content himself with going back from the existing celestial bodies to the nebular ball, and did not even dream of the self-equal state of matter! It may be remarked in passing that when contemporary natural science describes the Kantian nebular ball as primordial nebula, this, it goes without saying, is only to be understood in a relative sense. It is primordial nebula, on the one hand, in that it is the origin of the existing celestial bodies, and on the other hand because it is the earliest form of matter which we have up to now been able to work back to. This certainly does not exclude but rather implies the supposition that before the nebular stage matter passed through an infinite series of other forms.

Herr Dühring sees his advantage here. Where we, with science, stand still for the time being at what for the time being is deemed primordial nebula, his science of sciences helps him much further back to that

"state of the world medium which cannot be understood either as purely static in the present meaning of the idea, or as dynamic" [87]—

which therefore cannot be understood at all.

"The unity of matter and mechanical force which we call the world medium is what might be termed a logical-real formula for indicating the self-equal state of matter as the prerequisite of all innumerable stages of evolution" [87-88].

We are clearly not by a long shot rid of the self-equal primordial state of matter. Here it is spoken of as the unity of matter and mechanical force, and this as a logical-real formula, etc. Hence, as soon as the unity of matter and mechanical force comes to an end, motion begins.

The logical-real formula is nothing but a lame attempt to make the Hegelian categories "in itself" [*Ansich*] and "for itself" [*Fürsich*] usable in the philosophy of reality. With Hegel, "in itself" covers the original identity of the hidden, undeveloped contradictions within a thing, a process or an idea; and "for itself" contains the distinction and separation of these hidden elements and the starting-point of their conflict. We are therefore to think of the motionless primordial state as the unity of matter and mechanical force, and of the transition to movement as their separation and opposition. What we have gained by this is not any proof of the reality of that fantastic primordial state, but only the fact that it is possible to bring this state under the Hegelian category of "in itself", and its equally fantastic termination under the category of "for itself". Hegel help us!

Matter, Herr Dühring says, is the bearer of all reality; accordingly, there can be no mechanical force apart from matter. Mechanical force is furthermore a state of matter [See D. Ph. 73]. In the original state, when nothing happened, matter and its state, mechanical force, were one. Afterwards, when something began to happen, this state must apparently have become different from matter. So we are to let ourselves be dismissed with these mystical phrases and with the assurance that the self-equal state was neither static nor dynamic, neither in equilibrium nor in motion. We still do not know where mechanical force was in that state, and how we are to get from absolute immobility to motion without an impulse from outside, that is, without God.

The materialists before Herr Dühring spoke of matter and motion. He reduces motion to mechanical force as its supposed basic form, and thereby makes it impossible for himself to understand the real connection between matter and motion, which moreover was also unclear to all former materialists. And yet it is simple enough. *Motion is the mode of existence of matter.* Never anywhere has there been matter without motion, nor can there be. Motion in cosmic space, mechanical motion of smaller masses on the various celestial bodies, the vibration of molecules as heat or as electrical or magnetic currents, chemical disintegration and combination, organic life—at each given moment each individual atom of matter in the world is in one or other of these forms of motion, or in several forms at once. All rest, all equilibrium, is only relative, only has meaning in relation to one or other definite form of motion. On the earth, for example, a body may be in mechanical equilibrium, may be mechanically at rest; but this in no way prevents it from participating in the motion of the earth and in that of the whole solar system, just as little as it prevents its most minute physical particles from carrying out the vibrations determined by its temperature, or its atoms from passing through a chemical process. Matter without motion is just as inconceivable as motion without matter. Motion is therefore as uncreatable and indestructible as matter itself; as the older philosophy (Descartes) expressed it, the quantity of motion existing in the world is always the same. Motion therefore cannot be created; it can only be transferred. When motion is transferred from one body to another, it may be regarded, in so far as it transfers itself, is active, as the cause of motion, in so far as the latter is transferred, is passive. We call this active motion *force*, and the passive, the *manifestation of force*. Hence it is as clear as daylight that a force is as great as its manifestation, because in fact the *same* motion takes place in both.

A motionless state of matter is therefore one of the most empty and nonsensical of ideas—a "delirious fantasy" of the purest water. In order to arrive at such an idea it is necessary to conceive the relative mechanical equilibrium, a state in which a body on the earth may be, as absolute rest, and then to extend this equilibrium over the whole universe. This is certainly made easier if universal motion is reduced to purely mechanical force. And the restriction of motion to purely mechanical force has the further advantage that a force can be conceived as at rest, as tied up, and therefore for the moment inoperative. For if, as is very often the case, the transfer of a motion is a somewhat complex process containing a number of intermediate links, it is possible to postpone the actual transmission to any moment desired by omitting the last link in the chain. This is the case, for instance, if a man loads a gun and postpones the moment when, by the pulling of the trigger, the discharge, the transfer of the motion set free by the combustion of the powder, takes place. It is therefore possible to imagine that during its motionless, self-equal state, matter was loaded with force, and this, if anything at all, seems to be what Herr Dühring understands by the unity of matter and mechanical force. This conception is nonsensical, because it transfers to the entire universe a state as absolute, which by its nature is relative and therefore can only affect *a part* of matter at any one time. Even if we overlook this point, the difficulty still remains: first, how did the world come to be loaded, since nowadays guns do not load themselves; and second, whose finger was it then that pulled the trigger? We may turn and twist as much as we like, but under Herr Dühring's guidance we always come back again to—the finger of God.

From astronomy our philosopher of reality passes on to mechanics and physics, and voices the lament that the mechanical theory of heat has not, in the generation since its discovery, been materially advanced beyond the point to which Robert Mayer had himself developed it, bit by bit. Apart from this, the whole business is still very obscure;

we must "always remember that in the states of motion of matter, static relations are also present, and that these latter are not measurable by the mechanical work ... if previously we described nature as a great worker, and if we now construe this expression strictly, we must furthermore add that the self-equal states and static relations do not represent mechanical work. So once again we miss the bridge from the static to the dynamic, and if so-called latent heat has up to now remained a stumbling-block for the theory, we must recognise a defect in this too, which can least be denied in its cosmic applications" [D. Ph. 90].

This whole oracular discourse is once again nothing but the outpouring of a bad conscience, which is very well aware that with its creation of motion out of absolute immobility it got irretrievably stuck in the mud, but is nevertheless ashamed to appeal to the only possible saviour, namely, the creator of heaven and earth. If the bridge from the static to the dynamic, from equilibrium to motion, cannot be found even in mechanics, including the mechanics of heat, under what obligations is Herr Dühring to find the bridge from his motionless state to motion? That would be a fortunate way for him to get out of his plight.

In ordinary mechanics the bridge from the static to the dynamic is—the external impulse. If a stone weighing a hundredweight is raised from the ground ten yards into the air and is freely suspended in such a way that it remains hanging there in a self-equal state and in a condition of rest, it would be necessary to have an audience of sucklings to be able to maintain that the present position of this body does not represent any mechanical work, or that its distance from its previous position is not measurable by mechanical work. Any passer-by will easily explain to Herr Dühring that the stone did not rise of itself to the rope, and any manual of mechanics will tell him that if he lets the stone fall again it performs in falling just as much mechanical work as was necessary to raise it the ten yards in the air. Even the simple fact that the stone is hanging up there represents mechanical work, for if it remains hanging long enough the rope breaks, as soon as chemical decomposition makes it no longer strong enough to bear the weight of the stone. But it is to such simple basic forms, to use Herr Dühring's language, that all mechanical processes can be reduced, and the engineer is still to be born who cannot find the bridge from the static to the dynamic, so long as he has at his disposal a sufficient external impulse.

To be sure, it is a hard nut and a bitter pill for our metaphysician that motion should find its measure in its opposite, in rest. That is indeed a crying contradiction, and every *contradiction,* according to Herr Dühring, is *nonsense* [D. Ph. 30]. It is none the less a fact that a suspended stone represents a definite quantity of mechanical motion, which is measurable exactly by the stone's weight and its distance from the ground, and may be used in various ways at will, for example, by its direct fall, by sliding down an inclined plane, or by turning a shaft. The same is true of a loaded gun. From the dialectical standpoint, the possibility of expressing motion in its opposite, in rest, presents absolutely no difficulty. From the dialectical standpoint the whole antithesis, as we have seen, is only relative; there is no such thing as absolute rest, unconditional equilibrium. Each separate movement strives towards equilibrium, and the motion as a whole puts an end again to the equilibrium. When therefore rest and equilibrium occur they are the result of limited motion, and it is self-evident that this motion is measurable by its result, can be expressed in it, and can be restored out of it again in one form or another. But Herr Dühring cannot allow himself to be satisfied with such a simple presentation of the matter. As a good metaphysician he first tears open, between motion and equilibrium, a yawning gulf which does not exist in reality and is then surprised that he cannot find any bridge across this self-fabricated gulf. He might just as well mount his metaphysical Rosinante and chase the Kantian "thing-in-itself"; for it is that and nothing else which in the last analysis is hiding behind this undiscoverable bridge.

But what about the mechanical theory of heat and the tied-up or latent heat which "has remained a stumbling-block" for this theory?

If, under normal atmospheric pressure, a pound of ice at the temperature of the freezing point is transformed by heat into a pound of water of the same temperature, a quantity of heat disappears which would be sufficient to warm the same pound of water from 0° to 79.4° C, or to raise the temperature of 79.4 pounds of water by one degree. If this pound of water is heated to boiling point, that is, to 100° C, and is then transformed into steam of 100° C, the amount of heat that disappears, by the time the last of the water has changed into steam, is almost seven times greater, sufficient to raise the temperature of 537.2 pounds of water by one degree. The heat that disappears is called *tied-up*. If, by cooling, the steam is again transformed into water, and the water, in its turn, into ice, the same quantity of heat as was previously tied up is now again set *free*, i.e., can be felt and measured as heat. This setting free of heat on the condensation of steam and the freezing of water is the reason why steam, when cooled to 100°, is only gradually transformed into water, and why a mass of water of freezing point temperature is only very gradually transformed into ice. These are the facts. The question is, what happens to the heat while it is tied up?

The mechanical theory of heat, according to which heat consists in a greater or lesser vibration, depending on the temperature and state of aggregation, of the smallest physically active particles (molecules) of a body—a vibration which under certain conditions can change into any other form of motion—explains that the heat that has disappeared has done work, has been transformed into work. When ice melts, the close and firm connection between the individual molecules is broken, and transformed into a loose juxtaposition; when water at boiling point becomes steam a state is reached in which the individual molecules no longer have any noticeable influence on one another, and under the influence of heat even fly apart in all directions. It is clear that the single molecules of a body are endowed with far greater energy in the gaseous state than they are in the fluid state, and in the fluid state again more than in the solid state. The tied-up heat, therefore, has not disappeared; it has merely been transformed, and has assumed the form of molecular tension. As soon as the condition under which the separate molecules are able to maintain their absolute or relative freedom in regard to one another ceases to exist—that is, as soon as the temperature falls below the minimum of 100° or 0°, as the case may be, this tension relaxes, the molecules again press towards each other with the same force with which they had previously flown apart; and this force disappears, but only to reappear as heat, and as precisely the same quantity of heat as had previously been tied up. This explanation is of course a hypothesis, as is the whole mechanical theory of heat, inasmuch as no one has up to now ever seen a molecule, not to mention one in vibration. Just for this reason it is certain to be full of defects as this still very young theory is as a whole, but it can at least explain what happens without in any way coming into conflict with the indestructibility and uncreatability of motion, and it is even able to account for the whereabouts of heat during its transformations. Latent, or tied-up, heat is therefore in no way a stumbling-block for the mechanical theory of heat. On the contrary, this theory provides the first rational explanation of what takes place, and it involves no stumbling-block except in so far as physicists continue to describe heat which has been transformed into another form of molecular energy by means of the term "tied-up", which has become obsolete and unsuitable.

The self-equal states and conditions of rest in the solid, in the liquid and in the gaseous state of aggregation therefore represent, to be sure, mechanical work, in so far as mechanical work is the measure of heat. Both the solid crust of the earth and the water of the ocean, in their present aggregate states, represent a definite quantity of heat set free, to which of course corresponds an equally definite quantity of mechanical force. In the transition of the gaseous ball, from which the earth has developed, into the liquid and subsequently into the largely solid aggregate state, a definite quantity of molecular energy was radiated as heat into space. The difficulty about which Herr Dühring mumbles in his mysterious manner therefore does not exist, and though even in applying the theory cosmically we may come up against defects and gaps—which must be attributed to our imperfect means of knowledge—we nowhere come up against theoretically insuperable obstacles. The bridge from the static to the dynamic is here, too, the external impulse—the cooling or heating brought about by other bodies acting on an object which is in a state of equilibrium. The further we explore this natural philosophy of Dühring's, the more impossible appear all attempts to explain motion out of immobility or to find the bridge over which the purely static, the resting, can *by itself* pass to the dynamic, to motion.

With this we have fortunately rid ourselves for a time of the self-equal primordial state. Herr Dühring passes on to chemistry, and takes the opportunity to reveal to us three laws of nature's inertness which have so far been discovered by his philosophy of reality, viz.:

(1) the quantity of all matter in general, (2) that of the simple (chemical) elements, and (3) that of mechanical force are constant [D. Ph. 97].

Hence: the uncreatability and indestructibility of matter, and also of its simple component parts, in so far as it is made up of such, as well as the uncreatability and indestructibility of motion—these old facts known the world over and expressed most inadequately—is the only positive thing which Herr Dühring can provide us with as a result of his natural philosophy of the inorganic world. We knew all this long ago. But what we did not know was that they were "laws of inertness" and as such "schematic properties of the system of things". We are witnessing a repetition of what happened above to Kant[a]: Herr Dühring picks up some old familiar quip, sticks a Dühring label on it, and calls the result:

"from the ground up original conclusions and views ... system-creating ideas [525] ... deep-rooted science" [200, 219; D. C. 555-56].

But the need not by any means despair on this account. Whatever defects even the most deep-rooted science and the best-ordered society may have, Herr Dühring can at any rate assert one thing with confidence:

"The amount of gold existing in the universe must at all times have been the same, and it can have increased or diminished just as little as can matter in general" [D. Ph. 96].

Unfortunately Herr Dühring does not tell us what we can buy with this "existing gold".

VII. PHILOSOPHY OF NATURE. THE ORGANIC WORLD

"A single and uniform ladder of intermediate steps leads from the mechanics of pressure and impact to the linking together of sensations and ideas" [D. Ph. 104].

With this assurance Herr Dühring saves himself the trouble of saying anything further about the origin of life, although it might reasonably have been expected that a thinker who had traced the evolution of the world back to its self-equal state, and is so much at home on other celestial bodies, would have known exactly what's what also on this point. For the rest, however, the assurance he gives us is only half right unless it is completed by the Hegelian nodal line of measure relations which has already been mentioned.[b] In spite of all gradualness, the transition from one form of motion to another always remains a leap, a decisive change. This is true of the transition from the mechanics of celestial bodies to that of smaller masses on a particular celestial body; it is equally true of the transition from the mechanics of masses to the

---

[a] See this volume, pp. 44-46.— Ed.
[b] Ibid., pp. 42-43.— Ed.

mechanics of molecules—including the forms of motion investigated in physics proper: heat, light, electricity, magnetism. In the
same way, the transition from the physics of molecules to the
physics of atoms—chemistry—in turn involves a decided leap;
and this is even more clearly the case in the transition from
ordinary chemical action to the chemism of albumen which we call
life.[39] Then within the sphere of life the leaps become ever more
infrequent and imperceptible.—Once again, therefore, it is Hegel
who has to correct Herr Dühring.

The concept of purpose provides Herr Dühring with a
conceptual transition to the organic world. Once again, this is
borrowed from Hegel, who in his *Logic*—the Doctrine of the
Notion—makes the transition from chemism to life by means of
teleology, or the science of purpose. Wherever we look in Herr
Dühring we run into a Hegelian "crudity", which he quite
unblushingly dishes out to us as his own deep-rooted science. It
would take us too far afield to investigate here the extent to which
it is legitimate and appropriate to apply the ideas of means and
end to the organic world. In any case, even the application of the
Hegelian "inner purpose"—i.e., a purpose which is not imported
into nature by some third party acting purposively, such as the
wisdom of providence, but lies in the necessity of the thing
itself—constantly leads people who are not well versed in
philosophy to thoughtlessly ascribing to nature conscious and
purposive activity. That same Herr Dühring who is filled with
boundless moral indignation at the slightest "spiritistic" tendency
in other people assures us

"with certainty that the instinctive sensations were primarily created for the sake of
the satisfaction involved in their activity" [D. Ph. 158].

He tells us that poor nature

"is obliged incessantly to maintain order in the world of objects" [159] and in
doing so she has to settle more than one business "which requires more subtlety on
the part of nature than is usually credited to her" [165]. But nature not only *knows*
why she does one thing or another; she has not only to perform the duties of a
housemaid, she not only possesses subtlety, in itself a pretty good accomplishment
in subjective conscious thought; she has also a will. For what the instincts do in
addition, incidentally fulfilling real natural functions such as nutrition, propagation, etc., "we should not regard as directly but only indirectly *willed*" [169].

So we have arrived at a consciously thinking and acting nature,
and are thus already standing on the "bridge"—not indeed from
the static to the dynamic, but from pantheism to deism. Or is Herr
Dühring perhaps just for once indulging a little in "natural-
philosophical semi-poetry"?

Impossible! All that our philosopher of reality can tell us of organic nature is restricted to the fight against this natural-philosophical semi-poetry, against "charlatanism with its frivolous superficialities and pseudo-scientific mystifications", against the "poetising features" [109] of *Darwinism*.

The main reproach levelled against Darwin is that he transfer-red the Malthusian population theory from political economy to natural science, that he was held captive by the ideas of an animal breeder, that in his theory of the struggle for existence he pursued unscientific semi-poetry, and that the whole of Darwin-ism, after deducting what had been borrowed from Lamarck, is a piece of brutality directed against humanity.

Darwin brought back from his scientific travels the view that plant and animal species are not constant but subject to variation. In order to follow up this idea after his return home there was no better field available than that of the breeding of animals and plants. It is precisely in this field that England is the classical country; the achievements of other countries, for example Germany, fall far short of what England has achieved in this connection. Moreover, most of these successes have been won during the last hundred years, so that there is very little difficulty in establishing the facts. Darwin found that this breeding produced artificially, among animals and plants of the same species, differences greater than those found in what are generally recognised as different species. Thus was established on the one hand the variability of species up to a certain point, and on the other the possibility of a common ancestry for organisms with different specific characteristics. Darwin then investigated whether there were not possibly causes in nature which—without the conscious intention of the breeder—would nevertheless in the long run produce in living organisms changes similar to those produced by artificial selection. He discovered these causes in the disproportion between the immense number of germs created by nature and the insignificant number of organisms which actually attain maturity. But as each germ strives to develop, there necessarily arises a struggle for existence which manifests itself not merely as direct bodily combat or devouring, but also as a struggle for space and light, even in the case of plants. And it is evident that in this struggle those individuals which have some individual peculiarity, however insignificant, that gives them an advantage in the struggle for existence will have the best prospect of reaching maturity and propagating themselves. These individual peculiarities have thus the tendency to descend by heredity, and when they occur among many individuals of the same species, to become more pronounced through accumulated heredity in the direction once taken; while those individuals which do not possess these peculiarities succumb more easily in the struggle for existence and gradually disappear. In this way a species is altered through natural selection, through the survival of the fittest.

Against this Darwinian theory Herr Dühring now says that the origin of the idea of the struggle for existence, as, he claims, Darwin himself admitted, has to be sought in a generalisation of the views of the economist and theoretician of population, Malthus, and that the idea therefore suffers from all the defects inherent in the priestly Malthusian ideas of over-population [D. Ph. 101].—Now Darwin would not dream of saying that the *origin* of the idea of the struggle for existence is to be found in Malthus. He only says that his theory of the struggle for existence is the theory of Malthus applied to the animal and plant world as a whole. However great the blunder made by Darwin in accepting the Malthusian theory so naively and uncritically, nevertheless anyone can see at the first glance that no Malthusian spectacles are required to perceive the struggle for existence in nature—the contradiction between the countless host of germs which nature so lavishly produces and the small number of those which ever reach maturity, a contradiction which in fact for the most part finds its solution in a struggle for existence—often of extreme cruelty. And just as the law of wages has maintained its validity even after the Malthusian arguments on which Ricardo based it have long been consigned to oblivion, so likewise the struggle for existence can take place in nature, even without any Malthusian interpretation. For that matter, the organisms of nature also have their laws of population, which have been left practically uninvestigated, although their establishment would be of decisive importance for the theory of the evolution of species. But who was it that lent decisive impetus to work in this direction too? No other than Darwin.

Herr Dühring carefully avoids an examination of this positive side of the question. Instead, the struggle for existence is arraigned again and again. It is obvious, according to him, that there can be no talk of a struggle for existence among unconscious plants and good-natured plant-eaters:

"in the precise and definite sense the struggle for existence is found in the realm of brutality to the extent that animals live on prey and its devourment" [118].

And after he has reduced the idea of the struggle for existence to these narrow limits he can give full vent to his indignation at the brutality of this idea, which he himself has restricted to brutality. But this moral indignation only rebounds upon Herr Dühring himself, who is indeed the only author of the struggle for existence in this limited conception and is therefore solely responsible for it. It is consequently not Darwin who

"sought the laws and understanding of all nature's actions in the kingdom of the brutes" [117],—

Darwin had in fact expressly included the whole of organic nature in the struggle—but an imaginary bugbear dressed up by Herr Dühring himself. The *name*: the struggle for existence, can for that matter be willingly sacrificed to Herr Dühring's highly moral indignation. That the *fact* exists also among plants can be demonstrated to him by every meadow, every cornfield, every wood; and the question at issue is not what it is to be called, whether "struggle for existence" or "lack of conditions of life and mechanical effects" [118], but how this fact influences the preservation or variation of species. On this point Herr Dühring maintains an obstinate and self-equal silence. Therefore for the time being everything may remain as it was in natural selection.

But Darwinism "produces its transformations and differences out of nothing" [114].

It is true that Darwin, when considering natural selection, leaves out of account the *causes* which have produced the alterations in separate individuals, and deals in the first place with the way in which such individual deviations gradually become the characteristics of a race, variety or species. To Darwin it was of less immediate importance to discover these causes—which up to the present are in part absolutely unknown, and in part can only be stated in quite general terms—than to find a rational form in which their effects become fixed, acquire permanent significance. It is true that in doing this Darwin attributed to his discovery too wide a field of action, made it the sole agent in the alteration of species and neglected the causes of the repeated individual variations, concentrating rather on the form in which these variations become general; but this is a mistake which he shares with most other people who make any real advance. Moreover, if Darwin produces his individual transformations out of nothing, and in so doing applies exclusively "the wisdom of the breeder" [125], the breeder, too, must produce *out of nothing* his transformations in animal and plant forms which are not merely imaginary but real. But once again, the man who gave the impetus to investigate how exactly these transformations and differences arise is no other than Darwin.

In recent times the idea of natural selection was extended, particularly by Haeckel, and the variation of species conceived as a result of the mutual interaction of adaptation and heredity, in which process adaptation is taken as the factor which produces variations, and heredity as the preserving factor.[a] This is also not regarded as satisfactory by Herr Dühring.

"Real adaptation to conditions of life which are offered or withheld by nature presupposes impulses and actions determined by ideas. Otherwise the adaptation is only apparent, and the causality operative thereupon does not rise above the low grades of the physical, chemical and plant-physiological" [D. Ph. 115].

Once again it is the name which makes Herr Dühring angry. But whatever name he may give to the process, the question here is whether variations in the species of organisms are produced through such processes or not. And again Herr Dühring gives no answer.

"If, in growing, a plant takes the path along which it will receive most light, this effect of the stimulus is nothing but a combination of physical forces and chemical agents, and any attempt to describe it as adaptation—not metaphorically, but in the strict sense of the word—must introduce a *spiritistic* confusion into the concepts" [115].

Such is the severity meted out to others by the very man who knows exactly by whose *will* nature does one thing or another, who speaks of nature's *subtlety* and even of her *will*! Spiritistic confusion, yes—but where, in Haeckel or in Herr Dühring?

And not only spiritistic, but also logical confusion. We saw that Herr Dühring insists with might and main on establishing the validity in nature of the concept of purpose:

"The relation between means and end does not in the least presuppose a conscious intention" [102].

What, then, is adaptation without conscious intention, without the mediation of ideas, which he so zealously opposes, if not such unconscious purposive activity?

If therefore tree-frogs and leaf-eating insects are green, desert animals sandy-yellow, and animals of the polar regions mainly

---

[a] See E. Haeckel, *Natürliche Schöpfungsgeschichte,* p. 182 ff. On adaptation and heredity see this volume, pp. 582-83, 600-01.— *Ed.*

snow-white in colour, they have certainly not adopted these colours on purpose or in conformity with any ideas; on the contrary, the colours can only be explained on the basis of physical forces and chemical agents. And yet it cannot be denied that these animals, because of those colours, are purposively *adapted* to the environment in which they live, in that they have become far less visible to their enemies. In just the same way the organs with which certain plants seize and devour insects alighting on them are adapted to this action, and even purposively adapted. Consequently, if Herr Dühring insists that this adaptation must be effected through ideas, he as much as says, only in other words, that purposive activity must also be brought about through ideas, must be conscious and intentional. And this brings us, as is usually the case in his philosophy of reality, to a purposive creator, to God.

"An explanation of this kind used to be called deism, and was not thought much of"—Herr Dühring tells us—"but on this matter, too, views now seem to have been reversed" [111].

From adaptation we now pass on to heredity. Here likewise, according to Herr Dühring, Darwinism is completely on the wrong track. The whole organic world, Darwin is said to have asserted, descended from one primordial being, is so to speak the progeny of one single being. Dühring states that, in Darwin's view, there is no such thing as the independent parallel lines of homogeneous products of nature unless mediated by common descent; and that therefore Darwin and his retrospectively directed views had perforce to come to an end at the point where the thread of begetting, or other form of propagation, breaks off [111].

The assertion that Darwin traced all existing organisms back to *one* primordial being is, to put it politely, a product of Herr Dühring's "own free creation and imagination" [43]. Darwin expressly says on the last page but one of his *Origin of Species*,[a] sixth edition, that he regards

"all beings not as special creations, but as the lineal descendants *of some few beings*".[b]

And Haeckel even goes considerably further, assuming

"a quite independent stock for the vegetable kingdom, and a second for the animal kingdom", and between the two "a number of independent stocks of Protista, each

---

  [a] The title is given in English in the manuscript.— *Ed.*
  [b] Ch. Darwin, *The Origin of Species by Means of Natural Selection, or the Preservation of Favoured Races in the Struggle for Life*, p. 428. Italics by Engels.— *Ed.*

of which, quite independently of the former, has developed out of one special archegone of the moneron type" [40] (*Schöpfungsgeschichte,* p. 397).[a]

This primordial being was only invented by Dühring in order to bring it into as great disrepute as possible by drawing a parallel with the primordial Jew [D. Ph. 110] Adam; and in this he—that is to say, Herr Dühring—suffers the misfortune of not having the faintest idea that this primordial Jew had been shown by Smith's Assyrian discoveries [41] to have been a primordial Semite, and that the whole biblical history of creation and the flood turns out to be a part of the old heathen religious myths which the Jew have in common with the Babylonians, Chaldeans and Assyrians.

It is certainly a bitter reproach against Darwin, and one for which he has no defence, that he comes to an end at once at the point where the thread of descent breaks off. Unfortunately it is a reproach which has been earned by the whole of our natural science. Where the thread of descent breaks off for it, it "ends". It has not yet succeeded in producing organic beings without descent from others; indeed, it has not yet succeeded even in producing simple protoplasm or other albuminous bodies out of chemical elements. With regard to the origin of life, therefore, up to the present, natural science is only able to say with certainty that it must have been the result of chemical action. However, perhaps the philosophy of reality is in a position to give some help on this point as it has at its disposal independent parallel lines of products of nature not mediated by common descent. How can these have come into existence? By spontaneous generation? But up to now even the most audacious advocates of spontaneous generation have not claimed that this produced anything but bacteria, embryonic fungi and other very primitive organisms—no insects, fishes, birds or mammals. But if these homogeneous products of nature—organic, of course, as here we are only dealing with these—are not connected by descent, they or each of their ancestors must, at the point "where the thread of descent breaks off", have been put into the world by a separate act of creation. So we arrive once again at a creator and at what is called deism.

Herr Dühring further declares that it was very superficial on Darwin's part

"to make the mere act of the sexual composition of properties the fundamental principle of the origin of these properties" [116].

---

[a] E. Haeckel, *Natürliche Schöpfungsgeschichte,* p. 397.— *Ed.*

This is another free creation and imagination of our deep-rooted philosopher. Darwin definitely states the opposite: the expression natural selection only implies the *preservation* of variations, not their origin (p. 63). This new imputation to Darwin of things he never said nevertheless helps us to grasp the following depth of Dühringian mentality:

"If some principle of independent variation had been found in the inner schematism of generation, this idea would have been quite rational; for it is a natural idea to combine the principle of universal genesis with that of sexual propagation into a unity, and to regard so-called spontaneous generation, from a higher standpoint, not as the absolute antithesis of reproduction but just as a production" [116].

And the man who can write such rubbish is not ashamed to reproach Hegel for his "jargon" [D. K. G. 491]!

But enough of the peevish, contradictory grumbling and nagging through which Herr Dühring gives vent to his anger at the colossal impetus which natural science owes to the driving force of the Darwinian theory. Neither Darwin nor his followers among naturalists ever think of belittling in any way the great services rendered by Lamarck; in fact, they are the very people who first put him up again on his pedestal. But we must not overlook the fact that in Lamarck's time science was as yet far from being in possession of sufficient material to have enabled it to answer the question of the origin of species except in an anticipatory way, prophetically, as it were. In addition to the enormous mass of material, both of descriptive and anatomical botany and zoology, which has accumulated in the intervening period, two completely new sciences have arisen since Lamarck's time, and these are of decisive importance on this question: research into the development of plant and animal germs (embryology) and research into the organic remains preserved in the various strata of the earth's surface (palaeontology). There is in fact a peculiar correspondence between the gradual development of organic germs into mature organisms and the succession of plants and animals following each other in the history of the earth. And it is precisely this correspondence which has given the theory of evolution its most secure basis. The theory of evolution itself is however still in a very early stage, and it therefore cannot be doubted that further research will greatly modify our present conceptions, including strictly Darwinian ones, of the process of the evolution of species.

What, of a positive character, has the philosophy of reality to tell us concerning the evolution of organic life?

"The ... variability of species is a presupposition which can be accepted"
[D. Ph. 115]. But alongside it there hold also "the independent parallel lines of
homogeneous products of nature, not mediated by common descent" [111].

From this we are apparently to infer that the heterogeneous
products of nature, i.e., the species which show variations, descend
from each other but not so the homogeneous products. But this is
not altogether correct either; for even with species which show
variations,

"mediation by common descent is on the contrary quite a secondary act of nature"
[114].

So we get common descent after all, but only "second class". We
must rejoice that after Herr Dühring has attributed so much to it
that is evil and obscure, we nevertheless find it in the end
readmitted by the backdoor. It is the same with natural selection,
for after all his moral indignation over the struggle for existence
through which natural selection operates we suddenly read:

"The deeper basis of the constitution of organisms is thus to be sought in the
conditions of life and cosmic relations, while the natural selection emphasised by
Darwin can only come in as a secondary factor" [115].

So we get natural selection after all, though only second class;
and along with natural selection also the struggle,for existence,
and with that also the priestly Malthusian overpopulation! That is
all, and for the rest Herr Dühring refers us to Lamarck.
In conclusion he warns us against the misuse of the terms
metamorphosis and development. Metamorphosis, he maintains, is
an unclear concept [112], and the concept of development is
permissible only in so far as laws of development can be really
established [126]. In place of both these terms we should use the
term "composition" [114], and then everything would be all right.
It is the same old story over again: things remain as they were,
and Herr Dühring is quite satisfied as soon as we just alter the
names. When we speak of the development of the chicken in the
egg we are creating confusion, for we are able to prove the laws of
development only in an incomplete way. But if we speak of its
"composition" everything becomes clear. We shall therefore no
longer say: This child is developing finely but: It is composing
itself magnificently. We can congratulate Herr Dühring on being a
worthy peer of the author of the *Nibelungenring*[a] not only in his
noble self-esteem but also in his capacity of composer of the
future.[42]

---

[a] R. Wagner.— *Ed.*

VIII. PHILOSOPHY OF NATURE. THE ORGANIC WORLD

(Conclusion)

"Ponder ... what positive knowledge is required to equip our section on natural philosophy with all its scientific premises. Its basis is provided firstly by all the fundamental achievements of mathematics, and then the principal propositions established by exact science in mechanics, physics and chemistry, as well as the general conclusions of natural science in physiology, zoology and similar branches of inquiry" [D. Ph. 517].

Such is the confidence and assurance with which Herr Dühring speaks of the mathematical and naturalistic erudition of Herr Dühring. It is impossible to detect from the meagre section concerned, and still less from its even more paltry conclusions, what deep-rooted positive knowledge lies behind them. In any case, in order to create the Dühring oracle on physics and chemistry, it is not necessary to know any more of physics than the equation which expresses the mechanical equivalent of heat, or any more of chemistry than that all bodies can be divided into elements and combinations of elements. Moreover, a person who can talk of "gravitating atoms" [81], as Herr Dühring does (p. 131) [D. Ph.], only proves that he is completely "in the dark" as to the difference between atoms and molecules. As is well known, it is only chemical action, and not gravitation or other mechanical or physical forms of motion, that is explained by atoms. And if anyone should read as far as the chapter on organic nature, with its vacuous, self-contradictory and, at the decisive point, oracularly senseless meandering verbiage, and its absolutely futile final conclusion, he will not be able to avoid forming the opinion, from the very start, that Herr Dühring is here speaking of things of which he knows remarkably little. This opinion becomes absolute certainty when the reader reaches his suggestion that in the science of organic beings (biology) the term composition should be used instead of development [114]. The person who can put forward such a suggestion shows that he has not the faintest suspicion of the formation of organic bodies.

All organic bodies, except the very lowest, consist of cells, small granules of albumen which are only visible when considerably magnified, with a nucleus inside. As a rule the cells also develop an outer membrane and the contents are then more or less fluid. The lowest cellular bodies consist of a single cell; the immense majority of organic beings are multi-cellular, congruous complexes of many cells which in lower organisms remain of a homogeneous type, but in higher organisms develop more and more varied forms, groupings and functions. In the human body, for example, bones, muscles, nerves, tendons, ligaments, cartilages, skin, in a word, all tissues are either composed of cells or originated from them. But in all organic cellular structure, from the amoeba, which is a simple and most of the time skinless albuminous particle with a nucleus inside, up to man, and from the tiniest unicellular desmids up to the most highly developed plant, the manner in which the cells multiply is the same: by fission. The cell nucleus first becomes constricted in the middle, the constriction separating the two halves of the nucleus gets more and more pronounced, and at last they separate from each other and form two cell nuclei. The same process takes place in the cell itself; each of the two nuclei becomes the centre of an accumulation of cellular substance, linked to the other by a strip which is steadily growing narrower, until at last the two separate from each other and continue to exist as independent cells. Through such repeated cell fission the whole animal is gradually developed in full out of the embryonal vesicle of the animal egg, after it has been fertilised, and the replacement of used-up tissues is effected in the same way in the adult animal. To call such a process composition, and to say that to describe it as development is "pure imagination" [D. Ph. 126], certainly indicates a person who—however difficult this may be to believe at the present day—knows absolutely nothing of this process; here it is precisely and *exclusively* development that is going on, and indeed development in the most literal sense, and composition has absolutely nothing to do with it!

Later on we shall have something more to say about what Herr Dühring understands in general by life. In particular his conception of life is as follows:

"The inorganic world too is a system of self-executing impulses; but it is only at the point where there begins real differentiation, with the circulation of substances through special channels from one internal point and according to a germ-scheme transmissible to a smaller structure, that we may venture to speak of real life in the narrower and stricter sense" [141].

This sentence is, in the narrower and stricter sense, a system of self-executing impulses (whatever they may be) of nonsense, even apart from its hopelessly confused grammar. If life first begins where real differentiation commences, we must declare that the whole Haeckelian kingdom of Protista and perhaps much else are dead, depending on the meaning we attach to the idea of differentiation. If life first begins when this differentiation can be transmitted through a smaller germ-scheme, then at least all organisms up to and including unicellular ones cannot be regarded as living. If the circulation of substances through special channels is the hallmark of life, then, in addition to the foregoing, we must also strike from the ranks of the living the whole of the higher class of the Coelenterata (excepting however the Medusae), that is, all polyps and other zoophytes.[43] If the circulation of substances through special channels from one internal point is the essential hallmark of life, then we must declare that all those animals which have no heart and those which have more than one heart are dead. Under this heading would fall, in addition to those already enumerated, all worms, starfish and rotifers (Annuloida and Annulosa, Huxley's classification[44]), a section of the Crustacea (lobsters), and finally even a vertebrate animal, the lancelet (the Amphioxus). And moreover all plants.

In undertaking, therefore, to define real life in the narrower and stricter sense, Herr Dühring gives us four characteristics of life which totally contradict one another, one of which condemns to eternal death not only the whole vegetable kingdom but also about half the animal kingdom. Really no one can say that he misled us when he promised us "from the ground up original conclusions and views" [525]!

Another passage runs:

"In nature, too, one simple type is the basis of all organisms, from the lowest to the highest", and this type is "fully and completely present in its general essence even in the most subordinate impulse of the most undeveloped plant" [305].

This statement is again "full and complete" nonsense. The most simple type found in the whole of organic nature is the cell; and it certainly is the basis of the higher organisms. On the other hand, among the lowest organisms there are many which are far below the cell—the protamoeba, a simple albuminous particle without any differentiation whatever, and a whole series of other monera and all bladder seaweeds (Siphoneae). All of these are linked with the higher organisms only by the fact that their essential component is albumen and that they consequently perform functions of albumen, i.e., live and die.

Herr Dühring further tells us:

"Physiologically, sensation is bound up with the presence of some kind of nerve apparatus, however simple. It is therefore characteristic of all animal structures that they are capable of sensation, i.e., of a subjectively conscious awareness of their states. The sharp boundary line between plant and animal lies at the point where the leap to sensation takes place. Far from being obliterated by the known transitional structures, that line becomes a logical necessity precisely through these externally undecided or undecidable forms" [D. Ph. 141-42].

And again:

"On the other hand, plants are completely and for all time devoid of the slightest trace of sensation, and even lack any capacity for it" [140].

In the first place, Hegel says (*Naturphilosophie*, § 351, Addendum) that

"sensation is the *differentia specifica*,[a] the absolute distinguishing characteristic of the animal".

So once again we find a Hegelian "crudity" [D. K. G. 235], which through the simple process of appropriation by Herr Dühring is raised to the honourable position of a final and ultimate truth.

In the second place, we hear for the first time here of transitional structures, externally undecided or undecidable forms (fine gibberish!) between plant and animal. That these intermediate forms exist; that there are organisms of which we cannot say flatly whether they are plants or animals; that therefore we are wholly unable to draw a sharp dividing line between plant and animal—precisely this fact makes it a logical necessity for Herr Dühring to establish a criterion of differentiation which in the same breath he admits will not hold water! But we have absolutely no need to go back to the doubtful territory between plants and animals; are the sensitive plants which at the slightest touch fold their leaves or close their flowers, are the insect-eating plants devoid of the slightest trace of sensation and do they even lack any capacity for it? This cannot be maintained even by Herr Dühring without "unscientific semi-poetry" [D. Ph. 56, 142].

In the third place, it is once again a free creation and imagination on Herr Dühring's part when he asserts that sensation is physiologically bound up with the presence of some kind of nerve apparatus, however simple. Not only all primitive animals, but also the zoophytes, or at any rate the great majority of them, show no trace of a nerve apparatus. It is only from the worms on that such an apparatus is regularly found, and Herr Dühring is the first person to make the assertion that those animals have no sensation because they have no nerves. Sensation is not necessarily associated with nerves, but undoubtedly with certain albuminous bodies which up to now have not been more precisely determined.

---

[a] Specific difference.— *Ed.*

At any rate, Herr Dühring's biological knowledge is sufficiently characterised by the question which he does not hesitate to put to Darwin:

"Is it to be supposed that animals have developed out of plants?" [110].

Such a question could only be put by a person who has not the slightest knowledge of either animals or plants.

Of life in general Herr Dühring is only able to tell us:

"The metabolism which is carried out through a plastically creating schematisation" (what in the world can that be?) "remains always a distinguishing characteristic of the real life process" [141].

That is all we learn about life, while in the "plastically creating schematisation" we are left knee-deep in the meaningless gibberish of the purest Dühring jargon. If therefore we want to know what life is, we shall evidently have to look a little more closely at it ourselves.

That organic exchange of matter is the most general and most characteristic phenomenon of life has been said times out of number during the last thirty years by physiological chemists and chemical physiologists, and it is here merely translated by Herr Dühring into his own elegant and clear language. But to define life as organic metabolism is to define life as—life; for organic exchange of matter or metabolism with plastically creating schematisation is in fact a phrase which itself needs explanation through life, explanation through the distinction between the organic and the inorganic, that is, that which lives and that which does not live. This explanation therefore does not get us any further.

Exchange of matter as such takes place even without life. There is a whole series of processes in chemistry which, given an adequate supply of raw material, constantly reproduce their own conditions, and do so in such a way that a definite body is the carrier of the process. This is the case in the manufacture of sulphuric acid by the burning of sulphur. In this process sulphur dioxide, SO_2, is produced, and when steam and nitric acid are added, the sulphur dioxide absorbs hydrogen and oxygen and is converted into sulphuric acid, H_2SO_4. The nitric acid gives off oxygen and is reduced to nitric oxide; this nitric oxide immediately absorbs new oxygen from the air and is transformed into the higher oxides of nitrogen, but only to transfer this oxygen immediately to sulphur dioxide and to go through the same process again; so that theoretically an infinitely small quantity of nitric acid should suffice to change an unlimited quantity of sulphur dioxide, oxygen and water into sulphuric acid.— Exchange of matter also takes place in the passage of fluids through dead organic and even inorganic membranes, as in Traube's artificial cells.[45] Here too it is clear that we cannot get any further by means of exchange of matter; for the peculiar exchange of matter which is to explain life needs itself to be explained through life. We must therefore try some other way.

Life is the mode of existence of albuminous bodies, and this mode of existence essentially consists in the constant self-renewal of the chemical constituents of these bodies.

The term albuminous body is used here in the sense in which it is employed in modern chemistry, which includes under this name all bodies constituted similarly to ordinary white of egg, otherwise also known as protein substances. The name is an unhappy one, because ordinary white of egg plays the most lifeless and passive role of all the substances related to it, since, together with the yolk, it is merely food for the developing embryo. But while so little is yet known of the chemical composition of albuminous bodies, this name is better than any other because it is more general.

Wherever we find life we find it associated with an albuminous body, and wherever we find an albuminous body not in process of dissolution, there also without exception we find phenomena of life. Undoubtedly, the presence of other chemical combinations is also necessary in a living body in order to induce particular differentiations of these phenomena of life; but they are not requisite for naked life, except in so far as they enter the body as food and are transformed into albumen. The lowest living beings known to us are in fact nothing but simple particles of albumen, and they already exhibit all the essential phenomena of life.

But what are these universal phenomena of life which are equally present among all living organisms? Above all the fact that an albuminous body absorbs other appropriate substances from its environment and assimilates them, while other, older parts of the body disintegrate and are excreted. Other, non-living, bodies also change, disintegrate or enter into combinations in the natural course of events; but in doing this they cease to be what they were. A weather-worn rock is no longer a rock; metal which oxidises turns into rust. But what with non-living bodies is the cause of destruction, with albumen is *the fundamental condition of existence.* From the moment when this uninterrupted metamorphosis of its constituents, this constant alternation of nutrition and excretion, no longer takes place in an albuminous body, the albuminous body itself comes to an end, it decomposes, that is, *dies*. Life, the mode of existence of an albuminous body, therefore consists primarily in the fact that every moment it is itself and at the same time something else; and this does not take place as the result of a process to which it is subjected from without, as is the way in which this can occur also in the case of inanimate bodies. On the contrary, life, the metabolism which takes place through nutrition and excretion, is a self-implementing process which is inherent in, native to, its bearer, albumen, without which the latter cannot exist. And hence it follows that if chemistry ever succeeds in producing albumen artificially, this albumen must show the phenomena of life, however weak these may be. It is certainly open to question whether chemistry will at the same time also discover the right food for this albumen.

From the metabolism which takes place through nutrition and excretion, as the essential function of albumen, and from its peculiar plasticity proceed also all the other most simple factors of life: irritability, which is already included in the mutual interaction between the albumen and its food; contractibility, which is shown, even at a very low stage, in the consumption of food; the possibility of growth, which in the lowest forms includes propagation by fission; internal movement, without which neither the consumption nor the assimilation of food is possible.

Our definition of life is naturally very inadequate, inasmuch as, far from including *all* the phenomena of life, it has to be limited to those which are the most common and the simplest. From a scientific standpoint all definitions are of little value. In order to gain an exhaustive knowledge of what life is, we should have to go through all the forms in which it appears, from the lowest to the highest. But for ordinary usage such definitions are very convenient and in places cannot well be dispensed with; moreover, they can do no harm, provided their inevitable deficiencies are not forgotten.

But back to Herr Dühring. When things are faring badly with him in the sphere of earthly biology, he knows where to find consolation; he takes refuge in his starry heaven.

"It is not merely the special apparatus of an organ of sensation, but the whole objective world, which is adapted to the production of pleasure and pain. For this reason we take it for granted that the antithesis between pleasure and pain, and moreover *exactly* in the form with which we are familiar, is a universal antithesis, and must be represented *in the various worlds of the universe* by essentially homogeneous feelings... This conformity, however, is of *no little* significance, for it is the key to the *universe of sensations*... Hence the subjective cosmic world is to us not much more unfamiliar than the objective. The constitution of both spheres must be conceived according to one concordant type, and in this we have the beginnings of a science of consciousness whose range is wider than merely terrestrial" [D. Ph. 139-40].

What do a few gross blunders in terrestrial natural science matter to the man who carries in his pocket the key to the universe of sensations? *Allons donc!*[a]

IX. MORALITY AND LAW. ETERNAL TRUTHS

We refrain from giving samples of the mish-mash of platitudes and oracular sayings, in a word, of the simple *balderdash* with which Herr Dühring regales his readers for fifty full pages as the deep-rooted science of the elements of consciousness. We will cite only this:

"He who can think only by means of language has never yet learnt what is meant by *abstract* and *pure* thought" [D. Ph. 189].

On this basis animals are the most abstract and purest thinkers, because their thought is never obscured by the officious intrusion of language. In any case one can see from the Dühringian thoughts and the language in which they are couched how little suited these thoughts are to any language, and how little suited the German language is to these thoughts.

At last the fourth section brings us deliverance; apart from the liquefying pap of rhetoric, it does at least offer us, here and there, something tangible on the subject of *morality* and *law*. Right at the outset, on this occasion, we are invited to take a trip to the other celestial bodies:

the elements of morals "must occur in concordant fashion among all extra-human beings whose active reason has to deal with the conscious ordering of life impulses in the form of instincts... And yet our interest in such deductions will be small... Nevertheless it is an idea which *beneficently extends* our range of vision, when we think that on other celestial bodies individual and communal life must be based on a scheme which ... is unable to abrogate or escape from the general fundamental constitution of a rationally acting being" [192-93].

In this case, by way of exception, the validity of the Dühringian truths also for all other possible worlds is put at the beginning instead of the end of the chapter concerned; and for a sufficient reason. If the validity of the Dühringian conceptions of morality and justice is first etablished for all *worlds*, it is all the more easy beneficently to extend their validity to all *times*. But once again what is involved is nothing less than final and ultimate truth [2].

---

[a] Well, really!— *Ed.*

The world of morals, "just as much as the world of general knowledge", has "its permanent principles and simple elements". The moral principles stand "above history and also above the present differences in national characteristics... The special truths out of which, in the course of evolution, a more complete moral consciousness and, so to speak, conscience are built up, may, in so far as their ultimate basis is understood, claim a validity and range similar to the insights and applications of mathematics. *Genuine truths are absolutely immutable* ... so that it is altogether stupid to think that the correctness of knowledge is something that can be affected by time and changes in reality" [196]. Hence the certitude of strict knowledge and the adequacy of common cognition leave no room, when we are in possession of our senses, for doubting the absolute validity of the principles of knowledge. "Even persistent doubt is itself a diseased condition of weakness and only the expression of *hopeless confusion*, which sometimes seeks to contrive the appearance of something stable in the systematic consciousness of its *nothingness*. In the sphere of ethics, the denial of general principles clutches at the geographical and historical variety of customs and principles, and once the inevitable necessity of moral wickedness and evil is conceded, it believes itself so much the more to be above the recognition of the great importance and actual efficacy of concordant moral impulses. This *mordant scepticism*, which is not directed against particular false doctrines but against mankind's very capacity to develop conscious morality, resolves itself ultimately into a real Nothing, in fact into something that is worse than pure nihilism [194] ... It flatters itself that it can easily dominate within its *utter chaos* of disintegrated ethical ideas and open the gates to unprincipled arbitrariness. But it is greatly mistaken: for mere reference to the inevitable fate of reason in error and truth suffices to show by this analogy alone that natural fallibility does not necessarily exclude the attainment of accuracy" [195].

Up to now we have calmly put up with all these pompous phrases of Herr Dühring's about final and ultimate truths, the sovereignty of thought, absolute certainty of knowledge, and so forth, because it is only at the point which we have now reached that the matter can be settled. Up to this point it has been enough to enquire how far the separate assertions of the philosophy of reality had "sovereign validity" and "an unconditional claim to truth" [2]; now we come to the question whether any, and if so which, products of human knowledge ever can have sovereign validity and an unconditional claim to truth. When I say "of *human* knowledge" I do not use the phrase with the intention of insulting the inhabitants of other celestial bodies, whom I have not had the honour of knowing, but only for the reason that animals also have knowledge, though it is in no way sovereign. A dog acknowledges his master to be his God, though this master may be the biggest scoundrel on earth.

Is human thought sovereign? Before we can answer yes or no we must first enquire: what is human thought? Is it the thought of the individual man? No. But it exists only as the individual thought of many milliards of past, present and future men. If, then, I say that the total thought of all these human beings, including the future ones, which is embraced in my idea, is *sovereign,* able to know the world as it exists, if only mankind lasts long enough and in so far as no limits are imposed on its knowledge by its perceptive organs or the objects to be known, then I am saying something which is pretty banal and, in addition, pretty barren. For the most valuable result from it would be that it should make us extremely distrustful of our present knowledge, inasmuch as in all probability we are just about at the beginning of human history, and the generations which will put *us* right are likely to be far more numerous than those whose knowledge we—often enough with a considerable degree of contempt—have the opportunity to correct.

Herr Dühring himself proclaims it to be a necessity that consciousness, and therefore also thought and knowledge, can become manifest only in a series of individual beings. We can only ascribe sovereignty to the thought of each of these individuals in so far as we are not aware of any power which would be able to impose any idea forcibly on him, when he is of sound mind and wide awake. But as for the sovereign validity of the knowledge obtained by each individual thought, we all know that there can be no talk of such a thing, and that all previous experience shows that without exception such knowledge always contains much more that is capable of being improved upon than that which cannot be improved upon, or is correct.

In other words, the sovereignty of thought is realised in a series of extremely unsovereignly-thinking human beings; the knowledge which has an unconditional claim to truth is realised in a series of relative errors; neither the one nor the other can be fully realised except through an unending duration of human existence.

Here once again we find the same contradiction as we found above,[a] between the character of human thought, necessarily conceived as absolute, and its reality in individual human beings, all of whom think only limitedly. This is a contradiction which can be resolved only in the course of infinite progress, in what is—at least practically for us—an endless succession of generations of mankind. In this sense human thought is just as much sovereign as not sovereign, and its capacity for knowledge just as much unlimited as limited. It is sovereign and unlimited in its disposition, its vocation, its possibilities and its historical ultimate goal; it is not sovereign and it is limited in its individual realisation and in reality at any particular moment.

---

[a] See this volume, pp. 35-36.— *Ed.*

It is just the same with eternal truths. If mankind ever reached the stage at which it should work only with eternal truths, with results of thought which possess sovereign validity and an unconditional claim to truth, it would then have reached the point where the infinity of the intellectual world both in its actuality and in its potentiality had been exhausted, and thus the famous miracle of the counted uncountable would have been performed.

But are there any truths which are so securely based that any doubt of them seems to us to be tantamount to insanity? That twice two makes four, that the three angles of a triangle are equal to two right angles, that Paris is in France, that a man who gets no food dies of hunger, and so forth? Are there then nevertheless *eternal* truths, final and ultimate truths [D. Ph. 2]?

Certainly there are. We can divide the whole realm of knowledge in the traditional way into three great departments. The first includes all sciences that deal with inanimate nature and are to a greater or lesser degree susceptible of mathematical treatment: mathematics, astronomy, mechanics, physics, chemistry. If it gives anyone any pleasure to use mighty words for very simple things, it can be asserted that *certain* results obtained by these sciences are eternal truths, final and ultimate truths; for which reason these sciences are known as the *exact* sciences. But very far from all their results have this validity. With the introduction of variable magnitudes and the extension of their variability to the infinitely small and infinitely large, mathematics, usually so strictly ethical, fell from grace; it ate of the tree of knowledge, which opened up to it a career of most colossal achievements, but at the same time a path of error. The virgin state of absolute validity and irrefutable proof of everything mathematical was gone for ever; the realm of controversy was inaugurated, and we have reached the point where most people differentiate and integrate not because they understand what they are doing but from pure faith, because up to now it has always come out right. Things are even worse with astronomy and mechanics, and in physics and chemistry we are swamped by hypotheses as if attacked by a swarm of bees. And it must of necessity be so. In physics we are dealing with the motion of molecules, in chemistry with the formation of molecules out of atoms, and if the interference of light waves is not a myth, we have absolutely no prospect of ever seeing these interesting objects with our own eyes. As time goes on, final and ultimate truths become remarkably rare in this field.

We are even worse off in geology which, by its nature, has to deal chiefly with processes which took place not only in our absence but in the absence of any human being whatever. The gleaning here of final and ultimate truths is therefore a very troublesome business, and the crop is extremely scanty.

The second department of science is the one which covers the investigation of living organisms. In this field there is such a multiplicity of interrelationships and causalities that not only does the solution of each question give rise to a host of other questions, but each separate problem can in most cases only be solved piecemeal, through a series of investigations which often require centuries; and besides, the need for a systematic presentation of interconnections makes it necessary again and again to surround the final and ultimate truths with a luxuriant growth of hypotheses. What a long series of intermediaries from Galen to Malpighi was necessary for correctly establishing such a simple matter as the circulation of the blood in mammals, how slight is our knowledge of the origin of blood corpuscles, and how numerous are the missing links even today, for example, to be able to bring the symptoms of a disease into some rational relationship with its cause! And often enough discoveries, such as that of the cell, are made which compel us to revise completely all formerly established final and ultimate truths in the realm of biology, and to put whole piles of them on the scrap-heap once and for all. Anyone who wants to establish really genuine and immutable truths here will therefore have to be content with such platitudes as: all men are mortal, all female mammals have lacteal glands, and the like; he will not even be able to assert that the higher animals digest with their stomachs and intestines and not with their heads, for the nervous activity, which is centralised in the head, is indispensable to digestion.

But eternal truths are in an even worse plight in the third, the historical, group of sciences, which study in their historical sequence and in their present resultant state the conditions of human life, social relationships, forms of law and government, with their ideal superstructure in the shape of philosophy, religion, art, etc. In organic nature we are at least dealing with a succession of processes which, so far as our immediate observation is concerned, recur with fair regularity within very wide limits. Organic species have on the whole remained unchanged since the time of Aristotle. In social history, however, the repetition of conditions is the exception and not the rule, once we pass beyond the primitive state of man, the so-called Stone Age; and when such repetitions occur, they never arise under exactly similar circumstances. Such, for example, is the existence of an original common ownership of the land among all civilised peoples, or the way it was dissolved. In the sphere of human history our knowledge is therefore even more backward than in the realm of biology. Furthermore, when by way of exception the inner connection between the social and political forms of existence in any epoch comes to be known, this as a rule occurs only when these forms have already by half outlived themselves and are nearing extinction. Therefore, knowledge is here essentially relative, inasmuch as it is limited to the investigation of interconnections and consequences of certain social and state forms which exist only in a particular epoch and among particular peoples and are by their very nature transitory. Anyone therefore who here sets out to hunt down final and ultimate truths, genuine, absolutely immutable truths, will bring home but little, apart from platitudes and commonplaces of the sorriest kind—for example, that, generally speaking, men cannot live except by labour; that up to the present they for the most part have been divided into rulers and ruled; that Napoleon died on May 5, 1821, and so on.

Now it is a remarkable thing that it is precisely in this sphere that we most frequently encounter truths which claim to be eternal, final and ultimate and all the rest of it. That twice two makes four, that birds have beaks, and similar statements, are proclaimed as eternal truths only by those who aim at deducing, from the existence of eternal truths in general, the conclusion that there are also eternal truths in the sphere of human history— eternal morality, eternal justice, and so on—which claim a validity and scope similar to those of the insights and applications of mathematics. And then we can confidently rely on this same friend of humanity taking the first opportunity to assure us that all previous fabricators of eternal truths have been to a greater or lesser extent asses and charlatans, that they all fell into error and made mistakes; but that *their* error and *their* fallibility are in accordance with nature's laws, and prove the existence of truth and accuracy precisely in *his* case; and that he, the prophet who has now arisen, has in his bag, all ready-made, final and ultimate truth, eternal morality and eternal justice. This has all happened so many hundreds and thousands of times that we can only feel astonished that there should still be people credulous enough to believe this, not of others, oh no! but of themselves. Nevertheless we have here before us at least one more such prophet, who also, quite in the accustomed way, flies into highly moral indignation when other people deny that any individual whatsoever is in a position to deliver the final and ultimate truth. Such a denial, or indeed mere doubt of it, is weakness, hopeless confusion, nothingness, mordant scepticism, worse than pure nihilism, utter chaos and other such pleasantries. As with all prophets, instead of critical and scientific examination and judgment one encounters moral condemnation out of hand.

We might have made mention above also of the sciences which investigate the laws of human thought, i.e., logic and dialectics. In these, however, eternal truths do not fare any better. Herr Dühring declares that dialectics proper is pure nonsense; and the many books which have been and are still being written on logic provide abundant proof that here, too, final and ultimate truths are much more sparsely sown than some people believe.

For that matter, there is absolutely no need to be alarmed at the fact that the stage of knowledge which we have now reached is as little final as all that have preceded it. It already embraces a vast mass of judgments and requires very great specialisation of study on the part of anyone who wants to become conversant with any particular science. But a man who applies the measure of genuine, immutable, final and ultimate truth to knowledge which, by its very nature, must either remain relative for many generations and be completed only step by step, or which, as in cosmogony, geology and the history of mankind, must always contain gaps and be incomplete because of the inadequacy of the historical material— such a man only proves thereby his own ignorance and perversity, even if the real thing behind it all is not, as in this case, the claim to personal infallibility. Truth and error, like all thought-concepts which move in polar opposites, have absolute validity only in an extremely limited field, as we have just seen, and as even Herr Dühring would realise if he had any acquaintance with the first elements of dialectics, which deal precisely with the inadequacy of all polar opposites. As soon as we apply the antithesis between truth and error outside of that narrow field which has been referred to above it becomes relative and therefore unserviceable for exact scientific modes of expression; and if we attempt to apply it as absolutely valid outside that field we really find ourselves altogether beaten: both poles of the antithesis become transformed into their opposites, truth becomes error and error truth. Let us take as an example the well-known Boyle's law. According to it, if the temperature remains constant, the volume of a gas varies inversely with the pressure to which it is subjected. Regnault found that this law does not hold good in certain cases.

Had he been a philosopher of reality he would have had to say: Boyle's law is mutable, and is hence not a genuine truth, hence it is not a truth at all, hence it is an error. But had he done this he would have committed an error far greater than the one that was contained in Boyle's law; his grain of truth would have been lost sight of in a sand-hill of error; he would have distorted his originally correct conclusion into an error compared with which Boyle's law, along with the little particle of error that clings to it, would have seemed like truth. But Regnault, being a man of science, did not indulge in such childishness, but continued his investigations and discovered that in general Boyle's law is only approximately true, and in particular loses its validity in the case of gases which can be liquefied by pressure, namely, as soon as the pressure approaches the point at which liquefaction begins. Boyle's law therefore was proved to be true only within definite limits. But is it absolutely and finally true within those limits? No physicist would assert that. He would maintain that it holds good within certain limits of pressure and temperature and for certain gases; and even within these more restricted limits he would not exclude the possibility of a still narrower limitation or altered formulation as the result of future investigations.* This is how things stand with final and ultimate truths in physics, for example. Really scientific works therefore, as a rule, avoid such dogmatically moral expressions as error and truth, while these expressions meet us everywhere in works such as the philosophy of reality, in which empty phrasemongering attempts to impose itself on us as the most sovereign result of sovereign thought.

But, a naive reader may ask, where has Herr Dühring expressly stated that the content of his philosophy of reality is final and even ultimate truth [D. Ph. 2]? Where? Well, for example, in the dithyramb on his system (page 13), a part of which we cited in

---

* Since I wrote the above it would seem already to have been confirmed. According to the latest researches carried out with more exact apparatus by Mendeleyev and Boguski, all true gases show a variable relation between pressure and volume; the coefficient of expansion for hydrogen, at all the pressures so far applied, has been positive (that is, the diminution of volume was slower than the increase of pressure); in the case of atmospheric air and the other gases examined, there is for each a zero point of pressure, so that with pressure below this point the coefficient is positive, and with pressure above this point their coefficient is negative. So Boyle's law, which has always hitherto been usable for practical purposes, will have to be supplemented by a whole series of special laws. (We also know now—in 1885—that there are no "true" gases at all. They have all been reduced to a liquid form.)[46]

Chapter II.[a] Or when he says, in the passage quoted above[b]: Moral truths, in so far as their ultimate bases are understood, claim the same validity as mathematical insights. And does not Herr Dühring assert that, working from his really critical standpoint [D. Ph. 404] and by means of those researches of his which go to the root of things [200], he has forced his way through to these ultimate foundations, the basic schemata, and has thus bestowed final and ultimate validity on moral truths? Or, if Herr Dühring does not advance this claim either for himself or for his age, if he only meant to say that perhaps some day in the dark and nebulous future final and ultimate truths may be ascertained, if therefore he meant to say much the same, only in a more confused way, as is said by "mordant scepticism" and "hopeless confusion" [194]—then, in that case, what is all the noise about, what can we do for you, Herr Dühring?[c]

If, then, we have not made much progress with truth and error, we can make even less with good and evil. This opposition manifests itself exclusively in the domain of morals, that is, a domain belonging to the history of mankind, and it is precisely in this field that final and ultimate truths are most sparsely sown. The conceptions of good and evil have varied so much from nation to nation and from age to age that they have often been in direct contradiction to each other.—But all the same, someone may object, good is not evil and evil is not good; if good is confused with evil there is an end to all morality, and everyone can do as he pleases.—This is also, stripped of all oracular phrases, Herr Dühring's opinion. But the matter cannot be so simply disposed of. If it were such an easy business there would certainly be no dispute at all over good and evil; everyone would know what was good and what was bad. But how do things stand today? What morality is preached to us today? There is first Christian-feudal morality, inherited from earlier religious times; and this is divided, essentially, into a Catholic and a Protestant morality, each of which has no lack of subdivisions, from the Jesuit-Catholic and Orthodox-Protestant to loose "enlightened" moralities. Alongside these we find the modern-bourgeois morality and beside it also the proletarian morality of the future, so that in the most advanced European countries alone the past, present and future provide three great groups of moral theories which are in force

---

a See this volume, p. 28.— *Ed.*
b Ibid., p. 79.— *Ed.*
c Goethe, *Faust,* Act I, Scene III ("Faust's Study").— *Ed.*

simultaneously and alongside each other. Which, then, is the true one? Not one of them, in the sense of absolute finality; but certainly that morality contains the maximum elements promising permanence which, in the present, represents the overthrow of the present, represents the future, and that is proletarian morality.

But when we see that the three classes of modern society, the feudal aristocracy, the bourgeoisie and the proletariat, each have a morality of their own, we can only draw the one conclusion: that men, consciously or unconsciously, derive their ethical ideas in the last resort from the practical relations on which their class position is based—from the economic relations in which they carry on production and exchange.

But nevertheless there is great deal which the three moral theories mentioned above have in common—is this not at least a portion of a morality which is fixed once and for all?—These moral theories represent three different stages of the same historical development, have therefore a common historical background, and for that reason alone they necessarily have much in common. Even more. At similar or approximately similar stages of economic development moral theories must of necessity be more or less in agreement. From the moment when private ownership of movable property developed, all societies in which this private ownership existed had to have this moral injunction in common: Thou shalt not steal.[a] Does this injunction thereby become an eternal moral injunction? By no means. In a society in which all motives for stealing have been done away with, in which therefore at the very most only lunatics would ever steal, how the preacher of morals would be laughed at who tried solemnly to proclaim the eternal truth: Thou shalt not steal!

We therefore reject every attempt to impose on us any moral dogma whatsoever as an eternal, ultimate and for ever immutable ethical law on the pretext that the moral world, too, has its permanent principles which stand above history and the differences between nations. We maintain on the contrary that all moral theories have been hitherto the product, in the last analysis, of the economic conditions of society obtaining at the time. And as society has hitherto moved in class antagonisms, morality has always been class morality; it has either justified the domination and the interests of the ruling class, or ever since the oppressed class became powerful enough, it has represented its indignation against this domination and the future interests of the oppressed.

---

[a] Exodus 20 : 15; Deuteronomy 5 : 19.— *Ed.*

That in this process there has on the whole been progress in morality, as in all other branches of human knowledge, no one will doubt. But we have not yet passed beyond class morality. A really human morality which stands above class antagonisms and above any recollection of them becomes possible only at a stage of society which has not only overcome class antagonisms but has even forgotten them in practical life. And now one can gauge Herr Dühring's presumption in advancing his claim, from the midst of the old class society and on the eve of a social revolution, to impose on the future classless society an eternal morality independent of time and changes in reality. Even assuming—what we do not know up to now—that he understands the structure of the society of the future at least in its main outlines.

Finally, one more revelation which is "from the ground up original" [D. Ph. 525] but for that reason no less "going to the root of things" [200]: With regard to the origin of evil,

"the fact that the *type of the cat* with the guile associated with it is found in animal form, stands on an even plane with the circumstance that a similar type of character is found also in human beings... There is therefore nothing mysterious about evil, unless someone wants to scent out something mysterious in the existence of a *cat* or of any animal of prey" [210-11].

Evil is—the cat. The devil therefore has no horns or cloven hoof, but claws and green eyes. And Goethe committed an unpardonable error in presenting Mephistopheles as a black dog[a] instead of a black cat. Evil is the cat! That is morality, not only for all worlds, but also—for cats[b]

X. MORALITY AND LAW. EQUALITY

We have already had more than one occasion to make ourselves acquainted with Herr Dühring's method. It consists in dissecting each group of objects of knowledge to what is claimed to be their simplest elements, applying to these elements similarly simple and what are claimed to be self-evident axioms, and then continuing to operate with the aid of the results so obtained. Even a problem in the sphere of social life

---

[a] Goethe, *Faust*, Act I, Scenes II and III ("At the City Gates" and "Faust's Study").— *Ed.*

[b] In German a play on words: *für die Katze* (for the cat) denotes something utterly useless or wasted effort.— *Ed.*

"is to be decided axiomatically, in accordance with particular, simple basic forms, just as if we were dealing with the simple ... basic forms of mathematics" [D. Ph. 224].

And thus the application of the mathematical method to history, morals and law is to give us also in these fields mathematical certainty of the truth of the results obtained, to characterise them as genuine, immutable truths.

This is only giving a new twist to the old favourite ideological method, also known as the *a priori* method, which consists in ascertaining the properties of an object, by logical deduction from the concept of the object, instead of from the object itself. First the concept of the object is fabricated from the object; then the spit is turned round, and the object is measured by its reflexion, the concept. The object is then to conform to the concept, not the concept to the object. With Herr Dühring the simplest elements, the ultimate abstractions he can reach, do service for the concept, which does not alter matters; these simplest elements are at best of a purely conceptual nature. The philosophy of reality, therefore, proves here again to be pure ideology, the deduction of reality not from itself but from a concept.

And when such an ideologist constructs morality and law from the concept, or the so-called simplest elements of "society", instead of from the real social relations of the people round him, what material is then available for this construction? Material clearly of two kinds: first, the meagre residue of real content which may possibly survive in the abstractions from which he starts and, secondly, the content which our ideologist once more introduces from his own consciousness. And what does he find in his consciousness? For the most part, moral and juridical notions which are a more or less accurate expression (positive or negative, corroborative or antagonistic) of the social and political relations amidst which he lives; perhaps also ideas drawn from the literature on the subject; and, as a final possibility, some personal idiosyncrasies. Our ideologist may turn and twist as he likes, but the historical reality which he cast out at the door comes in again at the window, and while he thinks he is framing a doctrine of morals and law for all times and for all worlds, he is in fact only fashioning an image of the conservative or revolutionary tendencies of his day—an image which is distorted because it has been torn from its real basis and, like a reflection in a concave mirror, is standing on its head.

Herr Dühring thus dissects society into its simplest elements, and discovers in doing so that the simplest society consists of at least *two* people. With these two people he then proceeds to operate axiomatically. And so the basic moral axiom naturally presents itself:

"Two human wills are as such *entirely equal* to each other, and in the first place the one can demand nothing positive of the other" [D. Ph. 200]. This "characterises the basic form of moral justice" [201], and also that of legal justice, for "we need only the wholly simple and elementary relation of *two persons* for the development of the fundamental concepts of law" [228].

That two people or two human wills are as such *entirely* equal to each other is not only not an axiom but is even a great exaggeration. In the first place, two people, even as such, may be unequal in sex, and this simple fact leads us on at once to the idea that the simplest elements of society—if we accept this childishness for a moment—are not two men, but a man and a woman, who found a *family*, the simplest and first form of association for the purpose of production. But this cannot in any way suit Herr Dühring. For on the one hand the two founders of society must be made as equal as possible; and secondly even Herr Dühring could not succeed in constructing from the primitive family the moral and legal equality of man and woman. One thing or the other: either the Dühringian social molecule, by the multiplication of which the whole of society is to be built up, is doomed beforehand to disaster, because two men can never by themselves bring a child into the world; or we must conceive them as two heads of families. And in that case the whole simple basic scheme is turned into its opposite: instead of the equality of people it proves at most the equality of heads of families, and as women are not considered, it further proves that they are subordinate.

We have now to make an unpleasant announcement to the reader: that from this point on for some considerable time he will not get rid of these famous two men. In the sphere of social relations they play a similar role to that hitherto played by the inhabitants of other celestial bodies, with whom it is to be hoped we have now finished. Whenever a question of economics, politics, etc., is to be solved, the two men instantly march up and settle the matter in the twinkling of an eye "axiomatically" [224]. An excellent, creative and system-creating discovery on the part of our philosopher of reality. But unfortunately, if we want to pay due regard to truth, the two men are not his discovery. They are the common property of the whole eighteenth century. They are already to be found in Rousseau's discourse on inequality (1754),[47] where, by the way, they prove axiomatically the opposite of Herr Dühring's contentions. They play a leading part with the economists, from Adam Smith to Ricardo; but in these they are at least unequal in that each of the two carries on a different trade—as a rule one is a hunter and the other a fisherman—and that they mutually exchange their products. Besides, throughout the eighteenth century, they serve in the main as a purely illustrative example, and Herr Dühring's originality consists only in that he elevates this method of illustration into a basic method for all social science and a measure of all historical forms. Certainly it would be impossible to simplify further the "strictly scientific conception of things and men" [387].

In order to establish the fundamental axiom that two people and their wills are absolutely equal to each other and that neither lords it over the other, we cannot use any couple of men at random. They must be two people who are so thoroughly free from all reality, from all national, economic, political and religious relations which are found in the world, from all sexual and personal peculiarities, that nothing is left of either of them beyond the mere concept: human being, and then they are of course "entirely equal". They are therefore two complete phantoms conjured up by that very Herr Dühring who is everywhere scenting and denouncing "spiritistic" tendencies. These two phantoms are of course obliged to do everything which the man who conjured them into existence wants them to do, and for that very reason all their artifices are of no interest whatever to the rest of the world.

But let us pursue Herr Dühring's axiomatics a little further. The two wills can demand nothing positive of each other. If nevertheless one of them does so, and has its way by force, this gives rise to a state of injustice; and this fundamental scheme serves Herr Dühring to explain injustice, tyranny, servitude—in short, the whole reprehensible history of the past. Now Rousseau, in the essay referred to above, had already made use of two men to prove, likewise axiomatically, the very opposite: that is, given two men, A cannot enslave B by force, but only by putting B into a position in which the latter cannot do without A, a conception which, however, is much too materialistic for Herr Dühring. Let us put the same thing in a slightly different way. Two shipwrecked people are alone on an island, and form a society. Their wills are, formally, entirely equal, and this is acknowledged by both. But from a material standpoint there is great inequality. A has determination and energy, B is irresolute, lazy and flabby. A is quick-witted, B stupid. How long will it be before A regularly imposes his will on B, first by persuasion, subsequently by dint of habit, but always in form voluntarily? Servitude remains servitude, whether the voluntary form is retained or is trampled underfoot. Voluntary entry into servitude was known throughout the Middle Ages, in Germany until after the Thirty Years' War.[48] When serfdom was abolished in Prussia after the defeats of 1806 and 1807, and with it the obligation of the gracious lords to provide for their subjects in need, illness and old age, the peasants petitioned the king asking to be left in servitude—for otherwise who would look after them when in distress? The two-men scheme is therefore just as "appropriate" to inequality and servitude as to equality and mutual help; and inasmuch as we are forced, on pain of extinction of society, to assume that they are heads of families, hereditary servitude is also provided for in the idea from the start.

But let this entire matter rest for the moment. Let us assume that Herr Dühring's axiomatics have convinced us and that we are enthusiastic supporters of the entire equality of rights as between the two wills, of "general human sovereignty" [D. Ph. 229], of the "sovereignty of the individual" [268]—veritable verbal colossi, compared with whom Stirner's "Ego" together with his Own[49] is a mere dwarf, although he also could claim a modest part in them. Well, then, we are now all *entirely equal* [200] and independent. All? No, not quite all.

There are also cases of "permissible dependence", but these can be explained "on grounds which are to be sought not in the activity of the two wills as such, but in a third sphere, as for example in regard to children, in their inadequate self-determination" [200].

Indeed! The grounds of dependence are not to be sought in the activity of the two wills as such! Naturally not, for the activity of one of the wills is actually restricted. But in a third sphere! And what is this third sphere? The concrete determination of one, the subjected, will as inadequate! Our philosopher of reality has so far departed from reality that, as against the abstract term "will", which is devoid of content, he regards the real content, the characteristic determination of this will, as a "third sphere". Be that as it may, we are obliged to state that the equality of rights has an exception. It does not hold good for a will afflicted with inadequate self-determination. *Retreat No. 1.*

To proceed.

"Where beast and man are blended in one person the question may be asked, on behalf of a second, entirely human, person, whether his mode of action should be the same as if persons who, so to speak, are only human were confronting each other [201] ... our hypothesis of two morally unequal persons, one of whom in some sense or other has something of the real beast in his character, is therefore the typical basic form for all relations which, in accordance with this difference, may come about ... within and between groups of people" [202].

And now let the reader see for himself the pitiful diatribe that follows these clumsy subterfuges, in which Herr Dühring turns and twists like a Jesuit priest in order to determine casuistically how far the human man can go against the bestial man, how far he may show distrust and employ stratagems and harsh, even terrorist means, as well as deception against him, without himself deviating in any way from immutable morality.

So, when two persons are "morally unequal" [202], there again is no longer equality. But then it was surely not worth while to conjure up two entirely equal people, for there are no two persons who are morally entirely equal.—But the inequality is supposed to consist in this: that one person is human and the other has a streak of the beast in him. It is, however, inherent in the descent of man from the animal world that he can never entirely rid himself of the beast, so that it can always be only a question of more or less, of a difference in the degree of bestiality or of humanity. A division of mankind into two sharply differentiated groups, into human men and beast men, into good and bad, sheep and goats, is only found—apart from the philosophy of reality— in Christianity, which quite logically also has its judge of the universe to make the separation. But who is to be the judge of the universe in the philosophy of reality? Presumably the procedure will have to be the same as in Christian practice, in which the pious lambs themselves assume the office of judge of the universe in relation to their mundane goat-neighbours, and discharge this duty with notorious success. The sect of philosophers of reality, if it ever comes into being, will assuredly not yield precedence in this respect to the pious of the land. This, however, is of no concern to us; what interests us is the admission that, as a result of the moral inequality between men, equality has vanished once more. *Retreat No. 2.*

But, again, let us proceed.

"If one acts in accordance with truth and science, and the other in accordance with some superstition or prejudice, then ... as a rule mutual interference must occur [216]... At a certain degree of incompetence, brutality or perversity of character, conflict is always inevitable... It is not only children and madmen in relation to whom the ultimate resource is *force.* The character of whole natural groups and cultured classes in mankind may make the *subjection* of their will, which is hostile because of its perversity, an inevitable necessity, in order to guide it back to the ties held in common. Even in such cases the alien will is still recognised as *having equal rights*; but the perversity of its injurious and hostile activity has provoked an *equalisation*, and if it is subjected to force, it is only reaping the reaction to its own unrighteousness" [D. Ph. 217].

So not only moral but also mental inequality is enough to remove the "entire equality" of the two wills and to call into being a morality by which all the infamous deeds of civilised robber states against backward peoples, down to the Russian atrocities in Turkestan, can be justified. When in the summer of 1873, General Kaufmann ordered the Tatar tribe of the Yomuds to be attacked, their tents to be burnt and their wives and children butchered— "in the good old Caucasian way", as the order was worded—he, too, declared that the subjection of the hostile, because perverted, will of the Yomuds, with the object of guiding it back to the ties held in common, had become an inevitable necessity, that the means employed by him were best suited to the purpose,[50] and that whoever willed the end must also will the means. Only he was not so cruel as to insult the Yomuds on top of it all and to say that it was just by massacring them for purposes of equalisation that he was recognising their will as having equal rights. And once again in this conflict it is the elect, those who claim to be acting in accordance with truth and science and therefore in the last resort the philosophers of reality, who have to decide what are superstition, prejudice, brutality and perversity of character and when force and subjection are necessary for purposes of equalisation. Equality, therefore, is now—equalisation by force; and the second will is recognised by the first to have equal rights through subjection. *Retreat No. 3*, here already degenerating into ignominious flight.

Incidentally, the phrase that the alien will is recognised as having equal right precisely through equalisation by means of force is only a distortion of the Hegelian theory, according to which punishment is the right of the criminal;

"punishment is regarded as containing the criminal's right and hence by being punished he is honoured as a rational being" (*Rechtsphilosophie*, § 100, Note).

With that we can break off. It would be superfluous to follow Herr Dühring further in his piecemeal destruction of the equality which he set up so axiomatically [224], of his general human sovereignty [229] and so on; to observe how he manages to set up society with his two men, but in order to create the state he requires a third because—to put the matter briefly—without a third no majority decisions can be arrived at, and without these, and so also without the rule of the majority over the minority, no state can exist; and then how he gradually steers into calmer waters where he constructs his socialitarian state of the future, where one fine morning we shall have the honour to look him up. We have sufficiently observed that the entire equality of the two wills exists only so long as these two wills *will nothing*; that as soon as they cease to be human wills as such, and are transformed into real, individual wills, into the wills of two real people, equality comes to an end; that childhood, madness, so-called bestiality, supposed superstition, alleged prejudice and assumed incapacity on the one hand, and fancied humanity and knowledge of truth and science on the other hand—that therefore every difference in the quality of the two wills and in that of the intelligence associated with them—justifies an inequality of treatment which may go as far as subjection. What more can we ask, when Herr Dühring has so deep-rootedly, from the ground up, demolished his own edifice of equality?

But even though we have finished with Herr Dühring's shallow, botched treatment of the idea of equality, this does not mean that we have finished with the idea itself, which especially thanks to Rousseau played a theoretical, and during and since the great revolution[a] a practical political role, and even today still plays an important agitational role in the socialist movement of almost every country. The establishment of its scientific content will also determine its value for proletarian agitation.

The idea that all men, as men, have something in common, and that to that extent they are equal, is of course primeval. But the modern demand for equality is something entirely different from that; this consists rather in deducing from that common quality of being human, from that equality of men as men, a claim to equal political resp. social status for all human beings, or at least for all citizens of a state or all members of a society. Before that original conception of relative equality could lead to the conclusion that men should have equal rights in the state and in society, before that conclusion could even appear to be something natural and self-evident, thousands of years had to pass and did pass. In the most ancient, primitive communities, equality of rights could apply at most to members of the community; women, slaves and foreigners were excluded from this equality as a matter of course. Among the Greeks and Romans the inequalities of men were of much greater importance than their equality in any respect. It would necessarily have seemed insanity to the ancients that Greeks

---

[a] Reference by Engels to the French Revolution.— *Ed.*

and barbarians, freemen and slaves, citizens and peregrines, Roman citizens and Roman subjects (to use a comprehensive term) should have a claim to equal political status. Under the Roman Empire all these distinctions gradually disappeared, except the distinction between freemen and slaves, and in this way there arose, for the freemen at least, that equality as between private individuals on the basis of which Roman law developed—the completest elaboration of law based on private property which we know. But so long as the antithesis between freemen and slaves existed, there could be no talk of drawing legal conclusions from general equality of *men*; we saw this even recently, in the slave-owning states of the North American Union.

Christianity knew only *one* point in which all men were equal: that all were equally born in original sin—which corresponded perfectly to its character as the religion of the slaves and the oppressed. Apart from this it recognised, at most, the equality of the elect, which however was only stressed at the very beginning. The traces of community of goods which are also found in the early stages of the new religion can be ascribed to solidarity among the proscribed rather than to real equalitarian ideas. Within a very short time the establishment of the distinction between priests and laymen put an end even to this incipient Christian equality.—The overrunning of Western Europe by the Germans abolished for centuries all ideas of equality, through the gradual building up of such a complicated social and political hierarchy as had never existed before. But at the same time the invasion drew Western and Central Europe into the course of historical development, created for the first time a compact cultural area, and within this area also for the first time a system of predominantly national states exerting mutual influence on each other and mutually holding each other in check. Thereby it prepared the ground on which alone the question of the equal status of men, of the rights of man, could at a later period be raised.

The feudal Middle Ages also developed in their womb the class which was destined, in the course of its further development, to become the standard-bearer of the modern demand for equality: the bourgeoisie. Originally itself a feudal estate, the bourgeoisie developed the predominantly handicraft industry and the exchange of products within feudal society to a relatively high level, when at the end of the fifteenth century the great maritime discoveries opened to it a new career of wider scope. Trade beyond the confines of Europe, which had previously been carried on only between Italy and the Levant, was now extended to

America and India, and soon surpassed in importance both the mutual exchange between the various European countries and the internal trade within each individual country. American gold and silver flooded Europe and forced its way like a disintegrating element into every fissure, rent and pore of feudal society. Handicraft industry could no longer satisfy the rising demand; in the leading industries of the most advanced countries it was replaced by manufacture.

But this mighty revolution in the conditions of the economic life of society was, however, not followed by any immediate corresponding change in its political structure. The political order remained feudal, while society became more and more bourgeois. Trade on a large scale, that is to say, particularly international and, even more so, world trade, requires free owners of commodities who are unrestricted in their movements and as such enjoy equal rights; who may exchange their commodities on the basis of laws that are equal for them all, at least in each particular place. The transition from handicraft to manufacture presupposes the existence of a number of free workers—free on the one hand from the fetters of the guild and on the other from the means whereby they could themselves utilise their labour-power—workers who can contract with the manufacturer for the hire of their labour-power, and hence, as parties to the contract, have rights equal to his. And finally the equality and equal status of all human labour, because and in so far as it is *human* labour, found its unconscious but clearest expression in the law of value of modern bourgeois political economy, according to which the value of a commodity is measured by the socially necessary labour embodied in it.*—However, where economic relations required freedom and equality of rights, the political system opposed them at every step with guild restrictions and special privileges. Local privileges, differential duties, exceptional laws of all kinds affected in trade not only foreigners and people living in the colonies, but often enough also whole categories of the nationals of the country concerned; everywhere and ever anew the privileges of the guilds barred the development of manufacture. Nowhere was the road clear and the chances equal for the bourgeois competitors—and yet that this be so was the prime and ever more pressing demand.

* This derivation of the modern ideas of equality from the economic conditions of bourgeois society was first demonstrated by Marx in *Capital*.[a]

---

[a] See present edition, Vol. 35, Part I, Chapter I, Section 3, A, 3: "The Equivalent Form of Value".— *Ed.*

The demand for liberation from feudal fetters and the establishment of equality of rights by the abolition of feudal inequalities was bound soon to assume wider dimensions, once the economic advance of society had placed it on the order of the day. If it was raised in the interests of industry and trade, it was also necessary to demand the same equality of rights for the great mass of the peasantry who, in every degree of bondage, from total serfdom onwards, were compelled to give the greater part of their labour-time to their gracious feudal lord without compensation and in addition to render innumerable other dues to him and to the state. On the other hand, it was inevitable that a demand should also be made for the abolition of the feudal privileges, of the freedom from taxation of the nobility, of the political privileges of the separate estates. And as people were no longer living in a world empire such as the Roman Empire had been, but in a system of independent states dealing with each other on an equal footing and at approximately the same level of bourgeois development, it was a matter of course that the demand for equality should assume a general character reaching out beyond the individual state, that freedom and equality should be proclaimed *human rights.* And it is significant of the specifically bourgeois character of these human rights that the American constitution,[51] the first to recognise the rights of man, in the same breath confirms the slavery of the coloured races existing in America: class privileges are proscribed, race privileges sanctified.

As is well known, however, from the moment when the bourgeoisie emerged from feudal burgherdom, when this estate of the Middle Ages developed into a modern class, it was always and inevitably accompanied by its shadow, the proletariat. And in the same way bourgeois demands for equality were accompanied by proletarian demands for equality. From the moment when the bourgeois demand for the abolition of class *privileges* was put forward, alongside it appeared the proletarian demand for the abolition of the *classes themselves*—at first in religious form, leaning towards primitive Christianity, and later drawing support from the bourgeois equalitarian theories themselves. The proletarians took the bourgeoisie at its word: equality must not be merely apparent, must not apply merely to the sphere of the state, but must also be real, must also be extended to the social, economic sphere. And especially since the French bourgeoisie, from the great revolution on, brought civil equality to the forefront, the French proletariat has answered blow for blow with the demand for social, economic equality, and equality has become the battle-cry particularly of the French proletariat.

The demand for equality in the mouth of the proletariat has therefore a double meaning. It is either—as was the case especially at the very start, for example in the Peasant War—the spontaneous reaction against the crying social inequalities, against the contrast between rich and poor, the feudal lords and their serfs, the surfeiters and the starving; as such it is simply an expression of the revolutionary instinct, and finds its justification in that, and in that only. Or, on the other hand, this demand has arisen as a reaction against the bourgeois demand for equality, drawing more or less correct and more far-reaching demands from this bourgeois demand, and serving as an agitational means in order to stir up the workers against the capitalists with the aid of the capitalists' own assertions; and in this case it stands or falls with bourgeois equality itself. In both cases the real content of the proletarian demand for equality is the demand for the *abolition of classes*. Any demand for equality which goes beyond that, of necessity passes into absurdity. We have given examples of this, and shall find enough additional ones when we come to Herr Dühring's fantasies of the future.

The idea of equality, both in its bourgeois and in its proletarian form, is therefore itself a historical product, the creation of which required definite historical conditions that in turn themselves presuppose a long previous history. It is therefore anything but an eternal truth. And if today it is taken for granted by the general public—in one sense or another—if, as Marx says, it "already possesses the fixity of a popular prejudice",[52] this is not the effect of its axiomatic truth, but the effect of the general diffusion and the continued appropriateness of the ideas of the eighteenth century. If therefore Herr Dühring is able without more ado to let his famous two men conduct their economic relations on the basis of equality, this is so because it seems quite natural to popular prejudice. And in fact Herr Dühring calls his philosophy *natural* because it is derived solely from things which seem to him quite natural. But why they seem natural to him is a question which of course he does not ask.

XI. MORALITY AND LAW. FREEDOM AND NECESSITY

"In the sphere of politics and law the principles expounded in this course are based on the *most exhaustive specialised studies*. It is therefore ... necessary to proceed from the fact that what we have here ... is a consistent exposition of the *conclusions* reached in the sphere of legal and political science. Jurisprudence was my original special subject and I not only devoted to it the customary three years of theoretical university preparation, but also, during a further three years of court practice, continued to study it particularly with a view to the *deepening* of its scientific content... And *certainly* the critique of private law relationships and the corresponding legal inadequacies could not have been put forward with *such confidence* but the consciousness that all the weaknesses of the subject *were known* to it as well as its stronger sides" [D. Ph. 537].

A man who is justified in saying this of himself must from the outset inspire confidence, especially in contrast with the

"one-time, admittedly neglected, legal studies of Herr Marx"[a] [D. K. G. 503].

And for that reason it must surprise us to find that the critique of private law relationships which steps on to the stage with such confidence is restricted to telling us that

"the scientific character of jurisprudence has not developed far" [D. Ph. 222-23], that positive civil law is injustice in that it sanctions property based on force [219], and that the "natural basis" of criminal law is *revenge* [224],—

an assertion of which in any case the only thing new is its mystical wrapping of "natural basis". The conclusions in political science are limited to the transactions of the famous three men, one of whom has hitherto held down the others by force, with Herr Dühring in all seriousness conducting an investigation into whether it was the second or the third who first introduced violence and subjection [265-66].

However, let us go a little more deeply into our confident jurist's most exhaustive specialised studies and his erudition deepened by three years of court practice.

Herr Dühring tells us of Lassalle that

he was prosecuted for "*inciting* to an attempt to steal a cash-box" but that "no sentence by the court could be recorded, as the so-called *acquittal for lack of evidence*, which was *then still possible,* supervened ... this *half* acquittal" [D. K. G. 510].

The Lassalle case referred to here came up in the summer of 1848, before the assizes at Cologne,[53] where, as in almost the whole of the Rhine Province, French criminal law was in force. Prussian law had been introduced by way of exception only for political offences and crimes, but already in April 1848 this exceptional application had been abrogated by Camphausen.

---

[a] Cf. K. Marx, *Zur Kritik der politischen Oekonomie.* See present edition, Vol. 29.— *Ed.*

French law has no knowledge whatever of the loose Prussian legal category of "inciting" to a crime, let alone inciting to an attempt to commit a crime. It knows only *instigation* to crime, and this, to be punishable, must have been committed "by means of gifts, promises, threats, abuse of authority or of power, culpable incitements or artifices" (*Code pénal*, art. 60).[54] The Ministry of State, steeped in Prussian law, overlooked, just as Herr Dühring did, the essential difference between the sharply defined French code and the vague indefiniteness of Prussian law and, subjecting Lassalle to a tendentiously conducted trial, egregiously failed in the case. Only a person who is completely ignorant of modern French law can venture to assert that French criminal procedure permitted the Prussian legal form of an acquittal for lack of evidence, this *half* acquittal; criminal procedure under French law provides only for conviction or acquittal, nothing between.

And so we are forced to say that Herr Dühring would certainly not have been able to perpetrate this "historical depiction in the grand style" [556] against Lassalle if he had ever had the *Code Napoléon*[55] in his hands. We must therefore state as a fact that modern French law, the *only* modern civil code, which rests on the social achievements of the great French Revolution and translates them into legal form, is *completely unknown* to Herr Dühring.

In another place, in the criticism of trial by jury with majority decision which was adopted throughout the Continent in accordance with the French model, we are taught:

"Yes, it will *even* be possible to familiarise oneself with the idea, which for that matter is not without precedent in history, that a conviction *where opinion is divided* should be one of the impossible institutions in a perfect community [D. Ph. 402] ... This *important* and *profoundly intelligent* mode of thought, however, as already indicated above, must seem unsuitable for the traditional forms, because it is *too good* for them [D. Ph. 403].

Once again, Herr Dühring is ignorant of the fact that under English common law, i.e., the unwritten law of custom which has been in force since time immemorial, certainly at least since the fourteenth century, unanimity of the jury is absolutely essential, not only for convictions in criminal cases but also for judgments in civil suits. Thus the important and profoundly intelligent mode of thought, which according to Herr Dühring is *too good* for the present-day world, had had legal validity in England as far back as the darkest Middle Ages, and from England it was brought to Ireland, the United States of America and all the English colonies.

And yet the most exhaustive specialised studies failed to reveal to Herr Dühring even the faintest whisper of all this! The area in which a unanimous verdict by the jury is required is therefore not only infinitely greater than the tiny area where Prussian law is in force, but is also more extensive than all the areas taken together in which juries decide by majority vote. Not only is French law, the only modern law, totally unknown to Herr Dühring; he is equally ignorant of the only Germanic law which has developed independently of Roman authority up to the present day and spread to all parts of the world—English law. And why does Herr Dühring know nothing of it? Because the English brand of the juridical mode of thought

"would anyhow not be able to stand up against the schooling in the pure concepts of the classical Roman jurists given on German soil" [D. K. G. 456],

says Herr Dühring; and he says further:

"what is the English-speaking world with its childish hodgepodge language as compared with our natural language structure?" [D. Ph. 315.]

To which we might answer with Spinoza: *Ignorantia non est argumentum.* Ignorance is no argument.[56]

We can accordingly come to no other final conclusion than that Herr Dühring's most exhaustive specialised studies consisted in his absorption for three years in the theoretical study of the *Corpus juris,*[57] and for a further three years in the practical study of the noble Prussian law. That is certainly quite meritorious, and would be ample for a really respectable district judge or lawyer in old Prussia. But when a person undertakes to compose a legal philosophy for all worlds and all ages, he should at least have some degree of acquaintance with legal systems like those of the French, English and Americans, nations which have played quite a different role in history from that played by the little corner of Germany in which Prussian law flourishes. But let us follow him further.

"The variegated medley of local, provincial and national laws, which run counter to one another in the most various directions, in very arbitrary fashion, sometimes as common law, sometimes as written law, often cloaking the most important issues in a purely statutory form—this pattern-book of disorder and contradiction, in which particular points override general principles, and then at times general principles override particular points—is really not calculated to enable anyone to form a clear conception of jurisprudence" [278].

But where does this confusion exist? Once again, within the area where Prussian law holds sway, where alongside, over or under this law there are provincial laws and local statutes, here and there also common law and other trash, ranging through the most diverse degrees of relative validity and eliciting from all practising jurists that scream for help which Herr Dühring here so sympathetically echoes. He need not even go outside his beloved Prussia—he need only come as far as the Rhine to convince himself that all this ceased to be an issue there for the last seventy years—not to speak of other civilised countries, where these antiquated conditions have long since been abolished.

Further:

"In a less blunt form the natural responsibility of individuals is screened by means of secret and therefore anonymous collective decisions and actions on the part of *collegia* or other institutions of public authority, which mask the personal share of each separate member" [218].

And in another passage:

"In our present situation it will be regarded as an *astonishing* and extremely stern demand if one opposes the glossing over and covering up of individual responsibility through the medium of collective bodies" [402].

Perhaps Herr Dühring will regard it as an astonishing piece of information when we tell him that in the sphere of English law each member of a judicial bench has to give his decision separately and in open court, stating the grounds on which it is based; that administrative collective bodies which are not elected and do not transact business or vote publicly are essentially a *Prussian* institution and are unknown in most other countries, and that therefore his demand can be regarded as astonishing and extremely stern only—in *Prussia.*

Similarly, his complaints about the compulsory introduction of religious practices in birth, marriage, death and burial [407] apply to Prussia alone of all the greater civilised countries, and since the adoption of civil registration they no longer apply even there.[58] What Herr Dühring can accomplish only by means of a future "socialitarian" state of things, even Bismarck has meanwhile managed by means of a simple law.—It is just the same with his "plaint over the inadequate preparation of jurists for their profession" [501], a plaint which could be extended to cover the "administrative officials" [503]—it is a specifically Prussian jeremiad; and even his hatred of the Jews, which he carries to ridiculous extremes and exhibits on every possible occasion, is a feature which if not specifically Prussian is yet specific to the region east of the Elbe. That same philosopher of reality who has a sovereign contempt for all prejudices and superstitions is himself so deeply immersed in personal crotchets that he calls the popular prejudice against the Jews, inherited from the bigotry of the Middle Ages, a "natural judgment" based on "natural grounds", and he rises to the pyramidal heights of the assertion that

"socialism is the only power which can oppose population conditions with a rather strong Jewish admixture" [D. Ph. 393]. (Conditions with a Jewish admixture! What "natural" German!)

Enough of this. The grandiloquent boasts of legal erudition have as their basis—at best—only the most commonplace professional knowledge of quite an ordinary jurist of old Prussia. The sphere of legal and political science, the attainments in which Herr Dühring consistently expounds, "coincides" with the area where Prussian law holds sway. Apart from the Roman law, with which every jurist is fairly familiar, now even in England, his knowledge of law is confined wholly and entirely to Prussian law— that legal code of an enlightened patriarchal despotism which is written in a German such as Herr Dühring appears to have been trained in, and which, with its moral glosses, its juristic vagueness and inconsistency, its caning as a means of torture and punishment, belongs entirely to the pre-revolutionary epoch. Whatever exists beyond this Herr Dühring regards as evil[a]—both modern civil French law, and English law with its quite peculiar development and its safeguarding of personal liberty, unknown anywhere on the Continent. The philosophy which "does not allow the validity of any merely *apparent* horizon, but in its powerfully revolutionising movement unfolds all earths and heavens of outer and inner nature" [430]—has as its *real* horizon— the boundaries of the six eastern provinces of old Prussia,[59] and in addition perhaps the few other patches of land where the noble Prussian law holds sway; and beyond this horizon it unfolds neither earths nor heavens, neither outer nor inner nature, but only a picture of the crassest ignorance of what is happening in the rest of the world.

It is hard to deal with morality and law without coming up against the question of so-called free will, of man's mental responsibility, of the relation between necessity and freedom. And the philosophy of reality also has not only one but even two solutions of this problem.

---

[a] Matthew 5:37.—*Ed.*

"All false theories of freedom must be replaced by, what we know from experience is the nature of the relation between rational judgment on the one hand and instinctive impulses on the other, a relation which *so to speak* unites them into a resultant force. The fundamental facts of this form of dynamics must be drawn from observation, and for the calculation in advance of events which have not yet occurred must also be estimated, *as closely as possible,* in general both as to their nature and magnitude. In this manner the silly delusions of inner freedom, which people have chewed on and fed on for thousands of years, are not only cleared away in thoroughgoing fashion, but are replaced by something positive, which can be made use of for the practical regulation of life" [187].

Viewed thus freedom consists in rational judgment pulling a man to the right while irrational impulses pull him to the left, and in this parallelogram of forces the actual movement proceeds in the direction of the diagonal. Freedom is therefore the mean between judgment and impulse, reason and unreason, and its degree in each individual case can be determined on the basis of experience by a "personal equation", to use an astronomical expression.[60] But a few pages later on we find:

"We base moral responsibility on freedom, which however means nothing more to us than susceptibility to conscious motives in accordance with our natural and acquired intelligence. All such motives operate with the inevitability of natural law, notwithstanding an awareness of possible contrary actions; but it is precisely on this unavoidable compulsion that we rely when we apply the moral levers" [218].

This second definition of freedom, which quite unceremoniously gives a knock-out blow to the first one, is again nothing but an extreme vulgarisation of the Hegelian conception. Hegel was the first to state correctly the relation between freedom and necessity. To him, freedom is the insight into necessity [*die Einsicht in die Notwendigkeit*]. "Necessity is *blind* only *in so far as it is not understood* [*begriffen*]." [a] Freedom does not consist in any dreamt-of independence from natural laws, but in the knowledge of these laws, and in the possibility this gives of systematically making them work towards definite ends. This holds good in relation both to the laws of external nature and to those which govern the bodily and mental existence of men themselves— two classes of laws which we can separate from each other at most only in thought but not in reality. Freedom of the will therefore means nothing but the capacity to make decisions with knowledge of the subject. Therefore the *freer* a man's judgment is in relation to a definite question, the greater is the *necessity* with which the content of this judgment will be determined; while the

---

[a] G. W. F. Hegel, *Encyklopädie der philosophischen Wissenschaften,* § 147, Addendum. Italics by Engels.— *Ed.*

uncertainty, founded on ignorance, which seems to make an arbitrary choice among many different and conflicting possible decisions, shows precisely by this that it is not free, that it is controlled by the very object it should itself control. Freedom therefore consists in the control over ourselves and over external nature, a control founded on knowledge of natural necessity; it is therefore necessarily a product of historical development. The first men who separated themselves from the animal kingdom were in all essentials as unfree as the animals themselves, but each step forward in the field of culture was a step towards freedom. On the threshold of human history stands the discovery that mechanical motion can be transformed into heat: the production of fire by friction; at the close of the development so far gone through stands the discovery that heat can be transformed into mechanical motion: the steam-engine.— And, in spite of the gigantic liberating revolution in the social world which the steam-engine is carrying through, and which is not yet half completed, it is beyond all doubt that the generation of fire by friction has had an even greater effect on the liberation of mankind. For the generation of fire by friction gave man for the first time control over one of the forces of nature, and thereby separated him for ever from the animal kingdom. The steam-engine will never bring about such a mighty leap forward in human development, however important it may seem in our eyes as representing all those immense productive forces dependent on it—forces which alone make possible a state of society in which there are no longer class distinctions or anxiety over the means of subsistence for the individual, and in which for the first time there can be talk of real human freedom, of an existence in harmony with the laws of nature that have become known. But how young the whole of human history still is, and how ridiculous it would be to attempt to ascribe any absolute validity to our present views, is evident from the simple fact that all past history can be characterised as the history of the epoch from the practical discovery of the transformation of mechanical motion into heat up to that of the transformation of heat into mechanical motion.

True, Herr Dühring's treatment of history is different. In general, being a record of error, ignorance and barbarity, of violence and subjugation, history is a repulsive object to the philosophy of reality; but considered in detail it is divided into two great periods, namely (1) from the self-equal state of matter up to the French Revolution; (2) from the French Revolution up to Herr Dühring; the nineteenth century remains "still in essence reactionary, indeed from the intellectual standpoint even more so" (!) "than the eighteenth". Nevertheless, it bears socialism in its womb, and therewith "the germ of a mightier regeneration than was fancied" (!) "by the forerunners and the heroes of the French Revolution" [D. Ph. 301].

The philosophy of reality's contempt for all past history is justified as follows:

"The few thousand years, the historical retrospection of which has been facilitated by original documents, are, together with the constitution of mankind so far, *of little significance* when one thinks of the succession of thousands of years which are still to come... The human race as a whole is still very young, and when in time to come scientific retrospection has tens of thousands instead of thousands of years to reckon with, the intellectually immature childhood of our institutions becomes a self-evident premise undisputed in relation to our epoch, which will then be revered as hoary antiquity" [302].

Without dwelling on the really "natural language structure" of the last sentence, we shall note only two points. Firstly, that this "hoary antiquity" will in any case remain a historical epoch of the greatest interest for all future generations, because it forms the basis of all subsequent higher development, because it has for its starting-point the moulding of man from the animal kingdom, and for its content the overcoming of obstacles such as will never again confront associated mankind of the future. And secondly, that the close of this hoary antiquity—in contrast to which the future periods of history, which will no longer be kept back by these difficulties and obstacles, hold the promise of quite other scientific, technical and social achievements—is in any case a very strange moment to choose to lay down the law for these thousands of years that are to come, in the form of final and ultimate truths, immutable truths and deep-rooted conceptions discovered on the basis of the intellectually immature childhood of our so extremely "backward" and "retrogressive" century. Only a Richard Wagner in philosophy—but without Wagner's talents—could fail to see that all the depreciatory epithets slung at previous historical development remain sticking also on what is claimed to be its final outcome—the so-called philosophy of reality.

One of the most significant morsels of the new deep-rooted science [219] is the section on individualisation and increasing the value of life. In this section oracular commonplaces bubble up and gush forth in an irresistible torrent for three full chapters. Unfortunately we must limit ourselves to a few short samples.

"The deeper essence of all sensation and therefore of all subjective forms of life rests on the *difference* between states... But for a *full*" (!) "life it can be shown without much trouble" (!) "that its appreciation is heightened and the decisive stimuli are developed, not by persistence in a particular state, but by a transition from one situation in life to another... The approximately self-equal state which is *so to speak* in permanent inertia and *as it were* continues in the same position of equilibrium, whatever its nature may be, has but little significance for the testing of existence... Habituation and *so to speak* inurement makes it something of absolute indifference and unconcern, something which is not very distinct from deadness. At most the torment of boredom also enters into it as a kind of negative life impulse... A life of stagnation extinguishes all passion and all interest in existence, both for individuals and for peoples. *But it is our law of difference through which all these phenomena become explicable*" [D. Ph. 362-63].

The rapidity with which Herr Dühring establishes his from the ground up original conclusions passes all belief. The commonplace that the continued stimulation of the same nerve or the continuation of the same stimulus fatigues each nerve or each nervous system, and that therefore in a normal condition nerve stimuli must be interrupted and varied—which for years has been stated in every textbook of physiology and is known to every philistine from his own experience—is first translated into the language of the philosophy of reality. No sooner has this platitude, which is as old as the hills, been translated into the mysterious formula that the deeper essence of all sensation rests on the difference between states, than it is further transformed into "*our* law of difference". And this law of difference makes "absolutely explicable" a whole series of phenomena which in turn are nothing more than illustrations and examples of the pleasantness of variety and which require no explanation whatever even for the most common philistine understanding and gain not the breadth of an atom in clarity by reference to this alleged law of difference.

But this far from exhausts the deep-rootedness of "*our* law of difference" [219].

"The sequence of ages in life, and the emergence of different conditions of life bound up with it, furnish a very obvious example with which to illustrate *our* principle of difference... Child, boy, youth and man experience the intensity of their appreciation of life at each stage not so much when the state in which they find themselves has already become fixed, as in the periods of transition from one to another" [363].

Even this is not enough.

"*Our* law of difference can be given an even more extended application if we take into consideration the fact that a repetition of what has already been tried or done has no attraction" [365].

And now the reader can himself imagine the oracular twaddle for which sentences of the depth and deep-rootedness of those cited form the starting-point. Herr Dühring may well shout triumphantly at the end of his book:

"The law of difference has become decisive both in theory and in practice for the appraisement and heightening of the value of life!" [558]

This is likewise true of Herr Dühring's appraisement of the intellectual value of his public: he must believe that it is composed of sheer asses or philistines.

We are further given the following extremely practical rules of life:

"The method whereby total interest in life can be kept active" (a fitting task for philistines and those who want to become such!) "consists in allowing the particular and *so to speak* elementary interests, of which the total interest is composed, to develop or succeed each other in accordance with natural periods of time. Simultaneously, for the same state the succession of stages may be made use of by replacing the lower and more easily satisfied stimuli by higher and more permanently effective excitations in order to avoid the occurrence of any gaps that are entirely devoid of interest. However, it will be necessary to ensure that the natural tensions or those arising in the normal course of social existence are not arbitrarily accumulated or forced or—the opposite perversion—satisfied by the lightest stimulation, and thus prevented from developing a want which is capable of gratification. In this as in other cases the maintenance of the natural rhythm is the precondition of all harmonious and agreeable movement. Nor should anyone set before himself the insoluble problem of trying to prolong the stimuli of any situation beyond the period allotted them by nature or by the circumstances" [375]—and so on.

The simpleton who takes as his rule for the "testing of life" these solemn oracles of philistine pedantry subtilising over the shallowest platitudes will certainly not have to complain of "gaps entirely devoid of interest". It will take him all his time to prepare his pleasures and get them in the right order, so that he will not have a moment left to enjoy them.

We should try out life, full life. There are only two things which Herr Dühring prohibits us:

first "the uncleanliness of indulging in tobacco", and secondly drinks and foods which "have properties that rouse disgust or are in general obnoxious to the more refined feelings" [261].

In his course of political economy, however, Herr Dühring writes such a dithyramb on the distilling of spirits that it is impossible that he should include spirituous liquor in this category; we are therefore forced to conclude that his prohibition covers only wine and beer. He has only to prohibit meat, too, and then he will have raised the philosophy of reality to the same height as that on which the late Gustav Struve moved with such great success—the height of pure childishness.

For the rest, Herr Dühring might be slightly more liberal in regard to spirituous liquors. A man who, by his own admission, still cannot find the bridge from the static to the dynamic [D. Ph. 80] has surely every reason to be indulgent in judging some poor devil who has for once dipped too deep in his glass and as a result also seeks in vain the bridge from the dynamic to the static.

XII. DIALECTICS. QUANTITY AND QUALITY

"The first and most important principle of the basic logical properties of being refers to the *exclusion of contradiction.* Contradiction is a category which can only appertain to a combination of thoughts, but not to reality. There are no contradictions in things, or, to put it another way, contradiction accepted as reality is itself the apex of absurdity [D. Ph. 30] ... The antagonism of forces measured against each other and moving in opposite directions is in fact the basic form of all actions in the life of the world and its creatures. But this opposition of the directions taken by the forces of elements and individuals does not in the slightest degree coincide with the idea of absurd contradictions [31] ... We can be content here with having cleared the fogs which generally rise from the supposed mysteries of logic by presenting a clear picture of the actual absurdity of contradictions in reality, and with having shown the uselessness of the incense which has been burnt here and there in honour of the dialectics of contradiction—the very clumsily carved wooden doll which is substituted for the antagonistic world schematism" [32].

This is practically all we are told about dialectics in the *Cursus der Philosophie.* In his *Kritische Geschichte,* on the other hand, the dialectics of contradiction, and with it particularly Hegel, is treated quite differently.

"Contradiction, according to the Hegelian logic, or rather Logos doctrine, is objectively present not in thought, which by its nature can only be conceived as subjective and conscious, but in things and processes themselves and can be met with in so to speak corporeal form, so that absurdity does not remain an impossible combination of thought but becomes an actual force. The reality of the absurd is the first article of faith in the Hegelian unity of the logical and the illogical.... The more contradictory a thing the truer it is, or in other words, the more absurd the more credible it is. This maxim, which is not even newly invented but is borrowed from the theology of the Revelation and from mysticism, is the naked expression of the so-called dialectical principle" [D. K. G. 479-80].

The thought-content of the two passages cited can be summed up in the statement that contradiction=absurdity, and therefore cannot occur in the real world. People who in other respects show a fair degree of common sense may regard this statement as having the same self-evident validity as the statement that a straight line cannot be a curve and a curve cannot be straight. But, regardless of all protests made by common sense, the differential calculus under certain circumstances nevertheless equates straight lines and curves, and thus obtains results which common sense, insisting on the absurdity of straight lines being identical with curves, can never attain. And in view of the important role which the so-called dialectics of contradiction has played in philosophy from the time of the ancient Greeks up to the present, even a stronger opponent than Herr Dühring should have felt obliged to attack it with other arguments besides one assertion and a good many abusive epithets.

True, so long as we consider things as at rest and lifeless, each one by itself, alongside and after each other, we do not run up against any contradictions in them. We find certain qualities which are partly common to, partly different from, and even contradictory to each other, but which in the last-mentioned case are distributed among different objects and therefore contain no contradiction within. Inside the limits of this sphere of observation we can get along on the basis of the usual, metaphysical mode of thought. But the position is quite different as soon as we consider things in their motion, their change, their life, their reciprocal influence on one another. Then we immediately become involved in contradictions. Motion itself is a contradiction: even simple mechanical change of position can only come about through a body being at one and the same moment of time both in one place and in another place, being in one and the same place and also not in it. And the continuous origination and simultaneous solution of this contradiction is precisely what motion is.

Here, therefore, we have a contradiction which "is objectively present in things and processes themselves and can be met with in so to speak corporeal form". And what has Herr Dühring to say about it? He asserts that

up to the present there is "no bridge" whatever "in rational mechanics from the strictly static to the dynamic" [D. Ph. 80].

The reader can now at last see what is hidden behind this favourite phrase of Herr Dühring's—it is nothing but this: the mind which thinks metaphysically is absolutely unable to pass from the idea of rest to the idea of motion, because the contradiction pointed out above blocks its path. To it, motion is simply incomprehensible because it is a contradiction. And in asserting the incomprehensibility of motion, it admits against its will the existence of this contradiction, and thus admits the objective presence in things and processes themselves of a contradiction which is moreover an actual force.

If simple mechanical change of position contains a contradiction, this is even more true of the higher forms of motion of matter, and especially of organic life and its development. We saw above that life consists precisely and primarily in this—that a being is at each moment itself and yet something else.[a] Life is therefore also a contradiction which is present in things and processes themselves, and which constantly originates and resolves itself; and as soon as the contradiction ceases, life, too, comes to an end, and death steps in. We likewise saw that also in the sphere of thought we could not escape contradictions, and that for example the contradiction between man's inherently unlimited capacity for knowledge and its actual presence only in men who are externally limited and possess limited cognition finds its solution in what is—at least practically, for us—an endless succession of generations, in infinite progress.[b]

We have already noted that one of the basic principles of higher mathematics is the contradiction that in certain circumstances straight lines and curves may be the same. It also gets up this other contradiction: that lines which intersect each other before our eyes nevertheless, only five or six centimetres from their point of intersection, can be shown to be parallel, that is, that they will never meet even if extended to infinity. And yet, working with these and with even far greater contradictions, it attains results which are not only correct but also quite unattainable for lower mathematics.

But even lower mathematics teems with contradictions. It is for example a contradiction that a root of A should be a power of A, and yet $A^{\frac{1}{2}}=\sqrt{A}$. It is a contradiction that a negative quantity should be the square of anything, for every negative quantity multiplied by itself gives a positive square. The square root of minus one is therefore not only a contradiction, but even an absurd contradiction, a real absurdity. And yet $\sqrt{-1}$ is in many cases a necessary result of correct mathematical operations. Furthermore, where would mathematics—lower or higher—be, if it were prohibited from operation with $\sqrt{-1}$?

In its operations with variable quantities mathematics itself enters the field of dialectics, and it is significant that it was a

---

[a] See this volume, pp. 76-77.—*Ed.*
[b] Ibid., pp. 35-36 and 80.— *Ed.*

dialectical philosopher, Descartes, who introduced this advance. The relation between the mathematics of variable and the mathematics of constant quantities is in general the same as the relation of dialectical to metaphysical thought. But this does not prevent the great mass of mathematicians from recognising dialectics only in the sphere of mathematics, and a good many of them from continuing to work in the old, limited, metaphysical way with methods that were obtained dialectically.

It would be possible to go more closely into Herr Dühring's antagonism of forces and his antagonistic world schematism only if he had given us something more on this theme than the mere *phrase*. After accomplishing this feat this antagonism is not even once shown to us at work, either in his world schematism or in his natural philosophy—the most convincing admission that Herr Dühring can do absolutely nothing of a positive character with his "basic form of all actions in the life of the world and its creatures". When someone has in fact lowered Hegel's "Doctrine of Essence" to the platitude of forces moving in opposite directions but not in contradictions, certainly the best thing he can do is to avoid any application of this commonplace.

Marx's *Capital* furnishes Herr Dühring with another occasion for venting his anti-dialectical spleen.

"The absence of natural and intelligible logic which characterises these dialectical frills and mazes and conceptual arabesques... Even to the part that has already appeared we must apply the principle that in a certain respect and also in general" (!), "according to a well-known philosophical preconception, all is to be sought in each and each in all, and that therefore, according to this mixed and misconceived idea, it all amounts to one and the same thing in the end" [D. K. G. 496].

This insight into the well-known philosophical preconception also enables Herr Dühring to prophesy with assurance what will be the "end" of Marx's economic philosophising, that is, what the following volumes of *Capital* will contain, and this he does exactly seven lines after he has declared that

"speaking in plain human language it is really impossible to divine what is still to come in the two" (final) "volumes" [61] [496].

This, however, is not the first time that Herr Dühring's writings are revealed to us as belonging to the "things" in which "contradiction is objectively present and can be met with in so to speak corporeal form" [479-80]. But this does not prevent him from going on victoriously as follows:

"Yet sound logic will in all probability triumph over its caricature... This pretence of superiority and this mysterious dialectical rubbish will tempt no one who has even a modicum of sound judgment left to have anything to do ... with these deformities of thought and style. With the demise of the last relics of the dialectical follies this means of duping ... will lose its deceptive influence, and no one will any longer believe that he has to torture himself in order to get behind some profound piece of wisdom where the husked kernel of the abstruse things reveals at best the features of ordinary theories if not of absolute commonplaces... It is quite impossible to reproduce the" (Marxian) "maze in accordance with the Logos doctrine without prostituting sound logic" [D. K. G. 497]. Marx's method, according to Herr Dühring, consists in "performing dialectical miracles for his faithful followers" [498], and so on.

We are not in any way concerned here as yet with the correctness or incorrectness of the economic results of Marx's researches, but only with the dialectical method used by Marx. But this much is certain: most readers of *Capital* will have learnt for the first time from Herr Dühring what it is in fact that they have read. And among them will also be Herr Dühring himself, who in the year 1867 (*Ergänzungsblätter* III, No. 3) was still able to provide what for a thinker of his calibre was a relatively rational review of the book[a]; and he did this without first being obliged, as he now declares is indispensable, to translate the Marxian argument into Dühringian language. And though even then he committed the blunder of identifying Marxian dialectics with the Hegelian, he had not quite lost the capacity to distinguish between the method and the results obtained by using it, and to understand that the latter are not refuted in detail by lampooning the former in general.

At any rate, the most astonishing piece of information given by Herr Dühring is the statement that from the Marxian standpoint "it all amounts to one and the same thing in the end" [496], that therefore to Marx, for example, capitalists and wage-workers, feudal, capitalist and socialist modes of production are also "one and the same thing"—no doubt in the end even Marx and Herr Dühring are "one and the same thing". Such utter nonsense can only be explained if we suppose that the mere mention of the word dialectics throws Herr Dühring into such a state of mental irresponsibility that, as a result of a certain mixed and misconceived idea, what he says and does is "one and the same thing" in the end.

We have here a sample of what Herr Dühring calls

---

[a] E. Dühring, *Marx, Das Kapital, Kritik der politischen Oekonomie, 1. Band.—Ed.*

"*my* historical depiction in the grand style" [556], or "the summary treatment which settles with genus and type, and does not condescend to honour what a Hume called the learned mob with an exposure in micrological detail; this treatment in a higher and nobler style is the only one compatible with the interests of complete truth and with one's duty to the public which is free from the bonds of the guilds" [507].

Historical depiction in the grand style and the summary settlement with genus and type is indeed very convenient for Herr Dühring, inasmuch as this method enables him to neglect all known facts as micrological and equate them to zero, so that instead of proving anything he need only use general phrases, make assertions and thunder his denunciations. The method has the further advantage that it offers no real foothold to an opponent, who is consequently left with almost no other possibility of reply than to make similar summary assertions in the grand style, to resort to general phrases and finally thunder back denunciations at Herr Dühring—in a word, as they say, engage in a slanging match, which is not to everyone's taste. We must therefore be grateful to Herr Dühring for occasionally, by way of exception, dropping the higher and nobler style, and giving us at least two examples of the unsound Marxian Logos doctrine.

"How comical is the reference to the confused, hazy Hegelian notion that quantity changes into quality, and that therefore an advance, when it reaches a certain size, becomes capital by this quantitative increase alone" [498].

In this "expurgated" presentation by Herr Dühring that statement certainly seems curious enough. Let us see how it looks in the original, in Marx. On page 313 (2nd edition of *Capital*),[a] Marx, on the basis of his previous examination of constant and variable capital and surplus-value, draws the conclusion that "not every sum of money, or of value, is at pleasure transformable into capital. To effect this transformation, in fact, a certain minimum of money or of exchange-value must be presupposed in the hands of the individual possessor of money or commodities."[b] He takes as an example the case of a labourer in any branch of industry, who works daily eight hours for himself—that is, in producing the value of his wages—and the following four hours for the capitalist, in producing surplus-value, which immediately flows into the pocket of the capitalist. In this case, one would have to

---

[a] K. Marx, *Das Kapital, Kritik der politischen Oekonomie*, Hamburg, 1872. Further on Engels quotes according to this edition.— *Ed.*

[b] See present edition, Vol. 35, Part III, Chapter XI.— *Ed.*

have at his disposal a sum of values sufficient to enable one to provide two labourers with raw materials, instruments of labour, and wages, in order to pocket enough surplus-value every day to live on as well as one of his labourers. And as the aim of capitalist production is not mere subsistence but the increase of wealth, our man with his two labourers would still not be a capitalist. Now in order that he may live twice as well as an ordinary labourer, and turn half of the surplus-value produced again into capital, he would have to be able to employ eight labourers, that is, he would have to possess four times the sum of values assumed above. And it is only after this, and in the course of still further explanations elucidating and substantiating the fact that not every petty sum of values is enough to be transformable into capital, but that in this respect each period of development and each branch of industry has its definite minimum sum, that Marx observes: "Here, as in natural science, *is shown*[a] the correctness of the law discovered by Hegel in his *Logic*, that merely quantitative changes beyond a certain point pass into qualitative differences."[b]

And now let the reader admire the higher and nobler style, by virtue of which Herr Dühring attributes to Marx the opposite of what he really said. Marx says: The fact that a sum of values can be transformed into capital only when it has reached a certain size, varying according to the circumstances, but in each case definite, minimum size—this fact is a *proof of the correctness* of the Hegelian law. Herr Dühring makes him say: *Because*, according to the Hegelian law, quantity changes into quality, "*therefore*" "an advance, when it reaches a certain size, becomes capital" [D. K. G. 498]. That is to say, the very opposite.

In connection with Herr Dühring's examination of the Darwin case, we have already got to know his habit, "in the interests of complete truth" and because of his "duty to the public which is free from the bonds of the guilds" [507], of quoting incorrectly. It becomes more and more evident that this habit is an inner necessity of the philosophy of reality, and it is certainly a very "summary treatment" [507]. Not to mention the fact that Herr Dühring further makes Marx speak of any kind of "advance" whatsoever, whereas Marx only refers to an advance made in the form of raw materials, instruments of labour, and wages; and that in doing this Herr Dühring succeeds in making Marx speak pure nonsense. And then he has the cheek to describe

---

[a] Italics by Engels.— *Ed.*
[b] See present edition, Vol. 35, Part III, Chapter XI.— *Ed.*

as *comic* the nonsense which he himself has fabricated. Just as he built up a Darwin of his own fantasy in order to try out his strength against him, so here he builds up a fantastic Marx. "Historical depiction in the grand style" [556], indeed!

We have already seen earlier, when discussing world schematism,[a] that in connection with this Hegelian nodal line of measure relations—in which quantitative change suddenly passes at certain points into qualitative transformation—Herr Dühring had a little accident: in a weak moment he himself recognised and made use of this line. We gave there one of the best-known examples—that of the change of the aggregate states of water, which under normal atmospheric pressure changes at 0° C from the liquid into the solid state, and at 100° C from the liquid into the gaseous state, so that at both these turning-points the merely quantitative change of temperature brings about a qualitative change in the condition of the water.

In proof of this law we might have cited hundreds of other similar facts from nature as well as from human society. Thus, for example, the whole of Part IV of Marx's *Capital*—production of relative surplus-value—deals, in the field of co-operation, division of labour and manufacture, machinery and modern industry, with innumerable cases in which quantitative change alters the quality, and also qualitative change alters the quantity, of the things under consideration; in which therefore, to use the expression so hated by Herr Dühring, quantity is transformed into quality and vice versa. As for example the fact that the co-operation of a number of people, the fusion of many forces into one single force, creates, to use Marx's phrase, a "new power", which is essentially different from the sum of its separate forces.[b]

Over and above this, in the passage which, in the interests of complete truth, Herr Dühring perverted into its opposite, Marx had added a footnote: "The molecular theory of modern chemistry first scientifically worked out by Laurent and Gerhardt rests on no other law."[c] But what did that matter to Herr Dühring? He knew that:

"the eminently modern educative elements provided by the natural-scientific mode of thought are lacking precisely among those who, like Marx and his rival Lassalle,

---

[a] See this volume, pp. 42-43.— *Ed.*

[b] K. Marx, *Das Kapital,* p. 334. See present edition, Vol. 35, Part IV, Chapter XIII.— *Ed.*

[c] Ibid., p. 315. See present edition, Vol. 35, Part III, Chapter XI.— *Ed.*

make half-science and a little philosophistics the meagre equipment with which to vamp up their learning" [D. K. G. 504]—

while with Herr Dühring "the main achievements of exact knowledge in mechanics, physics and chemistry" [D. Ph. 517] and so forth serve as the basis—we have seen how. However, in order to enable third persons, too, to reach a decision in the matter, we shall look a little more closely into the example cited in Marx's footnote.

What is referred to here is the homologous series of carbon compounds, of which a great many are already known and each of which has its own algebraic formula of composition. If, for example, as is done in chemistry, we denote an atom of carbon by C, an atom of hydrogen by H, an atom of oxygen by O, and the number of atoms of carbon contained in each compound by n, the molecular formulas for some of these series can be expressed as follows:

C_nH_{2n+2} —the series of normal paraffins
$C_nH_{2n+2}O$—the series of primary alcohols
$C_nH_{2n}O_2$ —the series of the monobasic fatty acids.

Let us take as an example the last of these series, and let us assume successively that $n=1$, $n=2$, $n=3$, etc. We then obtain the following results (omitting the isomers):

CH_2O_2 —formic acid	—	boiling	point	100°	melting	point	1°
$C_2H_4O_2$ —acetic acid		"	"	118°	melting	point	17°
$C_3H_6O_2$ —propionic acid		"	"	140°	"	"	—
$C_4H_8O_2$ —butyric acid		"	"	162°	"	"	—
$C_5H_{10}O_2$—valerianic acid		"	"	175°	"	"	—

and so on to $C_{30}H_{60}O_2$, melissic acid, which melts only at 80° and has no boiling point at all, because it cannot evaporate without disintegrating.

Here therefore we have a whole series of qualitatively different bodies, formed by the simple quantitative addition of elements, and in fact always in the same proportion. This is most clearly evident in cases where the quantity of all the elements of the compound changes in the same proportion. Thus, in the normal paraffins C_nH_{2n+2}, the lowest is methane, CH_4, a gas; the highest known, hexadecane, $C_{16}H_{34}$, is a solid body forming colourless crystals which melts at 21° and boils only at 278°. Each new member of both series comes into existence through the addition of CH_2, one atom of carbon and two atoms of hydrogen, to the molecular formula of the preceding member, and this quantitative change in the molecular formula produces each time a qualitatively different body.

These series, however, are only one particularly obvious example; throughout practically the whole of chemistry, even in the various nitrogen oxides and oxygen acids of phosphorus or sulphur, one can see how "quantity changes into quality", and this allegedly confused, hazy Hegelian notion appears in so to speak corporeal form in things and processes—and no one but Herr Dühring is confused and befogged by it. And if Marx was the first to call attention to it, and if Herr Dühring read the reference without even understanding it (otherwise he would certainly not have allowed this unparalleled outrage to pass unchallenged), this is enough—even without looking back at the famous Dühringian philosophy of nature—to make it clear which of the two, Marx or Herr Dühring, is lacking in "the eminently modern educative elements provided by the natural-scientific mode of thought" [D. K. G. 504] and in acquaintance with the "main achievements of ... chemistry" [D. Ph. 517].

In conclusion we shall call one more witness for the transformation of quantity into quality, namely—Napoleon. He describes the combat between the French cavalry, who were bad riders but disciplined, and the Mamelukes, who were undoubtedly the best horsemen of their time for single combat, but lacked discipline, as follows:

"Two Mamelukes were undoubtedly more than a match for three Frenchmen; 100 Mamelukes were equal to 100 Frenchmen; 300 Frenchmen could generally beat 300 Mamelukes, and 1,000 Frenchmen invariably defeated 1,500 Mamelukes."[a]

Just as with Marx a definite, though varying, minimum sum of exchange-values was necessary to make possible its transformation into capital, so with Napoleon a detachment of cavalry had to be of a definite minimum number in order to make it possible for the force of discipline, embodied in closed order and planned utilisation, to manifest itself and rise superior even to greater numbers of irregular cavalry, in spite of the latter being better mounted, more dexterous horsemen and fighters, and at least as brave as the former. But what does this prove as against Herr Dühring? Was not Napoleon miserably vanquished in his conflict with Europe? Did he not suffer defeat after defeat? And why? Solely in consequence of having introduced the confused, hazy Hegelian notion into cavalry tactics!

---

[a] *Mémoires pour servir à l'histoire de France, sous Napoléon, écrits à Sainte-Hélène, par les généraux qui ont partagé sa captivité, et publiés sur les manuscrits entièrement corrigés de la main de Napoléon*, Vol. I, p. 262.— *Ed.*

XIII. DIALECTICS. NEGATION OF THE NEGATION

"This historical sketch" (of the genesis of the so-called primitive accumulation of capital in England) "is relatively the best part of Marx's book, and would be even better if it had not relied on the dialectical crutch to help out its scholarly crutch. The Hegelian negation of the negation, in default of anything better and clearer, has in fact to serve here as the midwife to deliver the future from the womb of the past. The abolition of 'individual property', which since the sixteenth century has been effected in the way indicated above, is the first negation. It will be followed by a second, which bears the character of a negation of the negation and hence of a restoration of 'individual property', but in a higher form, based on the common ownership of land and of the instruments of labour. Herr Marx calls this new 'individual property' also 'social property', and in this there appears the Hegelian higher unity, in which the contradiction is supposed to be sublated, that is to say, in the Hegelian verbal jugglery, both overcome and preserved... According to this, the expropriation of the expropriators is, as it were, the automatic result of historical reality in its materially external relations... It would be difficult to convince a sensible man of the necessity of the common ownership of land and capital, on the basis of credence in Hegelian word-juggling such as the negation of the negation [D. K. G. 502-03]... The nebulous hybrids of Marx's conceptions will not however appear strange to anyone who realises what nonsense can be concocted with Hegelian dialectics as the scientific basis, or rather what nonsense must necessarily spring from it. For the benefit of the reader who is not familiar with these artifices, it must be pointed out expressly that Hegel's first negation is the catechismal idea of the fall from grace and his second is that of a higher unity leading to redemption. The logic of facts can hardly be based on this nonsensical analogy borrowed from the religious sphere [504] ... Herr Marx remains cheerfully in the nebulous world of his property which is at once both individual and social and leaves it to his adepts to solve for themselves this profound dialectical enigma" [505].

Thus far Herr Dühring.

So Marx has no other way of proving the necessity of the social revolution, of establishing the common ownership of land and of the means of production produced by labour, except by citing the Hegelian negation of the negation; and because he bases his socialist theory on these nonsensical analogies borrowed from religion, he arrives at the result that in the society of the future there will be dominant an ownership at once both individual and social, as Hegelian higher unity of the sublated contradiction.

But let the negation of the negation rest for the moment and let us have a look at the "ownership" which is "at once both individual and social". Herr Dühring characterises this as a "nebulous world", and curiously enough he is really right on this point. Unfortunately, however, it is not Marx but again Herr Dühring himself who is in this nebulous world. Just as his dexterity in handling the Hegelian method of "delirious raving" [D. Ph. 227, 449] enabled him without any difficulty to determine what the still unfinished volumes of *Capital* are sure to contain, so here, too, without any great effort he can put Marx right *à la* Hegel, by imputing to him the higher unity of a property, of which there is not a word in Marx.

Marx says: "It is the negation of negation. This re-establishes individual property, but on the basis of the acquisitions of the capitalist era, i.e., on co-operation of free workers and their possession in common of the land and of the means of production produced by labour. The transformation of scattered private property, arising from individual labour, into capitalist private property is, naturally, a process, incomparably more protracted, arduous, and difficult, than the transformation of capitalistic private property, already practically resting on socialised production, into socialised property."[a] That is all. The state of things brought about by the expropriation of the expropriators is therefore characterised as the re-establishment of individual property, but *on the basis* of the social ownership of the land and of the means of production produced by labour itself. To anyone who understands plain talk this means that social ownership extends to the land and the other means of production, and individual ownership to the products, that is, the articles of consumption. And in order to make the matter comprehensible even to children of six, Marx assumes on page 56 "a community of free individuals, carrying on their work with the means of production in common, in which the labour-power of all the different individuals is consciously applied as the combined labour-power of the community", that is, a society organised on a socialist basis; and he continues: "The total product of our community is a social product. One portion serves as fresh means of production and *remains social.* But another portion is consumed by the members as means of subsistence. *A distribution of this portion amongst them is consequently necessary."*[b] And surely that is clear enough even for Herr Dühring, in spite of his having Hegel on his brain.

The property which is at once both individual and social, this confusing hybrid, this nonsense which necessarily springs from Hegelian dialectics, this nebulous world, this profound dialectical enigma, which Marx leaves his adepts to solve for themselves—is yet another free creation and imagination on the part of Herr

---

[a] K. Marx, *Das Kapital,* p. 793. See present edition, Vol. 35, Part VIII, Chapter XXXII.— *Ed.*

[b] Ibid., p. 56. See present edition, Vol. 35, Part I, Chapter I, Section 4. Italics by Engels.— *Ed.*

Dühring. Marx, as an alleged Hegelian, is obliged to produce a real higher unity, as the outcome of the negation of the negation, and as Marx does not do this to Herr Dühring's taste, the latter has to fall again into his higher and nobler style, and in the interests of complete truth impute to Marx things which are the products of Herr Dühring's own manufacture. A man who is totally incapable of quoting correctly, even by way of exception, may well become morally indignant at the "Chinese erudition" [D. K. G. 506] of other people, who always quote correctly, but precisely by doing this "inadequately conceal their lack of insight into the totality of ideas of the various writers from whom they quote". Herr Dühring is right. Long live historical depiction in the grand style [556]!

Up to this point we have proceeded from the assumption that Herr Dühring's persistent habit of misquoting is done at least in good faith, and arises either from his total incapacity to understand things or from a habit of quoting from memory—a habit which seems to be peculiar to historical depiction in the grand style, but is usually described as slovenly. But we seem to have reached the point at which, even with Herr Dühring, quantity is transformed into quality. For we must take into consideration in the first place that the passage in Marx is in itself perfectly clear and is moreover amplified in the same book by a further passage which leaves no room whatever for misunderstanding; secondly, that Herr Dühring had discovered the monstrosity of "property which is at once both individual and social" [505] neither in the critique of *Capital*, in the *Ergänzungsblätter*, which was referred to above,[a] nor even in the critique contained in the first edition of his *Kritische Geschichte*, but only in the second edition—that is, on the *third* reading of *Capital*; further, that in this second edition, which was rewritten in a socialist sense, it was deemed necessary by Herr Dühring to make Marx say the utmost possible nonsense about the future organisation of society, in order to enable him, in contrast, to bring forward all the more triumphantly—as he in fact does—"the economic commune as described by *me* in economic and juridical outline in my *Cursus*" [504]—when we take all this into consideration, we are almost forced to the conclusion that Herr Dühring has here deliberately made a "beneficent extension" of Marx's idea—beneficent for Herr Dühring.

But what role does the negation of the negation play in Marx?

---

[a] See this volume, p. 114.—*Ed.*

On page 791 and the following pages he sets out the final conclusions which he draws from the preceding fifty pages of economic and historical investigation into the so-called primitive accumulation of capital.[62] Before the capitalist era, petty industry existed, at least in England, on the basis of the private property of the labourer in his means of production. The so-called primitive accumulation of capital consisted there in the expropriation of these immediate producers, that is, in the dissolution of private property based on the labour of its owner. This became possible because the petty industry referred to above is compatible only with narrow and primitive bounds of production and society and at a certain stage brings forth the material agencies for its own annihilation. This annihilation, the transformation of the individual and scattered means of production into socially concentrated ones, forms the prehistory of capital. As soon as the labourers are turned into proletarians, their conditions of labour into capital, as soon as the capitalist mode of production stands on its own feet, the further socialisation of labour and further transformation of the land and other means of production, and therefore the further expropriation of private proprietors, takes a new form. "That which is now to be expropriated is no longer the labourer working for himself, but the capitalist exploiting many labourers. This expropriation is accomplished by the action of the immanent laws of capitalistic production itself, by the concentration of capitals. One capitalist always kills many. Hand in hand with this concentration, or this expropriation of many capitalists by few, develop, on an ever extending scale, the co-operative form of the labour-process, the conscious technical application of science, the methodical collective cultivation of the soil, the transformation of the instruments of labour into instruments of labour only usable in common, the economising of all means of production by their use as the jointly owned means of production of combined, socialised labour. Along with the constantly diminishing number of the magnates of capital, who usurp and monopolise all advantages of this process of transformation, grows the mass of misery, oppression, slavery, degradation, exploitation; but with this too grows the revolt of the working class, a class always increasing in numbers, and disciplined, united, organised by the very mechanism of the process of capitalist production itself. Capital[a] becomes a fetter upon the mode of production, which has sprung up and flourished along with, and under it. Concentration of the means

---

[a] Marx has: "Kapitalmonopol" K. Marx, *Das Kapital*, p. 793.— *Ed.*

of production and socialisation of labour at last reach a point where they become incompatible with their capitalist integument. This integument is burst asunder. The knell of capitalist private property sounds. The expropriators are expropriated."[a]

And now I ask the reader: where are the dialectical frills and mazes and conceptual arabesques; where the mixed and misconceived ideas according to which everything is all one and the same thing in the end; where the dialectical miracles for his faithful followers; where the mysterious dialectical rubbish and the maze in accordance with the Hegelian Logos doctrine, without which Marx, according to Herr Dühring, is unable to put his exposition into shape? Marx merely shows from history, and here states in a summarised form, that just as formerly petty industry by its very development necessarily created the conditions of its own annihilation, i.e., of the expropriation of the small proprietors, so now the capitalist mode of production has likewise itself created the material conditions from which it must perish. The process is a historical one, and if it is at the same time a dialectical process, this is not Marx's fault, however annoying it may be to Herr Dühring.

It is only at this point, after Marx has completed his proof on the basis of historical and economic facts, that he proceeds: "The capitalist mode of production and appropriation, hence the capitalist private property, is the first negation of individual private property founded on the labour of the proprietor. Capitalist production begets, with the inexorability of a process of nature, its own negation. It is the negation of the negation"—and so on (as quoted above).[b]

Thus, by characterising the process as the negation of the negation, Marx does not intend to prove that the process was historically necessary. On the contrary: only after he has proved from history that in fact the process has partially already occurred, and partially must occur in the future, he in addition characterises it as a process which develops in accordance with a definite dialectical law. That is all. It is therefore once again a pure distortion of the facts by Herr Dühring when he declares that the negation of the negation has to serve here as the midwife to deliver the future from the womb of the past [D. K. G. 502-03], or that Marx wants anyone to be convinced of the necessity of the common ownership of land and capital [503] (which is itself a

---

[a] K. Marx, *Das Kapital*, p. 793. See present edition, Vol. 35, Part VIII, Chapter XXXII.— *Ed.*

[b] Ibid. See this volume, p. 121.— *Ed.*

Dühringian contradiction in corporeal form) on the basis of credence in the negation of the negation [479-80].

Herr Dühring's total lack of understanding of the nature of dialectics is shown by the very fact that he regards it as a mere proof-producing instrument, as a limited mind might look upon formal logic or elementary mathematics. Even formal logic is primarily a method of arriving at new results, of advancing from the known to the unknown—and dialectics is the same, only much more eminently so; moreover, since it forces its way beyond the narrow horizon of formal logic, it contains the germ of a more comprehensive view of the world. The same correlation exists in mathematics. Elementary mathematics, the mathematics of constant quantities, moves within the confines of formal logic, at any rate on the whole; the mathematics of variables, whose most important part is the infinitesimal calculus, is in essence nothing other than the application of dialectics to mathematical relations. In it, the simple question of proof is definitely pushed into the background, as compared with the manifold application of the method to new spheres of research. But almost all the proofs of higher mathematics, from the first proofs of the differential calculus on, are from the standpoint of elementary mathematics, strictly speaking, wrong. And this is necessarily so, when, as happens in this case, an attempt is made to prove by formal logic results obtained in the field of dialectics. To attempt to prove anything by means of dialectics alone to a crass metaphysician like Herr Dühring would be as much a waste of time as was the attempt made by Leibniz and his pupils to prove the principles of the infinitesimal calculus to the mathematicians of their time. The differential gave them the same cramps as Herr Dühring gets from the negation of the negation, in which, moreover, as we shall see, the differential also plays a certain role. Finally these gentlemen—or those of them who had not died in the interval—grudgingly gave way, not because they were convinced, but because it always came out right. Herr Dühring, as he himself tells us, is only in his forties, and if he attains old age, as we hope he may, perhaps his experience will be the same.

But what then is this fearful negation of the negation, which makes life so bitter for Herr Dühring and with him plays the same role of the unpardonable crime as the sin against the Holy Ghost does in Christianity?—A very simple process which is taking place everywhere and every day, which any child can understand as soon as it is stripped of the veil of mystery in which it was enveloped by the old idealist philosophy and in which it is to the advantage of helpless metaphysicians of Herr Dühring's calibre to keep it enveloped. Let us take a grain of barley. Billions of such grains of barley are milled, boiled and brewed and then consumed. But if such a grain of barley meets with conditions which are normal for it, if it falls on suitable soil, then under the influence of heat and moisture it undergoes a specific change, it germinates; the grain as such ceases to exist, it is negated, and in its place appears the plant which has arisen from it, the negation of the grain. But what is the normal life-process of this plant? It grows, flowers, is fertilised and finally once more produces grains of barley, and as soon as these have ripened the stalk dies, is in its turn negated. As a result of this negation of the negation we have once again the original grain of barley, but not as a single unit, but ten-, twenty- or thirtyfold. Species of grain change extremely slowly, and so the barley of today is almost the same as it was a century ago. But if we take a plastic ornamental plant, for example a dahlia or an orchid, and treat the seed and the plant which grows from it according to the gardener's art, we get as a result of this negation of the negation not only more seeds, but also qualitatively improved seeds, which produce more beautiful flowers, and each repetition of this process, each fresh negation of the negation, enhances this process of perfection.—With most insects, this process follows the same lines as in the case of the grain of barley. Butterflies, for example, spring from the egg by a negation of the egg, pass through certain transformations until they reach sexual maturity, pair and are in turn negated, dying as soon as the pairing process has been completed and the female has laid its numerous eggs. We are not concerned at the moment with the fact that with other plants and animals the process does not take such a simple form, that before they die they produce seeds, eggs or offspring not once but many times; our purpose here is only to show that the negation of the negation *really does take place* in both kingdoms of the organic world. Furthermore, the whole of geology is a series of negated negations, a series of successive shatterings of old and deposits of new rock formations. First the original earth crust brought into existence by the cooling of the liquid mass was broken up by oceanic, meteorological and atmospherico-chemical action, and these fragmented masses were stratified on the ocean bed. Local upheavals of the ocean bed above the surface of the sea subject portions of these first strata once more to the action of rain, the changing temperature of the seasons and the oxygen and carbonic acid of the atmosphere. These same influences act on the molten masses of rock which issue from the interior of the earth, break through the strata and subsequently cool off. In this way, in the course of millions of centuries, ever new strata are formed and in turn are for the most part destroyed, ever anew serving as material for the formation of new strata. But the result of this process has been a very positive one: the creation of a soil composed of the most varied chemical elements and mechanically fragmented, which makes possible the most abundant and diversified vegetation.

It is the same in mathematics. Let us take any algebraic quantity whatever: for example, a. If this is negated, we get $-a$ (minus a). If we negate that negation, by multiplying $-a$ by $-a$, we get $+a^2$, i.e., the original positive quantity, but at a higher degree, raised to its second power. In this case also it makes no difference that we can obtain the same a^2 by multiplying the positive a by itself, thus likewise getting a^2. For the negated negation is so securely entrenched in a^2 that the latter always has two square roots, namely, a and $-a$. And the fact that it is impossible to get rid of the negated negation, the negative root of the square, acquires very obvious significance as soon as we come to quadratic equations.—The negation of the negation is even more strikingly obvious in higher analysis, in those "summations of indefinitely small magnitudes" [D. Ph. 418] which Herr Dühring himself declares are the highest operations of mathematics, and in ordinary language are known as the differential and integral calculus. How are these forms of calculus used? In a given problem, for example, I have two variables, x and y, neither of which can vary without the other also varying in a ratio determined by the facts of the case. I differentiate x and y, i.e., I take x and y as so infinitely small that in comparison with any real quantity, however small, they disappear, that nothing is left of x and y but their reciprocal relation without any, so to speak, material basis, a quantitative ratio in which there is no quantity. Therefore, $\dfrac{dy}{dx}$, the ratio between the differentials of x and y, is equal to $\dfrac{0}{0}$ but $\dfrac{0}{0}$ taken as the expression of $\dfrac{y}{x}$. I only mention in passing that this ratio between two quantities which have disappeared, caught at the moment of their disappearance, is a contradiction; however, it cannot disturb us any more than it has disturbed the whole of mathematics for almost two hundred years. And now, what have I done but negate x and y, though not in such a way that I need not bother about them any more, not in the way that metaphysics negates, but in the way that corresponds with the facts of the case? In place of x and y, therefore, I have their negation, dx and dy, in the formulas or equations before me. I continue then to operate with these formulas, treating dx and dy as quantities which are real, though subject to certain exceptional laws, and at a certain point *I negate the negation,* i.e., I integrate the differential formula, and in place of dx and dy again get the real quantities x and y, and am then not where I was at the beginning, but by using this method I have solved the problem on which ordinary geometry and algebra might perhaps have broken their jaws in vain.

It is the same in history, as well. All civilised peoples begin with the common ownership of the land. With all peoples who have passed a certain primitive stage, this common ownership becomes in the course of the development of agriculture a fetter on production. It is abolished, negated, and after a longer or shorter series of intermediate stages is transformed into private property. But at a higher stage of agricultural development, brought about by private property in land itself, private property conversely becomes a fetter on production, as is the case today both with small and large landownership. The demand that it, too, should be negated, that it should once again be transformed into common property, necessarily arises. But this demand does not mean the restoration of the aboriginal common ownership, but the institution of a far higher and more developed form of possession in common which, far from being a hindrance to production, on the contrary for the first time will free production from all fetters and enable it to make full use of modern chemical discoveries and mechanical inventions.

Or let us take another example: The philosophy of antiquity was primitive, spontaneously evolved materialism. As such, it was incapable of clearing up the relation between mind and matter. But the need to get clarity on this question led to the doctrine of a soul separable from the body, then to the assertion of the immortality of this soul, and finally to monotheism. The old materialism was therefore negated by idealism. But in the course of the further development of philosophy, idealism, too, became untenable and was negated by modern materialism. This modern materialism, the negation of the negation, is not the mere re-establishment of the old, but adds to the permanent foundations of this old materialism the whole thought-content of two thousand years of development of philosophy and natural science, as well as of the history of these two thousand years. It is no longer a philosophy at all, but simply a world outlook which has to establish its validity and be applied not in a science of sciences standing apart, but in the real sciences. Philosophy is therefore "sublated" here, that is, "both overcome and preserved" [D. K. G. 503]; overcome as regards its form, and preserved as regards its real content. Thus, where Herr Dühring sees only "verbal jugglery", closer inspection reveals an actual content.

Finally: Even the Rousseau doctrine of equality—of which Dühring's is only a feeble and distorted echo—could not have seen the light but for the midwife's services rendered by the Hegelian negation of the negation [502-03]—though it was nearly twenty years before Hegel was born.[63] And far from being ashamed of this, the doctrine in its first presentation bears almost ostentatiously the imprint of its dialectical origin. In the state of nature and savagery men were equal; and as Rousseau regards even language as a perversion of the state of nature, he is fully justified in extending the equality of animals within the limits of a single species also to the animal-men recently classified by Haeckel hypothetically as *Alali*: speechless.[a] But these equal animal-men had one quality which gave them an advantage over the other animals: perfectibility, the capacity to develop further; and this became the cause of inequality. So Rousseau regards the rise of inequality as progress. But this progress contained an antagonism: it was at the same time retrogression.

"All further progress" (beyond the original state) "meant so many steps seemingly towards the *perfection of the individual man,* but in reality towards the *decay of the race*... Metallurgy and agriculture were the two arts the discovery of which produced this great revolution" (the transformation of the primeval forest into cultivated land, but along with this the introduction of poverty and slavery through property). "For the poet it is gold and silver, but for the philosopher iron and corn, which have civilised *men* and ruined the human *race.*"[b]

Each new advance of civilisation is at the same time a new advance of inequality. All institutions set up by the society which has arisen with civilisation change into the opposite of their original purpose.

"It is an incontestable fact, and the fundamental principle of all public law, that the peoples set up their chieftains to safeguard their liberty and not to enslave them."

---

[a] E. Haeckel, *Natürliche Schöpfungsgeschichte*, p. 590-91.— *Ed.*
[b] Italics by Engels.— *Ed.*

And nevertheless the chiefs necessarily become the oppressors of the peoples, and intensify their oppression up to the point at which inequality, carried to the utmost extreme, again changes into its opposite, becomes the cause of equality: before the despot all are equal—equally ciphers.

"Here we have the extreme measure of inequality, *the final point which completes the circle and meets the point from which we set out*[a]: here all private individuals become equal once more, just because they are ciphers, and the subjects have no other law but their master's will." But the despot is only master so long as he is able to use force and therefore "when he is driven out", he cannot "complain of the use of force... Force alone maintained him in power, and force alone overthrows him; thus everything takes its natural course".

And so inequality once more changes into equality; not, however, into the former naive equality of speechless primitive men, but into the higher equality of the social contract. The oppressors are oppressed. It is the negation of the negation.

Already in Rousseau, therefore, we find not only a line of thought which corresponds exactly to the one developed in Marx's *Capital,* but also, in details, a whole series of the same dialectical turns of speech as Marx used: processes which in their nature are antagonistic, contain a contradiction; transformation of one extreme into its opposite; and finally, as the kernel of the whole thing, the negation of the negation. And though in 1754 Rousseau was not yet able to speak the Hegelian jargon [D. K. G. 491], he was certainly, sixteen years before Hegel was born, deeply bitten with the Hegelian pestilence, dialectics of contradiction, Logos doctrine, theologics, and so forth. And when Herr Dühring, in his shallow version of Rousseau's theory of equality, begins to operate with his victorious two men, he is himself already on the inclined plane down which he must slide helplessly into the arms of the negation of the negation. The state of things in which the equality of the two men flourished, which was also described as an ideal one, is characterised on page 271 of his *Philosophie* as the "primitive state". This primitive state, however, according to page 279, was necessarily sublated by the "robber system"—the first negation. But now, thanks to the philosophy of reality, we have gone so far as to abolish the robber system and establish in its stead the economic commune [504] based on equality which has been discovered by Herr Dühring—negation of the negation, equality on a higher plane. What a delightful spectacle, and how beneficently it extends our range of vision: Herr Dühring's

---

[a] Italics by Engels.— *Ed.*

eminent self committing the capital crime of the negation of the negation!

And so, what is the negation of the negation? An extremely general—and for this reason extremely far-reaching and important—law of development of nature, history, and thought; a law which, as we have seen, holds good in the animal and plant kingdoms, in geology, in mathematics, in history and in philosophy—a law which even Herr Dühring, in spite of all his stubborn resistance, has unwittingly and in his own way to follow. It is obvious that I do not say anything concerning the *particular* process of development of, for example, a grain of barley from germination to the death of the fruit-bearing plant, if I say it is a negation of the negation. For, as the integral calculus is also a negation of the negation, if I said anything of the sort I should only be making the nonsensical statement that the life-process of a barley plant was integral calculus or for that matter that it was socialism. That, however, is precisely what the metaphysicians are constantly imputing to dialectics. When I say that all these processes are a negation of the negation, I bring them all together under this one law of motion, and for this very reason I leave out of account the specific peculiarities of each individual process. Dialectics, however, is nothing more than the science of the general laws of motion and development of nature, human society and thought.

But someone may object: the negation that has taken place in this case is not a real negation: I negate a grain of barley also when I grind it, an insect when I crush it underfoot, or the positive quantity *a* when I cancel it, and so on. Or I negate the sentence: the rose is a rose, when I say: the rose is not a rose; and what do I get if I then negate this negation and say: but after all the rose is a rose?—These objections are in fact the chief arguments put forward by the metaphysicians against dialectics, and they are wholly worthy of the narrow-mindedness of this mode of thought. Negation in dialectics does not mean simply saying no, or declaring that something does not exist, or destroying it in any way one likes. Long ago Spinoza said: *Omnis determinatio est negatio*—every limitation or determination is at the same time a negation.[64] And further: the kind of negation is here determined, firstly, by the general and, secondly, by the particular nature of the process. I must not only negate, but also sublate the negation. I must therefore so arrange the first negation that the second remains or becomes possible. How? This depends on the particular nature of each individual case. If I grind a grain of barley, or crush an insect, I have carried out the first part of the action, but have made the second part impossible. Every kind of thing therefore has a peculiar way of being negated in such manner that it gives rise to a development, and it is just the same with every kind of conception or idea. The infinitesimal calculus involves a form of negation which is different from that used in the formation of positive powers from negative roots. This has to be learnt, like everything else. The bare knowledge that the barley plant and the infinitesimal calculus are both governed by negation of negation does not enable me either to grow barley successfully or to differentiate and integrate; just as little as the bare knowledge of the laws of the determination of sound by the dimensions of the strings enables me to play the violin.—But it is clear that from a negation of the negation which consists in the childish pastime of alternately writing and cancelling *a,* or in alternately declaring that a rose is a rose and that it is not a rose, nothing eventuates but the silliness of the person who adopts such a tedious procedure. And yet the metaphysicians try to make us believe that this is the right way to carry out a negation of the negation, if we ever should want to do such a thing.

Once again, therefore, it is no one but Herr Dühring who is mystifying us when he asserts that the negation of the negation is a stupid analogy invented by Hegel, borrowed from the sphere of religion and based on the story of the fall of man and his redemption [D. K. G. 504]. Men thought dialectically long before they knew what dialectics was, just as they spoke prose long before the term prose existed.[a] The law of negation of the negation, which is unconsciously operative in nature and history and, until it has been recognised, also in our heads, was only first clearly formulated by Hegel. And if Herr Dühring wants to operate with it himself on the quiet and it is only that he cannot stand the name, then let him find a better name. But if his aim is to banish the process itself from thought, we must ask him to be so good as first to banish it from nature and history and to invent a mathematical system in which $-a \times -a$ is not $+a^2$ and in which differentiation and integration are prohibited under severe penalties.

---

[a] An allusion to Molière's comedy *Le Bourgeois gentilhomme*, Act II, Scene 6.— *Ed.*

XIV. CONCLUSION

We have now finished with philosophy; such other fantasies of the future as the *Cursus* contains will de dealt with when we come to Herr Dühring's revolution in socialism. What did Herr Dühring promise us? Everything. And what promises has he kept? None. "The elements of a philosophy which is real and accordingly directed to the reality of nature and of life" [D. Ph. 430], the "strictly scientific [387] conception of the world", the "system-creating ideas" [525], and all Herr Dühring's other achievements, trumpeted forth to the world by Herr Dühring in high-sounding phrases, turned out, wherever we laid hold of them, to be *pure charlatanism.* The world schematism which, "without the slightest detraction from the profundity of thought, securely established the basic forms of being" [556-57], proved to be an infinitely vulgarised duplicate of Hegelian logic, and in common with the latter shares the superstition that these "basic forms" [9] or logical categories have led a mysterious existence somewhere before and outside of the world, to which they are "to be applied" [15]. The philosophy of nature offered us a cosmogony whose starting-point is a "self-equal state of matter" [87]—a state which can only be conceived by means of the most hopeless confusion as to the relation between matter and motion; a state which can, besides, only be conceived on the assumption of an extramundane personal God who alone can induce motion in this state of matter. In its treatment of organic nature, the philosophy of reality first rejected the Darwinian struggle for existence and natural selection as "a piece of brutality directed against humanity" [117], and then had to readmit both by the back-door as factors operative in nature, though of second rank. Moreover, the philosophy of reality found occasion to exhibit, in the biological domain, ignorance such as nowadays, when popular science lectures are no longer to be escaped, could hardly be found even among the daughters of the "educated classes". In the domain of morality and law, the philosophy of reality was no more successful in its vulgarisation of Rousseau than it had been in its previous shallow version of Hegel; and, so far as jurisprudence is concerned, in spite of all its assurances to the contrary, it likewise displayed a lack of knowledge such as is rarely found even among the most ordinary jurists of old Prussia. The philosophy "which cannot allow the validity of any merely apparent horizon" is content, in juridical matters, with a real horizon which is coextensive with the territory in which Prussian law exercises jurisdiction. We are still waiting for the "earths and heavens of outer and inner nature" [D. Ph. 430] which this philosophy promised to reveal to us in its mighty revolutionising sweep; just as we are still waiting for the "final and ultimate truths" [2] and the "absolutely fundamental" [150] basis. The philosopher whose mode of thought "excludes" any tendency to a "subjectively limited conception of the world" [13] proves to be subjectively limited not only by what has been shown to be his extremely defective knowledge, his narrowly construed metaphysical mode of thought and his grotesque conceit, but even by his childish personal crotchets. He cannot produce his philosophy of reality without dragging in his repugnance to tobacco, cats and Jews as a general law valid for all the rest of humanity, including the Jews. His "really critical standpoint" [404] in relation to other people shows itself by his insistently imputing to them things which they never said and which are of Herr Dühring's very own fabrication. His verbose lucubrations[a] on themes worthy of philistines, such as the value of life and the best way to enjoy life, are themselves so steeped in philistinism that they explain his anger at Goethe's *Faust* [112-13, 423]. It was really unpardonable of Goethe to make the unmoral Faust and not the serious philosopher of reality, Wagner, his hero.—In short, the philosophy of reality proves to be on the whole what Hegel would call "the weakest residue of the German would-be Enlightenment"—a residue whose tenuity and transparent commonplace character are made more substantial and opaque only by the mixing in of crumbs of oracular rhetoric. And now that we have finished the book we are just as wise as we were at the start; and we are forced to admit that the "new mode of thought" [543], the "from the ground up original conclusions and views" and the "system-creating ideas" [525], though they have certainly shown us a great variety of original nonsense, have not provided us with a single line from which we might have been able to learn something. And this man who praises his talents and his wares to the noisy accompaniment of cymbals and trumpets as loudly as any market quack, and behind whose great words there is nothing, absolutely nothing whatsoever—this man has the temerity to say of people like Fichte, Schelling and Hegel, the least of whom is a giant compared with him, that they are charlatans. Charlatan, indeed! But to whom had it best be applied?

---

[a] In the original: "breite Bettelsuppen" (thin gruel for the poor)—an expression from Goethe's *Faust,* Act I, Scene VI ("The Witch's Kitchen").— *Ed.*

Part II

POLITICAL ECONOMY

I. SUBJECT MATTER AND METHOD

Political economy, in the widest sense, is the science of the laws governing the production and exchange of the material means of subsistence in human society. Production and exchange are two different functions. Production may occur without exchange, but exchange—being necessarily an exchange of products—cannot occur without production. Each of these two social functions is subject to the action of external influences which to a great extent are peculiar to it and for this reason each has, also to a great extent, its own special laws. But on the other hand, they constantly determine and influence each other to such an extent that they might be termed the abscissa and ordinate of the economic curve.

The conditions under which men produce and exchange vary from country to country, and within each country again from generation to generation. Political economy, therefore, cannot be the same for all countries and for all historical epochs. A tremendous distance separates the bow and arrow, the stone knife and the acts of exchange among savages occurring only by way of exception, from the steam-engine of a thousand horse power, the mechanical loom, the railways and the Bank of England. The inhabitants of Tierra del Fuego have not got so far as mass production and world trade, any more than they have experience of bill-jobbing or a Stock Exchange crash. Anyone who attempted to bring the political economy of Tierra del Fuego under the same laws as are operative in present-day England would obviously produce nothing but the most banal commonplaces. Political economy is therefore essentially a *historical* science. It deals with material which is historical, that is, constantly changing; it must first investigate the special laws of each individual stage in the evolution of production and exchange, and only when it has completed this investigation will it be able to establish the few quite general laws which hold good for production and exchange in general. At the same time it goes without saying that the laws which are valid for definite modes of production and forms of exchange hold good for all historical periods in which these modes of production and forms of exchange prevail. Thus, for example, the introduction of metallic money brought into operation a series of laws which remain valid for all countries and historical epochs in which metallic money is a medium of exchange.

The mode of production and exchange in a definite historical society, and the historical conditions which have given birth to this society, determine the mode of distribution of its products. In the tribal or village community with common ownership of land—with which, or with the easily recognisable survivals of which, all civilised peoples enter history—a fairly equal distribution of products is a matter of course; where considerable inequality of distribution among the members of the community sets in, this is an indication that the community is already beginning to break up. —Both large- and small-scale agriculture admit of very diverse forms of distribution, depending upon the historical conditions from which they developed. But it is obvious that large-scale farming always gives rise to a distribution which is quite different from that of small-scale farming; that large-scale agriculture presupposes or creates a class antagonism—slave-owners and slaves, feudal lords and serfs, capitalists and wage-workers—while small-scale agriculture does not necessarily involve class differences between the individuals engaged in agricultural production, and that on the contrary the mere existence of such differences indicates the incipient dissolution of smallholding economy.—The introduction and extensive use of metallic money in a country in which hitherto natural economy was universal or predominant is always associated with a more or less rapid revolutionisation of the former mode of distribution, and this takes place in such a way that the inequality of distribution among the individuals and therefore the opposition between rich and poor becomes more and more pronounced.—The local guild-controlled handicraft production of the Middle Ages precluded the existence of big capitalists and lifelong wage-workers just as these are inevitably brought into existence by modern large-scale industry, the credit system of the present day, and the form of exchange corresponding to the development of both of them—free competition.

But with the differences in distribution, *class differences* emerge.

Society divides into classes: the privileged and the dispossessed, the exploiters and the exploited, the rulers and the ruled; and the state, which the natural groups of communities of the same tribe had at first arrived at only in order to safeguard their common interests (e.g., irrigation in the East) and for protection against external enemies, from this stage onwards acquires just as much the function of maintaining by force the conditions of existence and domination of the ruling class against the subject class.

Distribution, however, is not a merely passive result of production and exchange; it in its turn reacts upon both of these. Each new mode of production or form of exchange is at first retarded not only by the old forms and the political institutions which correspond to them, but also by the old mode of distribution; it can secure the distribution which is suitable to it only in the course of a long struggle. But the more mobile a given mode of production and exchange, the more capable it is of perfection and development, the more rapidly does distribution reach the stage at which it outgrows its progenitor, the hitherto prevailing mode of production and exchange, and comes into conflict with it. The old primitive communities which have already been mentioned could remain in existence for thousands of years—as in India and among the Slavs up to the present day—before intercourse with the outside world gave rise in their midst to the inequalities of property as a result of which they began to break up. On the contrary, modern capitalist production, which is hardly three hundred years old and has become predominant only since the introduction of modern industry, that is, only in the last hundred years, has in this short time brought about antitheses in distribution—concentration of capital in a few hands on the one side and concentration of the propertyless masses in the big towns on the other—which must of necessity bring about its downfall.

The connection between distribution and the material conditions of existence of society at any period lies so much in the nature of things that it is always reflected in popular instinct. So long as a mode of production still describes an ascending curve of development, it is enthusiastically welcomed even by those who come off worst from its corresponding mode of distribution. This was the case with the English workers in the beginnings of modern industry. And even while this mode of production remains normal for society, there is, in general, contentment with the distribution, and if objections to it begin to be raised, these come from within the ruling class itself (Saint-Simon, Fourier, Owen) and find no response whatever among the exploited masses. Only when the mode of production in question has already described a good part of its descending curve, when it has half outlived its day, when the conditions of its existence have to a large extent disappeared, and its successor is already knocking at the door—it is only at this stage that the constantly increasing inequality of distribution appears as unjust, it is only then that appeal is made from the facts which have had their day to so-called eternal justice. From a scientific standpoint, this appeal to morality and justice does not help us an inch further; moral indignation, however justifiable, cannot serve economic science as an argument, but only as a symptom. The task of economic science is rather to show that the social abuses which have recently been developing are necessary consequences of the existing mode of production, but at the same time also indications of its approaching dissolution; and to reveal, within the already dissolving economic form of motion, the elements of the future new organisation of production and exchange which will put an end to those abuses. The wrath which creates the poet[a] is absolutely in place in describing these abuses, and also in attacking those apostles of harmony in the service of the ruling class who either deny or palliate them; but how little it *proves* in any particular case is evident from the fact that in *every* epoch of past history there has been no lack of material for such wrath.

Political economy, however, as the science of the conditions and forms under which the various human societies have produced and exchanged and on this basis have distributed their products— political economy in this wider sense has still to be brought into being. Such economic science as we possess up to the present is limited almost exclusively to the genesis and development of the capitalist mode of production: it begins with a critique of the survivals of the feudal forms of production and exchange, shows the necessity of their replacement by capitalist forms, then develops the laws of the capitalist mode of production and its corresponding forms of exchange in their positive aspects, that is, the aspects in which they further the general aims of society, and ends with a socialist critique of the capitalist mode of production, that is, with an exposition of its laws in their negative aspects, with a demonstration that this mode of production, by virtue of its own development, drives towards the point at which it makes itself impossible. This critique proves that the capitalist forms of

---

[a] Juvenalis, *Satirae*, 1, 79 (si natura negat, facit indignatio versum).— *Ed.*

production and exchange become more and more an intolerable fetter on production itself, that the mode of distribution necessarily determined by those forms has produced a situation among the classes which is daily becoming more intolerable—the antagonism, sharpening from day to day, between capitalists, constantly decreasing in number but constantly growing richer, and propertyless wage-workers, whose number is constantly increasing and whose conditions, taken as a whole, are steadily deteriorating; and finally, that the colossal productive forces created within the capitalist mode of production which the latter can no longer master, are only waiting to be taken possession of by a society organised for co-operative work on a planned basis to ensure to all members of society the means of existence and of the free development of their capacities, and indeed in constantly increasing measure.

In order to complete this critique of bourgeois economics, an acquaintance with the capitalist form of production, exchange and distribution did not suffice. The forms which had preceded it or those which still exist alongside it in less developed countries, had also, at least in their main features, to be examined and compared. Such an investigation and comparison has up to the present been undertaken, in general outline, only by Marx, and we therefore owe almost exclusively to his researches[65] all that has so far been established concerning pre-bourgeois theoretical economics.

Although it first took shape in the minds of a few men of genius towards the end of the seventeenth century, political economy in the narrower sense, in its positive formulation by the physiocrats and Adam Smith, is nevertheless essentially a child of the eighteenth century, and ranks with the achievements of the contemporary great French philosophers of the Enlightenment, sharing with them all the merits and demerits of that period. What we have said of the philosophers[a] is also true of the economists of that time. To them, the new science was not the expression of the conditions and requirements of their epoch, but the expression of eternal reason; the laws of production and exchange discovered by this science were not laws of a historically determined form of those activities, but eternal laws of nature; they were deduced from the nature of man. But this man, when examined more closely, proved to be the average burgher of that epoch, on the way to becoming a bourgeois, and his nature consisted in

---

[a] See this volume, pp. 16, 19.— Ed.

manufacturing and trading in accordance with the historically determined conditions of that period.

Now that we have acquired sufficient knowledge of our "layer of critical foundations", Herr Dühring, and his method in the philosophical field, it will not be difficult for us to foretell the way in which he will handle political economy. In philosophy, in so far as his writings were not simply drivel (as in his philosophy of nature), his mode of outlook was a distortion of that of the eighteenth century. It was not a question of historical laws of development, but of laws of nature, eternal truths. Social relations such as morality and law were determined, not by the actual historical conditions of the age, but by the famous two men, one of whom either oppresses the other or does not—though the latter alternative, sad to say, has never yet come to pass. We are therefore hardly likely to go astray if we conclude that Herr Dühring will trace political economy also back to final and ultimate truths [D. Ph. 2], eternal natural laws, and the most empty and barren tautological axioms; that nevertheless he will smuggle in again by the backdoor the whole positive content of political economy, so far as this is known to him; and that he will not evolve distribution, as a social phenomenon, out of production and exchange, but will hand it over to his famous two men for final solution.[a] And as all these are tricks with which we are already familiar, our treatment of this question can be all the shorter.

In fact, already on page 2,[66] Herr Dühring tells us that

his economics links up with what has been "*established*" in his *Philosophie*, and "in certain essential points depends on *truths* of a higher order *which have already been consummated* [*ausgemacht*] in a higher field of investigation" [D. C. 2].

Everywhere the same importunate eulogy of himself; everywhere Herr Dühring is triumphant over what Herr Dühring has established and put out [*ausgemacht*]. Put out, yes, we have seen it to surfeit—but put out in the way that people put out a sputtering candle.[b]

Immediately afterwards we find

"the most general *natural laws* governing all economy" [4]—

so our forecast was right.

But these natural laws permit of a correct understanding of past history only if they are "investigated in that more precise determination which their results have experienced through the political forms of subjection and grouping. Institutions such

---

[a] See this volume, pp. 89-91.— *Ed.*

[b] In German an untranslatable play on words: *ausmachen* means consummate and also put out.— *Ed.*

as slavery and wage bondage, along with which is associated their twin-brother, property based on force, must be regarded as social-economic constitutional forms of a purely political nature, and have hitherto constituted the frame within which the consequences of the natural economic laws could alone manifest themselves" [4-5].

This sentence is the fanfare which, like a *leitmotif* in Wagner's operas, announces the approach of the famous two men. But it is more than this: it is the basic theme of Herr Dühring's whole book. In the sphere of law, Herr Dühring could not offer us anything except a bad translation of Rousseau's theory of equality into the language of socialism,[a] such as one has long been able to hear much more effectively rendered in any workers' tavern in Paris. Now he gives us an equally bad socialist translation of the economists' laments over the distortion of the eternal natural economic laws and of their effects owing to the intervention of the state, of force. And in this Herr Dühring stands, deservedly, absolutely alone among socialists. Every socialist worker, no matter of what nationality, knows quite well that force only protects exploitation, but does not cause it; that the relation between capital and wage-labour is the basis of his exploitation, and that this was brought about by purely economic causes and not at all by means of force.

Then we are further told that

in all economic questions "two processes, that of production and that of distribution, can be distinguished". Also that J. B. Say, notorious for his superficiality, mentioned in addition a third process, that of consumption, but that he was unable to say anything sensible about it, any more than his successors [7-8] and that exchange or circulation is, however, only a department of production, which comprises all the operations required for the products to reach the ultimate consumer, the consumer proper [11-12].

By confounding the two essentially different, though also mutually dependent, processes of production and circulation, and unblushingly asserting that the avoidance of this confusion can only "give rise to confusion", Herr Dühring merely shows that he either does not know or does not understand the colossal development which precisely circulation has undergone during the last fifty years, as indeed is further borne out by the rest of his book. But this is not all. After just lumping together production and exchange into one, as simply production, he puts distribution *alongside* production, as a second, wholly external process, which has nothing whatever to do with the first. Now we have seen that

---

[a] See this volume, pp. 89-95.— *Ed.*

distribution, in its decisive features, is always the necessary result of the production and exchange relations of a particular society, as well as of the historical conditions in which this society arose; so much so that when we know these relations and conditions, we can confidently infer the mode of distribution which prevails in this society. But we see also that if Herr Dühring does not want to be unfaithful to the principles "established" by him in his conceptions of morality, law and history, he is compelled to deny this elementary economic fact, especially if he is to smuggle his indispensable two men into economics. And once distribution has been happily freed of all connection with production and exchange, this great event can come to pass.

Let us first recall how Herr Dühring developed his argument in the field of morality and law. He started originally with *one* man, and he said:

"One man conceived as being alone, or, what is in effect the same, out of all connection with other men, can have no *obligations*; for such a man there can be no question of what he *ought*, but only of what he *wants*, to do" [D. Ph. 199].

But what is this man, conceived as being alone and without obligations, but the fateful "primordial Jew Adam" [110] in paradise, where he is without sin simply because there is no possibility for him to commit any?—However, even this Adam of the philosophy of reality is destined to fall into sin. Alongside this Adam there suddenly appears—not, it is true, an Eve with rippling tresses, but a second Adam. And instantly Adam acquires obligations and—breaks them. Instead of treating his brother as having equal rights and clasping him to his breast, he subjects him to his domination, he makes a slave of him—and it is the consequences of this first sin, the original sin of the enslavement of man, from which the world has suffered through the whole course of history down to the present day—which is precisely what makes Herr Dühring think world history is not worth a farthing.

Incidentally, Herr Dühring considered that he had brought the "negation of the negation" sufficiently into contempt by characterising it as a copy of the old fable of original sin and redemption [see D. K. G. 504]—but what are we to say of *his* latest version of the same story? (for, in due time, we shall, to use an expression of the reptile press,[67] "get down to brass tacks" on redemption as well). All we can say is that we prefer the old Semitic tribal legend, according to which it was worth while for the man and woman to abandon the state of innocence,[a] and that to Herr Dühring will be left the uncontested glory of having constructed his original sin with two men.

Let us now see how he translates this original sin into economic terms:

"We can get an appropriate cogitative scheme for the idea of production from the conception of a Robinson Crusoe who is facing nature alone with his own resources and has not to share with anyone else... Equally appropriate to illustrate what is most essential in the idea of distribution is the cogitative scheme of two persons, who combine their economic forces and must evidently come to a mutual understanding in some form as to their respective shares. In fact nothing more than this simple dualism is required to enable us accurately to portray some of the most important relations of distribution and to study their laws embryonically in their logical necessity... Co-operative working on an equal footing is here just as conceivable as the combination of forces through the complete subjection of one party, who is then compelled to render economic service as a slave or as a mere tool and is maintained also only as a tool... Between the state of equality and that of nullity on the one part and of omnipotence and solely-active participation on the other, there is a range of stages which the events of world history have filled in in rich variety. A universal survey of the various institutions of *justice* and *injustice* throughout history is here an essential presupposition" [D. C. 9-10] ...,

and in conclusion the whole question of distribution is transformed into an

"economic right of distribution" [10].

Now at last Herr Dühring has firm ground under his feet again. Arm in arm with his two men he can issue his challenge to his age.[b] But behind this trinity stands yet another, an unnamed man.

"Capital has not invented surplus-labour. Wherever a part of society possesses the monopoly of the means of production, the labourer, free or not free, must add to the working-time necessary for his own maintenance an extra working-time in order to produce the means of subsistence for the owners of the means of production, whether this proprietor be the Athenian καλὸς κἀγαθός,[c] Etruscan theocrat, civis Romanus (Roman citizen[d]), "Norman baron, American slave-owner, Wallachian Boyard, modern landlord or capitalist" (Marx, *Das Kapital*, Vol. 1, 2nd edition, p. 227).[e]

When Herr Dühring had thus learned what the basic form of exploitation common to all forms of production up to the present day

---

[a] Genesis 3: 5-7.— *Ed.*

[b] See this volume, p. 5, footnote.— *Ed.*

[c] Aristocrat.— *Ed.*

[d] The words in brackets are inserted into Marx's quotation by Engels.— *Ed.*

[e] See present edition, Vol. 35, Part III, Chapter X, Section 2.— *Ed.*

is—so far as these forms move in class antagonisms—all he had to do was to apply his two men to it, and the deep-rooted foundation of the economics of reality was completed. He did not hesitate for a moment to carry out this "system-creating idea" [D. Ph. 525]. Labour without compensation, beyond the labour-time necessary for the maintenance of the labourer himself—that is the point. The Adam, who is here called Robinson Crusoe, makes his second Adam—Man Friday—drudge for all he is worth. But why does Friday toil more than is necessary for his own maintenance? To this question, too, Marx step by step provides an answer. But this answer is far too long-winded for the two men. The matter is settled in a trice: Crusoe "oppresses" Friday, compels him "to render economic service as a slave or a tool" and maintains him "also only as a tool". With these latest "creative turns" [D. K. G. 462] of his, Herr Dühring kills as it were two birds with one stone. Firstly, he saves himself the trouble of explaining the various forms of distribution which have hitherto existed, their differences and their causes; taken in the lump, they are simply of no account—they rest on oppression, on force. We shall have to deal with this before long. Secondly, he thereby transfers the whole theory of distribution from the sphere of economics to that of morality and law, that is, from the sphere of established material facts to that of more or less vacillating opinions and sentiments. He therefore no longer has any need to investigate or to prove things; he can go on declaiming to his heart's content and demand that the distribution of the products of labour should be regulated, not in accordance with its real causes, but in accordance with what seems ethical and just to him, Herr Dühring. But what seems just to Herr Dühring is not at all immutable, and hence very far from being a genuine truth. For genuine truths [D. Ph. 196], according to Herr Dühring himself, are "absolutely immutable". In 1868 Herr Dühring asserted—*Die Schicksale meiner sozialen Denkschrift etc.*—that

it was "a tendency of all higher civilisation *to put more and more emphasis on property*, and in this, not in confusion of rights and spheres of sovereignty, lies the essence and the future of modern development".

And furthermore, he was quite unable to see

"*how a transformation of wage-labour into another manner of gaining a livelihood is ever to be reconciled with the laws of human nature and the naturally necessary structure of the body social*".[a]

---

[a] E. Dühring, *Die Schicksale meiner socialen Denkschrift für das Preussische Staatsministerium*, p. 5.— *Ed.*

Thus in 1868, private property and wage-labour are naturally necessary and therefore just; in 1876[a] both of these are the emanation of force and "robbery" and therefore unjust. And as we cannot possibly tell what in a few years' time may seem ethical and just to such a mighty and impetuous genius, we should in any case do better, in considering the distribution of wealth, to stick to the real, objective, economic laws and not to depend on the momentary, changeable, subjective conceptions of Herr Dühring as to what is just or unjust.

If for the impending overthrow of the present mode of distribution of the products of labour, with its crying contrasts of want and luxury, starvation and surfeit, we had no better guarantee than the consciousness that this mode of distribution is unjust, and that justice must eventually triumph, we should be in a pretty bad way, and we might have a long time to wait. The mystics of the Middle Ages who dreamed of the coming millennium were already conscious of the injustice of class antagonisms. On the threshold of modern history, three hundred and fifty years ago, Thomas Münzer proclaimed it to the world. In the English and the French bourgeois revolutions the same call resounded—and died away. And if today the same call for the abolition of class antagonisms and class distinctions, which up to 1830[68] had left the working and suffering classes cold, if today this call is re-echoed a millionfold, if it takes hold of one country after another in the same order and in the same degree of intensity that modern industry develops in each country, if in one generation it has gained a strength that enables it to defy all the forces combined against it and to be confident of victory in the near future—what is the reason for this? The reason is that modern large-scale industry has called into being on the one hand a proletariat, a class which for the first time in history can demand the abolition, not of this or that particular class organisation, or of this or that particular class privilege, but of classes themselves, and which is in such a position that it must carry through this demand on pain of sinking to the level of the Chinese coolie. On the other hand this same large-scale industry has brought into being, in the bourgeoisie, a class which has the monopoly of all the instruments of production and means of subsistence, but which in each speculative boom period and in each crash that follows it proves that it has become incapable of any longer controlling the

---

[a] I.e., in the second edition of Dühring's book *Cursus der National- und Socialökonomie.—Ed.*

productive forces, which have grown beyond its power; a class under whose leadership society is racing to ruin like a locomotive whose jammed safety-valve the driver is too weak to open. In other words, the reason is that both the productive forces created by the modern capitalist mode of production and the system of distribution of goods established by it have come into crying contradiction with that mode of production itself, and in fact to such a degree that, if the whole of modern society is not to perish, a revolution in the mode of production and distribution must take place, a revolution which will put an end to all class distinctions. On this tangible, material fact, which is impressing itself in a more or less clear form, but with insuperable necessity, on the minds of the exploited proletarians—on this fact, and not on the conceptions of justice and injustice held by any armchair philosopher, is modern socialism's confidence in victory founded.

II. THEORY OF FORCE

"In my system, the relation between general politics and the forms of economic law is determined in so definite a way and at the same time a way *so original* that it would not be superfluous, in order to facilitate study, to make special reference to this point. The formation of *political* relationships is *historically the fundamental thing,* and instances of *economic* dependence are only *effects* or special cases, and are consequently always *facts of a second order.* Some of the newer socialist systems take as their guiding principle the conspicuous semblance of a completely reverse relationship, in that they assume that political phenomena are subordinate to and, as it were, grow out of the economic conditions. It is true that these effects of the second order do exist as such, and are most clearly perceptible at the present time; but the *primary* must be sought in *direct political force* and not in any indirect economic power" [D. Ph. 538].

This conception is also expressed in another passage, in which Herr Dühring

"starts from the principle that the political conditions are the decisive cause of the economic situation and that the reverse relationship represents only a reaction of a second order ... so long as the political grouping is not taken for its own sake, as the starting-point, but is treated merely as a *stomach-filling agency,* one must have a portion of reaction stowed away in one's mind, however radical a socialist and revolutionary one may seem to be" [D. K. G. 230-31].

That is Herr Dühring's theory. In this and in many other passages it is simply set up, decreed, so to speak. Nowhere in the three fat tomes is there even the slightest attempt to prove it or to disprove the opposite point of view. And even if the arguments for it were as plentiful as blackberries,[a] Herr Dühring would give us none of them. For the whole affair has been already proved through the famous original sin, when Robinson Crusoe made Friday his slave. That was an act of force, hence a political act. And inasmuch as this enslavement was the starting-point and the basic fact underlying all past history and inoculated it with the original sin of injustice, so much so that in the later periods it was only softened down and "transformed into the more indirect forms of economic dependence" [D. C. 19]; and inasmuch as "property founded on force" [D. Ph. 242], which has asserted itself right up to the present day, is likewise based on this original act of enslavement, it is clear that all economic phenomena must be explained by political causes, that is, by force. And anyone who is not satisfied with that is a reactionary in disguise.

We must first point out that only one with as much self-esteem as Herr Dühring could regard this view as so very "original", which it is not in the least. The idea that political acts, grand performances of state, are decisive in history is as old as written history itself, and is the main reason why so little material has been preserved for us in regard to the really progressive evolution of the peoples which has taken place quietly, in the background, behind these noisy scenes on the stage. This idea dominated all the conceptions of historians in the past, and the first blow against it was delivered only by the French bourgeois historians[b] of the Restoration period[69]; the only "original" thing about it is that Herr Dühring once again knows nothing of all this.

Furthermore: even if we assume for a moment that Herr Dühring is right in saying that all past history can be traced back to the enslavement of man by man, we are still very far from having got to the bottom of the matter. For the question then arises: how did Crusoe come to enslave Friday? Just for the fun of it? By no means. On the contrary, we see that Friday "is compelled to render *economic* service as a slave or as a mere tool and is maintained also only as a tool" [D. C. 9]. Crusoe enslaved Friday only in order that Friday should work for Crusoe's benefit. And how can he derive any benefit for himself from Friday's labour? Only through Friday producing by his labour more of the necessaries of life than Crusoe has to give him to keep him fit to work. Crusoe, therefore, in violation of Herr Dühring's express orders, "takes the political grouping" arising out of Friday's enslavement "not

---

[a] Shakespeare, *King Henry IV*, Part I, Act II, Scene IV.— *Ed.*
[b] A. Thierry, F. Cuizot, F. Mignet, A. Thiers.— *Ed.*

for its own sake, as the starting-point, but merely *as a stomach-filling agency*"; and now let him see to it that he gets along with his lord and master, Dühring.

The childish example specially selected by Herr Dühring in order to prove that force is "historically the fundamental thing", therefore, proves that force is only the means, and that the aim, on the contrary, is economic advantage. And "the more fundamental" the aim is than the means used to secure it, the more fundamental in history is the economic side of the relationship than the political side. The example therefore proves precisely the opposite of what it was supposed to prove. And as in the case of Crusoe and Friday, so in all cases of domination and subjection up to the present day. Subjugation has always been—to use Herr Dühring's elegant expression—a "stomach-filling agency" (taking stomach-filling in a very wide sense), but never and nowhere a political grouping established "for its own sake". It takes a Herr Dühring to be able to imagine that state taxes are only "effects of a second order", or that the present-day political grouping of the ruling bourgeoisie and the ruled proletariat has come into existence "for its own sake", and not as a "stomach-filling agency" for the ruling bourgeois, that is to say, for the sake of making profits and accumulating capital.

However, let us get back again to our two men. Crusoe, "sword in hand" [D. C. 23], makes Friday his slave. But in order to manage this, Crusoe needs something else besides his sword. Not everyone can make use of a slave. In order to be able to make use of a slave, one must possess two kinds of things: first, the instruments and material for his slave's labour; and secondly, the means of bare subsistence for him. Therefore, before slavery becomes possible, a certain level of production must already have been reached and a certain inequality of distribution must already have appeared. And for slave-labour to become the dominant mode of production in the whole of a society, an even far higher increase in production, trade and accumulation of wealth was essential. In the ancient primitive communities with common ownership of the land, slavery either did not exist at all or played only a very subordinate role. It was the same in the originally peasant city of Rome; but when Rome became a "world city" and Italic landownership came more and more into the hands of a numerically small class of enormously rich proprietors, the peasant population was supplanted by a population of slaves. If at the time of the Persian wars the number of slaves in Corinth rose to 460,000 and in Aegina to 470,000 and there were ten slaves to every freeman,[70] something else besides "force" was required, namely, a highly developed arts and handicraft industry and an extensive commerce. Slavery in the United States of America was based far less on force than on the English cotton industry; in those districts where no cotton was grown or which, unlike the border states, did not breed slaves for the cotton-growing states, it died out of itself without any force being used, simply because it did not pay.

Hence, by calling property as it exists today property founded on force, and by characterising it as

"that form of domination *at the root of which lies* not merely the exclusion of fellow-men from the use of the natural means of subsistence, but also, what is far more important, the subjugation of man to make him do servile work" [5],

Herr Dühring is making the whole relationship stand on its head. The subjugation of a man to make him do servile work, in all its forms, presupposes that the subjugator has at his disposal the instruments of labour with the help of which alone he is able to employ the person placed in bondage, and in the case of slavery, in addition, the means of subsistence which enable him to keep his slave alive. In all cases, therefore, it presupposes the possession of a certain amount of property, in excess of the average. How did this property come into existence? In any case it is clear that it may in fact have been robbed, and therefore may be based on *force,* but that this is by no means necessary. It may have been got by labour, it may have been stolen, or it may have been obtained by trade or by fraud. In fact, it must have been obtained by labour before there was any possibility of its being robbed.

Private property by no means makes its appearance in history as the result of robbery or force. On the contrary. It already existed, though limited to certain objects, in the ancient primitive communities of all civilised peoples. It developed into the form of commodities within these communities, at first through barter with foreigners. The more the products of the community assumed the commodity form, that is, the less they were produced for their producers' own use and the more for the purpose of exchange, and the more the original spontaneously evolved division of labour was superseded by exchange also within the community, the more did inequality develop in the property owned by the individual members of the community, the more deeply was the ancient common ownership of the land undermined, and the more rapidly did the commune develop towards its dissolution and transformation into a village of smallholding peasants.

For thousands of years Oriental despotism and the changing rule of conquering nomad peoples were unable to injure these old communities; the gradual destruction of their primitive home industry by the competition of products of large-scale industry brought these communities nearer and nearer to dissolution. Force was as little involved in this process as in the dividing up, still taking place now, of the land held in common by the village communities [*Gehöferschaften*] on the Mosel and in the Hochwald; the peasants simply find it to their advantage that the private ownership of land should take the place of common ownership.[a] Even the formation of a primitive aristocracy, as in the case of the Celts, the Germans and the Indian Punjab, took place on the basis of common ownership of the land, and at first was not based in any way on force, but on voluntariness and custom. Wherever private property evolved it was the result of altered relations of production and exchange, in the interest of increased production and in furtherance of intercourse—hence as a result of economic causes. Force plays no part in this at all. Indeed, it is clear that the institution of private property must already be in existence for a robber to be able to *appropriate* another person's property, and that therefore force may be able to change the possession of, but cannot create, private property as such.

Nor can we use either force or property founded on force in explanation of the "subjugation of man to make him do servile work" in its most modern form—wage-labour. We have already mentioned the role played in the dissolution of the ancient communities, that is, in the direct or indirect general spread of private property, by the transformation of the products of labour into commodities, their production not for consumption by those who produced them, but for exchange. Now in *Capital,* Marx proved with absolute clarity—and Herr Dühring carefully avoids even the slightest reference to this—that at a certain stage of development, the production of commodities becomes transformed into capitalist production, and that at this stage "the laws of appropriation or of private property, laws that are based on the production and circulation of commodities, become by their own inner and inexorable dialectic changed into their[b] opposite. The exchange of equivalents, the original operation with which we

---

[a] Engels used: G. Hanssen, *Die Gehöferschaften (Erbgenossenschaften) im Regierungsbezirk Trier.—Ed.*

[b] Here Engels omitted the word "direktes". See K. Marx, *Das Kapital,* p. 607.— *Ed.*

started, has now become turned round in such a way that there is only an apparent exchange. This is owing to the fact, first, that the capital which is exchanged for labour-power is itself but a portion of the product of others' labour appropriated without an equivalent; and, secondly, that this capital must not only be replaced by its producer, but replaced together with an added surplus[a]... At first property seemed to us to be based on a man's own labour... Now, however" (at the end of Marx's analysis), "property turns out to be the right, on the part of the capitalist, to appropriate the unpaid labour of others, and to be the impossibility, on the part of the labourer, of appropriating his own product. The separation of property from labour has become the necessary consequence of a law that apparently originated in their identity."[b] In other words, even if we exclude all possibility of robbery, force and fraud, even if we assume that all private property was originally based on the owner's own labour, and that throughout the whole subsequent process there was only exchange of equal values for equal values, the progressive development of production and exchange nevertheless brings us of necessity to the present capitalist mode of production, to the monopolisation of the means of production and the means of subsistence in the hands of the one, numerically small, class, to the degradation into propertyless proletarians of the other class, constituting the immense majority, to the periodic alternation of speculative production booms and commercial crises and to the whole of the present anarchy of production. The whole process can be explained by purely economic causes; at no point whatever are robbery, force, the state or political interference of any kind necessary. "Property founded on force" [D. C. 4] proves here also to be nothing but the phrase of a braggart intended to cover up his lack of understanding of the real course of things.

This course of things, expressed historically, is the history of the development of the bourgeoisie. If "political conditions are the decisive cause of the economic situation" [D. K. G. 230-31], then the modern bourgeoisie cannot have developed in struggle with feudalism, but must be the latter's voluntarily begotten pet child. Everyone knows that what took place was the opposite. Originally an oppressed estate liable to pay dues to the ruling feudal nobility,

---

[a] In the original Marx has an English word "surplus", Engels also uses this word, but in brackets adds "Überschuß".— Ed.

[b] K. Marx, Das Kapital, pp. 607-08. See present edition, Vol. 35, Part VII, Chapter XXIV, Section 1.— Ed.

recruited from all manner of serfs and villains, the burghers conquered one position after another in their continuous struggle with the nobility, and finally, in the most highly developed countries, took power in its stead; in France, by directly overthrowing the nobility; in England, by making it more and more bourgeois and incorporating it as their own ornamental head. And how did they accomplish this? Simply through a change in the "economic situation", which sooner or later, voluntarily or as the outcome of combat, was followed by a change in the political conditions. The struggle of the bourgeoisie against the feudal nobility is the struggle of town against country, industry against landed property, money economy against natural economy; and the decisive weapon of the bourgeoisie in this struggle was its means of *economic* power, constantly increasing through the development of industry, first handicraft, and then, at a later stage, progressing to manufacture, and through the expansion of commerce. During the whole of this struggle political force was on the side of the nobility, except for a period when the Crown played the bourgeoisie against the nobility, in order to keep one estate in check by means of the other[71]; but from the moment when the bourgeoisie, still politically powerless, began to grow dangerous owing to its increasing economic power, the Crown resumed its alliance with the nobility, and by so doing called forth the bourgeois revolution, first in England and then in France. The "political conditions" in France had remained unaltered, while the "economic situation" had outgrown them. Judged by his political status the nobleman was everything, the burgher nothing; but judged by his social position the burgher now formed the most important class in the state, while the nobleman had been shorn of all his social functions and was now only drawing payment, in the revenues that came to him, for these functions which had disappeared. Nor was that all. Bourgeois production in its entirety was still hemmed in by the feudal political forms of the Middle Ages, which this production—not only manufacture, but even handicraft industry—had long outgrown; it had remained hemmed in by all the thousandfold guild privileges and local and provincial customs barriers which had become mere irritants and fetters on production. The bourgeois revolution put an end to this. Not, however, by adjusting the economic situation to suit the political conditions, in accordance with Herr Dühring's precept—this was precisely what the nobles and the Crown had been vainly trying to do for years—but by doing the opposite, by casting aside the old mouldering political rubbish and creating political conditions in which the new "economic situation" could exist and develop. And in this political and legal atmosphere which was suited to its needs it developed brilliantly, so brilliantly that the bourgeoisie has already come close to occupying the position held by the nobility in 1789[a]: it is becoming more and more not only socially superfluous, but a social hindrance; it is more and more becoming separated from productive activity, and, like the nobility in the past, becoming more and more a class merely drawing revenues; and it has accomplished this revolution in its own position and the creation of a new class, the proletariat, without any hocus-pocus of force whatever, in a purely economic way. Even more: it did not in any way will this result of its own actions and activities—on the contrary, this result established itself with irresistible force, against the will and contrary to the intentions of the bourgeoisie; its own productive forces have grown beyond its control, and, as if necessitated by a law of nature, are driving the whole of bourgeois society towards ruin, or revolution. And if the bourgeois now make their appeal to force in order to save the collapsing "economic situation" from the final crash, this only shows that they are labouring under the same delusion as Herr Dühring: the delusion that "political conditions are the decisive cause of the economic situation"; this only shows that they imagine, just as Herr Dühring does, that by making use of "the primary", "the direct political force", they can remodel those "facts of the second order" [D. Ph. 538], the economic situation and its inevitable development; and that therefore the economic consequences of the steam-engine and the modern machinery driven by it, of world trade and the banking and credit developments of the present day, can be blown out of existence by them with Krupp guns and Mauser rifles.[72]

III. THEORY OF FORCE

(Continuation)

But let us look a little more closely at this omnipotent "force" of Herr Dühring's. Crusoe enslaved Friday "sword in hand" [D. C. 23]. Where did he get the sword? Even on the imaginary islands of the Robinson Crusoe epic, swords have not, up to now, been known to grow on trees, and Herr Dühring provides no

---

[a] The year of the beginning of the French Revolution.— Ed.

answer to this question. If Crusoe could procure a sword for himself, we are equally entitled to assume that one fine morning Friday might appear with a loaded revolver in his hand, and then the whole "force" relationship is inverted. Friday commands, and it is Crusoe who has to drudge. We must apologise to the readers for returning with such insistence to the Robinson Crusoe and Friday story, which properly belongs to the nursery and not to the field of science—but how can we help it? We are obliged to apply Herr Dühring's axiomatic method conscientiously, and it is not our fault if in doing so we have to keep all the time within the field of pure childishness. So, then, the revolver triumphs over the sword; and this will probably make even the most childish axiomatician comprehend that force is no mere act of the will, but requires the existence of very real preliminary conditions before it can come into operation, namely, *instruments,* the more perfect of which gets the better of the less perfect; moreover, that these instruments have to be produced, which implies that the producer of more perfect instruments of force, *vulgo*[a] arms, gets the better of the producer of the less perfect instruments, and that, in a word, the triumph of force is based on the production of arms, and this in turn on production in general—therefore, on "economic power", on the "economic situation", on the *material* means which force has at its disposal.

Force, nowadays, is the army and navy, and both, as we all know to our cost, are "devilishly expensive". Force, however, cannot make any money; at most it can take away money that has already been made—and this does not help much either—as we have seen, also to our cost, in the case of the French milliards.[73] In the last analysis, therefore, money must be provided through the medium of economic production; and so once more force is conditioned by the economic situation, which furnishes the means for the equipment and maintenance of the instruments of force. But even that is not all. Nothing is more dependent on economic prerequisites than precisely army and navy. Armament, composition, organisation, tactics and strategy depend above all on the stage reached at the time in production and on communications. It is not the "free creations of the mind" [D. Ph. 43] of generals of genius that have had a revolutionising effect here, but the invention of better weapons and the change in the human material, the soldiers; at the very most the part played by generals

***

[a] Commonly speaking.— *Ed.*

of genius is limited to adapting methods of fighting to the new weapons and combatants.[a]

At the beginning of the fourteenth century, gunpowder came from the Arabs to Western Europe, and, as every school child knows, completely revolutionised the methods of warfare. The introduction of gunpowder and fire-arms, however, was not at all an act of force, but a step forward in industry, that is, an economic advance. Industry remains industry, whether it is applied to the production or the destruction of things. And the introduction of fire-arms had a revolutionising effect not only on the conduct of war itself, but also on the political relationships of domination and subjection. The procurement of powder and fire-arms required industry and money, and both of these were in the hands of the burghers of the towns. From the outset, therefore, fire-arms were the weapons of the towns, and of the rising town-supported monarchy against the feudal nobility. The stone walls of the noblemen's castles, hitherto unapproachable, fell before the cannon of the burghers, and the bullets of the burghers' arquebuses pierced the armour of the knights. With the defeat of the nobility's armour-clad cavalry, the nobility's supremacy was broken; with the development of the bourgeoisie, infantry and artillery became more and more the decisive types of arms; compelled by the development of artillery, the military profession had to add to its organisation a new and entirely industrial subsection, engineering.

The improvement of fire-arms was a very slow process. The pieces of artillery remained clumsy and the musket, in spite of a number of inventions affecting details, was still a crude weapon. It took over three hundred years for a weapon to be constructed that was suitable for the equipment of the whole body of infantry. It was not until the early eighteenth century that the flint-lock musket with a bayonet finally displaced the pike in the equipment of the infantry. The foot soldiers of that period were the mercenaries of princes; they consisted of the most demoralised elements of society, rigorously drilled but quite unreliable and only held together by the rod; they were often hostile prisoners of war who had been pressed into service. The only type of fighting

---

[a] Further on, instead of the six following paragraphs, in the first manuscript of Part II of *Anti-Dühring* (see Notes 1 and 332), there followed a more detailed variant of the text, which Engels subsequently entitled "Infantry Tactics, Derived from Material Causes. 1700-1870" as a separate manuscript (see this volume, pp. 623-29).— *Ed.*

in which these soldiers could apply the new weapons was the tactics of the line, which reached its highest perfection under Frederick II. The whole infantry of an army was drawn up in triple ranks in the form of a very long, hollow square, and moved in battle order only as a whole; at the very most, either of the two wings might move forward or keep back a little. This cumbrous mass could move in formation only on absolutely level ground, and even then only very slowly (seventy-five paces a minute); a change of formation during a battle was impossible, and once the infantry was engaged, victory or defeat was decided rapidly and at one blow.

In the American War of Independence,[74] these unwieldy lines were met by bands of rebels, who although not drilled were all the better able to shoot from their rifled guns; they were fighting for their vital interests, and therefore did not desert like the mercenaries; nor did they do the English the favour of encountering them also in line and on clear, even ground. They came on in open formation, a series of rapidly moving troops of sharpshooters, under cover of the woods. Here the line was powerless and succumbed to its invisible and inaccessible opponents. Skirmishing was reinvented—a new method of warfare which was the result of a change in the human war material.

What the American Revolution had begun the French Revolution[75] completed, also in the military sphere. It also could oppose to the well-trained mercenary armies of the Coalition only poorly trained but great masses of soldiers, the levy of the entire nation. But these masses had to protect Paris, that is, to hold a definite area, and for this purpose victory in open mass battle was essential. Mere skirmishes would not achieve enough; a form had to be found to make use of large masses and this form was discovered in the *column.* Column formation made it possible for even poorly trained troops to move with a fair degree of order, and moreover with greater speed (a hundred paces and more in a minute); it made it possible to break through the rigid forms of the old line formation; to fight on any ground, and therefore even on ground which was extremely disadvantageous to the line formation; to group the troops in any way if in the least appropriate; and, in conjunction with attacks by scattered bands of sharpshooters, to contain the enemy's lines, keep them engaged and wear them out until the moment came for masses held in reserve to break through them at the decisive point in the position. This new method of warfare, based on the combined action of skirmishers and columns and on the partitioning of the army into independent divisions or army corps, composed of all arms of the service—a method brought to full perfection by Napoleon in both its tactical and strategical aspects—had become necessary primarily because of the changed personnel: the soldiery of the French Revolution. Besides, two very important technical prerequisites had been complied with: first, the lighter carriages for field guns constructed by Gribeauval, which alone made possible the more rapid movement now required of them; and secondly, the slanting of the butt, which had hitherto been quite straight, continuing the line of the barrel. Introduced in France in 1777, it was copied from hunting weapons and made it possible to shoot at a particular individual without necessarily missing him. But for this improvement it would have been impossible to skirmish with the old weapons.

The revolutionary system of arming the whole people was soon restricted to compulsory conscription (with substitution for the rich, who paid for their release) and in this form it was adopted by most of the large states on the Continent. Only Prussia attempted, through its *Landwehr* system,[76] to draw to a greater extent on the military strength of the nation. Prussia was also the first state to equip its whole infantry—after the rifled muzzle-loader, which had been improved between 1830 and 1860 and found fit for use in war, had played a brief role—with the most up-to-date weapon, the rifled breech-loader. Its successes in 1866 were due to these two innovations.[77]

The Franco-German War was the first in which two armies faced each other both equipped with breech-loading rifles, and moreover both fundamentally in the same tactical formations as in the time of the old smoothbore flint-locks. The only difference was that the Prussians had introduced the company column formation in an attempt to find a form of fighting which was better adapted to the new type of arms. But when, at St. Privat on August 18,[78] the Prussian Guard tried to apply the company column formation seriously, the five regiments which were chiefly engaged lost in less than two hours more than a third of their strength (176 officers and 5,114 men). From that time on the company column, too, was condemned as a battle formation, no less than the battalion column and the line; all idea of further exposing troops in any kind of close formation to enemy gun-fire was abandoned, and on the German side all subsequent fighting was conducted only in those compact bodies of skirmishers into which the columns had so far regularly dissolved of themselves under a deadly hail of bullets, although this had been opposed by the higher commands as contrary to order; and in the same way the only form of movement when under fire from enemy rifles became the *double*. Once again the soldier had been shrewder than the officer; it was *he* who instinctively found the only way of fighting which has proved of service up to now under the fire of breech-loading rifles, and in spite of opposition from his officers he carried it through successfully.

The Franco-German War marked a turning-point of entirely new implications. In the first place the weapons used have reached such a stage of perfection that further progress which would have any revolutionising influence is no longer possible. Once armies have guns which can hit a battalion at any range at which it can be distinguished, and rifles which are equally effective for hitting individual men, while loading them takes less time than aiming, then all further improvements are of minor importance for field warfare. The era of evolution is therefore, in essentials, closed in this direction. And secondly, this war has compelled all continental powers to introduce in a stricter form the Prussian *Landwehr* system, and with it a military burden which must bring them to ruin within a few years. The army has become the main purpose of the state, and an end in itself; the peoples are there only to provide soldiers and feed them. Militarism dominates and is swallowing Europe. But this militarism also bears within itself the seed of its own destruction. Competition among the individual states forces them, on the one hand, to spend more money each year on the army and navy, artillery, etc., thus more and more hastening their financial collapse; and, on the other hand, to resort to universal compulsory military service more and more extensively, thus in the long run making the whole people familiar with the use of arms, and therefore enabling them at a given moment to make their will prevail against the warlords in command. And this moment will arrive as soon as the mass of the people—town and country workers and peasants—*will have* a will. At this point the armies of the princes become transformed into armies of the people; the machine refuses to work and militarism collapses by the dialectics of its own evolution. What the bourgeois democracy of 1848 could not accomplish, just because it was *bourgeois* and not proletarian, namely, to give the labouring masses a will whose content would be in accord with their class position—socialism will infallibly secure. And this will mean the bursting asunder *from within* of militarism and with it of all standing armies.

That is the first moral of our history of modern infantry. The second moral, which brings us back again to Herr Dühring, is that the whole organisation and method of warfare of the armies, and along with these victory or defeat, prove to be dependent on material, that is, economic conditions: on the human material and the armaments, and therefore on the quality and quantity of the population and on technical development. Only a hunting people like the Americans could rediscover skirmishing tactics—and they were hunters as a result of purely economic causes, just as now, as a result of purely economic causes, these same Yankees of the old States have transformed themselves into farmers, industrialists, seamen and merchants who no longer skirmish in the primeval forests, but instead all the more effectively in the field of speculation, where they have likewise made much progress in making use of large masses.—Only a revolution such as the French, which brought about the economic emancipation of the bourgeois and, especially, of the peasant, could find the mass armies and at the same time the free forms of movement which shattered the old rigid lines—the military counterparts of the absolutism which they were defending. And we have seen in case after case how advances in technique, as soon as they became applicable militarily and in fact were so applied, immediately and almost forcibly produced changes and even revolutions in the methods of warfare, often indeed against the will of the army command. And nowadays any zealous N.C.O. could explain to Herr Dühring how greatly, besides, the conduct of a war depends on the productivity and means of communication of the army's own hinterland as well as of the theatre of war. In short, always and everywhere it is the economic conditions and the instruments of economic power which help "force" to victory, without which force ceases to be force. And anyone who tried to reform methods of warfare from the opposite standpoint, on the basis of Dühringian principles, would certainly earn nothing but a beating.*

If we pass now from land to sea, we find that in the last twenty years alone an even more complete revolution has taken place

---

* This is already perfectly well known to the Prussian General Staff. "The *basis* of warfare is primarily the *economic* way of life of the peoples in general", said Herr Max Jähns, a captain of the General Staff, in a scientific lecture (*Kölnische Zeitung*, April 20, 1876, p. 3).[a]

---

[a] M. Jähns, *Machiavelli und der Gedanke der allgemeinen Wehrpflicht.* Italics by Engels.— *Ed.*

there. The warship of the Crimean War [79] was the wooden two- and three-decker of 60 to 100 guns; this was still mainly propelled by sail, with only a low-powered auxiliary steam-engine. The guns on these warships were for the most part 32-pounders, weighing approximately 50 centners, with only a few 68-pounders weighing 95 centners. Towards the end of the war, iron-clad floating batteries made their appearance; they were clumsy and almost immobile monsters, but to the guns of that period they were invulnerable. Soon warships, too, were swathed in iron armour-plating; at first the plates were still thin, a thickness of four inches being regarded as extremely heavy armour. But soon the progress made with artillery outstripped the armour-plating; each successive increase in the strength of the armour used was countered by a new and heavier gun which easily pierced the plates. In this way we have already reached armour-plating ten, twelve, fourteen and twenty-four inches thick (Italy proposes to have a ship built with plates three feet thick) on the one hand, and on the other, rifled guns of 25, 35, 80 and even 100 tons (at 20 centners[a]) in weight, which can hurl projectiles weighing 300, 400, 1,700 and up to 2,000 pounds to distances which were never dreamed of before. The warship of the present day is a gigantic armoured screw-driven steamer of 8,000 to 9,000 tons displacement and 6,000 to 8,000 horse power, with revolving turrets and four or at most six heavy guns, the bow being extended under water into a ram for running down enemy vessels. It is a single colossal machine, in which steam not only drives the ship at a high speed, but also works the steering-gear, raises the anchor, swings the turrets, changes the elevation of the guns and loads them, pumps out water, hoists and lowers the boats—some of which are themselves also steam-driven—and so forth. And the rivalry between armour-plating and the fire power of guns is so far from being at an end that nowadays a ship is almost always not up to requirements, already out of date, before it is launched. The modern warship is not only a product, but at the same time a specimen of modern large-scale industry, a floating factory—producing mainly, to be sure, a lavish waste of money. The country in which large-scale industry is most highly developed has almost a monopoly of the construction of these ships. All Turkish, almost all Russian and most German armoured vessels have been built in England; armour-plates that are at all serviceable are hardly made outside of Sheffield; of the three steelworks in

---

[a] German centner of 50 kilograms, i.e., half of the metric centner.—*Ed.*

Europe which alone are able to make the heaviest guns, two (Woolwich and Elswick) are in England, and the third (Krupp[80]) in Germany. In this sphere it is most palpably evident that the "direct political force" [D. Ph. 538] which, according to Herr Dühring, is the "decisive cause of the economic situation" [D. K. G. 231], is on the contrary completely subordinate to the economic situation, that not only the construction but also the operation of the marine instrument of force, the warship, has itself become a branch of modern large-scale industry. And that this is so distresses no one more than force itself, that is, the state, which has now to pay for one ship as much as a whole small fleet used to cost; which has to resign itself to seeing these expensive vessels become obsolete, and therefore worthless, even before they slide into the water; and which must certainly be just as disgusted as Herr Dühring that the man of the "economic situation", the engineer, is now of far greater importance on board than the man of "direct force", the captain. We, on the contrary, have absolutely no cause to be vexed when we see that, in this competitive struggle between armour-plating and guns, the warship is being developed to a pitch of perfection which is making it both outrageously costly and unusable in war,* and that this struggle makes manifest also in the sphere of naval warfare those inherent dialectical laws of motion on the basis of which militarism, like every other historical phenomenon, is being brought to its doom in consequence of its own development.

Here, too, therefore we see absolutely clearly that it is not by any means true that "the primary must be sought in direct political force and not in any indirect economic power" [D. Ph. 538]. On the contrary. For what in fact does "the primary" in force itself prove to be? Economic power, the disposal of the means of power of large-scale industry. Naval political force, which reposes on modern warships, proves to be not at all "direct" but on the contrary *mediated* by economic power, highly developed metallurgy, command of skilled technicians and highly productive coal-mines.

And yet what is the use of it all? If we put Herr Dühring in supreme command in the next naval war, he will destroy all fleets

---

* The perfecting of the latest product of modern industry for use in naval warfare, the self-propelled torpedo, seems likely to bring this to pass; it would mean that the smallest torpedo boat would be superior to the most powerful armoured warship. (It should be borne in mind that the above was written in 1878[81].)

of armoured ships, which are the slaves of the economic situation, without torpedoes or any other artifices, solely by virtue of his "direct force".

IV. THEORY OF FORCE

(Conclusion)

"It is a circumstance of great importance that as a matter of fact the domination over *nature*, generally speaking"(!), "only proceeded" (a domination proceeded!) "through the domination over *man*. The cultivation of landed property in tracts of considerable size never took place anywhere without the antecedent subjection of man in some form of slave-labour or corvée. The establishment of an economic domination over things has presupposed the political, social and economic domination of man over man. How could a large landed proprietor even be conceived without at once including in this idea also his domination over slaves, serfs, or others indirectly unfree? What could the efforts of an individual, at most supplemented by those of his family, have signified or signify in extensively practised agriculture? The exploitation of the land, or the extension of economic control over it on a scale exceeding the natural capacities of the individual, was only made possible in previous history by the establishment, either before or simultaneously with the introduction of dominion over land, of the enslavement of man which this involves. In the later periods of development this servitude was mitigated ... its present form in the more highly civilised states is wage-labour, to a greater or lesser degree carried on under police rule. Thus wage-labour provides the practical possibility of that form of contemporary wealth which is represented by dominion over wide areas of land and" (!) "extensive landed property. It goes without saying that all other types of distributive wealth must be explained historically in a similar way, and the indirect dependence of man on man, which is now the essential feature of the conditions which economically are most fully developed, cannot be understood and explained by its own nature, but only as a somewhat transformed heritage of an earlier direct subjugation and expropriation" [D. C. 18-19].

Thus Herr Dühring.

Thesis: The domination of nature (by man) presupposes the domination of man (by man).

Proof: The cultivation of landed *property in tracts of considerable size* never took place anywhere except by the use of bondmen.

Proof of the proof: How can there be large landowners without bondmen, as the large landowner, even with his family, could work only a tiny part of his property without the help of bondmen?

Therefore, in order to prove that man first had to subjugate man before he could bring nature under his control, Herr Dühring transforms "nature" without more ado into "landed property in tracts of considerable size", and then this landed property—ownership unspecified—is immediately further transformed into the property of a large landed proprietor, who naturally cannot work his land without bondmen.

In the first place "domination over nature" and the "cultivation of landed property" are by no means the same thing. In industry, domination over nature is exercised on quite another and much greater scale than in agriculture, which is still subject to weather conditions instead of controlling them.

Secondly, if we confine ourselves to the cultivation of landed property consisting of tracts of considerable size, the question arises: whose landed property is it? And then we find in the early history of all civilised peoples, not the "large landed proprietors" whom Herr Dühring interpolates here with his customary sleight of hand, which he calls "natural dialectics",[82] but tribal and village communities with common ownership of the land. From India to Ireland the cultivation of landed property in tracts of considerable size was originally carried on by such tribal and village communities; sometimes the arable land was tilled jointly for account of the community, and sometimes in separate parcels of land temporarily allotted to families by the community, while woodland and pastureland continued to be used in common. It is once again characteristic of "the most exhaustive specialised studies" made by Herr Dühring "in the domain of politics and law" [D. Ph. 537] that he knows nothing of all this; that all his works breathe total ignorance of Maurer's epoch-making writings on the primitive constitution of the German mark,[83] the basis of all German law, and of the ever-increasing mass of literature, chiefly stimulated by Maurer, which is devoted to proving the primitive common ownership of the land among all civilised peoples of Europe and Asia, and to showing the various forms of its existence and dissolution. Just as in the domain of French and English law Herr Dühring "himself acquired all his ignorance",[a] great as it was, so it is with his even much greater ignorance in the domain of German law. In this domain the man who flies into such a violent rage over the limited horizon of university professors is himself today, at the very most, still where the professors were twenty years ago.

It is a pure "free creation and imagination" [43] on Herr Dühring's part when he asserts that landed proprietors and bondmen were required for the cultivation of landed property in tracts of considerable size. In the whole of the Orient, where the village community or the state owns the land, the very term

---

[a] From Heine's poem *Kobes I.*— Ed.

landlord is not to be found in the various languages, a point on which Herr Dühring can consult the English jurists, whose efforts in India to solve the question: who is the owner of the land?—were as vain as those of the late Prince Heinrich LXXII of Reuss-Greiz-Schleiz-Lobenstein-Eberswalde [84] in his attempts to solve the question of who was the night-watchman. It was the Turks who first introduced a sort of feudal ownership of land in the countries conquered by them in the Orient. Greece made its entry into history, as far back as the heroic epoch, with a system of social estates which itself was evidently the product of a long but unknown prehistory; even there, however, the land was mainly cultivated by independent peasants; the larger estates of the nobles and tribal chiefs were the exception; moreover they disappeared soon after. Italy was brought under cultivation chiefly by peasants; when, in the final period of the Roman Republic, the great complexes of estates, the latifundia, displaced the small peasants and replaced them with slaves, they also replaced tillage with stockraising, and, as Pliny already realised, brought Italy to ruin (*latifundia Italiam perdidere*[a]). During the Middle Ages, peasant farming was predominant throughout Europe (especially in bringing virgin soil into cultivation); and in relation to the question we are now considering it is of no importance whether these peasants had to pay dues, and if so what dues, to any feudal lords. The colonists from Friesland, Lower Saxony, Flanders and the Lower Rhine, who brought under cultivation the land east of the Elbe which had been wrested from the Slavs, did this as free peasants under very favourable quit-rent tenures, and not at all under "some form of corvée" [D. C. 18].—In North America, by far the largest portion of the land was opened for cultivation by the labour of free farmers, while the big landlords of the South, with their slaves and their rapacious tilling of the land, exhausted the soil until it could grow only firs, so that the cultivation of cotton was forced further and further west. In Australia and New Zealand, all attempts of the British government to establish artificially a landed aristocracy came to nothing. In short, if we except the tropical and subtropical colonies, where the climate makes agricultural labour impossible for Europeans, the big landlord who subjugates nature by means of his slaves or serfs and brings the land under cultivation proves to be a pure figment of the imagination. The very reverse is the case. Where he makes his

---

[a] Plinius, *Naturalis historiae,* Liber XVIII, § 35.— *Ed.*

appearance in antiquity, as in Italy, he does not bring wasteland into cultivation, but transforms arable land brought under cultivation by peasants into stock pastures, depopulating and ruining whole countries. Only in a more recent period, when the increasing density of population had raised the value of land, and particularly since the development of agricultural science had made even poorer land more cultivable—it is only from this period that large landowners began to participate on an extensive scale in bringing wasteland and grass-land under cultivation—and this mainly through the robbery of common land from the peasants, both in England and in Germany. But there was another side even to this. For every acre of common land which the large landowners brought into cultivation in England, they transformed at least three acres of arable land in Scotland into sheep-runs and eventually even into mere big-game hunting-grounds.

We are concerned here only with Herr Dühring's assertion that the bringing into cultivation of tracts of land of considerable size and therefore of practically the whole area now cultivated, "never and nowhere" took place except through the agency of big landlords and their bondmen—an assertion which, as we have seen, "presupposes" a really unprecedented ignorance of history. It is not necessary, therefore, for us to examine here either to what extent, at different periods, areas which were already made entirely or mainly cultivable were cultivated by slaves (as in the hey-day of Greece) or serfs (as in the manors of the Middle Ages); or what was the social function of the large landowners at various periods.

And after Herr Dühring has shown us this masterpiece of the imagination—in which we do not know whether the conjuring trick of deduction or the falsification of history is more to be admired—he exclaims triumphantly:

"It goes without saying that all other types of distributive wealth *must be explained historically in similar manner!*" [19.]

Which of course saves him the trouble of wasting even a single word more on the origin, for example, of capital.

If, with his domination of man by man as a prior condition for the domination of nature by man, Herr Dühring only wanted to state in a general way that the whole of our present economic order, the level of development now attained by agriculture and industry, is the result of a social history which evolved in class antagonisms, in relationships of domination and subjection, he is saying something which long ago, ever since the *Communist*

Manifesto, became a commonplace. But the question at issue is how we are to explain the origin of classes and relations based on domination, and if Herr Dühring's only answer is the one word "force", we are left exactly where we were at the start. The mere fact that the ruled and exploited have at all times been far more numerous than the rulers and the exploiters, and that therefore it is in the hands of the former that the real force has reposed, is enough to demonstrate the absurdity of the whole force theory. The relationships based on domination and subjection have therefore still to be explained.

They arose in two ways.

As men originally made their exit from the animal world—in the narrower sense of the term—so they made their entry into history: still half animal, brutal, still helpless in face of the forces of nature, still ignorant of their own strength; and consequently as poor as the animals and hardly more productive than they. There prevailed a certain equality in the conditions of existence, and for the heads of families also a kind of equality of social position—at least an absence of social classes—which continued among the primitive agricultural communities of the civilised peoples of a later period. In each such community there were from the beginning certain common interests the safeguarding of which had to be handed over to individuals, true, under the control of the community as a whole: adjudication of disputes; repression of abuse of authority by individuals; control of water supplies, especially in hot countries; and finally when conditions were still absolutely primitive, religious functions. Such offices are found in aboriginal communities of every period—in the oldest German marks and even today in India. They are naturally endowed with a certain measure of authority and are the beginnings of state power. The productive forces gradually increase; the increasing density of the population creates at one point common interests, at another conflicting interests, between the separate communities, whose grouping into larger units brings about in turn a new division of labour, the setting up of organs to safeguard common interests and combat conflicting interests. These organs which, if only because they represent the common interests of the whole group, hold a special position in relation to each individual community—in certain circumstances even one of opposition— soon make themselves still more independent, partly through heredity of functions, which comes about almost as a matter of course in a world where everything occurs spontaneously, and partly because they become increasingly indispensable owing to the growing number of conflicts with other groups. It is not necessary for us to examine here how this independence of social functions in relation to society increased with time until it developed into domination over society; how he who was originally the servant, where conditions were favourable, changed gradually into the lord; how this lord, depending on the conditions, emerged as an Oriental despot or satrap, the dynast of a Greek tribe, chieftain of a Celtic clan, and so on; to what extent he subsequently had recourse to force in the course of this transformation; and how finally the individual rulers united into a ruling class. Here we are only concerned with establishing the fact that the exercise of a social function was everywhere the basis of political supremacy; and further that political supremacy has existed for any length of time only when it discharged its social functions. However great the number of despotisms which rose and fell in Persia and India, each was fully aware that above all it was the entrepreneur responsible for the collective maintenance of irrigation throughout the river valleys, without which no agriculture was possible there. It was reserved for the enlightened English to lose sight of this in India; they let the irrigation canals and sluices fall into decay, and are now at last discovering, through the regularly recurring famines, that they have neglected the one activity which might have made their rule in India at least as legitimate as that of their predecessors.

But alongside this process of formation of classes another was also taking place. The spontaneously evolved division of labour within the family cultivating the soil made possible, at a certain level of well-being, the incorporation of one or more strangers as additional labour forces. This was especially the case in countries where the old common ownership of the land had already disintegrated or at least the former joint cultivation had given place to the separate cultivation of parcels of land by the respective families. Production had developed so far that the labour-power of a man could now produce more than was necessary for its mere maintenance; the means of maintaining additional labour forces existed; likewise the means of employing them; labour-power acquired a *value*. But the community itself and the association to which it belonged yielded no available, superfluous labour forces. On the other hand, such forces were provided by war, and war was as old as the simultaneous existence alongside each other of several groups of communities. Up to that time one had not known what to do with prisoners of war, and had therefore simply killed them; at an even earlier period, eaten them. But at the stage of "economic situation" which had now been attained the prisoners acquired a value; one therefore let them live and made use of their labour. Thus force, instead of controlling the economic situation, was on the contrary pressed into the service of the economic situation. *Slavery* had been invented. It soon became the dominant form of production among all peoples who were developing beyond the old community, but in the end was also one of the chief causes of their decay. It was slavery that first made possible the division of labour between agriculture and industry on a larger scale, and thereby also Hellenism, the flowering of the ancient world. Without slavery, no Greek state, no Greek art and science; without slavery, no Roman Empire. But without the basis laid by Hellenism and the Roman Empire, also no modern Europe. We should never forget that our whole economic, political and intellectual development presupposes a state of things in which slavery was as necessary as it was universally recognised. In this sense we are entitled to say: Without the slavery of antiquity no modern socialism.

It is very easy to inveigh against slavery and similar things in general terms, and to give vent to high moral indignation at such infamies. Unfortunately all that this conveys is only what everyone knows, namely, that these institutions of antiquity are no longer in accord with our present conditions and our sentiments, which these conditions determine. But it does not tell us one word as to how these institutions arose, why they existed, and what role they played in history. And when we examine these questions, we are compelled to say—however contradictory and heretical it may sound—that the introduction of slavery under the conditions prevailing at that time was a great step forward. For it is a fact that man sprang from the beasts, and had consequently to use barbaric and almost bestial means to extricate himself from barbarism. Where the ancient communities have continued to exist, they have for thousands of years formed the basis of the cruellest form of state, Oriental despotism, from India to Russia. It was only where these communities dissolved that the peoples made progress of themselves, and their next economic advance consisted in the increase and development of production by means of slave labour. It is clear that so long as human labour was still so little productive that it provided but a small surplus over and above the necessary means of subsistence, any increase of the productive forces, extension of trade, development of the state and of law, or foundation of art and science, was possible only by means of a greater division of labour. And the necessary basis for this was the great division of labour between the masses discharging simple manual labour and the few privileged persons directing labour, conducting trade and public affairs, and, at a later stage, occupying themselves with art and science. The simplest and most natural form of this division of labour was in fact slavery. In the historical conditions of the ancient world, and particularly of Greece, the advance to a society based on class antagonisms could be accomplished only in the form of slavery. This was an advance even for the slaves; the prisoners of war, from whom the mass of the slaves was recruited, now at least saved their lives, instead of being killed as they had been before, or even roasted, as at a still earlier period.

We may add at this point that all historical antagonisms between exploiting and exploited, ruling and oppressed classes to this very day find their explanation in this same relatively undeveloped productivity of human labour. So long as the really working population were so much occupied with their necessary labour that they had no time left for looking after the common affairs of society—the direction of labour, affairs of state, legal matters, art, science, etc.—so long was it necessary that there should constantly exist a special class, freed from actual labour, to manage these affairs; and this class never failed, for its own advantage, to impose a greater and greater burden of labour on the working masses. Only the immense increase of the productive forces attained by modern industry has made it possible to distribute labour among all members of society without exception, and thereby to limit the labour-time of each individual member to such an extent that all have enough free time left to take part in the general—both theoretical and practical—affairs of society. It is only now, therefore, that every ruling and exploiting class has become superfluous and indeed a hindrance to social development, and it is only now, too, that it will be inexorably abolished, however much it may be in possession of "direct force".

When, therefore, Herr Dühring turns up his nose at Hellenism because it was founded on slavery, he might with equal justice reproach the Greeks with having had no steam-engines or electric telegraphs. And when he asserts that our modern wage bondage can only be explained as a somewhat transformed and mitigated heritage of slavery, and not by its own nature (that is, by the economic laws of modern society), this either means only that both wage-labour and slavery are forms of bondage and class domination, which every child knows to be so, or is false. For with equal justice we might say that wage-labour could only be explained as a mitigated form of cannibalism, which, it is now established, was the universal primitive form of utilisation of defeated enemies.

The role played in history by force as contrasted with economic development is therefore clear. In the first place, all political power is originally based on an economic, social function, and increases in proportion as the members of society, through the dissolution of the primitive community, become transformed into private producers, and thus become more and more divorced from the administrators of the common functions of society. Secondly, after the political force has made itself independent in relation to society, and has transformed itself from its servant into its master, it can work in two different directions. Either it works in the sense and in the direction of the natural economic development, in which case no conflict arises between them, the economic development being accelerated. Or it works against economic development, in which case, as a rule, with but few exceptions, force succumbs to it. These few exceptions are isolated cases of conquest, in which the more barbarian conquerors exterminated or drove out the population of a country and laid waste or allowed to go to ruin productive forces which they did not know how to use. This was what the Christians in Moorish Spain did with the major part of the irrigation works on which the highly developed agriculture and horticulture of the Moors depended. Every conquest by a more barbarian people disturbs of course the economic development and destroys numerous productive forces. But in the immense majority of cases where the conquest is permanent, the more barbarian conqueror has to adapt himself to the higher "economic situation" [D. K. G. 231] as it emerges from the conquest; he is assimilated by the vanquished and in most cases he has even to adopt their language. But where—apart from cases of conquest—the internal state power of a country becomes antagonistic to its economic development, as at a certain stage occurred with almost every political power in the past, the contest always ended with the downfall of the political power. Inexorably and without exception the economic development has forced its way through—we have already mentioned the latest and most striking example of this: the great French Revolution. If, in accordance with Herr Dühring's theory, the economic situation and with it the economic structure of a given country were dependent simply on political force, it is absolutely impossible to understand why Frederick William IV after 1848 could not succeed, in spite of his "magnificent army",[85] ingrafting the mediaeval guilds and other romantic oddities on to the railways, the steam-engines and the large-scale industry which was just then developing in his country; or why the tsar of Russia,[a] who is possessed of even much more forcible means, is not only unable to pay his debts, but cannot even maintain his "force" without continually borrowing from the "economic situation" of Western Europe.

To Herr Dühring force is the absolute evil; the first act of force is to him the original sin; his whole exposition is a jeremiad on the contamination of all subsequent history consummated by this original sin; a jeremiad on the shameful perversion of all natural and social laws by this diabolical power, force. That force, however, plays yet another role in history, a revolutionary role; that, in the words of Marx, it is the midwife of every old society pregnant with a new one,[b] that it is the instrument with the aid of which social movement forces its way through and shatters the dead, fossilised political forms—of this there is not a word in Herr Dühring. It is only with sighs and groans that he admits the possibility that force will perhaps be necessary for the overthrow of an economic system of exploitation—unfortunately, because all use of force demoralises the person who uses it. And this in spite of the immense moral and spiritual impetus which has been given by every victorious revolution! And this in Germany, where a violent collision—which may, after all, be forced on the people— would at least have the advantage of wiping out the servility which has penetrated the nation's mentality following the humiliation of the Thirty Years' War. And this parson's mode of thought—dull, insipid and impotent—presumes to impose itself on the most revolutionary party that history has known!

V. THEORY OF VALUE

It is now about a hundred years since the publication in Leipzig of a book which by the beginning of the nineteenth century had run through over thirty editions; it was circulated and distributed in town and country by the authorities, by preachers and philanthropists of all kinds, and was generally prescribed as a

---

[a] Alexander II.— Ed.
[b] K. Marx, Capital. See present edition, Vol. 35, Part VIII, Chapter XXXI.— Ed.

reader for use in the elementary schools. This book was Rochow's *Kinderfreund.*[a] Its purpose was to teach the youthful offspring of the peasants and artisans their vocation in life and their duties to their superiors in society and in the state, and likewise to inspire in them a beneficent contentment with their lot on earth, with black bread and potatoes, serf labour, low wages, paternal thrashings and other delectations of this sort, and all that by means of the system of enlightenment which was then in vogue. With this aim in view the youth of the towns and of the countryside was admonished how wisely nature had ordained that man must win his livelihood and his pleasures by labour, and how happy therefore the peasant or artisan should feel that it was granted to him to season his meal with bitter labour, instead of, like the rich glutton, suffering the pangs of indigestion or constipation, and having to gulp down the choicest tit-bits with repugnance. These same platitudes that old Rochow thought good enough for the peasant boys and girls of the electorate of Saxony of his time, are served up to us by Herr Dühring on page 14 and the following pages of his *Cursus*[b] as the "absolutely fundamental" [D. Ph. 150] basis of the most up-to-date political economy.

"Human wants as such have their natural laws, and their expansion is confined within limits which can be transgressed only by unnatural acts and only for a time, until these acts result in nausea, weariness of life, decrepitude, social mutilation and finally salutary annihilation... A game of life consisting purely of pleasures without any further serious aim soon makes one *blasé*, or, what amounts to the same thing, exhausts all capacity to feel. Real labour, in some form or other, is therefore the natural social law of healthy beings... If instincts and wants were not provided with counterbalances they could hardly bring us even infantile existence, let alone a historically intensified development of life. If they could find satisfaction without limit and without effort they would soon exhaust themselves, leaving an empty existence in the form of boring intervals lasting until the wants were felt again... In every respect, therefore, the fact that the satisfaction of the instincts and passions depends on the surmounting of economic obstacles is a salutary basic law of both the external arrangement of nature and the inner constitution of man" [D. C. 14, 15, 16]—and so on, and so forth.

It can be seen that the commonest commonplaces of the worthy Rochow are celebrating their centenary in Herr Dühring, and do so, moreover, as the "deeper foundation" [11] of the one and only really critical and scientific "socialitarian system" [IV].

---

[a] F. E. Rochow, *Der Kinderfreund. Ein Lesebuch zum Gebrauch in Landschulen.*— Ed.

[b] E. Dühring, *Cursus der National- und Socialökonomie.*—Ed.

With the foundations thus laid, Herr Dühring can proceed to build. Applying the mathematical method, he first gives us, following the ancient Euclid's example, a series of definitions.[a] This is all the more convenient because it enables him at once to contrive his definitions in such a way that what is to be proved with their help is already partially contained in them. And so we learn at the outset that

the governing concept in all prior political economy has been wealth and that wealth, as it really has been understood hitherto and as it has developed its sway in world history, is "economic power over men and things" [16-17].

This is doubly wrong. In the first place the wealth of the ancient tribal and village communities was in no sense a domination over men. And secondly, even in societies moving in class antagonisms, wealth, in so far as it includes domination over men, is mainly and almost exclusively a domination over men exercised *by virtue of*, and *through the agency of*, the domination over things. From the very early period when the capture of slaves and the exploitation of slaves became separate branches of business, the exploiters of slave-labour had to buy the slaves, acquiring control over men only through their prior control of things, of the purchase price of the slave and of his means of subsistence and instruments of labour. Throughout the Middle Ages large landed property was the prerequisite by means of which the feudal nobility came to have quit-rent peasants and corvée peasants. And nowadays even a six-year-old child sees that wealth dominates men exclusively by means of the things which it has at its disposal.

But what is it that makes Herr Dühring concoct this false definition of wealth, and why has he to sever the actual connection which existed in all former class societies? In order to drag wealth from the domain of economics over into that of morals. Domination over things is quite all right, but domination over men is an evil thing; and as Herr Dühring has forbidden himself to explain domination over men by domination over things, he can once again do an audacious trick and explain domination over men offhand by his beloved force. Wealth, as domination over men, is "robbery" [17]—and with this we are back again at a corrupted version of Proudhon's ancient formula: "Property is theft."[b]

---

[a] Euclides, *Elementa.*—*Ed.*

[b] P. J. Proudhon, *Qu'est-ce que la propriété? ou Recherches sur le principe du droit et du gouvernement,* p. 2.—*Ed.*

And so we have now safely brought wealth under two essential aspects, production and distribution: wealth as domination over things—production wealth, the good side; wealth as domination over men—distribution wealth up to the present day, bad side, away with it! Applied to the conditions of today, this means: The capitalist mode of production is quite good and may remain, but the capitalist mode of distribution is no good and must be abolished. Such is the nonsense which comes of writing on economics without even having grasped the connection between production and distribution.

After wealth, value is defined as follows:

"Value is the worth which economic things and services have in commerce." This worth corresponds to "the price or any other equivalent name, for example, wages" [D. C. 19].

In other words, value is the price. Or rather, in order not to do Herr Dühring an injustice and give the absurdity of his definition as far as possible in his own words: value are the prices. For he says on page 19:

"value, and the prices expressing it in money"

—thus himself stating that the same value has very different prices and consequently also just as many different values. If Hegel had not died long ago, he would hang himself; with all his theologics he could not have thought up this value which has as many different values as it has prices. It requires once more someone with the positive assurance of Herr Dühring to inaugurate a new and deeper foundation for economics with the declaration that there is no difference between price and value except that one is expressed in money and the other is not.

But all this still does not tell us what value is, and still less by what it is determined. Herr Dühring has therefore to come across with further explanations.

"Speaking absolutely in general, the basic law of comparison and evaluation, on which value and the prices expressing it in money depend, belongs in the first place to the sphere of pure production, apart from distribution, which introduces only a second element into the concept of value. The greater or lesser obstacles which the variety of natural conditions places in the way of efforts directed towards the procurement of things, and owing to which it necessitates a greater or lesser expenditure of economic energy, determine also ... the greater or lesser value", [19-20] and this is appraised according to "the resistance offered by nature and circumstances to the procuring of things [20] ... The extent to which we invest our own energy into them" (things) "is the immediate determining cause of the existence of value in general and of a particular magnitude of it" [21].

In so far as there is a meaning in this, it is: The value of a product of labour is determined by the labour-time necessary for its production; and we knew that long ago, even without Herr Dühring. Instead of stating the fact simply, he has to twist it into an oracular saying. It is simply wrong to say that the dimensions in which anyone invests his energies in anything (to keep to the bombastic style) is the immediate determining cause of value and of the magnitude of value. In the first place, it depends on what thing the energy is put into, and secondly, how the energy is put into it. If someone makes a thing which has no use-value for other people, his whole energy does not produce an atom of value; and if he is stiff-necked enough to produce by hand an object which a machine produces twenty times cheaper, nineteen-twentieths of the energy he put into it produces neither value in general nor any particular magnitude of value.

Moreover it is an absolute distortion to transform productive labour, which creates positive products, into a merely negative overcoming of a resistance. In order to come by a shirt we should then have to set about it somewhat as follows: Firstly we overcome the resistance of the cotton-seed to being sown and to growing, then the resistance of the ripe cotton to being picked and packed and transported, then its resistance to being unpacked and carded and spun, further the resistance of the yarn to being woven, then the resistance of the cloth to being bleached and sewn, and finally the resistance of the completed shirt to being put on.

Why all this childish perversion and perversity? In order, by means of the "resistance", to pass from the "production value", the true but hitherto only ideal value, to the "distribution value", the value, falsified by force, which alone was acknowledged in past history:

"In addition to the resistance offered by nature ... there is yet another, a purely social obstacle... An obstructive power steps in between man and nature, and this power is once again man. Man, conceived as alone and isolated, faces nature as a free being... The situation is different as soon as we think of a second man who, sword in hand, holds the approaches to nature and its resources and demands a price, whatever form it may take, for allowing access. This second man ..., so to speak, puts a tax on the other and is thus the reason why the value of the object striven for turns out greater than it might have been but for this political and social obstacle to the procuring or production of the object... The particular forms of this artificially enhanced worth of things are extremely manifold, and it naturally has its concomitant counterpart in a corresponding forcing down of the worth of labour [23] ... It is therefore an illusion to attempt to regard value in advance as an equivalent in the proper sense of this term, that is, as something which is of equal worth, or as a relation of exchange arising from the principle that service and counter-service are equal... On the contrary, the criterion of a correct theory of value will be that the most general cause of evaluation conceived in the theory does not coincide with the special form of worth which rests on compulsory distribution. This form varies with the social system, while economic value proper can only be a production value measured in relation to nature and in consequence of this will only change with changes in the obstacles to production of a purely natural and technical kind" [D. C. 24-25].

The value which a thing has in practice, according to Herr Dühring, therefore consists of two parts: first, the labour contained in it, and, secondly, the tax surcharge imposed "sword in hand". In other words, value in practice today is a monopoly price. Now if, in accordance with this theory of value, all commodities have such a monopoly price, only two alternatives are possible. Either each individual loses again as a buyer what he gained as a seller; the prices have changed nominally but in reality—in their mutual relationship—have remained the same; everything remains as before, and the far-famed distribution value is a mere illusion.—Or, on the other hand, the alleged tax surcharges represent a real sum of values, namely, that produced by the labouring, value-producing class but appropriated by the monopolist class, and then this sum of values consists merely of unpaid labour; in this event, in spite of the man with the sword in his hand, in spite of the alleged tax surcharges and the asserted distribution value, we arrive once again at the Marxian theory of *surplus-value*.

But let us look at some examples of the famous "distribution value". On page 135 and the following pages we find:

"The shaping of prices as a result of individual competition must also be regarded as a form of economic distribution and of the mutual imposition of tribute... If the stock of any necessary commodity is suddenly reduced to a considerable extent, this gives the sellers a disproportionate power of exploitation [135-36] ... what a colossal increase in prices this may produce is shown particularly by those abnormal situations in which the supply of necessary articles is cut off for any length of time" [137] and so on. Moreover, even in the normal course of things virtual monopolies exist which make possible arbitrary price increases, as for example the railway companies, the companies supplying towns with water and gas [see 153, 154], etc.

It has long been known that such opportunities for monopolistic exploitation occur. But that the monopoly prices these produce are not to rank as exceptions and special cases, but precisely as classical examples of the determination of values in operation today—this is new. How are the prices of the necessaries of life determined? Herr Dühring replies: Go into a beleaguered city from which supplies have been cut off, and find out! What effect has competition on the determination of market prices? Ask the monopolists—they will tell you all about it!

For that matter, even in the case of these monopolies, the man with the sword in his hand who is supposed to stand behind them is not discoverable. On the contrary: in cities under siege, if the man with the sword, the commandant, does his duty, he, as a rule, very soon puts an end to the monopoly and requisitions the monopolised stocks for the purpose of equal distribution. And for the rest, the men with the sword, when they have tried to fabricate a "distribution value", have reaped nothing but bad business and financial loss. With their monopolisation of the East Indian trade, the Dutch brought both their monopoly and their trade to ruin. The two strongest governments which ever existed, the North American revolutionary government and the French National Convention, ventured to fix maximum prices, and they failed miserably.[86] For some years now, the Russian government has been trying to raise the exchange rate of Russian paper money—which it is lowering in Russia by the continuous emission of irredeemable banknotes—by the equally continuous bying up in London of bills of exchange on Russia. It has had to pay for this pleasure in the last few years almost sixty million rubles, and the ruble now stands at under two marks instead of over three. If the sword has the magic economic powers ascribed to it by Herr Dühring, why is it that no government has succeeded in permanently compelling bad money to have the "distribution value" of good money, or *assignats* to have the "distribution value" of gold? And where is the sword which is in command of the world market?

There is also another principal form in which the distribution value facilitates the appropriation of other people's services without counter-services: this is possession-rent, that is to say, rent of land and the profit on capital. For the moment we merely record this, to enable us to state that this is all that we learn of this famous "distribution value".—All? No, not quite. Listen to this:

"In spite of the twofold standpoint which manifests itself in the recognition of a production value and a distribution value, there is nevertheless always underlying these *something in common, the thing of which all values consist* and by which they are therefore measured. The immediate, natural measure is the expenditure of energy, and the simplest unit is human energy in the crudest sense of the term. This latter can be reduced to the existence time whose *self*-maintenance in turn represents the overcoming of a certain sum of difficulties in nutrition and life. Distribution, or appropriation, value is present in pure and exclusive form only where the power to dispose of unproduced things, or, to use a commoner expression, where these things themselves are exchanged for services or things of real production value.

The homogeneous element, which is indicated and represented in every expression of value and therefore also in the component parts of value which are appropriated through distribution without counter-service consists in the expenditure of human energy, which ... finds embodiment ... in each commodity" [D. C. 27].

Now what should we say to this? If all commodity values are measured by the expenditure of human energy embodied in the commodities, what becomes of the distribution value, the price surcharge, the tax? True, Herr Dühring tells us that even unproduced things—things which consequently cannot have a real value—can be given a distribution value and exchanged against things which have been produced and possess value. But at the same time he tells us that *all values*—consequently also purely and exclusively distributive values—consist in the expenditure of energy embodied in them. Unfortunately we are not told how an expenditure of energy can find embodiment in an unproduced thing. In any case one point seems to emerge clearly from all this medley of values: that distribution value, the price surcharge on commodities extorted as a result of social position, and the tax levied by virtue of the sword all once more amount to nothing. The values of commodities are determined solely by the expenditure of human energy, *vulgo*[a] labour, which finds embodiment in them. So, apart from the rent of land and the few monopoly prices, Herr Dühring says the same, though in more slovenly and confused terms, as the much-decried Ricardo-Marxian theory of value said long ago in clearer and more precise form.

He says it, and in the same breath he says the opposite. Marx, taking Ricardo's investigations as his starting-point, says: The value of commodities is determined by the socially necessary general human labour embodied in them, and this in turn is measured by its duration. Labour is the measure of all values, but labour itself has no value. Herr Dühring, after likewise putting forward, in his clumsy way, labour as the measure of value, continues:

this "can be reduced to the existence time whose self-maintenance in turn represents the overcoming of a certain sum of difficulties in nutrition and life" [D. C. 27].

Let us ignore the confusion, due purely to his desire to be original, of labour-time, which is the only thing that matters here, with existence time, which has never yet created or measured values. Let us also ignore the false "socialitarian" pretence which

---

[a] Commonly speaking.—*Ed.*

the "*self*-maintenance" of this existence time is intended to introduce; so long as the world has existed and so long as it continues to exist every individual must maintain himself in the sense that he *himself* consumes his means of subsistence. Let us assume that Herr Dühring expressed himself in precise economic terms; then the sentence quoted either means nothing at all or means the following: The value of a commodity is determined by the labour-time embodied in it, and the value of this labour-time by the means of subsistence required for the maintenance of the labourer for this time. And, in its application to present-day society, this means: the value of a commodity is determined by the *wages* contained in it.

And this brings us at last to what Herr Dühring is really trying to say. The value of a commodity is determined, in the phraseology of vulgar economics, by the production outlays;

Carey, on the contrary, "brought out the truth that it is not the costs of production, but the costs of reproduction that determine value" (*Kritische Geschichte*, p. 401).

We shall see later what there is to these production or reproduction costs; at the moment we only note that, as is well known, they consist of wages and profit on capital. Wages represent the "expenditure of energy" embodied in commodities, the production value. Profit represents the tax or price surcharge extorted by the capitalist by virtue of his monopoly, the sword in his hand—the distribution value. And so the whole contradictory confusion of the Dühringian theory of value is ultimately resolved into the most beautiful and harmonious clarity.

The determination of the value of commodities by wages, which in Adam Smith still frequently appeared side by side with its determination by labour-time, has been banned from scientific political economy since Ricardo, and nowadays survives only in vulgar economics. It is precisely the shallowest sycophants of the existing capitalist order of society who preach the determination of value by wages, and along with this, describe the profit of the capitalist likewise as a higher sort of wages, as the wages of abstinence (reward to the capitalist for not playing ducks and drakes with his capital), as the premium on risk, as the wages of management, etc. Herr Dühring differs from them only in declaring that profit is robbery. In other words, Herr Dühring bases his socialism directly on the doctrines of the worst kind of vulgar economics. And his socialism is worth just as much as this vulgar economics. They stand and fall together.

After all, it is clear that what a labourer produces and what he costs are just as much different things as what a machine produces and what it costs. The value created by a labourer in a twelve-hour working-day has nothing in common with the value of the means of subsistence which he consumes in this working-day and the period of rest that goes with it. In these means of subsistence there may be embodied three, four or seven hours of labour-time, varying with the stage of development reached in the productivity of labour. If we assume that seven hours of labour were necessary for their production, then the theory of value of vulgar economics which Herr Dühring has accepted implies that the product of twelve hours of labour has the value of the product of seven hours of labour, that twelve hours of labour are equal to seven hours of labour, or that $12=7$. To put it even more plainly: A labourer working on the land, no matter under what social relationships, produces in a year a certain quantity of grain, say sixty bushels of wheat. During this time he consumes a sum of values amounting of forty-five bushels of wheat. Then the sixty bushels of wheat have the same value as the forty-five bushels, and that in the same market and with other conditions remaining absolutely identical; in other words, sixty=forty-five. And this styles itself political economy!

The whole development of human society beyond the stage of brute savagery begins on the day when the labour of the family created more products than were necessary for its maintenance, on the day when a portion of labour could be devoted to the production no longer of the mere means of subsistence, but of means of production. A surplus of the product of labour over and above the costs of maintenance of the labour, and the formation and enlargement, out of this surplus, of a social production and reserve fund, was and is the basis of all social, political and intellectual progress. In history, up to the present, this fund has been the possession of a privileged class, on which also devolved, along with this possession, political domination and intellectual leadership. The impending social revolution will for the first time make this social production and reserve fund—that is, the total mass of raw materials, instruments of production and means of subsistence—a really social fund, by depriving that privileged class of the disposal of it and transferring it to the whole of society as its common property.

Of two alternative courses, one. Either the value of commodities is determined by the costs of maintenance of the labour necessary for their production—that is, in present-day society, by the wages.

In that case each labourer receives *in his wages the value of the product of his labour*; and then the exploitation of the wage-earning class by the capitalist class is an impossibility. Let us assume that the costs of maintenance of a labourer in a given society can be expressed by the sum of three marks. Then the product of a day's labour, according to the above-cited theory of the vulgar economists, has the value of three marks. Let us assume that the capitalist who employs this labourer, adds a profit to this product, a tribute of one mark, and sells it for four marks. The other capitalists do the same. But from that moment the labourer can no longer cover his daily needs with three marks, but also requires four marks for this purpose. As all other conditions are assumed to have remained unchanged, the wages expressed in means of subsistence must remain the same, while the wages expressed in money must rise, namely, from three marks to four marks a day. What the capitalists take from the working class in the form of profit, they must give back to it in the form of wages. We are just where we were at the beginning: if wages determine value, no exploitation of the worker by the capitalist is possible. But the formation of a surplus of products is also impossible, for, on the basis of the assumption from which we started, the labourers consume just as much value as they produce. And as the capitalists produce no value, it is impossible to see how they expect to live. And if such a surplus of production over consumption, such a production and reserve fund, nevertheless exists, and exists in the hands of the capitalists, no other possible explanation remains but that the workers consume for their self-maintenance merely the *value* of the commodities, and have handed over the commodities themselves to the capitalist for further use.

Or, on the other hand, if this production and reserve fund does in fact exist in the hands of the capitalist class, if it has actually arisen through the accumulation of profit (for the moment we leave the land rent out of account), then it necessarily consists of the accumulated surplus of the product of labour handed over to the capitalist class by the working class, over and above the sum of wages paid to the working class by the capitalist class. In this case, however, it is not wages that determine value, but the quantity of labour; in this case the working class hands over to the capitalist class in the product of labour a greater quantity of value than it receives from it in the shape of wages; and then the profit on capital, like all other forms of appropriation without payment of the labour product of others, is explained as a simple component part of this surplus-value discovered by Marx.

Incidentally, in Dühring's whole *Cursus* of political economy there is no mention of that great and epoch-making discovery with which Ricardo opens his most important work:

"The value of a commodity ... depends on the quantity of labour which is necessary for its production, and not on the greater or lesser compensation which is paid for that labour." [a]

In the *Kritische Geschichte* it is dismissed with the oracular phrase:

"It is not considered" (by Ricardo) "that the greater or lesser proportion in which wages can be an allotment of the necessaries of life" (!) "must also involve ... different forms of the value relationships!" [D. K. G. 215.]

A phrase into which the reader can read what he pleases, and is on safest ground if he reads into it nothing at all.

And now let the reader select for himself, from the five sorts of value served up to us by Herr Dühring, the one that he likes best: the production value, which comes from nature; or the distribution value, which man's wickedness has created and which is distinguished by the fact that it is measured by the expenditure of energy, which is not contained in it; or thirdly, the value which is measured by labour-time; or fourthly, the value which is measured by the costs of reproduction; or lastly, the value which is measured by wages. The selection is wide, the confusion complete, and the only thing left for us to do is to exclaim with Herr Dühring:

"The theory of value is the touchstone of the worth of economic systems!" [499.]

VI. SIMPLE AND COMPOUND LABOUR

Herr Dühring has discovered in Marx a gross blunder in economics that a schoolboy would blush at, a blunder which at the same time contains a socialist heresy very dangerous to society.

Marx's theory of value is "nothing but the ordinary ... theory that labour is the cause of all values and labour-time is their measure. But the question of how the distinct value of so-called skilled labour is to be conceived is left in complete obscurity. It is true that in our theory also only the labour-time expended can be the measure of the natural cost and therefore of the absolute value of economic things; but here the labour-time of each individual must be considered absolutely equal, to start with, and it is only necessary to examine where, in skilled production, the labour-time of other persons ... for example in the tool used, is added to the separate labour-time of the individual. Therefore the position is not,

---

[a] D. Ricardo, *On the Principles of Political Economy, and Taxation*, p. 1.— *Ed.*

as in Herr Marx's hazy conception, that the labour-time of one person is in itself more valuable than that of another, because more average labour-time is condensed as it were within it, but all labour-time is in principle and without exception—and therefore without any need to take first an average—absolutely equal in value; and in regard to the work done by a person, as also in regard to every finished product, all that requires to be ascertained is how much of the labour-time of other persons may be concealed in what appears to be only his own labour-time. Whether it is a hand tool for production, or the hand, or even the head itself, which could not have acquired its special characteristics and capacity for work without the labour-time of others, is not of the slightest importance in the strict application of the theory. In his lucubrations on value, however, Herr Marx never rids himself of the ghost of a skilled labour-time which lurks in the background. He was unable to effect a thoroughgoing change here because he was hampered by the traditional mode of thought of the educated classes, to whom it necessarily appears monstrous to recognise the labour-time of a porter and that of an architect as of absolutely equal value from the standpoint of economics" [D. K. G. 499-500].

The passage in Marx which calls forth this "mightier wrath" [501] on Herr Dühring's part is very brief. Marx is examining what it is that determines the value of *commodities* and gives the answer: the human labour embodied in them. This, he continues, "is the expenditure of simple labour-power which, on an average, apart from any special development, exists in the organism of every ordinary individual... Skilled labour counts only as simple labour intensified, or rather, as multiplied simple labour, a given quantity of skilled being considered equal to a greater quantity of simple labour. Experience shows that this reduction is constantly being made. A commodity may be the product of the most skilled labour, but its value, by equating it to the product of simple unskilled labour, represents a definite quantity of the latter labour alone. The different proportions in which different sorts of labour are reduced to unskilled labour as their standard, are established by a social process that goes on behind the backs of the producers, and, consequently, appear to be fixed by custom".[a]

Marx is dealing here first of all only with the determination of the value of *commodities,* i.e., of objects which, within a society composed of private producers, are produced and exchanged against each other by these private producers for their private account. In this passage therefore there is no question whatever of "absolute value"—wherever this may be in existence—but of the value which is current in a definite form of society. This value, in this definite historical sense, is shown to be created and measured

---

[a] K. Marx, *Das Kapital,* p. 19. (See present edition, Vol. 35, Part I, Chapter I, Section 2.— Ed.

by the human labour embodied in the individual commodities, and this human labour is further shown to be the expenditure of simple labour-power. But not all labour is a mere expenditure of simple human labour-power; very many sorts of labour involve the use of capabilities or knowledge acquired with the expenditure of greater or lesser effort, time and money. Do these kinds of compound labour produce, in the same interval of time, the same commodity values as simple labour, the expenditure of mere simple labour-power? Obviously not. The product of one hour of compound labour is a commodity of a higher value—perhaps double or treble—in comparison with the product of one hour of simple labour. The values of the products of compound labour are expressed by this comparison in definite quantities of simple labour; but this reduction of compound labour is established by a social process which goes on behind the backs of the producers, by a process which at this point, in the development of the theory of value, can only be stated but not as yet explained.

It is this simple fact, taking place daily before our eyes in present-day capitalist society, which is here stated by Marx. This fact is so indisputable that even Herr Dühring does not venture to dispute it either in his *Cursus*[a] or in his history of political economy[b]; and the Marxian presentation is so simple and lucid that no one but Herr Dühring "is left in complete obscurity" by it. Because of his complete obscurity he mistakes the commodity value, which alone Marx was for the time being concerned with investigating, for "the natural cost", which makes the obscurity still more complete, and even for the "absolute value", which so far as our knowledge goes has never before had currency in political economy. But whatever Herr Dühring may understand by the natural cost, and whichever of his five kinds of value may have the honour to represent absolute value, this much at least is sure: that Marx is not discussing any of these things, but only the value of commodities; and that in the whole section of *Capital* which deals with value there is not even the slightest indication of whether or to what extent Marx considers this theory of the value of commodities[c] applicable also to other forms of society.

"Therefore the position is not," Herr Dühring proceeds, "as in Herr Marx's hazy conception, that the labour-time of one person is in itself more valuable than

---

[a] E. Dühring, *Cursus der National- und Socialökonomie.—Ed.*

[b] E. Dühring, *Kritische Geschichte der Nationalökonomie und des Sozialismus.—Ed.*

[c] See present edition, Vol. 35, Part I, Chapter I.—*Ed.*

that of another, because more average labour-time is condensed as it were within it, but all labour-time is in principle and without exception—and therefore without any need to take first an average—absolutely equal in value" [D. K. G. 500].

It is fortunate for Herr Dühring that fate did not make him a manufacturer, and thus saved him from fixing the value of his commodities on the basis of this new rule and thereby running infallibly into the arms of bankruptcy. But say, are we here still in the society of manufacturers? No, far from it. With his natural cost and absolute value Herr Dühring has made us take a leap, a veritable *salto mortale,* out of the present evil world of exploiters into his own economic commune of the future, into the pure, heavenly air of equality and justice; and so we must now, even though prematurely, take a glance at this new world.

It is true that, according to Herr Dühring's theory, only the labour-time expended can measure the value of economic things even in the economic commune; but as a matter of course the labour-time of each individual must be considered absolutely equal to start with, all labour-time is in principle and without exception absolutely equal in value, without any need to take first an average. And now compare with this radical equalitarian socialism Marx's hazy conception that the labour-time of one person is in itself more valuable than that of another, because more average labour-time is condensed as it were within it—a conception which held Marx captive by reason of the traditional mode of thought of the educated classes, to whom it necessarily appears monstrous that the labour-time of a porter and that of an architect should be recognised as of absolutely equal value from the standpoint of economics!

Unfortunately Marx put a short footnote to the passage in *Capital* cited above: "The reader must note that we are not speaking here of the *wages* or value that the labourer *gets* for a given labour-time, but of the *value of the commodity* in which that labour-time is *materialised.*" [a] Marx, who seems here to have had a presentiment of the coming of his Dühring, therefore safeguards himself against an application of his statements quoted above even to the wages which are paid in existing society for compound labour. And if Herr Dühring, not content with doing this all the same, presents these statements as the principles on which Marx would like to see the distribution of the necessaries of life

---

[a] K. Marx, *Das Kapital,* p. 19. See present edition, Vol. 35, Part I, Chapter I, Section 2. Italics by Engels.— *Ed.*

regulated in society organised socialistically, he is guilty of a shameless imposture, the like of which is only to be found in the gangster press.

But let us look a little more closely at the doctrine of equality in values. All labour-time is entirely equal in value, the porter's and the architect's. So labour-time, and therefore labour itself, has a value. But labour is the creator of all values. It alone gives the products found in nature value in the economic sense. Value itself is nothing else than the expression of the socially necessary human labour materialised in an object. Labour *can* therefore have *no* value. One might as well speak of the value of value, or try to determine the weight, not of a heavy body, but of heaviness itself, as speak of the value of labour, and try to determine it. Herr Dühring dismisses people like Owen, Saint-Simon and Fourier by calling them social alchemists [D. K. G. 237]. His subtilising over the value of labour-time, that is, of labour, shows that he ranks far beneath the real alchemists. And now let the reader fathom Herr Dühring's brazenness in imputing to Marx the assertion that the labour-time of one person is in itself more valuable than that of another [500], that labour-time, and therefore labour, has a value—to Marx, who first demonstrated that labour *can* have *no* value, and why it cannot!

For socialism, which wants to emancipate human labour-power from its status of a *commodity,* the realisation that labour has no value and can have none is of great importance. With this realisation all attempts—inherited by Herr Dühring from primitive workers' socialism—to regulate the future distribution of the necessaries of life as a kind of higher wages fall to the ground. And from it comes the further realisation that distribution, in so far as it is governed by purely economic considerations, will be regulated by the interests of production, and that production is most encouraged by a mode of distribution which allows *all* members of society to develop, maintain and exercise their capacities with maximum universality. It is true that, to the mode of thought of the educated classes which Herr Dühring has inherited, it must seem monstrous that in time to come there will no longer be any professional porters or architects, and that the man who for half an hour gives instructions as an architect will also act as a porter for a period, until his activity as an architect is once again required. A fine sort of socialism that would be—perpetuating professional porters!

If the equality of value of labour-time means that each labourer produces equal values in equal periods of time, without there being any need to take an average, then this is obviously wrong. If we take two workers, even in the same branch of industry, the value they produce in one hour of labour-time will always vary with the intensity of their labour and their skill—and not even an economic commune, at any rate not on our planet, can remedy this evil—which, however, is only an evil for people like Dühring. What, then, remains of the complete equality of value of any and every labour? Nothing but the purely braggart phrase, which has no other economic foundation than Herr Dühring's incapacity to distinguish between the determination of value by labour and determination of value by wages—nothing but the ukase, the basic law of the new economic commune: Equal wages for equal labour-time! Indeed, the old French communist workers and Weitling had much better reasons for the equality of wages which they advocated.

How then are we to solve the whole important question of the higher wages paid for compound labour? In a society of private producers, private individuals or their families pay the costs of training the qualified worker; hence the higher price paid for qualified labour-power accrues first of all to private individuals: the skilful slave is sold for a higher price, and the skilful wage-earner is paid higher wages. In a socialistically organised society, these costs are borne by society, and to it therefore belong the fruits, the greater values produced by compound labour. The worker himself has no claim to extra pay. And from this, incidentally, follows the moral that at times there is a drawback to the popular demand of the workers for "the full proceeds of labour".[87]

VII. CAPITAL AND SURPLUS-VALUE

"To begin with, Herr Marx does not hold the accepted economic view of capital, namely, that it is a means of production already produced; on the contrary, he tries to get up a more special, dialectical-historical idea that toys with metamorphoses of concepts and history. According to him, capital is born of money; it forms a historical phase opening with the sixteenth century, that is, with the first beginnings of a world market, which presumably appeared at that period. It is obvious that the keenness of national-economic analysis is lost in such a conceptual interpretation. In such barren conceptions, which are represented as half historical and half logical, but which in fact are only bastards of historical and logical fantasy, the faculty of discernment perishes, together with all honesty in the use of concepts" [D. K. G. 497-98]—

and so he blusters along for a whole page...

"Marx's definition of the concept of capital can only cause confusion in the strict theory of national economy ... frivolities which are palmed off as profound logical truths ... the fragility of foundations" [D. K. G. 498] and so forth.

So according to Marx, we are told, capital was born of money at the beginning of the sixteenth century. This is like saying that fully three thousand years ago metallic money was born of cattle, because once upon a time cattle, among other things, functioned as money. Only Herr Dühring is capable of such a crude and inept manner of expressing himself. In the analysis which Marx makes of the economic forms within which the process of the circulation of commodities takes place, money appears as the final form. "This final product of the circulation of commodities is the *first form in which* capital *appears*. As a matter of history, capital, as opposed to landed property, invariably takes the form at first of money; it appears as moneyed wealth, as the capital of the merchant and of the usurer... We can see it daily under our very eyes. All new capital, to commence with, comes on the stage, that is, on the market, whether of commodities, labour, or money, even in our days, in the shape of money that by a definite process has to be transformed into capital." [a] Here once again Marx is stating a fact. Unable to dispute it, Herr Dühring distorts it: Capital, he has Marx say, is born of money!

Marx then investigates the processes by which money is transformed into capital, and finds, first, that the form in which money circulates as capital is the inversion of the form in which it circulates as the general equivalent of commodities. The simple owner of commodities sells in order to buy; he sells what he does not need, and with the money thus procured he buys what he does need. The incipient capitalist starts by buying what he does *not* need himself; he buys in order to sell, and to sell at a higher price, in order to get back the value of the money originally thrown into the transaction, augmented by an increment in money; and Marx calls this increment *surplus-value*.

Whence comes this surplus-value? It cannot come either from the buyer buying the commodities under their value, or from the seller selling them above their value. For in both cases the gains and the losses of each individual cancel each other, as each individual is in turn buyer and seller. Nor can it come from cheating, for though cheating can enrich one person at the

---

[a] K. Marx, *Das Kapital*, p. 128. See present edition, Vol. 35, Part II, Chapter IV. Italics by Engels.— *Ed.*

expense of another, it cannot increase the total sum possessed by both, and therefore cannot augment the sum of the values in circulation. "The capitalist class, as a whole, in any country, cannot over-reach themselves." [a]

And yet we find that in each country the capitalist class as a whole is continuously enriching itself before our eyes, by selling dearer than it had bought, by appropriating to itself surplus-value. We are therefore just where we were at the start: whence comes this surplus-value? This problem must be solved, and it must be solved in a *purely economic* way, excluding all cheating and the intervention of any force—the problem being: how is it possible constantly to sell dearer than one has bought, even on the hypothesis that equal values are always exchanged for equal values?

The solution of this problem was the most epoch-making achievement of Marx's work. It spread the clear light of day through economic domains in which socialists no less than bourgeois economists previously groped in utter darkness. Scientific socialism dates from the discovery of this solution and has been built up around it.

This solution is as follows: The increase in the value of money that is to be converted into capital cannot take place in the *money* itself, nor can it originate in the *purchase*, as here this money does no more than realise the price of the commodity, and this price, inasmuch as we took as our premise an exchange of equivalents, is not different from its value. For the same reason, the increase in value cannot originate in the *sale* of the commodity. The change must, therefore, take place in the *commodity* bought; not however in its *value*, as it is bought and sold at its value, but in its *use-value* as such, that is, the change of value must originate in the consumption of the commodity. "In order to be able to extract value from the consumption of a commodity, our friend, Moneybags, must be so lucky as to find ... in the market, a commodity, whose use-value possesses the peculiar property of being a source of value, whose actual consumption, therefore, is itself an embodiment of labour, and, consequently, a *creation of value*. The possessor of money does find on the market such a special commodity in capacity for labour or *labour-power*." [b]

---

[a] K. Marx, *Das Kapital*, p. 147. See present edition, Vol. 35, Part II, Chapter V.— *Ed.*

[b] Ibid., p. 151-52. See present edition, Vol. 35, Part II, Chapter VI. Italics by Engels.— *Ed.*

Though, as we saw, labour as such can have no value, this is by no means the case with labour-*power*. This acquires a value from the moment that it becomes a *commodity,* as it is in fact at the present time, and this value is determined, "as in the case of every other commodity, by the labour-time necessary for the production, and consequently also the reproduction, of this special article"[a]; that is to say, by the labour-time necessary for the production of the means of subsistence which the labourer requires for his maintenance in a fit state to work and for the perpetuation of his race. Let us assume that these means of subsistence represent six hours of labour-time daily. Our incipient capitalist, who buys labour-power for carrying on his business, i.e., hires a labourer, consequently pays this labourer the full value of his day's labour-power if he pays him a sum of money which also represents six hours of labour. And as soon as the labourer has worked six hours in the employment of the incipient capitalist, he has fully reimbursed the latter for his outlay, for the value of the day's labour-power which he had paid. But so far the money would not have been converted into capital; it would not have produced any surplus-value. And for this reason the buyer of labour-power has quite a different notion of the nature of the transaction he has carried out. The fact that only six hours' labour is necessary to keep the labourer alive for twenty-four hours, does not in any way prevent him from working twelve hours out of the twenty-four. The value of the labour-power, and the value which that labour-power creates in the labour-process, are two different magnitudes. The owner of the money has paid the value of a day's labour-power; his, therefore, is the use of it for a day—a whole day's labour. The circumstance that the value which the use of it during one day *creates* is double its own value for a day is a piece of especially good luck for the buyer, but according to the laws of exchange of commodities by no means an injustice to the seller. On our assumption, therefore, the labourer each day *costs* the owner of money the value of the product of six hours' labour, but he *hands over* to him each day the value of the product of twelve hours' labour. The difference in favour of the owner of the money is six hours of unpaid surplus-labour, a surplus-product for which he does not pay and in which six hours' labour is embodied. The trick has been performed. Surplus-value has been produced; money has been converted into capital.

---

[a] K. Marx, *Das Kapital,* p. 155. See present edition, Vol. 35, Part II, Chapter VI.— *Ed.*

In thus showing how surplus-value arises, and how alone surplus-value can arise under the domination of the laws regulating the exchange of commodities, Marx exposed the mechanism of the existing capitalist mode of production and of the mode of appropriation based on it; he revealed the core around which the whole existing social order has crystallised.

However, this creation of capital requires that one essential prerequisite be fulfilled: "For the conversion of his money into capital the owner of money must meet in the market with the *free labourer*, free in the double sense, that as a free man he can dispose of his labour-power as his own commodity, and that on the other hand he has no other commodity for sale, is short of everything necessary for the realisation of his labour-power." [a] But this relation between the owners of money or of commodities on the one hand, and those who possess nothing beyond their own labour-power on the other, is not a natural relation, nor is it one that is common to all historical periods: "It is clearly the result of a past historical development, the product ... of the extinction of a whole series of older forms of social production." [b] And in fact we first encounter this free labourer on a mass scale in history at the end of the fifteenth and the beginning of the sixteenth century, as a result of the dissolution of the feudal mode of production. With this, however, and with the bringing into being of world trade and the world market dating from the same epoch, the basis was established on which the mass of the existing movable wealth was necessarily more and more converted into capital, and the capitalist mode of production, aimed at the creation of surplus-value, necessarily became more and more exclusively the prevailing mode.

Up to this point, we have been following the "barren conceptions" of Marx, these "bastards of historical and logical fantasy" in which "the faculty of discernment perishes, together with all honesty in the use of concepts". Let us contrast these "frivolities" with the "profound logical truths" and the "definitive and most strictly scientific treatment in the sense of the exact disciplines" [D. K. G. 498], such as Herr Dühring offers us.

So Marx "does not hold the accepted economic view of capital, namely, that it is a means of production already produced" [497];

---

[a] K. Marx, *Das Kapital*, p. 154. See present edition, Vol. 35, Part II, Chapter VI.— *Ed.*

[b] Ibid.— *Ed.*

he says, on the contrary, that a sum of values is converted into capital only when it *increases its value,* when it forms surplus-value. And what does Herr Dühring say?

"Capital is a basis of means of economic power for the continuation of production *and for the formation of shares in the fruits of the general labour-power* [D. C. 40].

However oracularly and slovenly that too is expressed, this much at least is certain: the basis of means of economic power may continue production to eternity, but according to Herr Dühring's own words it will not become capital so long as it does not form "shares in the fruits of the general labour-power"—that is to say, form surplus-value or at least surplus-product. Herr Dühring therefore not only himself commits the sin with which he charges Marx—of not holding the accepted economic view of capital—but besides commits a clumsy plagiarism of Marx, "badly concealed" [D. K. G. 506] by high-sounding phrases.

On page 262 [D. C.] this is further developed:

"Capital in the social sense" (and Herr Dühring still has to discover a capital in a sense which is not social) "is in fact specifically different from the mere means of production; for while the latter have only a technical character and are necessary under all conditions, the former is distinguished by its social power of appropriation and the formation of shares. It is true that social capital is to a great extent nothing but the technical means of production *in their social function*; but it is precisely this function which ... must disappear".

When we reflect that it was precisely Marx who first drew attention to the "social function" by virtue of which alone a sum of values becomes capital, it will certainly "at once be clear to every attentive investigator of the subject that Marx's definition of the concept of capital can only cause confusion" [D. K. G. 498]—not, however, as Herr Dühring thinks, in the strict theory of national economy but as is evident simply and solely in the head of Herr Dühring himself, who in the *Kritische Geschichte* has already forgotten how much use he made of the said concept of capital in his *Cursus.*[a]

However, Herr Dühring is not content with borrowing from Marx the latter's definition of capital, though in a "purified" form. He is obliged to follow Marx also in the "toying with metamorphoses of concepts and history" [497], in spite of his own better knowledge that nothing could come of it but "barren conceptions", "frivolities", "fragility of the foundations" [498] and so forth. Whence comes this "social function"

---

[a] E. Dühring, *Cursus der National- und Socialökonomie.*—*Ed.*

[D. C. 262] of capital, which enables it to appropriate the fruits of others' labour and which alone distinguishes it from mere means of production?

Herr Dühring says that it does not depend "on the nature of the means of production and their technical indispensability" [262].

It therefore arose historically, and on page 262 Herr Dühring only tells us again what we have heard ten times before, when he explains its origin by means of the old familiar adventures of the two men, one of whom at the dawn of history converted his means of production into capital by the use of force against the other. But not content with ascribing a historical beginning to the social function through which alone a sum of values becomes capital, Herr Dühring prophesies that it will also have a historical end. It is "precisely this which must disappear" [262]. In ordinary parlance it is customary to call a phenomenon which arose historically and disappears again historically, "a historical phase". Capital, therefore, is a historical phase not only according to Marx but also according to Herr Dühring, and we are consequently forced to the conclusion that we are among Jesuits here. When two persons do the same thing, then it is not the same.[a] When Marx says that capital is a historical phase, that is a barren conception, a bastard of historical and logical fantasy, in which the faculty of discernment perishes, together with all honesty in the use of concepts. When Herr Dühring likewise presents capital as a historical phase, that is proof of the keenness of his economic analysis and of his definitive and most strictly scientific treatment in the sense of the exact disciplines.

What is it then that distinguishes the Dühringian conception of capital from the Marxian?

"Capital," says Marx, "has not invented surplus-labour. Wherever a part of society possesses the monopoly of the means of production, the labourer, free or not free, must add to the working-time necessary for his own maintenance an extra working-time in order to produce the means of subsistence for the owners of the means of production."[b] Surplus-labour, labour beyond the time required for the labourer's own maintenance, and appropriation by others of the product of this surplus-labour, the

---

[a] A paraphrase of a dictum from the comedy *Adelphoe* by the Roman playwright Terentius (Act V, Scene 3).— *Ed.*

[b] K. Marx, *Das Kapital*, p. 227. See present edition, Vol. 35, Part III, Chapter X, Section 2.— *Ed.*

exploitation of labour, is therefore common to all forms of society that have existed hitherto, in so far as these have moved in class antagonisms. But it is only when the product of this surplus-labour assumes the form of surplus-value, when the owner of the means of production finds the free labourer—free from social fetters and free from possessions of his own—as an object of exploitation, and exploits him for the purpose of the production of *commodities*—it is only then, according to Marx, that the means of production assume the specific character of capital. And this first took place on a large scale at the end of the fifteenth and the beginning of the sixteenth century.

Herr Dühring on the contrary declares that *every* sum of means of production which "forms shares in the fruits of the general labour-power" [D. C. 40], that is, yields surplus-labour in any form, is capital. In other words, Herr Dühring annexes the surplus-labour discovered by Marx, in order to use it to kill the surplus-value, likewise discovered by Marx, which for the moment does not suit his purpose. According to Herr Dühring, therefore, not only the movable and immovable wealth of the Corinthian and Athenian citizens, built on a slave economy, but also the wealth of the large Roman landowners of the time of the empire, and equally the wealth of the feudal barons of the Middle Ages, in so far as it in any way served production—all this without distinction is capital.

So that Herr Dühring himself does not hold "the accepted view of capital, namely, that it is a means of production already produced" [D. K. G. 497], but rather one that is the very opposite of it, a view which includes in capital even means of production which have not been produced, the earth and its natural resources. The idea, however, that capital is simply "produced means of production" is once again the accepted view only in vulgar political economy. Outside of this vulgar economics, which Herr Dühring holds so dear, the "produced means of production" or any sum of values whatever, becomes capital only by yielding profit or interest, i.e., by appropriating the surplus-product of unpaid labour in the form of surplus-value, and, moreover, by appropriating it in these two definite subforms of surplus-value. It is of absolutely no importance that the whole of bourgeois economy is still labouring under the idea that the property of yielding profit or interest is inherent in every sum of values which is utilised under normal conditions in production or exchange. In classical political economy, capital and profit, or capital and interest, are just as inseparable, stand in the same reciprocal relations to each other, as cause and effect, father and son, yesterday and today. The word "capital" in its modern economic meaning is first met with, however, at the time when the thing itself makes its appearance, when movable wealth acquires, to a greater and greater extent, the function of capital, by exploiting the surplus-labour of free labourers for the production of commodities; and in fact it was introduced by the first nation of capitalists in history, the Italians of the fifteenth and sixteenth centuries. And if Marx was the first to make a fundamental analysis of the mode of appropriation characteristic of modern capital; if he brought the concept of capital into harmony with the historical facts from which, in the last analysis, it had been abstracted, and to which it owed its existence; if by so doing Marx cleared this economic concept of those obscure and vacillating ideas which still clung to it even in classical bourgeois political economy and among the former socialists—then it was Marx who applied that "definitive and most strictly scientific treatment" [498] about which Herr Dühring is so constantly talking and which we so painfully miss in his works.

In actual fact, Herr Dühring's treatment is quite different from this. He is not content with first inveighing against the presentation of capital as a historical phase by calling it a "bastard of historical and logical fantasy" [498] and then himself presenting it as a historical phase. He also roundly declares that *all* means of economic power, *all* means of production which appropriate "shares in the fruits of the general labour-power" [D. C. 40]—and therefore also landed property in all class societies—are capital; which however does not in the least prevent him, in the further course of his exposition, from separating landed property and land rent, quite in the traditional manner, from capital and profit, and designating as capital only those means of production which yield profit or interest, as he does at considerable length on page 156 and the following pages of his *Cursus*.[a] With equal justice Herr Dühring might first include under the name "locomotive" also horses, oxen, asses and dogs, on the ground that these, too, can be used as means of transport, and reproach modern engineers with limiting the name locomotive to the modern steam-engine and thereby setting it up as a historical phase, using barren conceptions, bastards of historical and logical fantasy and so forth; and then finally declare that horses, asses, oxen and dogs

---

[a] E. Dühring. *Cursus der National- und Socialökonomie.—Ed.*

are nevertheless excluded from the term locomotive, and that this term is applicable only to the steam-engine.—And so once more we are compelled to say that it is precisely the Dühringian conception of capital in which all keenness of economic analysis is lost and the faculty of discernment perishes, together with all honesty in the use of concepts; and that the barren conceptions, the confusion, the frivolities palmed off as profound logical truths and the fragility of the foundations are to be found in full bloom precisely in Herr Dühring's work.

But all that is of no consequence. For Herr Dühring's is the glory nevertheless of having discovered the axis on which all economics, all politics and jurisprudence, in a word, all history, has hitherto revolved. Here it is:

"Force and labour are the two principal factors which come into play in forming social connections" [D. C. 255].

In this one sentence we have the complete constitution of the economic world up to the present day. It is extremely short, and runs:

Article One: Labour produces.

Article Two: Force distributes.

And this, "speaking in plain human language" [D. K. G. 496], sums up the whole of Herr Dühring's economic wisdom.

VIII. CAPITAL AND SURPLUS-VALUE

(Conclusion)

"In Herr Marx's view, wages represent only the payment of that labour-time during which the labourer is actually working to make his own existence possible. But only a small number of hours is required for this purpose; all the rest of the working-day, often so prolonged, yields a surplus in which is contained what our author calls 'surplus-value', or, expressed in everyday language, the earnings of capital. If we leave out of account the labour-time which at each stage of production is already contained in the instruments of labour and in the pertinent raw material, this surplus part of the working-day is the share which falls to the capitalist entrepreneur. The prolongation of the working-day is consequently earnings of pure exploitation for the benefit of the capitalist" [D. K. G. 500-01].

According to Herr Dühring, therefore, Marx's surplus-value would be nothing more than what, expressed in everyday language, is known as the earnings of capital, or profit. Let us see what Marx says himself. On page 195 of *Capital,* surplus-value is explained in the following words placed in brackets after it:

"Interest, Profit, Rent".[a] On page 210, Marx gives an example in which a total surplus-value of £3.11.0. appears in the different forms in which it is distributed: tithes, rates and taxes, £1.10; rent £1.80; farmer's profit and interest, £1.20; together making a total surplus-value of £3.11.0.[b]—On page 542, Marx points out as one of Ricardo's main shortcomings that he "has not [...] investigated surplus-value as such, i.e., independently of its particular forms, such as profit, rent, etc", and that he therefore lumps together the laws of the rate of surplus-value and the laws of the rate of profit; against this Marx announces: "I shall show in Book III that, with a given rate of surplus-value, we may have any number of rates of profit, and that various rates of surplus-value may, under given conditions, express themselves in a single rate of profit.[c] On page 587 we find: "The capitalist who produces surplus-value—i.e., who extracts unpaid labour directly from the labourers, and fixes it in commodities, is, indeed, the first appropriator, but by no means the ultimate owner, of this surplus-value. He has to share it with capitalists, with landowners, etc., who fulfil other functions in the complex of social production. Surplus-value, therefore, splits up into various parts. Its fragments fall to various categories of persons, and take various forms, independent the one of the other, such as profit, interest, merchants' profit, rent, etc. It is only in Book III that we can take in hand these modified forms of surplus-value."[d] And there are many other similar passages.

It is impossible to express oneself more clearly. On each occasion Marx calls attention to the fact that his surplus-value must not be confounded with profit or the earnings of capital; that this latter is rather a subform and frequently even only a fragment of surplus-value. And if in spite of this Herr Dühring asserts that Marxian surplus-value, "expressed in everyday language, is the earnings of capital"; and if it is an actual fact that the whole of Marx's book turns on surplus-value—then there are only two possibilities: Either Herr Dühring does not know any better, and then it is an unparalleled act of impudence to decry a book of whose main content he is ignorant; or he knows what it is all

---

[a] See present edition, Vol. 35, Part III, Chapter VIII.— Ed.

[b] Ibid., Chapter IX, Section I.— Ed.

[c] K. Marx, Das Kapital, pp. 542-43. See present edition, Vol. 35, Part V, Chapter XVII, I.— Ed.

[d] See present edition, Vol. 35, Part VII.— Ed.

about, and in that case he has committed a deliberate act of falsification.

To proceed:

"The venomous hatred with which Herr Marx presents this conception of the business of extortion is only too understandable. But even mightier wrath and even fuller recognition of the exploitative character of the economic form which is based on wage-labour is possible without accepting the theoretical position expressed in Marx's doctrine of surplus-value" [D. K. G. 501].

The well-meant but erroneous theoretical position taken up by Marx stirs in him a venomous hatred against the business of extortion; but in consequence of his false "theoretical position" the emotion, in itself ethical, receives an unethical expression, manifesting itself in ignoble hatred and low venomousness, while the definitive and most strictly scientific treatment [498] by Herr Dühring expresses itself in ethical emotion of a correspondingly noble nature, in wrath which even in form is ethically superior and in venomous hatred is also quantitatively superior, is a mightier wrath. While Herr Dühring is gleefully admiring himself in this way, let us see where this mightier wrath stems from.

We read on: "Now the question arises, how the competing entrepreneurs are able constantly to realise the full product of labour, including the surplus-product, at a price so far above the natural outlays of production as is indicated by the ratio, already mentioned, of the surplus labour-hours. No answer to this is to be found in Marx's theory, and for the simple reason that there could be no place in it for even raising that question. The luxury character of production based on hired labour is not seriously dealt with at all, and the social constitution with its exploitatory features is in no way recognised as the ultimate basis of white slavery. On the contrary, political and social matters are always to be explained by economics" [501].

Now we have seen from the above passages that Marx does not at all assert that the industrial capitalist, who first appropriates the surplus-product, sells it regardless of circumstances on the average at its full value, as is here assumed by Herr Dühring. Marx says expressly that merchants' profit also forms a part of surplus-value, and on the assumptions made this is only possible when the manufacturer sells his product to the merchant *below* its value, and thus relinquishes to him a part of the booty. The way the question is put here, there clearly could be no place in Marx for even raising it. Stated in a rational way, the question is: How is surplus-value transformed into its subforms: profit, interest, merchants' profit, land rent, and so forth? And Marx, to be sure, promises to settle this question in the third book. But if Herr

Dühring cannot wait until the second volume of *Capital*[88] appears, he should in the meantime take a closer look at the first volume. In addition to the passages already quoted, he would then see, for example on p. 323, that according to Marx the immanent laws of capitalist production assert themselves in the external movements of individual masses of capital as coercive laws of competition, and in this form are brought home to the mind and consciousness of the individual capitalist as the directing motives of his operations; that therefore a scientific analysis of competition is not possible before we have a conception of the inner nature of capital, just as the apparent motions of the heavenly bodies are not intelligible to any but him who is acquainted with their real motions, which are not directly perceptible by the senses[a]; and then Marx gives an example to show how in a definite case, a definite law, the law of value, manifests itself and exercises its motive power in competition. Herr Dühring might see from this alone that competition plays a leading part in the distribution of surplus-value, and with some reflection the indications given in the first volume are in fact enough to make clear, at least in its main features, the transformation of surplus-value into its subforms.

But competition is precisely what absolutely prevents Herr Dühring from understanding the process. He cannot comprehend how the competing entrepreneurs are able constantly to realise the full product of labour, including the surplus-product, at prices so far above the natural outlays of production. Here again we find his customary "strictness" [D. C. 95] of expression, which in fact is simply slovenliness. In *Marx*, the surplus-product as such has *absolutely no outlays of production*; it is the part of the product which *costs nothing* to the capitalist. If therefore the competing entrepreneurs desired to realise the surplus-product at its natural outlays of production, they would have simply *to give it away*. But do not let us waste time on such "micrological details" [D. K. G. 507]. Are not the competing entrepreneurs every day selling the product of labour above its natural outlays of production? According to Herr Dühring, the natural outlays of production consist

"in the expenditure of labour or energy, and this in turn, in the last analysis, can be measured by the expenditure of food" [D. C. 274];

that is, in present-day society, these costs consist in the outlays really expended on raw materials, means of labour, and wages,

---

[a] See present edition, Vol. 35, Part IV, Chapter XII.— *Ed.*

as distinguished from the "tax" [D. C. 135], the profit, the surcharge levied sword in hand [23]. Now everyone knows that in the society in which we live the competing entrepreneurs do *not* realise their commodities at the natural outlays of production, but that they add on to these—and as a rule also receive—the so-called surcharge, the profit. The question which Herr Dühring thinks he has only to raise to blow down the whole Marxian structure—as Joshua once blew down the walls of Jericho[89]—this question also exists for Herr Dühring's economic theory. Let us see how he answers it.

"Capital ownership," he says, "has no practical meaning, and cannot be realised, unless indirect force against human material is simultaneously incorporated in it. The product of this force is earnings of capital, and the magnitude of the latter will therefore depend on the range and intensity in which this power is exercised [179] ... Earnings of capital are a political and social institution which exerts a more powerful influence than competition. In relation to this the capitalists act as a social estate, and each one of them maintains his position. A certain measure of earnings of capital is a necessity under the prevailing mode of economy" [180].

Unfortunately even now we do not know how the competing entrepreneurs are able constantly to realise the product of labour above the natural outlays of production. It cannot be that Herr Dühring thinks so little of his public as to fob it off with the phrase that earnings of capital are above competition, just as the King of Prussia[a] was above the law.[90] We know the manoeuvres by which the King of Prussia attained his position above the law; the manoeuvres by which the earnings of capital succeed in being more powerful than competition are precisely what Herr Dühring should explain to us, but what he obstinately refuses to explain. And it is of no avail, if, as he tells us, the capitalists act in this connection as an estate, and each one of them maintains his position. We surely cannot be expected to take his word for it that a number of people only need to act as an estate for each one of them to maintain his position. Everyone knows that the guildsmen of the Middle Ages and the French nobles in 1789 acted very definitely as estates and perished nevertheless. The Prussian army at Jena[91] also acted as an estate, but instead of maintaining their position they had on the contrary to take to their heels and afterwards even to capitulate in sections. Just as little can we be satisfied with the assurance that a certain measure of earnings of capital is a necessity under the prevailing mode of economy; for

---

[a] Frederick William IV.— *Ed.*

the point to be proved is precisely *why* this is so. We do not get a step nearer to the goal when Herr Dühring informs us:

"The domination of capital arose in close connection with the domination of land. Part of the agricultural serfs were transformed in the towns into craftsmen, and ultimately into factory material. After the rent of land, earnings of capital developed as a second form of rent of possession" [176].

Even if we ignore the historical inexactitude of this assertion, it nevertheless remains a mere assertion, and is restricted to assuring us over and over again of precisely what should be explained and proved. We can therefore come to no other conclusion than that Herr Dühring is incapable of answering his own question: how the competing entrepreneurs are able constantly to realise the product of labour above the natural outlays of production; that is to say, he is incapable of explaining the genesis of profit. He can only bluntly decree: earnings of capital shall be the product of *force*—which, true enough, is completely in accordance with Article 2 of the Dühringian constitution of society: Force distributes. This is certainly expressed very nicely; but now "the question arises" [D. K. G. 501]: Force distributes—what? Surely there must be something to distribute, or even the most omnipotent force, with the best will in the world, can distribute nothing. The earnings pocketed by the competing capitalists are something very tangible and solid. Force can *seize* them, but cannot *produce* them. And if Herr Dühring obstinately refuses to explain to us *how* force seizes the earnings of capitalists, the question of *whence* force takes them he meets only with silence, the silence of the grave. Where there is nothing, the king, like any other force, loses his rights. Out of nothing comes nothing, and certainly not profit. If capital ownership has no practical meaning, and cannot be realised, unless indirect force against human material is simultaneously embodied in it, then once again the question arises, first, how capital-wealth got this force—a question which is not settled in the least by the couple of historical assertions cited above; secondly, how this force is transformed into an accession of capital value, into profit; and thirdly, where it obtains this profit.

From whatever side we approach Dühringian economics, we do not get one step further. For every obnoxious phenomenon—profit, land rent, starvation wages, the enslavement of the workers—he has only one word of explanation: force, and ever again force, and Herr Dühring's "mightier wrath" [501] finally resolves itself into wrath at force. We have seen, first, that this invocation of force is a lame subterfuge, a relegation of the problem from the sphere of economics to that of politics, which is unable to explain a single economic fact; and secondly, that it leaves unexplained the origin of force itself—and very prudently so, for otherwise it would have to come to the conclusion that all social power and all political force have their source in economic preconditions, in the mode of production and exchange historically given for each society at each period.

But let us see whether we cannot wrest from the inexorable builder of "deeper foundations" [see D. C. 11] of political economy some further disclosures about profit. Perhaps we shall meet with success if we apply ourselves to his treatment of wages. On page 158[a] we find:

> "Wages are the hire paid for the maintenance of labour-power, and are at first taken into consideration only as a basis for the rent of land and earnings of capital. In order to get absolute clarity as to the relationships obtaining in this field, one must conceive the rent of land, and subsequently also earnings of capital, first historically, without wages, that is to say, on the basis of slavery or serfdom... Whether it is a slave or a serf, or a wage-labourer who has to be maintained, only gives rise to a difference in the mode of charging the costs of production. *In every case the net proceeds obtained by the utilisation of labour-power constitute the income of the master...* It can therefore be seen that ... the chief antithesis, by virtue of which there exists on the one hand some form of *rent of possession* and on the other hand propertyless hired labour, is not to be found exclusively in one of its members, but always only in both at the same time."

Rent of possession, however, as we learn on page 188, is a phrase which covers both land rent and earnings of capital. Further, we find on page 174:

> "The characteristic feature of earnings of capital is that they are an *appropriation of the most important part of the proceeds of labour-power.* They cannot be conceived except in correlation with some form of directly or indirectly subjected labour."

And on page 183:

> Wages "are in all circumstances nothing more than the hire by means of which, generally speaking, the labourer's maintenance and possibility of procreation must be assured".

And finally, on page 195:

> "The portion that falls to rent of possession must be lost to wages, and vice versa, the portion of the general productive capacity" (!) "that reaches labour must necessarily be taken from the revenues of possession."

---

[a] Here and below Engels cites Dühring's work *Cursus der National- und Socialökonomie.—Ed.*

Herr Dühring leads us from one surprise to another. In his theory of value and the following chapters up to and including the theory of competition, that is, from page 1 to page 155, the prices of commodities or values were divided, first, into natural outlays of production or the production value, i.e., the outlays on raw materials, instruments of labour and wages; and secondly, into the surcharge or distribution value [27], that tribute levied sword in hand [23] for the benefit of the monopolist class—a surcharge which, as we have seen, could not in reality make any change in the distribution of wealth, for what it took with one hand it would have to give back with the other, and which, besides, in so far as Herr Dühring enlightens us as to its origin and nature, arose out of nothing and therefore consists of nothing. In the two succeeding chapters, which deal with the kinds of revenue, that is, from page 156 to 217, there is no further mention of the surcharge. Instead of this, the value of every product of labour, that is, of every commodity, is now divided into the two following portions: first, the production costs, in which the wages paid are included; and secondly, the "*net proceeds* obtained by the utilisation of labour-power", which constitute the master's income. And these net proceeds have a very well-known physiognomy, which no tattooing and no house-painter's art can conceal. "In order to get absolute clarity as to the relationships obtaining in this field" [158], let the reader imagine the passages just cited from Herr Dühring printed opposite the passages previously cited from Marx, dealing with surplus-labour, surplus-product and surplus-value, and he will find that Herr Dühring is here, though in his own style, *directly copying* from *Capital*.

Surplus-labour, in any form, whether of slavery, serfdom or wage-labour, is recognised by Herr Dühring as the source of the revenues of all ruling classes up to now; this is taken from the much-quoted passage in *Capital*, p. 227: Capital has not invented surplus-labour, and so on.[a]—And the "net proceeds" which constitute "the income of the master"—what is that but the surplus of the labour product over and above the wages, which, even in Herr Dühring, in spite of his quite superfluous disguise of it in the term "hire", must assure, generally speaking, the labourer's maintenance and possibility of procreation? How can the "appropriation of the most important part of the proceeds of labour-power" [174] be carried out except by the capitalist, as

---

[a] See this volume, pp. 143 and 193.—*Ed.*

Marx shows, extorting from the labourer more labour than is necessary for the reproduction of the means of subsistence consumed by the latter; that is to say, by the capitalist making the labourer work a longer time than is necessary for the replacement of the value of the wages paid to the labourer? Thus the prolongation of the working-day beyond the time necessary for the reproduction of the labourer's means of subsistence—Marx's surplus-labour—this, and nothing but this, is what is concealed behind Herr Dühring's "utilisation of labour-power"; and his "net proceeds" [158] falling to the master—how can they manifest themselves otherwise than in the Marxian surplus-product and surplus-value? And what, apart from its inexact formulation, is there to distinguish the Dühringian rent of possession from the Marxian surplus-value? For the rest, Herr Dühring has taken the name "rent of possession" ["*Besitzrente*"] from Rodbertus, who included both the rent of land and the rent of capital, or earnings of capital, under the one term *rent*, so that Herr Dühring had only to add "possession" to it.* And so that no doubt may be left of his plagiarism, Herr Dühring sums up, in his own way, the laws of the changes of magnitude in the price of labour-power and in surplus-value which are developed by Marx in Chapter XV (page 539, *et seqq.*, of *Capital*),[b] and does it in such a manner that what falls to the rent of possession must be lost to wages, and vice versa, thereby reducing certain Marxian laws, so rich in content, to a tautology without content—for it is self-evident that of a given magnitude falling into two parts, one part cannot increase unless the other decreases. And so Herr Dühring has succeeded in appropriating the ideas of Marx in such a way that the "definitive and most strictly scientific treatment in the sense of the exact disciplines" [D. K. G. 498]—which is certainly present in Marx's exposition—is completely lost.

We therefore cannot avoid the conclusion that the strange commotion which Herr Dühring makes in the *Kritische Geschichte*[c] over *Capital*, and the dust he raises with the famous question that comes up in connection with surplus-value (a question which

---

* And not even this. Rodbertus says (*Sociale Briefe* Letter 2, p. 59): "Rent, according to this" (his) "theory, is all income obtained without personal labour, solely *on the ground of possession*."[a]

  [a] J. K. Rodbertus, *Sociale Briefe an von Kirchmann*. Letter 2: "Kirchmann's sociale Theorie und die meinige", p. 59.— *Ed.*
  [b] See present edition, Vol. 35, Part V, Chapter XVII.— *Ed.*
  [c] E. Dühring, *Kritische Geschichte der Nationalökonomie.*— *Ed.*

he had better have left unasked, inasmuch as he cannot answer it himself)—that all this is only a military ruse, a sly manoeuvre to cover up the gross plagiarism of Marx committed in the *Cursus*.[a] Herr Dühring had in fact every reason for warning his readers not to occupy themselves with "the intricate maze which Herr Marx calls *Capital*" [D. K. G. 497], with the bastards of historical and logical fantasy, the confused and hazy Hegelian notions and jugglery [498], etc. The Venus against whom this faithful Eckart warns the German youth had been taken by him stealthily from the Marxian preserves and brought to a safe place for his own use. We must congratulate him on these net proceeds derived from the utilisation of Marx's labour-power, and on the peculiar light thrown by his annexation of Marxian surplus-value under the name of rent of possession on the motives for his obstinate (repeated in two editions) and false assertion that by the term surplus-value Marx meant only profit or earnings of capital.

And so we have to portray Herr Dühring's achievements in Herr Dühring's own words as follows:

"In Herr" Dühring's "view wages represent only the payment of that labour-time during which the labourer is actually working to make his own existence possible. But only a small number of hours is required for this purpose; all the rest of the working-day, often so prolonged, yields a surplus in which is contained what our author calls" [500]—rent of possession.[a] "If we leave out of account the labour-time which at each stage of production is already contained in the instruments of labour and in the pertinent raw material, this surplus part of the working-day is the share which falls to the capitalist entrepreneur. The prolongation of the working-day is consequently earnings of pure extortion for the benefit of the capitalist. The venomous hatred with which Herr" Dühring "presents this conception of the business of exploitation is only too understandable" [501]...

But what is less understandable is how he will now arrive once more at his "mightier wrath" [501].

IX. NATURAL LAWS OF THE ECONOMY.
RENT OF LAND

Up to this point we have been unable, despite our sincerest efforts, to discover how Herr Dühring, in the domain of economics, can

---

[a] E. Dühring, *Cursus der National- und Socialökonomie.—Ed.*

[b] Here Engels uses Dühring's term "rent of possession" (*Besitzrente*) instead of Marx's term "surplus-value" (*Mehrwerth*) used by Dühring.— *Ed.*

"come forward with the claim to a new *system* which is not merely adequate for the epoch but *authoritative for the epoch*" [D. K. G. 1].

However, what we have not been able to discern in his theory of force and his doctrine of value and of capital, may perhaps become as clear as daylight to us when we consider the "natural laws of national economy" [D. C. 4] put forward by Herr Dühring. For, as he puts it with his usual originality and in his trenchant way,

"the triumph of the higher scientific method consists in passing beyond the mere description and classification of apparently static matter and attaining living intuitions which illumine the genesis of things. Knowledge of laws is therefore the most perfect knowledge, for it shows us how one process is conditioned by another" [59].

The very first natural law of any economy has been specially discovered by Herr Dühring.

Adam Smith, "curiously enough, not only did not bring out the leading part played by the most important factor in all economic development, but even completely failed to give it distinctive formulation, and thus unintentionally reduced to a subordinate role the power which placed its stamp on the development of modern Europe" [64]. This "fundamental law, to which the leading role must be assigned, is that of the technical equipment, one might even say armament, of the natural economic energy of man" [63].

This "fundamental law" [66] discovered by Herr Dühring reads as follows:

Law No. 1. "The productivity of the economic instruments, natural resources and human energy is increased *by inventions* and *discoveries*" [65].

We are overcome with astonishment. Herr Dühring treats us as Molière's newly baked nobleman is treated by the wag who announces to him the news that all through his life he has been speaking prose without knowing it.[a] That in a good many cases the productive power of labour is increased by inventions and discoveries (but also that in very many cases it is not increased, as is proved by the mass of waste-paper in the archives of every patent office in the world) we knew long ago; but we owe to Herr Dühring the enlightening information that this banality, which is as old as the hills, is the fundamental law of all economics. If "the triumph of the higher scientific method" in economics, as in philosophy, consists only in giving a high-sounding name to the first commonplace that comes to one's mind, and trumpeting it

---

[a] Molière, *Le Bourgeois gentilhomme*, Act II, Scene 6.— *Ed.*

forth as a natural law or even a fundamental law, then it becomes possible for anybody, even the editors of the Berlin *Volks-Zeitung*, to lay "deeper foundations" [11] and to revolutionise science. We should then "in all rigour" [9, 95] be forced to apply to Herr Duhring himself Herr Duhring's judgment on Plato:

"If however that is supposed to be political-economic wisdom, then the author of" the critical foundations[a] "shares it with every person who ever had occasion to conceive an idea" or even only to babble "about anything that was obvious on the face of it" [D. K. G. 20].

If, for example, we say animals eat, we are saying quite calmly, in our innocence, something of great import; for we only have to say that eating is the fundamental law of all animal life, and we have revolutionised the whole of zoology.

Law No. 2. Division of Labour: "The cleaving of trades and the dissection of activities raises the productivity of labour" [D. C. 73].

In so far as this is true, it also has been a commonplace since Adam Smith. *How* far it is true will be shown in Part III.

Law No. 3. "*Distance and transport* are the chief causes which hinder or facilitate the co-operation of the productive forces" [91].
Law No. 4. "The industrial state has an incomparably greater population capacity than the agricultural state" [107].
Law No. 5. "In the economy nothing takes place without a material interest" [126].

These are the "natural laws" [4, 5] on which Herr Dühring founds his new economics. He remains faithful to his method, already demonstrated in the section on Philosophy. In economics too a few self-evident statements of the utmost banality—moreover quite often very ineptly expressed—form the axioms which need no proof, the fundamental theorems, the natural laws. Under the pretext of developing the content of these laws, which have no content, he seizes the opportunity to pour out a wordy stream of economic twaddle on the various themes whose *names* occur in these pretended laws—inventions, division of labour, means of transport, population, interests, competition, and so forth—a verbal outpouring whose flat commonplaces are seasoned only with oracular grandiloquence, and here and there with inept formulations or pretentious hair-splitting over all kinds of casuistical subtleties. Then finally we reach rent of land, earnings

---

[a] This is an allusion to Dühring's *Kritische Grundlegung der Volkswirthschaftslehre.—Ed.*

of capital, and wages, and as we have dealt with only the two latter forms of appropriation in the preceding exposition, we propose now in conclusion to make a brief examination of the Dühringian conception of rent.

In doing this we shall not consider those points which Herr Dühring has merely copied from his predecessor Carey; we are not concerned with Carey, nor with defending Ricardo's views on rent of land against Carey's distortions and stupidities. We are only concerned with Herr Dühring, and he defines rent as

"that income which the proprietor *as such* draws from the land" [D. C. 156].

The economic concept of rent of land, which is what Herr Dühring is to explain, is straightaway transferred by him into the juridical sphere, so that we are no wiser than we were before. Our constructor of deeper foundations must therefore, whether he likes it or not, condescend to give some further explanation. He compares the lease of a farm to a tenant with the loan of capital to an entrepreneur, but soon finds that there is a hitch in the comparison, like in many others.

For, he says, "if one wanted to press the analogy further, the earnings left to the tenant after payment of rent must correspond to the balance of earnings of capital left with the entrepreneur who puts the capital to use after he has paid interest. *But it is not customary* to regard tenants' earnings as the main income and rent as a balance... A proof of this difference of conception is the *fact* that in the theory of land rent the case of management of land by the owner is not separately treated, and no special emphasis is laid on the difference between the amount of rent in the case of a lease and where the owner produces the rent himself. *At any rate no one has found it necessary* to conceive the rent resulting from such self-management of land as divided in such a way that one portion represents as it were the interest on the landed property and the other portion the surplus earnings of enterprise. Apart from the tenant's own capital which he brings into the business, it would *seem* that his specific *earnings are mostly regarded* as a kind of wages. It is however *hazardous* to assert anything on this subject, as the question has never been raised in this definite form. Wherever we are dealing with fairly large farms it can easily be seen that it will not do to treat what are specifically the farmer's earnings as wages. For these earnings are themselves based on the antithesis existing in relation to the rural labour-power, through whose exploitation that form of income is alone made possible. It is clearly *a part of the rent* which remains in the hands of the tenant and by which the *full rent,* which the owner managing himself would obtain, is reduced" [157-58].

The theory of land rent is a part of political economy which is specifically English, and necessarily so, because it was only in England that there existed a mode of production under which rent had in fact been separated from profit and interest. In England, as is well known, large landed estates and large-scale agriculture predominate. The landlords lease their land in large, often very large, farms, to tenant-farmers who possess sufficient capital to work them and, unlike our peasants, do not work themselves but employ the labour of hands and day-labourers on the lines of full-fledged capitalist entrepreneurs. Here, therefore, we have the three classes of bourgeois society and the form of income peculiar to each: the landlord, drawing rent of land; the capitalist, drawing profit; and the labourer, drawing wages. It has never occurred to any English economist to regard the farmer's earnings as a kind of wages, as *seems* to Herr Dühring to be the case; even less could it be *hazardous* for such an economist to assert that the farmer's profit is what it indisputably, obviously and tangibly is, namely, profit on capital. It is perfectly ridiculous to say that the question of what the farmer's earnings actually are has never been raised in this definite form. In England there has never been any necessity even to raise this question; both question and answer have long been available, derived from the facts themselves, and since Adam Smith there has never been any doubt about them.

The case of self-management, as Herr Dühring calls it—or rather, the management of farms by bailiffs for the landowner's account, as happens most frequently in Germany—does not alter the matter. If the landowner also provides the capital and has the farm run for his own account, he pockets the profit on capital in addition to the rent, as is self-understood and cannot be otherwise on the basis of the existing mode of production. And if Herr Dühring asserts that up to now no one has found it necessary to conceive the rent (he should say revenue) resulting from the owner's own management as divided into parts, this is simply untrue, and at best only proves his own ignorance once again. For example:

"The revenue derived from labour is called wages. That derived from stock, by the person who manages or employs it, is called profit... The revenue which proceeds altogether from land, is called rent, and belongs to the landlord... When those three different sorts of revenue belong to different persons, they are readily distinguished; but when they belong to the same they are sometimes confounded with one another, at least in common language. A gentleman *who farms* a part of his own estate, after paying the expense of cultivation, should *gain both the rent of the landlord and the profit of the farmer.* He is apt to denominate, however, his whole gain, profit, and thus confounds rent with profit, at least in common language. The greater part of our North American and West Indian planters are in this situation. They farm, the greater part of them, their own estates, and accordingly we seldom hear of the rent of a plantation, but frequently of its profit... A gardener who cultivates his own garden with his own hands, unites in his own person the three different characters, of landlord, farmer, and labourer. His produce, therefore, should pay him the rent of the first, the profit of the second, and the wages of the third. The whole, however, is commonly considered as the earnings of his labour. Both rent and profit are, in this case, confounded with wages."

This passage is from the sixth chapter of Book I of *Adam Smith*.[a] The case of self-management was therefore investigated a hundred years ago, and the doubts and uncertainties which so worry Herr Dühring in this connection are merely due to his own ignorance.

He eventually escapes from his quandary by an audacious trick:

The farmer's earnings come from the exploitation of the "rural labour-power" and are therefore obviously a "part of the rent" by which the "full rent", which really should flow into the landowner's pocket, "is reduced".

From this we learn two things. Firstly, that the farmer "reduces" the rent of the landowner, so that, according to Herr Dühring, it is not, as was considered hitherto, the farmer who pays rent to the landowner, but the *landowner* who *pays rent to the farmer*—certainly a "from the ground up original view" [D. Ph. 525]. And secondly, we learn at last what Herr Dühring thinks rent of land is: namely, the whole surplus-product obtained in farming by the exploitation of rural labour. But as this surplus-product in all economics hitherto—save perhaps for the works of a few vulgar economists—has been divided into land rent and profit on capital, we are compelled to note that Herr Dühring's view of rent also is "not the accepted one" [D. K. G. 497].

According to Herr Dühring, therefore, the only difference between rent of land and earnings of capital is that the former is obtained in agriculture and the latter in industry or commerce. And it was of necessity that Herr Dühring arrived at such an uncritical and confused view of the matter. We saw that his starting-point was the "really historical conception", that domination over the land could be based only on domination over man. As soon, therefore, as land is cultivated by means of any form of subjugated labour, a surplus for the landlord arises, and this surplus is the rent, just as in industry the surplus-labour product beyond what the labourer earns is the profit on capital.

"Thus it is clear that land rent exists on a considerable scale wherever and whenever agriculture is carried on by means of any of the forms of subjugation of labour" [D. C. 162].

---

a A. Smith, *An Inquiry into the Nature and Causes of the Wealth of Nations,* Vol. 1, pp. 63-64, 65. Italics by Engels.— *Ed.*

In this presentation of rent as the whole surplus-product obtained in agriculture, Herr Dühring comes up against both English farmer's profit and the division, based on English farming and recognised by all classical political economy, of that surplus-product into rent of land and farmer's profit, and hence against the *pure*, precise conception of rent. What does Herr Dühring do? He pretends not to have the slightest inkling of the division of the surplus-product of agriculture into farmer's profit and rent, and therefore of the whole rent theory of classical political economy; he pretends that the question of what farmer's profit really is has never yet been raised "in this definite form" [157], that at issue is a subject which has never yet been investigated and about which there is no knowledge but only illusion and uncertainty. And he flees from fatal England—where, without the intervention of any theoretical school, the surplus-product of agriculture is so remorselessly divided into its elements: rent of land and profit on capital—to the country so beloved by him, where the Prussian law exercises dominion, where self-management is in full patriarchal bloom, where "the landlord understands by rent the income from his plots of land" and the Junkers' views on rent still claim to be authoritative for science—where therefore Herr Dühring can still hope to slip through with his confused ideas of rent and profit and even to find credence for his latest discovery: that rent of land is paid not by the farmer to the landlord but by the landlord to the farmer.

X. FROM *KRITISCHE GESCHICHTE*[92]

Finally, let us take a glance at the *Kritische Geschichte der Nationalökonomie*, at "that enterprise" of Herr Dühring's which, as he says, "is absolutely without precedent" [9]. It may be that here at last we shall find the definitive and most strictly scientific treatment which he has so often promised us.

Herr Dühring makes a great deal of noise over his discovery that

"economic science" is "an enormously modern phenomenon" (p. 12).

In fact, Marx says in *Capital:* "Political economy ... as an independent science, first sprang into being during the period of manufacture"[a]; and in *Zur Kritik der politischen Oeko-*

---

[a] K. Marx, *Das Kapital,* p. 378. See present edition, Vol. 35, Part IV, Chapter XIV, Section 5.— *Ed.*

nomie, page 29, that "classical political economy ... dates from William Petty in England and Boisguillebert in France, and closes with Ricardo in the former country and Sismondi in the latter".[a] Herr Dühring follows the path thus laid down for him, except that in his view *higher* economics begins only with the wretched abortions brought into existence by bourgeois science after the close of its classical period. On the other hand, he is fully justified in triumphantly proclaiming at the end of his introduction:

"But if this enterprise, in its externally appreciable peculiarities and in the more novel portion of its content, is absolutely without precedent, in its inner critical approaches and its general standpoint, it is even more peculiarly mine" (p. 9).

It is a fact that, on the basis of both its external and its internal features, he might very well have announced his "enterprise" (the industrial term is not badly chosen) as: *The Ego and His Own.*[b]

Since political economy, as it made its appearance in history, is in fact nothing but the scientific insight into the economy in the period of capitalist production, principles and theorems relating to it, for example, in the writers of ancient Greek society, can only be found in so far as certain phenomena—commodity production, trade, money, interest-bearing capital, etc.—are common to both societies. In so far as the Greeks make occasional excursions into this sphere, they show the same genius and originality as in all other spheres. Because of this, their views form, historically, the theoretical starting-points of the modern science. Let us now listen to what the world-historic Herr Dühring has to say.

"We have, strictly speaking, really" (!) "absolutely nothing positive to report of antiquity concerning scientific economic theory, and the completely unscientific Middle Ages give still less occasion for this" (for this—for reporting *nothing*!). "As however the fashion of vaingloriously displaying a semblance of erudition ... has defaced the true character of modern science, notice must be taken of at least a few examples" [17].

And Herr Dühring then produces examples of a criticism which is in truth free from even the "semblance of erudition".
Aristotle's thesis, that

"twofold is the use of every object... The one is peculiar to the object as such, the other is not, as a sandal which may be worn, and is also exchangeable. Both are

---

a See present edition, Vol. 29.— *Ed.*
b An allusion to Max Stirner's book *Der Einzige und sein Eigenthum.— Ed.*

First page of K. Marx's manuscript *Randnoten zu Dührings Kritische Geschichte der Nationalökonomie*

uses of the sandal, for even he who exchanges the sandal for the money or food he is in want of, makes use of the sandal as a sandal. But not in its natural way. For it has not been made for the sake of being exchanged"[a] —

this thesis, Herr Dühring maintains, is "not only expressed in a really platitudinous and scholastic way" [18]; but those who see in it a "differentiation between use-value and exchange-value" fall besides into the "ridiculous frame of mind" [19] of forgetting that "in the most recent period" and "in the framework of the most advanced system"—which of course is Herr Dühring's own system—nothing has been left of use-value and exchange-value.

"In Plato's work on the state, people ... claim to have found the *modern* doctrine of the national-economic division of labour" [20].

This was apparently meant to refer to the passage in *Capital*, Ch. XII, 5 (p. 369 of the third edition), where the views of classical antiquity on the division of labour are on the contrary shown to have been "in most striking contrast" with the modern view.[b] Herr Dühring has nothing but sneers for Plato's presentation—one which, for his time, was full of genius—of the division of labour[c] as the natural basis of the city (which for the Greeks was identical with the state); and this on the ground that he did not mention—though the Greek Xenophon did,[d] Herr Dühring—the "limit"

"set by the given dimensions of the market to the further differentiation of professions and the technical subdivision of special operations... Only the conception of this limit constitutes the knowledge with the aid of which this idea, otherwise hardly fit to be called scientific, becomes a major economic truth" [20].

It was in fact "Professor" Roscher [14], of whom Herr Dühring is so contemptuous, who set up this "limit" at which the idea of the division of labour is supposed first to become "scientific", and who therefore expressly pointed to Adam Smith as the discoverer of the law of the division of labour.[e] In a society in which commodity production is the dominant form of production, "the market"—to adopt Herr Dühring's style for once—was always a

---

[a] Aristoteles, *De republica,* Liber I, Cap. 9. Marx also quotes this passage in his *Contribution to the Critique of Political Economy* and *Capital* (see present edition, Vol. 29 and Vol. 35, Part I, Chapter II).— *Ed.*

[b] K. Marx, *Das Kapital. Kritik der politischen Oekonomie,* 3rd enlarged ed. See present edition, Vol. 35, Part IV, Chapter XIV, Section 5.— *Ed.*

[c] Marx refers to Plato's *Res publica,* Liber II.— *Ed.*

[d] Marx refers to Xenophontis, *Cyropaedia,* Liber VIII, Cap. 2.— *Ed.*

[e] See W. Roscher, *System der Volkswirthschaft,* Bd. I, p. 86.— *Ed.*

"limit" very well known to "business people" [18]. But more than "the knowledge and instinct of routine" is needed to realise that it was not the market that created the capitalist division of labour, but that, on the contrary, it was the dissolution of former social connections, and the division of labour resulting from this, that created the market (see *Capital*, Vol. I, Ch. XXIV, 5: "Creation of the Home-Market for Industrial Capital").[a]

"The role of money has at all times provided the first and main stimulus to economic" (!) "ideas. But what did an Aristotle know of this role? No more, clearly, than was contained in the idea that exchange through the medium of money had followed the primitive exchange by barter" [21].

But when "an" Aristotle presumes to discover the two different *forms of the circulation* of money—the one in which it operates as a mere medium of circulation, and the other in which it operates as money capital,[b]

he is thereby—according to Herr Dühring—"only expressing a moral antipathy" [21].

And when "an" Aristotle carries his audacity so far as to attempt an analysis of money in its "role" of a *measure of value*, and actually states this problem, which has such decisive importance for the theory of money, correctly[c]—then "a" Dühring prefers (and for very good private reasons) to say nothing about such impermissible temerity.

Final result: Greek antiquity, as mirrored in the "notice taken" [21] by Dühring, in fact possessed "only quite ordinary ideas" (p. 25), if such *"niaiserie"* (p. 19) has anything whatever in common with ideas, whether ordinary or extraordinary.

It would be better to read Herr Dühring's chapter on mercantilism [93] in the "original", that is, in F. List's *Nationales System*, Chapter 29: "The Industrial System, Incorrectly Called the Mercantile System by the School". How carefully Herr Dühring manages to avoid here too any "semblance of erudition" [17] is shown by the following passage, among others:

List, Chapter 28: "The Italian Political Economists", says:

---

[a] See present edition, Vol. 35, Part VIII, Chapter XXX.—*Ed.*

[b] Aristoteles, *De republica*, Liber I, Cap. 8-10. Cf. present edition, Vol. 29 (*A Contribution to the Critique of Political Economy*) and Vol. 35, Part II, Chapters IV, V.—*Ed.*

[c] Marx refers to Aristotle's *Ethica Nicomachea*, Liber V, Cap. 8. He quotes corresponding passages from this book in *A Contribution to the Critique of Political Economy* and in *Capital* (see present edition, Vol. 29 and Vol. 35, Part I, Chapter I, Section 3, A, 3: "The Equivalent Form of Value").—*Ed.*

"Italy was in advance of all modern nations both in the practice and in the theory of political economy",

and then he cites, as

"the first work written in Italy, which deals especially with political economy, the book by Antonio Serra, of Naples, on the way to secure for the kingdoms an abundance of gold and silver (1613)".[a]

Herr Dühring confidently accepts this and is therefore able to regard Serra's *Breve trattato*[b]

"as a kind of inscription at the entrance of the more recent prehistory of economics" [34].

His treatment of the *Breve trattato* is in fact limited to this "piece of literary buffoonery" [506]. Unfortunately, the actual facts of the case were different: in 1609, that is four years before the *Breve trattato*, Thomas Mun's *A Discourse of Trade etc.*,[c] had appeared. The particular significance of this book was that, even in its first edition, it was directed against the original *monetary system* which was then still defended in England as being the policy of the state; hence it represented the conscious *self-separation* of the mercantile system from the system which gave it birth. Even in the form in which it first appeared the book had several editions and exercised a direct influence on legislation. In the edition of 1664 (*England's Treasure etc.*[d]), which had been completely rewritten by the author and was published after his death, it continued to be the mercantilist gospel for another hundred years. If mercantilism therefore has an epoch-making work "as a kind of inscription at the entrance", it is this book, and for this very reason it simply does not exist for Herr Dühring's "history which most carefully observes the distinctions of rank" [133].

Of *Petty*, the founder of modern political economy, Herr Dühring tells us that there was

"a fair measure of superficiality in his way of thinking" [54] and that "he had no sense of the intrinsic and nicer distinctions between concepts" [55] ... while he possessed "a versatility which knows a great deal but skips lightly from one thing to

---

[a] F. List, *Das nationale System der politischen Oekonomie*, Vol. I, pp. 451, 456.— *Ed.*

[b] A. Serra, *Breve trattato delle cause che possono far abbondare li regni d'oro et d'argento dove non sono miniere.— Ed.*

[c] T. M[un], *A Discourse of Trade, from England into the East-Indies: Answering to diverse Objections which are usually made against the same.* The title is given in English in the manuscript.— *Ed.*

[d] T. Mun, *England's Treasure by Forraign Trade. Or, the Ballance of our Forraign Trade is the Rule of our Treasure.* The title is given in English in the manuscript.— *Ed.*

another without taking root in any idea of a more profound character" [56]; ... his "national-economic ideas are still very crude", and "he achieves *naivetés,* whose contrasts ... a more serious thinker may well find amusing at times" [56].

What inestimable condescension, therefore, for the "more serious thinker" Herr Dühring to deign to take any notice at all of "a Petty" [60]! And what notice does he take of him?

Petty's propositions on

"labour and even labour-time as a measure of value, of which *imperfect traces* can be found in his writings" [62]

are not mentioned again apart from this sentence. Imperfect traces! In his *Treatise on Taxes and Contributions*[a] (first edition, 1662), Petty gives a perfectly clear and correct analysis of the magnitude of value of commodities. In illustrating this magnitude at the outset by the equal value of precious metals and corn on which the same quantity of labour has been expended, he says the first and the last "theoretical" word on the value of the precious metals. But he also lays it down in a definite and general form that the values of commodities must be measured by EQUAL LABOUR. He applies his discovery to the solution of various problems, some of which are very intricate, and on various occasions and in various works, even where he does not repeat the fundamental proposition, he draws important conclusions from it. But even in his very first work he says:

"This" (estimation by equal labour) "I say to be *the foundation of equalizing and balancing of values,* yet in the superstructures and practices hereupon, I confess there is much variety, and intricacy."[b]

Petty was thus conscious equally of the importance of his discovery and of the difficulty of applying it in detail. He therefore tried to find another way in certain concrete cases.

A NATURAL PAR should therefore be found between land and labour, so that value might be expressed at will "by either of them alone as well or better than by both"[c]

Even this error has genius.

Herr Dühring makes this penetrating observation on Petty's theory of value:

---

[a] The title is given in English in the manuscript.— *Ed.*

[b] W. Petty, *A Treatise of Taxes and Contributions,* pp. 24-25. Italics by Marx.— *Ed.*

[c] Ibid., p. 24.— *Ed.*

"Had his own thought been more penetrating it would not be possible to find, in other passages, traces of a contrary view, to which we have previously referred" [63-64];

that is to say, to which no "previous" reference has been made except that the "traces" are "imperfect". This is very characteristic of Herr Dühring's method—to allude to something "previously" in a meaningless phrase, in order "subsequently" to make the reader believe that he has "previously" been made acquainted with the main point, which in fact the author in question has slid over both previously and subsequently.

In Adam Smith, however, we can find not only "traces" of "contrary views" on the concept of value, not only two but even three, and strictly speaking even four sharply contrary opinions on value, running quite comfortably side by side and intermingled. But what is quite natural in a writer who is laying the foundations of political economy and is necessarily feeling his way, experimenting and struggling with a chaos of ideas which are only just taking shape, may seem strange in a writer who is surveying and summarising more than a hundred and fifty years of investigation whose results have already passed in part from books into the consciousness of the generality. And, to pass from great things to small: as we have seen, Herr Dühring himself gives us five different kinds of value to select from at will, and with them, an equal number of contrary views. Of course, "had his own thought been more penetrating", he would not have had to expend so much effort in trying to throw his readers back from Petty's perfectly clear conception of value into the uttermost confusion.

A smoothly finished work of Petty's which may be said to be cast in a single block, is his *Quantulumcunque concerning Money*,[a] published in 1682, ten years after his *Anatomy of Ireland*[a] (this "first" appeared in 1672, not 1691 as stated by Herr Dühring, who takes it second-hand from the "most current textbook compilations").[94] In this book the last vestiges of mercantilist views, found in other writings by him, have completely disappeared. In content and form it is a little masterpiece, and for this very reason Herr Dühring does not even mention its title. It is quite in the order of things that in relation to the most brilliant and original of economic investigators, our vainglorious and pedantic mediocrity should only snarl his displeasure, and take offence at the fact that the flashes of theoretical thought do not proudly parade about in

---

[a] The title is given in English in the manuscript.—*Ed.*

rank and file as ready-made "axioms" [D. Ph. 224], but merely rise sporadically to the surface from the depths of "crude" [D. K. G. 57] practical material, for example, of taxes.

Petty's foundations of *Political Arithmetic* [58], *vulgo*[a] statistics, are treated by Herr Dühring in the same way as that author's specifically economic works. He malevolently shrugs his shoulders at the odd methods used by Petty! Considering the grotesque methods still employed in this field a century later even by Lavoisier,[95] and in view of the great distance that separates even contemporary statistics from the goal which Petty assigned to them in broad outline, such self-satisfied superiority two centuries *post festum*[b] stands out in all its undisguised stupidity.

Petty's most important ideas—which received such scant attention in Herr Dühring's "enterprise" [9]—are, in the latter's view, nothing but disconnected conceits, chance thoughts, incidental comments, to which only in our day a significance is given, by the use of excerpts torn from their context, which in themselves they have not got; which therefore also play no part in the *real* history of political economy, but only in modern books below the standard of Herr Dühring's deep-rooted criticism and "historical depiction in the grand style" [556]. In his "enterprise", he seems to have had in view a circle of readers who would have implicit faith and would never be bold enough to ask for proof of his assertions. We shall return to this point soon (when dealing with Locke and North), but must first take a fleeting glance at Boisguillebert and Law.

In connection with the former, we must draw attention to the sole find made by Herr Dühring: he has discovered a connection between Boisguillebert and Law which had hitherto been missed. Boisguillebert asserts that the precious metals could be replaced, in the normal monetary functions which they fulfil in commodity circulation, by credit money (*un morceau de papier*[c]).[d] Law on the other hand imagines that any "increase" whatever in the number of these "pieces of paper" increases the wealth of a nation. Herr Dühring draws from this the conclusion that Boisguillebert's

"turn of thought already harboured a new turn in mercantilism" [83]

---

[a] Commonly speaking.— *Ed.*
[b] After the event.— *Ed.*
[c] A piece of paper.— *Ed.*
[d] P. Boisguillebert, *Dissertation sur la nature des richesses, de l'argent et des tributs*, Chapter II. In: *Économistes financiers du XVIII[e] siècle*, p. 397.— *Ed.*

in other words, already included Law. This is made as clear as daylight in the following:

"*All* that was necessary was to assign to the 'simple pieces of paper' the same role that the precious metals *should* have played, and a metamorphosis of mercantilism was thereby at once accomplished" [83].

In the same way it is possible to accomplish at once the metamorphosis of an uncle into an aunt. It is true that Herr Dühring adds appeasingly:

"Of course Boisguillebert had no such purpose in mind" [83].

But how, in the devil's name, could he intend to replace his own rationalist conception of the monetary function of the precious metals by the superstitious conception of the mercantilists for the sole reason that, according to him, the precious metals can be replaced in this role by paper money?

Nevertheless, Herr Dühring continues in his serio-comic style,

"nevertheless it may be conceded that here and there our author succeeded in making a really apt remark" (p. 83).

In reference to Law, Herr Dühring succeeded in making only this "really apt remark":

"Law too was naturally never able completely to *eradicate* the above-named basis" (namely, "the basis of the precious metals"), "but he pushed the issue of notes to its extreme limit, that is to say, to the collapse of the system" (p. 94).

In reality, however, these paper butterflies, mere money tokens, were intended to flutter about among the public, not in order to "eradicate" the basis of the precious metals, but to entice them from the pockets of the public into the depleted treasuries of the state.[96]

To return to Petty and the inconspicuous role in the history of economics assigned to him by Herr Dühring, let us first listen to what we are told about Petty's immediate successors, Locke and North. Locke's *Considerations on Lowering of Interest and Raising of Money*,[a] and North's *Discourses upon Trade*,[a] appeared in the same year, 1691.

"What he" (Locke) "wrote on interest and coin does not go beyond the range of the reflections, current under the dominion of mercantilism, in connection with the events of political life" (p. 64).

---

[a] The title is given in English in the manuscript.— *Ed.*

To the reader of this "report" it should now be clear as crystal why Locke's *Lowering of Interest*[a] had such an important influence, in more than one direction, on political economy in France and Italy during the latter half of the eighteenth century.

"Many businessmen thought the same" (as Locke) "on free play for the rate of interest, and the developing situation also produced the tendency to regard restrictions on interest as ineffective. At a period when a Dudley North could write his *Discourses upon Trade*[a] in the direction of free trade, a great deal must already have been in the air, as they say, which made the theoretical opposition to restrictions on interest rates seem something not at all extraordinary" (p. 64).

So Locke had only to cogitate the ideas of this or that contemporary "businessman", or to breathe in a great deal of what was "in the air, as they say" to be able to theorise on free play for the rate of interest without saying anything "extraordinary"! In fact, however, as early as 1662, in his *Treatise on Taxes and Contributions*,[a] Petty had counterposed interest, as RENT OF MONEY WHICH WE CALL USURY to RENT OF LAND AND HOUSES, and lectured the landlords, who wished to keep down by legislation not of course land rent, but the rent of money, on THE VANITY AND FRUITLESSNESS OF MAKING CIVIL POSITIVE LAW AGAINST THE LAW OF NATURE.[b] In his *Quantulumcunque* (1682) he therefore declared that legislative regulation of the rate of interest was as stupid as regulation of exports of precious metals or regulation of exchange rates. In the same work he made statements of unquestionable authority on the RAISING OF MONEY (for example, the attempt to give sixpence the name of one shilling by doubling the number of shillings coined from one ounce of silver).

As regards this last point, Locke and North did little more than copy him. In regard to interest, however, Locke followed Petty's parallel between rent of money and rent of land, while North goes further and opposes interest as RENT OF STOCK to land rent, and the STOCKLORDS to the LANDLORDS.[c] And while Locke accepts free play for the rate of interest, as demanded by Petty, only with reservations, North accepts it unconditionally.

Herr Dühring—himself still a bitter mercantilist in the "more subtle" [55] sense—surpasses himself when he dismisses Dudley North's *Discourses upon Trade*[a] with the comment that they were written "in the direction of free trade" [64]. It is rather like saying

---

[a] The title is given in English in the manuscript.— *Ed.*
[b] W. Petty, op. cit., pp. 28-29.— *Ed.*
[c] [D. North,] *Discourses upon Trade*, p. 4.— *Ed.*

of Harvey that he wrote "in the direction" of the circulation of the blood. North's work—apart from its other merits—is a classical exposition, driven home with relentless logic, of the doctrine of free trade, both foreign and internal—certainly "something extraordinary" [64] in the year 1691!

Herr Dühring, by the way, informs us that

North was a "merchant" and a bad type at that, also that his work "met with no approval" [64].

Indeed! How could anyone expect a book of this sort to have met with "approval" among the mob setting the tone at the time of the final triumph of protectionism in England? But this did not prevent it from having an immediate effect on theory, as can be seen from a whole series of economic works published in England shortly after it, some of them even before the end of the seventeenth century.

Locke and North gave us proof of how the first bold strokes which Petty dealt in almost every sphere of political economy were taken up one by one by his English successors and further developed. The traces of this process during the period 1691 to 1752 are obvious even to the most superficial observer from the very fact that all the more important economic writings of that time start from Petty, either positively or negatively. That period, which abounded in original thinkers, is therefore the most important for the investigation of the gradual genesis of political economy. The "historical depiction in the grand style" [556], which chalks up against Marx the unpardonable sin of making so much commotion in *Capital* about Petty and the writers of that period, simply strikes them right out of history. From Locke, North, Boisguillebert and Law it jumps straight to the physiocrats, and then, at the entrance to the real temple of political economy, appears—David Hume. With Herr Dühring's permission, however, we restore the chronological order, putting Hume before the physiocrats.

Hume's economic *Essays* appeared in 1752.[a] In the related essays: *Of Money, Of the Balance of Trade, Of Commerce*, Hume follows step by step, and often even in his personal idiosyncrasies, Jacob Vanderlint's *Money Answers All Things*,[b] published in London

---

[a] This is a reference to David Hume's *Political Discourses*. Marx quotes from the following edition: D. Hume, *Essays and Treatises on Several Subjects*. In two volumes, London, 1777, of which *Political Discourses* comprise the second half of Volume I. —*Ed.*

[b] The titles are given in English in the manuscript.—*Ed.*

in 1734. However unknown this Vanderlint may have been to Herr Dühring, references to him can be found in English economic works even at the end of the eighteenth century, that is to say, in the period after Adam Smith.

Like Vanderlint, Hume treated money as a mere token of value; he copied almost word for word (and this is important as he might have taken the theory of money as a token of value from many other sources) Vanderlint's argument on why the balance of trade cannot be permanently either favourable or unfavourable to a country; like Vanderlint, he teaches that the equilibrium of balances is brought about naturally, in accordance with the different economic situations in the different countries; like Vanderlint, he preaches free trade, but less boldly and consistently; like Vanderlint, though with less profundity, he emphasises wants as the motive forces of production; he follows Vanderlint in the influence on commodity prices which he erroneously attributes to bank money and government securities in general; like Vanderlint, he rejects credit money; like Vanderlint, he makes commodity prices dependent on the price of labour, that is, on wages; he even copies Vanderlint's absurd notion that by accumulating treasures commodity prices are kept down, etc., etc.

At a much earlier point Herr Dühring made an oracular allusion to how others had misunderstood Hume's monetary theory with a particularly minatory reference to Marx, who in *Capital* had, besides, pointed in a manner contrary to police regulations to the secret connections of Hume with Vanderlint and with J. Massie,[a] who will be mentioned later.

As for this misunderstanding, the facts are as follows. In regard to Hume's real theory of money (that money is a mere token of value, and therefore, other conditions being equal, commodity prices rise in proportion to the increase in the volume of money in circulation, and fall in proportion to its decrease), Herr Dühring, with the best intentions in the world—though in his own luminous way—can only repeat the errors made by his predecessors. Hume, however, after propounding the theory cited above, himself raises the objection (as Montesquieu,[b] starting from the same premises, had done previously) that

nevertheless "'tis certain" that since the discovery of the mines in America, "industry has encreased in all the nations of Europe, except in the possessors of

---

[a] See present edition, Vol. 35, Part I, Chapter III, Section 2, b, and Part V, Chapter XVI.— *Ed.*

[b] [Ch. Montesquieu,] *De l'esprit des loix.—Ed.*

those mines", and that this "may justly be ascribed, amongst other reasons, to the encrease of gold and silver".[a]

His explanation of this phenomenon is that

"though the high price of commodities be a necessary consequence of the, encrease of gold and silver, yet it follows not immediately upon that, encrease; but some time is required before the money circulate through the whole state, and make its effects be felt on all ranks of people". In this interval it has a beneficial effect on industry and trade.[b]

At the end of this analysis Hume also tells us why this is so, although in a less comprehensive way than many of his predecessors and contemporaries:

"'Tis easy to trace the money in its progress through the whole commonwealth; where we shall find, that it must first quicken the diligence of every individual, before *it encreases the price of labour.*"[c]

In other words, Hume is here describing the effect of a revolution in the value of the precious metals, namely, a depreciation, or, which is the same thing, a revolution in the *measure of value* of the precious metals. He correctly ascertains that, in the slow process of readjusting the prices of commodities, this depreciation "increases the price of labour"—*vulgo*, wages— only in the last instance; that is to say, it increases the profit made by merchants and industrialists at the cost of the labourer (which he, however, thinks is just as it should be), and thus "quickens diligence". But he does not set himself the task of answering the real scientific question, namely, whether and in what way an increase in the supply of the precious metals, their value remaining the same, affects the prices of commodities; and he lumps together *every* "increase of the precious metals" with their depreciation. Hume therefore does precisely what Marx says he does (*Zur Kritik etc.*, p. 141).[d] We shall come back once more to this point in passing, but we must first turn to Hume's essay on INTEREST.

Hume's arguments, expressly directed against Locke that the rate of interest is not regulated by the amount of available money but by the rate of profit, and his other explanations of the causes which determine rises or falls in the rate of interest, are all to be

---

[a] D. Hume, *Essays and Treatises on Several Subjects*, Vol. I, pp. 303-04.— *Ed.*

[b] Ibid.

[c] Ibid.

[d] K. Marx, *A Contribution to the Critique of Political Economy.* See present edition, Vol. 29.— *Ed.*

found, much more exactly though less cleverly stated, in *An Essay on the Governing Causes of the Natural Rate of Interest; wherein the sentiments of Sir W. Petty and Mr. Locke, on that head, are considered.*[a] This work appeared in 1750, two years before Hume's essay; its author was J. Massie, a writer active in various fields, who had a wide public, as can be seen from contemporary English literature. Adam Smith's discussion of the rate of interest is closer to Massie than to Hume. Neither Massie nor Hume know or say anything regarding the nature of "profit", which plays a role with both.

"In general," Herr Dühring sermonises us, "the attitude of most of Hume's commentators has been very prejudiced, and ideas have been attributed to him which he never entertained in the least" [131].

And Herr Dühring himself gives us more than one striking example of this "attitude".

For example, Hume's essay on interest begins with the following words:

"Nothing is esteemed a more certain sign of the flourishing condition of any nation than the lowness of interest: And with reason; though I believe the cause is somewhat different from what is commonly apprehended."[b]

In the very first sentence, therefore, Hume cites the view that the lowness of interest is the surest indication of the flourishing condition of a nation as a commonplace which had already become trivial in his day. And in fact this "idea" had already had fully a hundred years, since Child, to become generally current. But we are told:

"Among" (Hume's) "views on the rate of interest *we must particularly draw attention to the idea* that it is the true barometer of conditions" (conditions of what?) "and that its lowness is an almost infallible sign of the prosperity of a nation" (p. 130).

Who is the "prejudiced" and captivated "commentator" who says this? None other than Herr Dühring.

What arouses the naive astonishment of our critical historian is the fact that Hume, in connection with some felicitous idea or other, "does not even claim to have originated it" [131]. This would certainly not have happened to Herr Dühring.

We have seen how Hume confuses every increase of the precious metals with such an increase as is accompanied by a

---

[a] The title is given in English in the manuscript.— *Ed.*

[b] D. Hume, op. cit., p. 313.— *Ed.*

depreciation, a revolution in their own value, hence, in the measure of value of commodities. This confusion was inevitable with Hume because he had not the slightest understanding of the function of the precious metals as the *measure of value*. And he could not have it, because he had absolutely no knowledge of value itself. The word itself is to be found perhaps only once in his essays, namely, in the passage where, in attempting to "correct" Locke's erroneous notion that the precious metals had "only an imaginary value", he makes it even worse by saying that they had "merely a fictitious value".[a]

In this he is much inferior not only to Petty but to many of his English contemporaries. He shows the same "backwardness" in still proclaiming the old-fashioned notion that the *"merchant"* is the mainspring of production—an idea which Petty had long passed beyond. As for Herr Dühring's assurance that in his essays Hume concerned himself with the "chief economic relationships" [121], if the reader only compares Cantillon's work quoted by Adam Smith (which appeared the same year as Hume's essays, 1752, but many years after its author's death),[97] he will be surprised at the narrow range of Hume's economic writings. Hume, as we have said, in spite of the letters-patent issued to him by Herr Dühring, is nevertheless quite a respectable figure also in the field of political economy, but in this field he is anything but an original investigator, and even less an epoch-making one. The influence of his economic essays on the educated circles of his day was due not merely to his excellent presentation, but principally to the fact that the essays were a progressive and optimistic glorification of industry and trade, which were then flourishing— in other words, of the capitalist society which at that time was rapidly rising in England, and whose "approval" they therefore had to gain. Let one instance suffice here. Everyone knows the passionate fight that the masses of the English people were waging, just in Hume's day, against the system of indirect taxes which was being regularly exploited by the notorious Sir Robert Walpole for the relief of the landlords and of the rich in general. In his essay *Of Taxes*,[b] in which, without mentioning his name, Hume polemises against his indispensable authority Vanderlint— the stoutest opponent of indirect taxation and the most deter- mined advocate of a land tax—we read:

---

[a] Ibid., p. 314.— *Ed.*
[b] The title is given in English in the manuscript.— *Ed.*

"They" (taxes on consumption) "must be very heavy taxes, indeed, and very injudiciously levied, which the artisan will not, of himself, be enabled to pay, by superior industry and frugality, *without raising the price of his labour.*" [a]

It is almost as if Robert Walpole himself were speaking, especially if we also take into consideration the passage in the essay on "public credit" in which, referring to the difficulty of taxing the state's creditors, the following is said:

"The diminution of their revenue would not be *disguised* under the appearance of a branch of excise or customs." [b]

As might have been expected of a Scotchman, Hume's admiration of bourgeois acquisitiveness was by no means purely platonic. Starting as a poor man, he worked himself up to a very substantial annual income of many thousands of pounds; which Herr Dühring (as he is here not dealing with Petty) tactfully expresses in this way:

"Possessed of very small means to start with he succeeded, by good *domestic economy*, in reaching the position of not having to write to please anyone" [134].

Herr Dühring further says:

"He had never made the slightest concession to the influence of parties, princes or universities" [134].

There is no evidence that Hume ever entered into a literary partnership with a "Wagener",[98] but it is well known that he was an indefatigable partisan of the Whig oligarchy, which thought highly of "*Church* and state", and that in reward for these services he was given first a secretaryship in the Embassy in Paris and subsequently the incomparably more important and better-paid post of an Under-Secretary of State.

"In politics Hume was and always remained conservative and strongly monarchist in his views. For this reason he was never so bitterly denounced for heresy as Gibbon by the supporters of the established church,"

says old Schlosser.[c]

"This selfish Hume, this lying historian" reproaches the English monks with being fat, having neither wife nor family and living by begging; "but he himself never had a family or a wife, and was a great, fat fellow, fed, in considerable part, out of public money, without having merited it by any real public services"—this is what the "rude" plebeian Cobbett says. [d]

---

[a] D. Hume, op. cit., p. 367. Here and below italics by Marx.— *Ed.*

[b] Ibid., p. 379.— *Ed.*

[c] F. C. Schlosser, *Weltgeschichte für das deutsche Volk*, Vol. XVII, p. 76.— *Ed.*

[d] W. Cobbett, *A History of the Protestant "Reformation", in England and Ireland,* §§ 149, 116, 130.— *Ed.*

Hume was "in essential respects greatly superior to a Kant in the *practical management of life*" [122],

is what Herr Dühring says.

But why is Hume given such an exaggerated position in *Kritische Geschichte*? Simply because this "serious and subtle thinker" [121] has the honour of enacting the Dühring of the eighteenth century. Hume serves as proof that

"the creation of this whole branch of science" (economics) "is the achievement of a more enlightened philosophy" [123];

and similarly Hume as predecessor is the best guarantee that this whole branch of science will find its close, for the immediately foreseeable future, in that phenomenal man who has transformed the merely "more enlightened" philosophy into the absolutely luminous philosophy of reality, and with whom, just as was the case with Hume,

"the cultivation of philosophy in the narrow sense of the word is combined— something unprecedented on German soil—with scientific endeavours on behalf of the national economy" [D. Ph. 531].

Accordingly we find Hume, in any case respectable as an economist, inflated into an economic star of the first magnitude, whose importance has hitherto been denied only by the same envious people who have hitherto also so obstinately hushed up Herr Dühring's achievements, "authoritative for the epoch" [D. K. G. 1].

*   *   *

The *physiocratic* school left us in *Quesnay's Tableau économique*,[a] as everyone knows, a nut on which all former critics and historians of political economy have up to now broken their jaws in vain. This *Tableau*, which was intended to bring out clearly the physiocrats' conception of the production and circulation of a country's total wealth, remained obscure enough for the succeeding generations of economists. On this subject, too, Herr Dühring comes to finally enlighten us.

What this "economic image of the relations of production and distribution *means in Quesnay himself*," he says, can only be stated if one has "*first carefully examined* the leading ideas which are peculiar to him". All the more because these have hitherto been set forth only with "wavering indefiniteness", and their "essential features cannot be recognised" [105] even in Adam Smith.

---

a First published in 1758 in Versailles.— *Ed.*

Herr Dühring will now once and for all put an end to this traditional "superficial reporting". He then proceeds to pull the reader's leg through five whole pages, five pages in which all kinds of pretentious phrases, constant repetitions and calculated confusion are designed to conceal the awkward fact that Herr Dühring has hardly as much to tell us in regard to Quesnay's "leading ideas" [105], as the "most current textbook compilations" [109] against which he warns us so untiringly. It is "one of the most dubious sides" [111] of this introduction that here too the *Tableau*, which up to that point had only been mentioned by name, is just casually snuffled at, and then gets lost in all sorts of "reflections", such as, for example, "the difference between effort and result". Though the latter, "it is true, is not to be found completed in Quesnay's ideas", Herr Dühring will give us a fulminating example of it as soon as he comes from his lengthy introductory "effort" to his remarkably shortwinded "result" [109], that is to say, to his elucidation of the *Tableau* itself. We shall now give all, *literally all* that he feels it right to tell us of Quesnay's *Tableau*.

In his "effort" Herr Dühring says:

"It seemed to him" (Quesnay) "self-evident that the proceeds" (Herr Dühring had just spoken of the net product) "must be thought of and treated as a *money value* [105-06] ... He connected his deliberations" (!) "immediately with the *money values* which he assumed as the results of the sales of all agricultural products when they first change hands. In this way" (!) "he operates in the columns of his *Tableau* with several milliards" [106] (that is, with money values).

We have therefore learnt three times over that, in his *Tableau*, Quesnay operates with the "money values" of "agricultural products", including the money values of the "net product" or "net proceeds". Further on in the text we find:

Had Quesnay considered things from a really natural standpoint, and had he rid himself not only of regard for the precious metals and the amount of money, but also of regard for *money values*... But as it is he reckons solely with *sums of value*, and imagined" (!) "the net product in advance as *a money value*" [106].

So for the fourth and fifth time: there are only money values in the *Tableau!*

"He" (Quesnay) "obtained it" (the net product) "by deducting the expenses and *thinking*" (!) "principally" (not traditional but for that matter all the more superficial reporting) "of that value which would accrue to the landlord as rent" [106].

We have still not advanced a step; but now it is coming:

"On the other hand, *however, now also*"—this "however, now also" is a gem!—"the net product, as a natural object, enters into circulation, and in this way becomes an element which ... should serve ... to maintain the class which is described as sterile. In this the confusion can *at once*" (!) "be seen—the confusion arising from the fact that in one case it is the money value, and in the other the thing itself, which determines the course of thought" [106].

In general, it seems, *all* circulation of commodities suffers from the "confusion" that commodities enter into circulation simultaneously as "natural objects" and as "money values". But we are still moving in a circle about "money value", for

"Quesnay is anxious to avoid a double booking of the national-economic proceeds" [106].

With Herr Dühring's permission: In Quesnay's *Analysis*[a] at the foot of the *Tableau,* the various kinds of products figure as "natural objects" and above, in the *Tableau* itself, their money values are given. Subsequently Quesnay even made his famulus, the Abbé Baudeau, include the natural objects in the *Tableau* itself, *beside* their money values.[b]

After all this "effort", we at last get the "result". Listen and marvel at these words:

"Nevertheless, the inconsequence" (referring to the role assigned by Quesnay to the landlords) "*at once* becomes clear when we enquire *what becomes of the net product, which has been appropriated as rent, in the course of the national-economic circulation.* In regard to this the physiocrats and the *economic Tableau* could offer nothing but confused and arbitrary conceptions, ascending to mysticism" [110].

All's well that ends well. So Herr Dühring does not know "what becomes of the net product, which has been appropriated as rent, in the course of the national-economic circulation" (represented in the *Tableau*). To him, the *Tableau* is the "squaring of the circle" [110]. By his own confession, he does not understand the ABC of physiocracy. After all the beating about the bush, the dropping of buckets into an empty well, the hying hither and thither, the harlequinades, episodes, diversions, repetitions and stupefying mix-ups whose sole purpose was to prepare us for the imposing conclusion, "what the *Tableau* means in Quesnay

---

[a] F. Quesnay, *Analyse du Tableau économique.* It was first published in 1766 in the physiocrat *Journal de l'agriculture, du commerce et des finances.* Marx quotes from *Physiocrates. Avec une introduction sur la doctrine des physiocrates, des commentaires et des notices historiques,* par E. Daire. Part One, pp. 57-66.—*Ed.*

[b] Ibid., Part Two, pp. 864-67. Marx refers to the last paragraph of the Abbé Baudeau's *Explication du Tableau économique.* It was published for the first time in 1767 in the physiocrat journal *Éphémérides du citoyen.*—*Ed.*

himself" [105]—after all this Herr Dühring's shamefaced confession that *he himself does not know.*

Once he has shaken off this painful secret, this Horatian "black care"[a] which sat hunched on his back during his ride through the land of the physiocrats, our "serious and subtle thinker" blows another merry blast on his trumpet, as follows:

"The lines which Quesnay draws here and there" (in all there are just five of them!) "in his otherwise fairly simple" (!) "*Tableau,* and which are meant to represent the circulation of the net product", make one wonder whether "these whimsical combinations of columns" may not be suffused with fantastic mathematics; they are reminiscent of Quesnay's attempts to square the circle [110]—and so forth.

As Herr Dühring, by his own admission, was unable to understand these lines in spite of their simplicity, he had to follow his favourite procedure of *casting suspicion* on them. And now he can confidently deliver the *coup de grâce* to the vexatious *Tableau*:

"We have considered the net product in this its *most dubious aspect*" [111], etc.

So the confession he was constrained to make that he does not understand the first word about the *Tableau économique* and the "role" played by the net product which figures in it—that is what Herr Dühring calls "the most dubious aspect of the net product"! What grim humour!

But in order that our readers may not be left in the same cruel ignorance about Quesnay's *Tableau* as those necessarily are who receive their economic wisdom "first hand" from Herr Dühring, we will explain it briefly as follows[b]:

As is known, the physiocrats divide society into three classes: (1) The productive, i.e., the class which is actually engaged in agriculture—tenant-farmers and agricultural labourers; they are called productive, because their labour yields a surplus: rent. (2) The class which appropriates this surplus, including the landowners and their retainers, the prince and in general all officials paid by the state, and finally also the Church in its special character as appropriator of tithes. For the sake of brevity, in what follows we call the first class simply "farmers", and the second class "landlords". (3) The industrial or sterile class; sterile because, in the view of the physiocrats, it adds to the raw materials delivered

---

[a] "Black care" (atra Cura)—an expression from Horace's ode. (See Horatius, *Carmina,* Liber III, carmen I.)—*Ed.*

[b] See the diagram (formula) of Quesnay's *Tableau économique* on page 239 of this volume.—*Ed.*

to it by the productive class only as much value as it consumes in means of subsistence supplied to it by that same class. Quesnay's *Tableau* was intended to portray how the total annual product of a country (concretely, France) circulates among these three classes and facilitates annual reproduction.

The first premise of the *Tableau* was that the farming system and with it large-scale agriculture, in the sense in which this term was understood in Quesnay's time, had been generally introduced, Normandy, Picardy, Île-de-France and a few other French provinces serving as prototypes. The farmer therefore appears as the real leader in agriculture, as he represents in the *Tableau* the whole productive (agricultural) class and pays the landlord a rent in money. An invested capital or inventory of ten milliard livres is assigned to the farmers as a whole; of this sum, one-fifth, or two milliards, is the working capital which has to be replaced every year—this figure too was estimated on the basis of the best-managed farms in the provinces mentioned above.

Further premises: (1) that for the sake of simplicity constant prices and simple reproduction prevail; (2) that all circulation which takes place solely within one class is excluded, and that only circulation between class and class is taken into account; (3) that all purchases and sales taking place between class and class in the course of the industrial year are combined in a single total sum. Lastly, it must be borne in mind that in Quesnay's time in France, as was more or less the case throughout Europe, the home industry of the peasant families satisfied by far the greater portion of their needs other than food, and is therefore taken for granted here as supplementary to agriculture.

The starting-point of the *Tableau* is the total harvest, the gross product of the annual yield of the soil, which is consequently placed as the first item—or the "total reproduction" of the country, in this case France. The magnitude of value of this gross product is estimated on the basis of the average prices of agricultural products among the trading nations. It comes to five milliard livres, a sum which roughly expresses the money value of the gross agricultural production of France based on such statistical estimates as were then possible. This and nothing else is the reason why in his *Tableau* Quesnay "operates with several milliards" [106], to be precise, with five milliards, and not with five *livres tournois*.[99]

The whole gross product, of a value of five milliards, is therefore in the hands of the productive class, that is, in the first place the farmers, who have produced it by advancing an annual working capital of two milliards, which corresponds to an invested capital of ten milliards. The agricultural products—foodstuffs, raw materials, etc.—which are required for the replacement of the working capital, including therefore the maintenance of all persons directly engaged in agriculture, are taken *in natura*[a] from the total harvest and expended for the purpose of new agricultural production. Since, as we have seen, constant prices and simple reproduction on a given scale are assumed, the money value of the portion which is thus taken from the gross product is equal to two milliard livres. This portion, therefore, does not enter into general circulation. For, as we have noted, circulation which takes place only *within* a particular class, and not between one class and another, is excluded from the *Tableau*.

After the replacement of the working capital out of the gross product there remains a surplus of three milliards, of which two are in means of subsistence and one in raw materials. The rent which the farmers have to pay to the landlords is however only two-thirds of this sum, equal to two milliards. It will soon be seen why it is only these two milliards which figure under the heading of "net product" or "net income" [106].

But in addition to the "total reproduction" of agriculture amounting in value to five milliards, of which three milliards enter into general circulation, there is also in the hands of the farmers, *before* the movement described in the *Tableau* begins, the whole *"pécule"*[b] of the nation, two milliards of cash money. This comes about in the following way.

As the total harvest is the starting-point of the *Tableau,* this starting-point also forms the closing point of an economic year, for example, of the year 1758, from which point a new economic year begins. During the course of this new year, 1759, the portion of the gross product destined to enter into circulation is distributed among the two other classes through the medium of a number of individual payments, purchases and sales. These movements, separated, following each other in succession, and stretching over a whole year, are however—as was bound to happen in any case in the *Tableau*—combined into a few characteristic transactions each of which embraces a whole year's operations at once. This, then, is how at the close of the year 1758 there has flowed back to the farmer class the money paid by it to the landlords as rent for the year 1757 (the *Tableau* itself will show how this comes about),

---

[a] In kind.— *Ed.*
[b] Hoard.— *Ed.*

amounting to two milliards; so that the farmer class can again throw this sum into circulation in 1759. Since, however, that sum, as Quesnay observes, is much larger than is required in reality for the total circulation of the country (France), inasmuch as there is a constant succession of separate payments, the two milliard livres in the hands of the farmers represent the total money in circulation in the nation.

The class of landlords drawing rent first appears, as is the case sometimes even today, in the role of receivers of payments. On Quesnay's assumption the landlords proper receive only four-sevenths of the two milliards of rent: two-sevenths go to the government, and one -seventh to the receivers of tithes. In Quesnay's day the Church was the biggest landlord in France and in addition received the tithes on all other landed property.

The working capital (*avances annuelles*[a]) advanced by the "sterile" class in the course of a whole year .consists of raw materials to the value of one milliard—only raw materials, because tools, machinery, etc., are included among the products of that class itself. The many different roles, however, played by such products in the industrial enterprises of this class do not concern the *Tableau* any more than the circulation of commodities and money which takes place exclusively within that class. The wages for the labour by which the sterile class transforms the raw materials into manufactured goods are equal to the value of the means of subsistence which it receives in part directly from the productive class, and in part indirectly, through the landlords. Although it is itself divided into capitalists and wage-workers, it forms, according to Quesnay's basic conception, an integral class which is in the pay of the productive class and of the landlords. The total industrial production, and consequently also its total circulation, which is distributed over the year following the harvest, is likewise combined into a single whole. It is therefore assumed that at the beginning of the movement set out in the *Tableau* the annual commodity production of the sterile class is entirely in its hands, and consequently that its whole working capital, consisting of raw materials to the value of one milliard, has been converted into goods to the value of two milliards, one-half of which represents the price of the means of subsistence consumed during this transformation. An objection might be raised here: Surely the sterile class also uses up industrial products

---

[a] Annual advances.— *Ed.*

for its own domestic needs; where are these shown, if its own total product passes through circulation to the other classes? This is the answer we are given: The sterile class not only itself consumes a portion of its own commodities, but in addition it strives to retain as much of the rest as possible. It therefore sells the commodities thrown by it into circulation above their real value, and must do this, as we have evaluated these commodities at the total value of their production. This, however, does not affect the figures of the *Tableau*, for the two other classes receive manufactured goods only to the value of their total production.

So now we know the economic position of the three different classes at the beginning of the movement set out in the *Tableau*.

The productive class, after its working capital has been replaced in kind, still has three milliards of the gross product of agriculture and two milliards in money. The landlord class appears only with its rent claim of two milliards on the productive class. The sterile class has two milliards in manufactured goods. Circulation passing between only two of these three classes is called imperfect by the physiocrats; circulation which takes place between all three classes is called perfect.

Now for the economic *Tableau* itself.

First (imperfect) *Circulation:* The farmers pay the landlords the rent due to them with two milliards of money, without receiving anything in return. With one of these two milliards the landlords buy means of subsistence from the farmers, to whom one-half of the money expended by them in the payment of rent thus returns.

In his *Analyse du Tableau économique* Quesnay does not make further mention of the state, which receives two-sevenths, or of the Church, which receives one-seventh, of the land rent, as their social roles are generally known. In regard to the landlord class proper, however, he says that its expenditure (in which that of all its retainers is included) is, at least as regards the great bulk of it, unfruitful expenditure, with the exception of that small portion which is used "for the maintenance and improvement of their lands and the raising of their standard of cultivation". But by "natural law" their proper function consists precisely in "provision for the good management and expenditure for the maintenance of their patrimony in good repair",[a] or, as is explained further on, in making the *avances foncières*, that is, outlays for the preparation of the soil and provision of all equipment needed by the farms,

---

[a] F. Quesnay, *Analyse du Tableau économique.* In: *Physiocrates,* Part One, p. 68.— *Ed.*

which enable the farmer to devote his whole capital exclusively to the business of actual cultivation.

Second (perfect) *Circulation*: With the second milliard of money still remaining in their hands, the landlords purchase manufactured goods from the sterile class, and the latter, with the money thus obtained, purchases from the farmers means of subsistence for the same sum.

Third (imperfect) *Circulation*: The farmers buy from the sterile class, with one milliard of money, a corresponding amount of manufactured goods; a large part of these goods consists of agricultural implements and other means of production required in agriculture. The sterile class returns the same amount of money to the farmers, buying raw materials with it to the value of one milliard to replace its own working capital. Thus the two milliards expended by the farmers in payment of rent have flowed back to them, and the movement is closed. And therewith also the great riddle is solved:

"what becomes of the net product, which has been appropriated as rent, in the course of the economic circulation?" [110.]

We saw above that at the starting-point of the process there was a surplus of three milliards in the hands of the productive class. Of these, only two were paid as net product in the form of rent to the landlords. The third milliard of the surplus constitutes the interest on the total invested capital of the farmers, that is, ten per cent on ten milliards. They do not receive this interest—this should be carefully noted—from circulation; it exists *in natura* in their hands, and they realise it only in circulation, by thus converting it into manufactured goods of equal value.

If it were not for this interest, the farmer—the chief agent in agriculture—would not advance the capital for investment in it. Already from this standpoint, according to the physiocrats, the appropriation by the farmer of that portion of the agricultural *surplus proceeds* which represents interest is as necessary a condition of reproduction as the farmer class itself; and hence this element cannot be put in the category of the national "net product" or "net income"; for the latter is characterised precisely by the fact that it is consumable without any regard to the immediate needs of national reproduction. This fund of one milliard, however, serves, according to Quesnay, for the most part to cover the repairs which become necessary in the course of the year, and the partial renewals of invested capital; further, as a reserve fund against accidents, and lastly, where possible, for the enlargement of the invested and working capital, as well as for the improvement of the soil and extension of cultivation.

The whole process is certainly "fairly simple" [110]. There enter into circulation: from the farmers, two milliards in money for the payment of rent, and three milliards in products, of which two-thirds are means of subsistence and one-third raw materials; from the sterile class, two milliards in manufactured goods. Of the means of subsistence amounting to two milliards, one half is consumed by the landlords and their retainers, the other half by the sterile class in payment for its labour. The raw materials to the value of one milliard replace the working capital of this latter class. Of the manufactured goods in circulation, amounting to two milliards, one half goes to the landlords and the other to the farmers, for whom it is only a converted form of the interest, which accrues at first hand from agricultural reproduction, on their invested capital. The money thrown into circulation by the farmer in payment of rent flows back to him, however, through the sale of his products, and thus the same process can take place again in the next economic year.

And now we must admire Herr Dühring's "really critical" [D. Ph. 404] exposition, which is so infinitely superior to the "traditional superficial reporting" [D. K. G. 105]. After mysteriously pointing out to us five times in succession how hazardous it was for Quesnay to operate in the *Tableau* with mere money values—which moreover turned out not to be true—he finally reaches the conclusion that, when he asks,

"what becomes of the net product, which has been appropriated as rent, in the course of the national-economic circulation?"—the economic *Tableau* "could offer nothing but confused and arbitrary conceptions, ascending to mysticism" [110].

We have seen that the *Tableau*—this both simple and, for its time, brilliant depiction of the annual process of reproduction through the medium of circulation—gives a very exact answer to the question of what becomes of this net product in the course of national-economic circulation. Thus once again the "mysticism" and the "confused and arbitrary conceptions" are left simply and solely with Herr Dühring, as "the most dubious aspect" and the sole "net product" [111] of his study of physiocracy.

Herr Dühring is just as familiar with the historical influence of the physiocrats as with their theories.

"With Turgot," he teaches us, "physiocracy in France came to an end both in practice and in theory" [120].

Total reproduction: 5 milliards

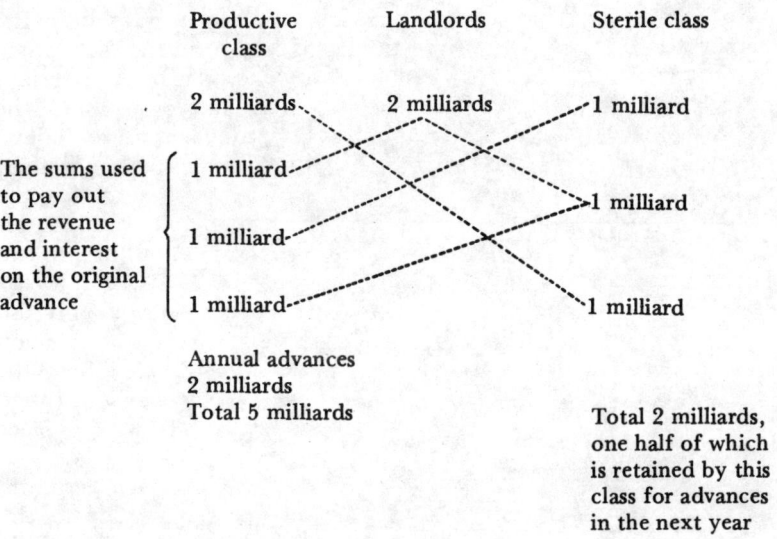

	Productive class	Landlords	Sterile class

The sums used to pay out the revenue and interest on the original advance

{ 2 milliards — 2 milliards — 1 milliard

1 milliard —

1 milliard —

1 milliard — 1 milliard

1 milliard — 1 milliard }

Annual advances
2 milliards
Total 5 milliards

Total 2 milliards, one half of which is retained by this class for advances in the next year

Diagram (formula) of Quesnay's *Tableau économique*

That Mirabeau, however, was essentially a physiocrat in his economic views; that he was the leading economic authority in the Constituent Assembly of 1789; that this Assembly in its economic reforms translated from theory into practice a substantial portion of the physiocrats' principles, and in particular laid a heavy tax also on land rent, the net product appropriated by the landowners "without consideration"—all this does not exist for "a" Dühring.—

Just as the long stroke drawn through the years 1691 to 1752 removed all of Hume's predecessors, so another stroke obliterated Sir James Steuart, who came between Hume and Adam Smith. There is not a syllable in Herr Dühring's "enterprise" [9] on Steuart's great work, which, apart from its historical importance, permanently enriched the domain of political economy.[a] But, instead, Herr Dühring applies to him the most abusive epithet in his vocabulary, and says that he was *"a professor"* [136] in Adam Smith's time. Unfortunately this insinuation is a pure invention. Steuart, as a matter of fact, was a large landowner in Scotland, who was banished from Great Britain for alleged complicity in the Stuart plot and through long residence and his journeys on the Continent made himself familiar with economic conditions in various countries.

In a word: according to the *Kritische Geschichte* the only value all earlier economists had was to serve either as "rudiments" [1] of Herr Dühring's "authoritative" [1] and deeper foundations, or, because of their unsound doctrines, as a foil to the latter. In political economy, however, there are also some heroes who represent not only "rudiments" of the "deeper foundation" [D. C. 11], but "principles" [5] from which this foundation, as was prescribed in Herr Dühring's natural philosophy, is not "developed" [353] but actually "composed": for example, the "incomparably great and eminent" [16] *List*, who, for the benefit of German manufacturers, puffed up the "more subtle" mercantilistic teachings of a Ferrier and others into "mightier" words; also *Carey* who reveals the true essence of his wisdom in the following sentence:

"Ricardo's system is one of discords ... its whole tends to the production of hostility among classes ... his book is the true manual of the demagogue, who seeks power by means of agrarianism, war, and plunder"[b];

---

[a] J. Steuart, *An Inquiry into the Principles of Political Oeconomy.*— Ed.
[b] H. C. Carey, *The Past, the Present, and the Future*, pp. 74-75.— Ed.

and, at long last, the London City Confucius,[a] *Macleod.*

People who want to study the history of political economy in the present and immediately foreseeable future will certainly be on much safer ground if they make themselves acquainted with the "watery products", "commonplaces" and "beggars' soup" [14] of the "most current text-book compilations" [109], rather than rely on Herr Dühring's "historical depiction in the grand style" [556].

* * *

What, then, is the final result of our analysis of Dühring's "very own system" of political economy? Nothing, except the fact that with all the great words and the still more mighty promises we are just as much duped as we were in the *Philosophy.* His theory of value, this "touchstone of the worth of economic systems" [499], amounts to this: that by value Herr Dühring understands five totally different and directly contradictory things, and, therefore, to put it at its best, himself does not know what he wants. The "natural laws of all economics" [D. C. 4], ushered in with such pomp, prove to be merely universally familiar and often not even properly understood platitudes of the worst description. The sole explanation of economic facts which his "very own" system can give us is that they are the result of "force", a term with which the philistine of all nations has for thousands of years consoled himself for everything unpleasant that happens to him, and which leaves us just where we were. Instead however of investigating the origin and effects of this force, Herr Dühring expects us to content ourselves gratefully with the mere *word* "force" as the last final cause and ultimate explanation of all economic phenomena. Compelled further to elucidate capitalist exploitation of labour, he first represents it in a general way as based on taxes and price surcharges, thereby completely appropriating the Proudhonian "deduction" (*prélèvement*), and then proceeding to explain it in detail by means of Marx's theory of surplus-labour, surplus-product and surplus-value. In this way he manages to bring about a happy reconciliation of two totally contradictory modes of outlook, by copying down both without taking his breath. And just

---

[a] Instead of Confucius, which appears in the MS of the tenth chapter written by Marx, the German printed edition of *Anti-Dühring* has the homophonous Confusius (confuser).— *Ed.*

as in philosophy he could not find enough hard words for the very Hegel whom he was so constantly exploiting and at the same time emasculating, so in the *Kritische Geschichte* the most baseless calumniation of Marx only serves to conceal the fact that everything in the *Cursus* about capital and labour which makes any sense at all is likewise an emasculated plagiarism of Marx. His ignorance, which in the *Cursus* puts the "large landowner" at the beginning of the history of the civilised peoples, and knows not a word of the common ownership of land in the tribal and village communities, which is the real starting-point of all history—this ignorance, at the present day almost incomprehensible, is well-nigh surpassed by the ignorance which, in the *Kritische Geschichte*, thinks not little of itself because of "the universal breadth of its historical survey" [2], and of which we have given only a few deterrent examples. In a word: first the colossal "effort" of self-admiration, of charlatan blasts on his own trumpet, of promises each surpassing the other; and then the "result" [109]— exactly nil.

Part III

SOCIALISM

I. HISTORICAL

We saw in the "Introduction"* how the French philosophers of the eighteenth century, the forerunners of the Revolution, appealed to reason as the sole judge of all that is. A rational government, rational society, were to be founded; everything that ran counter to eternal reason was to be remorselessly done away with. We saw also that this eternal reason was in reality nothing but the idealised understanding of the eighteenth century citizen, just then evolving into the bourgeois. The French Revolution had realised this rational society and government. But, the new order of things, rational enough as compared with earlier conditions, turned out to be by no means absolutely rational. The state based upon reason completely collapsed. Rousseau's Contrat Social had found its realisation in the Reign of Terror, from which the bourgeoisie, who had lost confidence in their own political capacity, had taken refuge first in the corruption of the Directorate, and, finally, under the wing of the Napoleonic despotism.[101] The promised eternal peace was turned into an endless war of conquest. The society based upon reason had fared no better. The antagonism between rich and poor, instead of dissolving into general prosperity, had become intensified by the removal of the guild and other privileges, which had to some extent bridged it over, and by the removal of the charitable institutions of the Church. The development of industry upon a capitalistic basis made poverty and misery of the working masses conditions of existence of society. The number of crimes increased

---

* Cf. *Philosophy* I.[100]

from year to year. Formerly, the feudal vices had openly stalked about in broad daylight; though not eradicated, they were now at any rate thrust into the background. In their stead, the bourgeois vices, hitherto practised in secret, began to blossom all the more luxuriantly. Trade became to a greater and greater extent cheating. The "fraternity" of the revolutionary motto [102] was realised in the chicanery and rivalries of the battle of competition. Oppression by force was replaced by corruption; the sword, as the first social lever, by gold. The right of the first night was transferred from the feudal lords to the bourgeois manufacturers. Prostitution increased to an extent never heard of. Marriage itself remained, as before, the legally recognised form, the official cloak of prostitution, and, moreover, was supplemented by rich crops of adultery. In a word, compared with the splendid promises of the philosophers, the social and political institutions born of the "triumph of reason" were bitterly disappointing caricatures. All that was wanting was the men to formulate this disappointment, and they came with the turn of the century. In 1802 Saint-Simon's Geneva letters appeared; in 1808 appeared Fourier's first work, [103] although the groundwork of his theory dated from 1799; on January 1, 1800, Robert Owen undertook the direction of New Lanark.[a]

At this time, however, the capitalist mode of production, and with it the antagonism between the bourgeoisie and the pro-letariat, was still very incompletely developed. Modern industry, which had just arisen in England, was still unknown in France. But modern industry develops, on the one hand, the conflicts which make absolutely necessary a revolution in the mode of production, conflicts not only between the classes begotten of it, but also between the very productive forces and the forms of exchange created by it. And, on the other hand, it develops, in these very gigantic productive forces, the means of ending these conflicts. If, therefore, about the year 1800, the conflicts arising from the new social order were only just beginning to take shape, this holds still more fully as to the means of ending them. The propertyless masses of Paris, during the Reign of Terror, were able for a moment to gain the mastery. But, in doing so, they only proved how impossible it was for their domination to last under the conditions then obtaining. The proletariat, which then for the first time evolved itself from these propertyless masses as the

---

[a] See this volume, p. 249.— Ed.

nucleus of a new class, as yet quite incapable of independent political action, appeared as an oppressed, suffering estate, to whom, in its incapacity to help itself, help could, at best, be brought in from without or down from above.

This historical situation also dominated the founders of socialism. To the crude conditions of capitalist production and the crude class conditions corresponded crude theories. The solution of the social problems, which as yet lay hidden in undeveloped economic conditions, the utopians attempted to evolve out of the human brain. Society presented nothing but wrongs; to remove these was the task of reason. It was necessary, then, to discover a new and more perfect system of social order and to impose this upon society from without by propaganda, and, wherever it was possible, by the example of model experiments. These new social systems were foredoomed as utopian; the more completely they were worked out in detail, the more they could not avoid drifting off into pure fantasies.

These facts once established, we need not dwell a moment longer upon this side of the question, now wholly belonging to the past. We can leave it to the literary small fry *à la* Dühring to solemnly quibble over these fantasies, which today only make us smile, and to crow over the superiority of their own bald reasoning, as compared with such "insanity" [D. K. G. 276, 278, 283]. For ourselves, we delight in the stupendously grand thoughts and germs of thought that everywhere break out through their fantastic covering, and to which these philistines are blind.

Already in his Geneva letters, Saint-Simon lays down the proposition that

"all men ought to work".[a]

In the same work he recognises also that the Reign of Terror was the reign of the non-possessing masses.

"See," says he to them, "what happened in France at the time when your comrades held sway there; they brought about a famine."

But to recognise the French Revolution as a class war between nobility, bourgeoisie, and the non-possessors, was, in the year 1802, a most pregnant discovery. In 1816, he declares that politics is the science of production, and foretells the complete absorption

---

[a] Here and below Engels quotes the second letter from H. Saint-Simon's *Lettres d'un habitant de Genève à ses contemporains* (see [N.] G. Hubbard, *Saint-Simon. Sa vie et ses travaux*, pp. 143 and 135).— *Ed.*

of politics by economics.[a] The knowledge that economic conditions are the basis of political institutions appears here only in embryo. Yet what is here already very plainly expressed is the idea of the future conversion of political rule over men into an administration of things and a direction of processes of production—that is to say, the "abolition of the state", about which recently there has been so much noise. Saint-Simon shows the same superiority over his contemporaries, when in 1814,[b] immediately after the entry of the allies into Paris,[104] and again in 1815,[c] during the Hundred Days' War,[105] he proclaims the alliance of France with England, and then of both these countries with Germany, as the only guarantee for the prosperous development and peace of Europe. To preach to the French in 1815 an alliance with the victors of Waterloo at any rate required somewhat more courage than to declare a war of tittle-tattle on German professors.[106]

If in Saint-Simon we find a comprehensive breadth of view, by virtue of which almost all the ideas of later Socialists, that are not strictly economic, are found in him in embryo, we find in Fourier a criticism of the existing conditions of society, genuinely French and witty, but not upon that account any the less thorough. Fourier takes the bourgeoisie, their inspired prophets before the Revolution, and their interested eulogists after it, at their own word. He lays bare remorselessly the material and moral misery of the bourgeois world. He confronts it with the philosophers' dazzling promises of a society in which reason alone should reign, of a civilisation in which happiness should be universal, of an illimitable human perfectibility, and with the rose-coloured phraseology of the bourgeois ideologists of his time. He points out how everywhere the most pitiful reality corresponds with the most high-sounding phrases, and he overwhelms this hopeless fiasco of phrases with his mordant sarcasm. Fourier is not only a critic; his imperturbably serene nature makes him a satirist, and assuredly one of the greatest satirists of all time. He depicts, with equal

---

[a] Engels refers to a passage from: H. Saint-Simon, *Lettres à un américain. Huitième lettre. Recherche d'un principe générale en politique.* In: [N.] G. Hubbard, op. cit., pp. 155-57.—*Ed.*

[b] Engels refers to the work written by H. Saint-Simon jointly with his pupil A. Thierry: *De la réorganisation de la société européenne, ou De la nécessité et des moyens de rassembler les peuples de l'Europe en un seul corps politique, en conservant à chacun son indépendance nationale* (see [N.] G. Hubbard, op. cit., pp. 149-54 and 68-76).— *Ed.*

[c] Engels refers to the work written by H. Saint-Simon and A. Thierry: *Opinion sur les mesures à prendre contre la coalition de 1815* (see [N.] G. Hubbard, op. cit., pp. 68-76).— *Ed.*

power and charm, the swindling speculations that blossomed out upon the downfall of the Revolution, and the shopkeeping spirit prevalent in, and characteristic of, French commerce at that time. Still more masterly is his criticism of the bourgeois form of the relations between the sexes, and the position of woman in bourgeois society. He was the first to declare that in any given society the degree of woman's emancipation is the natural measure of the general emancipation.[107] But Fourier is at his greatest in his conception of the history of society. He divides its whole course, thus far, into four stages of evolution—savagery, the patriarchate, barbarism, civilisation. This last is identical with the so-called bourgeois society of today. He proves

"that the civilised stage raises every vice practised by barbarism in a simple fashion into a form of existence, complex, ambiguous, equivocal, hypocritical",[a]

that civilisation moves in a "vicious circle", in contradictions which it constantly reproduces without being able to solve them; hence it constantly arrives at the very opposite to that which it wants to attain, or pretends to want to attain,[b] so that, e.g.,

"under civilisation *poverty is born of superabundance itself*".[c]

Fourier, as we see, uses the dialectic method in the same masterly way as his contemporary, Hegel. Using these same dialectics, he argues against the talk about illimitable human perfectibility, that every historical phase has its period of ascent and also its period of descent,[d] and he applies this observation to the future of the whole human race. As Kant introduced into natural science the idea of the ultimate destruction of the earth,[e] Fourier introduced into historical science that of the ultimate destruction of the human race.—

Whilst in France the hurricane of the Revolution swept over the land, in England a quieter, but not on that account less tremendous, revolution was going on. Steam and the new tool-making machinery were transforming manufacture into modern industry, and thus revolutionising the whole foundation of

---

[a] Ch. Fourier, *Théorie de l'unité universelle*, Vols. I and IV. In: *Oeuvres complètes*, Vol. 2, pp. 78-79 and Vol. 5, pp. 213-14.—*Ed.*

[b] See Ch. Fourier, *Le Nouveau Monde industriel et sociétaire, ou Invention du procédé d'industrie attrayante et naturelle distribuée en séries passionnées*. In: *Oeuvres complètes*, Vol. 6, pp. 27-46, 390; Vol. 1, p. 202.—*Ed.*

[c] *Ibid.*, Vol. 6, p. 35.—*Ed.*

[d] *Ibid.*, Vol. 1, p. 50 *et seqq.*—*Ed.*

[e] See this volume, p. 12.—*Ed.*

bourgeois society. The sluggish march of development of the manufacturing period changed into a veritable storm and stress period of production. With constantly increasing swiftness the splitting-up of society into large capitalists and non-possessing proletarians went on. Between these, instead of the former stable middle class, an unstable mass of artisans and small shopkeepers, the most fluctuating portion of the population, now led a precarious existence. The new mode of production was, as yet, only at the beginning of its period of ascent; as yet it was the normal method of production—the only one possible under existing conditions. Nevertheless, even then it was producing crying social abuses—the herding together of a homeless population in the worst quarters of the large towns; the loosening of all traditional moral bonds, of patriarchal subordination, of family relations; overwork, especially of women and children, to a frightful extent; complete demoralisation of the working class, suddenly flung into altogether new conditions. At this juncture there came forward as a reformer a manufacturer 29 years old—a man of almost sublime, child-like simplicity of character, and at the same time one of the few born leaders of men. Robert Owen had adopted the teaching of the materialistic philosophers: that man's character is the product, on the one hand, of heredity; on the other, of the environment of the individual during his lifetime, and especially during his period of development. In the industrial revolution most of his class saw only chaos and confusion, and the opportunity of fishing in these troubled waters and making large fortunes quickly. He saw in it the opportunity of putting into practice his favourite theory, and so of bringing order out of chaos. He had already tried it with success, as superintendent of more than five hundred men in a Manchester factory. From 1800 to 1829, he directed the great cotton-mill at New Lanark, in Scotland, as managing partner, along the same lines, but with greater freedom of action and with a success that made him a European reputation. A population, originally consisting of the most diverse and, for the most part, very demoralised elements, a population that gradually grew to 2,500, he turned into a model colony, in which drunkenness, police, magistrates, lawsuits, poor laws, charity, were unknown. And all this simply by placing the people in conditions worthy of human beings, and especially by carefully bringing up the rising generation. He was the founder of infant schools, and introduced them first at New Lanark. At the age of two the children came to school, where they enjoyed themselves so much that they could scarcely be got home again.

Whilst his competitors worked their people thirteen or fourteen hours a day, in New Lanark the working-day was only ten and a half hours. When a crisis in cotton stopped work for four months, his workers received their full wages all the time. And with all this the business more than doubled in value, and to the last yielded large profits to its proprietors.

In spite of all this, Owen was not content. The existence which he secured for his workers was, in his eyes, still far from being worthy of human beings.

"The people were slaves at my mercy."

The relatively favourable conditions in which he had placed them were still far from allowing a rational development of the character and of the intellect in all directions, much less of the free exercise of all their faculties.

"And yet the working part of this population of 2,500 persons was producing as much real wealth for society, as, less than half a century before, it would have required the working part of a population of 600,000 to create. I asked myself what became of the difference between the wealth consumed by 2,500 persons and that which would have been consumed by 600,000."

The answer was clear. It had been used to pay the proprietors of the establishment 5 per cent on the capital they had laid out, in addition to over £300,000 (6,000,000 marks) clear profit. And that which held for New Lanark held to a still greater extent for all the factories in England.

"If this new wealth had not been created, by machinery, the wars in opposition to Napoleon, and to support the aristocratic principles of society, could not have been maintained. And yet this new power was the creation of the working class." [108]

To them, therefore, the fruits of this new power belonged. The newly-created gigantic productive forces hitherto used only to enrich individuals and to enslave the masses, offered to Owen the foundations for a reconstruction of society; they were destined, as the common property of all, to be worked for the common good of all.

Owen's communism was based upon this purely business foundation, the outcome, so to say, of commercial calculation. Throughout, it maintained this practical character. Thus, in 1823, Owen proposed the relief of the distress in Ireland by communist colonies, and drew up complete estimates of costs of founding them, yearly expenditure, and probable revenue.ᵃ And in his definite plan for the future, the technical working out of details is managed with such practical knowledge that the Owen method of social reform once accepted, there is from the practical point of view little to be said against the actual arrangement of details.

His advance in the direction of communism was the turning-point in Owen's life. As long as he was simply a philanthropist, he was rewarded with nothing but wealth, applause, honour, and glory. He was the most popular man in Europe. Not only men of his own class, but statesmen and princes listened to him approvingly. But when he came out with his communist theories, that was quite another thing. Three great obstacles seemed to him especially to block the path to social reform: private property, religion, the present form of marriage. He knew what confronted him if he attacked these—outlawry, excommunication from official society, the loss of his whole social position. But nothing of this prevented him from attacking them without fear of consequences, and what he had foreseen happened. Banished from official society, with a conspiracy of silence against him in the press, ruined by his unsuccessful communist experiments in America, in which he sacrificed all his fortune, he turned directly to the working class and continued working in their midst for thirty years. Every social movement, every real advance in England on behalf of the workers links itself on to the name of Robert Owen. He forced through in 1819, after five years' fighting, the first law limiting the hours of labour for women and children in factories.[109] He was president of the first congress at which all the Trade Unions of England united in a single great trade association.[110] He introduced as transition measures to the complete communistic organisation of society, on the one hand, co-operative societies for retail trade and production. These have since that time, at least, given practical proof that the merchant and the manufacturer are socially quite unnecessary. On the other hand, he introduced labour bazaars for the exchange of the products of labour through the medium of labour-notes, whose unit was a single hour of work[111]; institutions necessarily doomed to failure, but completely anticipating Proudhon's bank of exchange[112] of a much later period, and differing entirely from this in that they did not claim to be the panacea for all social ills,

---

ᵃ R. Owen, *Report of the Proceedings at the Several Public.Meetings, held in Dublin ... On the 18th March, 12th April, 19th April and 3rd May*—Ed.

but only a first step towards a much more radical revolution of society.

These are the men on whom the sovereign Herr Dühring looks down, from the height of his "final and ultimate truth" [D. Ph. 2], with a contempt of which we have given a few examples in the Introduction. And in one respect this contempt is not devoid of adequate reason: for its basis is, in essence, a really frightful ignorance of the works of the three utopians. Thus Herr Dühring says of Saint-Simon that

"his basic idea was, in essentials, correct, and apart from some one-sided aspects, even today provides the directing impulse towards real creation" [D. K. G. 246].

But although Herr Dühring does actually seem to have had some of Saint-Simon's works in his hands, our search through the twenty-seven relevant printed pages for Saint-Simon's "basic idea" is just as fruitless as our earlier search for what Quesnay's *Tableau* "meant in Quesnay himself" [105], and in the end we have to allow ourselves to be put off with the phrase

"that imagination and philanthropic fervour ... along with the extravagant fantasy that goes with it, dominated the whole of Saint-Simon's thought complex" [252]!

As regards Fourier, all that Herr Dühring knows or takes into account is his fantasies of the future, painted in romantic detail. This of course "is far more important" for establishing Herr Dühring's infinite superiority over Fourier than an examination of how the latter "attempts *occasionally* to criticise actual conditions" [282]. Occasionally! In fact, almost every page of his works scintillates with sparkling satire and criticism aimed at the wretchedness of our vaunted civilisation. It is like saying that Herr Dühring only "occasionally" declares Herr Dühring to be the greatest thinker of all time. And as for the twelve pages devoted to Robert Owen, Herr Dühring has absolutely no other source for them than the miserable biography of the philistine Sargant,[a] who also did not know Owen's most important works—on marriage and the communist system.[b] Herr Dühring can therefore go the length of boldly asserting that we should not "assume any clear-cut communism" [301] in Owen. Had Herr Dühring ever even fingered Owen's *Book of the New Moral World*,[c] he

---

  [a] W. L. Sargant, *Robert Owen, and His Social Philosophy.—Ed.*

  [b] *The Marriage System of the New Moral World* (1838), *The Book of the New Moral World* (1836-44) and *The Revolution in the Mind and Practice of the Human Race* (1849).— *Ed.*

  [c] The title is given in English in the manuscript.— *Ed.*

would most assuredly have found clearly expressed in it not only
the most clear-cut communism possible, with equal obligation to
labour and equal rights in the product—equal according to age, as
Owen always adds—but also the most comprehensive building
project of the future communist community, with its groundplan,
front and side and bird's-eye views. But if one limits one's
"first-hand study of the writings of the representatives of socialist idea-complexes" [XIII] to a knowledge of the title and at
most the *motto* [294] of a small number of these works, like Herr
Dühring, the only thing left to do is make such a stupid and
purely fantastic assertion. Owen did not only preach "clear-cut
communism" [301]; for five years (at the end of the thirties and
beginning of the forties) he put it into practice in the Harmony
Hall Colony[113] in Hampshire, the clear-cut quality of whose
communism left nothing to be desired. I myself was acquainted
with several former members of this communist model experiment. But Sargant knew absolutely nothing of all this, or of any of
Owen's activities between 1836 and 1850, and consequently Herr
Dühring's "more profound historical work" [XIII] is also left in
pitch-black ignorance. Herr Dühring calls Owen "in every respect
a veritable monster of importunate philanthropy" [261]. But when
this same Herr Dühring starts to give us information about the
contents of books whose title and motto he hardly knows, we must
not on any account say that he is "in every respect a veritable
monster of importunate ignorance", for on *our* lips this would
certainly be "abuse".

The utopians, we saw, were utopians because they could be
nothing else at a time when capitalist production was as yet so little
developed. They necessarily had to construct the elements of a
new society out of their own heads, because within the old society
the elements of the new were not as yet generally apparent; for
the basic plan of the new edifice they could only appeal to reason,
just because they could not as yet appeal to contemporary history.
But when now, almost eighty years after their time, Herr Dühring
steps on to the stage and puts forward his claim to an
"authoritative" [1] system of a new social order—not evolved out
of the historically developed material at his disposal, as its
necessary result—oh, no!—but constructed in his sovereign head,
in his mind, pregnant with ultimate truths—then he, who scents
epigones everywhere, is himself nothing but the epigone of the
utopians, the latest utopian. He calls the great utopians "social
alchemists" [237]. That may be so. Alchemy was necessary in its
epoch. But since that time modern industry has developed the

contradictions lying dormant in the capitalist mode of production into such crying antagonisms that the approaching collapse of this mode of production is, so to speak, palpable; that the new productive forces themselves can only be maintained and further developed by the introduction of a new mode of production corresponding to their present stage of development; that the struggle between the two classes engendered by the hitherto existing mode of production and constantly reproduced in ever sharper antagonism has affected all civilised countries and is daily becoming more violent; and that these historical interconnections, the conditions of the social transformation which they make necessary, and the basic features of this transformation likewise determined by them, have also already been apprehended. And if Herr Dühring now manufactures a new utopian social order out of his sovereign brain instead of from the economic material available, he is not practising mere "social alchemy". He is acting rather like a person who, after the discovery and establishment of the laws of modern chemistry, attempts to restore the old alchemy and to use atomic weights, molecular formulas, the quantivalence of atoms, crystallography and spectral analysis for the sole purpose of discovering—*the philosopher's stone*.

II. THEORETICAL

The materialist conception of history starts from the proposition that the production and, next to production, the exchange of things produced, is the basis of all social structure; that in every society that has appeared in history, the manner in which wealth is distributed and society divided into classes or estates is dependent upon what is produced, how it is produced, and how the products are exchanged. From this point of- view the final causes of all social changes and political revolutions are to be sought, not in men's brains, not in man's better insight into eternal truth and justice, but in changes in the modes of production and exchange. They are to be sought, not in the *philosophy*, but in the *economics* of each particular epoch. The growing perception that existing social institutions are unreasonable and unjust, that reason has become unreason, and right wrong,[a] is only proof that in the modes of production and exchange changes have silently taken place with which the social order, adapted to earlier economic conditions, is

---

[a] Goethe, *Faust*, Act I, Scene 4 ("Faust's Study").—*Ed.*

no longer in keeping. From this it also follows that the means of getting rid of the incongruities that have been brought to light must also be present, in a more or less developed condition, within the changed modes of production themselves. These means are not to be *invented,* spun out of the head, but *discovered* with the aid of the head in the existing material facts of production.

What is, then, the position of modern socialism in this connection?

The present structure of society—this is now pretty generally conceded—is the creation of the ruling class of today, of the bourgeoisie. The mode of production peculiar to the bourgeoisie, known, since Marx, as the capitalist mode of production, was incompatible with the local privileges and the privileges of estate as well as with the reciprocal personal ties of the feudal system. The bourgeoisie broke up the feudal system and built upon its ruins the capitalist order of society, the kingdom of free. competition, of personal liberty, of the equality, before the law, of all commodity owners, of all the rest of the capitalist blessings. Thenceforward the capitalist mode of production could develop in freedom. Since steam, machinery, and the making of machines by machinery transformed the older manufacture into modern industry, the productive forces evolved under the guidance of the bourgeoisie developed with a rapidity and in a degree unheard of before. But just as the older manufacture, in its time, and handicraft, becoming more developed under its influence, had come into collision with the feudal trammels of the guilds, so now modern industry, in its more complete development, comes into collision with the bounds within which the capitalistic mode of production holds it confined. The new productive forces have already outgrown the capitalistic mode of using them. And this conflict between productive forces and modes of production is not a conflict engendered in the mind of man, like that between original sin and divine justice. It exists, in fact, objectively, outside us, independently of the will and actions even of the men that have brought it on. Modern socialism is nothing but the reflex, in thought, of this conflict in fact; its ideal reflection in the minds, first, of the class directly suffering under it, the working class.

Now, in what does this conflict consist?

Before capitalistic production, i.e., in the Middle Ages, the system of petty industry obtained generally, based upon the private property of the labourers in their means of production; [in the country,] the agriculture of the small peasant, freeman or serf; in the towns, the handicrafts. The instruments of labour—land, agricultural implements, the workshop, the tool—were the instruments of labour of single individuals, adapted for the use of one worker, and, therefore, of necessity, small, dwarfish, circumscribed. But, for this very reason they belonged, as a rule, to the producer himself. To concentrate these scattered, limited means of production, to enlarge them, to turn them into the powerful levers of production of the present day—this was precisely the historic role of capitalist production and of its upholder, the bourgeoisie. In Part IV of *Capital*[a] Marx has explained in detail, how since the fifteenth century this has been historically worked out through the three phases of simple co-operation, manufacture and modern industry. But the bourgeoisie, as is also shown there, could not transform these puny means of production into mighty productive forces without transforming them, at the same time, from means of production of the individual into *social* means of production only workable by a *collectivity of men*. The spinning-wheel, the hand-loom, the blacksmith's hammer, were replaced by the spinning-machine, the power-loom, the steam-hammer; the individual workshop by the factory implying the co-operation of hundreds and thousands of workmen. In like manner, production itself changed from a series of individual into a series of social acts, and the products from individual to social products. The yarn, the cloth, the metal articles that now came out of the factory were the joint product of many workers, through whose hands they had successively to pass before they were ready. No one person could say of them: "*I* made that; this is *my* product."

But where, in a given society, the fundamental form of production is that spontaneous division of labour, there the products take on the form of *commodities* whose mutual exchange, buying and selling, enable the individual producers to satisfy their manifold wants. And this was the case in the Middle Ages. The peasant, e.g., sold to the artisan agricultural products and bought from him the products of handicraft. Into this society of individual producers, of commodity producers, the new mode of production thrust itself. In the midst of the old division of labour, grown up spontaneously and upon *no definite plan,* which had governed the whole of society, now arose division of labour upon *a definite plan,* as organised in the factory; side by side with *individual* production appeared *social* production. The products of both were sold in the same market, and, therefore, at prices at

---

[a] See present edition, Vol. 35.— *Ed.*

least approximately equal. But organisation upon a definite plan was stronger than spontaneous division of labour. The factories working with the combined social forces of a collectivity of individuals produced their commodities far more cheaply than the individual small producers. Individual production succumbed in one department after another. Socialised production revolutionised all the old methods of production. But its revolutionary character was, at the same time, so little recognised that it was, on the contrary, introduced as a means of increasing and developing the production of commodities. When it arose, it found ready-made, and made liberal use of, certain machinery for the production and exchange of commodities: merchants' capital, handicraft, wage-labour. Socialised production thus introducing itself as a new form of the production of commodities, it was a matter of course that under it the old forms of appropriation remained in full swing, and were applied to its products as well.

In the mediaeval stage of evolution of the production of commodities, the question as to the owner of the product of labour could not arise. The individual producer, as a rule, had, from raw material belonging to himself, and generally his own handiwork, produced it with his own tools, by the labour of his own hands or of his family. There was no need for him to appropriate the new product. It belonged wholly to him, as a matter of course. His property in the product was, therefore, based *upon his own labour.* Even where external help was used, this was, as a rule, of little importance, and very generally was compensated by something other than wages. The apprentices and journeymen of the guilds worked less for board and wages than for education, in order that they might become master craftsmen themselves. Then came the concentration of the means of production in large workshops and manufactories, their transformation into actual socialised means of production. But the socialised means of production and their products were still treated, after this change, just as they had been before, i.e., as the means of production and the products of individuals. Hitherto, the owner of the instruments of labour had himself appropriated the product, because, as a rule, it was his own product and the assistance of others was the exception. Now the owner of the instruments of labour always appropriated to himself the product, although it was no longer *his* product but exclusively the product of the *labour of others.* Thus, the products now produced socially were not appropriated by those who had actually set in motion the means of production and actually produced the commodities, but by the *capitalists.* The means of production, and production itself, had become in essence socialised. But they were subjected to a form of appropriation which presupposes the private production of individuals, under which, therefore, everyone owns his own product and brings it to market. The mode of production is subjected to this form of appropriation, although it abolishes the conditions upon which the latter rests.* This contradiction, which gives to the new mode of production its capitalistic character, *contains the germ of the whole of the social antagonisms of today.* The greater the mastery obtained by the new mode of production over all decisive fields of production and in all economically decisive countries, the more it reduced individual production to an insignificant residium, *the more clearly was brought out the incompatibility of socialised production with capitalistic appropriation.*

The first capitalists found, as we have said, wage-labour ready-made for them. But it was exceptional, complementary, accessory, transitory wage-labour. The agricultural labourer, though, upon occasion, he hired himself out by the day, had a few acres of his own land on which he could at all events live at a pinch. The guilds were so organised that the journeyman of today became the master of tomorrow. But all this changed, as soon as the means of production became socialised and concentrated in the hands of capitalists. The means of production, as well as the product, of the individual producer became more and more worthless; there was nothing left for him but to turn wage-worker under the capitalist. Wage-labour, aforetime the exception and accessory, now became the rule and basis of all production; aforetime complementary, it now became the sole remaining function of the worker. The wage-worker for a time became a wage-worker for life. The number of these permanent wage-workers was further enormously increased by the breaking-up of the feudal system that occurred at the same time, by the disbanding of the retainers of the feudal lords, the eviction of the peasants from their homesteads, etc. The separation was made

---

* It is hardly necessary in this connection to point out that, even if the *form* of appropriation remains the same, the *character* of the appropriation is just as much revolutionised as production is by the changes described above. It is, of course, a very different matter whether I appropriate to myself my own product or that of another. Note in passing that wage-labour, which contains the whole capitalistic mode of production in embryo, is very ancient; in a sporadic, scattered form it existed for centuries alongside slave-labour. But the embryo could duly develop into the capitalistic mode of production only when the necessary historical preconditions had been furnished.

complete between the means of production concentrated in the hands of the capitalists, on the one side, and the producers, possessing nothing but their labour-power, on the other. *The contradiction between socialised production and capitalistic appropriation manifested itself as the antagonism of proletariat and bourgeoisie.*

We have seen that the capitalistic mode of production thrust its way into a society of commodity producers, of individual producers, whose social bond was the exchange of their products. But every society based upon the production of commodities has this peculiarity: that the producers have lost control over their own social interrelations. Each man produces for himself with such means of production as he may happen to have, and for such exchange as he may require to satisfy his remaining wants. No one knows how much of his particular article is coming on the market, nor how much of it will be wanted. No one knows whether his individual product will meet an actual demand, whether he will be able to make good his costs of production or even to sell his commodity at all. Anarchy reigns in socialised production. But the production of commodities, like every other form of production, has its peculiar, inherent laws inseparable from it; and these laws work, despite anarchy, in and through anarchy. They reveal themselves in the only persistent form of social interrelations, i.e., in exchange, and here they affect the individual producers as compulsory laws of competition. They are, at first, unknown to these producers themselves, and have to be discovered by them gradually and as the result of experience. They work themselves out, therefore, independently of the producers, and in antagonism to them, as inexorable natural laws of their particular form of production. The product governs the producers.

In mediaeval society, especially in the earlier centuries, production was essentially directed towards satisfying the wants of the individual. It satisfied, in the main, only the wants of the producer and his family. Where relations of personal dependence existed, as in the country, it also helped to satisfy the wants of the feudal lord. In all this there was, therefore, no exchange; the products, consequently, did not assume the character of commodities. The family of the peasant produced almost everything they wanted: clothes and furniture, as well as means of subsistence. Only when it began to produce more than was sufficient to supply its own wants and the payments in kind to the feudal lord, only then did it also produce commodities. This surplus, thrown into socialised exchange and offered for sale, became commodities. The artisans of the towns, it is true, had from the first to produce for exchange. But they, also, themselves supplied the greatest part of their own individual wants. They had gardens and plots of land. They turned their cattle out into the communal forest, which, also, yielded them timber and firing. The women spun flax, wool, and so forth. Production for the purpose of exchange, production of commodities, was only in its infancy. Hence, exchange was restricted, the market narrow, the methods of production stable; there was local exclusiveness without, local unity within; the mark [114] in the country; in the town, the guild.

But with the extension of the production of commodities, and especially with the introduction of the capitalist mode of production, the laws of commodity production, hitherto latent, came into action more openly and with greater force. The old bonds were loosened, the old exclusive limits broken through, the producers were more and more turned into independent, isolated producers of commodities. The anarchy of social production became apparent and grew to greater and greater height. But the chief means by aid of which the capitalist mode of production intensified this anarchy of socialised production was the exact opposite of anarchy. It was the increasing organisation of production, upon a social basis, in every individual productive establishment. By this, the old, peaceful, stable condition of things was ended. Wherever this organisation of production was introduced into a branch of industry, it brooked no other method of production by its side. Where it laid hold of a handicraft, that old handicraft was wiped out. The field of labour became a battle-ground. The great geographical discoveries, and the colonisation following upon them, multiplied markets and quickened the transformation of handicraft into manufacture. The war did not simply break out between the individual producers of particular localities. The local struggles begot in their turn national conflicts, the commercial wars of the seventeenth and the eighteenth centuries.[115] Finally, modern industry and the opening of the world market made the struggle universal, and at the same time gave it an unheard-of virulence. Advantages in natural or artificial conditions of production now decide the existence or non-existence of individual capitalists, as well as of whole industries and countries. He that falls is remorselessly cast aside. It is the Darwinian struggle of the individual for existence transferred from nature to society with intensified violence. The conditions of existence natural to the animal appear as the final term of human development. The contradiction between socialised production and capitalistic appropriation now presents itself as *an antagonism between the organisation of production in the individual workshop, and the anarchy of production in society generally.*

The capitalistic mode of production moves in these two forms of the antagonism immanent to it from its very origin. It is never able to get out of that "vicious circle" which Fourier had already discovered.[a] What Fourier could not, indeed, see in his time is that this circle is gradually narrowing; that the movement becomes more and more a spiral, and must come to an end, like the movement of the planets, by collision with the centre. It is the compelling force of anarchy in the production of society at large that more and more completely turns the great majority of men into proletarians; and it is the masses of the proletariat again who will finally put an end to anarchy in production. It is the compelling force of anarchy in social production that turns the limitless perfectibility of machinery under modern industry into a compulsory law by which every individual industrial capitalist must perfect his machinery more and more, under penalty of ruin. But the perfecting of machinery is making human labour superfluous. If the introduction and increase of machinery means the displacement of millions of manual by a few machine-workers, improvement in machinery means the displacement of more and more of the machine-workers themselves. It means, in the last instance, the production of a number of available wage-workers in excess of the average needs of capital, the formation of a complete industrial reserve army, as I called it in 1845,* available at the times when industry is working at high pressure, to be cast out upon the street when the inevitable crash comes, a constant dead-weight upon the limbs of the working class in its struggle for existence with capital, a regulator for the keeping of wages down to the low level that suits the interests of capital. Thus it comes about, to quote Marx, that machinery becomes the most powerful weapon in the war of capital against the working class; that the instruments of labour constantly tear the means of subsistence out of the hands of the labourer; that the very product of the worker is turned into an instrument for his subjugation.[c] Thus it comes about that the economising of the instruments of labour becomes

---

* *The Condition of the Working-Class in England*, p. 109.[b]

[a] See this volume, p. 248.— *Ed.*

[b] See present edition, Vol. 4, p. 384.— *Ed.*

[c] See K. Marx, *Das Kapital*, pp. 457, 513. See present edition, Vol. 35, Part IV, Chapter XV, Sections 5 and 9.— *Ed.*

at the same time, from the outset, the most reckless waste of labour-power, and robbery based upon the normal conditions under which labour functions[a]; that machinery, the most powerful instrument for shortening labour-time, becomes the most unfailing means for placing every moment of the labourer's time and that of his family at the disposal of the capitalist for the purpose of expanding the value of his capital. Thus it comes about that the overwork of some becomes the preliminary condition for the idleness of others, and that modern industry, which hunts after new consumers over the whole world, forces the consumption of the masses at home down to a starvation minimum, and in doing this destroys its own home market. "The law that always equilibrates the relative surplus-population, or industrial reserve army, to the extent and energy of accumulation, this law rivets the labourer to capital more firmly than the wedges of Vulcan did Prometheus to the rock. It establishes an accumulation of misery, corresponding with accumulation of capital. Accumulation of wealth at one pole is, therefore, at the same time accumulation of misery, agony of toil, slavery, ignorance, brutality, mental degradation, at the opposite pole, i.e., on the side of the class that *produces its own product in the form of capital.*" (Marx's *Capital,* p. 671.)[b] And to expect any other division of the products from the capitalistic mode of production is the same as expecting the electrodes of a battery not to decompose acidulated water, not to liberate oxygen at the positive, hydrogen at the negative pole, so long as they are connected with the battery.

We have seen that the ever increasing perfectibility of modern machinery is, by the anarchy of social production, turned into a compulsory law that forces the individual industrial capitalist always to improve his machinery, always to increase its productive force. The bare possibility of extending the field of production is transformed for him into a similar compulsory law. The enormous expansive force of modern industry, compared with which that of gases is mere child's play, appears to us now as a *necessity* for expansion, both qualitative and quantitative, that laughs at all resistance. Such resistance is offered by consumption, by sales, by the markets for the products of modern industry. But the capacity

---

[a] K. Marx, *Das Kapital,* p. 485. See present edition, Vol. 35, Part IV, Chapter XV, Section 8, b: "Reaction of the Factory System on Manufacture and Domestic Industries".— *Ed.*

[b] Ibid., pp. 671-72. See present edition, Vol. 35, Part VII, Chapter XXV, Section 4. Italics by Engels.— *Ed.*

for extension, extensive and intensive, of the markets is primarily governed by quite different laws that work much less energetically. The extension of the markets cannot keep pace with the extension of production. The collision becomes inevitable, and as this cannot produce any real solution so long as it does not break in pieces the capitalist mode of production, the collisions become periodic. Capitalist production has begotten another "vicious circle".

As a matter of fact, since 1825, when the first general crisis broke out, the whole industrial and commercial world, production and exchange among all civilised peoples and their more or less barbaric hangers-on, are thrown out of joint about once every ten years. Commerce is at a standstill, the markets are glutted, products accumulate, as multitudinous as they are unsaleable, hard cash disappears, credit vanishes, factories are closed, the mass of the workers are in want of the means of subsistence, because they have produced too much of the means of subsistence; bankruptcy follows upon bankruptcy, execution upon execution. The stagnation lasts for years; productive forces and products are wasted and destroyed wholesale, until the accumulated mass of commodities finally filters off, more or less depreciated in value, until production and exchange gradually begin to move again. Little by little the pace quickens. It becomes a trot. The industrial trot breaks into a canter, the canter in turn grows into the headlong gallop of a perfect steeplechase of industry, commercial credit, and speculation, which finally, after break-neck leaps, ends where it began—in the ditch of a crisis. And so over and over again. We have now, since the year 1825, gone through this five times, and at the present moment (1877) we are going through it for the sixth time. And the character of these crises is so clearly defined that Fourier hit all of them off when he described the first as *crise pléthorique*, a crisis from plethora.[a]

In these crises, the contradiction between socialised production and capitalist appropriation ends in a violent explosion. The circulation of commodities is, for the time being, stopped. Money, the means of circulation, becomes a hindrance to circulation. All the laws of production and circulation of commodities are turned upside down. The economic collision has reached its apogee. *The mode of production is in rebellion against the mode of exchange, the productive forces are in rebellion against the mode of production which they have outgrown.*

---

[a] See Ch. Fourier, *Le Nouveau Monde industriel et sociétaire.* In: *Oeuvres complètes,* Vol. 6, pp. 393-94.— *Ed.*

The fact that the socialised organisation of production within the factory has developed so far that it has become incompatible with the anarchy of production in society, which exists side by side with and dominates it, is brought home to the capitalists themselves by the violent concentration of capital that occurs during crises, through the ruin of many large, and a still greater number of small, capitalists. The whole mechanism of the capitalist mode of production breaks down under the pressure of the productive forces, its own creations. It is no longer able to turn all this mass of means of production into capital. They lie fallow, and for that very reason the industrial reserve army must also lie fallow. Means of production, means of subsistence, available labourers, all the elements of production and of general wealth, are present in abundance. But "abundance becomes the source of distress and want" (Fourier),[a] because it is the very thing that prevents the transformation of the means of production and subsistence into capital. For in capitalistic society the means of production can only function when they have undergone a preliminary transformation into capital, into the means of exploiting human labour-power. The necessity of this transformation into capital of the means of production and subsistence stands like a ghost between these and the workers. It alone prevents the coming together of the material and personal levers of production; it alone forbids the means of production to function, the workers to work and live. On the one hand, therefore, the capitalistic mode of production stands convicted of its own incapacity to further direct these productive forces. On the other, these productive forces themselves, with increasing energy, press forward to the removal of the existing contradiction, to the abolition of their quality as capital, *to the practical recognition of their character as social productive forces.*

This rebellion of the productive forces, as they grow more and more powerful, against their quality as capital, this stronger and stronger command that their social character shall be recognised, forces the capitalist class itself to treat them more and more as social productive forces, so far as this is possible under capitalist conditions. The period of industrial high pressure, with its unbounded inflation of credit, not less than the crash itself, by the collapse of great capitalist establishments, tends to bring about that form of the socialisation of great masses of means of production

---

a See Ch. Fourier, *Le Nouveau Monde industriel et sociétaire.* In: *Oeuvres complètes,* Vol. 6, p. 35.— *Ed.*

which we meet with in the different kinds of joint-stock companies. Many of these means of production and of communication are, from the outset, so colossal that, like the railways, they exclude all other forms of capitalistic exploitation. At a further stage of evolution this form also becomes insufficient: the official representative of capitalist society—the state—will ultimately have to* undertake the direction of production. This necessity for conversion into state property is felt first in the great institutions for intercourse and communication—the post office, the telegraphs, the railways.

If the crises demonstrate the incapacity of the bourgeoisie for managing any longer modern productive forces, the transformation of the great establishments for production and distribution into joint-stock companies and state property shows how unnecessary the bourgeoisie are for that purpose. All the social functions of the capitalist are now performed by salaried employees. The capitalist has no further social function than that of pocketing dividends, tearing off coupons, and gambling on the Stock Exchange, where the different capitalists despoil one another of their capital. At first the capitalist mode of production forces out the workers. Now it forces out the capitalists, and reduces them, just as it reduced the workers, to the ranks of the surplus population, although not immediately into those of the industrial reserve army.

But the transformation, either into joint-stock companies, or

---

* I say "have to". For only when the means of production and distribution have *actually* outgrown the form of management by joint-stock companies, and when, therefore, the taking them over by the state has become *economically* inevitable, only then—even if it is the state of today that effects this—is there an economic advance, the attainment of another step preliminary to the taking over of all productive forces by society itself. But of late, since Bismarck went in for state-ownership of industrial establishments, a kind of spurious socialism has arisen, degenerating, now and again, into something of flunkeyism, that without more ado declares *all* state ownership, even of the Bismarckian sort, to be socialistic. Certainly, if the taking over by the state of the tobacco industry is socialistic, then Napoleon and Metternich must be numbered among the founders of socialism. If the Belgian state, for quite ordinary political and financial reasons, itself constructed its chief railway lines; if Bismarck, not under any economic compulsion, took over for the state the chief Prussian lines, simply to be the better able to have them in hand in case of war, to bring up the railway employees as voting cattle for the government, and especially to create for himself a new source of income independent of parliamentary votes—this was, in no sense, a socialistic measure, directly or indirectly, consciously or unconsciously. Otherwise, the Royal Maritime Company,[116] the Royal porcelain manufacture, and even the regimental tailor of the army would also be socialistic institutions.

into state ownership, does not do away with the capitalistic nature of the productive forces. In the joint-stock companies this is obvious. And the modern state, again, is only the organisation that bourgeois society takes on in order to support the general external conditions of the capitalist mode of production against the encroachments as well of the workers as of individual capitalists. The modern state, no matter what its form, is essentially a capitalist machine, the state of the capitalists, the ideal personification of the total national capital. The more it proceeds to the taking over of productive forces, the more does it actually become the national capitalist, the more citizens does it exploit. The workers remain wage-workers—proletarians. The capitalist relation is not done away with. It is rather brought to a head. But, brought to a head, it topples over. State ownership of the productive forces is not the solution of the conflict, but concealed within it are the technical conditions that form the elements of that solution.

This solution can only consist in the practical recognition of the social nature of the modern forces of production, and therefore in the harmonising of the modes of production, appropriation, and exchange with the socialised character of the means of production. And this can only come about by society openly and directly taking possession of the productive forces which have outgrown all control except that of society as a whole. The social character of the means of production and of the products today reacts against the producers, periodically disrupts all production and exchange, acts only like a law of nature working blindly, forcibly, destructively. But with the taking over by society of the productive forces, the social character of the means of production and of the products will be utilised by the producers with a perfect understanding of its nature, and instead of being a source of disturbance and periodical collapse, will become the most powerful lever of production itself.

Active social forces work exactly like natural forces: blindly, forcibly, destructively, so long as we do not understand, and reckon with, them. But when once we understand them, when once we grasp their action, their direction, their effects, it depends only upon ourselves to subject them more and more to our own will, and by means of them to reach our own ends. And this holds quite especially of the mighty productive forces of today. As long as we obstinately refuse to understand the nature and the character of these social means of action—and this understanding goes against the grain of the capitalist mode of production and its defenders—so long these forces are at work in spite of us, in opposition to us, so long they master us, as we have shown above in detail. But when once their nature is understood, they can, in the hands of the producers working together, be transformed from master demons into willing servants. The difference is as that between the destructive force of electricity in the lightning of the storm, and electricity under command in the telegraph and the voltaic arc; the difference between a conflagration, and fire working in the service of man. With this recognition, at last, of the real nature of the productive forces of today, the social anarchy of production gives place to a social regulation of production upon a definite plan, according to the needs of the community and of each individual. Then the capitalist mode of appropriation, in which the product enslaves first the producer and then the appropriator, is replaced by the mode of appropriation of the products that is based upon the nature of the modern means of production: upon the one hand, direct social appropriation, as means to the maintenance and extension of production—on the other, direct individual appropriation, as means of subsistence and of enjoyment.

Whilst the capitalist mode of production more and more completely transforms the great majority of the population into proletarians, it creates the power which, under penalty of its own destruction, is forced to accomplish this revolution. Whilst it forces on more and more the transformation of the vast means of production, already socialised, into state property, it shows itself the way to accomplishing this revolution. *The proletariat seizes political power and turns the means of production in the first instance into state property.* But, in doing this, it abolishes itself as proletariat, abolishes all class distinctions and class antagonisms, abolishes also the state as state. Society thus far, based upon class antagonisms, had need of the state, that is, of an organisation of the particular class, which was *pro tempore* the exploiting class, for the maintenance of its external conditions of production, and, therefore, especially, for the purpose of forcibly keeping the exploited classes in the condition of oppression corresponding with the given mode of production (slavery, serfdom, wage-labour). The state was the official representative of society as a whole; the gathering of it together into a visible embodiment. But it was this only in so far as it was the state of that class which itself represented, for the time being, society as a whole: in ancient times, the state of slave-owning citizens; in the Middle Ages, the feudal lords; in our own time, the bourgeoisie. When at last it becomes the real representative of the whole of society, it renders itself unnecessary. As soon as there is no longer any social class to be held in subjection; as soon as class rule, and the individual struggle for existence based upon our present anarchy in production, with the collisions and excesses arising from these, are removed, nothing more remains to be repressed, and a special repressive force, a state, is no longer necessary. The first act by virtue of which the state really constitutes itself the representative of the whole of society—the taking possession of the means of production in the name of society—this is, at the same time, its last independent act as a state. State interference in social relations becomes, in one domain after another, superfluous, and then dies out of itself; the government of persons is replaced by the administration of things, and by the conduct of processes of production. The state is not "abolished". *It dies out.* This gives the measure of the value of the phrase "a free people's state", both as to its justifiable use at times by agitators, and as to its ultimate scientific insufficiency [117]; and also of the demands of the so-called anarchists for the abolition of the state out of hand.

Since the historical appearance of the capitalist mode of production, the appropriation by society of all the means of production has often been dreamed of, more or less vaguely, by individuals, as well as by sects, as the ideal of the future. But it could become possible, could become a historical necessity, only when the actual conditions for its realisation were there. Like every other social advance, it becomes practicable, not by men understanding that the existence of classes is in contradiction to justice, equality, etc., not by the mere willingness to abolish these classes, but by virtue of certain new economic conditions. The separation of society into an exploiting and an exploited class, a ruling and an oppressed class, was the necessary consequence of the deficient and restricted development of production in former times. So long as the total social labour only yields a produce which but slightly exceeds that barely necessary for the existence of all; so long, therefore, as labour engages all or almost all the time of the great majority of the members of society—so long, of necessity, this society is divided into classes. Side by side with the great majority, exclusively bond slaves to labour, arises a class freed from directly productive labour, which looks after the general affairs of society: the direction of labour, state business, law, science, art, etc. It is, therefore, the law of division of labour that lies at the basis of the division into classes. But this does not prevent this division into classes from being carried out by means of violence and robbery, trickery and fraud. It does not prevent the ruling class, once having the upper hand, from consolidating its power at the expense of the working class, from turning its social leadership into an exploitation of the masses.

But if, upon this showing, division into classes has a certain historical justification, it has this only for a given period, only under given social conditions. It was based upon the insufficiency of production. It will be swept away by the complete development of modern productive forces. And, in fact, the abolition of classes in society presupposes a degree of historical evolution at which the existence, not simply of this or that particular ruling class, but of any ruling class at all, and, therefore, the existence of class distinction itself has become an obsolete anachronism. It presupposes, therefore, the development of production carried out to a degree at which appropriation of the means of production and of the products, and, with this, of political domination, of the monopoly of culture, and of intellectual leadership by a particular class of society, has become not only superfluous but economically, politically, intellectually a hindrance to development. This point is now reached. Their political and intellectual bankruptcy is scarcely any longer a secret to the bourgeoisie themselves. Their economic bankruptcy recurs regularly every ten years. In every crisis, society is suffocated beneath the weight of its own productive forces and products, which it cannot use, and stands helpless face to face with the absurd contradiction that the producers have nothing to consume, because consumers are wanting. The expansive force of the means of production bursts the bonds that the capitalist mode of production had imposed upon them. Their deliverance from these bonds is the one precondition for an unbroken, constantly accelerated development of the productive forces, and therewith for a practically unlimited increase of production itself. Nor is this all. The socialised appropriation of the means of production does away, not only with the present artificial restrictions upon production, but also with the positive waste and devastation of productive forces and products that are at the present time the inevitable concomitants of production, and that reach their height in the crises. Further, it sets free for the community at large a mass of means of production and of products, by doing away with the senseless extravagance of the ruling classes of today and their political representatives. The possibility of securing for every member of society, by means of socialised production, an existence not only fully sufficient materially, and becoming day by day more full, but an existence guaranteeing to all the free development and exercise of their physical and mental faculties—this possibility is now for the first time here, but it *is here.**

With the seizing of the means of production by society, production of commodities is done away with, and, simultaneously, the mastery of the product over the producer. Anarchy in social production is replaced by systematic, definite organisation. The struggle for individual existence disappears. Then for the first time man, in a certain sense, is finally marked off from the rest of the animal kingdom, and emerges from mere animal conditions of existence into really human ones. The whole sphere of the conditions of life which environ man, and which have hitherto ruled man, now comes under the dominion and control of man, who for the first time becomes the real, conscious lord of nature, because he has now become master of his own social organisation. The laws of his own social action, hitherto standing face to face with man as laws of nature foreign to, and dominating him, will then be used with full understanding, and so mastered by him. Man's own social organisation, hitherto confronting him as a necessity imposed by nature and history, now becomes the result of his own free action. The extraneous objective forces that have hitherto governed history pass under the control of man himself. Only from that time will man himself, with full consciousness, make his own history—only from that time will the social causes set in movement by him have, in the main and in a constantly growing measure, the results intended by him. It is the humanity's leap from the kingdom of necessity to the kingdom of freedom.

To accomplish this act of universal emancipation is the historical mission of the modern proletariat. To thoroughly comprehend the historical conditions and thus the very nature of this act, to impart to the now oppressed class a full knowledge of the conditions and of the meaning of the momentous act it is called upon to

---

* A few figures may serve to give an approximate idea of the enormous expansive force of the modern means of production, even under capitalist pressure. According to Mr. Giffen,[118] the total wealth of Great Britain and Ireland amounted, in round numbers, in

$$
\begin{array}{llll}
1814 & \text{to } \pounds \ 2{,}200{,}000{,}000 = & 44 & \text{mld marks} \\
1865 & \text{to } \pounds \ 6{,}100{,}000{,}000 = & 122 & \text{»} \quad \text{»} \\
1875 & \text{to } \pounds \ 8{,}500{,}000{,}000 = & 170 & \text{»} \quad \text{»}
\end{array}
$$

As an instance of the squandering of means of production and of products during a crisis, the total loss in the *German iron industry* alone, in the recent crisis [of 1873-78], was given at the second German Industrial Congress (Berlin, February 21, 1878) as 455,000,000 marks.

accomplish, this is the task of the theoretical expression of the proletarian movement, scientific socialism.

III. PRODUCTION

After all that has been said above, the reader will not be surprised to learn that the exposition of the principal features of socialism given in the preceding part is not at all in accordance with Herr Dühring's view. On the contrary. He must hurl it into the abyss where lie all the other rejected "bastards of historical and logical fantasy", "barren conceptions", "confused and hazy notions" [D. K. G. 498], etc. To Herr Dühring, socialism in fact is not at all a necessary product of historical development and still less of the grossly material economic conditions of today, directed toward the filling of the stomach exclusively [231]. He's got it all worked out much better. His socialism is a final and ultimate truth;

it is "the natural system of society" [D. Ph. 282], whose roots are to be found in a "universal principle of justice" [D. C. 282],

and if he cannot avoid taking notice of the existing situation, created by the sinful history of the past, in order to remedy it, this must be regarded rather as a misfortune for the pure principle of justice. Herr Dühring creates his socialism, like everything else, through the medium of his famous two men.[a] Instead of these two puppets playing the part of master and servant, as they did in the past, they perform this once, for a change, the piece on the equality of rights—and the foundations of the Dühringian socialism have been laid.

It therefore goes without saying that to Herr Dühring the periodical crises in industry have not at all the historical significance which we were compelled to attribute to them.

In his view, crises are only occasional deviations from "normality" [218] and at most only serve to promote "the development of a more regulated order" [219]. The "common method" [227] of explaining crises by over-production is in no wise adequate for his "more exact conception of things" [343]. Of course such an explanation "may be permissible for specific crises in particular areas". As, for example, "a swamping of the book market with works suddenly released for republication and suitable for mass sale" [227].

---

[a] See this volume, pp. 89-91.— *Ed.*

Herr Dühring can at any rate go to sleep with the gratifying feeling that his immortal works will never bring on any such world disaster.

He claims, however, that in great crises, it is not over-production, but rather "the lagging behind of popular consumption ... artificially produced under-consumption ... interference with the natural growth of the *needs of the people*" (!) "which ultimately make the gulf between supply and demand so critically wide" [D. C. 227, 228].

And he has even had the good fortune to find a disciple for this crisis theory of his.

But unfortunately the under-consumption of the masses, the restriction of the consumption of the masses to what is necessary for their maintenance and reproduction, is not a new phenomenon. It has existed as long as there have been exploiting and exploited classes. Even in those periods of history when the situation of the masses was particularly favourable, as for example in England in the fifteenth century, they under-consumed. They were very far from having their own annual total product at their disposal to be consumed by them. Therefore, while under-consumption has been a constant feature in history for thousands of years, the general shrinkage of the market which breaks out in crises as the result of a surplus of production is a phenomenon only of the last fifty years; and so Herr Dühring's whole superficial vulgar economics is necessary in order to explain the new collision not by the *new* phenomenon of over-production but by the thousand-year-old phenomenon of under-consumption. It is like a mathematician attempting to explain the variation in the ratio between two quantities, one constant and one variable, not by the variation of the variable but by the fact that the constant quantity remains unchanged. The under-consumption of the masses is a necessary condition of all forms of society based on exploitation, consequently also of the capitalist form; but it is the capitalist form of production which first gives rise to crises. The under-consumption of the masses is therefore also a prerequisite condition of crises, and plays in them a role which has long been recognised. But it tells us just as little why crises exist today as why they did not exist before.

Herr Dühring's notions of the world market are altogether curious. We have seen how, like a typical German man of letters, he seeks to explain real industrial specific crises by means of imaginary crises on the Leipzig book market—the storm on the ocean by the storm in a teacup. He also imagines that present-day capitalist production must "depend for its market mainly *on the circles of the possessing classes* themselves" [221],

which does not prevent him, only sixteen pages later, from presenting, in the generally accepted way, the iron and cotton industries as the modern industries of decisive importance [236]—that is, precisely the two branches of production whose output is consumed only to an infinitesimally small degree within the circle of the possessing classes and is dependent more than any other on mass use. Wherever we turn in Herr Dühring's works there is nothing but empty and contradictory chatter. But let us take an example from the cotton industry. In the relatively small town of Oldham alone—it is one of a dozen towns round Manchester with fifty to a hundred thousand inhabitants engaged in the cotton industry—in this town alone, in the four years 1872 to 1875, the number of spindles spinning only Number 32 yarn increased from two and a half to five million; so that in one medium-sized English town there are as many spindles spinning one single count as the cotton industry of all Germany, including Alsace, possesses. And the expansion in the other branches and areas of the cotton industry in England and Scotland has taken place in approximately the same proportion. In view of these facts, it requires a strong dose of deep-rooted [555-56] effrontery to explain the present complete stagnation in the yarn and cloth markets by the under-consumption of the English masses and not by the over-production carried on by the English cotton-mill owners.*

But enough. One does not argue with people who are so ignorant of economics as to consider the Leipzig book market in the modern industrial sense. Let us therefore merely note that Herr Dühring has only one more piece of information for us on the subject of crises, that in crises we have nothing

"but the ordinary interplay of overstrain and relaxation" [228]; that over-speculation "is not only due to the planless multiplication of private enterprises", but that "the rashness of individual entrepreneurs and the lack of private circumspection must also be reckoned among the causes which give rise to oversupply" [229].

And what, again, is the "cause which gives rise" to the rashness and lack of private circumspection? Just precisely this very planlessness of capitalist production, which manifests itself in the

* The "under-consumption" explanation of crises originated with Sismondi, and in his exposition it still had a certain meaning. Rodbertus took it from Sismondi, and Herr Dühring has in turn copied it, in his usual vulgarising fashion, from Rodbertus.

planless multiplication of private enterprises. And to mistake the translation of an economic fact into moral reprobation as the discovery of a new cause is also a piece of extreme "rashness".

With this we can leave the question of crises. In the preceding section we showed that they were necessarily engendered by the capitalist mode of production, and explained their significance as crises of this mode of production itself, as means of compelling the social revolution, and it is not necessary to say another word in reply to Herr Dühring's superficialities on this subject. Let us pass on to his positive creations, the "natural system of society" [D. Ph. 282].

This system, built on a "universal principle of justice" [D. C. 320] and therefore free from all consideration of troublesome material facts, consists of a federation of economic communes among which there is

"freedom of movement and obligatory acceptance of new members on the basis of fixed laws and administrative regulations" [323].

The economic commune itself is above all

"a comprehensive schematism of great import in human history"[341] which is far superior to the "erroneous half-measures", for example, of a certain Marx [342]. It implies "a community of persons linked together by their public right to dispose of a definite area of land and a group of productive establishments for use in common, jointly participating in the proceeds" [322]. This public right is a "right to the object ... in the sense of a *purely publicistic relation to nature* and to the productive institutions" [342].

We leave it to the future jurists of the economic commune to cudgel their brains as to what this means; we give it up. The only thing we gather is that

it is not at all the same as the "corporative ownership of workers' associations" [342] which would not exclude mutual competition and even the exploitation of wage-labour.

In this connection he drops the remark that

the conception of a "collective ownership", such as is found also in Marx, is "to say the least unclear and open to question, as this conception of the future always gives the impression that it means nothing more than corporative ownership by groups of workers" [295].

This is one more instance of Herr Dühring's usual "vile habits" of passing off a thing for what it is not, "for whose vulgar nature"—to use his own words—"only the vulgar word snotty would be quite appropriate" [D. K. G. 506]; it is just as baseless a lie as Herr Dühring's other invention that by collective ownership

Marx means an "ownership which is at once both individual and social" [503, 505].

In any case this much seems clear: the publicistic right of an economic commune in its means of labour is an exclusive right of property at least as against every other economic commune and also as against society and the state.

But this right is not to entitle the commune "to cut itself off ... from the outside world, for among the various economic communes there is freedom of movement and obligatory acceptance of new members on the basis of fixed laws and administrative regulations ... like ... belonging to a political organisation at the present time, or participation in the economic affairs of the commune" [D. C. 322-23].

There will therefore be rich and poor economic communes, and the levelling out takes place through the population crowding into the rich communes and leaving the poor ones. So that although Herr Dühring wants to eliminate competition in products between the individual communes by means of national organisation of trade, he calmly allows competition among the producers to continue. Things are removed from the sphere of competition, but men remain subject to it.

But we are still very far from clear on the question of "publicistic right" [322]. Two pages further on Herr Dühring explains to us:

The trade commune "will at first cover the politico-social area whose inhabitants form a single legal entity and in this character have at their disposal the whole of the land, the dwellings and productive institutions" [325].

So after all it is not the individual commune at whose disposal these things are, but the whole nation. The "public right" [322], "right to the object", "publicistic relation to nature" [342] and so forth is therefore not merely "at least unclear and open to question" [295]: it is in direct contradiction with itself. It is in fact, at any rate in so far as each individual economic commune is likewise a legal entity, "an ownership which is at once both individual and social" [D. K. G. 503], and this latter "nebulous hybrid" [504] is once again, therefore, only to be met with in Herr Dühring's own works.

In any case the economic commune has at its disposal instruments of labour for the purpose of production. How is this production carried on? Judging by all Herr Dühring has told us, precisely as in the past, except that the commune takes the place of the capitalists. The most we are told is that everyone will then be free to choose his occupation, and that there will be equal obligation to work.

The basic form of all production hitherto has been the division of labour, on the one hand, within society as a whole, and on the other, within each separate productive establishment. How does the Dühring "sociality" [see D. C. 263, 277, 291] stand on this question?

The first great division of labour in society is the separation of town and country.

This antagonism, according to Herr Dühring, is "in the nature of things inevitable" [232]. But "it is in general doubtful to regard the gulf between agriculture and industry ... as unbridgeable. In fact, there already exists, to a certain extent, constancy of interconnection with promises to increase considerably in the future" [250]. Already, we learn, two industries have penetrated agriculture and rural production: "in the first place, distilling, and in the second, beet-sugar manufacturing ... the production of spirits is already of such importance that it is more likely to be under-estimated than over-estimated" [250-51]. And "if it were possible, as a result of some inventions, for a larger number of industries to develop in such a way that they should be compelled to localise their production in the country and carry it on in direct association with the production of raw materials" [251]—then this would weaken the antithesis between town and country and "provide the widest possible basis for the development of civilisation". Moreover, "a somewhat similar result might also be attained in another way. Apart from technical requirements, social needs are coming more and more to the forefront, and if the latter become the dominant consideration in the grouping of human activities it will no longer be possible to overlook those advantages which ensue from a close and systematic connection between the occupations of the countryside and the technical operations of working up raw materials" [252].

Now in the economic commune it is precisely social needs which are coming to the forefront; and so will it really hasten to take advantage, to the fullest possible extent, of the above-mentioned union of agriculture and industry? Will Herr Dühring not fail to tell us, at his accustomed length, his "more exact conceptions" [343] on the attitude of the economic commune to this question? The reader who expected him not to would be cruelly disillusioned. The above-mentioned meagre, stale commonplaces, once again not passing beyond the schnaps-distilling and beet-sugar-making sphere of the jurisdiction of Prussian law, are all that Herr Dühring has to say on the antithesis between town and country in the present and in the future.

Let us pass on to the division of labour in detail. Here Herr Dühring is a little "more exact". He speaks of

"a person who has to devote himself *exclusively* to *one* form of occupation" [D. C. 257]. If the point at issue is the introduction of a new branch of production, the problem simply hinges on whether a certain number of *entities,* who are to *devote themselves to the production of one single article,* can somehow be provided with the consumption (!) they require [278]. In the socialitarian system no branch of production would "*require* many *people*", and there, too, there would be "*economic species*" of men "distinguished by their way of life" [329].

Accordingly, within the sphere of production everything remains much the same as before. In society up to now, however, an "erroneous division of labour" [327] has obtained; but as to what this is, and by what it is to be replaced in the economic commune, we are only told:

"With regard to the division of labour itself, we have already said above that this question can be considered settled as soon as account is taken of the various natural conditions and personal capabilities" [259].

In addition to capabilities, personal likings are taken into account:

"The pleasure felt in rising to types of activity which involve additional capabilities and training would depend exclusively on the inclination felt for the occupation in question and on the joy produced in the *exercise of precisely this and no other thing*" [D. Ph. 283] (exercise of a thing!).

And this will stimulate competition within the socialitarian system, so that

"production itself will become interesting, and the dull pursuit of it, which sees in it nothing but a means of earning, will no longer put its heavy imprint on conditions" [D. C. 265].

In every society in which production has developed spontaneously—and our present society is of this type—the situation is not that the producers control the means of production, but that the means of production control the producers. In such a society each new lever of production is necessarily transformed into a new means for the subjection of the producers to the means of production. This is most of all true of that lever of production which, prior to the introduction of modern industry, was by far the most powerful—the division of labour. The first great division of labour, the separation of town and country, condemned the rural population to thousands of years of mental torpidity, and the people of the towns each to subjection to his own individual trade. It destroyed the basis of the intellectual development of the former and the physical development of the latter. When the peasant appropriates his land, and the townsman his trade, the land appropriates the peasant and the trade the townsman to the very same extent. In the division of labour, man is also divided. All other physical and mental faculties are sacrificed to the development of one single activity. This stunting of man grows in the same measure as the division of labour, which attains its highest development in manufacture. Manufacture splits up each trade into its separate partial operations, allots each of these to an individual labourer as his life calling, and thus chains him for life to a particular detail function and a particular tool. "It converts the labourer into a crippled monstrosity, by forcing his detail dexterity at the expense of a world of productive capabilities and instincts... The individual himself is made the automatic motor of a fractional operation" (Marx)[a]—a motor which in many cases is perfected only by literally crippling the labourer physically and mentally. The machinery of modern industry degrades the labourer from a machine to the mere appendage of a machine. "The life-long speciality of handling one and the same tool, now becomes the life-long speciality of serving one and the same machine. Machinery is put to a wrong use, with the object of transforming the workman, from his very childhood, into a part of a detail-machine" (Marx).[b] And not only the labourers, but also the classes directly or indirectly exploiting the labourers are made subject, through the division of labour, to the tool of their function: the empty-minded bourgeois to his own capital and his own insane craving for profits; the lawyer to his fossilised legal conceptions, which dominate him as an independent power; the "educated classes" in general to their manifold species of local narrow-mindedness and one-sidedness, to their own physical and mental short-sightedness, to their stunted growth due to their narrow specialised education and their being chained for life to this specialised activity—even when this specialised activity is merely to do nothing.

The utopians were already perfectly clear in their minds as to the effects of the division of labour, the stunting on the one hand of the labourer, and on the other of the labour function, which is restricted to the lifelong uniform mechanical repetition of one and the same operation. The abolition of the antithesis between town and country was demanded by Fourier, as by Owen, as the first basic prerequisite for the abolition of the old division of labour altogether. Both of them thought that the population should be scattered through the country in groups of sixteen hundred to three thousand persons; each group was to occupy a gigantic

---

[a] K. Marx, *Das Kapital,* pp. 373-74. See present edition, Vol. 35, Part IV, Chapter XIV, Section 5.— *Ed.*

[b] Ibid., p. 443. See present edition, Vol. 35, Part IV, Chapter XV, Section 4.— *Ed.*

palace, with a household run on communal lines, in the centre of their area of land. It is true that Fourier occasionally refers to towns, but these were to consist in turn of only four or five such palaces situated near each other. Both writers would have each member of society occupied in agriculture as well as in industry; with Fourier, industry covers chiefly handicrafts and manufacture, while Owen assigns the main role to modern industry and already demands the introduction of steam-power and machinery in domestic work. But within agriculture as well as industry both of them also demand the greatest possible variety of occupation for each individual, and in accordance with this, the training of the youth for the utmost possible all-round technical functions. They both consider that man should gain universal development through universal practical activity and that labour should recover the attractiveness of which the division of labour has despoiled it, in the first place through this variation of occupation, and through the correspondingly short duration of the "sitting"—to use Fourier's expression [a]—devoted to each particular kind of work. Both Fourier and Owen are far in advance of the mode of thought of the exploiting classes inherited by Herr Dühring, according to which the antithesis between town and country is inevitable in the nature of things; the narrow view that a number of "entities" [D. C. 257] must in any event be condemned to the production of *one single* article, the view that desires to perpetuate the "economic species" [329] of men distinguished by their way of life—people who take pleasure in the performance of precisely this and no other thing, who have therefore sunk so low that they *rejoice* in their own subjection and one-sidedness. In comparison with the basic conceptions even of the "idiot" [D. K. G. 286] Fourier's most recklessly bold fantasies; in comparison even with the paltriest ideas of the "crude, feeble, and paltry" [295, 296] Owen—Herr Dühring, himself still completely dominated by the division of labour, is no more than an impertinent dwarf.

In making itself the master of all the means of production to use them in accordance with a social plan, society puts an end to the former subjection of men to their own means of production. It goes without saying that society cannot free itself unless every individual is freed. The old mode of production must therefore be revolutionised from top to bottom, and in particular the former

---

[a] See Ch. Fourier, *Le Nouveau Monde industriel et sociétaire*, Chapters II, V and VI.— *Ed.*

division of labour must disappear. Its place must be taken by an organisation of production in which, on the one hand, no individual can throw on the shoulders of others his share in productive labour, this natural condition of human existence; and in which, on the other hand, productive labour, instead of being a means of subjugating men, will become a means of their emancipation, by offering each individual the opportunity to develop all his faculties, physical and mental, in all directions and exercise them to the full—in which, therefore, productive labour will become a pleasure instead of being a burden.

Today this is no longer a fantasy, no longer a pious wish. With the present development of the productive forces, the increase in production that will follow from the very fact of the socialisation of the productive forces, coupled with the abolition of the barriers and disturbances, and of the waste of products and means of production, resulting from the capitalist mode of production, will suffice, with everybody doing his share of work, to reduce the time required for labour to a point which, measured by our present conceptions, will be small indeed.

Nor is the abolition of the old division of labour a demand which could only be carried through to the detriment of the productivity of labour. On the contrary. Thanks to modern industry it has become a condition of production itself. "The employment of machinery does away with the necessity of crystallising the distribution of various groups of workmen among the different kinds of machines after the manner of Manufacture, by the constant annexation of a particular man to a particular function. Since the motion of the whole system does not proceed from the workman, but from the machinery, a change of persons can take place at any time without an interruption of the work... Lastly, the quickness with which machine work is learnt by young people, does away with the necessity of bringing up for exclusive employment by machinery, a special class of operatives." [a] But while the capitalist mode of employment of machinery necessarily perpetuates the old division of labour with its fossilised specialisation, although it has become superfluous from a technical standpoint, the machinery itself rebels against this anachronism. The technical basis of modern industry is revolutionary. "By means of machinery, chemical processes and other methods, it is continually causing changes not only in the technical basis of production, but also in the functions of

---

[a] K. Marx, *Das Kapital,* pp. 442-43. See present edition, Vol. 35, Part IV, Chapter XV, Section 4.— *Ed.*

the labourer, and in the social combinations of the labour-process. At the same time, it thereby also revolutionises the division of labour within the society, and incessantly launches masses of capital and of workpeople from one branch of production to another. Modern industry, by its very nature, therefore necessitates variation of labour, fluency of function, universal mobility of the labourer... We have seen how this absolute contradiction ... vents its rage in the incessant human sacrifices from among the working-class, in the most reckless squandering of labour-power, and in the devastation caused by social anarchy. This is the negative side. But if, on the one hand, variation of work at present imposes itself after the manner of an overpowering natural law, and with the blindly destructive action of a natural law that meets with resistance at all points, modern industry, on the other hand, through its catastrophes imposes the necessity of recognising, as a fundamental law of production, variation of work, consequently fitness of the labourer for varied work, consequently the greatest possible development of his varied aptitudes. It becomes a question of life and death for society to adapt the mode of production to the normal functioning of this law. Modern industry makes it a question of life and death to replace the monstrosity of a destitute working population kept in reserve at the disposal of capital for the changing needs of exploitation with the absolute availability of man for the changing requirements of labour; to replace what is virtually a mere fragment of the individual, the mere carrier of a social detail-function, with the fully developed individual, to whom the different social functions are so many alternating modes of activity" (Marx, *Capital*).[a]

Modern industry, which has taught us to convert the movement of molecules, something more or less universally feasible, into the movement of masses for technical purposes, has thereby to a considerable extent freed production from restrictions of locality. Water-power was local; steam-power is free. While water-power is necessarily rural, steam-power is by no means necessarily urban. It is capitalist utilisation which concentrates it mainly in the towns and changes factory villages into factory towns. But in so doing it at the same time undermines the conditions under which it operates. The first requirement of the steam-engine, and a main

---

[a] Ibid., pp. 513-14. See present edition, Vol. 35, Part IV, Chapter XV, Section 9.— *Ed.*

requirement of almost all branches of production in modern industry, is relatively pure water. But the factory town transforms all water into stinking manure. However much therefore urban concentration is a basic condition of capitalist production, each individual industrial capitalist is constantly striving to get away from the large towns necessarily created by this production, and to transfer his plant to the countryside. This process can be studied in detail in the textile industry districts of Lancashire and Yorkshire; modern capitalist industry is constantly bringing new large towns into being there by constant flight from the towns into the country. The situation is similar in the metal-working districts where, in part, other causes produce the same effects.

Once more, only the abolition of the capitalist character of modern industry can bring us out of this new vicious circle, can resolve this contradiction in modern industry, which is constantly reproducing itself. Only a society which makes it possible for its productive forces to dovetail harmoniously into each other on the basis of one single vast plan can allow industry to be distributed over the whole country in the way best adapted to its own development, and to the maintenance and development of the other elements of production.

Accordingly, abolition of the antithesis between town and country is not merely possible. It has become a direct necessity of industrial production itself, just as it has become a necessity of agricultural production and, besides, of public health. The present poisoning of the air, water and land can be put an end to only by the fusion of town and country; and only such fusion will change the situation of the masses now languishing in the towns, and enable their excrement to be used for the production of plants instead of for the production of disease.

Capitalist industry has already made itself relatively independent of the local limitations arising from the location of sources of the raw materials it needs. The textile industry works up, in the main, imported raw materials. Spanish iron ore is worked up in England and Germany and Spanish and South-American copper ores, in England. Every coalfield now supplies fuel to an industrial area far beyond its own borders, an area which is widening every year. Along the whole of the European coast steam-engines are driven by English and to some extent also by German and Belgian coal. Society liberated from the restrictions of capitalist production can go much further still. By generating a race of producers with an all-round development who understand the scientific basis of industrial production as a whole, and each of whom has had practical experience in a whole series of branches of production from start to finish, this society will bring into being a new productive force which will abundantly compensate for the labour required to transport raw materials and fuel from great distances.

The abolition of the separation of town and country is therefore not utopian, also, in so far as it is conditioned on the most equal distribution possible of modern industry over the whole country. It is true that in the huge towns civilisation has bequeathed us a heritage which it will take much time and trouble to get rid of. But it must and will be got rid of, however, protracted a process it may be. Whatever destiny may be in store for the German Empire of the Prussian nation,[119] Bismarck can go to his grave proudly aware that the desire of his heart is sure to be fulfilled: the great towns will perish.[120]

And now see how puerile is Herr Dühring's idea that society can take possession of all means of production in the aggregate without revolutionising from top to bottom the old method of production and first of all putting an end to the old division of labour; that everything will be in order once

"natural opportunities and personal capabilities are taken into account" [D. C. 259]—

that therefore whole masses of entities will remain, as in the past, subjected to the production of *one single* article; whole "populations" [275] will be engaged in a single branch of production, and humanity continue to be divided, as in the past, into a number of different crippled "economic species" [329], for there still are "porters" and "architects" [D. K. G. 500]. Society is to become master of the means of production as a whole, in order that each individual may remain the slave of his means of production, and have only a choice as to *which* means of production are to enslave him. And see also how Herr Dühring considers the separation of town and country as "inevitable in the nature of things" [D. C. 232], and can find only a tiny palliative in schnaps-distilling and beet-sugar manufacturing—two, in their connection specifically Prussian, branches of industry; how he makes the distribution of industry over the country dependent on certain future inventions and on the *necessity* of associating industry directly with the procurement of raw materials—raw materials which are already used at an ever increasing distance from their place of origin! And Herr Dühring finally tries to cover up his rear by assuring us that in the long run social wants will carry through the union between agriculture and industry even *against* economic considerations, as if this would be some economic sacrifice!

Certainly, to be able to see that the revolutionary elements, which will do away with the old division of labour, along with the separation of town and country, and will revolutionise the whole of production; see that these elements are already contained in embryo in the production conditions of modern large-scale industry and that their development is hindered by the existing capitalist mode of production—to be able to see these things, it is necessary to have a somewhat wider horizon than the sphere of jurisdiction of Prussian law, than the country where production of schnaps and beet-sugar are the key industries, and where commercial crises can be studied on the book market. To be able to see these things it is necessary to have some knowledge of real large-scale industry in its historical growth and in its present actual form, especially in the one country where it has its home and where alone it has attained its classical development. Then no one will think of attempting to vulgarise modern scientific socialism and to degrade it into Herr Dühring's *specifically Prussian socialism.*

IV. DISTRIBUTION

We have already seen [a] that Dühringian economics comes down to the following proposition: the capitalist mode of *production* is quite good, and can remain in existence, but the capitalist mode of *distribution* is of evil, and must disappear. We now find that Herr Dühring's "socialitarian" system is nothing more than the carrying through of this principle in fantasy. In fact, it turned out that Herr Dühring has practically nothing to take exception to in the mode of production—as such—of capitalist society, that he wants to retain the old division of labour in all its essentials, and that he consequently has hardly a word to say in regard to production within his economic commune. Production is indeed a sphere in which robust facts are dealt with, and in which, consequently, "rational fantasy" [D. Ph. 46] should give but little scope to the soaring of its free soul, because the danger of making a disgraceful blunder is too great. It is quite otherwise with distribution—which in Herr Dühring's view has no connection whatever with production and is determined not by production but by a pure act of the will—distribution is the predestined field of his "social alchemising" [D. K. G. 237].

---

[a] See this volume, p. 174.— *Ed.*

To the equal obligation to produce corresponds the equal right to consume, exercised in an organised manner in the economic commune and in the trading commune embracing a large number of economic communes. "Labour" is here "exchanged for other labour on the basis of equal valuation... Service and counterservice represent here real equality between quantities of labour" [D. C. 256]. And this "equalisation of human energies" applies "whether the individuals have in fact done more or less, or perhaps *even nothing at all*" [D. Ph. 281]; for all performances, in so far as they involve time and energy, can be regarded as labour done—therefore even playing bowls or going for a walk [see D. C. 266]. This exchange, however, does not take place between individuals as the community is the owner of all means of production and consequently also of all products; on the one hand it takes place between each economic commune and its individual members, and on the other between the various economic and trading communes themselves. "The individual economic communes in particular will replace retail trade within their own areas by completely planned sales" [326]. Wholesale trade will be organised on the same lines: "The system of the free economic society ... consequently remains a vast exchange institution, whose operations are carried out on the basis provided by the precious metals. It is insight into the inevitable necessity of this fundamental quality which distinguishes our scheme from all those foggy notions which cling even to the most rational forms of current socialist ideas" [324].

For the purposes of this exchange, the economic commune, as the first appropriator of the social products, has to determine, "for each type of articles, a uniform price" [277], based on the average production costs. "The significance which the so-called costs of production ... have for value and price today, will be provided" (in the socialitarian system) "...by the estimates of the quantity of labour to be employed. These estimates, by virtue of the principle of equal rights for each individual also in the economic sphere, can be traced back, in the last analysis, to consideration of the number of persons that participated in the labour; they will result in the relation of prices corresponding both to the natural conditions of production and to the social right of realisation. The output of the precious metals will continue, as now, to determine the value of money... It can be seen from this that in the changed constitution of society, one not only does not lose the determining factor and measure, in the first place of values, and, with value, of the exchange relations between products, but wins them good and proper for the first time" [326-327].

The famous "absolute value" [D. K. G. 499] is at last realised.

On the other hand, however, the commune must also put its individual members in a position to buy from it the articles produced, by paying to each, in compensation for his labour, a certain sum of money, daily, weekly or monthly, but necessarily the same for all. "From the socialitarian standpoint it is consequently a matter of indifference whether we say that wages disappear, or, that they must become the exclusive form of economic income" [D. C. 263]. Equal wages and equal prices, however, establish "quantitative, if not qualitative equality of consumption" [268], and thereby the "universal principle of justice" [282] is realised in the economic sphere.

As to how the level of this wage of the future is to be determined, Herr Dühring tells us only that here too, as in all other cases, there will be an exchange of "equal labour for equal labour" [D. C. 257]. For six hours of labour, therefore, a sum of money will be paid which also embodies in itself six hours of labour.

Nevertheless, the "universal principle of justice" must not in any way be confounded with that crude levelling down which makes the bourgeois so indignantly oppose all communism, and especially the spontaneous communism of the workers. It is by no means so inexorable as it would like to appear.

The "equality in principle of economic rights does not exclude the *voluntary* addition to what justice requires of an expression of special recognition and honour... Society *honours itself* in conferring distinction on the higher types of professional ability *by a moderate additional allocation* for consumption" [267].

And Herr Dühring, too, honours himself, when combining the innocence of a dove with the subtleness of a serpent,[a] he displays such touching concern for the moderate additional consumption of the Dührings of the future.

This will finally do away with the capitalist mode of distribution. For

"supposing under such conditions someone actually had a surplus of private means at his disposal, he would not be able to find any use for it as capital. No individual and no group would acquire it from him for production, except by way of exchange or purchase, but neither would ever have occasion to pay him interest or profit" [264-65]. Hence "inheritance conforming to the principle of equality" [289] would be permissible. It cannot be dispensed with, for "a certain form of inheritance will always be a necessary accompaniment of the family principle". But even the right of inheritance "will not be able to lead to any amassing of considerable wealth, as the building up of property ... can never again aim at the creation of means of production and purely rentiers' existences" [291].

And this fortunately completes the economic commune. Let us now have a look at how it works.

We assume that all of Herr Dühring's preliminary conditions are completely realised; we therefore take it for granted that the economic commune pays to each of its members, for six hours of labour a day, a sum of money, say twelve marks, in which likewise six hours of labour are embodied. We assume further that prices exactly correspond to values, and therefore, on our assumptions, cover only the costs of raw materials, the wear and tear of machinery, the consumption of instruments of labour and the wages paid. An economic commune of a hundred working members would then produce in a day commodities to the value

---

a Matthew 10:16.— *Ed.*

of twelve hundred marks; and in a year of 300 working-days, 360,000 marks. It pays the same sum to its members, each of whom does as he likes with his share, which is twelve marks a day or 3,600 marks a year. At the end of a year, and at the end of a hundred years, the commune is no richer than it was at the beginning. During this whole period it will never once be in a position to provide even the moderate additional allocation for Herr Dühring's consumption, unless it cares to take it from its stock of means of production. Accumulation is completely forgotten. Even worse: as accumulation is a social necessity and the retention of money provides a convenient form of accumulation, the organisation of the economic commune directly impels its members to accumulate privately, and thereby leads it to its own destruction.

How can this conflict in the nature of the economic commune be avoided? It might take refuge in his beloved "taxes" [24], the price surcharge, and sell its annual production for 480,000 instead of 360,000. But as all other economic communes are in the same position, and would therefore act in the same way, each of them, in its exchanges with the others, would have to pay just as much "taxes" as it pockets itself, and the "tribute" [374] would thus have to fall on its own members alone.

Or the economic commune might settle the matter without more ado by paying to each member, for six hours of labour, the product of less than six hours, say, of four hours, of labour; that is to say, instead of twelve marks only eight marks a day, leaving the prices of commodities, however, at their former level. In this case it does directly and openly what it strived to do in a hidden and indirect way in the former case: it forms Marxian surplus-value to the amount of 120,000 marks annually, by paying its members, on outright capitalist lines, less than the value of what they produce, while it sells them commodities, which they can only buy from it, at their full value. The economic commune can therefore secure a reserve fund only by revealing itself as an "ennobled" TRUCK SYSTEM* on the widest possible communist basis.

So have your choice: Either the economic commune exchanges "equal labour for equal labour" [257], and in this case it cannot accumulate a fund for the maintenance and extension of production, but only the individual members can do this; or it

* The TRUCK SYSTEM in England, also well known in Germany, is that system under which the manufacturers themselves run shops and compel their workers to buy their goods there.

does form such a fund, but in this case it does not exchange "equal labour for equal labour".

Such is the content of exchange in the economic commune. What of its form? The exchange is effected through the medium of metallic money, and Herr Dühring is not a little proud of the "world-historic import" [D. C. 341] of this reform. But in the trading between the commune and its members the money *is not* money at all, it does not function in any way as money. It serves as a mere labour certificate; to use Marx's phrase, it is "merely evidence of the part taken by the individual in the common labour, and of his right to a certain portion of the common produce destined for consumption", and in carrying out this function, it is "no more 'money' than a ticket for the theatre".[a] It can therefore be replaced by any other token, just as Weitling replaces it by a "ledger", in which the labour-hours worked are entered on one side and means of subsistence taken as compensation on the other.[121] In a word, in the trading of the economic commune with its members it functions merely as Owen's "labour money", that "phantom" which Herr Dühring looks down upon so disdainfully, but nevertheless is himself compelled to introduce into his economics of the future. Whether the token which certifies the measure of fulfilment of the "obligation to produce", and thus of the earned "right to consume" [320] is a scrap of paper, a counter or a gold coin is absolutely of no consequence for *this* purpose. For other purposes, however, it is by no means immaterial, as we shall see.

If therefore, in the trading of an economic commune with its members, metallic money does not function as money but as a disguised labour certificate, it performs its money function even less in exchange between the different economic communes. In this exchange, on the assumptions made by Herr Dühring, metallic money is totally superfluous. In fact, mere book-keeping would suffice, which would effect the exchange of products of equal labour for products of equal labour far more simply if it used the natural measure of labour-time, with the labour-hour as unit—than if it first converted the labour-hours into money. The exchange is in reality simple exchange in kind; all balances are easily and simply settled by drafts on other communes. But should a commune really have a deficit in its dealings with other communes, all "the gold existing in the universe" [D. Ph. 96],

---

[a] K. Marx, *Das Kapital,* p. 73. See present edition, Vol. 35, Part I, Chapter III, Section 1.— *Ed.*

"money by nature" [D. C. 39] though it be, could not save this commune from the fate of having to make good this deficit by increasing the quantity of its own labour, if it does not want to fall into a position of dependence on other communes on account of its debt. But let the reader always bear in mind that we are not ourselves constructing any edifice of the future; we are merely accepting Herr Dühring's assumptions and drawing the inevitable conclusions from them.

Thus neither in exchange between the economic commune and its members nor in exchange between the different communes can gold, which is "money by nature", get to realise this its nature. Nevertheless, Herr Dühring assigns to it the function of money even in the "socialitarian" system. Hence, we must see if there is any other field in which its money function can be exercised. And this field exists. Herr Dühring gives everyone a right to "quantitatively equal consumption" [268], but he cannot compel anyone to exercise it. On the contrary, he is proud that in the world he has created everyone can do what he likes with his money. He therefore cannot prevent some from setting aside a small money hoard, while others are unable to make ends meet on the wage paid to them. He even makes this inevitable by explicitly recognising in the right of inheritance that family property should be owned in common; whence comes also the obligation of the parents to maintain their children. But this makes a wide breach in quantitatively equal consumption. The bachelor lives like a lord, happy and content with his eight or twelve marks a day, while the widower with eight minor children finds it very difficult to manage on this sum. On the other hand, by accepting money in payment without any question, the commune leaves open the door to the possibility that this money may have been obtained otherwise than by the individual's own labour. *Non olet.*[122] The commune does not know where it comes from. But in this way all conditions are created permitting metallic money, which hitherto played the role of a mere labour certificate, to exercise its real money function. Both the opportunity and the motive are present, on the one hand to form a hoard, and on the other to run into debt. The needy individual borrows from the individual who builds up a hoard. The borrowed money, accepted by the commune in payment for means of subsistence, once more becomes what it is in present-day society, the social incarnation of human labour, the real measure of labour, the general medium of circulation. All the "laws and administrative regulations" [323] in the world are just as powerless against it as they are against the multiplication table or the chemical composition of water. And as the builder of the hoard is in a position to extort interest from people in need, usury is restored along with metallic money functioning as money.

Up to this point we have only considered the effects of a retention of metallic money within the field of operation of the Dühring economic commune. But outside this field the rest of the world, the profligate world, meanwhile carries on contentedly in the old accustomed way. On the world market gold and silver remain *world money,* a general means of purchase and payment, the absolute social embodiment of wealth. And this property of the precious metal gives the individual members of the economic communes a new motive to accumulate a hoard, get rich, exact usury; the motive to manoeuvre freely and independently with regard to the commune and beyond its borders, and to realise on the world market the private wealth which they have accumulated. The usurers are transformed into dealers in the medium of circulation, bankers, controllers of the medium of circulation and of world money, and thus into controllers of production, and thus into controllers of the means of production, even though these may still for many years be registered nominally as the property of the economic and trading communes. And so that hoarders and usurers, transformed into bankers, become the masters also of the economic and trading communes themselves. Herr Dühring's "socialitarian system" is indeed quite fundamentally different from the "hazy notions" [D. K. G. 498] of the other socialists. It has no other purpose but the recreation of high finance, under whose control and for whose pecuniary advantage it will labour valiantly—if it should ever happen to be established and to hold together. Its one hope of salvation would lie in the amassers of hoards preferring, by means of their world money, to run away from the commune with all possible speed.

Ignorance of earlier socialist thought is so widespread in Germany that an innocent youth might at this point raise the question whether, for example, Owen's labour-notes might not lead to a similar abuse. Although we are here not concerned with developing the significance of these labour-notes, space should be given to the following for the purpose of contrasting Dühring's "comprehensive schematism" [D. C. 341] with Owen's "crude, feeble and meagre ideas" [D. K. G. 295, 296]: In the first place, such a misuse of Owen's labour-notes would require their conversion into real money, while Herr Dühring presupposes real money, though attempting to prohibit it from functioning otherwise than as mere labour certificate. While in Owen's scheme there would have to be a real abuse, in Dühring's scheme the immanent nature of money, which is independent of human volition, would assert itself; the specific, correct use of money would assert itself in spite of the misuse which Herr Dühring tries to impose on it owing to his own ignorance of the nature of money. Secondly, with Owen the labour-notes are only a transitional form to complete community and free utilisation of the resources of society; and incidentally at most also a means designed to make communism plausible to the British public. If therefore any form of misuse should compel Owen's society to do away with the labour-notes, the society would take a step forward towards its goal, entering upon a more perfect stage of its development. But if the Dühringian economic commune abolishes money, it at one blow destroys its "world-historic import", it puts an end to its peculiar beauty, ceases to be the Dühring economic commune and sinks to the level of the befogged notions to lift it from which Herr Dühring has devoted so much of the hard labour of his rational fantasy.*

What, then, is the source of all the strange errors and entanglements amid which the Dühring economic commune meanders? Simply the fog which, in Herr Dühring's mind, envelops the concepts of value and money, and finally drives him to attempt to discover the value of labour. But as Herr Dühring has not by any means the monopoly of such fogginess for Germany, but on the contrary meets with many competitors, we will "overcome our reluctance for a moment and solve the knot" [497] which he has contrived to make here.

The only value known in economics is the value of commodities. What are commodities? Products made in a society of more or less separate private producers, and therefore in the first place private products. These private products, however, become commodities only when they are made, not for consumption by their producers, but for consumption by others, that is, for social consumption; they enter into social consumption through exchange. The private

---

* It may be noted in passing that the part played by labour-notes in Owen's communist society is completely unknown to Herr Dühring. He knows these notes—from Sargant[a]—only in so far as they figure in the LABOUR EXCHANGE BAZAARS [123] which of course were failures, inasmuch as they were attempts by means of the direct exchange of labour to pass from existing society into communist society.

---

[a] W. L. Sargant, *Robert Owen, and His Social Philosophy.—Ed.*

producers are therefore socially interconnected, constitute a society. Their products, although the private products of each individual, are therefore simultaneously but unintentionally and as it were involuntarily, also social products. In what, then, consists the social character of these private products? Evidently in two peculiarities: first, that they all satisfy some human want, have a use-value not only for the producers but also for others; and secondly, that although they are products of the most varied individual labour, they are at the same time products of human labour as such, of general human labour. In so far as they have a use-value also for other persons, they can, generally speaking, enter into exchange; in so far as general human labour, the simple expenditure of human labour-power is incorporated in all of them, they can be compared with each other in exchange, be assumed to be equal or unequal, according to the quantity of this labour embodied in each. In two equal products made individually, social conditions being equal, an unequal quantity of individual labour may be contained, but always only an equal quantity of general human labour. An unskilled smith may make five horseshoes in the time a skilful smith makes ten. But society does not form value from the accidental lack of skill of an individual; it recognises as general human labour only labour of a normal average degree of skill at the particular time. In exchange, therefore, one of the five horseshoes made by the first smith has no more value than one of the ten made by the other in an equal time. Individual labour contains general human labour only in so far as it is socially necessary.

Therefore when I say that a commodity has a particular value, I say (1) that it is a socially useful product; (2) that it has been produced by a private individual for private account; (3) that, although a product of individual labour, it is nevertheless at the same time and as it were unconsciously and involuntarily, also a product of social labour and, be it noted, of a definite quantity of this labour, ascertained in a social way, through exchange; (4) I express this quantity not in labour itself, in so and so many labour-hours, but *in another commodity*. If therefore I say that this clock is worth as much as that piece of cloth and each of them is worth fifty marks, I say that an equal quantity of social labour is contained in the clock, the cloth and the money. I therefore assert that the social labour-time represented in them has been socially measured and found to be equal. But not directly, absolutely, as labour-time is usually measured, in labour-hours or days, etc., but in a roundabout way, through the medium of exchange, relatively.

That is why I cannot express this definite quantity of labour-time in labour-hours—how many of them remains unknown to me—but also only in a roundabout way, relatively, in another commodity, which represents an equal quantity of social labour-time. The clock is worth as much as the piece of cloth.

But the production and exchange of commodities, while compelling the society based on them to take this roundabout way, likewise compel it to make the detour as short as possible. They single out from the commonalty of commodities one sovereign commodity in which the value of all other commodities can be expressed once and for all; a commodity which serves as the direct incarnation of social labour, and is therefore directly and unconditionally exchangeable for all commodities—money. Money is already contained in embryo in the concept of value; it is value, only in developed form. But since the value of commodities, as opposed to the commodities themselves, assumes independent existence in money, a new factor appears in the society which produces and exchanges commodities, a factor with new social functions and effects. We need only state this point at the moment, without going more closely into it.

The political economy of commodity production is by no means the only science which has to deal with factors known only relatively. The same is true of physics, where we do not know how many separate gas molecules are contained in a given volume of gas, pressure and temperature being also given. But we know that, so far as Boyle's law is correct, such a given volume of any gas contains as many molecules as an equal volume of any other gas at the same pressure and temperature. We can therefore compare the molecular content of the most diverse volumes of the most diverse gases under the most diverse conditions of pressure and temperature; and if we take as the unit one litre of gas at 0° C and 760 mm pressure, we can measure the above molecular content by this unit.—In chemistry the absolute atomic weights of the various elements are also not known to us. But we know them relatively, inasmuch as we know their reciprocal relations. Hence, just as commodity production and its economics obtain a relative expression for the unknown quantities of labour contained in the various commodities, by comparing these commodities on the basis of their relative labour content, so chemistry obtains a relative expression for the magnitude of the atomic weights unknown to it by comparing the various elements on the basis of their atomic weights, expressing the atomic weight of one element in multiples or fractions of the other (sulphur, oxygen, hydrogen). And just as commodity production elevates gold to the level of the absolute commodity, the general equivalent of all other commodities, the measure of all values, so chemistry promotes hydrogen to the rank of the chemical money commodity, by fixing its atomic weight at 1 and reducing the atomic weights of all other elements to hydrogen, expressing them in multiples of its atomic weight.

Commodity production, however, is by no means the only form of social production. In the ancient Indian communities and in the family communities of the southern Slavs, products are not transformed into commodities. The members of the community are directly associated for production; the work is distributed according to tradition and requirements, and likewise the products to the extent that they are destined for consumption. Direct social production and direct distribution preclude all exchange of commodities, therefore also the transformation of the products into commodities (at any rate within the community) and consequently also their transformation into *values*.

From the moment when society enters into possession of the means of production and uses them in direct association for production, the labour of each individual, however varied its specifically useful character may be, becomes at the start and directly social labour. The quantity of social labour contained in a product need not then be established in a roundabout way; daily experience shows in a direct way how much of it is required on the average. Society can simply calculate how many hours of labour are contained in a steam-engine, a bushel of wheat of the last harvest, or a hundred square yards of cloth of a certain quality. It could therefore never occur to it still to express the quantities of labour put into the products, quantities which it will then know directly and in their absolute amounts, in a third product, in a measure which, besides, is only relative, fluctuating, inadequate, though formerly unavoidable for lack of a better one, rather than express them in their natural, adequate and absolute measure, *time*. Just as little as it would occur to chemical science still to express atomic weight in a roundabout way, relatively, by means of the hydrogen atom, if it were able to express them absolutely, in their adequate measure, namely in actual weights, in billionths or quadrillionths of a gramme. Hence, on the assumptions we made above, society will not assign values to products. It will not express the simple fact that the hundred square yards of cloth have required for their production, say, a thousand hours of labour in the oblique and meaningless way, stating that they have the *value* of a thousand hours of labour. It is true that even then it will still be necessary for society to know how much labour each article of consumption requires for its production. It will have to arrange its plan of production in accordance with its means of production, which include, in particular, its labour-powers. The useful effects of the various articles of consumption, compared with one another and with the quantities of labour required for their production, will in the end determine the plan. People will be able to manage everything very simply, without the intervention of much-vaunted "value".*

The concept of value is the most general and therefore the most comprehensive expression of the economic conditions of commodity production. Consequently, this concept contains the germ, not only of money, but also of all the more developed forms of the production and exchange of commodities. The fact that value is the expression of the social labour contained in the privately produced products itself creates the possibility of a difference arising between this social labour and the private labour contained in these same products. If therefore a private producer continues to produce in the old way, while the social mode of production develops this difference will become palpably evident to him. The same result follows when the aggregate of private producers of a particular class of goods produces a quantity of them which exceeds the requirements of society. The fact that the value of a commodity is expressed only in terms of another commodity, and can only be realised in exchange for it, admits of the possibility that the exchange may never take place altogether, or at least may not realise the correct value. Finally, when the specific commodity labour-power appears on the market, its value is determined, like that of any other commodity, by the labour-time socially necessary for its production. The value form of products therefore already contains in embryo the whole capitalist form of production, the antagonism between capitalists and wage-workers, the industrial reserve army, crises. To seek to abolish the capitalist form of production by establishing "true value" [D. K. G. 78] is therefore tantamount to attempting to abolish Catholicism by establishing the

---

* As long ago as 1844 I stated that the above-mentioned balancing of useful effects and expenditure of labour on making decisions concerning production was all that would be left, in a communist society, of the politico-economic concept of value. (*Deutsch-Französische Jahrbücher*, p. 95.[a]) The scientific justification for this statement, however, as can be seen, was made possible only by Marx's *Capital*.

---

[a] Engels refers to his article "Umrisse zu einer Kritik der Nationaloekonomie" (see present edition, Vol. 3, pp. 418-43).— *Ed.*

"true" Pope, or to set up a society in which at last the producers control their product, by consistently carrying into life an economic category which is the most comprehensive expression of the enslavement of the producers by their own product.

Once the commodity-producing society has further developed the value form, which is inherent in commodities as such, to the money form, various germs still hidden in value break through to the light of day. The first and most essential effect is the generalisation of the commodity form. Money forces the commodity form even on the objects which have hitherto been produced directly for self-consumption; it drags them into exchange. Thereby the commodity form and money penetrate the internal husbandry of the communities directly associated for production; they break one tie of communion after another, and dissolve the community into a mass of private producers. At first, as can be seen in India, money replaces joint tillage of the soil by individual tillage; at a later stage it puts an end to the common ownership of the tillage area, which still manifests itself in periodical redistribution, by a final division (for example in the village communities on the Mosel^a; and it is now beginning also in the Russian village communes); finally, it forces the dividing-up of whatever woodland and pasturage is still owned in common. Whatever other causes arising in the development of production are also operating here, money always remains the most powerful means through which their influence is exerted on the communities. And, despite all "laws and administrative regulations" [D. C. 323], money would with the same natural necessity inevitably break up the Dühring economic commune, if it ever came into existence.

We have already seen above ("Political Economy", VI)^b that it is a contradiction in itself to speak of the value of labour. As under certain social relations labour produces not only products but also value, and this value is measured by labour, the latter can as little have a separate value as weight, as such, can have a separate weight, or heat, a separate temperature. But it is the characteristic peculiarity of all social confusion that ruminates on "true value" [D. K. G. 78] to imagine that in existing society the worker does not receive the full "value" of his labour, and that socialism is destined to remedy this. Hence it is necessary in the first place to discover what the value of labour is, and this is done by attempting to measure labour, not by its adequate measure, time,

---

^a See this volume, p. 150.— *Ed.*
^b Ibid., pp. 182-87.— *Ed.*

but by its product. The worker should receive the "full proceeds of labour" [D. C. 324].[124] Not only the labour product, but labour itself should be directly exchangeable for products; one hour's labour for the product of another hour's labour. This, however, gives rise at once to a very "serious" hitch. The *whole product* is distributed. The most important progressive function of society, accumulation, is taken from society and put into the hands, placed at the arbitrary discretion, of individuals. The individuals can do what they like with their "proceeds", but society at best remains as rich or poor as it was. The means of production accumulated in the past have therefore been centralised in the hands of society only in order that all means of production accumulated in the future may once again be dispersed in the hands of individuals. One knocks to pieces one's own premises; one has arrived at a pure absurdity.

Fluid labour, active labour-power, is to be exchanged for the product of labour. Then labour-power is a commodity, just like the product for which it is to be exchanged. Then the value of this labour-power is not in any sense determined by its product, but by the social labour embodied in it, according to the present law of wages.

But it is precisely this which must not be, we are told. Fluid labour, labour-power, should be exchangeable for its full product. That is to say, it should be exchangeable not for its *value*, but for its *use-value*; the law of value is to apply to all other commodities, but must be repealed so far as labour-power is concerned. Such is the self-destructive confusion that lies behind the "value of labour".

The "exchange of labour for labour on the principle of equal valuation" [256], in so far as it has any meaning, that is to say, the mutual exchangeability of products of equal social labour, hence the law of value, is the fundamental law of precisely commodity production, hence also of its highest form, capitalist production. It asserts itself in present-day society in the only way in which economic laws can assert themselves in a society of private producers: as a blindly operating law of nature inherent in things and relations, and independent of the will or actions of the producers. By elevating this law to the basic law of his economic commune and demanding that the commune should execute it in all consciousness, Herr Dühring converts the basic law of existing society into the basic law of his imaginary society. He wants existing society, but without its abuses. In this he occupies the same position as Proudhon. Like him, he wants to abolish the abuses which have arisen out of the development of commodity production into capitalist production, by giving effect against them to the basic law of commodity production, precisely the law to whose operation these abuses are due. Like him, he wants to abolish the real consequences of the law of value by means of fantastic ones.

Our modern Don Quixote, seated on his noble Rosinante, the "universal principle of justice" [D. C. 282], and followed by his valiant Sancho Panza, Abraham Enss,[a] sets out proudly on his knight errantry to win Mambrin's helmet, the "value of labour"; but we fear, fear greatly, he will bring home nothing but the old familiar barber's basin.[b]

V. STATE, FAMILY, EDUCATION

With the two last chapters we have about exhausted the economic content of Herr Dühring's "new socialitarian system" [D. Ph. 295]. The only point we might add is that his "universal range of historical survey" [D. K. G. 2] does not in the least prevent him from safeguarding his own special interests, even apart from the moderate surplus consumption referred to above. As the old division of labour continues to exist in the socialitarian system, the economic commune will have to reckon not only with architects and porters [500], but also with professional writers, and the question will then arise how authors' rights are to be dealt with. This question is one which occupies Herr Dühring's attention more than any other. Everywhere, for example, in connection with Louis Blanc and Proudhon [D. C. 302; D. K. G. 482-83], the reader stumbles across the question of authors' rights, until it is finally brought safely into the haven of "sociality", after a circumstantial discussion occupying nine full pages of the *Cursus,* in the form of a mysterious "remuneration of labour" [D. C. 307]—whether with or without moderate surplus consumption, is not stated. A chapter on the position of fleas in the natural system of society would have been just as appropriate and in any case far less tedious.

---

[a] Engels refers to the lampoon: A. Enss, *Engels Attentat auf den gesunden Menschenverstand oder Der wissenschaftliche Bankerott im Marxistischen Sozialismus. Ein offener Brief an meine Freunde in Berlin.—Ed.*

[b] M. Cervantes de Saavedra, *El ingenioso hidalgo Don Quijote de la Mancha,* Part I, Chapter XXI.—*Ed.*

The *Philosophie* gives detailed prescriptions for the organisation of the state of the future. Here Rousseau, although "the sole important forerunner" [D. Ph. 264] of Herr Dühring, nevertheless did not lay the foundations deep enough; his more profound successor puts this right by completely watering down Rousseau and mixing in remnants of the Hegelian philosophy of right, also reduced to a watery mess.[a] "The sovereignty of the individual" [268] forms the basis of the Dühringian state of the future; it is not to be suppressed by the rule of the majority, but to find its real culmination in it. How does this work? Very simply.

"If one presupposes agreements between each individual and every other individual in all directions, and if the object of these agreements is mutual aid against unjust offences—then the power required for the maintenance of right is only strengthened, and right is not deduced from the more superior strength of the many against the individual or of the majority against the minority" [268].

Such is the ease with which the living force of the hocus-pocus of the philosophy of reality surmounts the most impassable obstacles; and if the reader thinks that after that he is no wiser than he was before, Herr Dühring replies that he really must not think it is such a simple matter, for

"the *slightest error* in the conception of the role of the collective will would *destroy* the sovereignty of the individual, and this sovereignty is the only thing" (!) "conducive to the deduction of real rights" [268].

Herr Dühring treats his public as it deserves, when he makes game of it. He could have laid it on much thicker; the students of the philosophy of reality would not have noticed it anyhow.

Now the sovereignty of the individual consists essentially in that

"the individual is *subject to absolute compulsion* by the state"; this compulsion, however, can only be justified in so far as it "really serves natural justice" [271]. With this end in view there will be "legislative and judicial authority", which, however, "must remain in the hands of the community" [272]; and there will also be an alliance for defence, which will find expression in "joint action in the army or in an executive section for the maintenance of internal security" [273],

that is to say, there will also be army, police, gendarmerie. Herr Dühring has many times already shown that he is a good Prussian; here he proves himself a peer of that model Prussian, who, as the late Minister von Rochow put it, "carries his gendarme in his breast". This gendarmerie of the future, however, will not be so dangerous as the police thugs [125] of the present day. Whatever the

---

[a] See this volume, p. 134.— *Ed.*

sovereign individual may suffer at their hands, he will always have *one consolation*:

"the right or wrong which, according to the circumstances, may then be dealt to him by free society can never be *any worse* than that which the *state of nature* would have brought with it" [D. Ph. 274]!

And then, after Herr Dühring has once more tripped us up on those authors' rights of his which are always getting in the way, he assures us that in his world of the future

there will be, "of course, an absolutely free Bar available to all" [279].

"The free society, as it is conceived today" [304], gets steadily more and more mixed. Architects, porters, professional writers, gendarmes, and now also barristers! This "world of sober and critical thought" [D. C. 556-57] and the various heavenly king-doms of the different religions, in which the believer always finds in transfigured form the things which have sweetened his earthly existence, are as like as two peas. And Herr Dühring is a citizen of the state where "everyone can be happy in his own way".[126] What more do we want?

But it does not matter what we want. What matters is what Herr Dühring wants. And he differs from Frederick II in this, that in the Dühringian future state certainly not everyone will be able to be happy in his own way. The constitution of this future state provides:

"In the free society there can be no religious worship; *for* every member of it has got beyond the primitive childish superstition that there are beings, behind nature or above it, who can be influenced by sacrifices or prayers" [D. Ph. 285]. A "socialitarian system, rightly conceived, *has* therefore ... *to abolish* all the paraphernalia of religious magic, and therewith all the essential elements of religious worship" [D. C. 345].

Religion is being prohibited.

All religion, however, is nothing but the fantastic reflection in men's minds of those external forces which control their daily life, a reflection in which the terrestrial forces assume the form of supernatural forces. In the beginnings of history it was the forces of nature which were first so reflected, and which in the course of further evolution underwent the most manifold and varied personifications among the various peoples. This early process has been traced back by comparative mythology, at least in the case of the Indo-European peoples, to its origin in the Indian Vedas, and in its further evolution it has been demonstrated in detail among the Indians, Persians, Greeks, Romans, Germans and, so far as material is available, also among the Celts, Lithuanians and Slavs. But it is not long before, side by side with the forces of nature, social forces begin to be active—forces which confront man as equally alien and at first equally inexplicable, dominating him with the same apparent natural necessity as the forces of nature themselves. The fantastic figures, which at first only reflected the mysterious forces of nature, at this point acquire social attributes, become representatives of the forces of history.* At a still further stage of evolution, all the natural and social attributes of the numerous gods are transferred to *one* almighty god, who is but a reflection of the abstract man. Such was the origin of monotheism, which was historically the last product of the vulgarised philosophy of the later Greeks and found its incarnation in the exclusively national god of the Jews, Jehovah. In this convenient, handy and universally adaptable form, religion can continue to exist as the immediate, that is, the sentimental form of men's relation to the alien, natural and social, forces which dominate them, so long as men remain under the control of these forces. However, we have seen repeatedly that in existing bourgeois society men are dominated by the economic conditions created by themselves, by the means of production which they themselves have produced, as if by an alien force. The actual basis of the religious reflective activity therefore continues to exist, and with it the religious reflection itself. And although bourgeois political economy has given a certain insight into the causal connection of this alien domination, this makes no essential difference. Bourgeois economics can neither prevent crises in general, nor protect the individual capitalists from losses, bad debts and bankruptcy, nor secure the individual workers against unemployment and destitution. It is still true that man proposes and God (that is, the alien domination of the capitalist mode of production) disposes. Mere knowledge, even if it went much further and deeper than that of bourgeois economic science, is not enough to bring social forces under the domination of society. What is above all necessary for this, is a social *act*. And when this act has been accomplished, when society, by taking possession of all means of production and using

---

* This twofold character assumed later on by the divinities was one of the causes of the subsequently widespread confusion of mythologies—a cause which comparative mythology has overlooked, as it pays attention exclusively to their character as reflections of the forces of nature. Thus in some Germanic tribes the war-god is called Tyr (Old Nordic) or Zio (Old High German) and so corresponds to the Greek Zeus, Latin Jupiter for Diespiter; in other Germanic tribes, Er, Eor, corresponds therefore to the Greek Ares, Latin Mars.

them on a planned basis, has freed itself and all its members from
the bondage in which they are now held by these means of
production which they themselves have produced but which
confront them as an irresistible alien force; when therefore man
no longer merely proposes, but also disposes—only then will the
last alien force which is still reflected in religion vanish; and with it
will also vanish the religious reflection itself, for the simple reason
that then there will be nothing left to reflect.

Herr Dühring, however, cannot wait until religion dies this, its
natural, death. He proceeds in more deep-rooted fashion. He
out-Bismarcks Bismarck; he decrees sharper May laws [127] not
merely against Catholicism, but against all religion whatsoever; he
incites his gendarmes of the future against religion, and thereby
helps it to martyrdom and a prolonged lease of life. Wherever we
turn, we find specifically Prussian socialism.

After Herr Dühring has thus happily destroyed religion,

"man, made to rely solely on himself and nature, and matured in the knowledge of
his collective powers, can intrepidly enter on all the roads which the course of
events and his own being open to him" [D. Ph. 407].

Let us now consider for a change what "course of events" the
man made to rely on himself can intrepidly enter on, led by Herr
Dühring.

The first course of events whereby man is made to rely on
himself is: being born. Then,

for the period of natural minority, he remains committed to the "natural tutor of
children", his mother. "This period may last, as in ancient Roman law, until
puberty, that is to say, until about the fourteenth year." Only when badly brought
up older boys do not pay proper respect to their mother's authority will recourse
be had to paternal assistance, and particularly to the public educational regulations,
to remedy this. At puberty the child becomes subject to "the natural guardianship
of his father", if there is such a one "of real and uncontested paternity"
[293, 294]; otherwise the community appoints a guardian.

Just as Herr Dühring at an earlier point imagined that the
capitalist mode of production could be replaced by the social
without transforming production itself, so now he fancies that the
modern bourgeois family can be torn from its whole economic
foundations without changing its entire form. To him, this form is
so immutable that he even makes "ancient Roman law"
[293], though in a somewhat "ennobled" form, govern the
family for all time; and he can conceive a family only as a
"bequeathing" [D. C. 291], which means a possessing, unit. Here
the utopians are far in advance of Herr Dühring. They considered
that the socialisation of youth education and, with this, real

freedom in the mutual relations between members of a family, would directly follow from the free association of men and the transformation of private domestic work into a public industry. Moreover, Marx has already shown (*Capital*, [Vol. I,] p. 515 *et seqq.*) that "modern industry, by assigning as it does an important part in the socially organised process of production, outside the domestic sphere, to women, to young persons, and to children of both sexes, creates a new economic foundation for a higher form of the family and of the relations between the sexes".[a]

"Every dreamer of social reforms," says Herr Dühring, "naturally has ready a pedagogy corresponding to his new social life" [D. K. G. 295].

If we are to judge by this thesis, Herr Dühring is "a veritable monster" [261] among the dreamers of social reforms. For the school of the future occupies his attention at the very least as much as the author's rights, and this is really saying a great deal. He has his curricula for school and university all ready and complete, not only for the whole "foreseeable future" [D. Ph. 1] but also for the transition period. But we will confine ourselves to what will be taught to the young people of both sexes in the final and ultimate socialitarian system.

The universal people's school will provide

"everything which by itself and in principle can have any attraction for man", and therefore in particular the "foundations and main conclusions of all sciences touching on the understanding of the world and of life" [284]. In the first place, therefore, it teaches mathematics, and indeed to such effect that the field of all fundamental concepts and methods, from simple numeration and addition to the integral calculus, is "completely compassed" [418].

But this does not mean that in this school anyone will really differentiate or integrate. On the contrary. What is to be taught there will be, rather, entirely new elements of general mathematics, which contain in embryo both ordinary elementary and higher mathematics. And although Herr Dühring asserts that

he already has in his mind "schematically, in their main outlines", "the contents of the textbooks" [415] which the school of the future will use,

he has unfortunately not as yet succeeded in discovering these

"elements of general mathematics";

and what he cannot achieve

---

[a] K. Marx, *Das Kapital*, p. 516. See present edition, Vol. 35, Part IV, Chapter XV, Section 9.— *Ed.*

"can only really be expected from the free and enhanced forces of the new social order" [D. Ph. 418].

But if the grapes of the mathematics of the future are still very sour, future astronomy, mechanics and physics will present all the less difficulty and will

"provide the kernel of all schooling", while "the science of plants and animals, which, in spite of all theories, is mainly of a descriptive character" will serve "rather as topics for light conversation" [416-17].

There it is, in black and white, in the *Philosophie*, page 417. Even to the present day Herr Dühring knows no other botany and zoology than those which are mainly descriptive. The whole of organic morphology, which embraces the comparative anatomy, embryology, and palaeontology of the organic world, is entirely unknown to him even by name. While in the sphere of biology totally new sciences are springing up, almost by the dozen, behind his back, his puerile spirit still goes to Raff's *Naturgeschichte für Kinder* for "the eminently modern educative elements provided by the natural-scientific mode of thought" [D. K.G. 504], and this constitution of the organic world he decrees likewise for the whole "foreseeable future". Here, too, as is his wont, he entirely forgets chemistry.

As for the aesthetic side of education, Herr Dühring will have to fashion it all anew. The poetry of the past is worthless for this purpose. Where all religion is prohibited, it goes without saying that the "mythological or other religious trimmings" characteristic of poets up to now cannot be tolerated in this school. "Poetic mysticism", too, "such as, for example, Goethe practised so extensively", is to be condemned. Herr Dühring will therefore have to make up his mind to produce for us those poetic masterpieces which "are in accord with the higher claims of an imagination reconciled with reason", and represent the genuine ideal, which "denotes the consummation of the world" [D. Ph. 423]. Let him not tarry with it! The economic commune can achieve its conquest of the world only when it moves along at the Alexandrine double, reconciled with reason.

The adolescent citizen of the future will not be much troubled with philology.

"The dead languages will be entirely discarded ... the foreign living languages, however, ... will remain of secondary importance." Only where intercourse between nations extends to the movement of the masses of the peoples themselves would these languages be made accessible, according to needs and in an easy form. "Really educative study of language" will be provided by a kind of general grammar, and particularly by study of the "substance and form of one's own language" [426-27].

The national narrow-mindedness of modern man is still much too cosmopolitan for Herr Dühring. He wants also to do away with the two levers which in the world as it is today give at least the opportunity of rising above the narrow national standpoint: knowledge of the ancient languages, which opens a wider common horizon at least to those people of various nationalities who have had a classical education; and knowledge of modern languages, through the medium of which alone the people of different nations can make themselves understood by one another and acquaint themselves with what is happening beyond their own borders. On the contrary, the grammar of the mother tongue is to be thoroughly drilled in. "Substance and form of one's own language", however, become intelligible only when its origin and gradual evolution are traced, and this cannot be done without taking into account, first, its own extinct forms, and secondly, cognate languages, both living and dead. But this brings us back again to territory which has been expressly forbidden. If Herr Dühring strikes out of his curriculum all modern historical grammar, there is nothing left for his language studies but the old-fashioned technical grammar, cut to the old classical philological pattern, with all its casuistry and arbitrariness, based on the lack of any historical basis. His hatred of the old philology makes him elevate the very worst product of the old philology to "the central point of the really educative study of language" [427]. It is clear that we have before us a linguist who has never heard a word of the tremendous and successful development of the historical science of language which took place during the last sixty years, and who therefore seeks "the eminently modern educative elements" [D. K. G. 504] of linguistics, not in Bopp, Grimm and Diez, but in Heyse and Becker of blessed memory.

But all this would still fall far short of making the young citizen of the future "rely on himself". To achieve this, it is necessary here again to lay a deeper foundation, by means of

"the assimilation of the latest philosophical principles". "Such a deepening of the foundation, however, will not be ... at all a gigantic task", now that Herr Dühring has cleared the path. In fact, "if one purges of the spurious, scholastic excrescences those few strictly scientific truths of which the general schematics of being can boast, and determines to admit as valid only the reality authenticated" by Herr Dühring, elementary philosophy becomes perfectly accessible also to the youth of the future. "Recall to your mind the *extremely simple* methods by which we helped forward the concepts of infinity and their critique to a hitherto unknown import"—and then "you will not be able to see at all why the elements of the universal conception of space and time, which have been given such simple form by the deepening and sharpening now effected, should not eventually pass into the ranks of the elementary studies... The most deep-rooted ideas" of Herr Dühring "should play no secondary role in the universal educational scheme of the new society" [D. Ph. 427-28]. The self-equal state of matter and the counted uncountable are on the contrary destined "not merely to put man on his own feet but also to make him realise of himself that he *has the so-called absolute underfoot*".

The people's school of the future, as one can see, is nothing but a somewhat "ennobled" Prussian grammar school in which Greek and Latin are replaced by a little more pure and applied mathematics and in particular by the elements of the philosophy of reality, and the teaching of German is brought back to Becker, of blessed memory, that is, down to about a fourth-form level. And in fact, now that we have demonstrated Herr Dühring's mere schoolboy "knowledge" in all the spheres on which he has touched, the reader will "not be able to see at all" why it, or rather, such of it as is left after our preliminary thorough "purging", should not all and sundry "eventually pass into the ranks of the elementary studies"—inasmuch as in reality it has never left these ranks. True, Herr Dühring has heard something about the combination of work and instruction in socialist society, which is to ensure an all-round technical education as well as a practical foundation for scientific training; and this point, too, is therefore brought in, in his usual way, to help the socialitarian scheme [284, 414]. But because, as we have seen, the old division of labour, in its essentials, is to remain undisturbed in the Dühringian production of the future, this technical training at school is deprived of any practical application later on, or any significance for production itself; it has a purpose only within the school: it is to replace gymnastics, which our deep-rooted revolutioniser wants to ignore altogether. He can therefore offer us only a few phrases, as for example,

"young and old will work, in the serious sense of the word" [D. C. 328].

This spineless and meaningless ranting is really pitiful when one compares it with the passage in *Capital,* pages 508 to 515, in which Marx develops the thesis that "from the Factory system budded, as Robert Owen has shown us in detail, the germ of the education of the future, an education that will, in the case of every child over a given age, combine productive labour with instruction and gymnastics, not only as one of the methods of adding to the efficiency of production, but as the only method of producing fully developed human beings".[a]

We must skip the university of the future, in which the philosophy of reality will be the kernel of all knowledge, and where, alongside the Faculty of Medicine, the Faculty of Law will continue in full bloom; we must also omit the "special training institutions", about which all we learn is that they will be only "for a few subjects". Let us assume that the young citizen of the future has passed all his educational courses and has at last been "made to rely upon himself" sufficiently to be able to look about for a wife. What is the course of events which Herr Dühring offers him in this sphere?

"In view of the importance of propagation for the conservation, elimination, blending, and even new creative development of qualities, the ultimate roots of the human and unhuman must to a great extent be sought in sexual union and selection, and furthermore in the care taken for or against the ensuring of certain birth results. We must leave it practically to a later epoch to judge the brutality and stupidity now rife in this sphere. Nevertheless we must at least make clear from the outset, even in spite of the weight of prejudice, that far more important than the number of births is surely whether nature or human circumspection succeeded or failed in regard to their quality. It is true that at all times and under all legal systems monstrosities have been destroyed; but there is a wide range of degrees between the normal human being and deformities which lack all resemblance to the human being... It is obviously an advantage to prevent the birth of a human being who would only be a defective creature" [D. Ph. 246].

Another passage runs:

Philosophic thought can find no difficulty ... in comprehending the right of the unborn world to the best possible composition... Conception and, if need be, also birth offer the opportunity for preventive, or in exceptional cases selective, care in this connection" [395-96].

Again:

"Grecian art—the idealisation of man in marble—will not be able to retain its historical importance when the less artistic, and therefore, from the standpoint of the fate of the millions, far more important task of perfecting the human form in flesh and blood is taken in hand. This form of art does not merely deal with stone, and its aesthetics is not concerned with the contemplation of dead forms" [256]—and so on.

Our budding citizen of the future is brought to earth again. Even without Herr Dühring's help he certainly knew that marriage is not an art which merely deals with stone, or even with the

---

[a] K. Marx, *Das Kapital*, p. 509. See present edition, Vol. 35, Part IV, Chapter XV, Section 9.— *Ed.*

contemplation of dead forms; but after all, Herr Dühring had promised him that he would be able to strike out along all roads which the course of events and his own nature opened to him, in order to discover a sympathetic female heart together with the body belonging to it. Nothing of the kind—the "deeper and stricter morality" [D. Ph. 396] thunders at him. The first thing that he must do is to cast off the brutality and stupidity now rife in the sphere of sexual union and selection, and bear in mind the right of the new-born world to the best possible composition. At this solemn moment it is to him a matter of perfecting the human form in flesh and blood, of becoming a Phidias, so to speak, in flesh and blood. How is he to set about it? Herr Dühring's mysterious utterances quoted above give him not the slightest indication, although Herr Dühring himself says it is an "art". Has Herr Dühring perhaps "in his mind's eye, schematically", a textbook also on this subject—of the kind of which, in sealed wrappers, German bookshops are now so full? Indeed, we are no longer in socialitarian society, but rather in the *Magic Flute*[128]—the only difference being that Sarastro, the stout Masonic priest, would hardly rank as a "priest of the second order" [460] in comparison with our deeper and stricter moralist. The tests to which Sarastro put his couple of love's adepts are mere child's play compared with the terrifying examination through which Herr Dühring puts his two sovereign individuals before he permits them to enter the state of "free and ethical marriage" [296]. And so it may happen that our "made-to-be-self-reliant" Tamino of the future may indeed have the so-called absolute underfoot, but one of his feet may be a couple of rungs short of what it should be, so that evil tongues call him a club-foot. It is also within the realm of the possible that his best-beloved Pamina of the future does not hold herself quite straight on the above-said absolute, owing to a slight deviation in the direction of her right shoulder which jealous tongues might even call a little hump. What then? Will our deeper and stricter Sarastro forbid them to practise the art of perfecting humanity, in flesh and blood; will he exercise his "preventive care" at "conception", or his "selective care" at "birth" [396]? Ten to one, things will happen otherwise; the pair of lovers will leave Sarastro-Dühring where he stands and go off to the registry office.

Hold on there! Herr Dühring cries. This is not at all what was meant. Give me a chance to explain!

If the "higher, genuinely human motives of wholesome sexual unions ... the humanly ennobled form of sexual excitement, which in its intense manifestation is *passionate love,* when reciprocated is the best guarantee of a union which will be acceptable also in its result... it is only an effect of the second order that from a relation which in itself is harmonious a symphoniously composed product should result. From this in turn it follows that any compulsion must have harmful effects" [247]—and so on.

And thus all ends the very best way in the best of all possible socialitarian worlds: club-foot and hunchback love each other passionately, and therefore in their reciprocal relation offer the best guarantee for a harmonious "effect of the second order"; it is all just like a novel—they love each other, they get each other, and all the deeper and stricter morality [396] turns out as usual to be harmonious twaddle.

Herr Dühring's noble ideas about the female sex in general can be gathered from the following indictment of existing society:

"In a society of oppression based on the sale of human being to human being, prostitution is accepted as the natural complement of compulsory marriage ties in the men's favour, and it is one of the most comprehensible but also *most significant facts that nothing of the kind is possible for the women*" [291-92].

I would not care, for anything in the world, to have the thanks which might accrue to Herr Dühring from the women for this compliment. But has Herr Dühring really never heard of the form of income known as a petticoat-pension [*Schürzenstipendien*], which is now no longer quite an exceptional thing? Herr Dühring himself was once a referendary [129] and he lives in Berlin, where even in my day, thirty-six years ago, to say nothing of lieutenants *Referendarius* was used often enough to rhyme with *Schürzenstipendarius!*

* * *

May the reader permit us to take leave of our subject, which has often been dry and gloomy enough, on a note of facetiousness and reconciliation. So long as we had to deal with the separate issues raised, our judgment was bound by the objective, incontrovertible facts, and on the basis of these facts it was often enough necessarily sharp and even hard. Now when philosophy, economics and socialitarian system all lie behind us; when we have before us the picture of the author as a whole, which we had previously to judge in detail—now human considerations can come into the foreground; at this point we shall be permitted to trace back to personal causes many otherwise incomprehensible scientific errors and conceits, and to sum up our verdict against Herr Dühring in the words: *mental incompetence due to megalomania.*

Frederick Engels

DIALECTICS OF NATURE [130]

Written in the main from 1873 to 1882

First published in full in German and Russian in *Marx-Engels Archives,* Book II, 1925

Printed according to the manuscript

313

[PLAN OUTLINES]

[OUTLINE OF THE GENERAL PLAN] [131]

(1) Historical introduction: the metaphysical conception has become impossible in natural science owing to the very development of the latter.[a]

(2) Course of the theoretical development in Germany since Hegel (old preface).[b] The return to dialectics takes place unconsciously, hence contradictorily and slowly.

(3) Dialectics as the science of universal inter-connection. Main laws: transformation of quantity and quality—mutual penetration of polar opposites and transformation into each other when carried to extremes—development through contradiction or negation of the negation—spiral form of development.

(4) The inter-connection of the sciences. Mathematics, mechanics, physics, chemistry, biology. St. Simon (Comte), and Hegel.

(5) Aperçus[c] on the separate sciences and their dialectical content:

1. Mathematics: dialectical aids and expressions.—Mathematical infinite really occurring.

2. Celestial mechanics—now resolved into a *process.*—Mechanics: point of departure was inertia, which is only the negative expression of the indestructibility of motion.

3. Physics—transitions of molecular motions into one another. Clausius and Loschmidt.

---

[a] See this volume, pp. 318-35.— *Ed.*
[b] Ibid., pp. 336-44.— *Ed.*
[c] Reflections, remarks.— *Ed.*

12*

4. Chemistry: theories, energy.
5. Biology. Darwinism. Necessity and chance.
(6) The limits of knowledge. Du Bois-Reymond[a] and Nägeli.[b]—
Helmholtz, Kant, Hume.
(7) The mechanical theory. Haeckel.[c]
(8) The plastidule soul—Haeckel and Nägeli.[132]
(9) Science and teaching—Virchow.[133]
(10) The cell state—Virchow.[134]

(11) Darwinian politics and theory of society—Haeckel and
Schmidt.[135]—Differentiation of man through *labour* [Arbeit].[d]—
Application of economics to natural science. Helmholtz's *"work"*
[Arbeit] (*Populäre Vorträge,* II).[136]

---

[a] E. Du Bois-Reymond, *Über die Grenzen des Naturerkennens....*— *Ed.*
[b] C. Nägeli, "Die Schranken der naturwissenschaftlichen Erkenntniss," In:
Tageblatt der 50. Versammlung deutscher Naturforscher und Aerzte in München 1877.
Beilage. Zweite allgemeine Sitzung am 20. September 1877.— *Ed.*
[c] See this volume, pp. 530-34.— *Ed.*
[d] Ibid., pp. 452-64.— *Ed.*

Outline of the general plan of *Dialectics of Nature*

[OUTLINE OF THE PART PLAN] [137]

(1) Motion in general.
(2) Attraction and repulsion. Transference of motion.
(3) [Law of the] conservation of energy applied to this.
Repulsion + attraction.—Addition of repulsion = energy.
(4) Gravitation—heavenly bodies—terrestrial mechanics.
(5) Physics. Heat. Electricity.
(6) Chemistry.
(7) Summary.

(a) Before 4: Mathematics. Infinite line. + and − are equal.
(b) In astronomy: performance of work by the tides.
Double calculation in Helmholtz, II, [p.] 120.[a]
"Forces" in Helmholtz, II, [p.] 190.[b]

---

a Cf. this volume, pp. 373-77.— Ed.
b Ibid., pp. 372-74.— Ed.

318

[ARTICLES AND CHAPTERS]

INTRODUCTION [138]

Modern research into nature, which alone has achieved a scientific, systematic, all-round development, in contrast to the brilliant natural-philosophical intuitions of antiquity and the extremely important but sporadic discoveries of the Arabs, which for the most part vanished without results—this modern research into nature dates, like all more recent history, from that mighty epoch which we Germans term the Reformation, from the national misfortune that overtook us at that time, and which the French term the Renaissance and the Italians the *Cinquecento*,[a] although it is not fully expressed by any of these names. It is the epoch which had its rise in the latter half of the fifteenth century. Royalty, with the support of the burghers of the towns, broke the power of the feudal nobility and established the great monarchies, based essentially on nationality, within which the modern European nations and modern bourgeois society came to development. And while the burghers and nobles were still fighting one another, the German Peasant War pointed prophetically to future class struggles, by bringing on to the stage not only the peasants in revolt—that was no longer anything new—but behind them the beginnings of the modern proletariat, with the red flag in their hands and the demand for common ownership of goods on their lips. In the manuscripts saved from the fall of Byzantium, in the antique statues dug out of the ruins of Rome, a new world was revealed to the astonished West, that of ancient Greece; the ghosts of the Middle Ages vanished before its shining forms; Italy rose to

---

[a] Short for *milcinquecento*, 1500, used for the period A.D. 1500-1599.— *Ed.*

an undreamt-of flowering of art, which was like a reflection of classical antiquity and was never attained again. In Italy, France, and Germany a new literature arose, the first modern literature; shortly afterwards came the classical epochs of English and Spanish literature. The bounds of the old *orbis terrarum*[a] were pierced, only now for the first time was the world really discovered and the basis laid for subsequent world trade and the transition from handicraft to manufacture, which in its turn formed the starting-point for modern large-scale industry. The dictatorship of the Church over men's minds was shattered; it was directly cast off by the majority of the Germanic peoples, who adopted Protestantism, while among the Latins a cheerful spirit of free thought, taken over from the Arabs and nourished by the newly-discovered Greek philosophy, took root more and more and prepared the way for the materialism of the eighteenth century.

It was the greatest progressive revolution that mankind had so far experienced, a time which called for giants and produced giants—giants in power of thought, passion and character, in universality and learning. The men who founded the modern rule of the bourgeoisie had anything but bourgeois limitations. On the contrary, the adventurous character of the time inspired them to a greater or lesser degree. There was hardly any man of importance then living who had not travelled extensively, who did not speak four or five languages, who did not shine in a number of fields. Leonardo da Vinci was not only a great painter but also a great mathematician, mechanician, and engineer, to whom the most diverse branches of physics are indebted for important discoveries. Albrecht Dürer was painter, engraver, sculptor, and architect, and in addition invented a system of fortification embodying many of the ideas that much later were again taken up by Montalembert and the modern German science of fortification. Machiavelli was statesman, historian, poet, and at the same time the first notable military author of modern times. Luther not only cleaned the Augean stable of the Church but also that of the German language; he created modern German prose [139] and composed the text and melody of that triumphal hymn imbued with confidence in victory which became the Marseillaise of the sixteenth century.[140] The heroes of that time were not yet in thrall to the division of labour, the restricting effects of which, with its production of one-sidedness, we so often notice in their successors. But what is especially characteristic of them is that they almost all

---

[a] *Orbis terrarum*—the circle of lands, the whole world.—*Ed.*

live and pursue their activities in the midst of the contemporary movements, in the practical struggle; they take sides and join in the fight, one by speaking and writing, another with the sword, many with both. Hence the fullness and force of character that makes them complete men. Men of the study are the exception— either persons of second or third rank or cautious philistines who do not want to burn their fingers.

At that time natural science also developed in the midst of the general revolution and was itself thoroughly revolutionary; it had indeed to win in struggle its right of existence. Side by side with the great Italians from whom modern philosophy dates, it provided its martyrs for the stake and the dungeons of the Inquisition. And it is characteristic that Protestants outdid Catholics in persecuting the free investigation of nature. Calvin had Servetus burnt at the stake when the latter was on the point of discovering the circulation of the blood, and indeed he kept him roasting alive during two hours; for the Inquisition at least it sufficed to have Giordano Bruno simply burnt alive.

The revolutionary act by which natural science declared its independence and, as it were, repeated Luther's burning of the Papal Bull[141] was the publication of the immortal work by which Copernicus, though timidly and, so to speak, only from his death-bed, threw down the gauntlet to ecclesiastical authority in the affairs of nature.[142] The emancipation of natural science from theology dates from this, although the fighting out of particular mutual claims has dragged on down to our day and in many minds is still far from completion. Thenceforward, however, the development of the sciences proceeded with giant strides, and, it might be said, gained in force in proportion to the square of the distance (in time) from its point of departure. It was as if the world were to be shown that henceforth for the highest product of organic matter, the human mind, the law of motion holds good that is the reverse of that for inorganic matter.

The main work in the first period of natural science that now opened lay in mastering the material immediately at hand. In most fields a start had to be made from the very beginning. Antiquity had bequeathed Euclid and the Ptolemaic solar system; the Arabs had left behind the decimal notation, the beginnings of algebra, the modern numerals, and alchemy; the Christian Middle Ages nothing at all. Of necessity, in this situation the most fundamental natural science, the mechanics of terrestrial and heavenly bodies, occupied first place, and alongside of it, as handmaiden to it, the discovery and perfecting of mathematical methods. Great things were achieved here. At the end of the period characterised by Newton and Linnaeus we find these branches of science brought to a certain perfection. The basic features of the most essential mathematical methods were established; analytical geometry by Descartes especially, logarithms by Napier,[143] and the differential and integral calculus by Leibniz and perhaps Newton. The same holds good of the mechanics of rigid bodies, the main laws of which were made clear once for all. Finally in the astronomy of the solar system Kepler discovered the laws of planetary movement and Newton formulated them from the point of view of the general laws of motion of matter. The other branches of natural science were far removed even from this preliminary perfection. Only towards the end of the period did the mechanics of fluid and gaseous bodies receive further treatment.* Physics had still not gone beyond its first beginnings, with the exception of optics, the exceptional progress of which was due to the practical needs of astronomy. By the phlogistic theory,[a] chemistry for the first time emancipated itself from alchemy. Geology had not yet gone beyond the embryonic stage of mineralogy; hence palaeontology could not yet exist at all. Finally, in the field of biology the essential pre-occupation was still with the collection and first sifting of the immense material, not only botanical and zoological but also anatomical and properly physiological. There could as yet be hardly any talk of the comparison of the various forms of life, of the investigation of their geographical distribution and their climatic, etc., conditions of existence. Here only botany and zoology arrived at an approximate completion owing to Linnaeus.

But what especially characterises this period is the elaboration of a peculiar general outlook, the central point of which is the view *of the absolute immutability of nature.* In whatever way nature itself might have come into being, once present it remained as it was as long as it continued to exist. The planets and their satellites, once set in motion by the mysterious "first impulse", circled on and on in their predestined ellipses for all eternity, or at any rate until the end of all things. The stars remained for ever fixed and immovable in their places, keeping one another therein by "universal gravitation". The earth had remained the same without alteration from all eternity or, alternatively, from the first day of its creation. The "five continents" of the present day had always

---

* Torricelli in connection with the control of alpine rivers. [Marginal note.]

a See this volume, p. 344.— *Ed.*

existed, and they had always had the same mountains, valleys, and rivers, the same climate, and the same flora and fauna, except in so far as change or transplantation had taken place at the hand of man. The species of plants and animals had been established once for all when they came into existence; like continually produced like, and it was already a good deal for Linnaeus to have conceded that possibly here and there new species could have arisen by crossing. In contrast to the history of mankind, which develops in time, there was ascribed to the history of nature only an unfolding in space. All change, all development in nature, was denied. Natural science, so revolutionary at the outset, suddenly found itself confronted by an out-and-out conservative nature, in which even today everything was as it had been from the beginning and in which—to the end of the world or for all eternity—everything would remain as it had been since the beginning.

High as the natural science of the first half of the eighteenth century stood above Greek antiquity in knowledge and even in the sifting of its material, it stood just as deeply below Greek antiquity in the theoretical mastery of this material, in the general outlook on nature. For the Greek philosophers the world was essentially something that had emerged from chaos, something that had developed, that had come into being. For the natural scientists of the period that we are dealing with it was something ossified, something immutable, and for most of them something that had been created at one stroke. Science was still deeply enmeshed in theology. Everywhere it sought and found the ultimate cause in an impulse from outside that was not to be explained from nature itself. Even if attraction, by Newton pompously baptised as "universal gravitation", was conceived as an essential property of matter, whence comes the unexplained tangential force which first gives rise to the orbits of the planets? How did the innumerable species of plants and animals arise? And how, above all, did man arise, since after all it was certain that he was not present from all eternity? To such questions natural science only too frequently answered by making the creator of all things responsible. Copernicus, at the beginning of the period, shows theology the door; Newton closes the period with the postulate of a divine first impulse. The highest general idea to which this natural science attained was that of the purposiveness of the arrangements of nature, the shallow teleology of Wolff,[a] according to which cats were created to eat mice, mice to be eaten by cats, and the whole

---

[a] Christian Wolff.— *Ed.*

of nature to testify to the wisdom of the creator. It is to the highest credit of the philosophy of the time that it did not let itself be led astray by the restricted state of contemporary natural knowledge, and that—from Spinoza down to the great French materialists—it insisted on explaining the world from the world itself and left the justification in detail to the natural sciences of the future.

I include the materialists of the eighteenth century in this period because no natural-scientific material was available to them other than that above described. Kant's epoch-making work remained a secret to them, and Laplace came long after them.[144] We should not forget that this obsolete outlook on nature, although riddled through and through by the progress of science, dominated the entire first half of the nineteenth century,* and in substance is even now still taught in all schools.**

The first breach in this petrified outlook on nature was made not by a natural scientist but by a philosopher. In 1755 appeared Kant's *Allgemeine Naturgeschichte und Theorie des Himmels*. The question of the first impulse was done away with; the earth and the whole solar system appeared as something that had *come into being* in the course of time. If the great majority of the natural scientists had had a little less of the repugnance to thinking that Newton expressed in the warning: Physics, beware of metaphysics![145] they would have been compelled from this single brilliant discovery of Kant's to draw conclusions that would have spared them endless deviations and immeasurable amounts of time

---

* The rigidity of the old outlook on nature provided the basis for the general comprehension of all natural science as a single whole. The French encyclopaedists, still purely mechanically—alongside of one another; and then simultaneously St. Simon and German philosophy of nature, perfected by Hegel. [Marginal note.]

** How tenaciously even in 1861 this view could be held by a man whose scientific achievements had provided highly important material for abolishing it is shown by the following classic words:

"All [the arrangements of our solar system, so far as we are capable of comprehending them, aim at preservation of what exists and at unchanging continuance. Just as since the most ancient times no animal and no plant on the earth has become more perfect or in any way different, just as we find in all organisms only stages *alongside of* one another and not *following* one another, just as our own race has always remained the same in corporeal respects—so even the greatest diversity in the coexisting heavenly bodies does not justify us in assuming that these forms are merely different stages of development; it is rather that everything created is *equally* perfect] in itself." (Mädler, *Populäre Astronomie*, Berlin, 1861, 5th edition, p. 316).[a]

---

[a] J. H. Mädler, *Der Wunderbau des Weltalls, oder Populäre Astronomie.*—*Ed.*

and labour wasted in false directions. For Kant's discovery contained the point of departure for all further progress. If the earth was something that had come into being, then its present geological, geographical, and climatic state, and its plants and animals likewise, must be something that had come into being; it must have had a history not only of coexistence in space but also of succession in time. If at once further investigations had been resolutely pursued in this direction, natural science would now be considerably further advanced than it is. But what good could come of philosophy? Kant's work remained without immediate results, until many years later Laplace[a] and Herschel expounded its contents and gave them a deeper foundation, thereby gradually bringing the "nebular hypothesis" into favour.[146] Further discoveries finally brought it victory; the most important of these were: the discovery of proper motion of the fixed stars, the demonstration of a resistant medium in universal space, the proof furnished by spectral analysis of the chemical identity of the matter of the universe and of the existence of such glowing nebular masses as Kant had postulated.*

It is, however, permissible to doubt whether the majority of natural scientists would so soon have become conscious of the contradiction of a changing earth that bore immutable organisms, had not the dawning conception that nature does not just *exist,* but *comes into being* and *passes away,* derived support from another quarter. Geology arose and pointed out not only the terrestrial strata formed one after another and deposited one upon another, but also the shells and skeletons of extinct animals and the trunks, leaves, and fruits of no longer existing plants contained in these strata. The decision had to be taken to acknowledge that not only the earth as a whole but also its present surface and the plants and animals living on it possessed a history in time. At first the acknowledgement occurred reluctantly enough. Cuvier's theory of the revolutions of the earth was revolutionary in phrase and reactionary in substance. In place of a *single* divine creation, he put a whole series of repeated acts of creation, making the miracle an essential natural agent. Lyell first brought sense into geology by substituting for the sudden revolutions due to the moods of the

---

* Retardation of rotation by the tides, also from Kant, only now understood. [Marginal note.]

---

[a] P. S. Laplace, *Exposition du système du monde*, Vol. II.— *Ed.*

creator the gradual effects of a slow transformation of the earth.*

Lyell's theory[a] was even more incompatible than any of its predecessors with the assumption of constant organic species. Gradual transformation of the earth's surface and of all conditions of life led directly to gradual transformation of the organisms and their adaptation to the changing environment, to the mutability of species. But tradition is a power not only in the Catholic Church but also in natural science. For years, Lyell himself did not see the contradiction, and his pupils still less. This can only be explained by the division of labour that had meanwhile become dominant in natural science, which more or less restricted each person to his special sphere, there being only a few whom it did not rob of a comprehensive view.

Meanwhile physics had made mighty advances, the results of which were summed up almost simultaneously by three different persons in the year 1842, an epoch-making year for this branch of natural science. Mayer in Heilbronn[b] and Joule in Manchester[c] demonstrated the transformation of heat into mechanical force and of mechanical force into heat. The determination of the mechanical equivalent of heat put this result beyond question. Simultaneously, by simply working up the separate results of physics already arrived at, Grove[147]—not a natural scientist by profession, but an English lawyer—proved that all so-called physical forces, mechanical force, heat, light, electricity, magnetism, indeed even so-called chemical force, become transformed into one another under definite conditions without any loss of force occurring, and so proved additionally along physical lines Descartes' principle that the quantity of motion present in the world is constant. With that the special physical forces, the as it were immutable "species" of physics, were resolved into variously differentiated forms of the motion of matter, passing into one

---

* The defect of Lyell's view—at least in its first form—lay in conceiving the forces at work on the earth as constant, both in quality and quantity. The cooling of the earth does not exist for him; the earth does not develop in a definite direction but merely changes in an inconsequent fortuitous manner.

---

[a] Ch. Lyell, *Principles of Geology, Being an Attempt to Explain the Former Changes of the Earth's Surface, by Reference to Causes Now in Operation,* Vols. 1-3.— Ed.

[b] J. R. Mayer, "Bemerkungen über die Kräfte der unbelebten Natur". In: *Annalen der Chemie und Pharmacie,* Bd. 42, S. 233-40.— Ed.

[c] J. P. Joule, "On the Calorific Effects of Magneto-electricity and the Mechanical Value of Heat". In: *Report of the 13th Meeting of the British Association for the Advancement of Sciences; Held at Cork in August 1843.*— Ed.

another according to definite laws. The fortuitousness of the existence of such and such a number of physical forces was abolished from science by the proof of their inter-connections and transitions. Physics, like astronomy before it, had arrived at a result that necessarily pointed to the eternal cycle of matter in motion as the ultimate conclusion.

The wonderfully rapid development of chemistry, since Lavoisier and especially since Dalton, attacked the old ideas about nature from another aspect. The preparation by inorganic means of compounds that hitherto had been produced only in the living organism proved that the laws of chemistry have the same validity for organic as for inorganic bodies, and to a large extent bridged the gulf between inorganic and organic nature, a gulf that even Kant regarded as for ever impassable.

Finally, in the sphere of biological research also the scientific journeys and expeditions that had been systematically organised since the middle of the previous [i.e., 18th] century, the more thorough exploration of the European colonies in all parts of the world by specialists living there, and further the progress of palaeontology, anatomy, and physiology in general, particularly since the systematic use of the microscope and the discovery of the cell, had accumulated so much material that the application of the comparative method became possible and at the same time indispensable.* On the one hand the conditions of life of the various floras and faunas were established by means of comparative physical geography; on the other hand the various organisms were compared with one another according to their homologous organs, and this not only in the adult condition but at all stages of their development. The more deeply and exactly this research was carried on, the more did the rigid system of an immutably fixed organic nature crumble away at its touch. Not only did the separate species of plants and animals become more and more inextricably intermingled, but animals turned up, such as *Amphioxus* and *Lepidosiren*,[148] that made a mockery of all previous classification,** and finally organisms were encountered of which it was not possible to say whether they belonged to the plant or animal kingdom. More and more the gaps in the palaeontological record were filled up, compelling even the most reluctant to acknowledge the striking parallelism between the history of the development of the organic world as a whole and that of the

---

* Embryology. [Marginal note.]
** *Ceratodus.* Ditto *Archaeopteryx*, etc.[149] [Marginal note.]

individual organism, the Ariadne's thread that was to lead the way out of the labyrinth in which botany and zoology appeared to have become more and more deeply lost. It was characteristic that, almost simultaneously with Kant's attack on the eternity of the solar system, C. F. Wolff in 1759 launched the first attack on the fixity of species and proclaimed the theory of descent.[150] But what in his case was still only a brilliant anticipation took firm shape in the hands of Oken, Lamarck, Baer, and was victoriously carried through by Darwin in 1859, exactly a hundred years later.[a] Almost simultaneously it was established that protoplasm and the cell, which had already been shown to be the ultimate morphological constituents of all organisms, occurred independently, existing as the lowest forms of organic life. This not only reduced the gulf between inorganic and organic nature to a minimum but removed one of the most essential difficulties that had previously stood in the way of the theory of descent of organisms. The new outlook on nature was complete in its main features: all rigidity was dissolved, all fixity dissipated, all particularity that had been regarded as eternal became transient, the whole of nature was shown as moving in eternal flux and cyclical course.

Thus we have once again returned to the mode of outlook of the great founders of Greek philosophy, the view that the whole of nature, from the smallest element to the greatest, from grains of sand to suns, from Protista[151] to man, has its existence in eternal coming into being and passing away, in ceaseless flux, in unresting motion and change. Only with the essential difference that what in the case of the Greeks was a brilliant intuition, is in our case the result of strictly scientific research in accordance with experience, and hence also it emerges in a much more definite and clear form. It is true that the empirical proof of this cyclical course is not wholly free from gaps, but these are insignificant in comparison with what has already been firmly established, and with each year they become more and more filled up. And how could the proof in detail be other than one containing gaps when one bears in mind that the most important branches of science—transplanetary astronomy, chemistry, geology—have a scientific existence of barely a century, and the comparative method in physiology, one of barely fifty years, and that the basic form of

---

[a] Ch. Darwin, *On the Origin of Species by Means of Natural Selection, or the Preservation of Favoured Races in the Struggle for Life.—Ed.*

almost all organic development, the cell, is a discovery not yet forty years old?[a]

The innumerable suns and solar systems of our island universe, bounded by the outermost stellar rings of the Milky Way, developed by contraction and cooling from swirling, glowing masses of vapour, the laws of motion of which will perhaps be disclosed after the observations of some centuries have given us an insight into the proper motion of the stars. Obviously, this development did not proceed everywhere at the same rate. Astronomy is more and more being forced to recognise the existence of dark bodies, not merely planetary in nature, hence extinct suns in our stellar system (Mädler); on the other hand (according to Secchi) a part of the vaporous nebular patches belong to our stellar system as suns not yet fully formed, which does not exclude the possibility that other nebulae are, as Mädler maintains, distant independent island universes, the relative stage of development of which must be determined by the spectro-scope.[152]

How a solar system develops from an individual nebular mass has been shown in detail by Laplace in a manner still unsurpassed; subsequent science has more and more confirmed him.

On the separate bodies so formed—suns as well as planets and satellites—the form of motion of matter at first prevailing is that which we call heat. There can be no question of chemical compounds of the elements even at a temperature like that still possessed by the sun; the extent to which heat is transformed into electricity or magnetism under such conditions, continued solar observations will show; it is already as good as proved that the mechanical motion taking place in the sun arises solely from the conflict of heat with gravity.

The smaller the individual bodies, the quicker they cool down, the satellites, asteroids, and meteors first of all, just as our moon has long been extinct. The planets cool more slowly, the central body slowest of all.

With progressive cooling the interplay of the physical forms of motion which become transformed into one another comes more and more to the forefront until finally a point is reached from

---

[a] In Engels's manuscript, this paragraph is separated from the paragraphs which precede and follow it by horizontal lines, and is crossed out slantwise, as Engels usually did with the passages which he used in other works.—*Ed.*

when on chemical affinity begins to make itself felt, the previously chemically indifferent elements become differentiated chemically one after another, acquire chemical properties, and enter into combination with one another. These compounds change continually with the decreasing temperature, which affects differently not only each element but also each separate compound of the elements, changing also with the consequent passage of part of the gaseous matter first to the liquid and then the solid state, and with the new conditions thus created.

The time when the planet acquires a firm shell and accumulations of water on its surface coincides with that from when on its intrinsic heat diminishes more and more compared with the heat emitted to it from the central body. Its atmosphere becomes the arena of meteorological phenomena in the sense in which we now understand the term; its surface becomes the arena of geological changes in which the deposits resulting from atmospheric precipitation become of ever greater importance compared with the slowly decreasing external effects of the hot fluid interior.

If, finally, the temperature becomes so far equalised that over a considerable portion of the surface at least it no longer exceeds the limits within which protein is capable of life, then, if other chemical pre-conditions are favourable, living protoplasm is formed. What these preconditions are, we do not yet know, which is not to be wondered at since so far not even the chemical formula of protein has been established—we do not even know how many chemically different protein bodies there are—and since it is only about ten years ago that the fact became known that completely structureless protein exercises all the essential functions of life: digestion, excretion, movement, contraction, reaction to stimuli, and reproduction.

Thousands of years may have passed before the conditions arose in which the next advance could take place and this shapeless protein produce the first cell by formation of nucleus and cell membrane. But this first cell also provided the foundation for the morphological development of the whole organic world; the first to develop, as it is permissible to assume from the whole analogy of the palaeontological record, were innumerable species of non-cellular and cellular Protista, of which *Eozoon canadense*[153] alone has come down to us, and of which some were gradually differentiated into the first plants and others into the first animals. And from the first animals were developed, essentially by further differentiation, the numerous classes, orders, families, genera, and species of animals; and finally vertebrates, the form in which the nervous system attains its fullest development; and among these again finally that vertebrate in which nature attains consciousness of itself—man.

Man, too, arises by differentiation. Not only individually—by development from a single egg-cell to the most complicated organism that nature produces—but also historically. When after thousands of years of struggle the differentiation of hand from foot, and erect gait, were finally established, man became distinct from the ape and the basis was laid for the development of articulate speech and the mighty development of the brain that has since made the gulf between man and the ape an unbridgeable one. The specialisation of the hand—this implies the *tool*, and the tool implies specific human activity, the transforming reaction of man on nature, production. Animals in the narrower sense also have tools, but only as limbs of their bodies: the ant, the bee, the beaver; animals also produce, but their productive effect on surrounding nature, in relation to nature, amounts to nothing at all. Man alone has succeeded in impressing his stamp on nature, not only by shifting plant and animal species from one place to another, but also by so altering the aspect and climate of his dwelling-place, and even the plants and animals themselves, that the consequences of his activity can disappear only with the general extinction of the terrestrial globe. And he has accomplished this primarily and essentially by means of the *hand*. Even the steam-engine, so far his most powerful tool for the transformation of nature, depends, because it is a tool, in the last resort on the hand. But step by step with the development of the hand went that of the brain; first of all came consciousness of the conditions for separate practically useful actions, and later, among the more favoured peoples and arising from that consciousness, insight into the natural laws governing them. And with the rapidly growing knowledge of the laws of nature the means for reacting on nature also grew; the hand alone would never have achieved the steam-engine if, along with and parallel to the hand, and partly owing to it, the brain of man had not correspondingly developed.

With man we enter *history*. Animals also have a history, that of their descent and gradual evolution to their present position. This history, however, is made for them, and in so far as they themselves take part in it, this occurs without their knowledge and desire. On the other hand, the more the human beings become removed from animals in the narrower sense of the word, the more they make their history themselves, consciously, the less becomes the influence of unforeseen effects and uncontrolled forces on this history, and the more accurately does the historical result correspond to the aim laid down in advance. If, however, we apply this measure to human history, to that of even the most developed peoples of the present day, we find that there still exists here a colossal disproportion between the proposed aims and the results arrived at, that unforeseen effects predominate, and that the uncontrolled forces are far more powerful than those set into motion according to plan. And this cannot be otherwise as long as the most essential historical activity of men, the one which has raised them from the animal to the human state and which forms the material foundation of all their other activities, namely the production of their requirements of life, i.e., in our day social production, is above all subject to the interplay of unintended effects from uncontrolled forces and achieves its desired end only by way of exception, but much more frequently the exact opposite. In the most advanced industrial countries we have subdued the forces of nature and pressed them into the service of mankind; we have thereby infinitely multiplied production, so that a child now produces more than a hundred adults previously did. And what is the result? Increasing overwork and increasing misery of the masses, and every ten years a great collapse. Darwin did not know what a bitter satire he wrote on mankind, and especially on his countrymen, when he showed that free competition, the struggle for existence, which the economists celebrate as the highest historical achievement, is the normal state of the *animal kingdom*. Only conscious organisation of social production, in which production and distribution are carried on in a planned way, can lift mankind above the rest of the animal world as regards the social aspect, in the same way that production in general has done this for mankind in the specifically biological aspect. Historical development makes such an organisation daily more indispensable, but also with every day more possible. From it will date a new epoch of history, in which mankind itself, and with mankind all branches of its activity, and particularly natural science, will experience an advance that will put everything preceding it in the deepest shade.

Nevertheless, "all that comes into being deserves to perish".[a] Millions of years may elapse, hundreds of thousands of generations be born and die, but inexorably the time will come when the declining warmth of the sun will no longer suffice to melt the ice

---

[a] Mephistopheles' words in Goethe's *Faust*, Act I, Scene III ("Faust's Study").— *Ed.*

thrusting itself forward from the poles; when the human race, crowding more and more about the equator, will finally no longer find even there enough heat for life; when gradually even the last trace of organic life will vanish; and the earth, an extinct frozen globe like the moon, will circle in deepest darkness and in an ever narrower orbit about the equally extinct sun, and at last fall into it. Other planets will have preceded it, others will follow it; instead of the bright, warm solar system with its harmonious arrangement of members, only a cold, dead sphere will still pursue its lonely path through universal space. And what will happen to our solar system will happen sooner or later to all the other systems of our island universe; it will happen to all the other innumerable island universes, even to those the light of which will never reach the earth while there is a living human eye to receive it.

And when such a solar system has completed its life history and succumbs to the fate of all that is finite, death, what then? Will the sun's corpse roll on for all eternity through infinite space, and all the once infinitely diversely differentiated natural forces pass for ever into one single form of motion, attraction?

"Or"—as Secchi asks (p. 810)—"are there forces in nature which can reconvert the dead system into its original state of glowing nebula and re-awaken it to new life? We do not know."

Of course, we do not know it in the sense that we know that $2 \times 2 = 4$, or that the attraction of matter increases and decreases according to the square of the distance. In theoretical natural science, however, which as far as possible builds up its outlook on nature into a harmonious whole, and without which nowadays even the most unthinking empiricist cannot get anywhere, we have very often to calculate with incompletely known magnitudes, and consistency of thought must at all times help to get over defective knowledge. Modern natural science has had to take over from philosophy the principle of the indestructibility of motion; it cannot any longer exist without this principle. But the motion of matter is not merely crude mechanical motion, mere change of place, it is heat and light, electric and magnetic tension, chemical combination and dissociation, life and, finally, consciousness. To say that matter during the whole unlimited time of its existence has only once, and for what is an infinitesimally short period in comparison to its eternity, found itself able to differentiate its motion and thereby to unfold the whole wealth of this motion, and that before and after this it remains restricted for eternity to mere change of place—this is equivalent to maintaining that matter is mortal and motion transient. The indestructibility of motion cannot be conceived merely quantitatively; it must also be conceived qualitatively; matter whose purely mechanical change of place includes indeed the possibility under favourable conditions of being transformed into heat, electricity, chemical action, life, but which is not capable of producing these conditions from out of itself, such matter has *forfeited motion;* motion which has lost the capacity of being transformed into the various forms appropriate to it may indeed still have *dynamis*[a] but no longer *energeia,*[b] and so has become partially destroyed. Both, however, are unthinkable.

This much is certain: there was a time when the matter of our island universe had transformed into heat such an amount of motion—of what kind we do not yet know—that there could be developed from it the solar systems appertaining to (according to Mädler) at least twenty million stars,[c] the gradual extinction of which is likewise certain. How did this transformation take place? We know just as little as Father Secchi knows whether the future *caput mortuum*[d] of our solar system will once again be converted into the raw material of new solar systems. But here either we must have recourse to a creator, or we are forced to the conclusion that the incandescent raw material for the solar systems of our universe was produced in a natural way by transformations of motion which are *by nature inherent* in moving matter, and the conditions for which, therefore, must also be reproduced by matter, even if only after millions and millions of years and more or less by chance, but with the necessity that is also inherent in chance.

The possibility of such a transformation is more and more being conceded. The view is being arrived at that the heavenly bodies are ultimately destined to fall into one another, and calculations are even made of the amount of heat which must be developed on such collisions. The sudden flaring up of new stars, and the equally sudden increase in brightness of familiar ones, of which we are informed by astronomy, are most easily explained by such collisions. Moreover, not only does our group of planets move about the sun, and our sun within our island universe, but our whole island universe also moves in space in temporary, relative

---

[a] Power.— *Ed.*

[b] Activity.— *Ed.*

[c] J. H. Mädler, *Der Wunderbau des Weltalls...*, S. 451-52.— *Ed.*

[d] Literally: "dead head"; figuratively, waste remaining after a chemical reaction, etc.— *Ed.*

equilibrium with the other island universes, for even the relative equilibrium of freely floating bodies can only exist where the motion is reciprocally determined; and it is assumed by many that the temperature in space is not everywhere the same. Finally, we know that, with the exception of an infinitesimal portion, the heat of the innumerable suns of our island universe vanishes into space and fails to raise the temperature of space even by a millionth of a degree Centigrade. What becomes of all this enormous quantity of heat? Is it for ever dissipated in the attempt to heat universal space, has it ceased to exist practically, and does it only continue to exist theoretically, in the fact that universal space has become warmer by a decimal fraction of a degree beginning with ten or more noughts? Such an assumption denies the indestructibility of motion; it concedes the possibility that by the successive falling into one another of the heavenly bodies all existing mechanical motion will be converted into heat and the latter radiated into space, so that in spite of all "indestructibility of force" all motion in general would have ceased. (Incidentally, it is seen here how inaccurate is the term "indestructibility of force" instead of "indestructibility of motion"). Hence we arrive at the conclusion that in some way, which it will later be the task of scientific research to demonstrate, it must be possible for the heat radiated into space to be transformed into another form of motion, in which it can once more be stored up and become active. Thereby the chief difficulty in the way of the reconversion of extinct suns into incandescent vapour disappears.

For the rest, the eternally repeated succession of worlds in infinite time is only the logical complement to the coexistence of innumerable worlds in infinite space—a principle the necessity of which has forced itself even on the anti-theoretical Yankee brain of Draper.*

It is an eternal cycle in which matter moves, a cycle that certainly only completes its orbit in periods of time for which our terrestrial year is no adequate measure, a cycle in which the time of highest development, the time of organic life and still more that of the life of beings conscious of nature and of themselves, is just as narrowly restricted as the space in which life and self-

---

* "The multiplicity of worlds in infinite space leads to the conception of a succession of worlds in infinite time." (J. W. Draper, *History of the Intellectual Development of Europe*, Vol. II [p. 325].)ª

ª In the original Engels gives this quotation in English.— *Ed.*

consciousness come into operation; a cycle in which every finite mode of existence of matter, whether it be sun or nebular vapour, single animal or genus of animals, chemical combination or dissociation, is equally transient, and wherein nothing is eternal but eternally changing, eternally moving matter and the laws according to which it moves and changes. But however often, and however relentlessly, this cycle is completed in time and space; however many millions of suns and earths may arise and pass away; however long it may last before, in one solar system and only on *one* planet, the conditions for organic life develop; however innumerable the organic beings, too, that have to arise and to pass away before animals with a brain capable of thought are developed from their midst, and for a short span of time find conditions suitable for life, only to be exterminated later without mercy—we have the certainty that matter remains eternally the same in all its transformations, that none of its attributes can ever be lost, and therefore, also, that with the same iron necessity that it will exterminate on the earth its highest creation, the thinking mind, it must somewhere else and at another time again produce it.

OLD PREFACE TO [*ANTI-*]*DÜHRING*.
ON DIALECTICS [154]

The following work does not by any means owe its origin to an "inner urge". On the contrary, my friend Liebknecht can testify to the great effort it cost him to persuade me to turn the light of criticism on Herr Dühring's newest socialist theory. Once I made up my mind to do so I had no choice but to investigate this theory, which claims to be the latest practical fruit of a new philosophical system, in its connection with this system, and thus to examine the system itself. I was therefore compelled to follow Herr Dühring into that vast domain in which he speaks of all possible things and of some others as well. That was the origin of a series of articles which appeared in the Leipzig *Vorwärts* from the beginning of 1877 onwards and are here presented as a connected whole.

When, because of the nature of the subject, the critique of a system, so extremely insignificant despite all self-praise, is presented in such great detail, two circumstances may be cited in excuse. On the one hand this criticism afforded me the opportunity of setting forth in positive form in various fields my outlook on controversial issues that today are of quite general scientific or practical interest. And while it does not occur to me in the least to present another system as an alternative to Herr Dühring's, it is to be hoped that, notwithstanding the variety of material examined by me, the reader will not fail to observe the inter-connection inherent also in the views which I have advanced.

On the other hand the "system-creating" Herr Dühring is not an isolated phenomenon in contemporary Germany. For some time now in that country philosophical, especially natural-philosophical, systems have been springing up by the dozen overnight, like mushrooms, not to mention the countless new systems of politics, economics, etc. Just as in the modern state it is presumed that every citizen is competent to pass judgment on all the issues on which he is called to vote; and just as in political economy it is assumed that every buyer is a connoisseur of all the commodities which he has occasion to purchase for his maintenance—so similar assumptions are now to be made in science. Everybody can write about everything and "freedom of science"[a] consists precisely in people deliberately writing about things they have not studied and putting this forward as the only strictly scientific method. Herr Dühring, however, is one of the most characteristic types of this bumptious pseudo-science which in Germany nowadays is forcing its way to the front everywhere and is drowning everything with its resounding sublime nonsense. Sublime nonsense in poetry, in philosophy, in political economy, in historiography; sublime nonsense in the lecture room and on the platform, sublime nonsense everywhere; sublime nonsense which lays claim to a superiority and depth of thought distinguishing it from the simple, commonplace nonsense of other nations; sublime nonsense, the most characteristic mass product of Germany's intellectual industry—cheap but bad—just like other German-made goods, only that unfortunately it was not exhibited along with them at Philadelphia.[155] Even German socialism has lately, particularly since Herr Dühring's good example, gone in for a considerable amount of sublime nonsense; the fact that the practical Social-Democratic movement so little allows itself to be led astray by this sublime nonsense is one more proof of the remarkably healthy condition of our working class in a country where otherwise, with the exception of natural science, at the present moment almost everything goes ill.

When Nägeli, in his speech at the Munich meeting of natural scientists, voiced the idea that human knowledge would never acquire the character of omniscience,[b] he must obviously have been ignorant of Herr Dühring's achievements. These achievements have compelled me to follow him into a number of spheres in which I can move at best only in the capacity of a dilettante. This applies particularly to the various branches of natural science, where hitherto it was frequently considered more than presumptu-

---

[a] An allusion to the speech of R. Virchow, *Die Freiheit der Wissenschaft im modernen Staat.—Ed.*

[b] C. Nägeli, "Die Schranken der naturwissenschaftlichen Erkenntniss", *Tageblatt der 50. Versammlung deutscher Naturforscher...*, Beilage, S. 18.—*Ed.*

ous for a "layman" to want to have any say. I am encouraged
somewhat, however, by a dictum uttered, likewise in Munich, by
Herr Virchow and elsewhere discussed more in detail, that outside
of his own speciality every natural scientist is only a semi-initiate,[a]
vulgo: layman. Just as such a specialist may and must take the
liberty of encroaching from time to time on neighbouring fields,
and is granted indulgence there by the specialists concerned in
respect of minor inexactitudes and clumsiness of expression, so I
have taken the liberty of citing natural processes and laws of
nature as examples in proof of my general theoretical views, and I
hope that I can count on the same indulgence.[b] The results
obtained by modern natural science force themselves upon
everyone who is occupied with theoretical matters with the same
irresistibility with which the natural scientist today is willy-nilly
driven to general theoretical conclusions. And here a certain
compensation occurs. If theoreticians are semi-initiates in the
sphere of natural science, then natural scientists today are actually
just as much so in the sphere of theory, in the sphere of what
hitherto was called philosophy.

Empirical natural science has accumulated such a tremendous
mass of positive material for knowledge that the necessity of
classifying it in each separate field of investigation systematically
and in accordance with its inner inter-connection has become
absolutely imperative. It is becoming equally imperative to bring
the individual spheres of knowledge into the correct connection
with one another. In doing so, however, natural science enters the
field of theory and here the methods of empiricism will not work,
here only theoretical thinking can be of assistance.[c] But theoretical
thinking is an innate quality only as regards natural capacity. This
natural capacity must be developed, improved, and for its
improvement there is as yet no other means than the study of
previous philosophy.

In every epoch, and therefore also in ours, theoretical thought is
a historical product, which at different times assumes very
different forms and, therewith, very different contents. The
science of thought is therefore, like every other, a historical

---

[a] See this volume, p. 7.— *Ed.*

[b] Engels crossed out a part of his "Old Preface", from the beginning to this
sentence, by a vertical stroke, since he used this part in his preface to the first
edition of *Anti-Dühring* (see this volume, pp. 5-8).— *Ed.*

[c] In the manuscript this sentence and the one preceding it are underscored in
pencil.— *Ed.*

science, the science of the historical development of human thought. And this is of importance also for the practical application of thought in empirical fields. Because in the first place the theory of the laws of thought is by no means an "eternal truth" established once and for all, as philistine reasoning imagines to be the case with the word "logic". Formal logic itself has been the arena of violent controversy from the time of Aristotle to the present day. And dialectics has so far been fairly closely investigated by only two thinkers, Aristotle and Hegel. But it is precisely dialectics that constitutes the most important form of thinking for present-day natural science, for it alone offers the analogue for, and thereby the method of explaining, the evolutionary processes occurring in nature, inter-connections in general, and transitions from one field of investigation to another.

Secondly, an acquaintance with the historical course of development of human thought, with the views on the general inter-connections in the external world expressed at various times, is required by theoretical natural science for the additional reason that it furnishes a criterion of the theories propounded by this science itself. Here, however, lack of acquaintance with the history of philosophy is fairly frequently and glaringly displayed. Propositions which were advanced in philosophy centuries ago, which are often enough completely dead philosophically, are frequently put forward by theorising natural scientists as brand-new wisdom and even become fashionable for a while. It is certainly a great achievement of the mechanical theory of heat that it strengthened the principle of the conservation of energy by means of fresh proofs and put it once more in the forefront; but could this principle have appeared on the scene as something so absolutely new if the worthy physicists had remembered that it had already been formulated by Descartes?[a] Since physics and chemistry once more operate almost exclusively with molecules and atoms, the atomic philosophy of ancient Greece has of necessity come to the fore again. But how superficially it is treated even by the best of natural scientists! Thus Kekulé tells us *(Ziele und Leistungen der Chemie)* that Democritus, instead of Leucippus, originated it, and he maintains that Dalton was the first to assume the existence of qualitatively different elementary atoms and was the first to ascribe to them different weights characteristic of the different elements.[b] Yet anyone can read in Diogenes Laertius

---

[a] See this volume, p. 50.— *Ed.*

[b] A. Kekulé, *Die wissenschaftlichen Ziele und Leistungen der Chemie*, S. 13-15.— *Ed.*

(X, §§43-44 and 61)[a] that already Epicurus had ascribed to atoms differences not only of magnitude and form but also of *weight*,[b] that is, he was already acquainted in his own way with atomic weight and atomic volume.

The year 1848, which otherwise brought nothing to a conclusion in Germany, accomplished a complete revolution there only in the sphere of philosophy. By throwing itself into the field of the practical, here setting up the beginnings of large-scale industry and swindling, there initiating the mighty advance which natural science has since experienced in Germany and which was inaugurated by the caricature-like itinerant preachers Vogt, Büchner, etc., the nation resolutely turned its back on classical German philosophy that had lost itself in the sands of Berlin Old-Hegelianism. Berlin Old-Hegelianism had richly deserved that. But a nation that wants to climb the pinnacles of science cannot possibly manage without theoretical thought. Not only Hegelianism but dialectics too was thrown overboard—and that just at the moment when the dialectical character of natural processes irresistibly forced itself upon the mind, when therefore only dialectics could be of assistance to natural science in negotiating the mountain of theory—and so there was a helpless relapse into the old metaphysics. What prevailed among the public since then were, on the one hand, the vapid reflections of Schopenhauer, which were fashioned to fit the philistines, and later even those of Hartmann; and, on the other hand, the vulgar itinerant-preacher materialism of a Vogt and a Büchner. At the universities the most diverse varieties of eclecticism competed with one another and had only one thing in common, namely, that they were concocted from nothing but remnants of old philosophies and were all equally metaphysical. All that was saved from the remnants of classical philosophy was a certain neo-Kantianism, whose last word was the eternally unknowable thing-in-itself, that is, the bit of Kant that least merited preservation. The final result was the incoherence and confusion of theoretical thought now prevalent.

One can scarcely pick up a theoretical book on natural science without getting the impression that natural scientists themselves feel how much they are dominated by this incoherence and confusion, and that the so-called philosophy now current offers them absolutely no way out. And here there really is no other

---

[a] Diogenes Laertius, *De vitis philosophorum libri X.—Ed.*
[b] See this volume, pp. 470-71.—*Ed.*

way out, no possibility of achieving clarity, than by a return, in one form or another, from metaphysical to dialectical thinking.

This return can take place in various ways. It can come about spontaneously, by the sheer force of the natural-scientific discoveries themselves, which refuse any longer to allow themselves to be forced into the old Procrustean bed of metaphysics. But that is a protracted, laborious process during which a tremendous amount of unnecessary friction has to be overcome. To a large extent that process is already going on, particularly in biology. It could be greatly shortened if the theoreticians in the field of natural science were to acquaint themselves more closely with dialectical philosophy in its historically existing forms. Among these forms there are two which may prove especially fruitful for modern natural science.

The first of these is Greek philosophy. Here dialectical thought still appears in its pristine simplicity, still undisturbed by the charming obstacles [a] which the metaphysics of the seventeenth and eighteenth centuries—Bacon and Locke in England, Wolff in Germany—put in its own way, and with which it blocked its own progress, from an understanding of the part to an understanding of the whole, to an insight into the general inter-connection of things. Among the Greeks—just because they were not yet advanced enough to dissect, analyse nature—nature is still viewed as a whole, in general. The universal connection of natural phenomena is not proved in regard to particular; to the Greeks it is the result of direct contemplation. Herein lies the inadequacy of Greek philosophy, on account of which it had to yield later to other modes of outlook on the world. But herein also lies its superiority over all its subsequent metaphysical opponents. If in regard to the Greeks metaphysics was right in particulars, in regard to metaphysics the Greeks were right in general. That is the first reason why we are compelled in philosophy as in so many other spheres to return again and again to the achievements of that small people whose universal talents and activity assured it a place in the history of human development that no other people can ever claim. The other reason, however, is that the manifold forms of Greek philosophy contain in embryo, in the nascent state,

---

[a] An expression from the Prologue to Heine's cycle of poems, *Neuer Frühling*. —*Ed.*

almost all later modes of outlook on the world. Theoretical natural science is therefore likewise forced to go back to the Greeks if it desires to trace the history of the origin and development of the general principles it holds today. And this insight is forcing its way more and more to the fore. Instances are becoming increasingly rare of natural scientists who, while themselves operating with fragments of Greek philosophy, for example atomistics, as with eternal truths, look down upon the Greeks with Baconian superciliousness because the Greeks had no empirical natural science. It would be desirable only for this insight to advance to a real familiarity with Greek philosophy.

The second form of dialectics, which is the one that comes closest to the German naturalists, is classical German philosophy, from Kant to Hegel. Here a start has already been made in that it has again become fashionable to return to Kant, even apart from the neo-Kantianism mentioned above. Since the discovery that Kant was the author of two brilliant hypotheses, without which theoretical natural science today simply cannot make progress— the theory, formerly credited to Laplace, of the origin of the solar system and the theory of the retardation of the earth's rotation by the tides—Kant is again held in honour among natural scientists, as he deserves to be. But to study dialectics in the works of Kant would be a uselessly laborious and little-remunerative task, as there is now available, in *Hegel's* works, a comprehensive compendium of dialectics, developed though it be from an utterly erroneous point of departure.

After, on the one hand, the reaction against "philosophy of nature" had run its course and had degenerated into mere abuse—a reaction that was largely justified by this erroneous point of departure and the helpless degeneration of Berlin Hegelianism; and after, on the other hand, natural science had been so conspicuously left in the lurch by current eclectic metaphysics in regard to its theoretical requirements, it will perhaps be possible to pronounce once more the name of Hegel in the presence of natural scientists without provoking that St. Vitus's dance which Herr Dühring so entertainingly performs.

First of all it must be established that here it is not at all a question of defending Hegel's point of departure: that spirit, mind, the idea, is primary and that the real world is only a copy of the idea. Already Feuerbach abandoned that. We all agree that in every field of science, in natural as in historical science, one must proceed from the given *facts,* in natural science therefore from the various material forms and the various forms of motion of matter[a]; that therefore in theoretical natural science too the inter-connections are not to be built into the facts but to be discovered in them, and when discovered to be verified as far as possible by experiment.

Just as little can it be a question of maintaining the dogmatic content of the Hegelian system as it was preached by the Berlin Hegelians of the older and younger line. Hence, with the fall of the idealist point of departure, the system built upon it, in particular Hegelian philosophy of nature, also falls. It must however be recalled that the natural scientists' polemic against Hegel, in so far as they at all correctly understood him, was directed solely against these two points: viz., the idealist point of departure and the arbitrary, fact-defying construction of the system.

After allowance has been made for all this, there still remains Hegelian dialectics. It is the merit of Marx that, in contrast to the "peevish, arrogant, mediocre Επιγονοι who now talk large in Germany",[b] he was the first to have brought to the fore again the forgotten dialectical method, its connection with Hegelian dialectics and its distinction from the latter, and at the same time to have applied this method in *Capital* to the facts of an empirical science, political economy. And he did it so successfully that even in Germany the newer economic school rises above the vulgar free-trade system only by copying from Marx (often enough incorrectly), on pretence of criticising him.

In Hegel's dialectics there prevails the same inversion of all real inter-connection as in all other ramifications of his system. But, as Marx says: "The mystification which dialectics suffers in Hegel's hands by no means prevents him from being the first to present its general form of working in a comprehensive and conscious manner. With him it is standing on its head. It must be turned right side up again, if you would discover the rational kernel within the mystical shell."[c]

In natural science itself, however, we often enough encounter theories in which the real relation is stood on its head, the reflection is taken for the original form, and which consequently need to be turned right side up again. Such theories quite often

---

[a] After this comes the following sentence, crossed out in the manuscript: "We socialist materialists go even considerably further in this respect than the natural scientists by also...".— *Ed.*

[b] See present edition, Vol. 35. Afterword to the Second German Edition of Vol. I of *Capital.*— *Ed.*

[c] Ibid.— *Ed.*

dominate for a considerable time. When for almost two centuries heat was considered a special mysterious substance instead of a form of motion of ordinary matter, that was precisely such a case and the mechanical theory of heat carried out the inverting. Nevertheless physics dominated by the caloric theory discovered a series of highly important laws of heat and cleared the way, particularly through Fourier and Sadi Carnot,[a] for the correct conception, which now for its part had to put right side up the laws discovered by its predecessor, to translate them into its own language.* Similarly, in chemistry the phlogistic theory first supplied the material, by a hundred years of experimental work, with the aid of which Lavoisier was able to discover in the oxygen obtained by Priestley the real antipode of the fantastic phlogiston and thus could throw overboard the entire phlogistic theory.[156] But this did not in the least do away with the experimental results of phlogistics. On the contrary. They persisted, only their formulation was inverted, was translated from the phlogistic into the now valid chemical language and thus they retained their validity.

The relation of Hegelian dialectics to rational dialectics is the same as that of the caloric theory to the mechanical theory of heat and that of the phlogistic theory to the theory of Lavoisier.

---

* *Carnot's function* C literally inverted: $\frac{1}{C}$ = absolute temperature. Without this inversion nothing can be done with it. [Marginal note.]

[a] Engels means the following books: J. B. J. Fourier, *Théorie analytique de la chaleur,* and S. Carnot, *Réflexions sur la puissance motrice du feu et sur les machines propres à développer cette puissance.* The function C which is mentioned by Engels in his note in the margin occurs in a note on pp. 78-79 of Carnot's book.— *Ed.*

NATURAL SCIENCE IN THE SPIRIT WORLD [157]

The dialectics that has found its way into popular consciousness is expressed in the old saying that extremes meet. In accordance with this we should hardly err in looking for the most extreme degree of fantasy, credulity, and superstition, not in that trend of natural science which, like the German philosophy of nature, tries to force the objective world into the framework of its subjective thought, but rather in the opposite trend, which, exalting mere experience, treats thought with sovereign disdain and really has gone to the furthest extreme in emptiness of thought. This school prevails in England. Its father, the much lauded Francis Bacon, already advanced the demand that his new empirical, inductive method should be pursued to attain, above all, by its means: longer life, rejuvenation—to a certain extent, alteration of stature and features, transformation of one body into another, the production of new species, power over the air and the production of storms. He complains that such investigations have been abandoned, and in his natural history he gives definite recipes for making gold and performing various miracles.[158] Similarly Isaac Newton in his old age greatly busied himself with expounding the Revelation of St. John.[159] So it is not to be wondered at if in recent years English empiricism in the person of some of its representatives—and not the worst of them—should seem to have fallen a hopeless victim to the spirit-rapping and spirit-seeing imported from America.

The first natural scientist belonging here is the very eminent zoologist and botanist, Alfred Russel Wallace, the man who simultaneously with Darwin put forward the theory of the alteration of species by natural selection. In his little work, *On Miracles and Modern Spiritualism,* London, Burns, 1875, he relates that his first experiences in this branch of natural knowledge date from 1844, when he attended the lectures of Mr. Spencer Hall on mesmerism [160] and as a result carried out similar experiments on his pupils.

"I was intensely interested in the subject and pursued it with ARDOUR." [P. 119.]

He not only produced magnetic sleep together with the phenomena of articular rigidity and local loss of sensation, he also confirmed the correctness of Gall's map of the skull,[161] because on touching any one of Gall's organs the corresponding activity was aroused in the magnetised patient and exhibited by appropriate and lively gestures. Further, he established that his patient, merely by being touched, partook of all the sensations of the operator; he made him drunk with a glass of water as soon as he told him that it was brandy. He could make one of the young men so stupid, even in the waking condition, that he no longer knew his own name, a feat, however, that some schoolmasters are capable of accomplishing without any mesmerism. And so on.

Now it happens that I also saw this Mr. Spencer Hall in the winter of 1843-44 in Manchester. He was a very mediocre charlatan, who travelled the country under the patronage of some parsons and undertook magnetico-phrenological performances with a young woman in order to prove thereby the existence of God, the immortality of the soul, and the incorrectness of materialism, which was being preached at that time by the Owenites in all big towns. The lady was sent into a magnetic sleep and then, as soon as the operator touched any part of the skull corresponding to one of Gall's organs, she gave a bountiful display of theatrical, demonstrative gestures and poses representing the activity of the organ concerned; for instance, for the organ of PHILOPROGENITIVENESS she fondled and kissed an imaginary baby, etc. Moreover, the good Mr. Hall had enriched Gall's geography of the skull with a new island of Barataria [162]: right at the top of the skull he had discovered an organ of veneration, on touching which his hypnotic miss sank on to her knees, folded her hands in prayer, and depicted to the astonished, philistine audience an angel wrapt in veneration. That was the climax and conclusion of the exhibition. The existence of God had been proved.

The effect on me and one of my acquaintances was similar to that on Mr. Wallace: the phenomena interested us and we tried to find out how far we could reproduce them. A wide-awake young boy 12 years old offered himself as subject. Gently gazing into his eyes, or stroking, sent him without difficulty into the hypnotic condition. But since we were rather less credulous than Mr. Wallace and set to work with rather less fervour, we arrived at quite different results. Apart from muscular rigidity and loss of sensation, which were easy to produce, we found also a state of complete passivity of the will bound up with a peculiar hypersensitivity of sensation. The patient, when aroused from his lethargy by any external stimulus, exhibited very much greater liveliness than in the waking condition. There was no trace of any mysterious relation to the operator: anyone else could just as easily set the sleeper into activity. To put Gall's cranial organs into operation was a mere trifle for us; we went much further, we could not only exchange them for one another, or make their seat anywhere in the whole body, but we also fabricated any amount of other organs, organs of singing, whistling, piping, dancing, boxing, sewing, cobbling, tobacco-smoking, etc., and we could make their seat wherever we wanted. Wallace made his patients drunk on water, but we discovered in the great toe an organ of drunkenness which only had to be touched in order to cause the finest drunken comedy to be enacted. But it must be well understood, no organ showed a trace of action until the patient was given to understand what was expected of him; the boy soon perfected himself by practice to such an extent that the merest indication sufficed. The organs produced in this way then retained their validity for later occasions of putting to sleep, as long as they were not altered in the same way. The patient had indeed a double memory, one for the waking state and a second quite separate one for the hypnotic condition. As regards the passivity of the will and its absolute subjection to the will of a third person, this loses all its miraculous appearance when we bear in mind that the whole condition began with the subjection of the will of the patient to that of the operator, and cannot be produced without it. The most powerful magician of a magnetiser in the world will come to the end of his resources as soon as his patient laughs him in the face.

While we with our frivolous scepticism thus found that the basis of magnetico-phrenological charlatanry lay in a series of phenomena which for the most part differ only in degree from those of the waking state and require no mystical interpretation. Mr. Wallace's ARDOUR led him into a series of self-deceptions, in virtue of which he confirmed Gall's map of the skull in all its details and noted a

348 *Dialectics of Nature.* Articles and Chapters

mysterious relation between operator and patient.* Everywhere in Mr. Wallace's account, the sincerity of which reaches the degree of *naïveté*, it becomes apparent that he was much less concerned in investigating the factual background of charlatanry than in reproducing all the phenomena at all costs. Only this frame of mind is needed for one who was originally a scientist to be quickly converted into an adept by means of simple and facile self-deception. Mr. Wallace ended up with faith in magnetico-phrenological miracles and so already stood with one foot in the world of spirits.

He drew the other foot after him in 1865. On returning from his twelve years of travel in the tropics, experiments in table-turning introduced him to the society of various "mediums". How rapid his progress was, and how complete his mastery of the subject, is testified to by the above-mentioned booklet. He expects us to take for good coin not only all the alleged miracles of the Homes, the brothers Davenport, and other "mediums" who all more or less exhibit themselves for money and who have for the most part been frequently exposed as impostors, but also a whole series of allegedly authentic spirit histories from early times. The phythonesses of the Greek oracle and the witches of the Middle Ages, were all "mediums", and Iamblichus in his *De divinatione* already described quite accurately

"the most startling phenomena of modern spiritualism".

Just one example to show how lightly Mr. Wallace deals with the scientific establishment and authentication of these miracles. It is certainly a strong assumption that we should believe that the above-mentioned spirits would allow themselves to be photo-graphed, and we have surely the right to demand that such spirit photographs should be authenticated in the most indubitable manner before we accept them as genuine. Now Mr. Wallace recounts on p. 187 that in March 1872, a leading medium, Mrs. Guppy, *née* Nichol, had herself photographed together with her husband and small boy at Mr. Hudson's in Notting Hill, and on two photographs a tall female figure, FINELY draped in white gauzy robes, with somewhat Eastern features, was to be seen behind her in a pose as if giving a benediction.

---

* As already said, the patients perfect themselves by practice. It is therefore quite possible that when the subjection of the will has become habitual the relation between the participants becomes more intimate, individual phenomena are intensified and are reflected weakly even in the waking state.

"Here, then, one of two things *are*[a] absolutely certain.* Either there was a living, intelligent, but invisible being present, or Mr. and Mrs. Guppy, the photographer, and some fourth person planned a WICKED imposture, and have maintained it ever since. Knowing Mr. and Mrs. Guppy so well as I do, I feel an *absolute conviction* that they are as incapable of an imposture of this kind as any earnest inquirer after truth in the department of natural science." [P. 188.]

Consequently, either imposture or spirit photography. Quite so. And, if imposture, either the spirit was already on the photographic plates, or four persons must have been concerned, or three if we leave out as weak-minded or duped old Mr. Guppy who died in January 1875, at the age of 84 (it only needed that he should be sent behind the Spanish screen of the background). That a photographer could obtain a "model" for the spirit without difficulty does not need to be argued. But the photographer Hudson, shortly afterwards, was publicly prosecuted for habitual falsification of spirit photographs, so Mr. Wallace remarks in mitigation:

"One thing is clear; that if there has been imposture, it was at once detected by spiritualists themselves." [P. 189.]

Hence there is not much reliance to be placed on the photographer. Remains Mrs. Guppy, and for her there is only the "absolute conviction" of our friend Wallace and nothing more.— Nothing more? Not at all. The absolute trustworthiness of Mrs. Guppy is evidenced by her assertion that one evening, early in June 1871, she was carried through the air in a state of unconsciousness from her house in Highbury Hill Park to 69, Lamb's Conduit Street—three English miles as the crow flies—and deposited in the said house of No. 69 on the table in the midst of a spiritualistic *séance*. The doors of the room were closed, and although Mrs. Guppy was one of the stoutest women in London, which is certainly saying a good deal, nevertheless her sudden incursion did not leave behind the slightest hole either in the doors or in the ceiling. (Reported in the London *Echo*, June 8, 1871.)[c] And if anyone still does not believe in the genuineness of spirit photography, there's no helping him.

* HERE, THEN, ONE OF TWO THINGS *ARE* ABSOLUTELY CERTAIN. The spirit world is superior to grammar. A joker once caused the spirit of the grammarian Lindley Murray to testify. To the question whether he was there, he answered: "I ARE" (American for "I am"). The medium was from America.[b]

[a] Italics by Engels.— *Ed.*

[b] Here Engels uses the book by J. N. Maskelyne, *Modern Spiritualism*, p. 71.— *Ed.*

[c] J. N. Maskelyne, op. cit., pp. 99-101.— *Ed.*

The second eminent adept among English natural scientists is Mr. William Crookes, the discoverer of the chemical element thallium and of the radiometer (in Germany also called "Lichtmühle").[163] Mr. Crookes began to investigate spiritualistic manifestations about 1871, and employed for this purpose a number of physical and mechanical appliances, spring balances, electric batteries, etc. Whether he brought to his task the main apparatus required, a sceptically critical mind, or whether he kept it to the end in a fit state for working, we shall see. At any rate, within a not very long period, Mr. Crookes was just as completely captivated as Mr. Wallace.

"For some years," he relates, "a young lady, Miss Florence Cook, has exhibited remarkable mediumship, which latterly culminated in the production of an entire female form purporting to be of spiritual origin, and which appeared barefooted and in white flowing robes while she lay entranced, in dark clothing and securely bound in a CABINET or adjoining room." [P. 181.]

This spirit, which called itself Katie, and which looked remarkably like Miss Cook, was one evening suddenly seized round the waist by Mr. Volckman—the present husband of Mrs. Guppy— and held fast in order to see whether it was not indeed Miss Cook in another edition. The spirit proved to be a quite sturdy damsel, it defended itself vigorously, the onlookers intervened, the gas was turned out, and when, after some scuffling, peace was re-established and the room re-lit, spirit had vanished and Miss Cook lay bound and unconscious in her corner. Nevertheless, Mr. Volckman is said to maintain up to the present day that he had seized hold of Miss Cook and nobody else.[a] In order to establish this scientifically, Mr. Varley, a well-known electrician, on the occasion of a new experiment, arranged for the current from a battery to flow through the medium, Miss Cook, in such a way that she could not play the part of the spirit without interrupting the current. Nevertheless, the spirit made its appearance. It was, therefore, indeed a being different from Miss Cook. To establish this further was the task of Mr. Crookes. His first step was to win the *confidence* of the spiritualistic lady.

This confidence, so he says himself in the *Spiritualist,* June 5, 1874, "increased gradually to such an extent that she refused to give a *séance* unless *I made the arrangements.*[b] She said that she always wanted *me* to be near her and in the neighbourhood of the cabinet; I found that—when this confidence had been established and she was sure that *I would not break any promise made to her*—the

---

[a] Ibid., pp. 141-42.— *Ed.*
[b] In this and the next quotation italics are by Engels.— *Ed.*

phenomena increased considerably in strength and there was freely forthcoming evidence that would have been unobtainable in any other way. She frequently *consulted me* in regard to the persons present at the *séances* and the places to be given them, for she had recently become very NERVOUS as a result of certain ill-advised suggestions that, besides other more scientific methods of investigation, *force* also should be applied." [a]

The spirit lady rewarded this confidence, which was as kind as it was scientific, in the highest measure. She even made her appearance—which can no longer surprise us—in Mr. Crookes' house, played with his children and told them "anecdotes from her adventures in India", treated Mr. Crookes to an account of "some of the bitter experiences of her past life", allowed him to take her by the arm so that he could convince himself of her evident materiality, allowed him to take her pulse and count the number of her respirations per minute, and finally allowed herself to be photographed next to Mr. Crookes. [b]

"This figure," says Mr. Wallace, "after being seen, felt, conversed with, and photographed, *absolutely disappeared* from a small room from which there was no other exit than an adjoining room filled with spectators" [p. 183]

—which was not such a great feat, provided that the spectators were polite enough to show as much faith in Mr. Crookes, in whose house this happened, as Mr. Crookes did in the spirit.

Unfortunately these "fully authenticated phenomena" are not immediately credible even for spiritualists. We saw above how the very spiritualistic Mr. Volckman permitted himself to make a very material grab. And now a clergyman, a member of the committee of the "British National Association of Spiritualists", has also been present at a *séance* with Miss Cook, and he established the fact without difficulty that the room through the door of which the spirit came and disappeared communicated with the outer world by a *second door*. The behaviour of Mr. Crookes, who was also present, gave "the final death-blow to my belief that there might be 'something in' the face manifestations". (*Mystic London,* BY THE Rev. C. Maurice Davies, London, Tinsley Brothers.) [c] And, over and above that, it came to light in America how "Katies" were "materialised". A married couple named Holmes held *séances* in Philadelphia in which likewise a "Katie" appeared and received bountiful presents from the believers. However, one sceptic

---

[a] J. N. Maskelyne, op. cit., pp. 144-45.— *Ed.*

[b] This and the following two quotations are from Crookes' article "The Last of 'Katie King'...", *The Spiritualist Newspaper,* Vol. IV, No. 23, June 5, 1874.— *Ed.*

[c] Ch. M. Davies, *Mystic London,* p. 319.— *Ed.*

refused to rest until he got on the track of the said Katie, who, anyway, had already gone on strike once because of lack of pay; he discovered her in a BOARDING-HOUSE as a young lady of unquestionable flesh and bone, and in possession of all the presents that had been given to the spirit.[a]

Meanwhile the Continent also had its scientific spirit-seers. A scientific association at St. Petersburg—I do not know exactly whether the University or even the Academy itself—charged the Councillor of State, Aksakov, and the chemist, Butlerov, to examine the basis of the spiritualistic phenomena, but it does not seem that very much came of this.[164] On the other hand—if the noisy announcements of the spiritualists are to be believed—Germany has now also put forward its man in the person of Professor Zöllner in Leipzig.

For years, as is well known, Herr Zöllner has been hard at work on the "fourth dimension" of space, and has discovered that many things that are impossible in a space of three dimensions are a simple matter of course in a space of four dimensions. Thus, in the latter kind of space, a closed metal sphere can be turned inside out like a glove, without making a hole in it; similarly a knot can be tied in an endless string or one which has both ends fastened, and two separate closed rings can be interlinked without opening either of them, and many more such feats. Now, according to recent triumphant reports from the spirit world, Professor Zöllner has addressed himself to one or more mediums in order with their aid to determine more details of the locality of the fourth dimension. The success is said to have been surprising. After the session the arm of the chair, on which he rested his arm while his hand never left the table, was found to have become interlocked with his arm, a string that had both ends sealed to the table was found tied into four knots, and so on. In short, all the miracles of the fourth dimension are said to have been performed by the spirits with the utmost ease. It must be borne in mind: *relato refero*,[b] I do not vouch for the correctness of the spirit bulletins, and if they should contain any inaccuracy, Herr Zöllner ought to be thankful that I am giving him the opportunity to make a correction. If, however, they reproduce the experiences of Herr Zöllner without falsification, then they obviously signify a new era both in the science of spiritualism and that of mathematics. The

---

a J. N. Maskelyne, op. cit, pp. 118-19, 142-44, 146-53.— *Ed.*
b I am retelling what I have been told.— *Ed.*

spirits prove the existence of the fourth dimension, just as the fourth dimension vouches for the existence of spirits. And this once established, an entirely new, immeasurable field is opened to science. All previous mathematics and natural science will be only a preparatory school for the mathematics of the fourth and still higher dimensions, and for the mechanics, physics, chemistry, and physiology of the spirits dwelling in these higher dimensions. Has not Mr. Crookes scientifically determined how much weight is lost by tables and other articles of furniture on their passage into the fourth dimension—as we may now well be permitted to call it—and does not Mr. Wallace declare it proven that fire there does no harm to the human body? And now we have even the physiology of the spirit bodies! They breathe, they have a pulse, therefore lungs, heart, and a circulatory apparatus, and in consequence are at least as admirably equipped as our own in regard to the other bodily organs. For breathing requires carbo-hydrates which undergo combustion in the lungs, and these carbo-hydrates can only be supplied from without; hence, stomach, intestines, and their accessories—and if we have once established so much, the rest follows without difficulty. The existence of such organs, however, implies the possibility of their falling a prey to disease, hence it may still come to pass that Herr Virchow will have to compile a cellular pathology of the spirit world. And since most of these spirits are very handsome young ladies, who are not to be distinguished in any respect whatsoever from terrestrial damsels, other than by their supramundane beauty, it could not be very long before they come into contact with "men who feel the passion of love"[a]; and since, as established by Mr. Crookes from the beat of the pulse, "the female heart is not absent", natural selection also has opened before it the prospect of a fourth dimension, one in which it has no longer any need to fear of being confused with wicked Social-Democracy.[165]

Enough. Here it becomes palpably evident which is the most certain path from natural science to mysticism. It is not the extravagant theorising of the philosophy of nature, but the shallowest empiricism that spurns all theory and distrusts all thought. It is not *a priori* necessity that proves the existence of spirits, but the empirical observations of Messrs. Wallace, Crookes

---

[a] Here and below words of the duo of Pamina and Papageno from Mozart's opera, *The Magic Flute*, Act 1, Scene 14 (libretto by E. Schikaneder).— *Ed.*

& Co. If we trust the spectrum-analysis observations of Crookes, which led to the discovery of the metal thallium, or the rich zoological discoveries of Wallace in the Malay Archipelago, we are to place the same trust in the spiritualistic experiences and discoveries of these two scientists. And if we express the opinion that, after all, there is a little difference between the two, namely, that we can verify the one but not the other, then the spirit-seers retort that this is not the case, and that they are ready to give us the opportunity of verifying also the spirit phenomena.

Indeed, dialectics cannot be despised with impunity. However great one's contempt for all theoretical thought, nevertheless one cannot bring two natural facts into relation with each other, or understand the connection existing between them, without theoretical thought. The only question is whether one's thinking is correct or not, and contempt of theory is evidently the most certain way to think naturalistically, and therefore incorrectly. But, according to an old and well-known dialectical law, incorrect thinking, carried to its logical conclusion, inevitably arrives at the opposite of its point of departure. Hence, the empirical contempt for dialectics is punished by some of the most sober empiricists being led into the most barren of all superstitions, into modern spiritualism.

It is the same with mathematics. The ordinary, metaphysical mathematicians boast with enormous pride of the absolute irrefutability of the results of their science. But these results include also imaginary magnitudes, which thereby acquire a certain reality. When one has once become accustomed to ascribe some kind of reality outside of our minds to $\sqrt{-1}$, or to the fourth dimension, then it is not a matter of much importance if one goes a step further and also accepts the spirit world of the mediums. It is as Ketteler said about Döllinger:

"The man has defended so much nonsense in his life, he really could have accepted infallibility into the bargain!"[166]

In fact, mere empiricism is incapable of refuting the spiritualists. In the first place, the "higher" phenomena always show themselves only when the "investigator" concerned is already so far in the toils that he now only sees what he is meant to see or wants to see—as Crookes himself describes with such inimitable *naïveté*. In the second place, the spiritualists care nothing that hundreds of alleged facts are exposed as imposture and dozens of alleged mediums as ordinary tricksters. As long as *every* single alleged miracle has not been explained away, they have still room enough to carry on, as indeed Wallace says clearly enough in connection with the falsified spirit photographs. The existence of falsifications proves the genuineness of the genuine ones.

And so empiricism finds itself compelled to refute the importunate spirit-seers not by means of empirical experiments, but by theoretical considerations, and to say, with Huxley:

"The only good that I can see in the demonstration of the truth of 'spiritualism' is to furnish an additional argument against suicide. Better live a crossing-sweeper than die and be made to talk twaddle by a 'medium' hired at a guinea a *séance*."[167]

DIALECTICS [168]

(The general nature of dialectics to be developed as the science of interconnections, in contrast to metaphysics.)

It is, therefore, from the history of nature and human society that the laws of dialectics are abstracted. For they are nothing but the most general laws of these two stages of historical development, as well as of thought itself. And indeed they can be reduced in the main to three:

The law of the transformation of quantity into quality and vice versa;

The law of the interpenetration of opposites;

The law of the negation of the negation.

All three are developed by Hegel in his idealist fashion as mere laws of *thought*: the first, in the first part of his *Logik*, in "Die Lehre vom Seyn"; the second fills the whole of the second and by far the most important part of his *Logik*, "Die Lehre vom Wesen"; finally the third figures as the fundamental law for the construction of the whole system. The mistake lies in the fact that these laws are foisted on nature and history as laws of thought, and not deduced from them. This is the source of the whole forced and often outrageous treatment; the universe, willy-nilly, has to conform to a system of thought which itself is only the product of a definite stage of development of human thought. If we turn the thing round, then everything becomes simple, and the dialectical laws that look so extremely mysterious in idealist philosophy at once become simple and clear as noonday.

Moreover, anyone who is even only slightly acquainted with

Hegel will be aware that in hundreds of passages Hegel is capable of giving the most striking individual illustrations of the dialectical laws from nature and history.

We are not concerned here with writing a handbook of dialectics, but only with showing that the dialectical laws are real laws of development of nature, and therefore are valid also for theoretical natural science. Hence we cannot go into the inner inter-connection of these laws with one another.

I. The law of the transformation of quantity into quality and vice versa. For our purpose, we can express this by saying that in nature, in a manner exactly fixed for each individual case, qualitative changes can only occur by the quantitative addition or quantitative subtraction of matter or motion (so-called energy).

All qualitative differences in nature rest on differences of chemical composition or on different quantities or forms of motion (energy) or, as is almost always the case, on both. Hence it is impossible to alter the quality of a body without addition or subtraction of matter or motion, i.e., without quantitative altera-tion of the body concerned. In this form, therefore, Hegel's mysterious principle appears not only quite rational but even rather obvious.

It is surely hardly necessary to point out that the various allotropic and aggregational states of bodies, because they depend on various groupings of the molecules, depend on greater or lesser amounts [Mengen] of motion communicated to the bodies.

But what about change of form of motion, or so-called energy? If we change heat into mechanical motion or vice versa, is not the quality altered while the quantity remains the same? Quite correct. But it is with change of form of motion as with Heine's vices; anyone can be virtuous by himself, for vices two are always necessary.[a] Change of form of motion is always a process that takes place between at least two bodies, of which one loses a definite amount of motion of one quality (e.g., heat), while the other gains a corresponding quantity of motion of another quality (mechanical motion, electricity, chemical decomposition). Here, therefore, quantity and quality mutually correspond to each other. So far it has not been found possible to convert motion from one form to another inside a single isolated body.

We are concerned here in the first place with non-living bodies; the same law holds for living bodies, but it operates under very

---

[a] Heinrich Heine, *Ueber den Denunzianten.—Ed.*

complex conditions and at present quantitative measurement is still often impossible for us.

If we imagine any non-living body cut up into smaller and smaller portions, at first no qualitative change occurs. But this has a limit: if we succeed, as by evaporation, in obtaining the separate molecules in the free state, then it is true that we can usually divide these still further, yet only with a complete change of quality. The molecule is decomposed into its separate atoms, which have quite different properties from those of the molecule. In the case of molecules composed of different chemical elements, atoms or molecules of these elements themselves make their appearance in the place of the compound molecule; in the case of molecules of elements, the free atoms appear, which exert quite distinct qualitative effects: the free atoms of nascent oxygen are easily able to effect what the atoms of atmospheric oxygen, bound together in the molecule, can never achieve.

But the molecule is also qualitatively different from the mass of the body to which it belongs. It can carry out movements independently of this mass and while the latter remains apparently at rest, e.g., heat vibrations; by means of a change of position and of connection with neighbouring molecules it can change the body into an allotrope or a different state of aggregation.

Thus we see that the purely quantitative operation of division has a limit at which it becomes transformed into a qualitative difference: the mass consists solely of molecules, but it is something essentially different from the molecule, just as the latter is different from the atom. It is this difference that is the basis for the separation of mechanics, as the science of heavenly and terrestrial masses, from physics, as the mechanics of molecules, and from chemistry, as the physics of atoms.

In mechanics, no qualities occur; at most, states such as equilibrium, motion, potential energy, which all depend on measurable transference of motion and are themselves capable of quantitative expression. Hence, in so far as qualitative change takes place here, it is determined by a corresponding quantitative change.

In physics, bodies are treated as chemically unalterable or indifferent; we have to do with changes of their molecular states and with the change of form of motion, which in all cases, at least on one of the two sides, brings the molecule into action. Here every change is a transformation of quantity into quality, a consequence of the quantitative change of the amount of motion of one form or another that is inherent in the body or communicated to it.

"Thus the temperature of water is, in the first place, a point of no consequence in respect to its liquidity; still with the increase or diminution of the temperature of liquid water, there comes a point where this state of cohesion alters and the water is converted into steam or ice." (Hegel, *Encyclopädie, Gesamtausgabe,* Vol. VI, p. 217.)

Similarly, a definite minimum current strength is required to cause the platinum wire of an electric incandescent lamp to glow; and every metal has its temperature of incandescence and fusion, every liquid its definite freezing and boiling point at a given pressure—in so far as our means allow us to produce the temperature required; finally also every gas has its critical point at which it can be liquefied by pressure and cooling. In short, the so-called physical constants are for the most part nothing but designations of the nodal points at which quantitative addition or subtraction of motion produces qualitative change in the state of the body concerned, at which, therefore, quantity is transformed into quality.

The sphere, however, in which the law of nature discovered by Hegel celebrates its most important triumphs is that of chemistry. Chemistry can be termed the science of the qualitative changes of bodies as a result of changed quantitative composition. That was already known to Hegel himself. (*Logik, Gesamtausgabe,* III, p. 433).[a] As in the case of oxygen: if three atoms unite into a molecule, instead of the usual two, we get ozone, a body which is very considerably different from ordinary oxygen in its odour and reactions. And indeed the various proportions in which oxygen combines with nitrogen or sulphur, each of which produces a substance qualitatively different from any of the others! How different is laughing gas (nitrogen monoxide, N_2O) from nitric anhydride (nitrogen pentoxide, N_2O_5)! The first is a gas, the second at ordinary temperatures a solid crystalline substance. And yet the whole difference in composition is that the second contains five times as much oxygen as the first, and between the two of them are three more oxides of nitrogen (NO, N_2O_3, NO_2), each of which is qualitatively different from the first two and from one another.

This is seen still more strikingly in the homologous series of carbon compounds, especially of the simpler hydrocarbons. Of the normal paraffins, the lowest is methane, CH_4; here the four linkages of the carbon atom are saturated by four atoms of

---

a G. W. F. Hegel, *Wissenschaft der Logik,* Th. 1. Die objective Logik, Abth. 1. Die Lehre vom Seyn.— *Ed.*

hydrogen. The second, ethane, C_2H_6, has two atoms of carbon joined together and the six free linkages are saturated by six atoms of hydrogen. And so it goes on, with C_3H_8, C_4H_{10}, etc., according to the algebraic formula C_nH_{2n+2}, so that by each addition of CH_2, a body is formed that is qualitatively distinct from the preceding one. The three lowest members of the series are gases, the highest known, hexadecane, $C_{16}H_{34}$, is a solid body with a boiling point of 278° C. Exactly the same holds good for the series of primary alcohols with the formula $C_nH_{2n+2}O$, derived (theoretically) from the paraffins, and the series of monobasic fatty acids (formula $C_nH_{2n}O_2$). What qualitative difference can be caused by the quantitative addition of C_3H_6 is taught by experience if we consume ethyl alcohol, C_2H_6O, in any drinkable form without addition of other alcohols, and on another occasion take the same ethyl alcohol but with a slight addition of amyl alcohol, $C_5H_{12}O$, which forms the main constituent of the abominable fusel oil. One's head will certainly be aware of it the next morning, much to its detriment; so that one could even say that the intoxication, and subsequent "morning after" feeling, is also quantity transformed into quality, on the one hand of ethyl alcohol and on the other hand of this added C_3H_6.

In these series we encounter the Hegelian law in yet another form. The lower members permit only of a single mutual arrangement of the atoms. If, however, the number of atoms united into a molecule attains a size definitely fixed for each series, the grouping of the atoms in the molecule can take place in more than one way; so that two or more isomeric substances can be formed, having equal numbers of C, H, and O atoms in the molecule but nevertheless qualitatively distinct from one another. We can even calculate how many such isomers are possible for each member of the series. Thus, in the paraffin series, for C_4H_{10} there are two, for C_5H_{12} there are three; among the higher members the number of possible isomers mounts very rapidly. Hence once again it is the quantitative number of atoms in the molecule that determines the possibility and, in so far as it has been proved, also the actual existence of such qualitatively distinct isomers.

Still more. From the analogy of the substances with which we are acquainted in each of these series, we can draw conclusions as to the physical properties of the still unknown members of the series and, at least for the members immediately following the known ones, predict their properties, boiling point, etc., with fair certainty.

Finally, the Hegelian law is valid not only for compound substances but also for the chemical elements themselves. We now know that

"the chemical properties of the elements are a periodic function of their atomic weights" (Roscoe-Schorlemmer, *Ausführliches Lehrbuch der Chemie*, Vol. II, p. 823),

and that, therefore, their quality is determined by the quantity of their atomic weight. And the test of this has been brilliantly carried out. Mendeleyev proved that various gaps occur in the series of related elements arranged according to atomic weights indicating that here new elements remain to be discovered. He described in advance the general chemical properties of one of these unknown elements, which he termed eka-aluminium, because it follows after aluminium in the series beginning with the latter, and he predicted its approximate specific and atomic weight as well as its atomic volume. A few years later, Lecoq de Boisbaudran actually discovered this element, and Mendeleyev's predictions fitted with only very slight discrepancies. Eka-aluminium was realised in gallium (ibid., p. 828). By means of the—unconscious—application of Hegel's law of the transformation of quantity into quality, Mendeleyev achieved a scientific feat which it is not too bold to put on a par with that of Leverrier in calculating the orbit of the until then unknown planet Neptune.[169]

In biology, as in the history of human society, the same law holds good at every step, but we prefer to dwell here on examples from the exact sciences, since here the quantities are accurately measurable and traceable.

Probably the same gentlemen who up to now have decried the transformation of quantity into quality as mysticism and incomprehensible transcendentalism will now declare that it is indeed something quite self-evident, trivial, and commonplace, which they have long employed, and so they have been taught nothing new. But to have formulated for the first time in its universally valid form a general law of development of nature, society, and thought, will always remain an act of historic importance. And if these gentlemen have for years caused quantity and quality to be transformed into each other, without knowing what they did, then they will have to console themselves with Molière's Monsieur Jourdain who had spoken prose all his life without having the slightest inkling of it.[a]

---

[a] J. B. Molière, *Le Bourgeois gentilhomme*, Act II, Scene 6.— *Ed.*

362

BASIC FORMS OF MOTION [170]

Motion in the most general sense, conceived as the mode of existence, the inherent attribute, of matter, comprehends all changes and processes occurring in the universe, from mere change of place right up to thinking. The investigation of the nature of motion had as a matter of course to start from the lowest, simplest forms of this motion and to learn to grasp these before it could achieve anything in the way of explanation of the higher and more complicated forms. Hence, in the historical development of the natural sciences we see how first of all the theory of simplest change of place, the mechanics of heavenly bodies and terrestrial masses, was developed; it was followed by the theory of molecular motion, physics, and immediately afterwards, almost alongside of it and in some places in advance of it, the science of the motion of atoms, chemistry. Only after these different branches of the knowledge of the forms of motion governing non-living nature had attained a high degree of development could the explanation of the processes of motion representing the life process be successfully tackled. This advanced in proportion with the progress of mechanics, physics, and chemistry. Consequently, while mechanics has for a fairly long time already been able adequately to refer the effects in the animal body of the bony levers set into motion by muscular contraction to the laws that are valid also in non-living nature, the physico-chemical substantiation of the other phenomena of life is still pretty much at the beginning of its course. Hence, in investigating here the nature of motion, we are compelled to leave the organic forms of motion out of account. We are compelled to restrict ourselves—in accordance with the state of science—to the forms of motion of non-living nature.

All motion is bound up with some change of place, whether it be change of place of heavenly bodies, terrestrial masses, molecules, atoms, or ether particles. The higher the form of motion, the smaller this change of place. It in no way exhausts the nature of the motion concerned, but it is inseparable from the motion. It, therefore, has to be investigated before anything else.

The whole of nature accessible to us forms a system, an interconnected totality of bodies, and by bodies we understand here all material existences extending from stars to atoms, indeed right to ether particles, in so far as one grants the existence of the last named. In the fact that these bodies are interconnected is already included that they react on one another, and it is precisely this mutual reaction that constitutes motion. It already becomes evident here that matter is unthinkable without motion. And if, in addition, matter confronts us as something given, equally uncreatable as indestructible, it follows that motion also is as uncreatable as indestructible. It became impossible to reject this conclusion as soon as it was recognised that the universe is a system, an inter-connection of bodies. And since this recognition had been reached by philosophy long before it gained effective currency in natural science, one can understand why philosophy, fully two hundred years before natural science, drew the conclusion of the uncreatability and indestructibility of motion. Even the form in which it did so is still superior to the present-day formulation of natural science. Descartes' principle, that the amount [die Menge] of motion present in the universe is always the same, has only the formal defect of applying a finite expression to an infinite magnitude. On the other hand, two expressions of the same law are at present current in natural science: Helmholtz's law of the conservation of *force,* and the newer, more precise, one of the conservation of *energy.* Of these, the one, as we shall see, says the exact opposite of the other, and moreover each of them expresses only one side of the relation.

When two bodies act on each other so that a change of place of one or both of them results, this change of place can consist only in an approximation or a separation. They either attract each other or they repel each other. Or, as mechanics expresses it, the forces operating between them are central, acting along the line joining their centres. That this happens, that it is the case throughout the universe without exception, however complicated many movements may appear to be, is nowadays accepted as a matter of course. It would seem nonsensical to us to assume, when two bodies act on each other and their mutual interaction is not opposed by any obstacle or the influence of a third body, that this action should be effected otherwise than along the shortest and most direct path, i.e., along the straight line joining their centres.* It is well known, moreover, that Helmholtz (*Erhaltung der Kraft*, Berlin, 1847, Sections I and II[b]) has provided the mathematical proof that central action and unalterability of the amount of motion [Bewegungsmenge][171] are reciprocally conditioned and that the assumption of other than central actions leads to results in which motion could be either created or destroyed. Hence the basic form of all motion is approximation and separation, contraction and expansion—in short, the old polar opposites of *attraction* and *repulsion*.

It is expressly to be noted that attraction and repulsion are not regarded here as so-called "*forces*" but as *simple forms of motion*, just as Kant had already conceived matter as the unity of attraction and repulsion. What is to be understood by "forces" will be shown in due course.

All motion consists in the interplay of attraction and repulsion. Motion, however, is only possible when each individual attraction is compensated by a corresponding repulsion somewhere else. Otherwise in time one side would get the preponderance over the other and then motion would finally cease. Hence all attractions and all repulsions in the universe must mutually balance one another. Thus the law of the indestructibility and uncreatability of motion is expressed in the form that each movement of attraction in the universe must have as its complement an equivalent movement of repulsion and vice versa; or, as earlier philosophy—long before the natural-scientific formulation of the law of conservation of force or energy—expressed it: the sum of all attractions in the universe is equal to the sum of all repulsions.

However, it appears that there are here still two possibilities for all motion to cease at some time or other, either by repulsion and attraction finally cancelling each other out in actual fact, or by the total repulsion finally taking possession of one part of matter and the total attraction of the other part. For the dialectical conception, these possibilities are excluded from the outset. Dialectics has proved from the results of our experience of nature so far that all

---

* Kant [says], p. 22, that the three dimensions of space depend on the fact that this attraction or repulsion takes place in inverse proportion to the square of the distance.[a] [Marginal note.]

---

[a] I. Kant, *Sämmtliche Werke*, Bd. I, Leipzig, 1867.— *Ed.*
[b] H. Helmholtz, *Über die Erhaltung der Kraft...*, S. 10-20.— *Ed.*

polar opposites in general are determined by the mutual action of
the two opposite poles on each other, that the separation and
opposition of these poles exist only within their mutual connection
and union, and, conversely, that their union exists only in their
separation and their mutual connection only in their opposition.
This once established, there can be no question of a final
cancelling out of repulsion and attraction, or of a final partition
between the one form of motion in one half of matter and the
other form in the other half, consequently, there can be no
question of mutual penetration[a] or of absolute separation of the
two poles. It would be equivalent to demanding in the first case
that the north and south poles of a magnet should mutually cancel
themselves out or, in the second case, that dividing a magnet in
the middle between the two poles should produce on one side a
north half without a south pole, and on the other side a south half
without a north pole. Although, however, the impermissibility of
such assumptions follows at once from the dialectical nature of
polar opposites, nevertheless, thanks to the prevailing metaphysical
mode of thought of natural scientists, the second assumption at
least plays a certain part in physical theory. This will be dealt with
in its place.

How does motion present itself in the interaction of attraction
and repulsion? We can best investigate this in the separate forms
of motion itself. At the end, the general aspect of the matter will
show itself.

Let us take the motion of a planet about its central body.
Ordinary school astronomy follows Newton in explaining the
ellipse described as the result of the joint action of two forces, the
attraction of the central body and a tangential force driving the
planet along the normal to the direction of this attraction. Thus it
assumes, besides the form of motion directed centrally, also
another direction of motion, or so-called "force", perpendicular to
the line joining the centres. Thereby it contradicts the above-
mentioned basic law according to which all motion in our universe
can only take place along the line joining the centres of the bodies
acting on one another, or, as one says, is caused only by centrally
acting "forces". Thereby also it introduces into the theory an
element of motion which, as we have likewise seen, necessarily
leads to the creation and destruction of motion, and therefore
presupposes a creator. What had to be done, therefore, was to
reduce this mysterious tangential force to a form of motion acting

---

[a] In the sense of mutual equalisation and neutralisation.— *Ed.*

centrally, and this the Kant-Laplace theory of cosmogony accomplished. As is well known, according to this conception the whole solar system arose from a rotating, extremely tenuous, gaseous mass by gradual contraction. The rotational motion is obviously strongest at the equator of this gaseous sphere, and individual gaseous rings separate themselves from the mass and clump themselves together into planets, planetoids, etc., which revolve round the central body in the direction of the original rotation. This rotation itself is usually explained from the motion of the individual gaseous particles themselves. This motion takes place in all directions, but finally an excess in one particular direction makes itself evident and so causes the rotating motion, which is bound to become stronger and stronger with the progressive contraction of the gaseous sphere. But whatever hypothesis is assumed of the origin of the rotation, they all abolish the tangential force, dissolving it in a special form of the manifestation of centrally acting motion. If the one element of planetary motion, the directly central one, is represented by gravitation, the attraction between the planet and the central body, then the other, tangential, element appears as a relic, in a derivative or altered form, of the original repulsion of the individual particles of the gaseous sphere. Thus the life process of a solar system presents itself as an interplay of attraction and repulsion, in which attraction gradually more and more gets the upper hand owing to repulsion being radiated into space in the form of heat and thus more and more becoming lost to the system.

One sees at a glance that the form of motion here conceived as repulsion is the same as that which modern physics terms *"energy"*. By the contraction of the system and the resulting detachment of the individual bodies of which it consists today, the system has lost "energy", and indeed this loss, according to Helmholtz's well-known calculation, already amounts to $^{453}/_{454}$ of the total amount of motion [Bewegungsmenge] originally present in the form of repulsion.[172]

Let us take now a mass in the shape of a body on our earth itself. It is connected with the earth by gravitation, as the earth in turn is with the sun; but unlike the earth it is incapable of a free planetary motion. It can be set in motion only by an impulse from outside, and even then, as soon as the impulse ceases, its movement speedily comes to a standstill, whether by the effect of gravity alone or by the latter in combination with the resistance of the medium in which it moves. This resistance also is in the last resort an effect of gravity, in the absence of which the earth would not have on its surface any resistant medium, any atmosphere. Hence in pure mechanical motion on the earth's surface we are concerned with a situation in which gravitation, attraction, decisively predominates, where therefore the production of the motion shows both phases: first counteracting gravity and then allowing gravity to act—in a word, rising and falling.

Thus we have again mutual action between attraction on the one hand and a form of motion taking place in the opposite direction to it, hence a repelling form of motion, on the other hand. But within the sphere of terrestrial *pure* mechanics (which deals with masses of *given* states of aggregation and cohesion taken by it as unalterable) this repelling form of motion does not occur in nature. The physical and chemical conditions under which a lump of rock becomes separated from a mountain top, or a fall of water becomes possible, lie outside its sphere of action. Therefore, in terrestrial pure mechanics, the repelling, raising motion must be produced artificially: by human force, animal force, water or steam power, etc. And this circumstance, this necessity to combat the natural attraction artificially, causes the mechanicians to adopt the view that attraction, gravitation, or, as they say, the *force* of gravity, is the most important, indeed the basic, form of motion in nature.

When, for instance, a weight is raised and communicates motion to other bodies by falling directly or indirectly, then according to the usual view of mechanics it is not the *raising* of the weight which communicates this motion but the *force of gravity*. Thus Helmholtz, for instance, makes

"the force which is the simplest and the one with which we are best acquainted, viz., gravity, act as the driving force ... for instance in clocks that are actuated by a weight. The weight ... cannot comply with the pull of gravity without setting the whole clockwork in motion." But it cannot set the clockwork in motion without itself sinking and it goes on sinking until the string from which it hangs is completely unwound: "Then the clock comes to a stop, for the operative capacity of the weight is exhausted for the time being. Its weight is not lost or diminished, it remains attracted to the same extent by the earth, but the capacity of this weight to produce movements has been lost.... We can, however, wind up the clock by the power of the human arm, whereby the weight is once more raised up. As soon as this has happened, it regains its previous operative capacity and can again keep the clock in motion." (Helmholtz, *Populäre Vorträge*, II, p. 144[-45].)

According to Helmholtz, therefore, it is not the active communication of motion, the raising of the weight, that sets the clock into motion, but the passive heaviness of the weight, although this same heaviness is only withdrawn from its passivity by the raising, and once again returns to passivity after the string of the weight has unwound. If then according to the modern conception, as we saw above, *energy* is only another expression for *repulsion*, here in the older Helmholtz conception *force* appears as another expression for the opposite of repulsion, for *attraction*. For the time being we shall simply put this on record.

When, however, the process of terrestrial mechanics has reached its end, when the heavy mass has first of all been raised and then again has fallen through the same vertical distance, what becomes of the motion that constituted this process? For pure mechanics, it has disappeared. But we know now that it has by no means been destroyed. To a lesser extent it has been converted into the air vibrations of sound waves, to a much greater extent into heat—which has been communicated in part to the resisting atmosphere, in part to the falling body itself, and finally in part to the floor on which the weight comes to rest. The clock weight has also gradually given up its motion in the form of frictional heat to the separate driving wheels of the clockwork. But, although usually expressed in this way, it is not the *falling* motion, i.e., the attraction, that has passed into heat, and therefore into a form of repulsion. On the contrary, as Helmholtz correctly remarks, the attraction, the heaviness, remains what it previously was and, accurately speaking, becomes even greater. Rather it is the repulsion communicated to the raised body by raising that is *mechanically* destroyed by falling and reappears as heat. The repulsion of masses is transformed into molecular repulsion.

Heat, as already stated, is a form of repulsion. It sets the molecules of solid bodies into oscillation, thereby loosening the connection of the separate molecules until finally the transition to the liquid state takes place. In the liquid state also, on continued addition of heat, it increases the motion of the molecules until a degree is reached at which these split off altogether from the mass and, at a definite velocity determined for each molecule by its chemical constitution, they move away individually in the free state. With a still further addition of heat, this velocity is further increased, and so the molecules are more and more repelled from one another.

But heat is a form of so-called "energy"; here once again the latter proves to be identical with repulsion.

In the phenomena of static electricity and magnetism, we have a polar distribution of attraction and repulsion. Whatever hypothesis may be adopted of the *modus operandi* of these two forms of motion, in view of the facts no one has any doubt that attraction and repulsion, in so far as they are produced by static electricity or magnetism and are able to develop unhindered, completely compensate each other, as in fact necessarily follows from the very nature of the polar distribution. Two poles whose activities did not completely compensate each other would indeed not be poles, and also have so far not been met with in nature. For the time being we will leave galvanism out of account, because in its case the process is determined by chemical reactions, which makes it more complicated. Therefore, let us investigate rather the chemical processes of motion themselves.

When two parts by weight of hydrogen combine with 15.96 parts by weight of oxygen to form water vapour, an amount of heat of 68.924 heat-units is developed during the process. Conversely, if 17.96 parts by weight of water vapour are to be decomposed into two parts by weight of hydrogen and 15.96 parts by weight of oxygen, this is only possible on condition that the water vapour has communicated to it an amount of motion equivalent to 68.924 heat-units—whether in the form of heat itself or of electrical motion. The same thing holds for all other chemical processes. In the overwhelming majority of cases, motion is given off on combination and must be supplied on decomposition. Here, too, as a rule, repulsion is the active side of the process more endowed with motion or requiring the addition of motion, while attraction is the passive side producing a surplus of motion and giving off motion. On this account, the modern theory also declares that, on the whole, energy is set free on the combination of elements and is bound up on decomposition. Here, therefore, energy again stands for repulsion. And again Helmholtz declares:

"This force" (chemical affinity) "can be conceived as a force of *attraction*... This force of attraction between the atoms of carbon and oxygen performs work quite as much as that exerted on a raised weight by the earth in the form of gravitation... When carbon and oxygen atoms rush at one another and combine to form carbonic acid, the newly-formed particles of carbonic acid must be in very violent molecular motion, i. e., in heat motion... When later they have given up their heat to the environment, we still have in the carbonic acid all the carbon, all the oxygen, and in addition the affinity of both continuing to exist just as powerfully as before. But this affinity now expresses itself solely in the fact that the atoms of carbon and oxygen stick fast to one another, and do not allow of their being separated." (l. c., [p.] 169-[170].)

It is just as before: Helmholtz insists that in chemistry as in mechanics force consists only in *attraction*, and therefore is the exact opposite of what other physicists call energy and which is identical with *repulsion*.

Hence we have now no longer the two simple basic forms of attraction and repulsion, but a whole series of sub-forms in which the winding up and running down process of universal motion goes on within the opposition of attraction and repulsion. It is, however, by no means merely in our mind that these manifold forms of appearance are comprehended under the *single* expression of motion. On the contrary, they themselves prove in action that they are forms of one and the same motion by passing into one another under given conditions. Mechanical motion of masses passes into heat, into electricity, into magnetism; heat and electricity pass into chemical decomposition; chemical combination in turn again develops heat and electricity and, by means of the latter, magnetism; and finally, heat and electricity produce once more mechanical movement of masses. Moreover, these changes take place in such a way that a given amount of motion [Bewegungsmenge] of one form always has corresponding to it an exactly fixed amount of another form. Further, it is a matter of indifference which form of motion provides the unit by which the amount of motion is measured, whether it serves for measuring mass motion, heat, so-called electromotive force, or the motion undergoing transformation in chemical processes.

We base ourselves here on the theory of the "conservation of energy" established by J. R. Mayer in 1842* and afterwards worked out internationally with such brilliant success, and we have now to investigate the fundamental concepts nowadays made use of by this theory. These are the concepts of "force" or "energy", and "work".

---

* Helmholtz, in his *Populäre Vorlesungen*, II, p. 113, appears to ascribe a certain share in the natural-scientific proof of Descartes' principle of the quantitative immutability of motion to himself as well as to Mayer, Joule, and Colding. "I myself, without knowing anything of Mayer and Colding, and only becoming acquainted with Joule's experiments at the end of my work, *proceeded along the same path*; I occupied myself especially with searching out all the relations between the various processes of nature that could be deduced from the given mode of consideration, and I *published my investigations* in 1847 in a little work entitled *Über die Erhaltung der Kraft.*"[a]—But in this work there is to be found nothing new for the position in 1847 beyond the above-mentioned, mathematically very valuable, development that "conservation of force" and central action of the forces active between the various bodies of a system are only two different expressions for the same thing, and further a more accurate formulation of the law that the sum of the live and tensional forces in a given *mechanical* system is constant. In every other respect it was already superseded since Mayer's second paper of 1845. Already in 1842 Mayer maintained the "indestructibility of force", and from his new standpoint in 1845 he had much more brilliant things to say about the "relations between the various processes of nature" than Helmholtz had in 1847.[173]

---

a All italics in the quotation are by Engels.— *Ed.*

It has been shown above that according to the modern view, now fairly generally accepted, energy is the term used for repulsion, while Helmholtz mostly uses the word "force" to express attraction. One could regard this as an unimportant formal difference, inasmuch as attraction and repulsion compensate each other in the universe, and accordingly it would appear a matter of indifference which side of the relation is taken as positive and which as negative, just as it is of no importance in itself whether the positive abscissae are counted to the right or the left of a point in a given line. Nevertheless, this is not absolutely so.

For we are concerned here, first of all, not with the universe, but with phenomena occurring on the earth and conditioned by the exactly fixed position of the earth in the solar system, and of the solar system in the universe. At every moment, however, our solar system gives out enormous quantities of motion into space, and motion of a very definite quality, viz., the sun's heat, i. e., repulsion. But our earth itself allows of the existence of life on it only owing to the sun's heat, and the earth in turn finally radiates into space the sun's heat received, after it has converted a portion of this heat into other forms of motion. Consequently, in the solar system and above all on the earth, attraction already considerably preponderates over repulsion. Without the repulsive motion radiated to us from the sun, all motion on the earth would cease. If tomorrow the sun were to become cold, the attraction on the earth would still, other circumstances remaining the same, be what it is today. As before, a stone of 100 kilograms, wherever situated, would weigh 100 kilograms. But the motion, both of masses and of molecules and atoms, would come to what we would regard as an absolute standstill. Therefore it is clear that for processes occurring on the *earth* today it is by no means a matter of indifference whether attraction or repulsion is conceived as the active side of motion, hence as "force" or "energy". On the contrary, on the earth today attraction has already become *altogether passive* owing to its decisive preponderance over repulsion; we owe all active motion to the supply of repulsion from the sun. Therefore, the modern school—even if it remains unclear about the nature of the relation of motion [des Bewegungsverhältnisses]—nevertheless, in point of fact and for *terrestrial* processes, indeed for the whole solar system, is absolutely right in conceiving energy as repulsion.

The term "energy" by no means correctly expresses the entire relation of motion, for it comprehends only one aspect, the action but not the reaction. It still makes it appear as if "energy" was something external to matter, something implanted in it. But in all circumstances it is to be preferred to the expression "force".

As is generally conceded (from Hegel to Helmholtz), the notion of force is derived from the activity of the human organism within its environment. We speak of muscular force, of the lifting force of the arms, of the leaping power of the legs, of the digestive force of the stomach and intestinal tract, of the sensory force of the nerves, of the secretory force of the glands, etc. In other words, in order to save having to give the real cause of a change brought about by a function of our organism, we substitute a fictitious cause, a so-called force corresponding to the change. Then we carry this convenient method over to the external world also, and so invent as many forces as there are diverse phenomena.

In *Hegel's* time natural science (with the exception perhaps of celestial and terrestrial mechanics) was still in this naive state, and Hegel quite correctly attacks the prevailing way of denoting forces (passage to be quoted).[174] Similarly in another passage:

"It is better" (to say) "that a magnet has a *soul*" (as Thales expresses it) "than that it has an attracting force; force is a kind of property that, *separable from matter,* is put forward as a predicate—while soul, on the other hand, *is this movement itself, identical with the nature of matter.*" (*Geschichte der Philosophie,* I, p. 208.)[a]

Today we no longer make it so easy for ourselves in regard to forces. Let us listen to Helmholtz:

"If we are fully acquainted with a natural law, we must also demand that it should operate without exception... Thus the law confronts us as an objective power, and accordingly we term it a *force.* For instance, we objectivise the law of the refraction of light as a refractive power of transparent substances, the law of chemical affinities as a force of affinity of the various substances for one another. Thus we speak of the electrical force of contact of metals, of the force of adhesion, capillary force, and so on. These names objectivise laws which in the first place embrace only a limited series of natural processes, *the conditions for which are still rather complicated*[b]... Force is only the objectivised law of action... The abstract idea of force introduced by us only makes the addition that we have not arbitrarily invented this law but that it is a compulsory law of phenomena. Hence our demand to *understand* the phenomena of nature, i. e., to find out their *laws,* takes on another form of expression, viz., that we have to seek out the *forces* which are the

[a] G. W. F. Hegel, *Vorlesungen über die Geschichte der Philosophie, Werke,* Bd. XIII.— *Ed.*
[b] All italics in the quotation are by Engels.— *Ed.*

causes of the phenomena." (*Loc. cit.,* pp. [189-91]. Innsbruck lecture of 1869.)[a]

Firstly, it is certainly a peculiar manner of "objectivising" if the *purely subjective* notion of *force* is introduced into a natural law that has already been established as independent of our subjectivity and therefore completely *objective*. At most an Old-Hegelian of the strictest type might permit himself such a thing, but not a Neo-Kantian like Helmholtz. Neither the law, when once established, nor its objectivity or the objectivity of its action, acquires the slightest new objectivity by our interpolating a force into it; what is added is our *subjective assertion* that it acts in virtue of some so far entirely unknown force. The secret meaning, however, of this interpolating is seen as soon as Helmholtz gives us examples: refraction of light, chemical affinity, contact electricity, adhesion, capillarity, and raises the laws that govern these phenomena to the "objective" rank of nobility as *forces*. "These names objectivise laws which in the first place embrace only a limited series of natural processes, the conditions for which *are still rather complicated*." And it is just here that the "objectivising", which is rather subjectivising, gets its meaning; not because we have become fully acquainted with the law, but just because this is *not* the case. Just because we are *not* yet clear about the "rather complicated conditions" of these phenomena, we often take refuge here in the word force. We express thereby not our knowledge, but our *lack* of knowledge of the nature of the law and its mode of action. In this sense, as a short expression for a causal connection that has not yet been explained, as a makeshift expression, it may pass in current usage. Whatsoever is more than that cometh of evil. With just as much right as Helmholtz explains physical phenomena from so-called refractive force, electrical force of contact, etc., the mediaeval scholastics explained temperature changes by means of a *vis calorifica*[b] and a *vis frigifaciens*[c] and thus saved themselves all further investigation of heat phenomena.

And even in this sense it is unfortunate, for it expresses everything in a one-sided manner. All natural processes are two-sided, they are based on the relation of at least two operative parts, action and reaction. The notion of force, however, owing to

---

[a] H. Helmholtz, "Über das Ziel und die Fortschritte der Naturwissenschaft. Eröffnungsrede für die Naturforscherversammlung zu Innsbruck 1869". In: *Populäre wissenschaftliche Vorträge*, H. 2.— Ed.

[b] Heating force.— Ed.

[c] Cooling force.— Ed.

its origin from the action of the human organism on the external world, and further from terrestrial mechanics, implies that only one part is active, operative, the other part being passive, receptive; hence it lays down a not yet demonstrable extension of the difference between the sexes to non-living objects. The reaction of the second part, on which the force works, appears at most as a passive reaction, as a *resistance*. Now this mode of conception is permissible in a number of fields even outside pure mechanics, namely, where it is a matter of the simple transference of motion and its quantitative calculation. But already in the more complicated physical processes it is no longer adequate, as Helmholtz's own examples prove. The refractive force lies just as much in the light itself as in the transparent bodies. In the case of adhesion and capillarity, it is certain that the "force" is just as much situated in the surface of the solid as in the liquid. In contact electricity, at any rate, this much is certain, viz., that *both* metals contribute to it, and "chemical affinity" also is situated, if anywhere, in *both* the parts entering into combination. But a force which consists of two separated forces, an action which does not evoke its reaction, but which includes and bears this in itself, is no force in the sense of terrestrial mechanics, the only science in which one really knows what is meant by a force. For the basic conditions of terrestrial mechanics are, firstly, refusal to investigate the causes of the impulse, i. e., the nature of the particular force, and, secondly, the view of the one-sidedness of the force, it being everywhere opposed by an identical gravitational force, such that in comparison with any terrestrial distance of fall the earth's radius = ∞.

But let us see further how Helmholtz "objectivises" his "forces" into natural laws.

In a lecture of 1854 (*loc. cit.,* p. 119)[a] he examines the "store of working force" originally contained in the spherical nebula from which our solar system was formed.

"In point of fact it received an enormously large legacy in this respect, if only in the form of the general force of attraction of all its parts for one another."

This is indubitable. But it is equally indubitable that the whole of this legacy of gravity or gravitation is present undiminished in the solar system today, apart perhaps from the minute quantity

---

[a] H. Helmholtz, "Über die Wechselwirkung der Naturkräfte und die darauf bezüglichen neuesten Ermittlungen der Physik", *Populäre wissenschaftliche Vorträge,* H. II.— *Ed.*

that was lost together with the matter which possibly was flung out irrevocably into space. Further:

"Chemical forces too must have been already present and ready to act; but as these forces could become effective only on intimate contact of the various kinds of masses, condensation had to take place before they came into play." [P. 120.]

If, as Helmholtz does above, we regard these chemical forces as forces of affinity, hence as *attraction*, then again we are bound to say that the sum-total of these chemical forces of attraction still exists undiminished within the solar system.

But on the same page Helmholtz gives us as the result of his calculations

"that perhaps only the 454th part of the original mechanical force exists as such"—that is to say, in the solar system.

How is one to make sense of that? The force of attraction, general as well as chemical, is still present unimpaired in the solar system. Helmholtz does not mention any other certain source of force. In any case, according to Helmholtz, these forces have performed tremendous work. But they have neither increased nor diminished on that account. As it is with the clock weight mentioned above, so it is with every molecule in the solar system and the whole solar system itself. "Its weight is neither lost nor diminished". What happens to carbon and oxygen as previously mentioned holds good for all chemical elements: the total given quantity of each one remains, and "the total force of affinity continues to exist just as powerfully as before". What have we lost then? And what "force" has performed the tremendous work which is 453 times as great as that which, according to his calculation, the solar system is still able to perform? Up to this point Helmholtz has given no answer. But further on he says:

"Whether" [in the original spherical nebula] "a further *reserve of force in the shape of heat*[a] was present, we do not know." [P. 120.]

But, if we may be allowed to mention it, heat is a repulsive "force", it acts therefore *against* the direction of both gravitation and chemical attraction, being minus if these are put as plus. Hence if, according to Helmholtz, the original reserve of force is composed of general and chemical *attraction*, an extra reserve of heat would have to be, not added to that reserve of force, but subtracted from it. Otherwise the sun's heat would have to

---

[a] Italics by Engels.— *Ed.*

strengthen the force of attraction of the earth when it causes water to evaporate in direct *opposition* to this attraction, and the water vapour to rise; or the heat of an incandescent iron tube through which steam is passed would *strengthen* the chemical attraction of oxygen and hydrogen, whereas it puts it out of action. Or, to make the same thing clear in another form: let us assume that the spherical nebula with radius r, and therefore with volume $\frac{4}{3}\pi r^{3}$, has a temperature t. Let us further assume a second spherical nebula of equal mass having at the higher temperature T the larger radius R and volume $\frac{4}{3}\pi R^{3}$. Now it is obvious that in the second nebula the attraction, mechanical as well as physical and chemical, can act with the same force as in the first only when it has shrunk from radius R to radius r, i. e., when it has radiated into space heat corresponding to the temperature difference $T-t$. A hotter nebula will therefore condense later than a colder one; consequently the heat, considered from Helmholtz's standpoint as an obstacle to condensation, is no plus but a minus of the "reserve of force". Thus, Helmholtz, by presupposing the possibility of an amount of *repulsive* motion in the form of heat becoming added to the *attractive* forms of motion and increasing the total of these latter, commits a definite error of calculation.

Let us now bring the whole of this "reserve of force", possible as well as demonstrable, under the same mathematical sign so that an addition is possible. Since for the time being we cannot reverse the heat and replace its repulsion by the equivalent attraction, we shall have to perform this reversal with the two forms of attraction. Then, instead of the general force of attraction, instead of the chemical affinity, and instead of the heat, which moreover possibly already existed as such at the outset, we have simply to put the sum of the repulsive motion or so-called energy present in the gaseous sphere at the moment when it becomes independent. And by so doing Helmholtz's calculation will also hold, in which he wants to calculate "the heating that must arise from the assumed initial condensation of the heavenly bodies of our system from nebulously scattered matter". By thus reducing the whole "reserve of force" to heat, repulsion, he also makes it possible to add on the assumed "reserve of force of heat".[a] The calculation then means that $^{453}/_{454}$ of all the energy, i. e., repulsion, originally

---

    [a] H. Helmholtz, "Über die Wechselwirkung der Naturkräfte", *Populäre wissenschaftliche Vorträge*, H. II, S. 134.— *Ed.*

present in the gaseous sphere, has been radiated into space in the form of heat, or, to put it accurately, that the sum of all attraction in the present solar system is to the sum of all repulsion, still present in the same, as 454 : 1. But then it directly contradicts the text of the lecture to which it is added as proof.

If then the notion of force, even in the case of a physicist like Helmholtz, gives rise to such confusion of ideas, this is the best proof that it is altogether insusceptible of scientific use in all branches of investigation which go beyond mathematical mechanics. In mechanics the causes of motion are taken as given and their origin is disregarded, only their effects being taken into account. Hence if a cause of motion is termed a force, this does no damage to mechanics as such; but it becomes the custom to transfer this term also to physics, chemistry, and biology, and then confusion is inevitable. We have already seen this and shall frequently see it again more than once.

For the concept of work, see the next chapter.

THE MEASURE OF MOTION.—WORK [175]

"On the other hand, I have always found hitherto that the basic concepts in this field" (i. e., "the basic physical concepts of work and its unalterability") "seem very difficult to grasp for persons who have not gone through the school of mathematical mechanics, in spite of all zeal, all intelligence, and even a fairly high degree of natural-scientific knowledge. Moreover, it cannot be denied that they are abstractions of a quite peculiar kind. It was not without difficulty that even such an intellect as that of I. Kant succeeded in understanding them, as is proved by his polemic against Leibniz on this subject."

So says Helmholtz. (*Populäre wissenschaftliche Vorträge*, II, Preface.)

According to this, we are venturing now into a very dangerous field, the more so since we cannot very well take the liberty of guiding the reader "through the school of mathematical mechanics". Perhaps, however, it will turn out that, where it is a question of concepts, dialectical thinking will carry us at least as far as mathematical calculation.

Galileo discovered, on the one hand, the law of falling, according to which the distances traversed by falling bodies are proportional to the squares of the times taken in falling. On the other hand, as we shall see, he put forward the not quite compatible proposition that the quantity of motion of a body (its *impeto* or *momento*) is determined by the mass and the velocity in such a way that for constant mass it is proportional to the velocity. Descartes adopted this latter proposition and made the product of the mass and the velocity of a moving body quite generally into the measure of its motion.

Huyghens had already found that, on elastic impact, the sum of the products of the masses and the squares of their velocities remains the same before and after impact, and that an analogous law holds good in various other cases of motion of bodies united into a system.

Leibniz was the first to realise that the Cartesian measure of motion was in contradiction to the law of falling. On the other hand, it could not be denied that in many cases the Cartesian measure was correct. Accordingly, Leibniz divided motive forces into dead forces and living ones. The dead were the "pushes" or "pulls" of bodies at rest, and their measure the product of the mass and the velocity with which the body would move if it were to pass from a state of rest to one of motion. On the other hand, he put forward as the measure of *vis viva,* of the real motion of a body, the product of the mass and the square of the velocity. This new measure of motion he derived directly from the law of falling.

"The same force is required," so Leibniz concluded, "to raise a body of four pounds in weight one foot as to raise a body of one pound in weight four feet; but the distances are proportional to the square of the velocity, for when a body has fallen four feet, it attains twice the velocity reached on falling only one foot. However, bodies on falling acquire the force for rising to the same height as that from which they fell; hence the forces are proportional to the square of the velocity." (Suter, *Geschichte der mathematischen Wissenschaften,* II, p. 367.)

But he showed further that the measure of motion *mv* is in contradiction to the Cartesian law of the constancy of the quantity of motion, for if it was really valid the force (i.e., the amount of motion) in nature would continually increase or diminish. He even suggested an apparatus (*Acta Eruditorum,* 1690) which, if the measure *mv* were correct, would be bound to act as a *perpetuum mobile* with continual gain of force, which, however, would be absurd.[176] Recently, Helmholtz has again frequently employed this kind of argument.

The Cartesians protested with might and main and there developed a famous controversy lasting many years, in which Kant also participated in his very first work (*Gedanken von der wahren Schätzung der lebendigen Kräfte,* 1746),[177] without, however, seeing clearly into the matter. Mathematicians today look down with a certain amount of scorn on this "barren" controversy which

"dragged out for more than forty years and divided the mathematicians of Europe into two hostile camps, until at last d'Alembert by his *Traité de dynamique* (1743), as it were by a royal edict, put an end to the *useless verbal dispute,*[a] for it was nothing else". (Suter, *loc. cit,* p. 366.)

It would, however, seem that a controversy could not rest entirely on a useless verbal dispute when it had been initiated by a Leibniz against a Descartes, and had occupied a man like Kant to such an extent that he devoted to it his first work, a fairly large

---

[a] Italics by Engels.—*Ed.*

volume. And in point of fact, how is it to be understood that motion has two contradictory measures, that on one occasion it is proportional to the velocity, and on another to the square of the velocity? Suter makes it very easy for himself; he says both sides were right and both were wrong;

"nevertheless, the expression '*vis viva*' has endured up to the present day; *only it no longer serves as the measure of force*,[a] but is merely a term that was once adopted for the product of the mass and half the square of the velocity, a product so full of significance in mechanics." [P. 368.]

Hence, mv remains the measure of motion, and *vis viva* is only another expression for $\frac{mv^2}{2}$, concerning which formula we learn indeed that it is of great significance for mechanics, but now most certainly do not know what significance it has.

Let us, however, take up the salvation-bringing *Traité de dynamique* and look more closely at d'Alembert's "royal edict"; it is to be found in the *Preface.* In the text, it says, the whole question does not occur, on account of

"*l'inutilité parfaite dont elle est pour la mécanique*".[b] [P. XVII.]

This is quite correct for *purely mathematical* mechanics, in which, as in the case of Suter above, words used as designations are only other expressions or names for algebraic formulae, names in connection with which it is best not to think at all.

Nevertheless, since such important people have concerned themselves with the matter, he desires to examine it briefly in the Preface. Clearness of thought demands that by the force of moving bodies one should understand only their property of overcoming obstacles or resisting them. Hence, force is to be measured neither by mv nor by mv^2, but solely by the obstacles and the resistance they offer.

Now, there are, he says, three kinds of obstacles: (1) insuperable obstacles which totally destroy the motion, and for that very reason cannot be taken into account here; (2) obstacles whose resistance suffices to arrest the motion and to do so instantaneously: the case of equilibrium; (3) obstacles which only gradually arrest the motion: the case of retarded motion. [Pp. XVII-XVIII.]

"Everyone will agree that two bodies are in equilibrium when the products of their masses and virtual velocities, that is to say the velocities with which they tend to move, are equal on each side. Hence, in equilibrium the product of the mass and the velocity, or, what is the same thing, the quantity of motion, can represent the

---

[a] Italics by Engels.— *Ed.*
[b] "Its utter uselessness for the mechanics."— *Ed.*

force. Everyone will agree also that in retarded motion the number of obstacles overcome is as the square of the velocity, so that, for instance, a body which has compressed a spring with a certain velocity, could, with twice the velocity, compress simultaneously or successively not two, but four springs similar to the first, or nine with triple the velocity, and so on. Whence the partisans of *vis viva* (the Leibnizians) "conclude that the force of bodies actually in motion is in general proportional to the product of the mass and the square of the velocity. Basically, what inconvenience could there be in forces being measured differently in equilibrium and in retarded motion since, if one wants to use only clear views in reasoning, one should understand by the word *force* only the effect produced in surmounting the obstacle or resisting it?" [a] (Preface, pp. XIX-XX of the original edition.)

D'Alembert, however, is far too much of a philosopher not to realise that the contradiction of a twofold measure of one and the same force is not to be got over so easily. Therefore, after repeating what is basically only the same thing as Leibniz had already said—for his *équilibre* is precisely the same thing as the "dead pushes" of Leibniz—he suddenly goes over to the side of the Cartesians and finds the following way out:

The product *mv* can serve as a measure of force, even in the case of retarded motion,

"if in this last case the force is measured, not by the absolute magnitude of the obstacles, but by the sum of the resistances of these same obstacles. For it could not be doubted that this sum of the resistances would be proportional to the quantity of motion" (*mv*), "since, by general agreement, the quantity of motion lost by the body at each instant is proportional to the product of the resistance and the infinitely small duration of the instant, and the sum of these products evidently makes up the total resistance."

This latter mode of calculation seems to him the more natural one,

"for an obstacle is only such in as much as it offers resistance, and, properly speaking, it is the sum of the resistances that constitutes the obstacle overcome; moreover, in estimating the force in this way, one has the advantage of having a common measure for the equilibrium and for the retarded motion". [Pp. XX-XXI.]

Still, everyone can take that as he likes. And so, believing he has solved the question, by what, as Suter himself acknowledges, is a mathematical blunder, he concludes with unkind remarks on the confusion reigning among his predecessors, and asserts that after the above remarks there is possible only a very futile metaphysical discussion or a still more discreditable purely verbal dispute.

D'Alembert's proposal for reaching a reconciliation amounts to the following calculation:

---

[a] This and the two following quotations from d'Alembert are given by Engels in French.— *Ed.*

A mass 1, with velocity 1, compresses 1 spring in unit time.

A mass 1, with velocity 2, compresses 4 springs, but requires two units of time; i. e., only 2 springs per unit time.

A mass 1, with velocity 3, compresses 9 springs in three units of time, i. e., only 3 springs per unit of time.

Hence if we divide the effect by the time required for it, we again come from mv^2 to mv.

This is the same argument that Catelan[178] in particular had already employed against Leibniz; it is true that a body with velocity 2 rises against gravity four times as high as one with velocity 1, but it requires double the time for it; consequently the amount of motion (die Bewegungsmenge) must be divided by the time, and $= 2$, not 4. Curiously enough, this is also Suter's view, who indeed deprived the expression *"vis viva"* of all logical meaning and left it only a mathematical one. But this is natural. For Suter it is a question of saving the formula mv in its significance as sole measure of the amount of motion (Bewegungsmenge); hence logically mv^2 is sacrificed in order to arise again transfigured in the heaven of mathematics.

However, this much is correct: Catelan's argument provides one of the bridges connecting mv with mv^2, and so is of importance.

The mechanicians subsequent to d'Alembert by no means accepted his "royal edict", for his final verdict was indeed in favour of mv as the measure of motion. They adhered to his expression of the distinction which Leibniz had already made between dead and living forces: mv is valid for equilibrium, i. e., for statics; mv^2 is valid for motion against resistance, i. e., for dynamics. Although on the whole correct, the distinction in this form has, however, logically no more meaning than the famous decision of the N.C.O.: on duty always "to me", off duty always "me".[179] It is accepted tacitly, it just exists. We cannot alter it, and if a contradiction lurks in this double measure, what can we do about it?

Thus, for instance, Thomson and Tait say (*A Treatise on Natural Philosophy,* Oxford,[180] 1867, p. 162):

> "The *quantity of motion,* or the *momentum,* of a rigid body moving without rotation is proportional to its mass and velocity conjointly. Thus a double mass, or a double velocity, would correspond to double quantity of motion."[a]

And immediately below that they say:

---

[a] The quotations from Thomson and Tait are given by Engels in English.— *Ed.*

"The *Vis Viva* or *Kinetic energy* of a moving body is proportional to the mass and the square of the velocity conjointly."

The two contradictory measures of motion are put side by side in this very glaring form. Not so much as the slightest attempt is made to explain the contradiction, or even to disguise it. In the book by these two Scotsmen, thinking is forbidden, only calculation is permitted. No wonder that at least one of them, Tait, is accounted one of the most pious Christians of pious Scotland.

In Kirchhoff's lectures on mathematical mechanics,[a] the formulae mv and mv^2 do not occur at all *in this form*.

Perhaps Helmholtz will aid us. In his *Erhaltung der Kraft*[b] he proposes to express *vis viva* by $\dfrac{mv^2}{2}$—a point to which we shall return later. Then, on page 20 *et seq.*, he

enumerates briefly the cases in which so far the principle of the conservation of *vis viva* (hence of $\frac{mv^2}{2}$) has been used already and is recognised.

Included therein under No. 2 is

"the transference of motions by incompressible solid and fluid bodies, in so far as friction or impact of inelastic materials does not occur. For these cases our general principle is usually expressed in the rule that motion propagated and altered by mechanical powers always decreases in intensity of force in the same proportion as it increases in velocity. If, therefore, we imagine a weight m being raised with velocity c by a machine in which a force for performing work is produced uniformly by some process or other, then with a different mechanical arrangement the weight nm could be raised, but only with velocity $\frac{c}{n}$ so that in both cases the quantity of tensile force produced by the machine in unit time is represented by mgc, where g is the intensity of the gravitational force." [S. 21.]

Thus, here too we have the contradiction that an "intensity of force", which decreases and increases in simple proportion to the velocity, has to serve as proof for the conservation of an intensity of force which decreases and increases in proportion to the square of the velocity.

In any case, it becomes evident here that mv and $\dfrac{mv^2}{2}$ serve to determine two quite distinct processes, but we certainly knew that long ago, for mv^2 cannot equal mv, unless $v=1$. What has to be done is to make it comprehensible why motion should have a twofold measure, a thing which is surely just as impermissible in science as in commerce. Let us, therefore, attempt this in another way.

By mv, then, one measures "a motion propagated and altered by

[a] G. Kirchhoff, *Vorlesungen über mathematische Physik. Mechanik.*—*Ed.*

[b] H. Helmholtz, *Über die Erhaltung der Kraft...*, S. 9.—*Ed.*

mechanical powers"; hence this measure holds good for the lever and all its derivative forms, for wheels, screws, etc., in short, for all machinery for the transference of motion. But from a very simple and by no means new consideration it becomes evident that in so far as mv applies here, so also does mv^2. Let us take any mechanical contrivance in which the sums of the lever arms on the two sides are related to each other as 4 : 1, in which, therefore, a weight of 1 kg. holds a weight of 4 kg. in equilibrium. Hence, by a quite insignificant additional force on one arm of the lever we can raise 1 kg. by 20 metres; the same additional force, when applied to the other arm of the lever, raises 4 kg. a distance of 5 metres, and the preponderating weight sinks in the same time that the other weight requires for rising. Mass and velocity are inversely proportional to each other: mv, $1 \times 20 = m'v'$, 4×5. On the other hand, if we let each of the weights, after it has been raised, fall freely to the original level, then the one, 1 kg., after falling a distance of 20 metres (the acceleration due to gravity is put in round figures = 10 metres instead of 9.81 metres), attains a velocity of 20 metres; the other, 4 kg., after falling a distance of 5 metres, attains a velocity of 10 metres.

$$mv^2 = 1 \times 20 \times 20 = 400 = m'\, v'^{\,2} = 4 \times 10 \times 10 = 400.$$

On the other hand the times of fall are different: the 4 kg. traverse their 5 m. in 1 second, the 1 kg. traverses its 20 m. in 2 seconds. Friction and air resistance are, of course, neglected here.

But after each of the two bodies has fallen from its height, its motion ceases. Therefore, mv appears here as the measure of simply transferred, hence lasting, mechanical motion, and mv^2 as the measure of the vanished mechanical motion.

Further, the same thing applies to the impact of perfectly elastic bodies: the sum both of mv and of mv^2 is unaltered before and after impact. Both measures have the same validity.

This is not the case on impact of inelastic bodies. Here, too, the current elementary text-books (higher mechanics is hardly concerned at all any more with such trifles) teach that before and after impact the sum of mv remains the same. On the other hand a loss of *vis viva* occurs, for if the sum of mv^2 after impact is subtracted from the sum of mv^2 *before* impact, there is under all circumstances a positive remainder. By this amount (or the half of it, according to the point of view) the *vis viva* is diminished owing both to the mutual penetration and to the change of form of the colliding bodies.—The latter is now clear and obvious, but not so the first assertion that the sum of mv remains the same before and after impact. In spite of Suter, *vis viva* is motion, and if a part of it is lost, motion is lost. Consequently, either mv here incorrectly expresses the amount of motion [die Bewegungsmenge], or the above assertion is untrue. In general the whole theorem has been handed down from a period when there was as yet no inkling of the transformation of motion; when, therefore, a disappearance of mechanical motion was only conceded where there was no other way out. Thus, the equality here of the sum of mv before and after impact was taken as proved by the fact that no loss or gain of this sum had been introduced. If, however, the bodies lose *vis viva* in internal friction corresponding to their inelasticity, they also lose velocity, and the sum of mv after impact must be smaller than before. For it surely does not do to neglect internal friction in calculating mv, when it makes itself felt so clearly in calculating mv^2.

But this does not matter. Even if we admit the theorem, and calculate the velocity after impact, on the assumption that the sum of mv has remained the same, this decrease of the sum of mv^2 is still found. Here, therefore, mv and mv^2 conflict, and they do so by the difference of the mechanical motion that has actually disappeared. Moreover, the calculation itself shows that the sum of mv^2 expresses the amount of motion correctly, while the sum of mv expresses it incorrectly.

Such are pretty nearly all the cases in which mv is employed in mechanics. Let us now look at some cases in which mv^2 is employed.

When a cannon-ball is fired, it uses in its flight an amount of motion that is proportional to mv^2, irrespective of whether it encounters a solid target or comes to a standstill owing to air resistance and gravitation. If a railway train runs into a stationary one, the violence of the collision, and the corresponding destruction, is proportional to its mv^2. Similarly, mv^2 serves wherever it is necessary to calculate the mechanical force required for overcoming a resistance.

But what is the meaning of this convenient phrase, so current in mechanics: overcoming a resistance?

If we overcome the resistance of gravity by raising a weight, there disappears an amount of motion [Bewegungsmenge], an amount of mechanical force, equal to that which can be produced anew by the direct or indirect fall of the raised weight from the height reached back to its original level. The amount is measured by half the product of the mass and square of the final velocity after falling, $\frac{mv^2}{2}$. What then occurred on raising the weight?

Mechanical motion, or force, has disappeared as such. But it has not been annihilated; it has been converted into mechanical force of tension, to use Helmholtz's expression,[a] into potential energy, as the moderns say; into ergal as Clausius calls it[b] and this can at any moment, by any mechanically appropriate means, be reconverted into the same amount of mechanical motion as was necessary to produce it. The potential energy is only the negative expression of the *vis viva,* and vice versa.

A 24-lb. cannon-ball moving with a velocity of 400 m. per second strikes the one-metre-thick armour-plating of a warship and under these conditions has apparently no effect on the armour. Consequently an amount of mechanical motion has vanished equal to $\frac{mv^2}{2}$, i.e. since 24 lbs.=12 kg.[c] = =12 × 400 × 400 × $^1/_2$ = 960,000 kilogram-metres. What has become of it? A small portion has been expended in the concussion and molecular alteration of the armour-plate. A second portion goes in smashing the cannon-ball into innumerable fragments. But the greater part has been converted into heat and raises the temperature of the cannon-ball to red heat. When the Prussians, in making the crossing to Alsen in 1864, brought their heavy batteries into play against the armoured sides of the *Rolf Krake,*[181] after each hit they saw in the darkness the flare produced by the suddenly glowing shot. Even earlier, Whitworth had proved by experiment that explosive shells need no detonator when used against armoured warships; the glowing metal itself ignites the charge. Taking the mechanical motion as 424 kilogram-metres, the amount of heat corresponding to the above-mentioned amount of mechanical motion is 2,264 units. The specific heat of iron = 0.1140; that is to say, the amount of heat that raises the temperature of 1 kg. of water by 1° C. (which serves as the unit of heat) suffices to raise the temperature of $\frac{1}{0.1140}$=8.772 kg. of iron by 1° C. Therefore the 2,264 heat-units mentioned above raise the temperature of 1 kg. of iron by 8.772 × 2,264 = 19,860° or 19,860 kg. of iron by 1° C. Since this amount of heat is distributed uniformly in the armour and the shot, the latter has its temperature raised by $\frac{19,860°}{2 \times 12}$ =828°, amounting to quite a good

---

a See H. Helmholtz, *Über die Erhaltung der Kraft...*, S. 13-14.— *Ed.*
b R. Clausius, *Die mechanische Wärmetheorie...*, Bd. I, S. 12.— *Ed.*
c The German pound equals 500 grams.— *Ed.*

glowing heat. But since the foremost, striking end of the shot receives at any rate by far the greater part of the heat, certainly double that of the rear half, the former would be raised to a temperature of 1,104° C. and the latter to 552° C., which would fully suffice to explain the glowing effect even if we make a big deduction for the actual mechanical work performed on impact.

Mechanical motion also disappears in friction, to reappear as heat; it is well known that, by the most accurate possible measurement of the two mutually corresponding processes, Joule in Manchester and Colding in Copenhagen were the first to make an approximate experimental measurement of the mechanical equivalent of heat.

The same thing applies to the production of an electric current in a magneto-electrical machine by means of mechanical force, e.g., from a steam-engine. The amount of so-called electromotive force produced in a given time is proportional to the amount of mechanical motion used up in the same period, being equal to it if expressed in the same units. We can imagine this mechanical motion being produced, not by a steam-engine, but by a weight sinking under the pressure of gravity. The mechanical force that this is capable of supplying is measured by the *vis viva* that it would obtain on falling freely through the same distance, or by the force required to raise it again to the original height; in both cases $\frac{mv^2}{2}$.

Hence we find that mechanical motion has indeed a twofold measure, but also that each of these measures holds good for a very definitely demarcated series of phenomena. If already existing mechanical motion is transferred in such a way that it remains as mechanical motion, the transference takes place in proportion to the product of the mass and the velocity. If, however, it is transferred in such a way that it disappears as mechanical motion in order to reappear in the form of potential energy, heat, electricity, etc., in short, if it is converted into another form of motion, then the amount of this new form of motion is proportional to the product of the originally moving mass and the square of the velocity. In short, mv is mechanical motion measured by mechanical motion; $\frac{mv^2}{2}$ is mechanical motion measured by its capacity to become converted into a definite amount of another form of motion. And, as we have seen, these two measures, because different, do not contradict each other.

It becomes clear from this that Leibniz's dispute with the

Cartesians was by no means a mere verbal dispute, and that d'Alembert's "royal edict" in point of fact settled nothing at all. D'Alembert might have spared himself his tirades on the unclearness of his predecessors, for he was just as unclear as they were. In fact, as long as it was not known what becomes of the apparently annihilated mechanical motion, the absence of clarity was inevitable. And as long as mathematical mechanicians like Suter remain obstinately shut in by the four walls of their special science, they are bound to remain just as unclear as d'Alembert and to fob us off with empty and contradictory phrases.

But how does modern mechanics express this conversion of mechanical motion into another form of motion, proportional in quantity to the former?—It has *performed work,* and indeed a definite amount of work.

But this does not exhaust the concept of work in the physical sense of the word. If, as in a steam or heat engine, heat is converted into mechanical motion, i. e., molecular motion is converted into mass motion, if heat breaks up a chemical compound, if it becomes converted into electricity in a thermopile, if an electric current liberates the elements of water from dilute sulphuric acid, or, conversely, if the motion (alias energy) set free in the chemical process of a generating cell takes the form of electricity and this in the closed circuit once more becomes converted into heat—in all these processes the form of motion that initiates the process, and which is converted by it into another form, performs work, and indeed an amount of work corresponding to its own amount.

Work, therefore, is change of form of motion regarded in its quantitative aspect.

But how so? If a raised weight remains suspended and at rest, is its potential energy during the period of rest also a form of motion? Certainly. Even Tait arrives at the conviction that potential energy is subsequently resolved into a form of actual motion (*Nature*).[182] And, apart from that, Kirchhoff goes much further in saying (*Mathematische Mechanik,* p. 32):

"Rest is a special case of motion",[a]

and thus proves that he can not only calculate but can also think dialectically.

Hence, by a consideration of the two measures of mechanical motion, we arrive, incidentally, easily, and almost as a matter of

---

[a] G. Kirchhoff, *Vorlesungen über mathematische Physik. Mechanik.—Ed.*

course, at the concept of work, which was described to us as being so difficult to comprehend without mathematical mechanics. At any rate, we now know more about it than from Helmholtz's lecture *Über die Erhaltung der Kraft* (1862), which was intended precisely

"to make as clear as possible the basic physical concepts of work and its unalterability".[a]

All that we learn there about work is that it is something which is expressed in foot-pounds or in units of heat, and that the number of these foot-pounds or units of heat is invariable for a definite quantity of work; and, further, that besides mechanical forces and heat, chemical and electric forces can perform work, but that all these forces exhaust their capacity for work to the extent that they actually result in work. We learn also that it follows from this that the sum of all effective quantities of force in nature as a whole remains eternally and invariably the same throughout all the changes taking place in nature. The concept of work is neither developed, nor even defined.* And it is precisely the quantitative invariability of the magnitude of work which prevents him from realising that the qualitative alteration, the change of form, is the basic condition for all physical work. And so Helmholtz can go so far as to assert that

"friction and inelastic impact are processes in which *mechanical work is destroyed*[b] and heat is produced instead" (*Populäre Vorträge*, II, p. 166).

Just the contrary. Here mechanical work is not *destroyed,* here mechanical work is *performed.* It is mechanical *motion* that is *apparently* destroyed. But mechanical motion *can* never perform even a millionth part of a kilogram-metre of work, without apparently being destroyed as such, without becoming converted into another form of motion.

But, as we have seen, the capacity for work contained in a given amount of mechanical motion is what is known as its *vis viva,* and until recently was measured by mv^2. Here, however, a new contradiction arose. Let us listen to Helmholtz (*Erhaltung der Kraft,*

* We get no further by consulting Clerk Maxwell. He says (THEORY OF HEAT, 4TH ED., LONDON, 1875), p. 87: "WORK IS DONE WHEN RESISTANCE IS OVERCOME", and on p. 185, "THE ENERGY OF A BODY IS ITS CAPACITY FOR DOING WORK." That is all that we learn about it.

---

a H. Helmholtz, *Populäre wissenschaftliche Vorträge*, H. 2, S. VI.— *Ed.*
b Italics by Engels.— *Ed.*

p. 9). We read there that the magnitude of work can be expressed by a weight m being raised to a height h, when, if the force of gravity is put as g, the magnitude of work $= mgh$. For the body m to rise freely to the vertical height h, it requires a velocity $v = \sqrt{2\,gh}$, and it attains the same velocity on falling. Consequently, $mgh = \dfrac{mv^2}{2}$, and Helmholtz proposes

"to take the magnitude $\dfrac{mv^2}{2}$ as the quantity of *vis viva*, whereby it becomes identical with the measure of the magnitude of work. From the viewpoint of how the concept of *vis viva* has been applied hitherto ... this change has no significance, but it will offer us essential advantages in the future."

It is scarcely to be believed. In 1847, Helmholtz was so little clear about the mutual relations of *vis viva* and work, that he even fails to notice at all how he transforms the former proportional measure of *vis viva* into its absolute measure, and remains quite unconscious of the important discovery he has made by his audacious handling, recommending his $\dfrac{mv^2}{2}$ only because of its convenience as compared with mv^2! And it is as a matter of convenience that mechanicians have given general currency to $\dfrac{mv^2}{2}$. Only gradually was $\dfrac{mv^2}{2}$ also proved mathematically. Naumann (*Allgemeine Chemie*, p. 7)[a] gives an algebraical proof, Clausius (*Mechanische Wärmetheorie*, 2nd ed., I, p. 18),[b] an analytical one, which is then to be met with in another form and with a different method of deduction in Kirchhoff (*loc cit.*, p. 27).[c] Clerk Maxwell (*loc cit.*, p. 88)[d] gives an elegant algebraical deduction of $\dfrac{mv^2}{2}$ from mv.

This does not prevent our two Scotsmen, Thomson and Tait, from asserting (*loc cit.*, p. 163):

"The *vis viva*, or kinetic energy, of a moving body is proportional to the mass and the square of the velocity, conjointly. If we adopt the same units of mass [and velocity] as above" (namely, "UNIT OF MASS MOVING WITH UNIT VELOCITY"), "there is a *particular advantage* in defining kinetic energy as *half* the product of the mass and the square of the velocity."[e]

---

[a] A. Naumann, *Handbuch der allgemeinen und physikalischen Chemie.—Ed.*
[b] R. Clausius, *Die mechanische Wärmetheorie*, Bd. I.— *Ed.*
[c] G. Kirchhoff, *Vorlesungen über mathematische Physik. Mechanik.—Ed.*
[d] J. C., Maxwell, *Theory of Heat.—Ed.*
[e] W. Thomson and P. G. Tait, *Treatise on Natural Philosophy*, Vol. 1.— *Ed.*

Here, therefore, we find that not only the ability to think, but also to calculate, has come to a standstill in the two foremost mechanicians of Scotland. The particular advantage, the convenience of the formula, accomplishes everything in the most beautiful fashion.

For us, who have seen that *vis viva* is nothing but the capacity of a given amount of mechanical motion to perform work, it is obvious on the face of it that the expression in mechanical terms of this capacity for work and the work actually performed by the latter must be equal to each other; and that, consequently, if $\frac{mv^2}{2}$ measures the work, the *vis viva* must likewise be measured by $\frac{mv^2}{2}$. But that is what happens in science. Theoretical mechanics arrives at the concept of *vis viva,* the practical mechanics of the engineer arrives at the concept of work and forces it on the theoreticians. And, immersed in their calculations, the theoreticians have become so unaccustomed to thinking that for years they fail to recognise the connection between the two concepts, measuring one of them by mv^2, the other by $\frac{mv^2}{2}$, and finally accepting $\frac{mv^2}{2}$ for both, not from comprehension, but for the sake of simplicity of calculation!*

---

* The word "work" and the corresponding idea is derived from English engineers. But in English, practical work is called "work", while work in the economic sense is called "labour". Hence, physical work also is termed "work", thereby excluding all confusion with work in the economic sense. This is not the case in German; therefore it has been possible in recent pseudoscientific literature to make various peculiar applications of work in the physical sense to economic conditions of labour and vice versa. But we have also the word *"Werk"* which, like the English word "work", is excellently adapted for signifying physical work. Political economy, however, being a sphere far too remote from our natural scientists, they will scarcely decide to introduce it to replace the word *Arbeit,* which has already obtained general currency—unless, perhaps, when it is too late. Only Clausius has made the attempt to retain the expression " *Werk*", at least alongside the expression "*Arbeit*".[a]

---

[a] R. Clausius, *Über den zweiten Hauptsatz der mechanischen Wärmetheorie...*, S. 2-3.— Ed.

392

Thomson and Tait, *Natural Philosophy*, I,[a] p. 191 (§ 276):

"There are also indirect resistances,[184] owing to friction impeding the tidal motions, on all bodies which, like the earth, have portions of their free surfaces covered by liquid, which, as long as these bodies move relatively to neighbouring bodies, must keep drawing off energy from their relative motions. Thus, if we consider, in the first place, the action of the moon alone on the earth with its oceans, lakes, and rivers, we perceive that it must tend to equalize the periods of the earth's rotation about its axis, and of the revolution of the two bodies about their centre of inertia; because as long as these periods differ, the tidal action of the earth's surface must keep subtracting energy from their motions. To view the subject more in detail, and, at the same time, to avoid unnecessary complications, let us suppose the moon to be a uniform spherical body. The mutual action and reaction of gravitation between her mass and the earth's will be equivalent to a single force in some line through her centre; *and must be such as to impede the earth's rotation as long as this is performed in a shorter period than the moon's motion round the earth.*[b] It must, therefore, lie in some such direction as the line MQ in the diagram, which represents, necessarily with enormous exaggeration, its deviation, OQ, from the earth's centre. Now the actual force on the moon in the line MQ may be regarded as consisting of a force in the line MO towards the earth's centre, sensibly equal in amount to the whole force, and a comparatively very small force in the line MT perpendicular to

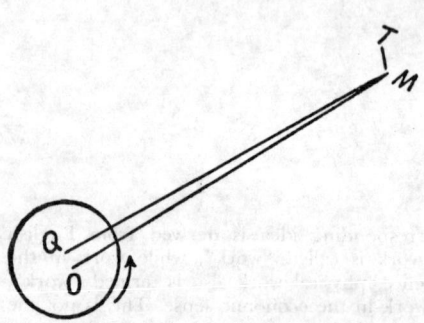

---

[a] W. Thomson and P. G. Tait, *Treatise on Natural Philosophy*, Vol. I. Engels gives this quotation in English.— *Ed.*

[b] Italics by Engels.— *Ed.*

MO. This latter is very nearly tangential to the moon's path, and is in the direction *with* her motion. Such a force, if suddenly commencing to act, would, in the first place, increase the moon's velocity; but after a certain time she would have moved so much farther from the earth, in virtue of this acceleration, as to have lost, by moving against the earth's attraction, as much velocity as she had gained by the tangential accelerating force. The effect of a continued tangential force, acting with the motion, but so small in amount as to make only a small deviation at any moment from the circular form of the orbit, is to gradually increase the distance from the central body, and to cause as much again as its own amount of work to be done against the attraction of the central mass, by the kinetic energy of motion lost. The circumstances will be readily understood by considering this motion round the central body in a very gradual spiral path tending outwards. Provided the law of force is the inverse square of the distance, the tangential component of gravity against the motion will be twice as great as the disturbing tangential force in the direction with the motion; and therefore one-half of the amount of work done against the former is done by the latter, and the other half by kinetic energy taken from the motion. The integral effect on the moon's motion, of the particular disturbing cause now under consideration, is most easily found by using the principle of moments of momenta. Thus we see that as much moment of momentum is gained in any time by the motions of the centres of inertia of the moon and earth relatively to their common centre of inertia, as is lost by the earth's rotation about its axis. The sum of the moments of momentum of the centres of inertia of the moon and earth as moving at present, is about 4.45 times the present moment of momentum of the earth's rotation. The average plane of the former is the ecliptic; and therefore the axes of the two momenta are inclined to one another at the average angle of 23°27.5′, which, as we are neglecting the sun's influence on the plane of the moon's motion, may be taken as the actual inclination of the two axes at present. The resultant, or whole moment of momentum, is therefore 5.38 times that of the earth's present rotation, and its axis is inclined 19°13′ to the axis of the earth. Hence the ultimate tendency of the *tides*[a] is to reduce the earth and moon to a simple uniform rotation with this resultant moment round this resultant axis, as if they were two parts of one rigid body: in which condition the moon's distance would be increased (approximately) in the ratio of 1 : 1.46, being the ratio of the square of the present moment of momentum of the centres of inertia to the square of the whole moment of momentum; and the period of revolution in the ratio of 1 : 1.77, being that of the cubes of the same quantities. The distance would therefore be increased to 347,100 miles, and the period lengthened to 48.36 days. Were there no other bodies in the universe but the earth and the moon, these two bodies might go on moving thus for ever, in circular orbits round their common centre of inertia, and the earth rotating about its axis in the same period, so as always to turn the same face to the moon, and, therefore, to have all the liquids at its surface at rest relatively to the solid. But the existence of the sun would prevent any such state of things from being permanent. There would be solar tides—twice high water and twice low water—in the period of the earth's revolution relatively to the sun (that is to say, twice in the solar day, or, which would be the same thing, in the month). This could not go on without *loss of energy by fluid friction.* It is not easy to trace the whole course of the disturbance in the earth's and moon's motion which this cause would produce, but its ultimate effect must be to bring the earth, moon, and sun to rotate round their common centre of inertia, like parts of one rigid body."

---

[a] Italics here and below by Engels.— *Ed.*

Kant, in 1754, was the first to put forward the view that the rotation of the earth is retarded by tidal friction and that this effect will only reach its conclusion

"when its" (the earth's) "surface will be at relative rest in relation to the moon, i.e., when it will rotate on its axis in the same period that the moon takes to revolve round the earth, and consequently will always turn the same side to the latter".[a]

He held the view that this retardation had its origin in tidal friction alone, arising, therefore, from the presence of fluid masses on the earth:

"If the earth were a quite solid mass without any fluid, neither the attraction of the sun nor of the moon would do anything to alter its free axial rotation; for it draws with equal force both the eastern and western parts of the terrestrial sphere and so does not cause any inclination either to the one or to the other side; consequently it allows the earth full freedom to continue this rotation unhindered as if there were no external influence on it."[a]

Kant could rest content with this result. All scientific prerequisites were lacking at that time for penetrating deeper into the effect of the moon on the rotation of the earth. Indeed, it required almost a hundred years before Kant's theory obtained general recognition, and still longer before it was discovered that the ebb and flow of the tides are only the *visible* aspect of the effect exercised by the attraction of the sun and moon on the rotation of the earth.

This more general conception of the matter is just that which has been developed by Thomson and Tait. The attraction of the moon and sun affects not only the fluids of the terrestrial body or its surface, but the whole mass of the earth in general in a manner that hinders the rotation of the earth. As long as the period of the earth's rotation does not coincide with the period of the moon's revolution round the earth, so long the attraction of the moon—to deal with this alone first of all—has the effect of bringing the two periods closer and closer together. If the rotational period of the (relative) central body were longer than the period of revolution of the satellite, the former would be gradually shortened; if it were shorter, as is the case for the earth, it would be lengthened. But neither in the one case will kinetic energy be created out of nothing, nor in the other will it be annihilated. In the first case, the satellite would approach closer to the central body and shorten

---

[a] I. Kant, *"Untersuchung der Frage, ob die Erde in ihrer Umdrehung um die Achse...", Sämmtliche Werke,* Bd. I, S. 185.— *Ed.*

[b] Ibid., S. 182-83.— *Ed.*

its period of revolution, in the second it would increase its distance from it and acquire a longer period of revolution. In the first case, the satellite by approaching the central body loses exactly as much potential energy as the central body gains in kinetic energy from the accelerated rotation; in the second case the satellite, by increasing its distance, gains exactly the same amount of potential energy as the central body loses in kinetic energy of rotation. The total amount of dynamic energy, potential and kinetic, present in the earth-moon system remains the same; the system is fully conservative.

One sees that this theory is entirely independent of the physico-chemical constitution of the bodies concerned. It is derived from the general laws of motion of free heavenly bodies, the connection between them being produced by attraction in proportion to their masses and in inverse proportion to the square of the distances between them. The theory has obviously arisen as a generalisation of Kant's theory of tidal friction, and is even presented here by Thomson and Tait as its substantiation on mathematical lines. But in reality—and remarkably enough the authors have simply no inkling of this—in reality it excludes the special case of tidal friction.

Friction is hindrance to the motion of masses, and for centuries it was regarded as the destruction of such motion, and therefore of kinetic energy. We now know that friction and impact are the two forms in which kinetic energy is converted into molecular energy, into heat. In all friction, therefore, kinetic energy as such is lost in order to reappear, not as potential energy in the sense of dynamics, but as molecular motion in the definite form of heat. The kinetic energy lost by friction is, therefore, in the first place *really lost* for the dynamic aspects of the system concerned. It can only become dynamically effective again if it is *reconverted* from the form of heat into kinetic energy.

How then does the matter stand in the case of tidal friction? It is obvious that here also the whole of the kinetic energy communicated to the masses of water on the earth's surface by lunar attraction is converted into heat, whether by friction of the water particles among themselves in virtue of the viscosity of the water, or by friction at the rigid surface of the earth and the comminution of rocks which stand up against the tidal motion. Of this heat there is reconverted into kinetic energy only the infinitesimally small part that contributes to evaporation at the surface of the water. But even this infinitesimally small amount of kinetic energy, ceded by the total earth-moon system to a part of the earth's surface, remains first of all at the earth's surface and is subject to the conditions prevailing there, and these conditions lead to all energy active there reaching one and the same final destiny: final conversion into heat and radiation into space.

Consequently, to the extent that tidal friction indisputably has an impeding effect on the rotation of the earth, the kinetic energy used for this purpose is absolutely lost to the dynamic earth-moon system. It can therefore not reappear within this system as dynamic potential energy. In other words, of the kinetic energy expended in impeding the earth's rotation by means of the attraction of the moon, only that part that acts on the *solid mass* of the earth's body can entirely reappear as dynamic potential energy, and hence be compensated for by a corresponding increase of the distance of the moon. On the other hand, the part that acts on the fluid masses of the earth can do so only in so far as it does not set these masses themselves into a motion opposite in direction to that of the earth's rotation, for such a motion is *wholly* converted into heat and is finally lost to the system by radiation.

What holds good for tidal friction at the surface of the earth is equally valid for the often hypothetically assumed tidal friction of a supposed fluid core of the earth.

The peculiar part of the matter is that Thomson and Tait do not notice that in order to establish the theory of tidal friction they are putting forward a theory that proceeds from the tacit assumption that the earth is an *entirely rigid* body, and so excludes any possibility of tides and hence also of tidal friction.

HEAT[185]

As we have seen, there are two forms in which mechanical motion, *vis viva*, disappears. The first is its conversion into mechanical potential energy, for instance on lifting a weight. This form has the peculiarity that not only can it be retransformed into mechanical motion—this mechanical motion, moreover, having the same *vis viva* as the original one—but also that it is capable only of this change of form. Mechanical potential energy can never produce heat or electricity, unless it has been converted first into real mechanical motion. To use Clausius' term, it is a "reversible process".

The second form in which mechanical motion disappears is in friction and impact—which differ only in degree. Friction can be conceived as a series of small impacts occurring successively and side by side, impact as friction concentrated at one spot and in a single moment of time. Friction is chronic impact, impact is acute friction. The mechanical motion that disappears here, disappears *as such*. It cannot be restored immediately out of itself. The process is not directly reversible. The mechanical motion has been transformed into qualitatively different forms of motion, into heat, electricity—into forms of molecular motion.

Hence, friction and impact lead from the motion of masses, the subject-matter of mechanics, to molecular motion, the subject-matter of physics.

In calling physics the mechanics of molecular motion,[a] it has not been overlooked that this expression by no means covers the

---

[a] See this volume, pp. 358, 362, see also p. 61.— *Ed.*

entire field of contemporary physics. On the contrary. Ether vibrations, which are responsible for the phenomena of light and radiant heat, are certainly not molecular motions in the modern sense of the word. But their terrestrial actions concern molecules first and foremost: refraction of light, polarisation of light, etc., are determined by the molecular constitution of the bodies concerned. Similarly the most important scientists now almost unanimously regard electricity as a motion of ether particles, and Clausius even says of heat that

in "the movement of ponderable atoms" (it would be better to say molecules) "... the ether within the body can also participate". (*Mechanische Wärmetheorie*, I, p. 22.)

But in the phenomena of electricity and heat, once again it is primarily molecular motions that have to be considered; it could not be otherwise, so long as our knowledge of the ether is so small. But when we have got so far as to be able to present the mechanics of the ether, this subject will include, of course, a great deal that is now of necessity allocated to physics.

The physical processes in which the structure of the molecules is altered, or even destroyed, will be dealt with later on. They form the transition from physics to chemistry.

Only with molecular motion does the change of form of motion acquire complete freedom. Whereas at the boundary of mechanics the motion of masses can assume only a few other forms—heat or electricity—here, a quite different, lively capacity for change of form is to be seen. Heat passes into electricity in the thermopile, it becomes identical with light at a certain stage of radiation, and in its turn reproduces mechanical motion. Electricity and magnetism, a twin pair like heat and light, not only become transformed into each other, but also into heat and light as well as mechanical motion. And this takes place in such definite measure relations that a given amount of any one of these forms can be expressed in any other—in kilogram-metres, in heat-units, in volts,[186] and similarly any unit of measurement can be translated into any other.

The practical discovery of the conversion of mechanical motion into heat is so very ancient that it can be taken as marking the beginning of human history. Whatever discoveries, in the way of tools and domestication of animals, may have preceded it, the making of fire by friction was the first instance of men pressing a non-living force of nature into their service. Popular superstitions today still show how greatly the almost immeasurable import of this gigantic advance impressed itself on the mind of mankind. Long after the introduction of the use of bronze and iron the invention of the stone knife, the first tool, continued to be celebrated, all religious sacrifices being performed with stone knives. According to the Jewish legend, Joshua decreed that men born in the wilderness should be circumcised with stone knives[a]; the Celts and Germans used only stone knives in their human sacrifices. But all this long ago passed into oblivion. It was different with the making of fire by friction. Long after other methods of producing fire had become known, every sacred fire among the majority of peoples had to be obtained by friction. But even today, in the majority of the European countries the popular superstition persists that fire with miraculous powers (e.g., our German bonfire against epidemics) may be lighted only by means of friction. Thus, down to our own day, the grateful memory of the first great victory of mankind over nature lives on—half unconsciously—in popular superstition, in the relics of heathen-mythological recollections among the most educated peoples in the world.

However, the process of making fire by friction is still one-sided. By it mechanical motion is converted into heat. To complete the process, it must be reversed; heat must be converted into mechanical motion. Only then is justice done to the dialectics of the process, the cycle of the process being completed—for the first stage, at least. But history has its own pace, and however dialectical its course may be in the last analysis, dialectics has often to wait for history a fairly long time. Many thousands of years must have elapsed between the discovery of fire by friction and the time when Heron of Alexandria (ca. 120 B. C.) invented a machine which was set in rotary motion by the steam issuing from it. And almost another two thousand years elapsed before the first steam-engine was built, the first apparatus for the conversion of heat into really usable mechanical motion.

The steam-engine was the first really international invention, and this fact, in turn, testifies to a mighty historical advance. The Frenchman, Papin, invented the steam-engine, and he invented it in Germany. It was the German, Leibniz, scattering around him, as always, brilliant ideas, without caring whether the

---

[a] Joshua 5 : 2 - 3.— *Ed.*

merit for them would be awarded to him or someone else, who, as we know now from Papin's correspondence (published by Gerland),[a] gave him the main idea of the machine: the employment of a cylinder and piston. Soon after that, the Englishmen, Savery and Newcomen, invented similar machines; finally, their fellow-countryman, Watt, by introducing a separate condenser, brought the steam-engine in principle up to the level of today. The cycle of inventions in this sphere was completed; the conversion of heat into mechanical motion was achieved. What came afterwards were improvements in details.

Practice, therefore, solved after its own fashion the problem of the relations between mechanical motion and heat. It had, to begin with, converted the first into the second, and then it converted the second into the first. But how did matters stand in regard to theory?

The situation was pitiable enough. Although it was just in the seventeenth and eighteenth centuries that innumerable accounts of travel appeared, teeming with descriptions of savage peoples who knew no way of producing fire other than by friction, yet physicists were almost uninterested in it; they were equally indifferent to the steam-engine during the whole of the eighteenth century and the first decades of the nineteenth. For the most part they were satisfied simply to record the facts.

Finally, in the twenties [of the nineteenth century], Sadi Carnot took the matter in hand, and indeed so very skilfully that his best calculations, afterwards presented by Clapeyron in geometrical form, have retained their validity to the present day in the works of Clausius and Clerk Maxwell. Sadi Carnot almost got to the bottom of the question. It was not the lack of factual data that prevented him from completely solving it, but solely a preconceived *false theory.* Moreover, this false theory was not one which had been forced upon physicists by some variety of malicious philosophy, but was one concocted by the physicists themselves, by means of their own naturalistic mode of thought, allegedly so very superior to the metaphysical-philosophical mode of thought.

In the seventeenth century heat was regarded, at any rate in England, as a property of bodies (as "A MOTION [b] OF A PARTICULAR KIND, THE NATURE OF WHICH HAS NEVER BEEN EXPLAINED IN A SATISFACTORY MANNER").[c]

---

[a] *Leibnizens und Huyghens' Briefwechsel mit Papin....* —*Ed.*
[b] Italics by Engels.— *Ed.*
[c] Th. Thomson, *An Outline of the Sciences...,* p. 281.— *Ed.*

That is what Th. Thomson called it, two years before the discovery of the mechanical theory of heat. (*Outline of the Sciences of Heat and Electricity*, 2nd edition, London, 1840.) But in the eighteenth century the view came more and more to the forefront that heat, as also light, electricity, and magnetism, is a special substance, and that all these peculiar substances differ from ordinary matter in having no weight, in being imponderable.

ELECTRICITY *

Electricity, like heat, only in a different way, has also a certain omnipresent character. Hardly any change can occur on the earth without being accompanied by electrical phenomena. If water evaporates, if a flame burns, if two different metals, or two metals of different temperature, touch, or if iron comes into contact with a solution of copper sulphate, and so on, electrical processes take place simultaneously with the more apparent physical and chemical phenomena. The more exactly we investigate natural processes of the most diverse nature, the more do we find evidence of electricity. In spite of its omnipresence, in spite of the fact that for half a century electricity has become more and more pressed into the industrial service of mankind, it remains precisely that form of motion the nature of which is still enveloped in the greatest obscurity. The discovery of the galvanic current is approximately 25 years younger than that of oxygen and is at least as significant for the theory of electricity as the latter discovery was for chemistry. Yet what a difference obtains even today between the two fields! In chemistry, thanks especially to Dalton's discovery of atomic weights, there is order, relative certainty about what has been achieved, and systematic, almost planned, attack on

* For the factual material in this chapter we rely mainly on Wiedemann's *Lehre vom Galvanismus und Elektromagnetismus*, 2 B-de in 3 Abt., 2. Auflage, Braunschweig, [1872-]74.

In *Nature*, June 15, 1882, there is a reference to this "admirable treatise, which in its forthcoming shape, with electrostatics added, will be the greatest experimental treatise on electricity in existence."[a] [187]

---

[a] Engels quotes in English.— *Ed.*

the territory still unconquered, comparable to the regular siege of a fortress. In the theory of electricity there is a barren lumber of ancient, doubtful experiments, neither definitely confirmed nor definitely refuted; and uncertain fumbling in the dark; unco-ordinated research, and experiment on the part of numerous isolated individuals, who attack the unknown territory with their scattered forces like the attack of a swarm of nomadic horsemen. It must be admitted, indeed, that in the sphere of electricity a discovery like that of Dalton, giving the whole science a central point and a firm basis for research, is still to seek. It is essentially this confused state of the theory of electricity, which for the time being makes it impossible to establish a comprehensive theory, that is responsible for the fact that a one-sided empiricism prevails in this sphere, an empiricism which as far as possible forbids itself thought, and which precisely for that reason not only thinks incorrectly but also is incapable of faithfully pursuing the facts or even of reporting them faithfully, and which, therefore, becomes transformed into the opposite of true empiricism.

If in general Messrs natural scientists who cannot say anything bad enough of the crazy *a priori* speculations of the German philosophy of nature are to be recommended to read the theoretico-physical works of the empirical school, not only of the contemporary but even of a much later period, this holds good quite especially for the theory of electricity. Let us take a work of the year 1840: *An Outline of the Sciences of Heat and Electricity,* by Thomas Thomson. Old Thomson was indeed an authority in his day; moreover he had already at his disposal a very considerable part of the work of the greatest electrician so far—Faraday. Yet his book contains at least just as crazy things as the corresponding section of the much older Hegelian philosophy of nature.[a] The description of the electric spark, for instance, might have been translated directly from the corresponding passage in Hegel. Both enumerate all the wonders that people sought to discover in the electric spark, prior to knowledge of its real nature and manifold diversity, and which have been shown to be mainly special cases or errors. More than that, Thomson recounts quite seriously on p. 416 Dessaigne's cock-and-bull stories, such as that, with a rising barometer and falling thermometer, glass, resin, silk, etc., become negatively electrified on immersion in mercury, but positively if instead the barometer is falling and the temperature rising; that

---

a G. W. F. Hegel, *Vorlesungen über die Naturphilosophie...*, *Werke,* Bd. VII, Abt. I.— *Ed.*

in summer gold and several other metals become positive on warming and negative on cooling, but in winter the reverse; that with a high barometer and northerly wind they are strongly electric, positive if the temperature is rising and negative if it is falling, etc. So much for the treatment of the facts. As regards *a priori* speculation, Thomson favours us with the following theory of the electric spark, derived from no lesser person than Faraday himself:

"The spark is a discharge or lowering of the polarised inductive state of many dielectric particles, by a particular action of a few of the particles occupying a very small and limited space. Faraday conceives that the few particles where the discharge occurs are not merely pushed apart, but assume a peculiar state, a HIGHLY EXALTED condition for the time; that is to say, have thrown upon them all the surrounding forces in succession, and rising up to proportionate intensity of condition perhaps equal to that of chemically combining atoms; discharge the powers, possibly in the same manner as they do theirs, by some operation at present unknown to us; AND SO THE END OF THE WHOLE. The ultimate effect is exactly as if a metallic particle had been put into the place of the discharging particle, and it does not seem impossible that the principles of action, in both cases, may hereafter prove to be the same." "I have," adds Thomson, "given this explanation of Faraday's in his own words, because I do not clearly understand it." [188]

This will certainly have been the experience of other persons also, quite as much as when they read in Hegel that in the electric spark

"the special materiality of the changed body does not as yet enter into the process but is determined within it only in an elementary and spiritual way", and that electricity is "the anger, the effervescence, proper to the body," its "angry self" that "is exhibited by every body when excited". (*Naturphilosophie*, § 324, addendum.) [a]

Yet the basic thought of both Hegel and Faraday is the same. Both oppose the idea that electricity is not a state of matter but a special, distinct variety of matter. [b] And since in the spark electricity is apparently exhibited as independent, free, separated from any foreign material substratum, and yet perceptible to the senses, they arrive at the necessity, in the state of science at the time, of having to conceive of the spark as the transient phenomenal form of a "force" momentarily freed from all matter. For us, of course, the riddle is solved, since we know that on the

---

[a] G. W. F. Hegel, *Vorlesungen über Naturphilosophie...,* *Werke,* Bd. VII, Abt. I, S. 346, 348 and 349.— *Ed.*

[b] Ibid., S. 347-48.— *Ed.*

spark discharge between metal electrodes real "metallic particles" leap across, and hence "the special materiality of the charged body" in actual fact "enters into the process".

As is well known, electricity and magnetism, like heat and light, were at first regarded as special IMPONDERABLE substances. As far as electricity is concerned, it is well known that the view soon developed that there are two opposing substances, two "fluids", one positive and one negative, which in the normal state neutralise each other, until they are forced apart by a so-called "electric force of separation". It is then possible to charge two bodies, one with positive, the other with negative electricity; on uniting them by a third conducting body equalisation occurs, either suddenly or by means of a continuous current, according to circumstances. The sudden equalisation appeared very simple and comprehensible, but the current offered difficulties. The simplest hypothesis, that the current in every case is a movement of either purely positive or purely negative electricity, was opposed by Fechner, and in more detail by Weber, with the view that in every closed circuit two equal currents of positive and negative electricity flow in opposite directions in channels lying side by side between the ponderable molecules of the bodies. Weber's detailed mathematical working out of this theory finally arrives at the result that a function, of no interest to us here, is multiplied by a magnitude $\frac{1}{r}$, where $\frac{1}{r}$ denotes "*the ratio ... of the unit of electricity to the milligram*".[a] (Wiedemann, *Lehre vom Galvanismus, etc.*, 2nd ed., III, p. 569.) The ratio to a measure of weight can naturally only be a weight ratio. Hence one-sided empiricism had already to such an extent forgotten the practice of thought in calculating that here it even makes the imponderable ·electricity ponderable and introduces its weight into the mathematical calculation.

The formulae derived by Weber sufficed only within certain limits, and Helmholtz, in particular, only a few years ago calculated from them results that come into conflict with the principle of the conservation of energy. In opposition to Weber's hypothesis of the double current flowing in opposite directions, C. Neumann in 1871 put forward the other hypothesis that in the current only one of the two electricities,[b] for instance the positive, moves, while the other, negative one, remains firmly bound up

---

[a] Italics by Engels.— *Ed.*

[b] Engels gives this data according to G. Wiedemann, *Die Lehre vom Galvanismus...*, Bd. 2, Abt. 2, S. 576.— *Ed.*

with the mass of the body. On this Wiedemann includes the remark:

"This hypothesis could be linked up with that of Weber if to Weber's supposed double current of electric masses $\pm \frac{1}{2} e$ flowing in opposite directions there was added a further *current of neutral electricity*,[a] externally inactive, which carried with it amounts of electricity $\pm \frac{1}{2} e$ in the direction of the positive current." (III, p. 577).[b]

This proposition is once again characteristic of one-sided empiricism. In order to bring about the flow of electricity at all, it is decomposed into positive and negative. All attempts, however, to explain the current with these two substances meet with difficulties: both the assumption that only one of them is present in every case in the current and that the two of them flow in opposite directions simultaneously, and, finally, the third assumption also that one flows and the other is at rest. If we adopt this last assumption how are we to explain the inexplicable idea that negative electricity, which is mobile enough in the electrical machine and the Leyden jar, in the current is firmly united with the mass of the body? Quite simply. Besides the positive current $+e$, flowing through the wire to the right, and the negative current, $-e$, flowing to the left, we make yet another current, this time of neutral electricity, $\pm \frac{1}{2} e$, flow to the right. First we assume that the two electricities, to be able to flow at all, must be separated from each other; and then, in order to explain the phenomena that occur on the flow of the separated electricities, we assume that they can also flow unseparated. First we make a supposition to explain a particular phenomenon, and at the first difficulty encountered we make a second supposition which directly negates the first one. What must be the sort of philosophy that these gentlemen have the right to complain of?

However, alongside this view of the material nature of electricity, there soon appeared a second view, according to which it is to be regarded as a mere state of the body, a "force", or, as we would say today, a special form of motion. We saw above that Hegel, and later Faraday, adhered to this view. After the discovery of the mechanical equivalent of heat had finally disposed of the idea of a special "heat stuff", and heat was shown to be a molecular motion, the next step was to treat electricity also

---

[a] Italics by Engels.— *Ed.*
[b] G. Wiedemann, op. cit., Bd. 2, Abt. 2, S. 576-77.— *Ed.*

according to the new method and to attempt to determine its mechanical equivalent. This attempt was fully successful. Particularly owing to the experiments of Joule, Favre, and Raoult, not only was the mechanical and thermal equivalent of the so-called "electromotive force" of the galvanic current established, but also its complete equivalence with the energy liberated by chemical processes in the generating cell or used up in the electrolytic cell. This made the assumption that electricity is a special material fluid more and more untenable.

The analogy, however, between heat and electricity was not perfect. The galvanic current still differed in very essential respects from the conduction of heat. It was still not possible to say *what* it was that moved in the electrically affected bodies. The assumption of a mere molecular vibration as in the case of heat seemed insufficient. In view of the enormous velocity of motion of electricity, even exceeding that of light, it remained difficult to overcome the view that here some material substance is in motion between the molecules of the body. Here the most recent theories put forward by Clerk Maxwell (1864), Hankel (1865), Reynard (1870), and Edlund (1872) are in complete agreement with the assumption, already advanced for the first time in 1846 as a suggestion by Faraday, that electricity is a motion of an elastic medium permeating the whole of space and hence all bodies as well, the discrete particles of which medium repel one another according to the law of the inverse square of the distance. In other words, it is a motion of ether particles, and the molecules of the body take part in this motion. As to the manner of this motion, the various theories are divergent; those of Maxwell, Hankel, and Reynard, taking as their basis modern investigations of vortex motion, explain it, too, in various ways from vortices, so that the vortex of old Descartes also once more comes into favour in an increasing number of new fields. We refrain from going more closely into the details of these theories. They differ strongly from one another and they will certainly still experience many transformations. But a decisive advance appears to lie in their common basic conception: that electricity is a motion of the particles of the luminiferous ether that penetrates all ponderable matter, this motion reacting on the molecules of the body. This conception reconciles the two earlier ones. According to it, in electrical phenomena it is indeed something substantial that moves, something different from ponderable matter. But this substance is not electricity itself, which in fact proves rather to be a form of motion, although not a form of the immediate, direct motion of ponderable matter. While, on the one hand, the ether theory shows a way of getting over the primitive clumsy idea of two opposed electrical fluids, on the other hand it gives a prospect of explaining *what* the real, material substratum of electrical motion is, *what* sort of a thing it is whose motion produces electrical phenomena.

The ether theory has already had *one* decisive success. As is well known, there is at least one point where electricity directly alters the motion of light: it rotates the latter's plane of polarisation. On the basis of his theory mentioned above, Clerk Maxwell calculates that the electric specific inductive capacity of a body is equal to the square of its index of refraction. Boltzmann has investigated dielectric constants of various nonconductors and he found that in sulphur, rosin, and paraffin, the square roots of these constants were respectively equal to their indices of refraction. The highest deviation—in sulphur—amounted to only 4 per cent.[a] Consequently, the Maxwellian ether theory in this particular has hereby been experimentally confirmed.

It will, however, require a lengthy period and cost much labour before new series of experiments extract a firm kernel from these mutually contradictory hypotheses. Until then, or until the ether theory, too, is perhaps supplanted by an entirely new one, the theory of electricity finds itself in the uncomfortable position of having to employ a mode of expression which it itself admits to be false. Its whole terminology is still based on the idea of two electric fluids. It still speaks quite unashamedly of "electric masses flowing in the bodies", of "a division of electricities in every molecule", etc. This is a misfortune which for the most part, as already said, follows inevitably from the present transitional state of science, but which also, with the one-sided empiricism that prevails especially in this branch of investigation, contributes not a little to preserving the existing confusion of thought.

The opposition between so-called static or frictional electricity and dynamic electricity or galvanism can now be regarded as bridged over, since we have learned to produce continuous currents by means of the electrical machine and, conversely, by means of the galvanic current to produce so-called static electricity, to charge Leyden jars, etc. We shall not here touch on the sub-form of static electricity, or on magnetism, which is now recognised to be also a sub-form of electricity. In any case, the

---

[a] Engels gives this data according to G. Wiedemann, op. cit., Bd. 2, Abt. 2, S. 612 and 649-50.— *Ed.*

theoretical explanation of the phenomena belonging here will have to be sought in the theory of the galvanic current, and consequently we shall keep mainly to this.

A continuous current can be produced in many different ways. Mechanical mass motion produces *directly*, by friction, in the first place only static electricity, and a continuous current only with great dissipation of energy; for the major part, at least, to become transformed into electric motion, the intervention of magnetism is required, as in the well-known magneto-electric machines of Gramme, Siemens, and others. Heat can be converted directly into an electric current, as occurs, for instance, at the soldered joint of two different metals. The energy set free by chemical action, which under ordinary circumstances appears in the form of heat, is converted under appropriate conditions into electric motion. Conversely, the latter form of motion, as soon as the requisite conditions are present, passes into any other form of motion: into mass motion (to a very small extent directly into electro-dynamic attractions and repulsions; to a large extent, however, by the intervention again of magnetism in the electro-magnetic motor); into heat—throughout a closed circuit, unless other changes are brought about; into chemical energy—in electrolytic cells and voltameters introduced into the circuit, where the current dissociates compounds that are attacked in vain by other means.[a]

All these transformations are governed by the basic law of the quantitative equivalence of motion through all its changes of form. Or, as Wiedemann expresses it:

"by the law of conservation of force the mechanical work exerted in any way for the production of the current must be equivalent to the work exerted in producing all the effects of the current." [II, p. 472.]

The conversion of mass motion or heat into electricity[*] offers us no difficulties here; it has been proved that the so-called "electromotive force" in the first case is equal to the work expended on that motion, and in the second case it is "at every soldered joint of the thermopile directly proportional to its

* (Note:) I use the term "electricity" in the sense of electric motion with the same justification that the general term "heat" is used to express the form of motion that our senses perceive as heat. This is the less open to objection in as much as any possible confusion with the state of *tension* of electricity is here expressly excluded in advance.

a Engels gives these data according to G. Wiedemann, op. cit., Bd. 2, Abt. 2, S. 230-65.— *Ed.*

absolute temperature" (Wiedemann, III, p. 482), i.e., to the quantity of heat present at every soldered joint measured in absolute units. The same law has in fact been proved valid also for electricity produced from chemical energy. But here the matter seems to be not so simple, at least for the theory now current. Let us, therefore, consider it more closely.

One of the most beautiful series of experiments on the transformations of form of motion as a result of the action of a galvanic pile is that of Favre (1857-58).[a] He put a Smee pile of five elements in a calorimeter; in a second calorimeter he put a small electro-magnetic motor, with the main axle and pulley wheel projecting so as to be available for any kind of coupling. Each production in the pile of one gram of hydrogen, or solution of 32.6 grams of zinc (the old chemical equivalent of zinc, equal to half the now accepted atomic weight 65.2, and expressed in grams), gave the following results:

A. The pile enclosed in the calorimeter, excluding the motor: heat production 18,682 or 18,674 units of heat.

B. Pile and motor linked in the closed circuit, but the motor prevented from moving: heat in the pile 16,448, in the motor 2,219, together 18,667 units of heat.

C. As B, but the motor in motion without, however, lifting a weight: heat in the pile 13,888, in the motor 4,769, together 18,657 units of heat.

D. As C, but the motor raises a weight and so performs mechanical work = 131.24 kilogram-metres; heat in the pile 15,427, in the motor 2,947, total 18,374 units of heat; loss in contrast to the above 18,682 equals 308 units of heat. But the mechanical work performed amounting to 131.24 kilogram-metres, multiplied by 1,000 (in order to bring the kilograms into line with the grams of the chemical results) and divided by the mechanical equivalent of heat = 423.5 kilogram-metres, gives 309 units of heat, hence exactly the loss mentioned above as the heat equivalent of the mechanical work performed.

The equivalence of motion in all its transformations is, therefore, strikingly proved for electric motion also, within the limits of unavoidable error. And it is likewise proved that the "electromotive force" of the galvanic battery is nothing but chemical energy converted into electricity, and the battery itself nothing but a device, an apparatus, that converts chemical energy

---

[a] Engels describes Favre's experiments according to G. Wiedemann *Die Lehre vom Galvanismus...*, Bd. 2, Abt. 2, S. 521-22.— *Ed.*

on its liberation into electricity, just as a steam-engine transforms the heat supplied to it into mechanical motion, without in either case the converting apparatus supplying further energy on its own account.

A difficulty arises here, however, in relation to the traditional mode of conception. The latter ascribes an *"electric force of separation"* to the battery in virtue of the conditions of contact present in it between the fluids and metals, which force is proportional to the electromotive force and therefore for a given battery represents a definite quantity of energy. What then is the relation of this electric force of separation, of this source of energy which, according to the traditional mode of conception, is inherent in the battery as such even without chemical action, to the energy set free by chemical action? And if it is a source of energy independent of the latter, whence comes the energy furnished by it?

This question in a more or less unclear form constitutes the point of dispute between the contact theory founded by Volta and the chemical theory of the galvanic current that arose immediately afterwards.

The contact theory explained the current from the electric tensions arising in the battery on contact of the metals with one or more of the liquids, or even merely on contact of the liquids themselves, and from their neutralisation or that of the opposing electricities thus generated in the circuit. The pure contact theory regarded any chemical changes that might thereby occur as quite secondary. On the other hand, as early as 1805, Ritter maintained that a current could only be formed if the excitants reacted chemically even *before* closing the circuit. In general this older chemical theory is summarised by Wiedemann (I, p. 784) to the effect that according to it so-called contact electricity

"makes its appearance only if at the same time there comes into play a real chemical action of the bodies in contact, or at any rate a disturbance of the chemical equilibrium, even if not directly bound up with chemical processes, a 'tendency towards chemical action' between the bodies in contact".

It is seen that both sides put the question of the source of energy of the current only indirectly, as indeed could hardly be otherwise at the time. Volta and his successors found it quite in order that the mere contact of heterogeneous bodies should produce a continuous current, and consequently be able to perform definite work without equivalent return. Ritter and his supporters are just as little clear how the chemical action makes the battery capable of producing the current and its performance of work. But if this point has long ago been cleared up for chemical theory by Joule, Favre, Raoult, and others, the opposite is the case for the contact theory. In so far as it has persisted, it remains essentially at the point where it started. Notions belonging to a period long outlived, a period when one had to be satisfied to ascribe a particular effect to the first available apparent cause that showed itself on the surface, regardless of whether motion was thereby made to arise out of nothing—notions that directly contradict the law of the conservation of energy—thus continue to exist in the theory of electricity of today. And if the most objectionable aspects of these ideas are shorn off, weakened, watered down, castrated, glossed over, this does not improve matters at all: the confusion is bound to become only so much the worse.

As we have seen, even the older chemical theory of the current declares the contact relations of the battery to be absolutely indispensable for the formation of the current: it maintains only that these contacts can never achieve a continuous current without simultaneous chemical action. And even today it is taken as a matter of course that the contact arrangements of the battery provide precisely the apparatus by means of which liberated chemical energy is transformed into electricity, and that it depends essentially on these contact arrangements whether and how much chemical energy actually passes into electric motion.

Wiedemann, as a one-sided empiricist, seeks to save what can be saved of the old contact theory. Let us follow what he has to say.

"In contrast to what was formerly believed," says Wiedemann (I, p. 799), "the effect of contact of chemically indifferent bodies, e.g., of metals, is *neither indispensable for the theory of the pile*,[a] nor proved by the facts that *Ohm* derived his law from it, a law that can be derived without this assumption, and that *Fechner*, who confirmed this law experimentally, likewise defended the contact theory. Nevertheless, the excitation of electricity by *metallic* contact, at least according to the experiments now available, is not to be denied, even though the quantitative results, obtainable in this respect may always be tainted with an inevitable uncertainty owing to the impossibility of keeping absolutely clean the surfaces of the bodies in contact."

It is seen that the contact theory has become very modest. It concedes that it is not at all indispensable for explaining the current, and neither proved theoretically by Ohm nor experimentally by Fechner. It even concedes that the so-called fundamental experiments, on which alone it can still rest, can never furnish

---

a Italics by Engels.— *Ed.*

other than uncertain results in a quantitative respect, and finally it asks us merely to recognise that in general it is by contact— although only of *metals!*—that electric motion occurs.

If the contact theory remained content with this, there would not be a word to say against it. It will certainly be granted that on the contact of two metals electrical phenomena occur, by means of which a preparation of a frog's leg can be made to twitch, an electroscope charged, and other movements brought about. The only question that arises in the first place is: whence comes the energy required for this?

To answer this question, we shall, according to Wiedemann (I, p. 14):

"adduce *more or less the following*[a] considerations: if the heterogeneous metal plates A and B are brought within a close distance of each other, they attract each other in consequence of the forces of adhesion. On mutual contact they lose the *vis viva* of motion imparted to them by this attraction. (If we assume that the molecules of the metals are in a state of permanent vibration, it *could* also happen that, if on contact of the heterogeneous metals the molecules not vibrating simultaneously come into contact, an alteration of their vibration is thereby brought about with loss of *vis viva*.) The lost *vis viva* is *to a large extent* converted into heat. A *small portion* of it, however, is expended in bringing about a different distribution of the electricities previously unseparated. As we have already mentioned above, the bodies brought together become charged with equal quantities of positive and negative electricity, *possibly* as the result of an unequal attraction for the two electricities."

The modesty of the contact theory becomes greater and greater. At first it is admitted that the powerful electric force of separation, which has later such a gigantic work to perform, in itself possesses no energy of its own, and that it cannot function if energy is not supplied to it from outside. And then it has allotted to it a more than diminutive source of energy, the *vis viva* of adhesion, which only comes into play at scarcely measurable distances and which allows the bodies to travel a scarcely measurable length. But it does not matter: it undeniably exists and equally undeniably vanishes on contact. But even this minute source still furnishes too much energy for our purpose: a *large* part is converted into heat and only a *small* portion serves to evoke the electric force of separation. Now, although it is well known that cases enough occur in nature where extremely minute impulses bring about extremely powerful effects, Wiedemann himself seems to feel that his hardly trickling source of energy can with difficulty suffice here, and he seeks a possible second source in the assumption of an interference of the molecular vibrations of the two metals at

---

[a] Here and below italics by Engels.— *Ed.*

the surfaces of contact. Apart from other difficulties encountered here, Grove and Gassiot have shown that for exciting electricity actual contact is not at all indispensable, as Wiedemann himself tells us on the previous page.[a] In short, the more we examine it the more does the source of energy for the electric force of separation dwindle to nothing.

Yet up to now we hardly know of any other source for the excitation of electricity on metallic contact. According to Naumann (*Allgemeine und physikalische Chemie,*[b] Heidelberg, 1877, p. 675), "the contact-electromotive forces convert heat into electricity"; he finds "the assumption natural that the ability of these forces to produce electric motion depends on the quantity of heat present, or, in other words, that it is a function of the temperature", as has also been proved experimentally by Le Roux. Here, too, we find ourselves groping in the dark. The law of the voltaic series of metals forbids us to have recourse to the chemical processes that to a small extent are continually taking place at the contact surfaces, which are always covered by a thin layer of air and impure water, a layer as good as inseparable as far as we are concerned; hence it forbids us to explain the excitation of electricity by the presence of an invisible active electrolyte between the contact surfaces. An electrolyte should produce a continuous current in the closed circuit, but the electricity of mere metallic contact, on the contrary, disappears on closing the circuit. And here we come to the real point: whether, and in what manner, the production of a continuous current on the contact of chemically indifferent bodies is made possible by this "electric force of separation", which Wiedemann himself first of all restricted to metals, declaring it incapable of functioning without energy being supplied from outside, and then referred exclusively to a truly microscopic source of energy.

The voltaic series arranges the metals in such a sequence that each one behaves as electro-negative in relation to the preceding one and as electro-positive in relation to the one that follows it. Hence if we arrange a series of pieces of metal in this order, e. g., zinc, tin, iron, copper, platinum, we shall be able to obtain an electric tension at each end. If, however, we arrange the series of metals to form a closed circuit so that the zinc and platinum are in contact, the electric tension is at once neutralised and disappears.

"Therefore the production of a continuous current of electricity is not possible in a closed circuit of bodies belonging to the voltaic series.." [I, p. 45.]

---

[a] G. Wiedemann, op. cit., Bd. 1, S. 13.— *Ed.*
[b] A. Naumann, *Handbuch der allgemeinen und physikalischen Chemie.*— *Ed.*

Wiedemann further supports this statement by the following theoretical consideration:

"In fact, if a continuous electric current were to make its appearance in the circuit, it would produce heat in the metallic conductors themselves, and this heating could at the most be counterbalanced by cooling at the metallic junctions. In any case it would give rise to an uneven distribution of heat; moreover an electro-magnetic motor could be driven continuously by the current without [any sort of] supply from outside, and thus work would be performed, which is impossible, since on firmly joining the metals, for instance by soldering, no further changes to compensate for this work could take place even at the contact surfaces." [I, pp. 44-45.]

And not content with the theoretical and experimental proof that the contact electricity of metals by itself cannot produce any current, we shall see too that Wiedemann finds himself compelled to put forward a special hypothesis to abolish its activity even where it might perhaps make itself evident in the current.

Let us, therefore, try another way of passing from contact electricity to the current. Let us imagine, with Wiedemann,

"two metals, such as a zinc rod and a copper rod, soldered together at one end, but with their free ends connected by a third body which does *not* act electromotively in relation to the two metals, but only conduct the opposing electricities collected on their surfaces, so that they are neutralised in it. Then the electric force of separation would always restore the previous potential difference, thus a continuous electric current would make its appearance in the circuit, a current that would be able to perform work without any compensation, which again is impossible. Accordingly, there cannot be a body which only conducts electricity without electromotive activity in relation to the other bodies." [I, p. 45.]

We are no better off than before: the impossibility of creating motion again bars the way. By the contact of chemically indifferent bodies, hence by contact electricity as such, we shall never produce a current. Let us therefore go back again and try a third way pointed out by Wiedemann:

"Finally, if we immerse a zinc plate and a copper plate in a liquid that contains a so-called *binary* compound, which therefore can be decomposed into two chemically distinct constituents that completely saturate one another, e.g., dilute hydrochloric acid (H + Cl), etc., then according to paragraph 27 the zinc becomes negatively charged and the copper positively. On joining the metals, these electricities neutralise each other through the place of contact, through which, *therefore, a current of positive electricity* flows from the copper to the zinc. Moreover, since the electric force of separation making its appearance on the contact of these two metals *conveys* the positive electricity *in the same direction*, the effects of the electric forces of separation are *not* abolished as in a closed metallic circuit. *Hence there arises a continuous current of positive electricity*, flowing in the closed circuit from the copper through its place of contact with the zinc, in the direction of the latter, and through the liquid from the zinc to the copper. We shall return in a moment (paragraph 34, et seq.) to the question how far the individual electric forces of separation present in the circuit *really* participate in the formation of the current.—A combination of conductors providing such a 'galvanic current' we term a galvanic element or also a galvanic battery." [I, p. 45.][a]

Thus the miracle has been accomplished. By the mere electric force of separation of the contact which, according to Wiedemann himself, cannot be effective without energy being supplied from outside, a continuous current has been produced. And if we were offered nothing more for its explanation than the above passage from Wiedemann, it would indeed remain an absolute miracle. What have we learned here about the process?

1. If zinc and copper are immersed in a liquid containing a so-called *binary* compound, then, according to § 27, the zinc becomes negatively charged and the copper positively charged.—But in the whole of § 27 there is no word of any binary compound. It describes only a simple voltaic element of a zinc plate and a copper plate, with a piece of cloth moistened by an *acid* liquid interposed between them, and then investigates, without mentioning any chemical processes, the resulting static-electric charges of the two metals. Hence, the so-called *binary* compound has been smuggled in here by the backdoor.[b]

2. What this binary compound is doing here remains a complete mystery. The circumstance that it "*can*[c] be decomposed into two chemical constituents that fully saturate each other" (fully saturate each other after they have been decomposed?!) could at most teach us something new if it were *actually to decompose.* But we are not told a word about that, hence for the time being we have to assume that it does *not* decompose, e. g., in the case of paraffin.

3. When the zinc in the liquid has been negatively charged, and the copper positively charged, we bring them into contact (outside the liquid). At once "these electricities neutralise each other through the place of contact, through which, *therefore,* a current of *positive* electricity flows from the copper to the zinc". Again, we do not learn why only a current of "positive" electricity flows in the one direction, and not also a current of "negative" electricity in the opposite direction. We do not learn at all what becomes of the negative electricity, which, hitherto, was just as necessary as the positive; the effect of the electric force of separation consisted precisely in setting them free to oppose each other. Now it has been suddenly suppressed, as it were eliminated, and it is made to

---

[a] All italics by Engels.—*Ed.*

[b] G. Wiedemann, op. cit., Bd. 1, S. 40-41.—*Ed.*

[c] Italics by Engels.—*Ed.*

appear as if there exists only positive electricity.

But then again, on p. 51, the precise opposite is said, for here "*the electricities unite*[a] in one current"; consequently both negative and positive flow in it! Who will rescue us from this confusion?

4. "Moreover, *since* the electric force of separation making its appearance on the contact of these two metals *conveys* the positive electricity *in the same direction*, the effects of the electric forces of separation are not abolished as in a closed metallic circuit. *Hence*, there arises a continuous current," etc.[b]

This is a bit thick. For, as we shall see, Wiedemann proves to us a few pages later (p. 52) that

on the "formation of a continuous current ... the electric force of separation at the place of contact of the metals ... *must be inactive*[c]",

that not only does a current occur even when this force, instead of conveying the positive electricity in the same direction, acts in opposition to the direction of the current, but that in this case too it is not compensated by a definite share of the force of separation of the battery and, hence, once again is inactive. Consequently, how can Wiedemann on p. 45 make an electric force of separation participate as a necessary factor in the formation of the current, when on p. 52 he puts it out of action for the duration of the current, and that, moreover, by a hypothesis erected specially for this purpose?

5. "Hence there arises a *continuous current*[c] of positive electricity, flowing in the closed circuit from the copper through its place of contact with the zinc, in the direction of the latter, and through the liquid from the zinc to the copper."

But in the case of such a continuous electric current, "heat would be produced by it in the conductors themselves", and also it would be possible for "an electromagnetic motor to be driven by it and thus work performed", which, however, is impossible without supply of energy. Since Wiedemann up to now has not breathed a syllable as to whether such a supply of energy occurs, or whence it comes, the continuous current so far remains just as much an impossibility as in both the previously investigated cases.

No one feels this more than Wiedemann himself. So he finds it desirable to hurry, as quickly as possible over the many ticklish points of this remarkable explanation of current formation, and instead to entertain the reader throughout several pages with all

---

[a] Italics by Engels.— *Ed.*
[b] G. Wiedemann, op. cit., Bd. 1, S. 45. All italics by Engels.— *Ed.*
[c] Italics by Engels.— *Ed.*

kinds of elementary anecdotes about the thermal, chemical, magnetic, and physiological effects of this still mysterious current, in the course of which by way of exception he even adopts a quite popular tone. Then he suddenly continues (p. 49):

"We have now to investigate in what way the electric forces of separation are active in a closed circuit of two metals and a liquid, e.g., zinc, copper, and hydrochloric acid.

"*We know* that when the current flows through the liquid the constituents of the binary compound (HCl) contained in it become separated in such a manner that one constituent (H) *is set free* on the copper, and an equivalent amount of the other (Cl) on the zinc, *whereby* the latter constituent combines with an equivalent amount of zinc to form ZnCl." [a]

We know! If we know this, we certainly do not know it from Wiedemann who, as we have seen, so far has not breathed a syllable about this process. Further, *if* we do know anything of this process, it is that it cannot proceed in the way described by Wiedemann.

On the formation of a molecule of HCl from gaseous hydrogen and gaseous chlorine, an amount of energy = 22,000 units of heat is liberated (Julius Thomsen).[189] Therefore, to break away the chlorine from its combination with hydrogen, the same quantity of energy must be supplied from outside for each molecule of HCl. Where does the battery derive this energy? Wiedemann's description does not tell us, so let us look for ourselves.

When chlorine combines with zinc to form zinc chloride a considerably greater quantity of energy is liberated than is necessary to separate chlorine from hydrogen; (Zn, Cl$_2$) develops 97,210 and 2 (H, Cl) 44,000 units of heat (Julius Thomsen). With that the process in the battery becomes comprehensible. Hence it is not, as Wiedemann relates, that hydrogen without more ado is liberated on the copper, and chlorine on the zinc, "whereby" then subsequently and accidentally the zinc and chlorine enter into combination. On the contrary, the combination of the zinc with the chlorine is the essential, basic condition for the whole process, and as long as this does not take place, one would wait in vain for hydrogen on the copper.

The excess of energy liberated on formation of a molecule of ZnCl$_2$ over that expended on liberating two atoms of H from two molecules of HCl, is converted in the battery into electric motion and provides the entire "electromotive force" that makes its appearance in the current circuit. Hence it is not a mysterious

---

[a] All italics by Engels.— *Ed.*

"electric force of separation" that tears asunder hydrogen and chlorine without any demonstrable source of energy, it is the total chemical process taking place in the battery that endows all the "electric forces of separation" and "electromotive forces" of the closed circuit with the energy necessary for their existence.

For the time being, therefore, we put on record that Wiedemann's *second* explanation of the current gives us just as little assistance as his first one, and let us proceed further with the text:

"This process proves that the behaviour of the binary substance between the metals does not consist merely in a simple predominant attraction of its entire mass for one electricity or the other, as in the case of metals, but that in addition a special action of its constituents is exhibited. Since the constituent Cl is given off where the current of positive electricity enters the fluid, and the constituent H where the negative electricity enters, *we assume*[a] that each equivalent of chlorine in the compound HCl is charged with a definite amount of negative electricity determining its attraction by the entering positive electricity. It is the *electro-negative constituent* of the compound. Similarly the equivalent of H must be charged with positive electricity and so represent the electro-positive constituent of the compound. These charges *could* be produced on the combination of H and Cl in just the same way as on the contact of zinc and copper. Since the compound HCl as such is non-electric, *we must assume*[b] accordingly that in it the atoms of the positive and negative constituents contain equal quantities of positive and negative electricity.

"If now a zinc plate and a copper plate are dipped in dilute hydrochloric acid, *we can suppose* that the zinc has a stronger attraction towards the electro-negative constituent (Cl) than towards the electro-positive one (H). Consequently, the molecules of hydrochloric acid in contact with the zinc *would* dispose themselves so that their electro-negative constituents are turned towards the zinc, and their electro-positive constituents towards the copper. Owing to the constituents when so arranged exerting their electrical attraction on the constituents of the next molecules of HCl, the whole series of molecules between the zinc and copper plates becomes arranged as follows:

---

[a] Italics by Engels.— *Ed.*
[b] Here and below in this quotation italics by Engels.— *Ed.*

If the second metal acted on the positive hydrogen as the zinc does on the negative chlorine, it would help to promote the arrangement. If it acted in the opposite manner, only more weakly, at least the direction would remain unaltered.

"By the influence exerted by the negative electricity of the electronegative constituent Cl adjacent to the zinc, the electricity *would* be so distributed in the zinc that places on it which are close to the Cl of the immediately adjacent atom [190] of acid would become charged positively, those farther away negatively. Similarly, negative electricity would accumulate in the copper next to the electro-positive constituent (H) of the adjacent atom of hydrochloric acid, and the positive electricity would be driven to the more remote parts.

"*Next*, the positive electricity in the zinc *would* combine with the negative electricity of the immediately adjacent atom of Cl, and the latter itself with the zinc [to form non-electric ZnCl]. The electropositive atom H, which was previously combined with this atom of Cl, *would* combine with the atom of Cl turned towards it belonging to the second atom of HCl, with simultaneous combination of the electricities contained in these atoms; similarly, the H of the second atom of HCl *would combine* with the Cl of the third atom, and so on, until finally on the copper an atom of H *would* be set free, the positive electricity of which would unite with the distributed negative electricity of the copper, so that it would escape in a non-electrified state." This process would "repeat itself until the repulsive action of the electricities accumulated in the metal plates on the electricities of the hydrochloric acid constituents turned towards them balances the chemical attraction of the latter by the metals. If, however, the metal plates are joined by a conductor, the free electricities of the metal plates unite with one another and the above-mentioned processes can recommence. *In this way* a constant flow of electricity would come into being. "It is evident that thereby a continual loss of *vis viva* occurs, owing to the constituents of the binary compound on their migration to the metals moving to the latter with a definite velocity and then coming to rest, either with formation of a compound (ZnCl) or by escaping in the free state (H)." (*Note* [by Wiedemann]: "Since the gain in *vis viva* on separation of the constituents Cl and H ... is compensated by the *vis viva* lost on the union of these constituents with the constituents of the adjacent atoms, the influence of this process can be neglected.") "This loss of *vis viva* is equivalent to the quantity of heat which is set free in the visibly occurring chemical process, essentially, therefore, that produced on the solution of an equivalent of zinc in the dilute acid. This value must be the same as that of the work expended on separating the electricities. If, therefore, the electricities unite to form a current, then, during the solution of an equivalent of zinc and the giving off of an equivalent of hydrogen from the liquid, there must make its appearance in the whole circuit, whether in the form of heat or in the form of external performance of work, an amount of work that is likewise equivalent to the development of heat corresponding to this chemical process." [I, pp. 49-51.]

"Let us assume—could—we must assume—we can suppose—would be distributed—would become charged", etc., etc. Sheer conjecture and subjunctives from which only three actual indicatives can be definitely extracted: firstly, that the combination of the zinc with the chlorine is *now* pronounced to be the condition for the liberation of hydrogen; secondly, as we now learn right at the end and as it were incidentally, that the energy herewith liberated is the source, and indeed the exclusive source, of all energy required for the formation of the current; and thirdly, that this explanation of the current formation is as directly in contradiction to both those previously given as the latter are themselves mutually contradictory.

Further it is said:

"For the formation of a continuous current, therefore, there is active *purely and solely*[a] the electric force of separation which is derived from the unequal attraction and polarisation of the atoms of the binary compound in the exciting liquid of the battery by the metal electrodes; at the place of contact of the metals, at which no further mechanical changes can occur, the electric force of separation *must on the other hand be inactive*. That this force, if perchance it *counteracts* the electromotive excitation of the metals by the liquid (as on immersion of tin and lead in potassium cyanide solution), is not compensated by a definite share of the force of separation at the place of contact, is proved by the above-mentioned complete proportionality of the total electric force of separation (and electromotive force) in the closed circuit, with the above-mentioned heat equivalent of the chemical processes. Hence it must be neutralised in another way. This would most simply occur on the assumption that on contact of the exciting liquid with the metals the electromotive force is produced in a double manner; on the one hand by an unequally strong attraction of the *mass* of the liquid as a whole towards one or the other electricity, on the other hand by the unequal attraction of the metals towards the *constituents* of the liquid charged with opposite electricities.... Owing to the former unequal mass attraction towards the electricities, the liquids would fully conform to the law of the voltaic series of metals, and in a closed circuit ... complete neutralisation to zero of the electric forces of separation (and electromotive forces) take place; the second (*chemical*) action ... on the other hand would *by itself* supply the electric force of separation necessary for the formation of the current and the corresponding electromotive force." (I, pp. 52-53.)

Herewith the last relics of the contact theory are now happily eliminated from formation of the current, and simultaneously also the last relics of Wiedemann's first explanation of current formation given on p. 45.[b] It is finally conceded without reservation that the galvanic battery is a simple apparatus for converting chemical energy in process of liberation into electric motion, into so-called electric force of separation and electromotive force, just as the steam-engine is an apparatus for converting heat energy into mechanical motion. In the one case, as in the other, the apparatus provides only the conditions for liberation and further transformation of the energy, but supplies no energy on its own account. This once established, it remains for us now to make a closer examination of this third version of Wiedemann's explana-

---

[a] All italics by Engels.— *Ed.*
[b] See this volume, pp. 415-16.— *Ed.*

tion of the current. How are the energy transformations in the closed circuit of the battery represented here?

It is evident, he says, that in the battery "a continual loss of *vis viva* occurs, owing to the constituents of the binary compound on their migration to the metals moving to the latter with a definite velocity and then coming to rest, either with formation of a compound (ZnCl) or by escaping in the free state (H). This loss is equivalent to the quantity of heat which is set free in the visibly occurring chemical process, essentially, therefore, that produced on the solution of an equivalent of zinc in the dilute acid."[a]

Firstly, if the process goes on in *pure* form, no heat at all is set free in the battery on solution of the zinc; the liberated energy is indeed converted directly into electricity and only from this converted further into heat by the resistance of the whole circuit.

Secondly, *vis viva* is half the product of the mass and the square of the velocity. Hence the above statement would read: the energy set free on solution of an equivalent of zinc in dilute hydrochloric acid, equalling so many calories, is likewise equivalent to half the product of the mass of the ions and the square of the velocity with which they migrate to the metals. Expressed in this way, the statement is obviously false; the *vis viva* appearing on the migration of the ions is far from being equivalent to the energy set free by the chemical process.* But if it were to be so, no current

---

* F. Kohlrausch has recently calculated *(Wiedemanns Annalen,* VI,[p.] 206)[b] that "immense forces" are required to drive the ions through the water solvent. To cause one milligram to move through a distance of one millimetre requires a force of attraction which for $H = 32,500$ kg., for $Cl = 5,200$ kg., hence for $HCl = 37,700$ kg.—Even if these figures are absolutely correct, they do not affect what has been said above. But the calculation contains the hypothetical factors hitherto inevitable in the sphere of electricity and therefore requires control by experiment. Such control appears possible. In the first place, these "immense forces" must reappear as a definite quantity of heat in the place where they are consumed, i.e., in the above case in the battery. Secondly, the energy consumed by them must be smaller than that supplied by the chemical processes of the battery, and there should be a definite difference. Thirdly, this difference must be used up in the rest of the closed circuit and likewise be quantitatively demonstrable there. Only after confirmation by this control can the above figures be regarded as final. The demonstration in the electrolytic cell appears still more susceptible of realisation.

---

[a] G. Wiedemann, op. cit., Bd. 1, S. 51.— *Ed.*
[b] F. Kohlrausch, "Das elektrische Leitungsvermögen *der* wässerigen Lösungen von den Hydraten und Salzen der leichten Metalle...", *Annalen der Physik und Chemie,* Neue Folge, Bd. VI, No. 1, S. 206-07.— *Ed.*

would be possible, since there would be no energy remaining over for the current in the remainder of the closed circuit. Hence the further remark is introduced that the ions come to rest "either with formation of a compound or by escaping in the free state". But if the loss of *vis viva* is to include also the energy transformations taking place on these two processes, then we have indeed arrived at a dead-lock. For it is precisely to these two processes taken together that we owe the whole liberated energy, so that there can be absolutely no question here of a *loss* of *vis viva*, but at most of a *gain*.

It is therefore obvious that Wiedemann himself did not mean anything definite by this proposition; rather the "loss of *vis viva*" represents only the *deus ex machina*[a] which is to enable him to make the fatal leap from the old contact theory to the chemical explanation of the current. In point of fact, the loss of *vis viva* has now performed its function and is dismissed; henceforth the chemical process in the battery is recognised indisputably as the sole source of energy for current formation, and the only remaining anxiety of our author is as to how he can politely rid the current of the last relic of excitation of electricity on the contact of chemically indifferent bodies, namely, the force of separation active at the place of contact of the two metals.

Reading the above explanation of current formation given by Wiedemann, one could believe oneself in the presence of a specimen of the kind of *apologia* that wholly- and semi-orthodox theologians of almost forty years ago employed to meet the philologico-historical bible criticism[191] of Strauss, Wilke, Bruno Bauer, and others. The method is exactly the same, and it is bound to be so. For in both cases it is a question of saving the *inherited tradition* from scientific thought. Exclusive empiricism, which at most allows itself thinking in the form of mathematical calculation, imagines that it operates only with undeniable facts. In reality, however, it operates predominantly with traditional notions, with the largely obsolete products of thought of its predecessors, and such are positive and negative electricity, the electric force of separation, the contact theory. These serve it as the foundation of endless mathematical calculations in which, owing to the strictness of the mathematical formulation, the hypothetical nature of the premises gets comfortably forgotten. This kind of empiricism is as credulous towards the results of the thought of its predecessors as it is sceptical in its attitude to the

---

[a] Literally: "a deity from a machine"; hence, any person or thing artificially introduced, as in a story, to solve a difficulty.— *Ed.*

results of contemporary thought. For it even the experimentally established facts have gradually become inseparable from their traditional interpretations; the simplest electric phenomenon is presented falsely, e.g., by smuggling in the two electricities; this empiricism *cannot* any longer describe the facts correctly, because the traditional interpretation is woven into the description. In short, we have here in the field of the theory of electricity a tradition just as highly developed as that in the field of theology. And since in both fields the results of recent research, the establishment of hitherto unknown or disputed facts and of the necessarily following theoretical conclusions, run pitilessly counter to the old traditions, the defenders of these traditions find themselves in the direct dilemma. They have to resort to all kinds of subterfuges and untenable expedients, to the glossing over of irreconcilable contradictions, and thus finally land themselves into a medley of contradictions from which they have no escape. It is this faith in all the old theory of electricity that entangles Wiedemann here into most inextricably contradicting himself, simply owing to the hopeless attempt to reconcile rationally the old explanation of the current by "contact force" with the modern one by liberation of chemical energy.

It will perhaps be objected that the above criticism of Wiedemann's explanation of the current rests on juggling with words; that although at the beginning Wiedemann expresses himself somewhat carelessly and inaccurately, still he does finally give the correct account in accord with the principle of the conservation of energy and so sets everything right. As against this view, we give below another example, his description of the process in the battery: zinc—dilute sulphuric acid—copper:

"If, however, the two plates are joined by a wire, a galvanic current arises.... *By the electrolytic process,*[a] one equivalent of hydrogen is given off on the copper from the *water* of the dilute sulphuric acid, this hydrogen escaping in bubbles. On the zinc there is formed one equivalent of oxygen which oxidises the zinc to form zinc oxide, the latter becoming dissolved in the surrounding acid to form sulphuric zinc oxide." (I, p. 593.)

To break up water into gaseous hydrogen and gaseous oxygen requires an amount of energy of 68,924 heat-units for each molecule of water. Whence then comes the energy in the above battery? "By the electrolytic process." And where does the electrolytic process get it from? No answer is given.

_____

[a] All italics in this quotation by Engels.— *Ed.*

But Wiedemann further tells us, not once, but at least twice (I, p. 472 and p. 614), that "according to recent experiments [in electrolysis] the water itself is not decomposed", but that in our case it is the sulphuric acid H_2SO_4 that splits up into H_2 on the one hand and into $SO_3 + O$ on the other hand, whereby under suitable conditions H_2 and O can escape in gaseous form. But this alters the whole nature of the process. The H_2 of the H_2SO_4 is directly replaced by the bivalent zinc, forming zinc sulphate, $ZnSO_4$. There remains over, on the one side H_2, on the other $SO_3 + O$. The two gases escape in the proportions in which they unite to form water, the SO_3 unites with the water H_2O of the solution to reform H_2SO_4, i.e., sulphuric acid. The formation of $ZnSO_4$, however, develops sufficient energy not only to displace and liberate the hydrogen of the sulphuric acid, but also to leave over a considerable excess, which in our case is expended in forming the current. Hence the zinc does not wait until the electrolytic process puts free oxygen at its disposal, in order first to become oxidised and then to become dissolved in the acid. On the contrary, it enters directly into the process, which only comes into being at all *by this participation of the zinc.*

We see here how obsolete chemical notions come to the aid of the obsolete contact notions. According to modern views, a salt is an acid in which hydrogen has been replaced by a metal. The process under investigation confirms this view; the direct replacement of the hydrogen of the acid by the zinc fully explains the transformations of energy. The old view, adhered to by Wiedemann, regards a salt as a compound of a metallic oxide with an acid and therefore speaks of sulphuric zinc oxide instead of zinc sulphate. But to arrive at sulphuric zinc oxide in our battery of zinc and sulphuric acid, the zinc must first be oxidised. In order to oxidise the zinc fast enough, we must have free oxygen. In order to get free oxygen, we must assume—since hydrogen appears on the copper—that the water is decomposed. In order to decompose water, we need tremendous energy. How are we to get this? Simply "by the electrolytic process" which itself cannot come into operation as long as its chemical end product, the "sulphuric zinc oxide", has not begun to be formed. The child gives birth to the mother.

Consequently, here again Wiedemann puts the whole process absolutely the wrong way round and upside down. And the reason is that he lumps together active and passive electrolysis, two directly opposite processes, simply as electrolysis.

So far we have only examined the events in the battery, i.e., that process in which an excess of energy is set free by chemical action and is converted into electricity by the arrangements of the battery. But it is well known that this process can also be reversed: the electricity of a continuous current produced in the battery from chemical energy can, in its turn, be reconverted into chemical energy in an electrolytic cell inserted in the closed circuit. The two processes are obviously the opposites of each other; if the first is regarded as chemico-electric, then the second is electro-chemical. Both can take place in the same circuit with the same substances. Thus, the voltaic pile from gas elements, the current of which is produced by the union of hydrogen and oxygen to form water, can, in an electrolytic cell inserted in the circuit, furnish gaseous hydrogen and gaseous oxygen in the proportion in which they form water. The usual view lumps these two opposite processes together under the *single* expression: electrolysis, and does not even distinguish between active and passive electrolysis, between an exciting liquid and a passive electrolyte. Thus Wiedemann treats of electrolysis in general for 143 pages[a] and then adds at the end some remarks on "electrolysis in the battery", in which, moreover, the processes in actual batteries only occupy the lesser part of the seventeen pages of this section.[b] Also in the "theory of electrolysis" that follows, this contrast of battery and electrolytic cell is not even mentioned,[c] and anyone who looked for some treatment of the transformations of energy in the closed circuit in the next chapter, "The Influence of Electrolysis on the Conduction Resistance and the Electromotive Force in the Circuit", would be bitterly disappointed.[d]

Let us now consider the irresistible "electrolytic process" which is able to separate H_2 from O without visible supply of energy, and which plays the same role in these sections of the book as did previously the mysterious "electric force of separation".

"Alongside the *primary, purely electrolytic*[e] process of separation of the ions, a number of *secondary, purely chemical* processes, quite independent of the first, take place by the action of the ions split off by the current. This action can take place on the material of the electrodes and on the bodies that are decomposed, and in the case of solutions also on the solvent." (I, p. 481.)

---

[a] G. Wiedemann, op. cit., Bd. 1, S. 459-91.— *Ed.*
[b] Ibid., S. 592-609.— *Ed.*
[c] Ibid., S. 609-34.— *Ed.*
[d] Ibid., S. 635-737.— *Ed.*
[e] Italics by Engels.— *Ed.*

Let us return to the above-mentioned battery: zinc and copper in dilute sulphuric acid. Here, according to Wiedemann's own statement, the separated ions are the H_2 and O of the water. Consequently, for him the oxidation of the zinc and the formation of $ZnSO_4$ is a secondary, purely chemical process, independent of the electrolytic process, in spite of the fact that it is only through it that the primary process becomes possible. Let us now examine somewhat in detail the confusion that must necessarily arise from this inversion of the true course of events.

Let us consider in the first place the so-called secondary processes in the electrolytic cell, of which Wiedemann puts forward some examples* (pp. 481-82):

I. The electrolysis of sodium sulphate (Na_2SO_4) dissolved in water.

This "breaks up ... into 1 equivalent of SO_3+O ... and 1 equivalent of Na.... The latter, however, reacts on the water solvent and splits off from it 1 equivalent of H, while 1 equivalent of caustic soda (NaOH) is formed and becomes dissolved in the surrounding water."

The equation is:

$$Na_2SO_4+2H_2O = O+SO_3+2NaOH+2H.$$

In fact, in this example the decomposition

$$Na_2SO_4 = Na_2+SO_3+O$$

could be regarded as the primary, electro-chemical process, and the further transformation

$$Na_2+2H_2O = 2NaOH+2H$$

as the secondary, purely chemical one. But this secondary process is effected immediately at the electrode where the hydrogen appears, the very considerable quantity of energy (111,810 heat-units for Na, O, H, aq. according to Julius Thomsen) thereby liberated is therefore, at least for the most part, converted into electricity, and only a portion in the cell is transformed directly into heat. But the latter can also happen to the chemical energy directly or primarily liberated in the *battery*. The quantity of

---

* It may be noted here once for all that Wiedemann employs throughout the old chemical equivalent values, writing HO, ZnCl, etc.[192] In my equations, the modern atomic weights are everywhere employed, putting, therefore, H_2O, $ZnCl_2$, etc.

energy which has thus become available and converted into electricity, however, is to be subtracted from that which the current has to supply for continued decomposition of the Na_2SO_4. If the conversion of sodium into hydrated oxide appeared in the *first* moment of the total process as a secondary process, from the second moment onwards it becomes an essential factor of the total process and so ceases to be secondary.

But yet a third process takes place in this electrolytic cell: SO_3 combines with H_2O to form H_2SO_4, sulphuric acid, provided the SO_3 does not enter into combination with the metal of the positive electrode, in which case again energy would be liberated. But this change does not necessarily proceed immediately at the electrode, and consequently the quantity of energy (21,320 heat-units, J. Thomsen) thereby liberated becomes converted wholly or mainly into heat in the cell itself, and provides at most a very small portion of the electricity in the current. The only really secondary process occurring in this cell is therefore not mentioned at all by Wiedemann.

II. "If a solution of copper sulphate [$CuSO_4+5H_2O$] is electrolysed between a positive copper electrode and a negative one of platinum, 1 equivalent of copper separates out for 1 equivalent of water decomposed at the negative platinum electrode, with simultaneous decomposition of sulphuric acid in the same current circuit; at the positive electrode, 1 equivalent of SO_4 should make its appearance; but this combines with the copper of the electrode to form 1 equivalent of $CuSO_4$, which becomes dissolved in the water of the electrolysed solution." [I, p. 481.]

In the modern chemical mode of expression we have, therefore, to represent the process as follows: copper is deposited on the platinum; the liberated SO_4, which cannot exist as such, splits up into SO_3+O, the latter escaping in the free state; the SO_3 takes up H_2O from the aqueous solvent and forms H_2SO_4, which again combines with the copper of the electrode to form $CuSO_4$, H_2 being set free. Strictly speaking, we have here three processes: (1) the separation of Cu and SO_4; (2) $SO_3+O+H_2O = H_2SO_4+O$; (3) $H_2SO_4+Cu = H_2+CuSO_4$. It is natural to regard the first as primary, the two others as secondary. But if we inquire into the energy transformations, we find that the first process is completely compensated by a part of the third: the separation of copper from SO_4 by the reuniting of both at the other electrode. If we leave out of account the energy required for shifting the copper from one electrode to the other, and likewise the inevitable, not accurately determinable, loss of energy in the battery by conversion into heat, we have here a case where the so-called primary process withdraws no energy from the current. The current provides energy exclusively to make possible the separation of H_2 and O, which moreover is indirect, and this proves to be the real chemical result of the whole process—hence, for carrying out a *secondary,* or even tertiary, process.

Nevertheless, in both the above examples, as in other cases also, it is undeniable that the distinction of primary and secondary processes has a relative justification. Thus in both cases, among other things, water also is apparently decomposed and the elements of water given off at the opposite electrodes. Since, according to the most recent experiments, absolutely pure water comes as near as possible to being an ideal non-conductor, hence also a non-electrolyte, it is important to show that in these and similar cases it is not the water that is directly electro-chemically decomposed, but that the elements of water are separated from the acid, in the formation of which here it is true the water of the solution must participate.

III. "If one electrolyses simultaneously in two U-tubes ... hydrochloric acid [$HCl+8H_2O$] ... using in one tube a zinc positive electrode and in the other tube one of copper, then in the first tube a quantity of zinc 32.53 is dissolved, in the other a quantity of copper 2×31.7." [I, p. 482.]

For the time being let us leave the copper out of account and consider the zinc. The decomposition of HCl is regarded here as the primary process, the solution of Zn as secondary.

According to this conception, therefore, the current brings to the electrolytic cell from outside the energy necessary for the separation of H and Cl, and after this separation is completed, the Cl combines with the Zn, whereby a quantity of energy is set free that is subtracted from that required for separating H and Cl; the current needs only therefore to supply the difference. So far everything agrees beautifully; but if we consider the two amounts of energy more closely we find that the one liberated on the formation of $ZnCl_2$ is *larger* than that used up in separating 2HCl; consequently, that the current not only does not need to supply energy, but on the contrary *receives energy.* We are no longer confronted by a passive electrolyte, but by an exciting fluid, not an electrolytic cell but a *battery,* which strengthens the current-forming voltaic pile by a new element; the process which we are supposed to conceive as secondary becomes absolutely primary, becoming the source of energy of the whole process and making the latter independent of the current supplied by the voltaic pile.

We see clearly here the source of the whole confusion prevailing in Wiedemann's theoretical description. Wiedemann's point of departure is electrolysis; whether this is active or passive, battery or electrolytic cell, is all one to him: saw-bones is saw-bones, as the old Major said to the Doctor of Philosophy[193] doing his year's military service. And since it is easier to study electrolysis in the electrolytic cell than in the battery, he does, in fact, take the electrolytic cell as his point of departure, and he makes the processes taking place in it, and the partly justifiable division of them into primary and secondary, the measure of the altogether reverse processes in the battery, not even noticing when his electrolytic cell becomes surreptitiously transformed into a battery. Hence he is able to put forward the proposition:

"The chemical affinity that the separated substances have for the electrodes has no influence on the electrolytic process as such" (I, p. 471),

a proposition which in this absolute form, as we have seen, is totally false. Hence, further, his threefold theory of current formation: firstly, the old traditional one, by means of pure contact; secondly, that derived by means of the abstractly conceived electric force of separation, which in an inexplicable manner obtains for itself or for the "electrolytic process" the requisite energy for splitting apart the H and Cl in the battery and for forming a current as well; and finally, the modern, chemico-electric theory which demonstrates the source of this energy in the algebraic sum of all the chemical reactions in the battery. Just as he does not notice that the second explanation overthrows the first, so also he has no idea that the third in its turn overthrows the second. On the contrary, the principle of the conservation of energy is merely added in a quite superficial way to the old theory handed down from routine, just as a new geometrical theorem is appended to the earlier ones. He has no inkling that this principle makes necessary a revision of the whole traditional point of view in this as in all other fields of natural science. Hence Wiedemann confines himself to noting the principle in his explanation of the current, and then calmly puts it on one side, taking it up again only right at the end of the book, in the chapter on the work performed by the current.[a] Even in the theory of the excitation of electricity by contact (I, p. 781 et seq.) the conservation of energy plays no role at all in relation to the chief subject dealt with, and is

---

[a] G. Wiedemann, op. cit., Bd. 2, Abt. 2, S. 472.— *Ed.*

only incidentally brought in for throwing light on subsidiary matters: it is and remains a "secondary process".[a]

Let us return to the above example III. There the same current was used to electrolyse hydrochloric acid in two U-tubes, but in one there was a positive electrode of zinc, in the other the positive electrode used was of copper. According to Faraday's basic law of electrolysis, the same galvanic current decomposes in each cell equivalent quantities of electrolyte, and the quantities of the substances liberated at the two electrodes are also in proportion to the equivalents. (I, p. 470.) In the above case it was found that in the first tube a quantity of zinc 32.53 was dissolved, and in the other a quantity of copper 2×31.7.

"Nevertheless," continues Wiedemann, "this is no proof for the equivalence of these values. They are observed only in the case of very weak currents with the formation of zinc chloride ... on the one hand, and of copper chloride ... on the other. In the case of stronger currents, with the same amount of zinc dissolved, the quantity of dissolved copper would sink ... down to 31.7 with formation of increasing quantities of chloride."[b]

It is well known that zinc forms only a single compound with chlorine, zinc chloride, $ZnCl_2$; copper on the other hand forms two compounds, cupric chloride, $CuCl_2$, and cuprous chloride, Cu_2Cl_2. Hence the process is that the weak current splits off two copper atoms from the electrode for each two chlorine atoms, the two copper atoms remaining united by *one* of their two valencies, while their two free valencies unite with the two chlorine atoms:

$$\begin{array}{c} Cu\!-\!Cl \\ | \\ Cu\!-\!Cl \end{array}$$

On the other hand, if the current becomes stronger, it splits the copper atoms apart altogether, and each one unites with two chlorine atoms:

$$Cu\!\!\diagup\!\!\diagdown\begin{array}{c} Cl \\ Cl \end{array}$$

In the case of currents of medium strength, both compounds are formed side by side. Thus it is solely the strength of the current

---

[a] G. Wiedemann, op. cit., Bd. 1, S. 781-800.— *Ed.*

[b] Ibid., S. 482.— *Ed.*

that determines the formation of one or the other compound, and therefore the process is essentially *electro*-chemical, if this word has any meaning at all. Nevertheless Wiedemann declares explicitly that it is secondary, hence not electro-chemical, but purely chemical.

The above experiment is one performed by Renault (1867) and is one of a whole series of similar experiments in which the same current is led in one U-tube through salt solution (positive electrode—zinc), and in another cell through a varying electrolyte with various metals as the positive electrode. The amounts of the other metals dissolved here for each equivalent of zinc diverged very considerably, and Wiedemann gives the results of the whole series of experiments which, however, in point of fact, are mostly self-evident chemically and could not be otherwise. Thus, for 1 equivalent of zinc, only $^2/_3$ of an equivalent of gold is dissolved in hydrochloric acid.[a] This can only appear remarkable if, like Wiedemann, one adheres to the old equivalent weights and writes ZnCl for zinc chloride, according to which both the chlorine and the zinc appear in the chloride with only a *single* valency. In reality two chlorine atoms stick to one zinc atom ($ZnCl_2$), and as soon as we know this formula we see at once that in the above determination of equivalents, the chlorine atom is to be taken as the unit and not the zinc atom. The formula for gold chloride, however, is $AuCl_3$, from which it is at once seen that $3ZnCl_2$ contains exactly as much chlorine as $2AuCl_3$, and so all primary, secondary, and tertiary processes in the battery or cell are compelled to transform, for each part by weight of zinc converted into zinc chloride, neither more nor less than $^2/_3$ of a part by weight of gold into gold chloride. This holds absolutely unless the compound AuCl also could be prepared by galvanic means, in which case even 2 equivalents of gold would have to be dissolved for 1 equivalent of zinc, when also similar variations according to the current strength could occur as in the case of copper and chlorine mentioned above. The value of Renault's experiments consists in the fact that they show how Faraday's law is confirmed by facts that appear to contradict it. But what they are supposed to contribute in throwing light on secondary processes in electrolysis is not evident.

Wiedemann's third example led us again from the electrolytic cell to the battery. And in fact the battery offers by far the greatest interest when one investigates the electrolytic processes in

---

[a] G. Wiedemann, op. cit., Bd. 1, S. 483.— *Ed.*

relation to the transformations of energy taking place here. Thus we not infrequently encounter batteries in which the chemico-electric processes seem to take place in direct contradiction to the law of the conservation of energy and in opposition to chemical affinity.

According to Poggendorff's [194] measurements, the battery: zinc—concentrated salt solution—platinum, provides a current of strength 134.6. Hence we have here quite a respectable quantity of electricity, $\frac{1}{3}$ more than in the Daniell cell.[195] What is the source of the energy appearing here as electricity? The "primary" process is the replacement of sodium in the chlorine compound by zinc. But in ordinary chemistry it is not zinc that replaces sodium, but vice versa, sodium replacing zinc from chlorine and other compounds. The "primary" process, far from being able to give the current the above quantity of energy, on the contrary requires itself a supply of energy from outside in order to come into being. Hence, with the mere "primary" process we are again at a standstill. Let us look, therefore, at the real process. Then we find that the change is not

$$Zn + 2NaCl = ZnCl_2 + 2Na,$$

but

$$Zn + 2NaCl + 2H_2O = ZnCl_2 + 2NaOH + H_2.$$

In other words, the sodium is not split off in the free state at the negative electrode, but forms a hydroxide as in the above example I (pp. ....).[a]

To calculate the energy transformations taking place here, Julius Thomsen's determinations provide us at least with certain important data. According to them, the energy liberated on combination is as follows:

$$(Zn,\ Cl_2) = 97,210$$
$$(ZnCl_2,\ aqua) = 15,630$$

making a total for dissolved

zinc chloride	= 112,840	heat-units.
2 (Na, O, H, aqua)	= 223,620	" "
	336,460	" "

---

[a] See this volume, p. 427.— Ed.

Deducting consumption of energy on the separations:

$$2 \text{ (Na, Cl, aq.)} = 193,020 \text{ heat-units.}$$
$$2 \text{ (H}_2\text{O)} = 136,720 \text{ ”   ”}$$
$$\overline{329,740 \text{ ”   ”}}$$

The excess of liberated energy equals 6,720 heat-units.

This amount is obviously small for the current strength obtained, but it suffices to explain, on the one hand, the separation of the sodium from chlorine, and on the other hand, the current formation in general.

We have here a striking example of the fact that the distinction of primary and secondary processes is purely relative and leads us *ad absurdum* as soon as we take it absolutely. The primary electrolytic process, taken alone, not only cannot produce any current, but cannot even take place itself. It is only the secondary, ostensibly purely chemical process that makes the primary one possible and, moreover, supplies the whole surplus energy for current formation. In reality, therefore, it proves to be the primary process and the other the secondary one. When the rigid differences and opposites, as imagined by the metaphysicians and metaphysical natural scientists, were dialectically turned into their opposites by Hegel, it was said that he had twisted the words in their mouths. But if nature itself proceeds exactly like old Hegel, it is surely time to examine the matter more closely.

With greater justification one can regard as secondary those processes which, while taking place *in consequence* of the chemico-electric process of the battery or the electro-chemical process of the electrolytic cell, do so independently and separately, occurring therefore at some distance from the electrodes. Hence the energy transformations taking place in such secondary processes likewise do not enter into the electric process; directly they neither withdraw energy from it nor supply energy to it. Such processes occur very frequently in the electrolytic cell; we saw an instance in the example I above on the formation of sulphuric acid during electrolysis of sodium sulphate. They are, however, of lesser interest here. Their occurrence in the battery, on the other hand, is of greater practical importance. For although they do not directly supply energy to, or withdraw it from, the chemico-electric process, nevertheless they alter the total available energy present in the battery and thus affect it indirectly.

There belong here, besides subsequent chemical changes of the ordinary kind, the phenomena that occur when the ions are liberated at the electrodes in a different condition from that in which they usually occur in the free state, and when they pass over to the latter only after moving away from the electrodes. In such cases the ions can assume a different density or a different state of aggregation. They can also undergo considerable changes in regard to their molecular constitution, and this case is the most interesting. In all these cases, an analogous heat change corresponds to the secondary chemical or physical change of the ions taking place at a certain distance from the electrodes; usually heat is set free, in some cases it is consumed. This heat change is, of course, restricted primarily to the place where it occurs: the liquid in the battery or electrolytic cell becomes warmer or cooler while the rest of the circuit remains unaffected by this change. Hence this heat is called *local* heat. The liberated chemical energy available for conversion into electricity is, therefore, diminished or increased by the equivalent of this positive or negative local heat produced in the battery. According to Favre, in a battery with hydrogen peroxide and hydrochloric acid two-thirds of the total energy set free is consumed as local heat; the Grove cell, on the other hand, on closing the circuit became considerably cooler and therefore supplied energy from outside to the circuit by absorption of heat. Hence we see that these secondary processes also react on the primary one. We can make whatever approach we like, the distinction between primary and secondary processes remains merely a relative one and is regularly suspended in the interaction of the one with the other.[a] If this is forgotten and such relative opposites are treated as absolute, one finally gets hopelessly involved in contradictions, as we have seen above.

As is well known, on the electrolytic liberation of gases the metal electrodes become covered with a thin layer of gas; in consequence the current strength decreases until the electrodes are saturated with gas, whereupon the weakened current again becomes constant. Favre and Silbermann have shown that local heat arises also in such an electrolytic cell; this local heat, therefore, can only be due to the fact that the gases are not liberated at the electrodes in the state in which they usually occur, but that they are only brought into this usual state after their separation from the electrodes, by a further process bound up with the development of heat.[b] But what is the state in which the gases are given off at the electrodes? One cannot express oneself more cautiously on this

---

[a] Engels gives this data according to G. Wiedemann, op. cit., Bd. 2. Abt. 2, S. 499.— *Ed.*

[b] G. Wiedemann, op. cit., Bd. 2. Abt. 2, S. 500-08.— *Ed.*

than Wiedemann does. He terms it a "certain", an "allotropic", an "active", and finally, in the case of oxygen, several times an "ozonised" state. In the case of hydrogen his statements are still more mysterious. Incidentally, the view comes out that ozone and hydrogen peroxide are the forms in which this "active" state is realised. Our author is so keen in his pursuit of ozone that he even explains the extreme electro-negative properties of certain peroxides from the fact that they "possibly contain a part of the oxygen *in the ozonised state*"![a] (I, p. 57). Certainly both ozone and hydrogen peroxide are formed on the so-called decomposition of water, but only in small quantities. There is no basis at all for assuming that in the case mentioned local heat is produced first of all by the origin and then by the decomposition of any large quantities of the above two compounds. We do not know the heat of formation of ozone (O_3) from *free* oxygen atoms. According to Berthelot[196] the heat of formation of hydrogen peroxide from H_2O (liquid) $+ O = 21,480$; the origin of this compound in any large amount would therefore give rise to a large excess of energy (about 30 per cent of the energy required for the separation of H_2 and O), which could not but be evident and demonstrable. Finally, ozone and hydrogen peroxide would take only oxygen into account (apart from current reversals, where both gases would come together at the same electrode), but not hydrogen. Yet the latter also escapes in an "active" state, in such a way that in the combination: potassium nitrate solution between platinum electrodes, it combines directly with the nitrogen split off from the acid to form ammonia.

In point of fact, all these difficulties and doubts have no existence. The electrolytic process has no monopoly of splitting off bodies "in an active state". Every chemical decomposition does the same thing. It splits off the liberated chemical element in the first place in the form of free atoms of O, H, N, etc., which only after their liberation can unite to form molecules O_2, H_2, N_2, etc., and on thus uniting give off a definite, though up-to-now still undetermined, quantity of energy which appears as heat. But during the infinitesimal moment of time when the atoms are free, they are the bearers of the total quantity of energy that they can take up at all; while possessed of their maximum energy they are free to enter into any combination offered them. Hence they are "in an active state" in contrast to the molecules O_2, H_2, N_2, which have already surrendered a part of this energy and cannot enter

---

[a] Italics by Engels.— *Ed.*

into combination with other elements without this quantity of energy surrendered being re-supplied from outside. We have no need, therefore, to resort only to ozone and hydrogen peroxide, which themselves are merely products of this active state. For instance, we can undertake the above-mentioned formation of ammonia on electrolysis of potassium nitrate even without a battery, simply by chemical means, by adding nitric acid or a nitrate solution to a liquid in which hydrogen is set free by a chemical process. In both cases the active state of the hydrogen is the same. But the interesting point about the electrolytic process is that here the transitory existence of the free atoms becomes as it were tangible. The process here is divided into two phases: the electrolysis provides free atoms at the electrodes, but their combination to form molecules occurs at some distance from the electrodes. However infinitesimally minute this distance may be compared to measurements relating to masses, it suffices to prevent the energy liberated on formation of the molecules being used for the electric process, at least for the most part, and so determines its conversion into heat—the local heat in the battery. But it is owing to this that the fact is established that the elements have been split off as free atoms and for a moment have existed in the battery as free atoms. This fact, which in pure chemistry can only be established by theoretical conclusions, is here proved experimentally, in so far as this is possible without sensuous perception of the atoms and molecules themselves. Herein lies the high scientific importance of the so-called local heat of the battery.

The conversion of chemical energy into electricity by means of the battery is a process about whose course we know next to nothing, and we shall become more closely acquainted with it only when the *modus operandi* of electric motion itself becomes better known.

The battery has ascribed to it an "electric force of separation" which is given for each particular battery. As we saw at the outset, Wiedemann conceded that this electric force of separation is not a definite form of energy. On the contrary, it is primarily nothing more than the capacity, the property, of a battery to convert a definite quantity of liberated chemical energy into electricity in unit time. Throughout the whole process, this chemical energy itself never assumes the form of an "electric force of separation", but, on the contrary, at once and immediately takes on the form of so-called "electromotive force", i.e., of electric motion. If in ordinary life we speak of the force of a steam-engine in the sense that it is capable in unit time of converting a definite quantity of heat into the motion of masses, this is not a reason for introducing the same confusion of ideas into scientific thought also. We might just as well speak of the varying force of a pistol, a carbine, a smooth-bored gun, and a rifle, because, with equal gunpowder charges and projectiles of equal weight, they shoot varying distances. But here the wrongness of the expression is quite obvious. Everyone knows that it is the ignition of the gunpowder charge that drives the bullet, and that the varying range of the weapon is only determined by the greater or lesser dissipation of energy according to the length of the barrel, the clearance of the projectile,[197] and the form of the latter. But it is the same for the force of steam and for the electric force of separation. Two steam-engines—other conditions being equal, i.e., assuming the quantity of energy liberated in equal periods of time to be equal in both—or two galvanic batteries, of which the same thing holds good, differ as regards performance of work only owing to their greater or lesser dissipation of energy. And if until now all armies have been able to develop the technique of fire-arms without the assumption of a special shooting force of weapons, the science of electricity has absolutely no excuse for assuming an "electric force of separation" analogous to this shooting force, a force which embodies absolutely no energy and which therefore of itself cannot perform a millionth of a milligram-millimetre of work.

The same thing holds good for the second form of this "force of separation", the "electric force of contact of metals" mentioned by Helmholtz. It is nothing but the property of metals to convert on their contact the existing energy of another form into electricity. Hence it is likewise a force that does not contain a particle of energy. If we assume with Wiedemann that the source of energy of contact electricity lies in the *vis viva* of the motion of adhesion, then this energy exists in the first in the form of this mass motion and on its vanishing becomes converted immediately into electric motion, without even for a moment assuming the form of an "electric force of contact".

And now we are assured in addition that the electromotive force, i.e., the chemical energy, reappearing as electric motion is proportional to this "electric force of separation", which not only contains no energy, but owing to the very conception of it *cannot* contain any! This proportionality between non-energy and energy obviously belongs to the same mathematics as that in which there figures the "ratio of the unit of electricity to the milligram".[a] But the absurd form, which owes its existence only to the conception of a simple *property* as a mystical *force*, conceals a quite simple tautology: the capacity of a given battery to convert liberated chemical energy into electricity is measured—by what? By the quantity of the energy reappearing in the closed circuit as electricity in relation to the chemical energy consumed in the battery. That is all.

In order to arrive at an electric force of separation, one must take seriously the emergency device of the two electric fluids. To convert these from their neutrality to their polarity, hence to split them apart, requires a certain expenditure of energy—the electric force of separation. Once separated, the two electricities can, on being reunited, again give off the same quantity of energy—electromotive force. But since nowadays no one, not even Wiedemann, regards the two electricities as having a real existence, it means that one is writing for a defunct public if one deals at length with such a point of view.

The basic error of the contact theory consists in the fact that it cannot divorce itself from the idea that contact force or electric force of separation is a *source of energy*, which of course was difficult when the mere property of an apparatus to bring about transformation of energy had been converted into a *force*; for indeed, a *force* ought precisely to be a definite form of energy. Because Wiedemann cannot rid himself of this unclear notion of force, although side by side with it the modern ideas of indestructible and uncreatable energy have been forced upon him, he falls into his nonsensical explanation No. 1, of the current, and into all the later demonstrated contradictions.

If the expression "electric force of separation" is directly contrary to reason, the other "electromotive force" is at least superfluous. We had heat engines long before we had electromotors, and yet the theory of heat has been developed quite well without any special thermo-motor force. Just as the simple expression "heat" includes all phenomena of motion that belong to this form of energy, so also can the expression "electricity" in its own sphere. Moreover, very many forms of action of electricity are not at all directly "motor"; the magnetisation of iron, chemical decomposition, conversion into heat. And finally, in every natural science, even in mechanics, it is always an advance if the word *force* can somewhere be got rid of.

---

[a] See this volume, p. 405.— *Ed.*

We saw that Wiedemann did not accept the chemical explanation of the processes in the battery without a certain reluctance. This reluctance continually attacks him; where he can blame anything on the so-called chemical theory, this is certain to occur. Thus,

"it is by no means established that electromotive force is proportional to the intensity of chemical action". (I, p. 791.)

Certainly not in every case; but where this proportionality does not occur, it is only a proof that the battery has been badly constructed, that dissipation of energy takes place in it. For that reason Wiedemann is quite right in paying absolutely no attention in his theoretical deductions to such subsidiary circumstances which falsify the purity of the process, but in simply assuring us that the electromotive force of a cell is equal to the mechanical equivalent of the chemical action taking place in it in unit time with unit intensity of current.

In another passage we read:

"That further, in the acid-alkali battery, the combination of acid and alkali is not the cause of current formation follows from the experiments, paragraph 61 (Becquerel and Fechner), paragraph 260 (Du-Bois-Reymond), and paragraph 261 (Worm-Müller), according to which in certain cases when these are present in equivalent quantities no current makes its appearance, and likewise from the experiment (Henrici) mentioned in paragraph 62, that on interposing a solution of potassium nitrate between the potassium hydroxide and nitric acid, the electromotive force makes its appearance in the same way as without this interposition." [a] (I, pp. 791-[792].)

The question whether the combination of acid and alkali is the cause of current formation is a matter of very serious concern for our author. Put in this form it is very easy to answer. The combination of acid and alkali is first of all the cause of a *salt* being formed with liberation of energy. Whether this energy wholly or partly takes the form of electricity depends on the circumstances under which it is liberated. For instance, in the battery: nitric acid and potassium hydroxide between platinum electrodes, this will be at least partially the case, and it is a matter of indifference for the *formation* of the current whether a potassium nitrate solution is interposed between the acid and alkali or not, since this can at most slow down the salt formation but not prevent it. If, however, a battery is formed like one of Worm-Müller's, to which Wiedemann constantly refers, where the

---

[a] Names included in brackets are added by Engels. They were taken from corresponding passages of Wiedemann's book.— *Ed.*

acid and the alkali solutions are in the middle, but a solution of their salt at both ends, and in the same concentration as the solution that is formed in the battery, then it is obvious that no current can arise, because on account of the end members—since everywhere identical bodies are formed—*no ions can be produced.* Hence the conversion of the liberated energy into electricity has been prevented in as direct a manner as if the circuit had not been closed at all; it is therefore not to be wondered at that no current is obtained. But that acid and alkali can in general produce a current is proved by the battery: carbon, sulphuric acid (one part in ten of water), potassium hydroxide (one part in ten of water), carbon, which according to Raoult has a current strength of 73.* And that, with suitable arrangement of the battery, acid and alkali can provide a current strength corresponding to the large quantity of energy set free on their combination, is seen from the fact that the most powerful batteries known depend almost exclusively on the formation of alkali salts, e.g., that of Wheatstone: platinum, platinic chloride, potassium amalgam—current strength 230; lead peroxide, dilute sulphuric acid, potassium amalgam—326; manganese peroxide instead of lead peroxide—280; in each case, if zinc amalgam was employed instead of potassium amalgam, the current strength fell almost exactly by 100. Similarly in the battery: manganese dioxide, potassium permanganate solution, potassium hydroxide, potassium, Beetz obtained the current strength 302, and further: platinum, dilute sulphuric acid, potassium—293,8; Joule: platinum, nitric acid, potassium hydroxide, potassium amalgam—302.[a] The "cause" of these exceptionally high current strengths is certainly the combination of acid and alkali, or alkali metal, and the large quantity of energy thereby liberated.

A few pages further on it is again stated:

"It must, however, be carefully borne in mind that the equivalent in work of the whole chemical action occurring at the place of contact of the heterogeneous bodies is not to be directly regarded as the measure of the electromotive force in the closed circuit. When, for instance, in the acid-alkali battery" (*iterum Crispinus!*[b]) "of Becquerel, these two substances combine; when carbon is consumed in the battery: platinum, molten potassium nitrate, carbon; when zinc is rapidly dissolved in an

---

* In all the following data relating to current strength, the Daniell cell is put = 100.

---

[a] Engels gives all data according to G. Wiedemann, op. cit., Bd. 1. S. 375-76, 385, 390.— *Ed.*

[b] "Again Crispin!"—in a figurative sense "again the same person!" or "again the same theme!" (Juvenal, *Satirae*, I, 4).— *Ed.*

ordinary cell of copper, impure zinc, dilute sulphuric acid, with formation of local currents, then a large part of the work produced" (it should read: energy liberated) "in these chemical processes ... is converted into heat and is thus lost for the total current circuit." (I, p. 798.)

All these processes are to be referred to loss of energy in the battery; they do not affect the fact that the electric motion arises from transformed chemical energy, but only affect the quantity of energy transformed.

Electricians have devoted an endless amount of time and trouble to composing the most diverse batteries and measuring their "electromotive force". The experimental material thus accumulated contains very much of value, but certainly still more that is valueless. For instance, what is the scientific value of experiments in which "water" is employed as the electrolyte, when, as has now been proved by F. Kohlrausch, water is the worst conductor and therefore also the worst electrolyte,* and where, therefore, it is not the water but its unknown impurities that caused the process? And yet, for instance, almost half of all Fechner's experiments depend on such employment of water, even his "*experimentum crucis*",[198] by which he sought to establish the contact theory impregnably on the ruins of the chemical theory. As is already evident from this, in almost all experiments, a few only excepted, the chemical processes in the battery, which however form the source of the so-called electromotive force, remain practically disregarded. There are, however, a number of batteries whose chemical composition does not allow of any certain conclusion being drawn as to the chemical changes proceeding in them when the current circuit is closed. On the contrary, as Wiedemann (I, p. 797) says, it is

"not to be denied that we are by no means in all cases able to obtain an insight into the chemical attractions in the battery".

Hence, from the ever more important chemical aspect, all such experiments are valueless unless they are repeated with these processes under control.

In these experiments it is indeed only quite by way of exception that any account is taken of the energy transformations taking

---

* A column of the purest water prepared by Kohlrausch 1 mm. in length offered the same resistance as a copper conductor of the same diameter and a length approximately that of the moon's orbit. (Naumann, *Allgemeine Chemie*,[a] p. 729.)

---

[a] A. Naumann, *Handbuch der allgemeinen und physikalischen Chemie.—Ed.*

place in the battery. Many of them were made before the law of the equivalence of motion was recognised in natural science, but as a matter of custom they continue to be dragged from one textbook into another without having been checked or brought to a finish. It has been said that electricity has no inertia (which has about as much sense as saying velocity has no specific gravity), but this certainly cannot be said of the *theory* of electricity.

So far, we have regarded the galvanic cell as an apparatus in which, in consequence of the contact relations established, chemical energy is liberated in some way for the time being unknown, and converted into electricity. We have likewise described the electrolytic cell as an apparatus in which the reverse process is set up, electric motion being converted into chemical energy and used up as such. In so doing we had to put in the foreground the chemical aspect of the process, the aspect that has been so much neglected by electricians, because this was the only way of getting rid of the lumber of notions handed down from the old contact theory and the theory of the two electric fluids. This once accomplished, the question was whether the chemical process in the battery takes place under the same conditions as outside it, or whether special phenomena make their appearance that are dependent on the electric excitation.

In every science, incorrect notions are, in the last resort, apart from errors of observation, incorrect notions of correct facts. The latter remain even when the former are shown to be false. Although we have discarded the old contact theory, the established facts remain, of which this theory was supposed to be the explanation. Let us consider these and with them the electric aspect proper of the process in the battery.

It is not disputed that on the contact of heterogeneous bodies, with or without chemical changes, an excitation of electricity occurs which can be demonstrated by means of an electroscope or a galvanometer. As we have already seen at the outset, it is difficult to establish in a particular case the source of energy of these in themselves extremely minute phenomena of motion; it suffices that the existence of such an external source is generally conceded.

In 1850-53, Kohlrausch published a series of experiments in which he assembled the separate components of a battery in pairs and tested the static electric tensions produced in each case; the electromotive force of the cell should then be composed of the algebraic sum of these tensions. Thus, taking the tension of $Zn/Cu = 100$, he calculates the relative strengths of the Daniell and Grove cells as follows:

Daniell:

$$Zn/Cu + \text{amalg. } Zn/H_2SO_4 + Cu/SO_4Cu = 100 + 149 - 21 = 228;$$

Grove:

$$Zn/Pt + \text{amalg. } Zn/H_2SO_4 + Pt/HNO_3 = 107 + 149 + 149 = 405,$$

which closely agrees with the direct measurement of the current strengths of these cells. These results, however, are by no means certain. In the first place, Wiedemann himself calls attention to the fact that Kohlrausch only gives the final result but

"unfortunately no figures for the results of the separate experiments". [I, p. 104.]

In the second place, Wiedemann himself repeatedly recognises that all attempts to determine quantitatively the electric excitations on contact of metals, and still more on contact of metal and liquid, are at least very uncertain on account of the numerous unavoidable sources of error. If, nevertheless, he repeatedly uses Kohlrausch's figures in his calculations, we shall do better not to follow him here, the more so as another means of determination is available which is not open to these objections.

If the two exciting plates of a battery are immersed in the liquid and afterwards joined into a closed circuit by the terminals of a galvanometer, then, according to Wiedemann,

"the initial deflection of its magnetic needle, before chemical changes have altered the strength of the electric excitation, is a measure of the sum of the electromotive forces in the closed circuit". [I, p. 62.]

Batteries of various strengths, therefore, give initial deflections of various strengths, and the magnitude of these initial deflections is proportional to the current strength of the corresponding batteries.

It looks as if we had here tangibly before our eyes the "electric force of separation", the "contact force", which causes motion independently of any chemical action. And this in fact is the opinion of the whole contact theory. In reality we are confronted here by a relation between electric excitation and chemical action that we have not yet investigated. In order to pass to this subject, we shall first of all examine rather more closely the so-called electromotive law; in so doing, we shall find that here also the traditional contact notions not only provide no explanation, but once again directly bar the way to an explanation.

If in any cell consisting of two metals and a liquid, e. g., zinc, dilute hydrochloric acid, and copper, one inserts a third metal such as a platinum plate, without connecting it to the external circuit by a wire, then the initial deflection of the galvanometer will be exactly the same as *without* the platinum plate. Consequently it has no effect on the excitation of electricity. But it is not permissible to express this so simply in electromotive language. Hence one reads:

"The sum of the electromotive forces of zinc and platinum and platinum and copper now takes the place of the electromotive force of zinc and copper in the liquid. Since the path of the electricities is not perceptibly altered by the insertion of the platinum plate, we can conclude from the identity of the galvanometer readings in the two cases, that the electromotive force of zinc and copper in the liquid is equal to that of zinc and platinum plus that of platinum and copper in the same liquid. This would correspond to Volta's theory of the excitation of electricity between the metals as such. The result, which holds good for all liquids and metals, is expressed by saying:

On their electromotive excitation by liquids, metals follow the law of the voltaic series. This law is also given the name of the *electromotive law*." (Wiedemann, I, p. 62.)

In saying that in this combination the platinum does not act at all as an exciter of electricity, one expresses what is simply a fact. If one says that it does act as an exciter of electricity, but in two opposite directions with equal strength so that the effect is neutralised, the fact is converted into a hypothesis merely for the sake of doing honour to the "electromotive force". In both cases the platinum plays the role of a supernumerary.

During the first deflection there is still no closed circuit. The acid, being undecomposed, does not conduct; it can only conduct by means of the ions. If the third metal has no influence on the first deflection, this is simply because it is still *isolated.*

How does the third metal behave *after* the establishment of the continuous current and during the latter?

In the voltaic series of metals in most liquids, zinc lies after the alkali metals fairly close to the positive end and platinum at the negative end, copper being between the two. Hence, if platinum is put as above between copper and zinc it is negative to them both. If the platinum had any effect at all, the current in the liquid would have to flow to the platinum both from the zinc and from the copper, that is away from both electrodes to the unconnected platinum, which would be a *contradictio in adjecto*.[a] The basic condition for the efficacy of several different metals in the battery consists precisely in their being connected among themselves externally into a closed circuit. An unconnected, superfluous metal in the battery acts as a nonconductor; it can neither form ions nor allow them to pass through, and without ions we know of no conduction in electrolytes. Hence it is no mere supernumerary, it even stands in the way by forcing the ions to go round it.

The same thing holds good if we connect the zinc and platinum, leaving the copper unconnected in the middle; here the latter, if it had any effect at all, would produce a current from the zinc to the copper and another from the copper to the platinum; hence it would have to act as a sort of intermediary electrode and give off gaseous hydrogen on the side turned towards the zinc, which again is impossible.

If we discard the traditional electromotive mode of expression the case becomes extremely simple. As we have seen, the galvanic battery is an apparatus in which chemical energy is liberated and transformed into electricity. It consists as a rule of one or more liquids and two metals as electrodes, which must be connected together by a conductor outside the liquids. That constitutes the apparatus. Anything else that is dipped unconnected into the exciting liquid, whether metal, glass, resin, or anything else, cannot participate in the chemico-electric process taking place in the battery, in the formation of the current, so long as the liquid is not chemically altered by it; it can at most *hinder* the process. Whatever the capacity for exciting electricity of a third metal dipped into the liquid may be in relation to the liquid or to one or both electrodes of the battery, it cannot have any effect so long as this metal is not connected to the closed circuit outside the liquid.

Consequently, not only is Wiedemann's *derivation,* as given above, of the so-called electromotive law false, but the interpretation which he gives to this law is also false. One cannot speak of a compensating electromotive activity of the unconnected metal, since the sole condition for such activity is cut off from the outset; nor can the so-called electromotive law be deduced from a fact which lies outside the sphere of this law.

In 1845, old Poggendorff published a series of experiments in which he measured the electromotive force of the most various batteries, that is to say the quantity of electricity supplied by each of them in unit time. Of these experiments, the first twenty-seven

---

[a] A contradiction in definition, illogical statement, nonsense.— *Ed.*

are of special value, in each of which three given metals were one after another connected in the same exciting liquid to three different batteries, and the latter investigated and compared as regards the quantity of electricity produced. As a good adherent of the contact theory, Poggendorff also put the third metal unconnected in the battery in each experiment and so had the satisfaction of convincing himself that in all eighty-one batteries this "third in the alliance"[a] remained a pure supernumerary. But the significance of these experiments by no means consists in this fact but rather in the confirmation and establishment of the correct meaning of the so-called electromotive law.

Let us consider the above series of batteries in which zinc, copper, and platinum were connected together in pairs in dilute hydrochloric acid. Here Poggendorff found the quantities of electricity produced to be as follows, taking that of a Daniell cell as 100:

Zinc-copper	78.8
Copper-platinum	74.3
Total	153.1
Zinc-platinum	153.7

Thus, zinc in direct connection with platinum produced almost exactly the same quantity of electricity as zinc-copper + copper-platinum. The same thing occurred in all other batteries, whatever liquids and metals were employed.[b] When, from a series of metals in the same exciting liquid, batteries are formed in such a way that, according to the voltaic series valid for this liquid, the second, third, fourth, etc., one after the other are made to serve as negative electrodes for the preceding one and as positive electrodes for the one which follows, then the sum of the quantities of electricity produced by all these batteries is equal to the quantity of electricity produced by a battery formed directly between the two end members of the whole metallic series. For instance, in dilute hydrochloric acid the sum-total of the quantities of electricity produced by the batteries zinc-tin, tin-iron, iron-copper, copper-silver, and silver-platinum, would be equal to that produced by the battery: zinc-platinum. A pile formed from all the cells of the above series would, other things being equal, be

---

[a] Schiller, *Die Bürgschaft.—Ed.*
[b] See G. Wiedemann, op. cit., Bd. 1, S. 370.—*Ed.*

exactly neutralised by the introduction of a zinc-platinum cell with a current of the opposite direction.

In this form, the so-called electromotive law has a real and considerable significance. It reveals a new aspect of the interconnection between chemical and electrical action. Hitherto, on investigating mainly the *source* of energy of the galvanic current, this source, the chemical change, appeared as the active side of the process; the electricity was produced from it and therefore appeared primarily as passive. Now this is reversed. The electric excitation determined by the constitution of the heterogeneous bodies put into contact in the battery can neither add energy to nor subtract energy from the chemical action (other than by conversion of liberated energy into electricity). It can, however, according as the battery is made up, accelerate or slow down this action. If the battery, zinc—dilute hydrochloric acid—copper, produced in unit time only half as much electricity for the current as the battery, zinc—dilute hydrochloric acid—platinum, this means in chemical terms that the first battery produces in unit time only half as much zinc chloride and hydrogen as the second. *Hence the chemical action has been doubled, although the purely chemical conditions have remained the same.* The electric excitation has become the regulator of the chemical action; it appears now as the active side, and the chemical action as the passive side.

Thus, it becomes comprehensible that a number of processes previously regarded as purely chemical now appear as electrochemical. Chemically pure zinc is not attacked at all by dilute acid, or only very weakly; ordinary commercial zinc, on the other hand, is rapidly dissolved with formation of a salt and production of hydrogen; it contains an admixture of other metals and carbon, which make their appearance in unequal amounts at various places of the surface. Local currents are formed in the acid between them and the zinc itself, the zinc areas forming the positive electrodes and the other metals the negative electrodes, the hydrogen bubbles being given off on the latter. Likewise the phenomenon that when iron is dipped into a solution of copper sulphate it becomes covered with a layer of copper is now seen to be an electro-chemical phenomenon, one determined by the currents which arise between the heterogeneous areas of the surface of the iron.

In accordance with this we find also that the voltaic series of metals in liquids corresponds on the whole to the series in which metals replace one another from their compounds with halogens and acid radicals. At the extreme negative end of the voltaic series we regularly find the metals of the gold group: gold, platinum, palladium, rhodium, which oxidise with difficulty, are little or not at all attacked by acids, and which are easily precipitated from their salts by other metals. At the extreme positive end are the alkali metals, which exhibit exactly the opposite behaviour: they are scarcely to be split off from their oxides even with the greatest expenditure of energy; they occur in nature almost exclusively in the form of salts, and of all the metals they have by far the greatest affinity for halogens and acid radicals. Between these two come the other metals in somewhat varying sequence, but in such a way that on the whole electrical and chemical behaviour correspond to one another. The sequence of the separate members varies according to the liquids and has hardly been finally established for any single liquid. It is even permissible to doubt whether there exists such an *absolute* voltaic series of metals for any single liquid. Given suitable batteries and electrolytic cells, two pieces of the same metal can act as positive and negative electrodes respectively, hence the same metal can be both positive and negative towards itself. In thermo-cells which convert heat into electricity, with large temperature differences at the two junctions, the direction of the current is reversed; the previously positive metal becomes negative and vice versa. Similarly, there is no absolute series according to which the metals replace one another from their chemical compounds with a particular halogen or acid radical; in many cases by supplying energy in the form of heat we are able almost at will to alter and reverse the series valid for ordinary temperatures.

Hence we find here a peculiar interaction between chemism and electricity. The chemical action in the battery, which provides the electricity with the total energy for current formation, is in many cases first brought into operation, and in all cases quantitatively regulated, by the electric tensions developed in the battery. If previously the processes in the battery seemed to be chemico-electric in nature, we see here that they are just as much electrochemical. From the point of view of formation of the *continuous* current, chemical action appears to be primary; from the point of view of *excitation* of current it appears as secondary and accessory. The reciprocal action excludes any absolute primary or absolute secondary; but it is just as much a double-sided process which from its very nature can be regarded from two different standpoints; to be understood in its totality it must even be investigated from both standpoints one after the other, before the total result can be arrived at. If, however, we adhere one-sidedly to a single standpoint as the absolute one in contrast to the other, or if we arbitrarily jump from one to the other according to the momentary needs of our argument, we shall remain entangled in the one-sidedness of metaphysical thinking; the inter-connection escapes us and we become involved in one contradiction after another.

We saw above that, according to Wiedemann, the initial deflection of the galvanometer, immediately after dipping the exciting plates into the liquid of the battery and before chemical changes have altered the strength of the electric excitation,

"is a measure of the sum of the electromotive forces in the closed circuit".[a]

So far we have become acquainted with the so-called electromotive force as a form of energy, which in our case was produced in an equivalent amount from chemical energy, and which in the further course of the process became converted again into equivalent quantities of heat, mass motion, etc. Here all at once we learn that the "sum of the electromotive forces in the closed circuit" is already in existence *before* this energy has been liberated by chemical changes; in other words, that the electromotive force is nothing but the capacity of a particular battery to liberate a particular quantity of chemical energy in unit time and to convert it into electric motion. As previously in the case of the electric force of separation, so here also the electromotive force appears as a force which does not contain a single spark of energy. Consequently, Wiedemann understands by "electromotive force" two totally different things: on the one hand, the capacity of a battery to liberate a definite quantity of given chemical energy and to convert it into electric motion, and, on the other hand, the quantity of electric motion itself that is developed. The fact that the two are proportional, that the one is a measure for the other, does not do away with the difference between them. The chemical action in the battery, the quantity of electricity developed, and the heat in the circuit derived from it, when otherwise no work is performed, are even more than proportional, they are even equivalent; but that does not do away with the difference between them. The capacity of a steam-engine with a given cylinder bore and piston stroke to produce a given quantity of mechanical motion from the heat supplied is very different from this mechanical motion itself, however proportional to the latter it may be. And while such a mode of speech was tolerable at a time

---

[a] See this volume, p. 444.— *Ed.*

when in natural science nothing had yet been said of the conservation of energy, nevertheless it is obvious that since the recognition of this basic law it is no longer permissible to confuse real active energy in any form with the capacity of any apparatus to impart this form to energy which is being liberated. This confusion is a corollary of the confusion of force and energy in the case of the electric force of separation; these two confusions provide a harmonious background for Wiedemann's three mutually contradictory explanations of the current, and in the last resort are the basis in general for all his errors and confusions in regard to so-called "electromotive force".

Besides the above-considered peculiar interaction between chemism and electricity there is also a second point that they have in common, which likewise indicates a closer kinship between these two forms of motion. Both can exist only while they *disappear*. The chemical process takes place suddenly for each group of atoms undergoing it. It can be prolonged only by the presence of new material that continually enters into it. The same thing holds for electric motion. Hardly has it been produced from some other form of motion than it is once more converted into a third form; only the continual readiness of available energy can produce the continuous current, in which at each moment new amounts of motion [Bewegungsmengen] assume the form of electricity and lose it again.

An insight into this close connection of chemical with electric action and vice versa will lead to important results in both spheres of investigation. Such an insight is already becoming more and more widespread. Among chemists, Lothar Meyer, and after him Kekulé, have plainly stated that a revival of the electro-chemical theory in a rejuvenated form is impending. Among electricians also, as indicated especially by the latest works of F. Kohlrausch, the conviction seems finally to have taken hold that only exact attention to the chemical processes in the battery and electrolytic cell can help their science to emerge from the blind alley of old traditions.

And in fact one cannot see how else a firm foundation is to be given to the theory of galvanism and so secondarily to that of magnetism and static electricity, other than by a chemically exact general revision of all traditional, uncontrolled experiments made from an obsolete scientific standpoint, with exact attention to establishing the energy transformations and preliminary rejection of all traditional theoretical notions about electricity.

THE PART PLAYED BY LABOUR
IN THE TRANSITION
FROM APE TO MAN [199]

Labour is the source of all wealth, the political economists assert. And it really is the source—next to nature, which supplies it with the material that it converts into wealth. But it is even infinitely more than this. It is the prime basic condition for all human existence, and this to such an extent that, in a sense, we have to say that labour created man himself.

Many hundreds of thousands of years ago, during an epoch, not yet definitely determinable, of that period of the earth's history known to geologists as the Tertiary period, most likely towards the end of it, a particularly highly-developed race of anthropoid apes lived somewhere in the tropical zone—probably on a great continent that has now sunk to the bottom of the Indian Ocean.[200] Darwin has given us an approximate description of these ancestors of ours. They were completely covered with hair, they had beards and pointed ears, and they lived in bands in the trees.[a]

First, owing to their way of living which meant that the hands had different functions than the feet when climbing, these apes began to lose the habit of using their hands to walk and adopted a more and more erect posture. This was *the decisive step in the transition from ape to man.*

All extant anthropoid apes can stand erect and move about on their feet alone, but only in case of urgent need and in a very clumsy way. Their natural gait is in a half-erect posture and includes the use of the hands. The majority rest the knuckles of the fist on the ground and, with legs drawn up, swing the body

---

[a] See Ch. Darwin, *The Descent of Man, and Selection in Relation to Sex*, Vol. 1, Ch. VI.— *Ed.*

through their long arms, much as a cripple moves on crutches. In general, all the transition stages from walking on all fours to walking on two legs are still to be observed among the apes today. The latter gait, however, has never become more than a makeshift for any of them.

It stands to reason that if erect gait among our hairy ancestors became first the rule and then, in time, a necessity, other diverse functions must, in the meantime, have devolved upon the hands. Already among the apes there is some difference in the way the hands and the feet are employed. In climbing, as mentioned above, the hands and feet have different uses. The hands are used mainly for gathering and holding food in the same way as the fore paws of the lower mammals are used. Many apes use their hands to build themselves nests in the trees or even to construct roofs between the branches to protect themselves against the weather, as the chimpanzee, for example, does. With their hands they grasp sticks to defend themselves against enemies, or bombard their enemies with fruits and stones. In captivity they use their hands for a number of simple operations copied from human beings. It is in this that one sees the great gulf between the undeveloped hand of even the most man-like apes and the human hand that has been highly perfected by hundreds of thousands of years of labour. The number and general arrangement of the bones and muscles are the same in both hands, but the hand of the lowest savage can perform hundreds of operations that no simian hand can imitate—no simian hand has ever fashioned even the crudest stone knife.

The first operations for which our ancestors gradually learned to adapt their hands during the many thousands of years of transition from ape to man could have been only very simple ones. The lowest savages, even those in whom regression to a more animal-like condition with a simultaneous physical degeneration can be assumed, are nevertheless far superior to these transitional beings. Before the first flint could be fashioned into a knife by human hands, a period of time probably elapsed in comparison with which the historical period known to us appears insignificant. But the decisive step had been taken, *the hand had become free* and could henceforth attain ever greater dexterity; the greater flexibility thus acquired was inherited and increased from generation to generation.

Thus the hand is not only the organ of labour, *it is also the product of labour*. Only by labour, by adaptation to ever new operations, through the inheritance of muscles, ligaments, and, over longer periods of time, bones that had undergone special development and the ever-renewed employment of this inherited finesse in new, more and more complicated operations, have given the human hand the high degree of perfection required to conjure into being the pictures of a Raphael, the statues of a Thorwaldsen, the music of a Paganini.

But the hand did not exist alone, it was only one member of an integral, highly complex organism. And what benefited the hand, benefited also the whole body it served; and this in two ways.

In the first place, the body benefited from the law of correlation of growth, as Darwin called it. This law states that the specialised forms of separate parts of an organic being are always bound up with certain forms of other parts that apparently have no connection with them.[a] Thus all animals that have red blood cells without cell nuclei, and in which the head is attached to the first vertebra by means of a double articulation (condyles), also without exception possess lacteal glands for suckling their young. Similarly, cloven hoofs in mammals are regularly associated with the possession of a multiple stomach for rumination. Changes in certain forms involve changes in the form of other parts of the body, although we cannot explain the connection. Perfectly white cats with blue eyes are always, or almost always, deaf. The gradually increasing perfection of the human hand, and the commensurate adaptation of the feet for erect gait, have undoubtedly, by virtue of such correlation, reacted on other parts of the organism. However, this action has not as yet been sufficiently investigated for us to be able to do more here than to state the fact in general terms.

Much more important is the direct, demonstrable influence of the development of the hand on the rest of the organism. It has already been noted that our simian ancestors were gregarious; it is obviously impossible to seek the derivation of man, the most social of all animals, from non-gregarious immediate ancestors. Mastery over nature began with the development of the hand, with labour, and widened man's horizon at every new advance. He was continually discovering new, hitherto unknown properties in natural objects. On the other hand, the development of labour necessarily helped to bring the members of society closer together by increasing cases of mutual support and joint activity, and by making clear the advantage of this joint activity to each individual.

---

[a] Ch. Darwin, *On the Origin of Species...*, Ch. 1-5.— *Ed.*

In short, men in the making arrived at the point where *they had something to say* to each other. Necessity created the organ; the undeveloped larynx of the ape was slowly but surely transformed by modulation to produce constantly more developed modulation, and the organs of the mouth gradually learned to pronounce one articulate sound after another.

Comparison with animals proves that this explanation of the origin of language from and in the process of labour is the only correct one. The little that even the most highly-developed animals need to communicate to each other does not require articulate speech. In its natural state, no animal feels handicapped by its inability to speak or to understand human speech. It is quite different when it has been tamed by man. The dog and the horse, by association with man, have developed such a good ear for articulate speech that they easily learn to understand any language within their range of concept. Moreover they have acquired the capacity for feelings such as affection for man, gratitude, etc., which were previously foreign to them. Anyone who has had much to do with such animals will hardly be able to escape the conviction that in many cases they *now* feel their inability to speak as a defect, although, unfortunately, it is one that can no longer be remedied because their vocal organs are too specialised in a definite direction. However, where vocal organs exist, within certain limits even this inability disappears. The buccal organs of birds are as different from those of man as they can be, yet birds are the only animals that can learn to speak; and it is the bird with the most hideous voice, the parrot, that speaks best of all. Let no one object that the parrot does not understand what it says. It is true that for the sheer pleasure of talking and associating with human beings, the parrot will chatter for hours at a stretch, continually repeating its whole vocabulary. But within the limits of its range of concepts it can also learn to understand what it is saying. Teach a parrot swear words in such a way that it gets an idea of their meaning (one of the great amusements of sailors returning from the tropics); tease it and you will soon discover that it knows how to use its swear words just as correctly as a Berlin costermonger. The same is true of begging for titbits.

First labour, after it and then with it speech—these were the two most essential stimuli under the influence of which the brain of the ape gradually changed into that of man, which for all its similarity is far larger and more perfect. Hand in hand with the development of the brain went the development of its most immediate instruments—the senses. Just as the gradual development of speech is inevitably accompanied by a corresponding refinement of the organ of hearing, so the development of the brain as a whole is accompanied by a refinement of all the senses. The eagle sees much farther than man, but the human eye discerns considerably more in things than does the eye of the eagle. The dog has a far keener sense of smell than man, but it does not distinguish a hundredth part of the odours that for man are definite signs denoting different things. And the sense of touch, which the ape hardly possesses in its crudest initial form, has been developed only side by side with the development of the human hand itself, through the medium of labour.

The reaction on labour and speech of the development of the brain and its attendant senses, of the increasing clarity of consciousness, power of abstraction and of conclusion, gave both labour and speech an ever-renewed impulse to further development. This development did not reach its conclusion when man finally became distinct from the ape, but on the whole made further powerful progress, its degree and direction varying among different peoples and at different times, and here and there even being interrupted by local or temporary regression. This further development has been strongly urged forward, on the one hand, and guided along more definite directions, on the other, by a new element which came into play with the appearance of fully-fledged man, namely, *society.*

Hundreds of thousands of years—of no greater significance in the history of the earth than one second in the life of man*—certainly elapsed before human society arose out of a troupe of tree-climbing monkeys. Yet it did finally appear. And what do we find once more as the characteristic difference between the troupe of monkeys and human society? *Labour.* The ape herd was satisfied to browse over the feeding area determined for it by geographical conditions or the resistance of neighbouring herds; it undertook migrations and struggles to win new feeding grounds, but it was incapable of extracting from them more than they offered in their natural state, except that it unconsciously fertilised the soil with its own excrement. As soon as all possible

---

* A leading authority in this respect, Sir William Thomson, has calculated that *little more than a hundred million years* could have elapsed since the time when the earth had cooled sufficiently for plants and animals to be able to live on it.[a]

---

[a] W. Thomson, "Review of evidence regarding physical condition of the earth...". In: *Nature*, Vol. XIV, No. 359, September 14, 1876, pp. 427-31.— *Ed.*

feeding grounds were occupied, there could be no further increase in the ape population; the number of animals could at best remain stationary. But all animals waste a great deal of food, and, in addition, destroy in the germ the next generation of the food supply. Unlike the hunter, the wolf does not spare the doe which would provide it with the young the next year; the goats in Greece, that eat away the young bushes before they grow to maturity, have eaten bare all the mountains of the country. This "predatory economy" of animals plays an important part in the gradual transformation of species by forcing them to adapt themselves to other than the usual food, thanks to which their blood acquires a different chemical composition and the whole physical constitution gradually alters, while species that have remained unadapted die out. There is no doubt that this predatory economy contributed powerfully to the transition of our ancestors from ape to man. In a race of apes that far surpassed all others in intelligence and adaptability, this predatory economy must have led to a continual increase in the number of plants used for food and the consumption of more and more edible parts of food plants. In short, food became more and more varied, as did also the substances entering the body with it, substances that were the chemical premises for the transition to man. But all that was not yet labour in the proper sense of the word. Labour begins with the making of tools. And what are the most ancient tools that we find—the most ancient judging by the heirlooms of prehistoric man that have been discovered, and by the mode of life of the earliest historical peoples and of the rawest of contemporary savages? They are hunting and fishing implements, the former at the same time serving as weapons. But hunting and fishing presuppose the transition from an exclusively vegetable diet to the concomitant use of meat, and this is another important step in the process of transition from ape to man. A *meat diet* contained in an almost ready state the most essential ingredients required by the organism for its metabolism. By shortening the time required for digestion, it also shortened the other vegetative bodily processes that correspond to those of plant life, and thus gained further time, material and desire for the active manifestation of animal life proper. And the farther man in the making moved from the vegetable kingdom the higher he rose above the animal. Just as becoming accustomed to a vegetable diet side by side with meat converted wild cats and dogs into the servants of man, so also adaptation to a meat diet, side by side with a vegetable diet, greatly contributed towards giving bodily strength and independence to man in the making. The meat diet, however, had its greatest effect on the brain, which now received a far richer flow of the materials necessary for its nourishment and development, and which, therefore, could develop more rapidly and perfectly from generation to generation. With all due respect to the vegetarians man did not come into existence without a meat diet, and if the latter, among all peoples known to us, has led to cannibalism at some time or other (the forefathers of the Berliners, the Weletabians or Wilzians, used to eat their parents as late as the tenth century),[201] that is of no consequence to us today.

The meat diet led to two new advances of decisive importance— the harnessing of fire and the domestication of animals. The first still further shortened the digestive process, as it provided the mouth with food already, as it were, half-digested; the second made meat more copious by opening up a new, more regular source of supply in addition to hunting, and moreover provided, in milk and its products, a new article of food at least as valuable as meat in its composition. Thus both these advances were, in themselves, new means for the emancipation of man. It would lead us too far afield to dwell here in detail on their indirect effects notwithstanding the great importance they have had for the development of man and society.

Just as man learned to consume everything edible, he also learned to live in any climate. He spread over the whole of the habitable world, being the only animal fully able to do so of its own accord. The other animals that have become accustomed to all climates—domestic animals and vermin—did not become so independently, but only in the wake of man. And the transition from the uniformly hot climate of the original home of man to colder regions, where the year was divided into summer and winter, created new requirements—shelter and clothing as protection against cold and damp, and hence new spheres of labour, new forms of activity, which further and further separated man from the animal.

By the combined functioning of hand, speech organs and brain, not only in each individual but also in society, men became capable of executing more and more complicated operations, and were able to set themselves, and achieve, higher and higher aims. The work of each generation itself became different, more perfect and more diversified. Agriculture was added to hunting and cattle raising; then came spinning, weaving, metalworking, pottery and navigation. Along with trade and industry, art and science finally appeared. Tribes developed into nations and states. Law and politics arose, and with them that fantastic reflection of human things in the human mind—religion. In the face of all these images, which appeared in the first place to be products of the mind and seemed to dominate human societies, the more modest productions of the working hand retreated into the background, the more so since the mind that planned the labour was able, at a very early stage in the development of society (for example, already in the primitive family), to have the labour that had been planned carried out by other hands than its own. All merit for the swift advance of civilisation was ascribed to the mind, to the development and activity of the brain. Men became accustomed to explain their actions as arising out of thought instead of their needs (which in any case are reflected and perceived in the mind); and so in the course of time there emerged that idealistic world outlook which, especially since the fall of the world of antiquity, has dominated men's minds. It still rules them to such a degree that even the most materialistic natural scientists of the Darwinian school are still unable to form any clear idea of the origin of man, because under this ideological influence they do not recognise the part that has been played therein by labour.

Animals, as has already been pointed out, change the environment by their activities in the same way, even if not to the same extent, as man does, and these changes, as we have seen, in turn react upon and change those who made them. In nature nothing takes place in isolation. Everything affects and is affected by every other thing, and it is mostly because this manifold motion and interaction is forgotten that our natural scientists are prevented from gaining a clear insight into the simplest things. We have seen how goats have prevented the regeneration of forests in Greece; on the island of St. Helena, goats and pigs brought by the first arrivals have succeeded in exterminating its old vegetation almost completely, and so have prepared the ground for the spreading of plants brought by later sailors and colonists. But animals exert a lasting effect on their environment unintentionally and, as far as the animals themselves are concerned, accidentally. The further removed men are from animals, however, the more their effect on nature assumes the character of premeditated, planned action directed towards definite preconceived ends. The animal destroys the vegetation of a locality without realising what it is doing. Man destroys it in order to sow field crops on the soil thus released, or to plant trees or vines which he knows will yield many times the amount planted. He transfers useful plants and domestic animals from one country to another and thus changes the flora and fauna of whole continents. More than this. Through artificial breeding both plants and animals are so changed by the hand of man that they become unrecognisable. The wild plants from which our grain varieties originated are still being sought in vain. There is still some dispute about the wild animals from which our very different breeds of dogs or our equally numerous breeds of horses are descended.[202]

It goes without saying that it would not occur to us to dispute the ability of animals to act in a planned, premeditated fashion. On the contrary, a planned mode of action exists in embryo wherever protoplasm, living albumen, exists and reacts, that is, carries out definite, even if extremely simple, movements as a result of definite external stimuli. Such reaction takes place even where there is yet no cell at all, far less a nerve cell. There is something of the planned action in the way insect-eating plants capture their prey, although they do it quite unconsciously. In animals the capacity for conscious, planned action is proportional to the development of the nervous system, and among mammals it attains a fairly high level. While fox-hunting in England one can daily observe how unerringly the fox makes use of its excellent knowledge of the locality in order to elude its pursuers, and how well it knows and turns to account all favourable features of the ground that cause the scent to be lost. Among our domestic animals, more highly developed thanks to association with man, one can constantly observe acts of cunning on exactly the same level as those of children. For, just as the development history of the human embryo in the mother's womb is only an abbreviated repetition of the history, extending over millions of years, of the bodily development of our animal ancestors, starting from the worm, so the mental development of the human child is only a still more abbreviated repetition of the intellectual development of these same ancestors, at least of the later ones. But all the planned action of all animals has never succeeded in impressing the stamp of their will upon the earth. That was left for man.

In short, the animal merely *uses* its environment, and brings about changes in it simply by its presence; man by his changes makes it serve his ends, *masters* it. This is the final, essential distinction between man and other animals, and once again it is labour that brings about this distinction.*

Let us not, however, flatter ourselves overmuch on account of our human victories over nature. For each such victory nature

---

* Ennoblement. [Marginal note.]

takes its revenge on us. Each victory, it is true, in the first place brings about the results we expected, but in the second and third places it has quite different, unforeseen effects which only too often cancel the first. The people who, in Mesopotamia, Greece, Asia Minor and elsewhere, destroyed the forests to obtain cultivable land, never dreamed that by removing along with the forests the collecting centres and reservoirs of moisture they were laying the basis for the present forlorn state of those countries. When the Italians of the Alps used up the pine forests on the southern slopes, so carefully cherished on the northern slopes, they had no inkling that by doing so they were cutting at the roots of the dairy industry in their region; they had still less inkling that they were thereby depriving their mountain springs of water for the greater part of the year, and making it possible for them to pour still more furious torrents on the plains during the rainy seasons. Those who spread the potato in Europe were not aware that with these farinaceous tubers they were at the same time spreading scrofula. Thus at every step we are reminded that we by no means rule over nature like a conqueror over a foreign people, like someone standing outside nature—but that we, with flesh, blood and brain, belong to nature, and exist in its midst, and that all our mastery of it consists in the fact that we have the advantage over all other creatures of being able to learn its laws and apply them correctly.[a]

And, in fact, with every day that passes we are acquiring a better understanding of these laws and getting to perceive both the more immediate and the more remote consequences of our interference with the traditional course of nature. In particular, after the mighty advances made by the natural sciences in the present century, we are more than ever in a position to realise, and hence to control, also the more remote natural consequences of at least our day-to-day production activities. But the more this progresses the more will men not only feel but also know their oneness with nature, and the more impossible will become the senseless and unnatural idea of a contrast between mind and matter, man and nature, soul and body, such as arose after the decline of classical antiquity in Europe and obtained its highest elaboration in Christianity.

It required the labour of thousands of years for us to learn a little of how to calculate the more remote *natural* effects of our

---

[a] See also this volume, pp. 105-06.— *Ed.*

actions in the field of production, but it has been still more difficult in regard to the more remote *social* effects of these actions. We mentioned the potato and the resulting spread of scrofula. But what is scrofula compared to the effects which the reduction of the workers to a potato diet had on the living conditions of the popular masses in whole countries, or compared to the famine the potato blight brought to Ireland in 1847, which consigned to the grave a million Irishmen, nourished solely or almost exclusively on potatoes, and forced the emigration overseas of two million more? When the Arabs learned to distil spirits, it never entered their heads that by so doing they were creating one of the chief weapons for the annihilation of the aborigines of the then still undiscovered American continent. And when afterwards Columbus discovered this America, he did not know that by doing so he was giving a new lease of life to slavery, which in Europe had long ago been done away with, and laying the basis for the Negro slave trade. The men who in the seventeenth and eighteenth centuries laboured to create the steam-engine had no idea that they were preparing the instrument which more than any other was to revolutionise social relations throughout the world. Especially in Europe, by concentrating wealth in the hands of a minority and dispossessing the huge majority, this instrument was destined at first to give social and political domination to the bourgeoisie, but later, to give rise to a class struggle between bourgeoisie and proletariat which can end only in the overthrow of the bourgeoisie and the abolition of all class antagonisms.—But in this sphere too, by long and often cruel experience and by collecting and analysing historical material, we are gradually learning to get a clear view of the indirect, more remote social effects of our production activity, and so are afforded an opportunity to control and regulate these effects as well.

This regulation, however, requires something more than mere knowledge. It requires a complete revolution in our hitherto existing mode of production, and simultaneously a revolution in our whole contemporary social order.

All hitherto existing modes of production have aimed merely at achieving the most immediately and directly useful effect of labour. The further consequences, which appear only later and become effective through gradual repetition and accumulation, were totally neglected. The original common ownership of land corresponded, on the one hand, to a level of development of human beings in which their horizon was restricted in general to what lay immediately available, and presupposed, on the other hand, a certain superfluity of land that would allow some latitude for correcting the possible bad results of this primeval type of economy. When this surplus land was exhausted, common ownership also declined. All higher forms of production, however, led to the division of the population into different classes and thereby to the antagonism of ruling and oppressed classes. Thus the interests of the ruling class became the driving factor of production, since production was no longer restricted to providing the barest means of subsistence for the oppressed people. This has been put into effect most completely in the capitalist mode of production prevailing today in Western Europe. The individual capitalists, who dominate production and exchange, are able to concern themselves only with the most immediate useful effect of their actions. Indeed, even this useful effect—inasmuch as it is a question of the usefulness of the article that is produced or exchanged—retreats far into the background, and the sole incentive becomes the profit to be made on selling.

Classical political economy, the social science of the bourgeoisie, in the main examines only social effects of human actions in the fields of production and exchange that are actually intended. This fully corresponds to the social organisation of which it is the theoretical expression. As individual capitalists are engaged in production and exchange for the sake of the immediate profit, only the nearest, most immediate results must first be taken into account. As long as the individual manufacturer or merchant sells a manufactured or purchased commodity with the usual coveted profit, he is satisfied and does not concern himself with what afterwards becomes of the commodity and its purchasers. The same thing applies to the natural effects of the same actions. What cared the Spanish planters in Cuba, who burned down forests on the slopes of the mountains and obtained from the ashes sufficient fertiliser for *one* generation of very highly profitable coffee trees—what cared they that the heavy tropical rainfall afterwards washed away the unprotected upper stratum of the soil, leaving behind only bare rock! In relation to nature, as to society, the present mode of production is predominantly concerned only about the immediate, the most tangible result; and then surprise is expressed that the more remote effects of actions directed to this end turn out to be quite different, are mostly quite the opposite in character; that the harmony of supply and demand is transformed into the very reverse opposite, as shown by the course of each ten years' industrial cycle—even Germany has had a little preliminary experience of it in the "crash"[203]; that private ownership based on one's own labour must of necessity develop into the expropriation of the workers, while all wealth becomes more and more concentrated in the hands of non-workers; that [...][a]

_____

[a] Here the manuscript breaks off.—*Ed.*

[NOTES AND FRAGMENTS]

[FROM THE HISTORY OF SCIENCE][204]

* * *

The successive development of the separate branches of natural science should be studied.—First of all, *astronomy,* which, if only on account of the seasons, was absolutely indispensable for pastoral and agricultural peoples. Astronomy can only develop with the aid of *mathematics.* Hence this also had to be tackled.—Further, at a certain stage of agriculture and in certain regions (raising of water for irrigation in Egypt), and especially with the origin of towns, big building structures and the development of handicrafts, *mechanics* also arose. This was soon needed also for *navigation* and *war.*—Moreover, it requires the aid of mathematics and so promotes the latter's development. Thus, from the very beginning the origin and development of the sciences has been determined by production.

Throughout antiquity, scientific investigation proper remained restricted to these three branches, and indeed in the form of exact, systematic research it occurs for the first time in the post-classical period (the Alexandrines,[205] Archimedes, etc.). In physics and chemistry, which were as yet hardly separated in men's minds (theory of the elements, absence of the concept of a chemical element), in botany, zoology, human and animal anatomy, it had only been possible until then to collect facts and arrange them as systematically as possible. Physiology was sheer guess-work, as soon as one went beyond the most tangible things—e.g., digestion and excretion—and it could not be otherwise when even the circulation of the blood was not known.—At the end of the period, chemistry makes its appearance in the primitive form of alchemy.

If, after the dark night of the Middle Ages was over, the sciences suddenly arose anew with undreamt-of force, developing at a miraculous rate, once again we owe this miracle to production.* In the first place, following the crusades, industry developed enormously and brought to light a quantity of new mechanical (weaving, clockmaking, milling), chemical (dyeing, metallurgy, alcohol), and physical (spectacles) facts, and this not only gave enormous material for observation, but also itself provided quite other means for experimenting than previously existed, and allowed the construction of *new* instruments; it can be said that really systematic experimental science now became possible for the first time. Secondly, the whole of West and Middle Europe, including Poland, now developed in a connected fashion, even though Italy was still at the head owing to its old-inherited civilisation. Thirdly, geographical discoveries—made purely for the sake of gain and, therefore, in the last resort, of production—opened up an infinite and hitherto inaccessible amount of material of a meteorological, zoological, botanical, and physiological (human) bearing. Fourthly, there was the *printing press.*

Now—apart from mathematics, astronomy, and mechanics, which were already in existence—physics becomes definitely separate from chemistry (Torricelli, Galileo—the former in connection with industrial waterworks studied first of all the movement of liquids, see Clerk Maxwell[a]). Boyle put chemistry on a stable basis as a science. Harvey did the same for physiology (human and animal) by the discovery of the blood circulation. Zoology and botany remain at first collecting sciences, until paleontology appeared on the scene—Cuvier—and shortly afterwards came the discovery of the cell and the development of organic chemistry. Therewith comparative morphology and physiology became possible and from then on both are true sciences. Geology was founded at the end of the last century, and recently anthropology, badly so-called, enabling the transition from the morphology and physiology of man and human races to history. This to be studied further in detail and to be developed.

---

* Hitherto, what has been boasted of is what production owes to science, but science owes infinitely more to production. [Marginal note.]

---

[a] J. C. Maxwell, *Theory of Heat.*—*Ed.*

* * *

THE ANCIENTS' OUTLOOK ON NATURE[206]

(Hegel, *Geschichte der Philosophie,*
Bd. I.— *Griechische Philosophie*)

Of the first philosophers, Aristotle says (*Metaphysica,* I, 3), that they assert:

"That of which all things consist, from which they first come and into which they are ultimately resolved... of which the essence (ουτία) persists although modified by its affections (πάθεσι)—this is the element (στοιχεῖον) and principle (αρχή) of all being... Hence they believe that nothing is either generated (ουτε γίγνεσθαι ουδέν) or destroyed, since this kind of primary entity always persists." (P. 198.)

Here, therefore, is already the whole original spontaneous materialism which at its beginning quite naturally regards the unity of the infinite diversity of natural phenomena as a matter of course, and seeks it in something definitely corporeal, a particular thing, as Thales does in water.

Cicero says:

"*Thales*[a] Milesius ... aquam dixit esse initium rerum, Deum autem eam mentem, quae ex aqua cuncta fingeret."[b] (*De Natura Deorum,* I, p. 10.)

Hegel quite rightly declares that this is an addition of Cicero's and says:

"However, we are not concerned here with this question whether, in addition, Thales believed in God; it is not a matter here of supposition, belief, popular religion ... and even if he spoke of God as having created all things from that water, we would not thereby know anything more of this being ... it is an empty word without its idea." P[p]. 209[−10] (ca. 600 [B. C.]).

---

[a] Italics by Engels.— *Ed.*
[b] "*Thales* of Miletos ... declared that water is the basis of things, and God that mind that forms everything out of water."

The oldest Greek philosophers were at the same time investigators of nature: *Thales,* a geometrician, fixed the year at 365 days, and is said to have predicted a solar eclipse.—*Anaximander* constructed a sun clock, a kind of map (περίμετρον) of land and sea, and various astronomical instruments.—Pythagoras was a mathematician.

Anaximander of Miletus, according to Plutarch (*Quaestiones convivales,* VIII, p. 8), makes "*man come from a fish, emerging from the water on to the land,*" [a] ([p.] 213). For him the αρχὴ καὶ στοιχεῖον τὸ απειρον,[b] without determining (διορίζων) it as air or water or anything else (Diogenes Laertius II, 1). This infinite correctly reproduced by Hegel (p. 215) as "undetermined matter" (ca. 580).

Anaximenes of Miletos takes *air* as principle and basic element, declaring it to be infinite (Cicero, *De Natura Deorum,* I, p. 10) and that

"everything arises from it, in it everything is again dissolved" (Plutarch, *De placitis philosophorum,* I, p. 3).

Here air αήρ=πνεῦμα.[c]

"Just as our soul, which is air, holds us together, so also a spirit (πνεῦμα) and air hold the whole world together. Spirit and air have the same meaning" (Plutarch).[207] [Pp. 215-16.]

Soul and air conceived as a general medium (ca. 555).

Aristotle already says that these ancient philosophers put the primordial essence in a form of matter: air and water (and perhaps Anaximander in something midway between both), later Heraclitus in fire, but none in earth on account of its multiple composition (διὰ τὴν μεγαλομέρειαν), *Metaphysica,* I, 8. (P. 217.)

Aristotle correctly remarks of all of them that they leave the origin of motion unexplained (p. 218 et seq.).

Pythagoras of Samos (ca. 540): *number* is the basic principle:

"That *number* is the essence of all things, and the organisation of the universe as a whole in its determinations is a *harmonious system of numbers and their relations.*" [d] (Aristotle, *Metaphysica,* I. [Ch.] 5 passim).

Hegel justly points out

---

[a] Italics by Engels.—*Ed.*
[b] Beginning and element is *the infinite.*—*Ed.*
[c] Breath, spirit.—*Ed.*
[d] Italics by Engels.—*Ed.*

"the audacity of such language, which at one blow strikes down all that is regarded by the imagination as being or as essential (true), and annihilates the sensuous essence", and puts the essence in a thought determination, even if it is a very restricted and one-sided one. [Pp. 237-38.]

Just as number is subject to definite laws, so also the universe; hereby its obedience to law was expressed for the first time. To Pythagoras is ascribed the reduction of musical harmonies to mathematical relations [pp. 261-64].
Likewise:

"The Pythagoreans put fire in the centre, but the earth as a star which revolves in a circle around this central body." (Aristotle, De coelo, II, 13). [P. 265.]

This fire, however, is not the sun; nevertheless this is the first inkling that *the earth moves* [p. 265].
Hegel on the planetary system:

"...the harmonious element, which determines the distances [between the planets]—all mathematics has still not been able to give any basis for it. The empirical numbers are accurately known; but it has all the appearance of chance, not of necessity. An approximate regularity in the distances is known, and thus with luck planets between Mars and Jupiter have been guessed at, where later Ceres, Vesta, Pallas, etc., were discovered; but astronomy still did not find a consistent series in which there was any sense, any reason. Rather it looks with contempt on the regular presentation of this series; for itself, however, it is an extremely important point which must not be surrendered." (Pp. 267-[68].)

For all the naive materialism of the total outlook, the kernel of the later split is already to be found among the ancient Greeks. For Thales, the soul is already something special, something different from the body (just as he ascribes a soul also to the magnet), for Anaximenes it is air (as in *Genesis*),[a] for the Pythagoreans it is already immortal and migratory, the body being purely accidental to it. For the Pythagoreans, also, the soul is "a chip of the ether (ἀπόσπασμα αἰθέρος)" (Diogenes Laertius, VIII, 26-28), where the cold ether is the air, the dense ether the sea and moisture. [Pp. 279-80.]
Aristotle correctly reproaches the Pythagoreans also:

With their numbers "they do not say how motion comes into being, and how, without motion and change, there is coming into being and passing away, or states and activities of heavenly things". (*Metaphysica*, I, 8). [P. 277.]

Pythagoras is supposed to have discovered the identity of the morning and evening star, that the moon gets its light from the sun, and finally the Pythagorean theorem.

---

[a] Genesis 2:7.—*Ed.*

"Pythagoras is said to have slaughtered a hecatomb on discovering this theorem ... and however remarkable it may be that his joy went so far on that account as to order a great feast, to which the rich and the whole people were invited, it was worth the trouble. It is joyousness, joy of the spirit (knowledge)—at the expense of the oxen." [P. 279.]

The Eleatics.

* * *

Leucippus and Democritus.[208]

"Leucippus, however, and his disciple Democritus hold that the elements are the *Full* and the Void—calling the one 'what is' and the other 'what is not'. Of these they identify the *full* or *solid* with 'what is' (i.e., τὰ ατομα [a]) and the void or *rare* with 'what is not'. Hence they hold that what is not is no less real than what is ... and they say that these are the material causes of things. And just as those who make the underlying substance of unity generate all other things by means of its modification ... so these thinkers hold that the '*differences*'" (namely, of the atoms) "are the causes of everything else. These differences, *they say, are three: shape, arrangement,* and position... Thus, e.g., *A* differs from *N* in·*shape, AN* from *NA* in *arrangement,* and *Z* from *N* in position." (Aristotle, *Metaphysica,* Book I, Chapter IV.)

Leucippus

"was the first to set up atoms as general principles ... and these he calls elements. Out of them arise the worlds unlimited in number and into them they are dissolved. This is how the worlds are formed: *In a given section* many atoms of all manner of shapes are carried *from the unlimited* into the vast empty space. These collect together and *form a single vortex,* in which they jostle against each other and, circling round in every possible way, separate off, by like atoms joining like. And, the atoms being so numerous that they can no longer revolve *in equilibrium, the light ones pass into the empty space outside,* as if they were being winnowed; the remainder keep together and, becoming entangled, go on their circuit together, and form a primary spherical system." (Diogenes Laertius, Book IX, Chap. 6.)[b]

The following about Epicurus.

"The atoms are in continual *motion* through all eternity. Further, he says below that the atoms move *with equal speed,* since the *void* makès way *for the lightest and heaviest alike...* Atoms have no quality at all except *shape, size,* and *weight... They are not of any and*

---

[a] The atoms.— *Ed.*

[b] Diogenes Laertius, *De vitis philosophorum libri X.* Cum indice rerum IX, 6, §§ 30-31.— *Ed.*

every size; at any rate no atom has ever been seen by our sense." (Diogenes Laertius, Book X, Ch. 1, §§ 43-44.) "When they are travelling through the void and meet with no resistance, the atoms must move with equal speed. Neither will heavy atoms travel more quickly than small and light ones, so long as nothing meets them, nor will small atoms travel more quickly than large ones, *provided they always find a suitable passage,* and provided also that they meet with no obstruction." (Ibid., § 61.)

"Thus it is clear that in every kind [of things] the *one* is of a definite nature and that in none of them does this, the one, have its nature." (Aristotle, *Metaphysica*, Book IX, Chap. 2.)

* * *

Aristarchus of Samos, 270 B.C., already held the *Copernican theory of the Earth and Sun.* (Mädler, p. 44,[a] Wolf, pp. 35-37.[b])

Democritus had already surmised that the *Milky Way* sheds on us the combined light of innumerable small stars. (Wolf, p[p]. 313 [-14].)

* * *

DIFFERENCE BETWEEN THE SITUATION AT THE END
OF THE ANCIENT WORLD, CA. 300—AND THE END
OF THE MIDDLE AGES—1453 [209]

1. Instead of a thin strip of civilisation along the coast of the Mediterranean, stretching its arms sporadically into the interior and as far as the Atlantic coast of Spain, France, and England, which could thus easily be broken through and rolled back by the Germans and Slavs from the North, and by the Arabs from the South-East, there was now a closed area of civilisation—the whole of West Europe with Scandinavia, Poland, and Hungary as outposts.

2. Instead of the contrast between the Greeks, or Romans, and the barbarians, there were now six civilised peoples with civilised languages, not counting the Scandinavian etc., all of whom had developed to such an extent that they could participate in the mighty rise of literature in the fourteenth century, and guaranteed a far more diversified culture than that of the Greek and Latin languages, which were already in decay and dying out at the end of ancient times.

---

[a] J. H. Mädler, *Der Wunderbau des Weltalls...,* § 31, S. 43-44.— *Ed.*
[b] R. Wolf, *Geschichte der Astronomie.— Ed.*

3. An infinitely higher development of industrial production and trade, created by the burghers of the Middle Ages; on the one hand, production more perfected, more varied and on a larger scale, and, on the other hand, commerce much stronger, navigation being infinitely more enterprising since the time of the Saxons, Frisians, and Normans, and on the other hand also an amount of inventions and importation of oriental inventions, which not only for the first time made possible the importation and diffusion of Greek literature, the maritime discoveries, and the bourgeois religious revolution, but also gave them a quite different and quicker range of action. In addition they produced a mass of scientific facts, although as yet unsystematised, such as antiquity never had: the magnetic needle, printing, type, flax paper (used by the Arabs and Spanish Jews since the twelfth century, cotton paper gradually making its appearance since the tenth century, and already more widespread in the thirteenth and fourteenth centuries, papyrus quite obsolete in Egypt since the Arabs), gunpowder, *spectacles, m e c h a n i c a l   c l o c k s,* great progress both of *chronology* and of *mechanics.*

(See No. 11 concerning inventions.)[a]

In addition material provided by *travels* (Marco Polo, ca. 1272, etc.).

General education, even though still bad, much more widespread owing to the universities.[210]

With the rise of Constantinople and the fall of Rome, antiquity comes to an end.[211] The end of the Middle Ages is indissolubly linked with the fall of Constantinople. The new age begins with the return to the Greeks.—Negation of the negation!

* * *

HISTORICAL MATERIAL.—INVENTIONS[212]

B.C.:

Fire-hose, water-clock, ca. 200 B.C. Street paving (Rome).

Parchment, ca. 160.

A.D.:

Watermills *on the Mosel,* ca. 340, in Germany in the time of Charles the Great.

---

[a] Engels is referring to the eleventh sheet of his notes. The chronological table of inventions given in that sheet is printed below: "Historical Material.—Inventions".— *Ed.*

First signs of glass windows, street lighting in Antioch, ca. 370.
Silk-worms from China, ca. 550 in Greece.
Quill pens in the sixth century.
Cotton paper from China to the Arabs in the seventh century,
in the ninth in Italy.
Water-powered organs in France in the eighth century.
Silver mines in the Harz worked since the tenth century.
Windmills, about 1000.
Notes, Guido of Arezzo's musical scale, about 1000.
Sericulture introduced in Italy, about 1100.
Clocks with wheels—ditto.
Magnetic needle from the Arabs to the Europeans, ca. 1180.
Street paving in Paris, 1184.
Spectacles in Florence. Glass mirrors. ⎰Second half of
Herring-salting. Sluices. ⎱ thirteenth
Striking clocks. Cotton paper in France. ⎰ century.
Rag-paper—beginning of fourteenth century.
Bills of exchange—middle of ditto.
First paper mill in Germany (Nuremberg), 1390.
Street lighting in London—beginning of fifteenth century.
Post in Venice—ditto.
Wood-cuts and printing—ditto.
Copper-engraving—middle ditto.
Horse post in France, 1464.
Silver mines in the Saxon Erzgebirge, 1471.
Pedal clavichord invented, 1472.
Pocket watches. Air-guns. Flintlock—end of fifteenth century.
Spinning-wheel, 1530.
Diving bell, 1538.

* * *

HISTORICAL[213]

Modern natural science—the only one which can come into
consideration *qua* science as against the brilliant intuitions of the
Greeks and the sporadic unconnected investigations of the
Arabs—begins with that mighty epoch when feudalism was
smashed by the burghers. In the background of the struggle
between the burghers of the towns and the feudal nobility this
epoch showed the peasant in revolt; and behind the peasant the
revolutionary beginnings of the modern proletariat, already red

flag in hand and with communism on its lips. It was the epoch which brought into being the great monarchies in Europe, broke the spiritual dictatorship of the Pope, evoked the revival of Greek antiquity and with it the highest artistic development of the new age, broke through the boundaries of the old *orbis,*[a] and for the first time really discovered the world.

It was the greatest revolution that the world had so far experienced. Natural science also flourished in this revolution, was revolutionary through and through, advanced hand in hand with the awakening modern philosophy of the great Italians, and provided its martyrs for the stake and the prisons. It is characteristic that Protestants and Catholics vied with one another in persecuting them. The former burned Servetus, the latter Giordano Bruno. It was a time that called for giants and produced giants, giants in learning, intellect, and character, a time that the French correctly called the Renaissance and Protestant Europe with one-sided prejudice called that of the Reformation.

At that time natural science also had its declaration of independence,[214] though it is true it did not come right at the beginning, any more than that Luther was the first Protestant. What Luther's burning of the papal bull was in the religious field,[215] in the field of natural science was the great work of Copernicus, in which he, although timidly after thirty-six years' hesitation and so to say on his death-bed, threw down a challenge to ecclesiastical superstition.[216] From then on natural science was in essence emancipated from religion, although the complete settlement of accounts in all details has gone on to the present day and in many minds is still far from being complete. But from then on the development of science went forward with giant strides, increasing, so to speak, proportionately to the square of the distance in time from its point of departure, as if it wanted to show the world that for the motion of the highest product of organic matter, the human mind, the law that holds good is the reverse of that for the motion of inorganic matter.

The first period of modern natural science ends—in the inorganic sphere—with Newton. It is the period in which the available subject-matter was mastered; it performed a great work in the fields of mathematics, mechanics and astronomy, statics and dynamics, especially owing to Kepler and Galileo, from whose work Newton drew the conclusions. In the organic sphere, however, there was no progress beyond the first beginnings. The

---

[a] *Orbis terrarum*—the circle of lands, the whole world.— *Ed.*

investigation of the forms of life historically succeeding one another and replacing one another, as well as the changing conditions of life corresponding to them—palaeontology and geology—did not yet exist. Nature was not at all regarded as something that developed historically, that had a history in time; only extension in space was taken into account; the various forms were grouped not one after the other, but only one beside the other; natural history was valid for all periods, like the elliptical orbits of the planets. For any closer analysis of organic structure both the immediate bases were lacking, viz., chemistry and knowledge of the essential organic structure, the cell. Natural science, at the outset revolutionary, was confronted by an out-and-out conservative nature, in which everything remained today as it was at the beginning of the world, and in which right to the end of the world everything would remain as it had been in the beginning.

It is characteristic that this conservative outlook on nature both in the inorganic and in the organic sphere [...] [a]

Astronomy	Physics	Geology	Plant physiology	Therapeutics
Mechanics	Chemistry	Palaeontology	Animal physiology	Diagnostics
Mathematics		Mineralogy	Anatomy	

The first breach: Kant and Laplace. The second: geology and palaeontology (Lyell, slow development). The third: organic chemistry, which prepares organic bodies and shows the validity of chemical laws for living bodies. The fourth: 1842, mechanical [theory of] heat, Grove. The fifth: Lamarck, the cell, etc. Darwin (struggle, Cuvier and Agassiz). The sixth: the *comparative element* in anatomy, climatology (isotherms), animal and plant geography (scientific travel expeditions since the middle of the eighteenth century), physical geography in general (Humboldt), the assembling of the material in its inter-connection. Morphology (embryology, Baer).[b]

The old teleology has gone to the devil, but it is now firmly established that matter in its eternal cycle moves according to laws

---

[a] The sentence was not finished.— *Ed.*

[b] Up to this point the text of the note has been crossed out in the manuscript by a vertical stroke as having been used by Engels in the first part of the "Introduction" (see this volume, pp. 318-28). The two further paragraphs, partially used in the second part of the "Introduction" (pp. 328-35), were not crossed out.— *Ed.*

which at a definite stage—now here, now there—necessarily give
rise to the thinking mind in organic beings.

The normal existence of animals is given by the contemporary
conditions in which they live and to which they adapt themselves—those of man, as soon as he differentiates himself from
the animal in the narrower sense, have as yet never been present,
and are only to be elaborated by the ensuing historical development. Man is the sole animal capable of working his way out of
the merely animal state—his normal state is one appropriate to his
consciousness, *one that has to be created by himself.*

* * *

OMITTED FROM "FEUERBACH" [217]

[The vulgarising peddlers who dealt in materialism in the
Germany of the fifties in no wise went beyond these limits of their
teachers.[a] All the advances made by natural science since then served
them merely] as fresh arguments against the belief in a creator of the
universe; and in fact the further development of theory was quite
outside their line of business. Idealism was hard hit owing to 1848
but materialism in this renovated form of it sank still lower.
Feuerbach was absolutely right in repudiating responsibility for *this*
materialism; only he had no right to confuse the doctrine of the
itinerant preachers with materialism in general.[b]

At about the same time, however, empirical natural science
made such an advance and arrived at such brilliant results that not
only did it become possible to overcome completely the mechanical
one-sidedness of the eighteenth century, but also natural science
itself, owing to the proof of the inter-connections existing in
nature itself between the various fields of investigation (mechanics,
physics, chemistry, biology, etc.), was transformed from an
empirical into a theoretical science and, by generalising the results
achieved, into a system of the materialist knowledge of nature.
The mechanics of gases; newly created organic chemistry, which
stripped the last remnants of incomprehensibility from one
so-called organic compound after another by preparing them from

---

[a] I.e., the French materialists of the eighteenth century.— *Ed.*

[b] K. Grün, *Ludwig Feuerbach in seinem Briefwechsel und Nachlass sowie in seiner Philosophischen Charakterentwicklung,* Bd. 2, S. 307-08.— *Ed.*

inorganic substances; scientific embryology dating from 1818; geology and palaeontology; comparative anatomy of plants and animals—all these furnished new material in an unprecedented measure. Three great discoveries, however, were of decisive importance.

The first was the proof of the transformation of energy arising out of the discovery of the mechanical equivalent of heat (by Robert Mayer, Joule and Colding). All the innumerable acting causes in nature, which had hitherto led a mysterious, inexplicable existence as so-called forces—mechanical force, heat, radiation (light and radiant heat), electricity, magnetism, chemical force of association and dissociation—have now been proved to be special forms, modes of existence of one and the same energy, i.e., motion. We can not only demonstrate its conversion from one form into another, which continually takes place in nature, but we can carry out this conversion in the laboratory and in industry, and indeed in such a way that a given quantity of energy in one form always corresponds to a given quantity of energy in some other form. Thus we can express the unit of heat in kilogramm-metres and the units of any quantity of electrical or chemical energy once more in heat-units and vice versa; we can likewise measure the energy consumption and energy intake of a living organism and express it in any desired unit, e.g., in heat-units. The unity of all motion in nature is no longer a philosophical assertion, but a natural-scientific fact.

The second discovery—earlier in point of time—was that of the organic cell by Schwann and Schleiden, as being the unit out of which, by its multiplication and differentiation, all organisms with the exception of the lowest are formed and develop. This discovery for the first time gave a firm basis to the investigation of the organic, living products of nature—both comparative anatomy and physiology, and embryology. The origin, growth and structure of organisms were deprived of their mysterious character; the hitherto incomprehensible miracle was merged in a process which takes place according to a law that is essentially identical for all multicellular organisms.

But an essential gap still remained. If all multicellular organisms—both plants and animals, including man—in each case grow out of a single cell according to the law of cell division, what then is the source of the infinite diversity of these organisms? This question was answered by the third great discovery, the theory of evolution, which for the first time was comprehensively worked out and substantiated by Darwin. However many transformations this theory will still undergo as regards details, in the main it has already solved the problem in a more than adequate manner. The evolutionary series of organisms from a few simple forms to increasingly multifarious and complicated ones, as it confronts us today, and extending right up to man, has been established as far as its main features are concerned. Thanks to this, not only has it become possible to explain the existing stock of organic products of nature but the basis has also been provided for the pre-history of the human mind, for tracing the various stages of its development, from the simple protoplasm—structureless but sensitive to stimuli—of the lowest organisms right up to the thinking human brain. Without this pre-history, however, the existence of the thinking human brain remains a miracle.

By means of these three great discoveries, the main processes of nature were explained and referred to natural causes. One thing still remains to be done here: to explain the origin of life from inorganic nature. At the present stage of science that implies nothing less than the preparation of protein bodies from inorganic substances. Chemistry is approaching closer and closer to the solution of this task, but it is still a long way from it. If, however, we bear in mind that it was only in 1828 that Wöhler prepared the first organic body, urea, from inorganic materials, and what an innumerable number of so-called organic compounds are now artificially prepared without any organic materials, we shall not be inclined to bid chemistry halt when confronted by protein. So far chemistry has been able to prepare every organic substance, the composition of which is accurately known. As soon as the composition of the protein bodies becomes known, chemistry will be able to set about the preparation of living protein. But to demand that it should achieve overnight what nature itself succeeds in doing only under very favourable circumstances on a few cosmic bodies after millions of years, would be to demand a miracle.

Thus the materialist outlook on nature rests today on a much firmer foundation than it did in the previous century. At that time only the motion of the heavenly bodies and that of terrestrial solid bodies under the influence of gravity was at all exhaustively understood; almost the entire field of chemistry and the whole of organic nature remained mysterious and not understood. Today the whole of nature lies spread out before us as a system of inter-connections and processes that, at least in its main features, has been explained and understood. At all events, the materialist outlook on nature means nothing more than the simple conception of nature just as it is, without alien addition, and hence among the Greek philosophers it was originally understood in this way as a matter of course. But between those ancient Greeks and us lie more than two thousand years of an essentially idealist outlook on the world, and so the return to self-evident understanding is more difficult than it appears to be at first sight. For it is by no means a matter of simply throwing overboard the entire thought content of those two thousand years, but of a criticism of it, of extracting the results—that had been won within a form that was false but which was inevitably idealistic for its time and for the course of evolution itself—from this transitory form. And how difficult that is, is proved for us by those numerous natural scientists who are inexorable materialists within their science but outside it are not merely idealists, but even pious and indeed orthodox Christians.

All these epoch-making advances of natural science passed Feuerbach by without affecting him in any essential respect. This was not so much his fault as that of the miserable German conditions, owing to which the university chairs were occupied by empty-headed, eclectic hair-splitters, while Feuerbach, who towered high above them, was compelled almost to rusticate in lonely village isolation.[218] That is why, on the subject of nature, he wastes so much labour—except for a few brilliant generalisations—on empty belletristic writing. Thus he says:

"Life is, of course, not the product of a chemical process, nor in general is it the product of an isolated natural force or phenomenon, to which the metaphysical materialist reduces it; it is a result of the whole of nature."[a]

That life is a result of the whole of nature in no way contradicts the fact that protein, which is the exclusive independent bearer of life, arises under definite conditions determined by the whole inter-connection of nature, but arises precisely as the product of a chemical process. <Had Feuerbach lived in conditions which permitted him to follow even superficially the development of natural science, it would never have happened that he would speak of a chemical process as the effect of an isolated force of nature.>[b] To the same solitariness must be ascribed the fact that Feuerbach loses himself in a circle of barren speculations on the

---

[a] C. N. Starcke, *Ludwig Feuerbach*, S. 154-55. The quotation is taken from Feuerbach's "Die Unsterblichkeitsfrage vom Standpunkt der Anthropologie", *Sämmtliche Werke*, Bd. III, S. 331.—*Ed.*

[b] This sentence was crossed out in the manuscript.—*Ed.*

relations of thought to the thinking organ, the brain[a]—a sphere in which Starcke follows him willingly.[b]

Enough, Feuerbach revolts against the name materialism.[c] And not entirely without reason; for he never completely ceases to be an idealist. In the field of nature he is a materialist; but in the human field [...][d]

* * *

God is nowhere treated worse than by the natural scientists who believe in him. Materialists simply explain the *facts,* without making use of such phrases, they do this first when importunate pious believers try to force God upon them, and then they answer curtly, either like Laplace: *Sire, je n'avais pas, etc.,*[219] or more rudely in the manner of the Dutch merchants who, when German commercial travellers press their shoddy goods on them, are accustomed to turn them away with the words: *Ik kan die zaken niet gebruiken,*[e] and that is the end of the matter. But what God has had to suffer at the hands of his defenders! In the history of modern natural science, God is treated by his defenders as Frederick William III was treated by his generals and officials in the Jena campaign.[220] One division of the army after another lays down its arms, one fortress after another capitulates before the march of science, until at last the whole infinite realm of nature is conquered by science, and there is no place left in it for the Creator. Newton still allowed Him the "first impulse" but forbade Him any further interference in his solar system. Father Secchi bows Him out of the solar system altogether, with all canonical honours it is true, but none the less categorically for all that, and he only allows Him a creative act as regards the primordial nebula. And so in all spheres. In biology, his last great Don Quixote, Agassiz, even ascribes positive nonsense to Him: He is supposed to have created not only the actual animals but also abstract animals,

---

[a] K. Grün, *Ludwig Feuerbach in seinem Briefwechsel...,* S. 307-08.—*Ed.*

[b] C. N. Starcke, op. cit., S. 165-66.—*Ed.*

[c] K. Grün, op. cit., S. 308.—*Ed.*

[d] Page 19 of the original manuscript of *Ludwig Feuerbach* ends here. The end of this sentence occurs on the following page, which has not come down to us. On the basis of the printed text of *Ludwig Feuerbach* it may be supposed that this sentence read approximately as follows: "In the human field he is an idealist."—*Ed.*

[e] I have no use for the things.—*Ed.*

the fish as such! *ᵃ And finally Tyndall totally forbids Him any entry into nature and relegates Him to the world of emotional processes, only admitting Him because, after all, there must be somebody who knows more about all these things (nature) than John Tyndall! ²²² What a distance from the old God—the Creator of heaven and earth, the maintainer of all things—without whom not a hair can fall from the head!

Tyndall's emotional need proves nothing. The Chevalier des Grieux also had an emotional need to love and possess Manon Lescaut, who sold herself and him over and over again; for her sake he became a cardsharper and pimp, and if Tyndall wants to reproach him, he would reply with his "emotional need"!

---

* God=nescio [I do not know]; but *ignorantia non est argumentum* [ignorance is no argument] (Spinoza).²²¹ [Marginal note.]

ᵃ See this volume, p. 488.—*Ed.*

[NATURAL SCIENCE AND PHILOSOPHY]

* * *

BÜCHNER[223]

Rise of the tendency. The passing of German philosophy into materialism—control over science abolished—outbreak of shallow materialist popularisation, in which the materialism had to make up for the lack of science. Its flourishing at the time of the deepest degradation of bourgeois Germany and official German science—1850-60. Vogt, Moleschott, Büchner. Mutual assurance.[224]—New impetus by the coming into fashion of Darwinism, which was immediately monopolised by these gentlemen.[225]

One could let them alone and leave them to their not unpraiseworthy if narrow occupation of teaching atheism, etc., to the German philistine but for: 1, abuse directed against philosophy (passages to be quoted),* which in spite of everything is the glory of Germany, and 2, the presumption of applying the theories about nature to society and of reforming socialism. Thus they compel us to take note of them.

---

* Büchner is acquainted with philosophers only as dogmatists, just as he himself is a dogmatist of the shallowest reflection of the German would-be Enlightenment, which missed the spirit and movement of the great French materialists (Hegel on this) [a]—just as Nicolai had that of Voltaire. Lessing's "dead dog Spinoza". ([Hegel] Encyclopädie, Preface, p. 19.[226])

---

[a] See G. W. F. Hegel, Vorlesungen über die Geschichte der Philosophie, Bd. 3, S. 506-34.—Ed.

First page of the first folder of *Dialectics of Nature*

First of all, what do they achieve in their own sphere? Quotations.

2. Turning point, pages 170-71. Whence this sudden Hegelianism?[227] Transition to dialectics.

Two philosophical tendencies, the metaphysical with fixed categories, the dialectical (Aristotle and especially Hegel) with fluid categories; the proofs that these fixed opposites of basis and consequence, cause and effect, identity and difference, appearance and essence are untenable, that analysis shows one pole already present in the other *in nuce*,[a] that at a definite point the one pole becomes transformed into the other, and that all logic develops only from these progressing contradictions.—This mystical in Hegel himself, because the categories appear as pre-existing and the dialectics of the real world as their mere reflection. In reality it is the reverse: the dialectics of the mind is only the reflection of the forms of motion of the real world, both of nature and of history. Until the end of the last century, indeed until 1830, natural scientists could manage pretty well with the old metaphysics, because real science did not go beyond mechanics—terrestrial and cosmic. Nevertheless confusion had already been introduced by higher mathematics, which regards the eternal truth of lower mathematics as a superseded point of view, often asserting the contrary, and putting forward propositions which appear sheer nonsense to the lower mathematician. The rigid categories disappeared here; mathematics arrived at a field where even such simple relations as those of mere abstract quantity, bad infinity, assumed a completely dialectical form and compelled the mathematicians to become dialectical, unconsciously and against their will. There is nothing more comical than the twistings, subterfuges, and expedients employed by the mathematicians to solve this contradiction, to reconcile higher and lower mathematics, to make clear to their understanding that what they had arrived at as an undeniable result is not sheer nonsense, and in general rationally to explain the starting-point, method, and result of the mathematics of the infinite.

Now, however, everything is quite different. Chemistry—atomistics. The abstract divisibility in physics—bad infinity. Physiology—the cell (the organic process of development, both of the individual and of species, by differentiation, the most striking test of rational dialectics), and finally the identity of the forces of nature and their mutual convertibility, which put an end to all

---

[a] In embryo.— *Ed.*

fixity of categories. Nevertheless, the bulk of natural scientists are still held fast in the old metaphysical categories and helpless when these modern facts, which so to say prove the dialectics in nature, have to be rationally explained and brought into relation with one another. And here *thinking* is necessary: atoms and molecules, etc., cannot be observed under the microscope, but only by the process of thought. Compare the chemists (except for Schorlemmer, who is acquainted with Hegel) and Virchow's *Cellularpathologie,* where in the end the helplessness has to be concealed by general phrases. Dialectics divested of mysticism becomes an absolute necessity for natural science, which has forsaken the field where rigid categories sufficed, which represent as it were the lower mathematics of logic, its everyday weapons. Philosophy takes its revenge posthumously on natural science for the latter having deserted it; and yet the scientists could have seen even from the successes in natural science achieved by philosophy that the latter possessed something that was superior to them even in their own special sphere (Leibniz—the founder of the mathematics of the infinite, in contrast to whom the inductive ass Newton [a] appears as a plagiarist and corrupter [228]; Kant—the theory of the origin of the universe *before* Laplace [b]; Oken—the first in Germany to accept the theory of evolution [229]; Hegel—whose encyclopaedic comprehensive treatment and rational grouping of the natural sciences is a greater achievement than all the materialistic nonsense put together).

———

On Büchner's claim to pronounce judgment on socialism and political economy on the basis of the struggle for existence: Hegel (*Encyclopädie,* I, p. 9), on cobbling. [230]

On politics and socialism: The understanding for which the world has waited (p. 11). [231]

Separation, coexistence, and succession. Hegel, *Encyclopädie,* p. 35! as determination of the sensuous, of the idea.

Hegel, *Encyclopädie,* p. 40. Natural phenomena—but in Büchner not *thought about,* merely copied out, hence it is superfluous.

Page 42. Solon's laws were "produced out of his head"— Büchner is able to do the same for modern society.

Page 45. Metaphysics—the science of *things*—not of movements.

Page 53. "In experience [everything depends upon the mind we

———

bring to bear upon actuality. A great mind is great in its experience; and in the motley play of phenomena at once perceives the point of real significance]."

Page 56. The parallelism between the human individual and history [232] = the parallelism between embryology and palaeontology.

* * *

Just as Fourier is A MATHEMATICAL POEM and yet still used,[233] so Hegel A DIALECTICAL POEM.

* * *

The incorrect *theory of porosity* (according to which the various false matters, caloric, etc., are situated in the pores of one another and yet do not penetrate one another) is presented by Hegel as a pure *figment of the mind* (*Encyclopädie*, I, p. 259. See also his *Logik*[a]).

* * *

Hegel, *Encyclopädie*, I, pp. 205-206, a prophetic passage on atomic weights in contrast to the physical views of the time, and on atoms and molecules as *thought* determinations, on which *thinking* has to decide.

* * *

If Hegel regards nature as a manifestation of the eternal "idea" in its alienation,[b] and if this is such a serious crime, what are we to say of the morphologist Richard Owen:

"The archetypal idea was manifested in the flesh under diverse modifications upon this planet, long prior to the existence of those animal species that actually exemplify it." (*Nature of Limbs*, 1849.)[c]

---

[a] G. W. F. Hegel, *Wissenschaft der Logik*, Th. 1, Die objective Logik, Abth. 2. Die Lehre vom Wesen, S. 135-39.— *Ed.*

[b] G. W. F. Hegel, *Encyclopädie der philosophischen Wissenschaften...*, § 18, S. 26-27, and *Vorlesungen über die Naturphilosophie...*, § 247, S. 23-28.— *Ed.*

[c] Richard Owen, *On the Nature of Limbs*, p. 86. Engels quotes in English.— *Ed.*

If that is said by a mystical natural scientist, who means nothing by it, it is calmly allowed to pass, but if a philosopher says the same thing, and one who means something by it, and indeed *au fond*[a] something correct, although in inverted form, then it is mysticism and a terrible crime.

* * *

Natural-scientific thought. Agassiz's plan of creation, according to which God proceeded in creation from the general to the particular and individual, first creating the vertebrate as such, then the mammal as such, the animal of prey as such, the cat as such, and only finally the lion, etc.! That is to say, first of all abstract ideas in the shape of concrete things and then concrete things! (See Haeckel, p. 59).[234]

* * *

In *Oken* (Haeckel, p. 85 et seq.) the nonsense that has arisen from the dualism between natural science and philosophy is evident. By the path of thought, Oken discovers protoplasm and the cell, but it does not occur to anyone to follow up the matter along the lines of natural-scientific investigation—it is to be accomplished by *thinking*! And when protoplasm and the cell were discovered, Oken was in general disrepute!

* * *

Hofmann (*Ein Jahrhundert Chemie unter den Hohenzollern*) cites the philosophy of nature. A quotation from Rosenkranz, the belletrist, whom no real Hegelian recognises. To make the philosophy of nature responsible for Rosenkranz is as foolish as Hofmann making the Hohenzollerns responsible for Marggraf's discovery of beet sugar.[235]

* * *

Theory and empiricism. The oblateness of the earth was theoretically established by Newton. The Cassinis[236] and other Frenchmen

---

[a] Basically.— *Ed.*

maintained a long time afterwards, on the basis of their empirical measurements, that the earth is ellipsoidal and the polar axis the longest one.

* * *

The contempt of the empiricists for the Greeks receives a peculiar illustration if one reads, for instance, Th. Thomson (*On Electricity*[a]), where people like Davy and even Faraday grope in the dark (the electric spark, etc.), and make experiments that quite remind one of the stories of Aristotle and Pliny about physico-chemical phenomena. It is precisely in this new science that the empiricists entirely reproduce the blind groping of the ancients. And when Faraday with his genius gets on the right track, the philistine Thomson has to protest against it. (P. 397.)

* * *

Haeckel, *Anthropogenie*, p[p]. 707-[08].

"According to the materialist outlook on the world, *matter or substance* was present *earlier than motion*[b] or *vis viva*, matter created force." This is just as false as that force created matter, since force and matter are inseparable.

Where does he get his materialism from?

* * *

Causae finales and efficientes transformed by Haeckel (pp. 89, 90) into *purposively* acting and *mechanically* acting causes, because for him *causa finalis* = God! Likewise for him "mechanical", adopted out of hand from Kant, = monistic, not = mechanical in the sense of mechanics. With such confusion of language, nonsense is inevitable. What Haeckel says here of Kant's *Kritik der Urteilskraft* does not agree with Hegel. (*Geschichte der Philosophie*, p. 603.[237])

* * *

Another example of polarity[238] in Haeckel: mechanism = monism, and vitalism or teleology = dualism.[c] Already in Kant and Hegel

---

[a] Th. Thomson, *An Outline of the Sciences of Heat and Electricity.—Ed.*

[b] Italics by Engels.— *Ed.*

[c] E. Haeckel, *Natürliche Schöpfungsgeschichte*, S. 1, 19.— *Ed.*

inner purpose is a protest against dualism. Mechanism applied to life is a helpless category, at the most we could speak of chemism, if we do not want to renounce all understanding of names. Purpose: Hegel, V, p. 205:

"Thus mechanism manifests itself as a tendency of totality in that it seeks to seize nature for itself as a whole which requires no other for its notion—a totality which is *not found in end and the extra-mundane understanding which is associated therewith*." [a]

The point is, however, that mechanism (and also the materialism of the eighteenth century) does not get away from abstract necessity, and hence not from chance either. That matter evolves out of itself the thinking human brain is for mechanism a pure accident, although necessarily determined, step by step, where it happens. But the truth is that it is the nature of matter to advance to the evolution of thinking beings, hence this always necessarily occurs wherever the conditions for it (not necessarily identical at all places and times) are present.

Further, Hegel, V. p. 206:

"Consequently, in its connection of external necessity, this principle" (of mechanism) "affords the consciousness of infinite freedom as against teleology, which sets up as something absolute whatever it contains that is trivial or even contemptible; and here a more universal thought can only feel infinitely cramped or even nauseated."

Here, again, the colossal waste of matter and motion in nature. In the solar system there are perhaps three planets at most on which life and thinking beings could exist—under present conditions. And the whole enormous apparatus for their sake!

The *inner purpose* in the organism, according to Hegel (V, p. 244), operates through *impulse*. *Pas trop fort.*[b] Impulse is supposed to bring the single living being more or less into harmony with the idea of it. From this it is seen how much the whole *inner purpose* is itself an ideological determination. And yet Lamarck is contained in this.

* * *

Natural scientists believe that they free themselves from philosophy by ignoring it or abusing it. They cannot, however,

---

[a] G. W. F. Hegel, *Wissenschaft der Logik*, Th. 2. Die subjective Logik, oder: Die Lehre vom Begriff. Italics by Engels.— *Ed.*

[b] Not too convincing.— *Ed.*

make any headway without thought, and for thought they need thought determinations. But they take these categories unreflectingly from the common consciousness of so-called educated persons, which is dominated by the relics of long obsolete philosophies, or from the little bit of philosophy compulsorily listened to at the University (which is not only fragmentary, but also a medley of views of people belonging to the most varied and usually the worst schools), or from uncritical and unsystematic reading of philosophical writings of all kinds. Hence they are no less in bondage to philosophy, but unfortunately in most cases to the worst philosophy, and those who abuse philosophy most are slaves to precisely the worst vulgarised relics of the worst philosophies.

* * *

Natural scientists may adopt whatever attitude they please, they are still under the domination of philosophy. It is only a question whether they want to be dominated by a bad, fashionable philosophy or by a form of theoretical thought which rests on acquaintance with the history of thought and its achievements.

"Physics, beware of metaphysics!"[239] is quite right, but in a different sense.

Natural scientists allow philosophy to prolong an illusory existence by making shift with the dregs of the old metaphysics. Only when natural and historical science has become imbued with dialectics will all the philosophical rubbish—other than the pure theory of thought—be superfluous, disappearing in positive science.[a]

---

[a] See this volume, p. 24.— Ed.

[DIALECTICS]

[a) GENERAL QUESTIONS OF DIALECTICS.
THE FUNDAMENTAL LAWS OF DIALECTICS]

* * *

Dialectics, so-called *objective* dialectics, prevails throughout nature, and so-called subjective dialectics, dialectical thought, is only the reflection of the motion through opposites which asserts itself everywhere in nature, and which by the continual conflict of the opposites and their final passage into one another, or into higher forms, determines the life of nature. Attraction and repulsion. Polarity begins with magnetism,[a] it is exhibited in one and the same body; in the case of electricity it distributes itself over two or more bodies which become oppositely charged. All chemical processes reduce themselves to processes of chemical attraction and repulsion. Finally, in organic life the formation of the cell nucleus is likewise to be regarded as a polarisation of the living protein material, and from the simple cell onwards the theory of evolution demonstrates how each advance up to the most complicated plant on the one side, and up to man on the other, is effected by the continual conflict between heredity and adaptation.[b] In this connection it becomes evident how little applicable to such forms of development are categories like "positive" and "negative". One can conceive of heredity as the positive, conservative side, adaptation as the negative side that continually destroys what has been inherited, but one can just as well take adaptation as the creative, active, positive activity, and heredity as the resisting, passive, negative activity. But just as in history progress makes its appearance as the negation of the existing state of things, so here also—on purely *practical* grounds—adaptation

---

[a] See this volume, pp. 489-90, 494, 497.— *Ed.*
[b] See also ibid., p. 66.— *Ed.*

is better conceived as negative activity. In history, motion through opposites is most markedly exhibited in all critical epochs of the foremost peoples. At such moments a people has only the choice between the two horns of a dilemma: "either—or!" and indeed the question is always put in a way quite different from that in which the philistines, who dabble in politics in every age, would have liked it put. Even the liberal German philistine of 1848 found himself in 1849 suddenly, unexpectedly, and against his will confronted by the question: a return to the old reaction in an intensified form, or continuance of the revolution up to the republic, perhaps even the one and indivisible republic with a socialist background. He did not spend long in reflection and helped to create the Manteuffel reaction as the flower of German liberalism.[240] Similarly, in 1851, the French bourgeois when faced with the dilemma which he certainly did not expect: a caricature of the empire, pretorian rule, and the exploitation of France by a gang of scoundrels, or a social-democratic republic—and he bowed down before the gang of scoundrels so as to be able, under their protection, to go on exploiting the workers.[241]

* * *

HARD AND FAST LINES are incompatible with the theory of evolution. Even the border-line between vertebrates and invertebrates is now no longer rigid, just as little is that between fishes and amphibians, while that between birds and reptiles dwindles more and more every day. Between *Compsognathus* and *Archaeopteryx*[242] only a few intermediate links are wanting, and birds' beaks with teeth crop up in both hemispheres. "Either—or" becomes more and more inadequate. Among lower animals the concept of the individual cannot be established at all sharply. Not only as to whether a particular animal is an individual or a colony, but also where in development *one* individual ceases and the other begins (nurses).[243]—For a stage in the outlook on nature where all differences become merged in intermediate steps, and all opposites pass into one another through intermediate links, the old metaphysical method of thought no longer suffices. Dialectics, which likewise knows no HARD AND FAST LINES, no unconditional, universally valid "either—or" and which bridges the fixed metaphysical differences, and besides "either—or" recognises also in the right place "both this—and that" and reconciles the opposites, is the sole method of thought appropriate in the highest degree to this stage. Of course, for everyday use, for the small change of science, the metaphysical categories retain their validity.

* * *

The transformation of quantity into quality = "mechanical" world outlook, quantitative change alters quality. The gentlemen never suspected that!

* * *

The character of mutual opposites belonging to the thought determinations of reason: *polarisation.* Just as electricity, magnetism, etc., become polarised and move in opposites, so do thoughts. Just as in the former it is not possible to maintain any one-sidedness, and no natural scientist would think of doing so, so also in the latter.[a]

* * *

The true nature of the determinations of "essence" is expressed by Hegel himself (*Encyclopädie,* I, § 111, addendum): "In essence everything is *relative*"[b] (e.g., positive and negative, which have meaning only in their relation, not each for itself).

* * *

Part and whole, for instance, are already categories which become inadequate in organic nature. The ejection of seeds—the embryo—and the new-born animal are not to be conceived as a "part" that is separated from the "whole"; that would give a distorted treatment. It becomes a part only in a *dead body.* (*Encyclopädie,* I, p. 268.[244])

* * *

Simple and compound. Categories which even in organic nature likewise lose their meaning and become inapplicable. An animal is

---

[a] See this volume, pp. 489-90, 497-98.— *Ed.*
[b] Italics by Engels.— *Ed.*

expressed neither by its mechanical composition from bones, blood, gristle, muscles, tissues, etc., nor by its chemical composition from the elements. Hegel, *Encyclopädie*, I, [p.] 256. The organism is *neither* simple *nor* compound, however complex it may be.

* * *

Abstract identity (*a* = *a*; and negatively, *a* cannot be simultaneously equal and unequal to *a*) is likewise inapplicable in organic nature. The plant, the animal, every cell is at every moment of its life identical with itself and yet becoming distinct from itself, by absorption and excretion of substances, by respiration, by cell formation and death of cells, by the process of circulation taking place, in short, by a sum of incessant molecular changes which make up life and the sum-total of whose results is evident to our eyes in the phases of life—embryonic life, youth, sexual maturity, process of reproduction, old age, death. The further physiology develops, the more important for it become these incessant, infinitely small changes, and hence the more important for it also the consideration of difference *within* identity, and the old abstract formal identity standpoint, that an organic being is to be treated as something simply identical with itself, as something constant, becomes out of date.* Nevertheless, the mode of thought based thereon, together with its categories, persists. But even in inorganic nature identity as such is in reality non-existent. Every body is continually exposed to mechanical, physical, and chemical influences, which are always changing it and modifying its identity. Abstract identity, with its opposition to difference, is in place only in mathematics—an abstract science which is concerned with creations of thought, even though they are reflections of reality—and even there it is continually being sublated. Hegel, *Encyclopädie*, I, p. 235. The fact that identity contains difference within itself is expressed in *every s e n t e n c e,* where the predicate is necessarily different from the subject; the *lily* is a *plant,* the *rose* is *red,* where, either in the subject or in the predicate, there is something that is not covered by the predicate or the subject. Hegel, Vol. VI, p. 231.[245] That from the outset *identity with itself* requires *difference from everything else* as its complement, is self-evident.

---

* *Apart, moreover, from the evolution of species.* [Marginal note.]

Identity. Addition. Continual change, i. e., sublation of abstract identity with itself, is also found in so-called inorganic nature. Geology is its history. On the surface, mechanical changes (denudation, frost), chemical changes (weathering); internally, mechanical changes (pressure), heat (volcanic), chemical (water, acids, binding substances); on a large scale—upheavals, earthquakes, etc. The slate of today is fundamentally different from the ooze from which it is formed, the chalk from the loose microscopic shells that compose it, even more so limestone, which indeed according to some is of purely organic origin, and sandstone from the loose sea sand, which again is derived from disintegrated granite, etc., not to speak of coal.

* * *

The law of identity in the old metaphysical sense is the fundamental law of the old outlook: $a = a$. Each thing is equal to itself. Everything was permanent, the solar system, stars, organisms. This law has been refuted by natural science bit by bit in each separate case, but theoretically it still prevails and is still put forward by the supporters of the old in opposition to the new: a thing cannot simultaneously be itself and something else. And yet the fact that true, concrete identity includes difference, change, has recently been shown in detail by natural science (see above).—Abstract identity, like all metaphysical categories, suffices for *everyday* use, where small dimensions or brief periods of time are in question; the limits within which it is usable differ in almost every case and are determined by the nature of the object; for a planetary system, where in ordinary astronomical calculation the ellipse can be taken as the basic form for practical purposes without error, they are much wider than for an insect that completes its metamorphosis in a few weeks. (Give other examples, e.g., alteration of species, which is reckoned in periods of thousands of years.) For natural science in its comprehensive role, however, even in each single branch, abstract identity is totally inadequate, and although on the whole it has now been abolished in practice, theoretically it still dominates people's minds, and most natural scientists imagine that identity and difference are irreconcilable opposites, instead of one-sided poles which represent the truth only in their reciprocal action, in the inclusion of difference *within* identity.

* * *

Identity and difference—necessity and chance—cause and effect—the two main opposites which, treated separately, become transformed into one another. And then "first principles" must help.

* * *

Positive and negative. Can also be given the reverse names: in electricity, etc.; North and South ditto. If one reverses this and alters the rest of the terminology accordingly, everything remains correct. We can call West East and East West. The sun rises in the West, and planets revolve from East to West, etc., the names alone are changed. Indeed, in physics we call the real South pole of the magnet, which is attracted by the North pole of the earth's magnetism, the *North pole*, and it does not matter.

* * *

That positive and negative are equivalent, irrespective of which side is positive and which negative, [holds good] not only in analytical geometry, but still more in physics (see Clausius, p. 87 et seq.).[a]

* * *

Polarity. A magnet, on being cut through, polarises the neutral middle portion, but in such a way that the old poles remain. On the other hand a worm, on being cut into two, retains the receptive mouth at the positive pole and forms a new negative pole at the other end with excretory anus; but the old negative pole (the anus) now becomes positive, becoming a mouth, and a new anus or negative pole is formed at the cut end. *Voilà* transformation of positive into negative.

* * *

Polarisation. For. J. Grimm it was still a firmly established law that a German dialect must be either High German or Low

---

a R. Clausius, *Die mechanische Wärmetheorie*, Bd. 1.—*Ed.*

German. In this he totally lost sight of the Frankish dialect.[246] Because the written Frankish of the later Carlovingian period was High German (since the High German shifting of consonants had taken possession of the Frankish South-East), he imagined that Frankish passed in one place into old High German, in another place into French. It then remained absolutely impossible to explain the source of the Netherland dialect in the ancient Salic regions. Frankish was only rediscovered after Grimm's death: Salic in its rejuvenation as the Netherland dialect, Ripuaric in the Middle and Lower Rhine dialects, which in part have been shifted to various stages of High German, and in part have remained Low German, so that Frankish is a dialect that is *both* High German *and* Low German.

* * *

CHANCE AND NECESSITY

Another opposition in which metaphysics is entangled is that of chance and necessity. What can be more sharply contradictory than these two thought determinations? How is it possible that both are identical, that the accidental is necessary, and the necessary is also accidental? Common sense, and with it the majority of natural scientists, treats necessity and chance as determinations that exclude each other once for all. A thing, a circumstance, a process is either accidental or necessary, but not both. Hence both exist side by side in nature; nature contains all sorts of objects and processes, of which some are accidental, the others necessary, and it is only a matter of not confusing the two sorts with each other. Thus, for instance, one assumes the decisive specific characters to be necessary, other differences between individuals of the same species being termed accidental, and this holds good of crystals as it does for plants and animals. Then again the lower group becomes accidental in relation to the higher, so that it is declared to be a matter of chance how many different species are included in the *genus felis*[a] or *equus*[b], or how many genera and orders there are in a class, and how many individuals of each of these species exist, or how many different species of animals occur in a given region, or what in general the

---

[a] Cat.— *Ed.*
[b] Horse.— *Ed.*

fauna and flora are like. And then it is declared that the necessary is the sole thing of scientific interest and that the accidental is a matter of indifference to science. That is to say: what can be brought under laws, hence what one *knows,* is interesting; what cannot be brought under laws, and therefore what one does not know, is a matter of indifference and can be ignored. Thereby all science comes to an end, for it has to investigate precisely that which we do *not* know. That is to say: what can be brought under general laws is regarded as necessary, and what cannot be so brought as accidental. Anyone can see that this is the same sort of science as that which proclaims natural what it can explain, and ascribes what it cannot explain to supernatural causes; whether I term the cause of the inexplicable chance, or whether I term it God, is a matter of complete indifference as far as the thing itself is concerned. Both are only equivalents for: I do not know, and therefore do not belong to science. The latter ceases where the requisite connection is wanting.

In opposition to this view there is determinism, which passed from French materialism into natural science, and which tries to dispose of chance by denying it altogether. According to this conception only simple, direct necessity prevails in nature. That a particular pea-pod contains five peas and not four or six, that a particular dog's tail is five inches long and not a whit longer or shorter, that this year a particular clover flower was fertilised by a bee and another not, and indeed by precisely one particular bee and at a particular time, that a particular windblown dandelion seed has sprouted and another not, that last night I was bitten by a flea at four o'clock in the morning, and not at three or five o'clock, and on the right shoulder and not on the left calf—these are all facts which have been produced by an irrevocable concatenation of cause and effect, by an unshatterable necessity of such a nature indeed that the gaseous sphere, from which the solar system was derived, was already so constituted that these events had to happen thus and not otherwise. With this kind of necessity we likewise do not get away from the theological conception of nature. Whether with Augustine and Calvin we call it the eternal decree of God, or Kismet [247] as the Turks do, or whether we call it necessity, is all pretty much the same for science. There is no question of tracing the chain of causation in any of these cases; so we are just as wise in one as in another, the so-called necessity remains an empty phrase, and with it—chance also remains what it was before. As long as we are not able to show on what the number of peas in the pod depends, it remains just a matter of chance, and the assertion that the case was foreseen already in the primordial constitution of the solar system does not get us a step further. Still more. A science which was to set about the task of following back the *casus* of this individual pea-pod in its causal concatenation would be no longer science but pure trifling; for this same pea-pod alone has in addition innumerable other individual, accidentally appearing qualities; shade of colour, thickness and hardness of the pod, size of the peas, not to speak of the individual peculiarities revealed by the microscope. The *one* pea-pod, therefore, would already provide more causal connections for following up than all the botanists in the world could solve.

Hence chance is not here explained by necessity, but rather necessity is degraded to the production of what is merely accidental. If the fact that a particular pea-pod contains six peas, and not five or seven, is of the same order as the law of motion of the solar system, or the law of the transformation of energy, then as a matter of fact chance is not elevated into necessity, but rather necessity degraded into chance. Furthermore, however much the diversity of the organic and inorganic species and individuals existing side by side in a given area may be asserted to be based on irrefragable necessity, for the separate species and individuals it remains what it was before, a matter of chance. For the individual animal it is a matter of chance, where it happens to be born, what environment it finds for living, what enemies and how many of them threaten it. For the mother plant it is a matter of chance whither the wind scatters its seeds, and, for the daughter plant, where the seed finds soil for germination; and to assure us that here also everything rests on irrefragable necessity is a poor consolation. The jumbling together of natural objects in a given region, still more in the whole world, for all the primordial determination from eternity, remains what it was before—a matter of chance.

In contrast to both conceptions, Hegel came forward with the hitherto quite unheard-of propositions that the accidental has a cause because it is accidental, and just as much also has no cause because it is accidental; that the accidental is necessary, that necessity determines itself as chance, and, on the other hand, this chance is rather absolute necessity. (*Logik*, II, Book III, 2: "Die Wirklichkeit".)[a] Natural science has simply ignored these proposi-

---

[a] G. W. F. Hegel, *Wissenschaft der Logik*, Th. 1. Die objective Logik, Abth. 2. Die Lehre vom Wesen, S. 199, 209.— *Ed.*

tions as paradoxical trifling, as self-contradictory nonsense, and, as regards theory, has persisted on the one hand in the barrenness of thought of Wolffian metaphysics, according to which a thing is *either* accidental *or* necessary, but not both at once; or, on the other hand, in the hardly less thoughtless mechanical determinism which in words denies chance in general only to recognise it in practice in each particular case.

While natural science continued to think in this way, what *did it do* in the person of Darwin?

Darwin, in his epoch-making work,[a] set out from the widest existing basis of chance. Precisely the infinite, accidental differences between individuals within a single species, differences which become accentuated until they break through the character of the species, and whose immediate causes even can be demonstrated only in extremely few cases (the material on chance occurrences accumulated in the meantime has suppressed and shattered the old idea of necessity), compelled him to question the previous basis of all regularity in biology, viz., the concept of species in its previous metaphysical rigidity and unchangeability. Without the concept of species, however, all science was nothing. All its branches needed the concept of species as basis: human anatomy and comparative anatomy—embryology, zoology, palaeontology, botany, etc., what were they without the concept of species? All their results were not only put in question but directly set aside. Chance overthrows necessity, as conceived hitherto. The previous idea of necessity breaks down. To retain it means dictatorially to impose on nature as a law a human arbitrary determination that is in contradiction to itself and to reality, it means to deny thereby all inner necessity in living nature, it means generally to proclaim the chaotic kingdom of chance to be the sole law of living nature.

"*Gilt nichts mehr der Tausves-Jontof*,"[248] cried out quite logically the biologists of all schools.

Darwin.[b]

---

[a] Ch. Darwin, *On the Origin of Species*...— *Ed.*
[b] Cf. this volume, p. 582.— *Ed.*

* * *

HEGEL, *LOGIK*, BD. I.[a]

"Nothing that is opposed to something, the *nothing of any something*, is a *determinate nothing*." (P. 74.)[b]

"In view of the mutually determinant connection of the" (world) "whole, metaphysics could make the assertion *(which is really a tautology)* that if the least grain of dust were destroyed the whole universe must collapse." (P. 78.)

Negation, main passage. "Introduction", p. 38:

"that the self-contradictory resolves itself not into nullity, into abstract Nothingness, but essentially only *into the negation of its particular content*", etc.

Negation of the negation. Phänomenologie, Preface, p. 4. Bud, flower, fruit, etc.[249]

[b) DIALECTICAL LOGIC AND THE THEORY OF KNOWLEDGE. ON THE "LIMITS OF KNOWLEDGE"]

* * *

Unity of nature and mind. To the Greeks it was self-evident that nature could not be unreasonable, but even today the stupidest empiricists prove by their reasoning (however wrong it may be) that they are convinced from the outset that nature cannot be unreasonable or reason contrary to nature.

* * *

The development of a concept, or of a conceptual relation (positive and negative, cause and effect, substance and accidency) in the history of thought, is related to its development in the mind of the individual dialectician, just as the development of an organism in palaeontology is related to its development in embryology (or rather in history and in the single embryo). That this is so was first discovered for concepts by Hegel. In historical development, chance plays its part, which in dialectical thinking, as in the development of the embryo, *is summed up in necessity.*

---

[a] G. W. F. Hegel, *Wissenschaft der Logik,* Th. 1. Die objective Logik, Abth. 1. Die Lehre vom Seyn. Italics in the quotations are by Engels.— *Ed.*

[b] Engels used this quotation in the note on zero and the preparatory works for *Anti-Dühring* (see this volume, pp. 540, 607).— *Ed.*

* * *

Abstract and concrete. The general law of the change of form of motion is much more concrete than any single "concrete" example of it.

* * *

Understanding and reason. This Hegelian distinction, according to which only dialectical thinking is reasonable, has a definite meaning.[a] We have in common with animals all activity of the understanding: *induction, deduction,* and hence also *abstraction* (Dido's [250] generic concepts: quadrupeds and bipeds), *analysis* of unknown objects (even the cracking of a nut is a beginning of analysis), *synthesis* (in animal tricks), and, as the union of both, *experiment* (in the case of new obstacles and unfamiliar situations). In their nature all these modes of procedure—hence all means of scientific investigation that ordinary logic recognises—are absolutely the same in men and the higher animals. They differ only in degree (of development of the method in each case). The basic features of the method are the same and lead to the same results in man and animals, so long as both operate or make shift merely with these elementary methods.—On the other hand, dialectical thought—precisely because it presupposes investigation of the nature of concepts themselves—is only possible for man, and for him only at a comparatively high stage of development (Buddhists and Greeks), and it attains its full development much later still through modern philosophy—and *yet* we have the colossal results already among the Greeks which by far anticipate investigation![b]

* * *

[ON THE CLASSIFICATION OF JUDGMENTS]

Dialectical logic, in contrast to the old, merely formal logic, is not, like the latter, content with enumerating the forms of motion

---

[a] See G. W. F. Hegel, *Wissenschaft der Logik*, Th. 1. Die objective Logik, Abth. 1. Die Lehre vom Seyn, S. 6-7, 26-27; Th. 2. Die subjective Logik, oder: Die Lehre vom Begriff, S. 245-53.— *Ed.*

[b] See G. W. F. Hegel, *Vorlesungen über die Geschichte der Philosophie*, Bd. 1 and also this volume, pp. 467-70.— *Ed.*

of thought, i.e., the various forms of judgment and conclusion, and placing them side by side without any connection. On the contrary, it derives these forms out of one another, it makes one subordinate to another instead of putting them on an equal level, it develops the higher forms out of the lower. Faithful to his division of the whole of logic, Hegel groups judgments as [251]:

1. Judgment of inherence, the simplest form of judgment, in which a general property is affirmatively or negatively predicated of a single thing (positive judgment: the rose is red; negative judgment: the rose is not blue; infinite judgment: the rose is not a camel);

2. Judgment of subsumption, in which a relation determination is predicated of the subject (singular judgment: this man is mortal; particular judgment: some, many men are mortal; universal judgment: all men are mortal, or man is mortal);

3. Judgment of necessity, in which its substantial determination is predicated of the subject (categorical judgment: the rose is a plant; hypothetical judgment: when the sun rises it is day-time; disjunctive judgment: *Lepidosiren* is either a fish or an amphibian);

4. Judgment of the notion, in which is predicated of the subject how far it corresponds to its general nature or, as Hegel says, to the notion of it (assertoric judgment: this house is bad; problematic judgment: if a house is constituted in such and such a way, it is good; apodeictic judgment: the house that is constituted in such and such a way is good.

1. *Individual Judgment.* 2 and 3. *Special.* 4. *General.*

However dry this sounds here, and however arbitrary at first sight this classification of judgments may here and there appear, yet the inner truth and necessity of this grouping will become clear to anyone who studies the brilliant exposition in Hegel's *Larger Logic* (*Werke*, V, pp. 63-115).[a] To show how much this grouping is based not only on the laws of thought but also on the laws of nature, we should like to put forward here a very well-known example outside this connection.

That friction produces heat was already known practically to prehistoric man, who discovered the making of fire by friction perhaps more than 100,000 years ago, and who still earlier warmed cold parts of the body by rubbing. But from that to the discovery that friction is in general a source of heat, who knows how many thousands of years elapsed? Enough that the time came

---

[a] G. W. F. Hegel, *Wissenschaft der Logik*, Th. 2. Die subjective Logik, oder: Die Lehre vom Begriff.— *Ed.*

when the human brain was sufficiently developed to be able to formulate the judgment: *friction is a source of heat*, a judgment of inherence, and indeed a positive one.

Still further thousands of years passed until, in 1842, Mayer, Joule, and Colding investigated this special process in its relation to other processes of a similar kind that had been discovered in the meantime,[a] i.e., as regards its immediate general conditions, and formulated the judgment: all mechanical motion is capable of being converted into heat by means of friction. So much time and an enormous amount of empirical knowledge were required before we could make the advance in knowledge of the object from the above positive judgment of inherence to this universal judgment of subsumption.

But from now on things went quickly. Only three years later, Mayer was able, at least in substance, to raise the judgment of subsumption to the level at which it now stands: any form of motion, under conditions fixed for each case, is both able and compelled to undergo transformation, directly or indirectly, into any other form of motion—a judgment of the notion, and moreover an apodeictic one, the highest form of judgment altogether.[b]

What, therefore, in Hegel appears as a development of the thought form of judgment as such, confronts us here as the development of our *empirically* based theoretical knowledge of the nature of motion in general. This shows, however, that laws of thought and laws of nature are necessarily in agreement with one another, if only they are correctly known.

We can regard the first judgment as that of individuality; the isolated fact that friction produces heat is registered. The second judgment is that of particularity: a special form of motion, mechanical motion, exhibits the property, under special conditions (through friction), of passing into another special form of motion, viz., heat. The third judgment is that of universality: any form of motion proves able and compelled to undergo transformation into any other form of motion. In this form the law attains its final expression. By new discoveries we can give new illustrations of it, we can give it a new and richer content. But we cannot add anything to the law itself as here formulated. In its universality, equally universal in form and content, it is not susceptible of further extension: it is an absolute natural law.

---

[a] J. R. Mayer, *Die Mechanik der Wärme*, S. 3-12.— *Ed.*
[b] Ibid., S. 13-126.— *Ed.*

Unfortunately we are in a difficulty about the form of motion of protein, ALIAS life, so long as we are not able to make protein.

* * *

Above, however, it has also been proved that to make judgments involves not merely Kant's "power of judgment", but a [...][a]

* * *

Individuality, particularity, universality—these are the three determinations in which the whole "Doctrine of the Notion"[b] moves. Under these heads, progression from the individual to the particular and from the particular to the universal takes place not in one but in many modalities, and this is often enough exemplified by Hegel as the progression: individual, species, genus. And now the Haeckels come forward with their induction and trumpet it as a great fact—against Hegel—that progression must be from the individual to the particular and then to the universal (!), from the individual to the species and then to the genus—and then permit *deductive* conclusions which are supposed to lead further. These people have got into such a dead-lock over the opposition between induction and deduction that they reduce all logical forms of conclusion to these two, and in so doing do not notice that they (1) unconsciously employ quite different forms of conclusion under those names, (2) deprive themselves of the whole wealth of forms of conclusion in so far as it cannot be forced under these two, and (3) thereby convert both forms, induction and deduction, into sheer nonsense.

* * *

Induction and deduction. Haeckel, p. 75 et seq., where Goethe draws the inductive conclusion that man, who *does not normally*

---

[a] This unfinished note closes the fourth page of the double sheet of which the second and third pages and the beginning of the fourth page constitute the preceding large fragment on the classification of judgments.— *Ed.*

[b] G. W. F. Hegel, *Wissenschaft der Logik,* Th. 2. Die subjective Logik, oder: Die Lehre vom Begriff.— *Ed.*

have a premaxillary bone, *must* have one, hence by *incorrect* induction arrives at something correct! [252]

* * *

Haeckel's nonsense: induction against deduction. As if it were not the case that deduction = conclusion, and therefore induction is also a deduction. This comes from polarisation. Haeckel, *Schöpfungsgeschichte*; pp. 76-77. The conclusion polarised into induction and deduction!

* * *

By induction it was discovered 100 years ago that crayfish and spiders were insects and all lower animals were worms. By induction it has now been found that this is nonsense and there exist *x* classes. Wherein then lies the advantage of the so-called inductive conclusion, which can be just as false as the so-called deductive conclusion, the basis of which is nevertheless classification? [253]

Induction can never prove that there will never be a mammal without lacteal glands. Formerly nipples were the mark of a mammal. But the platypus has none.

The whole swindle of induction [is derived] from the Englishmen; Whewell, INDUCTIVE SCIENCES, comprising the purely mathematical sciences,[254] and so the antithesis to deduction invented. Logic, old or new, knows nothing of this. All forms of conclusion that start from the individual are experimental and based on experience, indeed the inductive conclusion even starts from U—I—P [255] (universal).

It is also characteristic of the thinking capacity of our natural scientists that Haeckel fanatically champions induction at the very moment when the *results* of induction—the classifications—are everywhere put in question (*Limulus* a spider, *Ascidia* a vertebrate or *chordate*, the *Dipnoi*, however, being fishes, in opposition to all original definitions of amphibia[a]) and daily new facts are being discovered which overthrow the *entire* previous classification by induction. What a beautiful confirmation Hegel's thesis that the

---

[a] H. A. Nicholson, *A Manual of Zoology*, 5 ed., 1878, pp. 283-85, 303-70, and 481-84.— *Ed.*

inductive conclusion is essentially a problematic one![a] Indeed, owing to the theory of evolution, even the whole classification of organisms has been taken away from induction and brought back to "deduction", to descent—one species being literally *deduced* from another by descent—and it is impossible to prove the theory of evolution by induction alone, since it is quite anti-inductive. The concepts with which induction operates: species, genus, class, have been rendered fluid by the theory of evolution and so have become *relative*: but cannot use relative concepts for induction.

* * *

To the Pan-Inductionists. With all the induction in the world we would never have got to the point of becoming clear about the *process* of induction. Only the *analysis* of this process could accomplish this.— Induction and deduction belong together as necessarily as synthesis and analysis.* Instead of one-sidedly lauding one to the skies at the expense of the other, we should seek to apply each of them in its place, and that can only be done by bearing in mind that they belong together, that they supplement each other.— According to the inductionists, induction is an infallible method. It is so little so that its apparently surest results are every day overthrown by new discoveries. Light corpuscles and caloric were results of induction. Where are they now? Induction taught us that all vertebrates have a central nervous system differentiated into brain and spinal cord, and that the spinal cord is enclosed in cartilaginous or bony vertebrae— whence indeed the name is derived. Then *Amphioxus*[256] was revealed as a vertebrate with an undifferentiated central nervous strand and *without* vertebrae. Induction established that fishes are those vertebrates which throughout life breathe exclusively by means of gills. Then animals come to light whose fish character is almost universally recognised, but which, besides gills, have also well-developed lungs, and it turns out that every fish carries a potential lung in the swim bladder. Only by audacious application of the theory of evolution did Haeckel rescue the inductionists,

---

* Chemistry, in which *analysis* is the predominant form of investigation, is nothing without its opposite— *synthesis*. [Marginal note.]

---

[a] G. W. F. Hegel, *Wissenschaft der Logik*, Th. 2. Die subjective Logik, oder: Die Lehre vom Begriff, S. 149.— *Ed.*

who were feeling quite comfortable in these contradictions.—If induction were really so infallible, whence come the rapid successive revolution in classification of the organic world? They are the most characteristic product of induction, and yet they annihilate one another.

* * *

Induction and analysis. A striking example of how little induction can claim to be the sole or even the predominant form of scientific discovery occurs in thermodynamics: the steam-engine provided the most striking proof that one can impart heat and obtain mechanical motion. 100,000 steam-engines did not prove this more than *one*, but only more and more forced the physicists into the necessity of explaining it. Sadi Carnot was the first seriously to set about the task. But not by induction.[a] He studied the steam-engine, analysed it, and found that in it the process which mattered does not appear *in pure form* but is concealed by all sorts of subsidiary processes. He did away with these subsidiary circumstances that have no bearing on the essential process, and constructed an ideal steam-engine (or gas engine), which it is true is as little capable of being realised as, for instance, a geometrical line or surface, but in its way performs the same service as these mathematical abstractions: it presents the process in a pure, independent, and unadulterated form. And he came right up against the mechanical equivalent of heat (see the significance of his function C),[b] which he only failed to discover and see because he believed in *caloric*. Here also proof of the damage done by false theories.[c]

* * *

The empiricism of observation alone can never adequately prove necessity. *Post hoc* but not *propter hoc*.[d] (*Encyclopädie*, I, S. 84.)[257]

---

[a] S. Carnot, *Réflexions sur la puissance motrice du feu et sur les machines propres à développer cette puissance.*—*Ed.*

[b] Cf. this volume, p. 344.—*Ed.*

[c] See this volume, pp. 400-01.—*Ed.*

[d] After this but not because of this. *Post hoc, ergo propter hoc* (after this, therefore because of this) denotes a fallacious reasoning that the preceding (event or phenomenon) is taken to be the cause of the subsequent.—*Ed.*

This is so very correct that it does not follow from the continual rising of the sun in the morning that it will rise again tomorrow, and in fact we know now that a time will come when one morning the sun will *not rise.* But the proof of necessity lies in human activity, in experiment, in work: if I am able to *make* the *post hoc,* it becomes identical with the *propter hoc.*

* * *

Causality. The first thing that strikes us in considering matter in motion is the inter-connection of the individual motions of separate bodies, their *being determined* by one another. But not only do we find that a particular motion is followed by another, we find also that we can evoke a particular motion by setting up the conditions in which it takes place in nature, that we can even produce motions which do not occur at all in nature (industry), at least not in this way, and that we can give these motions a predetermined direction and extent. *In this way,* by the *activity of human beings,* the idea of *causality* becomes established, the idea that one motion is the *cause* of another. True, the regular sequence of certain natural phenomena can by itself give rise to the idea of causality: the heat and light that come with the sun; but this affords no proof, and to that extent Hume's scepticism was correct in saying that a regular *post hoc* can never establish a *propter hoc.*[a] But the activity of human beings *forms the test* of causality. If we bring the sun's rays to a focus by means of a concave mirror and make them act like the rays of an ordinary fire, we thereby prove that heat comes from the sun. If we bring together in a rifle the priming, the explosive charge, and the bullet and then fire it, we count upon the effect known in advance from previous experience, because we can follow in all its details the whole process of ignition, combustion, explosion by the sudden conversion into gas and pressure of the gas on the bullet. And here the sceptic cannot even say that because of previous experience it does not follow that it will be the same next time. For, as a matter of fact, it does sometimes happen that it is *not* the same, that the priming or the gunpowder fails to work, that the barrel bursts, etc. But it is precisely this which *proves* causality instead of refuting it, because we can find out the cause of each such deviation from the rule by appropriate investigation:

---

[a] D. Hume, *Philosophical Essays Concerning Human Understanding.—Ed.*

chemical decomposition of the priming, dampness, etc., of the gunpowder, defect in the barrel, etc., etc., so that here the test of causality is so to say a *double* one.

Natural science, like philosophy, has hitherto entirely neglected the influence of men's activity on their thought; both know only nature on the one hand and thought on the other. But it is precisely the *alteration of nature by men,* not solely nature as such, which is the most essential and immediate basis of human thought, and it is in the measure that man has learned to change nature that his intelligence has increased. The naturalistic conception of history, as found, for instance, to a greater or lesser extent in Draper[a] and other scientists, as if nature exclusively reacts on man, and natural conditions everywhere exclusively determined his historical development, is therefore one-sided and forgets that man also reacts on nature, changing it and creating new conditions of existence for himself. There is devilishly little left of "nature" as it was in Germany at the time when the Germanic peoples immigrated into it. The earth's surface, climate, vegetation, fauna, and the human beings themselves have infinitely changed, and all this owing to human activity, while the changes of nature in Germany which have occurred in this period of time without human interference are incalculably small.

* * *

Reciprocal action is the first thing that we encounter when we consider matter in motion as a whole from the standpoint of modern natural science.* We see a series of forms of motion, mechanical motion, heat, light, electricity, magnetism, chemical compound and decomposition, transitions of states of aggregation, organic life, all of which, if *at present* we *still* make an exception of organic life, pass into one another, mutually determine one another, are in one place cause and in another effect, the sum-total of the motion in all its changing forms remaining the same. Mechanical motion becomes transformed into heat, electricity, magnetism, light, etc., and vice versa. Thus natural science confirms

* (Spinoza: *substance is causa sui*[b] strikingly expresses the reciprocal action.)[c] [Marginal note.]

---

[a] J. W. Draper, *History of the Intellectual Development of Europe.—Ed.*
[b] Cause of itself.— *Ed.*
[c] B. Spinoza, *Ethica...*, Pars I. De Deo. Definitiones 1, 3.— *Ed.*

what Hegel has said (where?), that reciprocal action is the true *causa finalis* of things. We cannot go back further than to knowledge of this reciprocal action, for the very reason that there is nothing behind to know. If we know the forms of motion of matter (for which it is true there is still very much lacking, in view of the short time that natural science has existed), then we know matter itself, and therewith our knowledge is complete. (Grove's whole misunderstanding about causality rests on the fact that he does not succeed in arriving at the category of reciprocal action; he has the thing, but not the abstract thought, and hence the confusion—pp. 10-14.ª) Only from this universal reciprocal action do we arrive at the real causal relation. In order to understand the separate phenomena, we have to tear them out of the general inter-connection and consider them in isolation, and *then* the changing motions appear, one as cause and the other as effect.

* * *

For one who denies causality every natural law is a hypothesis, among others also the chemical analysis of heavenly bodies by means of the prismatic spectrum. What shallowness of thought to remain at such a viewpoint.

* * *

ON NÄGELI'S INCAPACITY TO KNOW THE INFINITE[258]

Nägeli, pp. 12, 13

Nägeli first of all says that we cannot know real qualitative differences, and immediately afterwards says that such "absolute differences" do not occur in nature! (P. 12.)

Firstly, every quality has infinitely many quantitative gradations, e. g., shades of colour, hardness and softness, length of life, etc., and these, although qualitatively distinct, are measurable and knowable.

Secondly, qualities do not exist but only things *with* qualities and indeed with infinitely many qualities. Two different things always have certain qualities (properties of corporeality at least) in common, others differing in degree, while still others may be

---

ª W. R. Grove, *The Correlation of Physical Forces.—Ed.*

entirely absent in one of them. If we consider two such extremely different things—e. g., a meteorite and a man—in separation, we get very little out of it, at most that heaviness and other general properties of bodies are common to both. But an infinite series of other natural objects and natural processes can be put between the two things, permitting us to complete the series from meteorite to man and to allocate to each its place in the inter-connection of nature and thus to *know* them. Nägeli himself admits this.

Thirdly, our various senses might give us impressions differing absolutely as regards quality. In that case, properties which we experience by means of sight, hearing, smell, taste, and touch would be absolutely different. But even here the differences disappear with the progress of investigation. Smell and taste have long ago been recognised as allied senses belonging together, which perceive conjoint if not identical properties. Sight and hearing both perceive wave oscillations. Touch and sight supplement each other to such an extent that from the appearance of an object we can often enough predict its tactile properties. And, finally, it is always the same *"I* that receives and elaborates all these different sense impressions, that therefore comprehends them into a unity, and likewise these various impressions are provided by the same thing, appearing as its *common* properties, and therefore helping us to know it. To explain these different properties accessible only to different senses, to bring out their internal interconnection, is precisely the task of science, which so far has not complained because we have not a general sense in place of the five special senses, or because we are not able to see or hear tastes and smells.

Wherever we look, nowhere in nature are there to be found such "qualitatively or absolutely distinct fields", [p. 12] which are alleged to be incomprehensible. The whole confusion springs from the confusion about quality and quantity. In accordance with the prevailing mechanical view, Nägeli regards all qualitative differences as explained only in so far as they can be reduced to quantitative differences (on which what is necessary is said elsewhere),[a] or because quality and quantity are for him absolutely distinct categories. Metaphysics.

"We can know *only the finite*",[b] etc. [P. 13.]

---

[a] See this volume, pp. 529-32.— *Ed.*
[b] Italics by Engels.— *Ed.*

This is quite correct in so far as only finite objects enter the sphere of our knowledge. But the proposition needs to be supplemented by this: "fundamentally we can know *only the infinite.*" In fact all real, exhaustive knowledge consists solely in raising the individual thing in thought from individuality into particularity and from this into universality, in seeking and establishing the infinite in the finite, the eternal in the transitory. The form of universality, however, is the form of self-completeness, hence of infinity; it is the comprehension of the many finites in the infinite. We know that chlorine and hydrogen, within certain limits of temperature and pressure and under the influence of light, combine with an explosion to form hydrochloric acid gas, and as soon as we know this, we know also that this takes place *everywhere* and *at all times* where the above conditions are present, and it can be a matter of indifference, whether this occurs once or is repeated a million times, or on how many heavenly bodies. The form of universality in nature is *law,* and no one talks more of the *eternal character of the laws of nature* than the natural scientists. Hence when Nägeli says that the finite is made impossible to understand by not desiring to investigate merely this finite, but instead adding something eternal to it, then he denies either the possibility of knowing the laws of nature or their eternal character. All true knowledge of nature is knowledge of the eternal, the infinite, and hence essentially absolute.

But this absolute knowledge has an important drawback. Just as the infinity of knowable matter is composed of the purely finite things, so the infinity of the thought which knows the absolute is composed of an infinite number of finite human minds, working side by side and successively at this infinite knowledge, committing practical and theoretical blunders, setting out from erroneous, one-sided, and false premises, pursuing false, tortuous, and uncertain paths, and often not even finding what is right when they run their noses against it (Priestley[259]). The cognition of the infinite is therefore beset with double difficulty and from its very nature can only take place in an infinite asymptotic progress. And that fully suffices us in order to be able to say: the infinite is just as much knowable as unknowable, and that is all that we need.

Curiously enough, Nägeli says the same thing:

"We can know only the finite, but we can know *all the finite*[a] that comes into the sphere of our sensuous perception." [P. 13.]

---

[a] Italics by Engels.— *Ed.*

The finite that comes into the sphere, etc., constitutes in sum precisely the infinite, for *it is just from this that Nägeli has derived his idea of the infinite!* Without this finite, etc., he would have indeed no idea of the infinite!

(Bad infinity, as such, to be dealt with elsewhere.) [a]

Before this investigation of infinity comes the following:

(1) The "insignificant sphere" in regard to space and time.
(2) The "probably defective development of the sense organs".
(3) That we "only know the finite, changing, transitory, only what is different in degree and relative, because we can only transfer mathematical concepts to natural objects and judge the latter only by measures obtained from them themselves. We have no notions for all that is infinite or eternal, for all that is permanent, for all absolute differences. We know exactly the meaning of an hour, a metre, a kilogram, but we do not know what time, space, force and matter, motion and rest, cause and effect are." [P. 13.]

It is the old story. First of all one makes sensuous things into abstractions and then one wants to know them through the senses, to see time and smell space. The empiricist becomes so steeped in the habit of empirical experience, that he believes that he is still in the field of sensuous experience when he is operating with abstractions. We know what an hour is, or a metre, but not what time and space are! As if time was anything other than just hours, and space anything but just cubic metres! The two forms of existence of matter are naturally nothing without matter, empty concepts, abstractions which exist only in our minds. But, of course, we are supposed not to know what matter and motion are! Of course not, for matter as such and motion as such have not yet been seen or otherwise experienced by anyone, but only the various, actually existing material things and forms of motion. Matter is nothing but the totality of material things from which this concept is abstracted, and motion as such nothing but the totality of all sensuously perceptible forms of motion; words like matter and motion are nothing but *abbreviations* in which we comprehend many different sensuously perceptible things according to their common properties. Hence matter and motion *can* be known in no other way than by investigation of the separate material things and forms of motion, and by knowing these, we also *pro tanto* know matter and motion *as such.* Consequently, in saying that we do not know what time, space, matter, motion, cause and effect are, Nägeli merely says that first of all we make

---

[a] See this volume, pp. 516-17.— *Ed.*

abstractions of the real world through our minds, and then cannot know these self-made abstractions because they are creations of thought and not sensuous objects, while all knowing is *sensuous measurement*! This is just like the difficulty mentioned by Hegel; we can eat cherries and plums, but not *fruit,* because no one has so far eaten fruit as such.[a]

When Nägeli asserts that there are probably a whole number of forms of motion in nature which we cannot perceive by our senses, that is a poor apology, equivalent to the suspension— *at least for our knowledge*—of the law of the uncreatability of motion. For they could certainly be *transformed into motion perceptible to us*! That would be an easy explanation of, for instance, contact electricity.

* * *

Ad vocem Nägeli. Impossibility of conceiving the infinite. When we say that matter and motion are not created and are indestructible, we are saying that the world exists as infinite progress, i. e., in the form of bad infinity, and thereby we have understood all of this process that is to be understood. At the most the question still arises whether this process is an eternal repetition—in great cycles—or whether the cycles have descending and ascending branches.

* * *

Bad infinity. True infinity was already correctly put by Hegel in *filled* space and time, in the process of nature and in history.[b] The whole of nature also is now merged in history, and history is only differentiated from natural history as the evolutionary process of *self-conscious* organisms. This infinite complexity of nature and history has within it the infinity of space and time—bad infinity—only as a sublated factor, essential but not predominant.

---

[a] G. W. F. Hegel, *Encyclopädie der philosophischen Wissenschaften...*, § 13, S. 21-22.— *Ed.*
[b] Ibid., § 126, Addendum; see also *Wissenschaft der Logik*, Th. 1. Die objective Logik, Abth. 1. Die Lehre vom Seyn, 2. Absch., 2. Kap.— *Ed.*

The extreme limit of our natural science until now has been *our* universe, and we do not need the infinitely numerous universes outside it to have knowledge of nature. Indeed, only a *single* sun among millions, with its solar system, forms the essential basis of our astronomical researches. For terrestrial mechanics, physics, and chemistry we are more or less restricted to our little earth, and for organic science entirely so. Yet this does not do any essential injury to the practically infinite diversity of phenomena and natural knowledge, any more than history is harmed by the similar, even greater limitation to a comparatively short period and small portion of the earth.

* * *

1. According to Hegel, infinite progress is a barren waste because it appears only as *eternal repetition of the same thing:* $1+1+1$, etc.

2. In reality, however, it is no repetition, but a development, an advance or regression, and thereby it becomes a necessary form of motion. This apart from the fact that it is not infinite: the end of the earth's lifetime can already be foreseen. But then, the earth is not the whole universe. In Hegel's system, any development was excluded from the temporal history of nature, otherwise nature would not be the being-beyond-self of spirit. But in human history infinite progress is recognised by Hegel as the sole true form of existence of "spirit", except that fantastically this development is assumed to have an end—in the production of the Hegelian philosophy.

3. There is also infinite knowing: *questa infinita che le cose non hanno in progresso, la hanno in giro.*[a][260] (Quantity, p. 259. Astronomy).[261] Thus the law of the change of form of motion is an infinite one, including itself in itself. Such infinities, however, are in their turn smitten with finiteness, and only occur piecemeal. So also $\frac{1}{r^2}$.[262]

* * *

The eternal laws of nature also become transformed more and more into historical ones. That water is fluid from 0°-100° C. is an

---

[a] This infinite, which things do not have in progress, they have in circling.— *Ed.*

eternal law of nature, but for it to be valid, there must be (1) water, (2) the given temperature, (3) normal pressure. On the moon there is no water, in the sun only its elements, and the law does not exist for these two heavenly bodies.—The laws of meteorology are also eternal, but only for the earth or for a body of the size, density, axial inclination, and temperature of the earth, and on condition that it has an atmosphere of the same mixture of oxygen and nitrogen and with the same amounts of water vapour being evaporated and precipitated. The moon has no atmosphere, the sun one of glowing metallic vapours; the former has no meteorology, that of the latter is quite different from ours.—Our whole official physics, chemistry, and biology are exclusively *geocentric,* calculated only for the earth. We are still quite ignorant of the conditions of electric and magnetic tensions on the sun, fixed stars, and nebulae, even on the planets of a different density from ours. On the sun, owing to high temperature, the laws of chemical combination of the elements are suspended or only momentarily operative at the limits of the solar atmosphere, the compounds becoming dissociated again on approaching the sun. The chemistry of the sun is just in process of arising, and is necessarily quite different from that of the earth not overthrowing the latter but standing outside it. In the nebulae perhaps there do not exist even those of the 65 elements which are possibly themselves of compound nature. Hence, if we wish to speak of general laws of nature that are uniformly applicable to *all* bodies—from the nebula to man—we are left only with gravity and perhaps the most general form of the theory of the transformation of energy, *vulgo* the mechanical theory of heat. But, on its general, consistent application to all phenomena of nature, this theory itself becomes converted into a historical presentation of the successive changes occurring in a system of the universe from its origin to its passing away, hence into a history in which at each stage different laws, i. e., different phenomenal forms of the same universal motion, predominate, and so nothing remains as absolutely universally valid except— *motion.*

* * *

The *geocentric* standpoint in astronomy is prejudiced and has rightly been abolished. But as we go deeper in our investigations, it comes more and more into its own. The sun, etc., *serve* the earth (Hegel, *Naturphilosophie,* p. 155).[263] (The whole huge sun exists merely for the sake of the little planets.) Anything other than geocentric physics, chemistry, biology, meteorology, etc., is impossible for us, and these sciences lose nothing by saying that they only hold good for the earth and are therefore only relative. If one takes that seriously and demands a centreless science, one puts a stop to *all* science. It suffices us to know that under the same conditions everywhere the same must take place, at a distance to the right or the left of us that is a million million times as great as the distance from the earth to the sun.

* * *

Cognition. Ants have eyes different from ours, they can see chemical (?) light-rays (*Nature,* June 8, 1882, Lubbock), but as regards knowledge of these rays that are invisible to us, we are considerably more advanced than the ants, and the very fact that we are able to demonstrate *that* ants can see things invisible to us, and that this proof is based solely on perceptions made with *our* eyes, shows that the special construction of the human eye sets no absolute barrier to human cognition.[264]

In addition to the eye, we have not only the other senses but also our thought activity. With regard to the latter, matters stand exactly as with the eye. To know what can be discovered by our thinking, it is no use, a hundred years after Kant, to try and find out the range of thought from the critique of reason or the investigation of the instrument of knowing. It is as little use as when Helmholtz uses the imperfection of our sight (indeed a necessary imperfection, for an eye that could see *all* rays would for that very reason see *nothing at all*), and the construction of our eye—which restricts sight to definite limits and even so does not give quite correct reproduction—as proof that the eye acquaints us incorrectly or unreliably with the nature of what is seen.[a] What can be discovered by our thought is more evident from what it has already discovered and is every day still discovering. And that is already enough both as regards quantity and quality. On the other hand, the investigation of the *forms* of thought, the thought determinations, is very profitable and necessary, and since Aristotle this has been systematically undertaken only by Hegel.

---

[a] H. Helmholtz, "Die neuen Fortschritte in der Theorie des Sehens", *Populäre wissenschaftliche Vorträge,* H. II, S. 1-98.— *Ed.*

In any case we shall never find out *how* chemical rays appear to ants. Anyone who is distressed by this is simply beyond help.

* * *

The form of development of natural science, in so far as it thinks, is the *hypothesis*.[265] A new fact is observed which makes impossible the previous method of explaining the facts belonging to the same group. From this moment onwards new methods of explanation are required—at first based on only a limited number of facts and observations. Further observational material weeds out these hypotheses, doing away with some and correcting others, until finally the law is established in a pure form. If one should wait until the material for a law was *in a pure form,* it would mean suspending the process of thought in investigation until then and, if only for this reason, the law would never come into being.

The number and succession of hypotheses supplanting one another—given the lack of logical and dialectical education among natural scientists—easily gives rise to the idea that we cannot know the *essence* of things (Haller and Goethe).[266] This is not peculiar to natural science since all human knowledge develops in a much twisted curve; and in the historical sciences also, including philosophy, theories displace one another, from which, however, nobody concludes that formal logic, for instance, is nonsense.— The last form of this outlook is the "thing-in-itself". In the first place, this assertion that we cannot know the thing-in-itself (Hegel, *Encyclopädie,* § 44)[a] passes out of the realm of science into that of fantasy. Secondly, it does not add a word to our scientific knowledge, for if we cannot occupy ourselves with things, they do not exist for us. And, thirdly, it is a mere phrase and is never applied. Taken in the abstract it sounds quite sensible. But suppose one applies it. What would one think of a zoologist who said: "A dog *seems* to have four legs, but we do not know whether in reality it has four million legs or none at all"? Or of a mathematician who first of all defines a triangle as having three sides, and then declares that he does not know whether it might not have 25? That 2×2 *seems* to be 4? But scientists take care not to apply the phrase about the thing-in-itself in natural science, they permit themselves this only in passing into philosophy. This is the best proof how little seriously they take it and what little value

---

[a] G. W. F. Hegel, *Encyclopädie der philosophischen Wissenschaften...*, S. 95.— *Ed.*

it has itself. If they did take it seriously, *à quoi bon*[a] of investigating anything?

Taken historically the thing would have a certain meaning: we can only know under the conditions of our epoch and *as far as these allow.*

* * *

The thing-in-itself: Hegel, *Logik,* II, p. 10, also later a whole section on it[b]:

"Scepticism did not dare to affirm *it is;* modern idealism" (i.e., Kant and Fichte) "did not dare to regard cognition as a knowledge of the thing-in-itself*.... But at the same time, scepticism admitted manifold determinations of its show, or rather its show had for content all the manifold riches of the world. In the same manner the *appearance*[c] of idealism" (i.e., WHAT idealism CALLS appearance) "comprehends the whole range of these manifold determinatenesses.... The content may then have no basis in any being nor in any thing nor thing-in-itself: *for itself it remains as it is; it has only been translated from being into show.*"[d]

Hegel, therefore, is here a much more resolute materialist than the modern natural scientists.

* * *

Valuable self-criticism of the Kantian *thing-in-itself,* which shows that Kant suffers shipwreck also on the thinking ego and likewise discovers in it an unknowable thing-in-itself. (Hegel, V, p. 256 et seq.)[e]

---

* Cf. *Encyclopädie,* I, p. 252. [See § 124.] [Marginal note.]

---

[a] What would be the good.— *Ed.*

[b] G. W. F. Hegel, *Wissenschaft der Logik,* Th. 1, Die objective Logik, Abth. 2. Die Lehre vom Wesen, I. Absch., 1. Kap. Der Schein, B. Der Schein and 2. Absch., 1. Kap. Die Existenz.— *Ed.*

[c] Italics by Engels.— *Ed.*

[d] G. W. F. Hegel, *Encyclopädie der philosophischen Wissenschaften...,* S. 125-29, 131-32. Italics by Engels.— *Ed.*

[e] G. W. F. Hegel, *Wissenschaft der Logik,* Th. 2. Die subjective Logik, oder: Die Lehre vom Begriff.— *Ed.*

[FORMS OF MOTION OF MATTER.
CLASSIFICATION OF THE SCIENCES]

Causa finalis—matter and its inherent motion. This matter is *no abstraction*. Even in the sun the different substances are dissociated and without distinction in their action. But in the *gaseous sphere of the nebula* all substances, although separately present, *become merged in pure matter as such*, acting only as matter, not according to their specific properties.

(Moreover already in Hegel the antithesis of *causa efficiens* and *causa finalis* is sublated in reciprocal action.)[a]

* * *

Primordial matter.

"The conception of matter as original and pre-existent, and as naturally formless, is a very ancient one; it meets us even among the Greeks, at first in the mythical shape of chaos, which is supposed to represent the unformed substratum of the existing world." (Hegel, *Encyclopädie*, I, [S.] 258.)[b]

We find this chaos again in Laplace, and approximately in the nebula which also has only the *beginning* of form. Differentiation comes afterwards.

* * *

Gravity as *the most general determination of materiality* is commonly accepted. That is to say, attraction is a necessary property of

---

[a] G. W. F. Hegel, *Wissenschaft der Logik*, Th. 1. Die objective Logik, Abth. 2. Die Lehre vom Wesen, S. 231-35.— *Ed.*

[b] G. W. F. Hegel, *Encyclopädie der philosophischen Wissenschaften*, § 128, Zusatz.— *Ed.*

matter, but not repulsion. But attraction and repulsion are as inseparable as positive and negative, and hence from dialectics itself it can already be predicted that the true theory of matter must assign as important a place to repulsion as to attraction, and that a theory of matter based on mere attraction is false, inadequate, and one-sided. In fact sufficient phenomena occur that demonstrate this in advance. If only on account of light, the ether is not to be dispensed with. Is the ether of material nature? If it *exists* at all, it must be of material nature, it must come under the concept of matter. But it is not affected by gravity. The tail of a comet is granted to be of material nature. It shows a powerful repulsion. Heat in a gas produces repulsion, etc.[a]

* * *

Attraction and gravitation. The whole theory of gravitation rests on saying that attraction is the essence of matter. This is necessarily false. Where there is attraction, it must be complemented by repulsion. Hence already Hegel was quite right in saying that the essence of matter is attraction *and* repulsion.[b] And in fact we are more and more becoming forced to recognise that the dissipation of matter has a limit where attraction is transformed into repulsion, and conversely the condensation of the repelled matter has a limit where it becomes attraction.

* * *

The transformation of attraction into repulsion and vice versa is mystical in Hegel, but in substance he anticipated by it[c] the scientific discovery that came later. Even in a gas there is repulsion of the molecules, still more so in more finely-divided matter, for instance in the tail of a comet, where it even operates with enormous force. Hegel shows his genius even in the fact that he derives attraction as something secondary from repulsion as something preceding it: a solar system is only formed by the

---

a See also this volume, pp. 363-77.— *Ed.*

b G. W. F. Hegel, *Vorlesungen über die Naturphilosophie...*, § 262, S. 67-68 and also *Wissenschaft der Logik,* Th. 1. Die objective Logik, Abth. 1. Die Lehre vom Seyn, S. 181-200.— *Ed.*

c G. W. F. Hegel, *Encyclopädie der philosophischen Wissenschaften,* § 97, S. 192.— *Ed.*

gradual preponderance of attraction over the originally prevailing repulsion.—Expansion by heat = repulsion. The kinetic theory of gases.

* * *

The divisibility of matter. For science the question is in practice a matter of indifference. We know that in chemistry there is a definite limit to divisibility, beyond which bodies can no longer act chemically—the atom; and that several atoms are always in combination—the molecule. Ditto in physics we are driven to the acceptance of certain—for physical analysis—smallest particles, the arrangement of which determines the form and cohesion of bodies, their vibrations becoming evident as heat, etc. But whether the physical and chemical molecules are identical or different, we do not yet know.—Hegel very easily gets over this question of divisibility by saying that matter is both divisible and continuous, and at the same time neither of the two,[a] which is no answer but is now almost proved (see sheet 5, 3 below: Clausius[b]).

* * *

Divisibility.—The mammal is indivisible, the reptile can regrow a foot.—Ether waves, divisible and measurable to the infinitesimally small.—Every body divisible, in practice, within certain limits, e.g., in chemistry.

* * *

"Its essence" (of motion) "is to be the immediate unity of space and time ... to motion belong space and time; velocity, the quantum of motion, is space in relation to a definite time that has elapsed." (*Naturphilosophie,* [p.] 65.) "... Space and time are filled with matter.... Just as there is no motion without matter, so there is no matter without motion." ([P.] 67.)[c]

---

[a] G. W. F. Hegel, *Wissenschaft der Logik,* Th. 1. Die objective Logik, Abth. 1. Die Lehre vom Seyn, S. 208-20.— *Ed.*

[b] Engels is referring to the Note "Kinetic Theory of Gases", which is at the end of page 3 of the 5th double sheet of *Dialectics of Nature* (see this volume, pp. 564-65).— *Ed.*

[c] G. W. F. Hegel, *Vorlesungen über die Naturphilosophie...,* § 261, Zusatz.— *Ed.*

* * *

The indestructibility of motion in *Descartes'* principle that *the universe always contains the same quantity of motion.*[a] Natural scientists express this imperfectly as the "indestructibility of force". The merely quantitative expression of Descartes is likewise inadequate: motion as such, as essential activity, the form of existence of matter, is indestructible as the latter itself, this formulation includes the quantitative element. So here again the philosopher has been confirmed by the natural scientist after 200 years.

* * *

The indestructibility of motion. A pretty passage in Grove—p. 20 et seq.[b]

* * *

Motion and equilibrium. Equilibrium is inseparable from motion.* In the motion of the heavenly bodies there is *motion in equilibrium* and *equilibrium in motion* (relative). But all specifically relative motion, i.e., here all separate motion of individual bodies on one of the heavenly bodies in motion, is an effort to establish relative rest, equilibrium. The possibility of bodies being at relative rest, the possibility of temporary states of equilibrium, is the essential condition for the differentiation of matter and hence for life. On the sun there is no equilibrium of the various substances, only of the mass as a whole, or at any rate only a very restricted one, determined by considerable differences of density; on the surface there is eternal motion and unrest, dissociation. On the moon, equilibrium appears to prevail exclusively, without any relative motion—death (moon = negativity). On the earth motion has become differentiated into interchange of motion and equilibrium: the individual motion strives towards equilibrium, the motion as a whole once more destroys the individual equilibrium. The rock

* Equilibrium=predominance of attraction over repulsion. [Marginal note.]

---

[a] R. Descartes, *Principia philosophiae,* Pars 2, XXXVI; see this volume, p. 50.— *Ed.*

[b] W. R. Grove, *The Correlation of Physical Forces,* pp. 20-29. See also this volume, pp. 325-26.— *Ed.*

comes to rest, but weathering, the ACTION of the ocean surf, of rivers and glacier ice continually destroy the equilibrium. Evaporation and rain, wind, heat, electric and magnetic phenomena offer the same spectacle. Finally, in the living organism we see continual motion of all the smallest particles as well as of the larger organs, resulting in the continual equilibrium of the total organism during the normal period of life, which yet always remains in motion, the living unity of motion and equilibrium.

All equilibrium is only *relative* and *temporary.*[a]

* * *

(1) Motion of the heavenly bodies.[267] Approximate equilibrium of attraction and repulsion in motion.

(2) Motion on one heavenly body. Mass. In so far as this motion comes from pure mechanical causes, here also there is equilibrium. The masses *are at rest* on their foundation. On the moon this is apparently complete. Mechanical attraction has overcome mechanical repulsion. From the standpoint of pure mechanics, we do not know what has become of the repulsion, and pure mechanics just as little explains whence come the "forces", by which nevertheless masses on the earth, for example, are set in motion *against* gravity. It takes the fact for granted. Here therefore there is simple communication of repelling, displacing motion from mass to mass, with equality of attraction and repulsion.

(3) The overwhelming majority of all terrestrial motions, however, are made up of the conversion of one form of motion into another—mechanical motion into heat, electricity, chemical motion—and of each form into any other; hence either[b] the transformation of attraction into repulsion—mechanical motion into heat, electricity, chemical decomposition (the transformation is the conversion of the original *lifting* mechanical motion into heat, not of the *falling* motion, which is only the semblance) [—or transformation of repulsion into attraction].

(4) All energy now active on the earth is transformed heat from the sun.

---

[a] See this volume, pp. 55-58.— *Ed.*

[b] The sentence is not finished. This "either" is not followed by "or". Engels probably intended to mention the reverse transformation of repulsion into attraction. The presumable ending of the sentence is given in brackets.— *Ed.*

* * *

Mechanical motion. Among natural scientists motion is always as a matter of course taken to mean mechanical motion, change of place. This has been handed down from the pre-chemical eighteenth century and makes a clear conception of the processes much more difficult. Motion, as applied to matter, is *change in general.* From the same misunderstanding is derived also the craze to reduce everything to mechanical motion—even Grove is

"strongly inclined to believe that the other affections of matter ... are, and will ultimately be resolved into, modes of motion" (p. 16),[268]—

which obliterates the specific character of the other forms of motion. This is not to say that each of the higher forms of motion is not always necessarily connected with some real mechanical (external or molecular) motion, just as the higher forms of motion simultaneously also produce other forms, and just as chemical action is not possible without change of temperature and electric changes, organic life without mechanical, molecular, chemical, thermal, electric, etc., changes. But the presence of these subsidiary forms does not exhaust the essence of the main form in each case. One day we shall certainly "reduce" thought experimentally to molecular and chemical motion in the brain; but does that exhaust the essence of thought?

* * *

Dialectics of natural science[269]: Subject-matter—matter in motion. The different forms and varieties of matter itself can likewise only be known through motion, only in this are the properties of bodies exhibited; of a body that does not move there is nothing to be said. Hence the nature of bodies in motion results from the forms of motion.

1. The first, simplest form of motion is the mechanical form, pure change of place:

(a) Motion of a single body does not exist—[it can be spoken of][a] only in a relative sense—falling.

---

[a] The words in brackets have been taken from Engels' letter to Marx of May 30, 1873 (see present edition, Vol. 44).— *Ed.*

(b) The motion of separated bodies: trajectory, astronomy—apparent equilibrium—the end always *contact.*

(c) The motion of bodies in contact in relation of one another—pressure. Statics. Hydrostatics and gases. The lever and other forms of mechanics proper—which all in their simplest form of contact amount to friction or impact, which are different only in degree. But friction and impact, IN FACT contact, have also other consequences never pointed out here by natural scientists: they produce, according to circumstances, sound, heat, light, electricity, magnetism.

2. These different forces (with the exception of sound)—physics of heavenly bodies—

(a) pass into one another and mutually replace one another, and

(b) on a certain quantitative development of each force, different for each body, applied to the bodies, whether they are chemically compound or several chemically simple bodies, *chemical* changes take place, and we enter the realm of chemistry.*

3. Physics had to leave out of consideration the living organic body, or could do so; chemistry finds only in the investigation of organic compounds the real key to the true nature of the most important bodies, and, on the other hand, it synthesises bodies which only occur in organic nature. Here chemistry leads to organic life, and it has gone far enough to assure us that *it alone* will explain to us the dialectical transition to the organism.

4. The *real* transition, however, is in *history*—of the solar system, the earth; the *real* pre-condition for organic nature.

5. Organic nature.

* * *

Classification of the sciences, each of which analyses a single form of motion, or a series of forms of motion that belong together and pass into one another, is therefore the classification, the arrangement, of these forms of motion themselves according to their inherent sequence, and herein lies its importance.

* * *

At the end of the last century, after the French materialists, who were predominantly mechanical, the need became evident for an *encyclopaedic summing up* of the entire

* Chemistry of heavenly bodies. Crystallography—part of chemistry. [Marginal note.]

natural science of the *old* Newton-Linnaeus school, and two men of the greatest genius undertook this, *Saint-Simon* (uncompleted) and *Hegel*. Today, when the new outlook on nature is complete in its basic features, the same need makes itself felt, and attempts are being made in this direction. But since the general evolutionary connection in nature has now been demonstrated, an external side by side arrangement is as inadequate as Hegel's artificially constructed dialectical transitions. The transitions must make themselves, they must be natural. Just as one form of motion develops out of another, so their reflections, the various sciences, must arise necessarily out of one another.

* * *

How little Comte can have been the author of his encyclopaedic arrangement of the natural sciences,[a] which he copied from Saint-Simon, is already evident from the fact that it only serves him for the purpose of *arranging the means of instruction* and *course of instruction,* and so leads to the crazy *enseignement intégral,*[b] where one science is always exhausted before another is even broached, where a basically correct idea is pushed to a mathematical absurdity.

* * *

Hegel's division (the original one) into mechanics, chemics, and organics,[270] fully adequate for the time. Mechanics: the movement of masses. Chemics: molecular (for physics is also included in this and, indeed, both—physics as well as chemistry—belong to the same order) motion and atomic motion. Organics: the motion of bodies in which the two are inseparable.* For the organism is certainly *the higher unity which within itself unites mechanics, physics, and chemistry into a whole* where the trinity can no longer be separated. In the organism, mechanical motion is effected directly by physical and chemical change, in the form of nutrition,

---

* Each group in turn is twofold. Mechanics: (1) celestial, (2) terrestrial. Molecular motion: (1) physics, (2) chemistry. Organics: (1) plant, (2) animal. [Marginal note.]

---

[a] A. Comte, *Cours de philosophie positive,* t. 1, pp. 47-88.— *Ed.*
[b] Integral instruction.— *Ed.*

respiration, secretion, etc., just as much as pure muscular movement.

* * *

Physiography. After the transition from chemistry to life has been made, then in the first place it is necessary to analyse the conditions in which life has been produced and continues to exist, i.e., first of all geology, meteorology, and the rest. Then the various forms of life themselves, which indeed without this are incomprehensible.

* * *

ON THE "MECHANICAL" CONCEPTION OF NATURE[271]

Re page 46[a]: The Various Forms of Motion and the Sciences Dealing with Them

Since the above article appeared (*Vorwärts*, February 9, 1877),[272] Kekulé (*Die wissenschaftlichen Ziele und Leistungen der Chemie*) has defined mechanics, physics, and chemistry in a quite similar way:

"If this idea of the nature of matter is made the basis, one could define chemistry as the *science of atoms* and physics as the *science of molecules*, and then it would be natural to separate that part of modern physics which deals with *masses* as a special science, reserving for it the name of *mechanics*. Thus mechanics appears as the basic science of physics and chemistry, in so far as in certain aspects and especially in certain calculations both of these have to treat their molecules or atoms as masses." [P. 12.]

It will be seen that this formulation differs from that in the text and in the previous note[b] only being rather less definite. But when' an English journal *(Nature)* put the above statement of Kekulé in the form that mechanics is the statics and dynamics of masses, physics the statics and dynamics of molecules, and chemistry the statics and dynamics of Atoms,[273] then it seems to me that this unconditional reduction of even chemical processes to merely mechanical ones unduly restricts the field, at least of chemistry. And yet it is so much the fashion that, for instance, Haeckel

---

[a] Engels is referring to the Leipzig 1878 edition of his *Herrn Eugen Dühring's Umwälzung der Wissenschaft;* see also this volume, p. 62.— *Ed.*

[b] I.e., in the text of *Anti-Dühring* and in the Note "On the Prototypes of the Mathematical Infinite in the Real World" (see this volume, pp. 62 and 544-50.— *Ed.*

continually uses "mechanical" and "monistic" as having the same meaning, and in his opinion

"modern physiology ... in its field allows only of the operation of physico-chemical—or *in the wider sense*, mechanical—forces". (*Perigenesis*.)[a]

If I term *first of all* physics the mechanics of molecules, chemistry the physics of atoms, and furthermore biology the chemistry of proteins, I wish thereby to express the passing of each of these sciences into another, hence both the connection, the continuity, and the distinction, the discrete separation, between the two of them. To go further and to define chemistry as likewise a kind of mechanics seems to me inadmissible. Mechanics—in the wider or narrower sense—knows only quantities, it calculates with velocities and masses, and at most with volumes. Where the quality of bodies comes across its path, as in hydrostatics and aerostatics, it cannot achieve anything without going into molecular states and molecular motions, it is itself only an auxiliary science, the prerequisite for physics. In physics, however, and still more in chemistry, not only does continual qualitative change take place in consequence of quantitative change, the transformation of quantity into quality, but there are also many qualitative changes to be taken into account whose dependence on quantitative change is by no means proven. That the present tendency of science goes in this direction can be readily granted, but does not prove that this direction is the exclusively correct one, that the pursuit of this tendency will *exhaust* the whole of physics and chemistry. All motion includes mechanical motion, change of place of the largest or smallest portions of matter, and the *first* task of science, but only the *first*, is to obtain knowledge of this motion. But this mechanical motion does not exhaust motion as a whole. Motion is not merely change of place, in fields higher than mechanics it is also change of quality. The discovery that heat is a molecular motion was epoch-making. But if I have nothing more to say of heat than that it is a certain displacement of molecules, I should best be silent. Chemistry seems to be well on the way to explaining a number of chemical and physical properties of elements from the ratio of the atomic volumes to the atomic weights. But no chemist would assert that all the properties of an element are exhaustively expressed by its position in the Lothar Meyer curve,[274] that it will ever be possible by this alone to explain, for instance, the peculiar

---

[a] E. Haeckel, *Die Perigenesis der Plastidule...*, S. 13. Italics by Engels.—*Ed.*

constitution of carbon that makes it the essential bearer of organic life, or the necessity for phosphorus in the brain. Yet the "mechanical" conception amounts to nothing else. It explains all change from change of place, all qualitative differences from quantitative ones, and overlooks that the relation of quality and quantity is reciprocal, that quality transforms into quantity just as much as quantity into quality, that, in fact, reciprocal action takes place.[a] If all differences and changes of quality are to be reduced to quantitative differences and changes, to mechanical displacement, then we inevitably arrive at the proposition that all matter consists of *identical* smallest particles, and that all qualitative differences of the chemical elements of matter are caused by quantitative differences in number and by the spatial grouping of those smallest particles to form atoms. But we have not got so far yet.

It is our modern natural scientists' lack of acquaintance with any other philosophy than the most mediocre vulgar philosophy, like that now rampant in the German universities, which allows them to use expressions like "mechanical" in this way, without taking into account, or even suspecting, the consequences with which they thereby necessarily burden themselves. The theory of the absolute qualitative identity of matter has its supporters—empirically it is equally impossible to refute it or to prove it. But if one asks these people who want to explain everything "mechanically" whether they are conscious of this consequence and accept the identity of matter, what a variety of answers will be heard!

The most comical part about it is that to make "materialist" equivalent to "mechanical" derives from *Hegel,* who wanted to throw contempt on materialism by the addition "mechanical".[b] Now the materialism criticised by Hegel—the French materialism of the eighteenth century—was in fact exclusively *mechanical,* and indeed for the very natural reason that at that time physics, chemistry, and biology were still in their infancy, and were very far from being able to offer the basis for a general outlook on nature. Similarly Haeckel takes from Hegel the translation: *causae efficientes* = "mechanically acting causes", and *causae finales* = "purposively acting causes"[c]; where Hegel, therefore, puts "mechanical" as equivalent to blindly acting, unconsciously acting, and not as equivalent to mechanical in Haeckel's sense of the

---

[a] See this volume, pp. 512-13.— *Ed.*

[b] G. W. F. Hegel, *Encyclopädie der philosophischen Wissenschaften...,* § 99, Zusatz, S. 199-200.— *Ed.*

[c] See this volume, p. 522.— *Ed.*

word. But this whole antithesis is for Hegel himself so much a superseded standpoint that he *does not even mention* it in either of his two expositions of causality in his *Logik*—but only in his *Geschichte der Philosophie*, in the place where it comes historically[a] (hence a sheer misunderstanding on Haeckel's part due to superficiality!) and quite incidentally in dealing with teleology (*Logik*, III, II, 3)[b] where he mentions it as the form in which the *old metaphysics* conceived the antithesis of mechanism and teleology, but otherwise treating it as a long superseded standpoint. Hence Haeckel copied incorrectly in his joy at finding a confirmation of his "mechanical" conception and so arrived at the beautiful result that if a particular change is produced in an animal or plant by natural selection it has been effected by a *causa efficiens,* but if the same change arises by *artificial* selection then it has been effected by a *causa finalis!* The breeder a *causa finalis!* Of course a dialectician of Hegel's calibre could not be caught in the vicious circle of the narrow antithesis of *causa efficiens* and *causa finalis.* And for the modern standpoint the whole hopeless rubbish about this antithesis is put an end to because we *know* from experience and from theory that both matter and its mode of existence, motion, are uncreatable and are, therefore, their own final cause; while to give the name *effective* causes to the individual causes which momentarily and locally become isolated in the mutual interaction of the motion of the universe, or which are isolated by our reflecting mind, adds absolutely no new determination but only a confusing element. A cause that is not effective is no cause.

N.B. Matter as such is a pure creation of thought and an abstraction. We leave out of account the qualitative differences of things in lumping them together as corporeally existing things under the concept matter. Hence matter as such, as distinct from definite existing kinds of matter, is not anything sensuously existing. When natural science directs its efforts to seeking out uniform matter as such, to reducing qualitative differences to merely quantitative differences in combining identical smallest particles, it is doing the same thing as demanding to see fruit as such instead of cherries, pears, apples,[c] or the mammal as such

---

[a] G. W. F. Hegel, *Vorlesungen über die Geschichte der Philosophie*, Bd. 2, S. 190-91.— *Ed.*

[b] G. W. F. Hegel, *Wissenschaft der Logik*, Th. 2. Die subjective Logik, oder: Die Lehre vom Begriff, S. 203.— *Ed.*

[c] See this volume, p. 516.— *Ed.*

instead of cats, dogs, sheep, etc., gas as such, metal, stone, chemical compound as such, motion as such. The Darwinian theory demands such a primordial mammal, Haeckel's pro-mammal,[a] but, at the same time, it has to admit that if this pro-mammal contained within itself in *germ* all future and existing mammals, it was in reality lower in rank than all existing mammals and primitively crude, hence more transitory than any of them. As Hegel has already shown (*Encyclopädie*, I, S. 199), this view, this "one-sided mathematical view", according to which matter must be looked upon as having only quantitative determina-tion, but, qualitatively, as identical originally, is "no other standpoint than that" of the French materialism of the eighteenth century. It is even a retreat to Pythagoras who regarded number, quantitative determination as the essence of things.[b]

* * *

In the first place, Kekulé.[275] Then: the systematising of natural science, which is now becoming more and more necessary, cannot be found in any other way than in the inter-connections of phenomena themselves. Thus the mechanical motion of small masses on any heavenly body ends in the contact of two bodies, which has two forms, differing only in degree, viz., friction and impact. So we investigate first of all the mechanical effect of friction and impact. But we find that the effect is not thereby exhausted: friction produces heat, light, and electricity, impact produces heat and light if not electricity also—hence conversion of motion of masses into molecular motion. We enter the realm of molecular motion, physics, and investigate further. But here too we find that molecular motion does not represent the conclusion of the investigation. Electricity passes into and arises from chemical transformation. Heat and light, ditto. Molecular motion becomes transformed into motion of atoms—chemistry. The investigation of chemical processes is confronted by the organic world as a field for research, that is to say, a world in which chemical processes take place, although under different condi-tions, according to the same laws as in the inorganic world, for the explanation of which chemistry suffices. In the organic world, on the other hand, all chemical investigations lead back in the last

---

a E. Haeckel, *Natürliche Schöpfungsgeschichte*, S. 588.— *Ed.*
b See this volume, pp. 468-69.— *Ed.*

resort to a body—protein—which, while being the result of ordinary chemical processes, is distinguished from all others by being a self-acting, permanent chemical process. If chemistry succeeds in preparing this protein, in the specific form in which it obviously arose, that of a so-called protoplasm, a specificity, or rather absence of specificity, such that it contains potentially within itself all other forms of protein (though it is not necessary to assume that there is only one kind of protoplasm), then the dialectical transition will have been proved in reality, hence completely proved. Until then, it remains a matter of thought, ALIAS of hypothesis. When chemistry produces protein, the chemical process will reach out beyond itself, as in the case of the mechanical process above, that is, it will come into a more comprehensive realm, that of the organism. Physiology is, of course, the physics and especially the chemistry of the living body, but with that it ceases to be specially chemistry: on the one hand its domain becomes restricted but, on the other hand, inside this domain it becomes raised to a higher power.

[MATHEMATICS]

* * *

The so-called axioms of mathematics are the few thought determinations which mathematics needs for its point of departure. Mathematics is the science of magnitudes; its point of departure is the concept of magnitude.[a] It defines this lamely and then adds the other elementary determinations of magnitude, not contained in the definition, from outside as axioms, so that they appear as unproved, and naturally also as *mathematically* unprovable. The analysis of magnitude would yield all these axiom determinations as necessary determinations of magnitude. Spencer is right in as much as what thus appears to us to be the *self-evidence* of these axioms is *inherited*. They are provable dialectically, in so far as they are not pure tautologies.

* * *

Mathematics. Nothing appears more solidly based than the difference between the four species of arithmetical operations, the elements of all mathematics. Yet right at the outset multiplication is seen to be an abbreviated addition, and division an abbreviated subtraction, of a definite number of equal numerical magnitudes; and in one case—when the divisor is a fraction—division is even carried out by multiplying by the inverted fraction. In algebraic calculation the thing is carried much further. Every subtraction $(a-b)$ can be represented as an addition $(-b+a)$, every division

---

[a] See also this volume, pp. 36-38 and 545.— *Ed.*

$\dfrac{a}{b}$ as a multiplication $a \times \dfrac{1}{b}$. In calculations with powers of magnitudes one goes much further still. All rigid differences between the kinds of calculation disappear, everything can be presented in the opposite form. A power can be put as a root $(x^2 = \sqrt{x^4})$, a root as a power $(\sqrt{x} = x^{\frac{1}{2}})$. Unity divided by a power or root can be put as a power of the denominator $(\dfrac{1}{\sqrt{x}} = x^{-\frac{1}{2}}; \dfrac{1}{x^3} = x^{-3})$. Multiplication or division of the powers of a magnitude becomes converted into addition or subtraction of their exponents. Any number can be conceived and expressed as the power of any other number (logarithms, $y = a^x$). And this transformation of one form into the opposite one is no idle trifling, it is one of the most powerful levers of mathematical science, without which today hardly any of the more difficult calculations are carried out. If negative and fractional powers alone were abolished from mathematics, how far could one get?

$(-.- = +, \overline{=} = +, \sqrt{-1}$, etc, to be expounded earlier.)

The turning point in mathematics was Descartes' *variable magnitude*. With that came *motion* and *hence dialectics* in mathematics, and *at once, too, of necessity the differential and integral calculus*, which moreover immediately begins, and which on the whole was completed by Newton and Leibniz, not discovered by them.

* * *

Quantity and quality. Number is the purest quantitative determination that we know. But it is chock-full of qualitative differences. 1. Hegel, number and unity, multiplication, division, raising to a higher power, extraction of roots. Thereby, and this is not shown in Hegel,[a] qualitative differences already make their appearance: prime numbers and products, simple roots and powers. 16 is not merely the sum of 16 ones, it is also the square of 4, the fourth power of 2. Still more. Prime numbers communicate new, definitely determined qualities to numbers derived from them by multiplication with other numbers; only even numbers are divisible by 2, and there is a similar determination in the case of 4 and 8. For 3 there is the rule of the sum of the figures, and the same thing for 9 and also for 6, in the last case in combination with the even number.

---

[a] G. W. F. Hegel, *Wissenschaft der Logik*, Th. 1. Die objective Logik, Abth. 1. Die Lehre vom Seyn, S. 228.— *Ed.*

For 7 there is a special rule. These form the basis for tricks with numbers which seem incomprehensible to the uninitiated. Hence what Hegel says ("Quantität", P. 237) on the absence of thought in arithmetic is incorrect. Compare, however, "Maß".[276]

When mathematics speaks of the infinitely large and infinitely small, it introduces a qualitative difference which even takes the form of an unbridgeable qualitative opposition: quantities so enormously different from one another that every rational relation, every comparison, between them ceases, that they become quantitatively incommensurable. Ordinary incommensurability, for instance of the circle and the straight line, is also a dialectical qualitative difference; but here[a] it is the difference in *quantity* of *similar* magnitudes that increases the difference of *quality* to the point of incommensurability.

* * *

Number. The individual number becomes endowed with quality already in the numerical system itself, and the quality depends on the system used. 9 is not only 1 added together 9 times, but also the basis for 90, 99, 900,000, etc. All numerical laws depend upon and are determined by the system adopted. In dyadic and triadic systems 2 multiplied by 2 does not equal 4, but = 100 or = 11. In all systems with an odd basic number, the difference between odd and even numbers falls to the ground, e.g., in the system based on 5, $5 = 10$, $10 = 20$, $15 = 30$. Likewise in the same system the sums of digits $3n$ of products of 3 or 9 ($6 = 11$, $9 = 14$). Hence the basic number determines not only its own quality but also that of all the other numbers.

With powers of numbers, the matter goes still further: any number can be conceived as the power of any other number—there are as many logarithmic systems as there are whole and fractional numbers.

* * *

One. Nothing looks simpler than quantitative unity, and nothing is more manifold than it, as soon as we investigate it in connection with the corresponding plurality and according to its various modes of origin from plurality. First of all, one is the basic

---

[a] I. e., in the mathematics of the infinite.— *Ed.*

number of the whole positive and negative system of numbers, all other numbers arising by the successive addition of one to it-self.—One is the expression of all positive, negative, and fractional powers of one: 1^2, $\sqrt{1}$, 1^{-2} are all equal to one.—It is the content of all fractions in which the numerator and denominator prove to be equal.—It is the expression of every number that is raised to the power of zero, and therewith the sole number the logarithm of which is the same in all systems, viz., $= 0$. Thus one is the boundary that divides all possible systems of logarithms into two parts: if the base is greater than one, then the logarithms of all numbers more than one are positive, and of all numbers less than one negative; if it is smaller than one, the reverse is the case.

Hence, if every number contains unity in itself in as much as it is compounded entirely of ones added together, unity likewise contains all other numbers in itself. This is not only a possibility, in as much as we can construct any number solely of ones, but also a reality, in as much as one is a definite power of every other number. But the very same mathematicians who, without turning a hair, interpolate into their calculations, wherever it suits them, $x^0 = 1$, or a fraction whose numerator and denominator are equal and which therefore likewise represents one, who therefore apply mathematically the plurality contained in unity, turn up their noses and grimace if they are told in general terms that unity and plurality are inseparable, mutually penetrating concepts and that plurality is not less contained in unity than unity is in plurality. How much this is the case we see as soon as we forsake the field of pure numbers. Already in the measurement of lines, surfaces, and the volumes of bodies it becomes apparent that we can take any desired magnitude of the appropriate order as unity, and the same thing holds for measurement of time, weight, motion, etc. For the measurement of cells even millimetres and milligrams are too large, for the measurement of stellar distances or the velocity of light even the kilometre is uncomfortably small, just as the kilogram for planetary or, even more so, solar masses. Here is seen very clearly what diversity and multiplicity is contained in the concept of unity, at first sight so simple.

* * *

Zero, because it is the negation of any definite quantity, is not therefore devoid of content. On the contrary, zero has a very definite content. As the border-line between all positive and negative magnitudes, as the sole really neutral number, which can be neither positive nor negative, it is not only a very definite number, but also in itself more important than all other numbers bounded by it. In fact, zero is richer in content than any other number. Put on the right of any other number, it gives to the latter, in our system of numbers, the tenfold value. Instead of zero one could use here any other sign, but only on the condition that this sign taken by itself signifies zero, $= 0$. Hence it is part of the nature of zero itself that it finds this application and that it alone *can* be applied in this way. Zero annihilates every other number with which it is multiplied; united with any other number as divisor or dividend, in the former case it makes this infinitely large, in the latter infinitely small; it is the only number that stands in a relation of infinity to every other number $\frac{0}{0}$ can express every number between $-\infty$ and $+\infty$, and in each case represents a real magnitude.—The real content of an equation first clearly emerges when all its members have been brought to one side, and the equation is thus reduced to zero value, as already happens for quadratic equations, and is almost the general rule in higher algebra. The function $F(x, y) = 0$ can then also be put equal to z, and this z, although it is $= 0$, differentiated like an ordinary dependent variable and its partial derivative determined.

The nothing of every quantity, however, is itself quantitatively determined, and only on that account is it possible to calculate with zero. The very same mathematicians who are quite unembarrassed in reckoning with zero in the above manner, i.e., in operating with it as a definite quantitative concept, bringing it into quantitative relation to other quantitative concepts, clutch their heads in desperation when they read this in Hegel generalised as: the nothing of a something is a *determinate* nothing.[a]

But now for (analytical) geometry. Here zero is a definite point from which measurements are taken along a line, in one direction positively, in the other negatively. Here, therefore, the zero point has not only just as much significance as any point denoted by a positive or negative magnitude, but a much greater significance than all of them: it is the point on which they are all dependent, to which they are all related, and by which they are all determined. In many cases it can even be taken quite arbitrarily. But once adopted, it remains the central point of the whole operation, often determining even the direction of the line along which the other points—the end points of the abscissae—are to be

---

[a] See this volume, p. 502.— *Ed.*

inserted. If, for example, in order to arrive at the equation of the circle, we choose any point of the periphery as the zero point, then the line of the abscissae must go through the centre of the circle. All this finds just as much application in mechanics, where likewise in the calculation of the motions the point taken as zero in each case forms the main point and pivot for the entire operation. The zero point of the thermometer is the very definite lower limit of the temperature section that is divided into any desired number of degrees, thereby serving as a measure both for temperature stages within the section as also for higher or lower temperatures. Hence in this case also it is a very essential point. And even the absolute zero of the thermometer in no way represents pure abstract negation, but a very definite state of matter: the limit at which the last trace of independent molecular motion vanishes and matter acts only as mass. Wherever we come upon zero, it represents something very definite, and its practical application in geometry, mechanics, etc., proves that—as limit—it is more important than all the real magnitudes bounded by it.

* * *

Zero powers. Of importance in the logarithmic series:
$$\overset{0}{10^0} \; \overset{1}{10^1} \; \overset{2}{10^2} \; \overset{3}{10^3} \; {\scriptstyle \text{log}}.$$
All variables pass somewhere through unity; hence also a constant raised to a variable power $(a^x) = 1$, if $x = 0$, $a^0 = 1$ means nothing more than conceiving unity in its connection with the other members of the series of powers of a, only there has it any meaning and can lead to results $(\Sigma x^0 = \frac{x}{\omega})$,[277] otherwise not at all. From this it follows that unity also, however much it may appear identical with itself, includes within it an infinite manifoldness, since it can be the zero power of any other possible number, and that this manifoldness is not merely imaginary is proved on each occasion where unity is conceived as a determined unity, as one of the variable results of a process (as a momentary magnitude or form of a variable) in connection with this process.

* * *

$\sqrt{-1}$.—The negative magnitudes of algebra are real only in so far as they are connected with positive magnitudes and only within the relation to the latter; outside this relation, taken by themselves, they are purely imaginary. In trigonometry and analytical geometry, together with the branches of higher mathematics of which these are the basis, they express a definite direction of motion, opposite to the positive direction. But the sine and tangent of the circle can be reckoned from the upper right-hand quadrant just as well as from the lower right-hand quadrant, thus directly reversing plus and minus. Similarly, in analytical geometry, abscissae can be calculated from the periphery or from the centre of the circle, indeed in all curves they can be reckoned from the curve in the direction usually denoted as minus, [or] in any desired direction, and still give a correct rational equation of the curve. Here plus exists only as the complement of minus, and vice versa. But algebraic abstraction treats them [negative magnitudes] as real and independent, even outside the relation to a *larger*, positive magnitude.

* * *

Mathematics. To common sense it appears an absurdity to resolve a definite magnitude, e.g., a binomial expression, into an infinite series, that is, into something indefinite. But where would we be without infinite series and the binomial theorem?

* * *

Asymptotes. Geometry begins with the discovery that straight and curved are absolute opposites, that straight is absolutely inexpressible in curved, and curved in straight, that the two are incommensurable. Yet even the calculation of the circle is only possible by expressing its periphery in straight lines. For curves with asymptotes, however, straight becomes completely merged in curved, and curved in straight, just as much as the notion of parallelism: the lines are not parallel, they continually approach one another and yet never meet; the arm of the curve becomes more and more straight, without ever becoming entirely so, just as in analytical geometry the straight line is regarded as a curve of the first order with an infinitely small curvature. However large the $-x$ of the logarithmic curve may become, y can never $= 0$.

* * *

Straight and curved in the differential calculus are in the last resort put as equal: in the differential triangle, the hypotenuse of which forms the differential of the arc (in the tangent method), this hypotenuse can be regarded

"comme une petite ligne droite qui est tout à la fois l'élément de l'arc et celui de la tangente"—no matter whether the curve is regarded as composed of an infinite number of straight lines, or also, "lorsqu'on la considère comme rigoureuse; puisque le détour à chaque point M étant infiniment petit, la raison dernière de l'élément de la courbe à celui de la tangente *est évidemment une raison d'égalité*".[a]

Here, therefore, although the ratio continually *approaches* equality, but *asymptotically* in accordance with the nature of the curve, yet, since the contact is limited to a single *point* which has no length, it is finally assumed that equality of straight and curved has been reached (Bossut, *Calcul différentiel et intégral*, Paris, An VI, I, p. 149). In polar curves[278] the differential imaginary abscissae are even taken as parallel to the real abscissae and operations based on this, although both meet at the pole; indeed, from it is deduced the similarity of two triangles, one of which has an angle precisely at the point of intersection of the two lines, the parallelism of which is the whole basis of the similarity! (Fig. 17.)[279]

When the mathematics of straight and curved lines has thus pretty well reached exhaustion a new almost infinite field is opened up by the mathematics *that conceives curved as straight* (the differential triangle) and *straight as curved* (curve of the first order with infinitely small curvature). O metaphysics!

* * *

Trigonometry. After synthetic geometry has exhausted the properties of a triangle, regarded as such, and has nothing new to say, a more extensive horizon is opened up by a very simple, thoroughly dialectical procedure. The triangle is no longer considered in and for itself but in connection with another figure, the circle. Every right-angled triangle can be regarded as belonging to a circle: if the hypotenuse $= r$, then the sides enclosing the right angle are sin and cos; if one of these sides $= r$, then the other $=$ tan, the hypotenuse $=$ sec. In this way the sides and angles are given quite different, definite relationships which without this

---

[a] "as a small, quite straight line which is at the same time the element of the arc and that of the tangent"... "whether one considers it as a strict curve; since the curvature at each point *M* is infinitely small, the last ratio of the element of the curve to that of the tangent *is evidently a ratio of equality*". Italics by Engels.— *Ed.*

relation of the triangle to the circle would be impossible to discover and use, and quite a new theory of the triangle arises, far surpassing the old and universally applicable, because every triangle can be resolved into two right-angled triangles. This development of trigonometry from synthetic geometry is a good example of dialectics, of the way in which it comprehends things in their interconnection instead of in isolation.

* * *

Identity and difference—the dialectical relation is already seen in the differential calculus, where *dx* is infinitely small, but yet is effective and does everything.

* * *

Molecule and differential. Wiedemann (III, p. 636)[a] puts *finite* and *molecular* distances as directly opposed to one another.

* * *

ON THE PROTOTYPES OF THE MATHEMATICAL INFINITE IN THE REAL WORLD[280]

Re pp. 17-18.[b] Concordance of Thought and Being.— The Infinite in Mathematics

The fact that our subjective thought and the objective world are subject to the same laws, and hence, too, that in the final analysis they cannot contradict each other in their results, but must coincide, governs absolutely our whole theoretical thought. It is the unconscious and unconditional premise for our theoretical thought. Eighteenth-century materialism, owing to its essentially metaphysical character, investigated this premise only as regards content. It restricted itself to the proof that the content of all thought and knowledge must derive from sensuous experience,

---

[a] G. Wiedemann, *Die Lehre vom Galvanismus und Elektromagnetismus,* Bd. II, Abt. 1.— *Ed.*

[b] Engels is referring to the Leipzig 1878 edition of his *Herrn Eugen Dühring's Umwälzung der Wissenschaft;* see also this volume, pp. 33-35.— *Ed.*

and revived the principle: *nihil est in intellectu, quod non fuerit in sensu.*[281] It was modern idealistic, but at the same time dialectical, philosophy, and especially Hegel, which for the first time investigated it also as regards *form*. In spite of all the innumerable arbitrary constructions and fantasies that we encounter here, in spite of the idealist, topsy-turvy form of its result—the unity of thought and being—it is undeniable that this philosophy proved the analogy of the processes of thought to those of nature and history and vice versa, and the validity of similar laws for all these processes,[a] in numerous cases and in the most diverse fields. On the other hand, modern natural science has extended the principle of the origin of all thought content from experience in a way that breaks down its old metaphysical limitation and formulation. By recognising the inheritance of acquired characters, it extends the subject of experience from the individual to the genus; the single individual that must have experience is no longer necessary, its individual experience can be replaced to a certain extent by the results of the experiences of a number of its ancestors. If, for instance, among us the mathematical axioms seem self-evident to every eight-year-old child, and in no need of proof from experience, this is solely the result of "accumulated inheritance". It would be difficult to teach them by a proof to a bushman or Australian Negro.

In the present work[b] dialectics is conceived as the science of the most general laws of *all* motion. This implies that its laws must be valid just as much for motion in nature and human history as for the motion of thought. Such a law can be recognised in two of these three spheres, indeed even in all three, without the metaphysical philistine being clearly aware that it is one and the same law that he has come to know.

Let us take an example. Of all theoretical advances there is surely none that ranks so high as a triumph of the human mind as the discovery of the infinitesimal calculus in the last half of the seventeenth century. If anywhere, it is here that we have a pure and exclusive feat of human intelligence. The mystery which even today surrounds the magnitudes employed in the infinitesimal calculus, the differentials and infinites of various degrees, is the best proof that it is still imagined that what are dealt with here are pure "free creations and imaginations"[c] of the human mind, to

---

[a] Cf. this volume, pp. 34-35.— *Ed.*

[b] F. Engels, *Herrn Eugen Dühring's Umwälzung der Wissenschaft,* S. 20; see also this volume, p. 131.— *Ed.*

[c] See this volume, p. 36.— *Ed.*

which there is nothing corresponding in the objective world. Yet the contrary is the case. Nature offers prototypes for all these imaginary magnitudes.

Our geometry takes as its starting-point space relations, and our arithmetic and algebra numerical magnitudes, which correspond to our terrestrial conditions, which therefore correspond to the magnitude of bodies that mechanics terms masses—masses such as occur on earth and are moved by men. In comparison with these masses, the mass of the earth seems infinitely large and indeed terrestrial mechanics treats it as infinitely large. The radius of the earth $= \infty$, this is the basic principle of all mechanics in the law of falling. But not merely the earth but the whole solar system and the distances occurring in the latter in their turn appear infinitely small as soon as we have to deal with the distances reckoned in light years in the stellar system visible to us through the telescope. We have here, therefore, already an infinity, not only of the first but of the second degree, and we can leave it to the imagination of our readers to construct further infinities of a higher degree in infinite space, if they feel inclined to do so.

According to the view prevailing in physics and chemistry today, however, the terrestrial masses, the bodies with which mechanics operates, consist of molecules, of smallest particles which cannot be further divided without abolishing the physical and chemical identity of the body concerned. According to W. Thomson's calculations, the diameter of the smallest of these molecules cannot be smaller than a fifty-millionth of a millimetre.[a] But even if we assume that the largest molecule itself attains a diameter of a twenty-five-millionth of a millimetre, it still remains an infinitesimally small magnitude compared with the smallest mass dealt with by mechanics, physics, or even chemistry. Nevertheless, it is endowed with all the properties peculiar to the mass in question, it can represent the mass physically and chemically, and does actually represent it in all chemical equations. In short, it has the same properties in relation to the corresponding mass as the mathematical differential has in relation to its variables. The only difference is that what seems mysterious and inexplicable to us in the case of the differential, in the mathematical abstraction, here seems a matter of course and as it were obvious.

Nature operates with these differentials, the molecules, in exactly the same way and according to the same laws as

---

[a] See W. Thomson, "The Size of Atoms", *Nature,* Vol. I, No. 22, March 31, 1870, p. 553.—*Ed.*

mathematics does with its abstract differentials. Thus, for instance, the differential of $x^3=3x^2dx$, where $3xdx^2$ and dx^3 are neglected. If we put this in geometrical form, we have a cube with sides of length x, the length being increased by the infinitely small amount dx. Let us suppose that this cube consists of a sublimated element, say sulphur; and that three of the surfaces around one corner are protected, the other three being free. Let us now expose this sulphur cube to an atmosphere of sulphur vapour and lower the temperature sufficiently; sulphur will be deposited on the three free sides of the cube. We remain quite within the ordinary mode of procedure of physics and chemistry in supposing, in order to picture the process in its pure form, that in the first place a layer of the thickness of a single molecule is deposited on each of these three sides. The length x of the sides of the cube has increased by the diameter of a molecule dx. The content of the cube x^3 has increased by the difference between x^3 and $x^3 + 3x^2dx + 3xdx^2 + dx^3$, where dx^3, a *single* molecule, and $3xdx^2$, three rows of length $x + dx$, consisting simply of lineally arranged molecules, can be neglected with the same justification as in mathematics. The result is the same, the increase in mass of the cube is $3x^2dx$.

Strictly speaking dx^3 and $3xdx^2$ do not occur in the case of the sulphur cube, because two or three molecules cannot occupy the same space, and the cube's increase of bulk is therefore exactly $3x^2dx + 3xdx + dx$. This is explained by the fact that in mathematics dx is a linear magnitude, while it is well known that such lines, without thickness or breadth, do not occur independently in nature, hence also the mathematical abstractions have unrestricted validity only in pure mathematics. And since the latter neglects $3xdx^2 + dx^3$, it makes no difference.

Similarly in evaporation. When the uppermost molecular layer in a glass of water evaporates, the height of the water layer, x, is decreased by dx, and the continual flight of one molecular layer after another is actually a continued differentiation. And when the hot vapour is once more condensed to water in a vessel by pressure and cooling, and one molecular layer is deposited on another (it is permissible to leave out of account secondary circumstances that make the process an impure one) until the vessel is full, then literally an integration has been performed which differs from the mathematical one only in that the one is consciously carried out by the human brain, while the other is unconsciously carried out by nature.

But it is not only in the transition from the liquid to the gaseous state and vice versa that processes occur which are completely analogous to those of the infinitesimal calculus. When mass motion, as such, is abolished—by impact—and becomes transformed into heat, molecular motion, what is it that happens but that the mass motion is differentiated? And when the movements of the molecules of steam in the cylinder of the steam-engine become added together so that they lift the piston by a definite amount, so that they become transformed into mass motion, have they not been integrated? Chemistry dissociates molecules into atoms, magnitudes of lesser mass and spatial extension, but magnitudes of the same order, so that the two stand in definite, finite relations to one another. Hence, all the chemical equations which express the molecular composition of bodies are in their form differential equations. But in reality they are already integrated owing to the atomic weights which figure in them. For chemistry calculates with differentials, the mutual relation of the magnitudes of which is known.

Atoms, however, are in no wise regarded as simple, or in general as the smallest known particles of matter. Apart from chemistry itself, which is more and more inclining to the view that atoms are compound, the majority of physicists assert that the universal ether, which transmits light and heat radiations, likewise consists of discrete particles, which, however, are so small that they have the same relation to chemical atoms and physical molecules as these have to mechanical masses, that is to say as d^2x to dx. Here, therefore, in the now usual notion of the constitution of matter, we have likewise a differential of the second degree, and there is no reason at all why anyone, to whom it would give satisfaction, should not imagine that analogies of d^3x, d^4x, etc., also occur in nature.

Hence, whatever view one may hold of the constitution of matter, this much is certain, that it is divided up into a series of big, well-defined groups of a relatively different mass character in such a way that the members of each separate group stand to one another in definite finite mass ratios, in contrast to which those of the next group stand to them in the ratio of the infinitely large or infinitely small in the mathematical sense. The visible system of stars, the solar system, terrestrial masses, molecules and atoms, and finally ether particles, form each of them such a group. It does not alter the case that intermediate links can be found between the separate groups. Thus, between the masses of the solar system and terrestrial masses come the asteroids (some of which have a diameter no greater than, for example, that of the younger branch of the Reuss principality [282]), meteorites, etc. Thus, in the organic world the cell stands between terrestrial masses and molecules. These intermediate links prove only that there are no leaps in nature, *precisely because* nature is composed entirely of leaps.

In so far as mathematics calculates with real magnitudes, it also employs this mode of outlook without hesitation. For terrestrial mechanics the mass of the earth is regarded as infinitely large, just as for astronomy terrestrial masses and the meteorites corresponding to them are regarded as infinitely small, and just as the distances and masses of the planets of the solar system dwindle to nothing as soon as astronomy investigates the constitution of our stellar system extending beyond the nearest fixed stars. As soon, however, as the mathematicians withdraw into their impregnable fortress of abstraction, so-called pure mathematics, all these analogies are forgotten, infinity becomes something totally mysterious, and the manner in which operations are carried out with it in analysis appears as something absolutely incomprehensible, contradicting all experience and all reason. The stupidities and absurdities by which mathematicians have rather excused than explained their mode of procedure, which remarkably enough always leads to correct results, exceed the worst apparent and real fantasies, e.g., of the Hegelian philosophy of nature, about which mathematicians and natural scientists can never adequately express their horror. What they charge Hegel with doing, viz., pushing abstractions to the extreme limit, they do themselves on a far greater scale. They forget that the whole of so-called pure mathematics is concerned with abstractions, that *all* its magnitudes, strictly speaking, are imaginary, and that all abstractions when pushed to extremes are transformed into nonsense or into their opposite. Mathematical infinity is taken from reality, although unconsciously, and therefore can only be explained from reality and not from itself, from mathematical abstraction. And, as we have seen, if we investigate reality in this regard we come also upon the real relations from which the mathematical relation of infinity is taken, and even the natural analogies of the mathematical way in which this relation operates. And thereby the matter is explained.

(Haeckel's bad reproduction of the identity of thinking and being.[283] But also *the contradiction between continuous and discrete matter*; see Hegel.[a])

---

[a] G. W. F. Hegel, *Wissenschaft der Logik*, Th. 1. Die objective Logik, Abth. 1. Die Lehre vom Seyn, S. 208-20. See also the Note "The Divisibility of Matter", this volume, p. 524.— *Ed.*

* * *

The differential calculus for the first time makes it possible for natural science to represent mathematically *processes* and not only *states*: motion.

* * *

Application of mathematics: in the mechanics of solid bodies it is absolute, in that of gases approximate, in that of fluids already more difficult; in physics more tentative and relative; in chemistry, simple equations of the first order and of the simplest nature; in biology = 0.

[MECHANICS AND ASTRONOMY]

* * *

An example of the necessity of dialectical thought and of the non-rigid categories and relations in nature; the law of falling, which already in the case of a period of fall of some minutes becomes incorrect, since then the radius of the earth can no longer without error be put $=\infty$, and the attraction of the earth increases instead of remaining constant as Galileo's law of falling assumes. Nevertheless, this law is still continually taught, but the reservation omitted!

* * *

Newtonian attraction and centrifugal force—an example of metaphysical thinking: the problem not solved but only *posed,* and this preached as the solution.—Ditto Clausius' dissipation of heat.[284]

* * *

Newtonian gravitation. The best that can be said of it is that it does not explain but *pictures* the present state of planetary motion. The motion is given. Ditto the force of attraction of the sun. With these data, how is the motion to be explained? By the parallelo-gram of forces, by a tangential force which now becomes a necessary postulate that we *must* accept. That is to say, assuming the *eternal character* of the existing state, we need a *first impulse,*

God. But neither is the existing planetary state eternal nor is the motion originally compound, but *simple rotation,* and the parallelogram of forces applied here is wrong, because it did not merely make evident the unknown magnitude, the *x,* that had still to be found, that is to say in so far as Newton claimed not merely to put the question but to solve it.

* * *

Newton's parallelogram of forces in the solar system is true at best *for the moment when the annular bodies separate,* because then the rotational motion comes into contradiction with itself, appearing on the one hand as attraction, and on the other hand as tangential force. As soon as the separation is complete, however, the motion is again a unity. That this separation must occur is a proof of the dialectical process.

* * *

Laplace's theory presupposes only matter in motion—rotation necessary for all bodies suspended in universal space.

* * *

MÄDLER, THE FIXED STARS[285]

Halley, at the beginning of the eighteenth century, from the difference between the data of Hipparchus and Flamsteed on three stars, first arrived at the idea of proper motion (p. 410).— Flamsteed's British Catalogue,[a] the first fairly accurate and comprehensive one (p. 420), then ca. 1750, Bradley, Maskelyne, and Lalande.

Crazy *theory of the range of light rays in the case of enormous bodies* and Mädler's calculation based on this—as crazy as anything in Hegel's *Naturphilosophie*[b] (pp. 424-25).

The strongest (apparent) proper motion of a star $= 701''$ in a century $= 11'41'' =$ one-third of the sun's diameter; smallest

---

[a] J. Flamsteed, *Historia coelestris Britannica complectens stellar....—Ed.*

[b] G. W. F. Hegel, *Vorlesungen über die Naturphilosophie...,* Th. 2, Abth. 1.—*Ed.*

average of 921 telescopic stars 8″, 65, some of them 4″ [pp. 425-26].

Milky Way is a series of rings, all with a common centre of gravity (p. 434).

The Pleiades Group, and in it Alcyone, η Tauri, the centre of motion of our island universe "as far as the most remote regions of the Milky Way" (p. 448). Periods of revolution within the Pleiades Group on the average ca. two million years (p. 449). About the Pleiades are annular groups alternately poor in stars and rich in stars.—Secchi contests the possibility of fixing a centre at the present time [p. 799].

According to Bessel, *Sirius* and *Procyon* describe an orbit about a *dark* body, as well as the general motion (p. 450).

Eclipse of Algol every 3 days, duration 8 hours, *confirmed by spectral analysis* (Secchi, p. 786).

In the region of the *Milky Way,* but deep *within* it, a dense ring of stars of magnitudes 7-11; a long way outside this ring are the concentric Milky Way rings, of which we see two. In the Milky Way, according to Herschel, ca. 18 million stars visible through his telescope, those lying *within* the ring being ca. 2 million or more, hence over 20 million in all. In addition there is still a non-resolvable glow in the Milky Way, even behind the resolved stars, hence perhaps still further rings concealed owing to perspective? (Pp. 451-52.)

Alcyone distant from the sun 573 light years. *Diameter of the Milky Way ring* of separate visible stars, at least 8,000 light years (pp. 462-63).

The *mass* of the bodies moving within the sun-Alcyone radius of 573 light years is calculated at 118 million sun masses (p. 462), not at all in agreement with the at most 2 million stars moving therein. Dark bodies? At any rate SOMETHING WRONG. A proof of how imperfect our observational bases still are.

For the outermost ring of the Milky Way, Mädler assumes a distance of thousands, perhaps of hundreds of thousands, of light years (p. 464).

A *beautiful argument* against the so-called absorption of light:

"At any rate, there does exist a distance from which no further light can reach us, but the reason is quite a different one. The velocity of light is *finite*; from the beginning of creation to our day a *finite* time has elapsed, and therefore we can only become aware of the heavenly bodies up to the distance which light has travelled in this finite time!" ([P.] 466.)

That light, decreasing in intensity according to the square of the distance, must reach a point where it is no longer visible to our eyes, however much the latter may be strengthened and equipped, is quite obvious, and suffices for refuting the view of Olbers that only light absorption is capable of explaining the darkness of the sky [286] that nevertheless is filled in all directions with shining stars to an infinite distance. That is not to say that there does not exist a distance at which the ether *allows no further light to penetrate.*

* * *

Nebulae. Of all forms, strictly circular, elliptical, or irregular and jagged. All degrees of resolvability, merging into total non-resolvability, where only a thickening towards the centre can be distinguished. In some of the resolvable nebulae, up to ten thousand stars are perceptible, the middle mostly denser, very rarely a central star of greater brilliance. Rosse's giant telescope has, however, resolved many of them. Herschel I enumerates 197 star aggregations and 2,300 nebulae, to which must be added those catalogued by Herschel II in the southern heavens.—The irregular ones *must be distant island universes* since masses of vapour can only exist in equilibrium in globular or ellipsoidal form. Most of them, moreover, are only just visible even through the most powerful telescopes. At any rate the circular ones *can* be vapour masses: there are 78 of them among the above 2,500. Herschel assumes 2 million, Mädler—on the assumption of a true diameter equal to 8,000 light years—30 million light years distant from us. Since the distance of each astronomical system of bodies from the next one amount to at least a hundredfold the diameter of the system, the distance of our island universe from the next one would be *at least* 50 times 8,000 light years = 400,000 light years, in which case with the several thousands of nebulae we get far beyond Herschel I's 2 million ([Mädler, loc cit., p. 484-] 492).

Secchi:

The resolvable nebulae give a continuous and an ordinary stellar spectrum. The nebulae proper, however, "in part give a continuous spectrum like the nebula in Andromeda, but mostly they give a spectrum consisting of one or only very few bright lines, like the nebulae in Orion, in Sagittarius, in Lyra, and the majority of those that are known by the name of *planetary*" (circular) "nebulae" ([S.] 787).

(The nebula in Andromeda according to Mädler, p. 495, is unresolvable.—The nebula in Orion is irregular, flocculent and, as it were, puts out arms, p. 495.—Those of Lyra are ring-shaped, only slightly elliptical, p. 498.)

Huggins found in the spectrum of Herschel's nebula No. 4374 three bright lines, "from this it follows immediately that this nebula does not consist of an aggregate of separate stars, but is a *true nebula*, a glowing substance in the gaseous state" [S. 787-88].

The lines belong to nitrogen (1) and hydrogen (1), the third is unknown. Similarly for the nebula in Orion [pp. 787-88]. Even nebulae that contain gleaming points (Hydra, Sagittarius) have these bright lines, so that star masses in course of aggregation are still not solid or liquid (p. 789). The nebula in Lyra has only a nitrogen line (p. 789).—The densest place of the nebula in Orion is 1°, its whole extension 4° [pp. 790-91].

* * *

Secchi: *Sirius:*

"Eleven years later" (subsequent to Bessel's calculation, Mädler, p. 450) "... not only was the satellite of Sirius discovered in the form of a self-luminous star of the sixth magnitude, but it was also shown that its orbit coincides with that calculated by Bessel. Since then the orbit also for Procyon and its companion has been determined by Auwers, although the satellite itself has not yet been seen" ([S.] 793).

Secchi: Fixed stars.

"Since the fixed stars, with the exception of two or three, have no perceptible parallax, they are at least" some 30 light years distant from us ([p.] 799).

According to Secchi, the stars of the 16th magnitude (still distinguishable in Herschel's big telescope) are 7,560 light years distant, those distinguishable in Rosse's telescope are at least 20,900 light years distant (p. 802).

Secchi (p. 810) himself asks:

When the sun and the whole system are extinct, "are there forces in nature which can reconvert the dead system into its original state of glowing nebula and reawaken it to new life? We do not know." [a]

* * *

Secchi and the Pope.[287]

---

[a] Cf. this volume, pp. 331-33.— *Ed.*

* * *

Descartes discovered that the ebb and flow of tides are caused by the attraction of the moon. He also discovered simultaneously with Snell the basic law of the refraction of light (contested by Wolf, p. 325)[288] and this in a form peculiar to himself and different from that of Snell.

* * *

Mayer, Mechanische Theorie der Wärme, p. 328. *Kant has already stated* that the ebb and flow of tides exert a retarding pressure on the rotating earth. (Adam's calculation that the duration of the sidereal day is now increasing by $1/_{100}$ second in 1,000 years.)[a]

---

[a] J. R. Mayer, *Die Mechanik der Wärme*, S. 328, 330.— *Ed.*

[PHYSICS]

* * *

Impact and friction. Mechanics regards the effect of impact as *taking place in a pure form*. But in reality things are different. On every impact part of the mechanical motion is transformed into heat, and friction is nothing more than a form of impact that continually converts mechanical motion into heat (fire by friction known from primeval times).

* * *

The consumption of kinetic energy as such in the field of dynamics is always of a twofold nature and has a twofold result: (1) the kinetic work done, production of a corresponding quantity of potential energy, which, however, is always less than the applied kinetic energy; (2) overcoming—besides gravity—frictional and other resistances that convert the remainder of the used-up kinetic energy into *heat*.—Likewise on reconversion: according to the way this takes place, a part of the loss through friction, etc., is dissipated as heat—and that is all very ancient!

* * *

The first, naïve outlook is as a rule more correct than the later, metaphysical one. Thus already *Bacon* (and after him Boyle, Newton, and almost all the Englishmen) said heat is motion [a]

---
[a] F. Bacon, *Novum Organum*, Book II.— *Ed.*

(Boyle even said molecular motion). It was only in the eighteenth century that the caloric theory arose in France and became more or less accepted on the Continent.

* * *

Conservation of energy. The *quantitative* constancy of motion was already enunciated by Descartes,[a] and indeed almost in the same words as now by? (Clausius, Robert Mayer, Maxwell?). On the other hand, the transformation of the *form* of motion was only discovered in 1842 and this, not the law of quantitative constancy, is what is new.[b]

* * *

Force and conservation of force. The passages of J. R. Mayer in his two first papers[c] to be cited against Helmholtz.

* * *

Force.[d]—Hegel (*Geschichte der Philosophie,* I, S. 208) says:

"It is better to say that a magnet has a *soul*" (as Thales expresses it) "than that it has an attracting *force*; force is a kind of property that, *separable from matter,* is put forward as a predicate—while soul, on the other hand, is *this movement itself, identical with the nature of matter.*" [e]

* * *

Hegel's conception of force and its manifestation, of cause and effect as identical, is proved in the change of form of matter, where the equivalence is proved mathematically. This had already been recognised in measurement: force is measured by its manifestation, cause by effect.

---

[a] See this volume, pp. 50 and 525.— *Ed.*

[b] Ibid., p. 370.— *Ed.*

[c] G. R. Mayer, "Bemerkungen über die Kräfte der unbelebten Natur", *Annalen der Chemie und Pharmacie,* Bd. 42, and *Die organische Bewegung in ihrem Zusammenhang mit dem Stoffwechsel.—Ed.*

[d] Engels used this note in the Chapter "Basic Forms of Motion" (see this volume, p. 372).— *Ed.*

[e] G. W. F. Hegel, *Vorlesungen über die Geschichte der Philosophie.* Italics by Engels.— *Ed.*

* * *

Force. If any kind of motion is transferred from one body to another, then one can regard the motion, *in so far as it transfers itself,* i.e., is active, as the cause of motion, *in so far as the latter becomes transferred,* i.e., is passive, and then this cause, the active motion, appears as *force* and the passive as its *manifestation.* From the law of the indestructibility of motion, it follows automatically that the force is exactly as great as its manifestation since indeed it is *the same motion* in both cases.[a] Motion that transfers itself, however, is more or less quantitatively determinable, because it appears in two bodies, of which one can serve as a unit of measurement in order to measure the motion in the other. The measurability of motion gives the category *force* its value, otherwise it has none. Hence the more this is the case, the more are the categories of force, and its manifestation usable in research. Hence this is so especially in mechanics, where one resolves the forces still further, regarding them as compound, and thereby often arriving at new results, although one should not forget that this is merely a mental operation; by applying the analogy of forces that are really compound, as expressed in the parallelogram of forces, to forces that are really simple, the latter still do not thereby really become compound.—Similarly in statics. Then, again, in the transformation of other forms of motion into mechanical motion (heat, electricity, magnetism in the attraction of iron), where the original motion can be measured by the mechanical effect produced. But here, where various forms of motion are considered simultaneously, the limitation of the category or abbreviation, *force,* already stands revealed. No regular physicist any longer terms electricity, magnetism, or heat mere *forces,* any more than *substances* or *imponderabilia.* When we know into how much mechanical motion a definite quantity of heat motion is converted, we still do not know anything of the nature of heat, however much the examination of these transformations may be necessary for investigating this nature of heat. To conceive heat as a form of motion is the latest advance of physics, and by so doing the category of force is sublated in it: in certain connections—those of transition—they[b] can appear as forces and so be measured. Thus heat is measured by the expansion of a

---

[a] Cf. this volume, pp. 55-56.— *Ed.*

[b] I.e., the various forms of motion: mechanical motion, heat, electricity, etc.— *Ed.*

body on warming. If heat did not pass here from one body to the other—the measuring rod—i.e., if the heat of the body acting as a measuring rod did not alter, there could be no talk of measurement, of a change of magnitude. One says simply: heat expands a body, whereas to say: heat has the force to expand a body, would be a mere tautology, and to say: heat is the force which expands bodies, would not be correct, since 1. expansion, e.g., in gases, is produced also by other means, and 2. heat is not exhaustively characterised in this way.

Some chemists speak also of chemical force, as the force that makes and maintains compounds. Here, however, there is no real transference, but a combination of the motion of various bodies into a single whole, and so "force" here reaches its limit. It is, however, still measurable by the heat production, but so far without much result. Here it becomes a phrase, as everywhere where, instead of investigating the uninvestigated forms of motion, one *invents* a so-called force for their explanation (as, for instance, explaining the floating of wood in water by a buoyancy force—the refraction of light by a refractive force, etc.), in which case as many forces are obtained as there are unexplained phenomena, the external phenomenon being indeed merely translated into an internal phrase.[289] (Attraction and repulsion are easier to excuse; here a number of phenomena inexplicable to the physicist are embraced under a common name, which gives an inkling of an inner connection.)

Finally in organic nature the category of force is completely inadequate and yet continually applied. True, it is possible to characterise the action of the muscles, in accordance with its mechanical effect, as muscular force, and also to measure it. One can even conceive of other measurable functions as forces, e.g., the digestive capacity of various stomachs, but one quickly arrives *ad absurdum* (e.g., nervous force), and in any case one can speak here of forces only in a very restricted and figurative sense (the ordinary phrase: to regain one's forces). This misuse, however, has led to speaking of a vital force. If by this is meant that the form of motion in the organic body is different from the mechanical, physical, or chemical form, and contains them all sublated in itself, then it is a very lax manner of expression, and especially so because the force—presupposing transference of motion—appears here as something pumped into the organism from outside, not as inherent in it and inseparable from it, and therefore this vital force has been the last refuge of all supernaturalists.

The defect: (1) Force usually treated as having independent existence. (Hegel, *Naturphilosophie*, S. 79.[a])

(2) *Latent, dormant* force—this to be explained from the relation of motion and rest (inertia, equilibrium), where also arousing of forces to be dealt with.

* * *

Force (see above). The transference of motion takes place, of course, only in the presence of *all* the various conditions, which are often multiple and complex, especially in machines (the steam-engine, the shotgun with lock, trigger, percussion cap, and gunpowder). If *one* of them is missing, then the transference does not take place until this condition is supplied. In that case one can imagine this as if the force must first be *aroused* by the introduction of this last condition, as if it lay *latent* in a body, the so-called carrier of force (gunpowder, charcoal), whereas in reality not only this body but all the other conditions must be present in order to evoke precisely this special transference.—

The notion of force comes to us quite automatically in that we possess in our own body means for transferring motion, which within certain limits can be brought into action by our will; especially the muscles of the arms through which we produce mechanical change of place and motion of other bodies, lifting, carrying, throwing, hitting, etc., resulting in definite useful effects. The motion is here apparently *produced,* not transferred, and this gives rise to the notion of force in general *producing motion.* That muscular force is also merely transference has only now been proved physiologically.

* * *

Force. The negative side also has to be analysed: the resistance which is opposed to the transference of motion.

* * *

Radiation of heat into universal space. All the hypotheses cited by Lavrov of the renewal of extinct heavenly bodies (p. 109)[290] *involve*

---

[a] G. W. F. Hegel, *Vorlesungen über die Naturphilosophie...*, § 266.— *Ed.*

loss of motion. The heat once radiated, i.e., the infinitely greater part of the original motion, is and remains lost. Helmholtz says, up to now, $\frac{453}{454}$.[a] Hence one finally arrives after all at the exhaustion and cessation of motion. The question is only finally solved when it has been shown how the heat radiated into universal space becomes *utilisable* again. The theory of the transformation of motion puts this question categorically, and it cannot be got over by postponing the answer or by evasion. That, however, with the posing of the question the conditions for its solution are simultaneously given—*c'est autre chose.*[b] The transformation of motion and its indestructibility were first discovered hardly thirty years ago, and it is only quite recently that the consequences have been further elaborated and worked out. The question as to what becomes of the apparently lost heat has, as it were, only been *nettement posée*[c] since 1867 (Clausius).[d] No wonder that it has not yet been solved; it may still be a long time before we arrive at a solution with our small means. But it will be solved, just as surely as it is certain that there are no miracles in nature and that the original heat of the nebular ball is not communicated to it miraculously from outside the universe. The general assertion that the *total amount* (die *Masse*) *of motion is infinite,* and hence inexhaustible, is of equally little assistance in overcoming the difficulties of each individual case; it too does not suffice for the revival of extinct universes, except in the cases provided for in the above hypotheses, which are always bound up with loss of force and are therefore only temporary cases. The cycle has not been traced and will not be until the possibility of the re-utilisation of the radiated heat is discovered.

* * *

Clausius—IF CORRECT—proves that the universe has been created, *ergo* that matter is creatable, *ergo* that it is destructible, *ergo* that also force, or motion, is creatable and destructible, *ergo* that the whole theory of the "conservation of force" is nonsense, *ergo* that all his conclusions from it are also nonsense.

---

[a] H. Helmholtz, *Populäre wissenschaftliche Vorträge,* H. II, S. 119-21; see also this volume, pp. 375-77.— *Ed.*
[b] That is quite another thing.— *Ed.*
[c] Clearly posed.— *Ed.*
[d] R. Clausius, *Über den zweiten Hauptsatz der mechanischen Wärmetheorie.*— *Ed.*

* * *

Clausius' second law, etc., however it may be formulated, shows energy as lost, qualitatively if not quantitatively. *Entropy cannot be destroyed by natural means but it can certainly be created.* The world clock has to be wound up, then it goes on running until it arrives at a state of equilibrium from which only a miracle can set it going again. The energy expended in winding has disappeared, at least qualitatively, and can only be restored by an *impulse from outside.* Hence, an impulse from outside was necessary at the beginning also, hence, the quantity of motion, or energy, existing in the universe was not always the same, hence, energy must have been created, i.e., it must be creatable, and therefore destructible. *Ad absurdum!*

* * *

Conclusion for Thomson, Clausius, Loschmidt: *The reversion consists in repulsion repelling itself and thereby returning out of the medium into extinct heavenly bodies.* But just therein lies also the proof that repulsion is the really *active* aspect of motion, and attraction the *passive* aspect.[a]

---

* * *

In the motion of gases—in the process of evaporation—the motion of masses passes directly into molecular motion. Here, therefore, the transition has to be made.

* * *

States of aggregation—nodal points where quantitative change is transformed into qualitative.

* * *

Cohesion—already negative in gases—transformation of attraction into *repulsion,* the latter only real in gas and ether (?).

---

[a] See also this volume, pp. 362-77 and 523.— *Ed.*

* * *

At absolute 0° no gas is possible, all motion of the molecules ceases; the slightest pressure, and hence their own attraction, forces them together. *Consequently, a permanent gas is an impossibility.*

* * *

mv^2 has been proved also for gas molecules by the kinetic theory of gases. Hence there is the same law for molecular motion as for the motion of masses; the difference between the two is here abolished.

* * *

The kinetic theory has to show how molecules that strive upwards can at the same time exert a downward pressure and—assuming the atmosphere as more or less permanent in relation to universal space—how in spite of gravity they can move to a distance from the centre of the earth, but nevertheless, at a certain distance, although the force of gravity has decreased according to the *square* of the distance, are yet compelled by this force to come to a stop or to return.

* * *

The kinetic theory of gases:

"In a perfect gas ... the molecules are already so far distant from one another that their mutual interaction can be neglected." (Clausius, p. 6.[a])

What fills up the spaces between them? Ditto ether.[291] Hence here *the postulate of a matter that is not articulated into molecular or atomic cells.*

* * *

The character of mutual opposites belonging to theoretical development; from the *horror vacui*[292] the transition was made at once to absolutely empty universal space, only afterwards the *ether*.

---

[a] R. Clausius, *Über den zweiten Hauptsatz der mechanischen Wärmetheorie.—Ed.*

* * *

Ether. If the ether offers resistance at all, it must also offer resistance to *light,* and so at a certain distance be impenetrable to light. That however ether *propagates* light, being its *medium,* necessarily involves that it should also offer resistance to light, otherwise light could not set it in vibration.—This is the solution of the controversial questions raised by Mädler[a] and mentioned by Lavrov.[293]

* * *

Light and darkness are certainly the most conspicuous and definite opposites in nature; they have always served as a rhetorical phrase for religion and philosophy from the time of the fourth Gospel[b] to the *lumières*[c] of the eighteenth century.

Fick, p. 9: "the law long ago rigidly demonstrated in physics ... that the form of motion called radiant heat is identical in all essential respects with the form of motion that we call *light.*"[d] Clerk Maxwell, p. 14: "These rays" (of radiant heat) "have all the physical properties of rays of light, and are capable of reflection, etc.... Some of the heat-rays are identical with the rays of light, while other kinds of heat-rays make no impression upon our eyes."[e]

Hence there exist *dark* light-rays, and the famous opposition between light and darkness disappears from natural science as an absolute opposition. Incidentally, the deepest darkness and the brightest, most glaring light have the same effect of *dazzling* our eyes, and in this way are *for us* identical.—The fact is, the sun's rays have different effects according to the length of the vibration; those with the greatest wave-length communicate heat, those with medium wave-length, light, and those with the shortest wave-length, chemical action (Secchi, p. 632 et seq.), the maxima of the three actions being closely approximated, the *inner* minima of the outer groups of rays, as regards their action, coming within the light-ray group.[294] What is light and what is non-light depends on the structure of the eye. Night animals may be able to see even a part, not of the heat-rays, but of the chemical rays, since their eyes

---

[a] See this volume, pp. 553-54.— *Ed.*
[b] John 1.— *Ed.*
[c] Enlightenment.— *Ed.*
[d] A. Fick, *Die Naturkräfte in ihrer Wechselbeziehung.* Italics by Engels.— *Ed.*
[e] J. C. Maxwell, *Theory of Heat.* Engels quotes in English.— *Ed.*

are adapted for shorter wave-lengths than ours.[a] The difficulty disappears if one assumes, instead of three kinds, only a single kind of ray (and scientifically we know only *one* and everything else is a premature conclusion), which has different, but within narrow limits compatible, effects according to the wave-length.

* * *

Hegel constructs the theory of light and colour out of pure thought, and in so doing falls into the *grossest empiricism* of home-bred philistine experience (although with a certain justification, since this point had not been cleared up at that time), e.g., where he adduces against Newton the mixtures of colours used by painters (p. 314, below).[b]

* * *

Electricity. In regard to Thomson's cock-and-bull stories, cf. Hegel, pp. 346-47, where there is exactly the same thing.[c]—On the other hand, Hegel already conceives frictional electricity quite clearly as *tension,* in contrast to the fluid theory and the electrical matter theory (p. 347).

* * *

When Coulomb says that "PARTICLES OF ELECTRICITY WHICH REPEL EACH OTHER INVERSELY AS THE SQUARE OF THEIR DISTANCE", Thomson calmly takes this as proved (p. 358).[295] Ditto (p. 366) the hypothesis that electricity consists of "2 FLUIDS, POSITIVE AND NEGATIVE", whose "PARTICLES REPEL EACH OTHER". It is said (p. 360) that electricity in a charged body is retained merely by the pressure of the atmosphere.

Faraday put the seat of electricity in the opposed poles of the atoms (or molecules, there is still confusion about it), and thus for the first time expressed the idea that electricity is not a fluid but a form of motion, a "force" (p. 378). What old Thomson cannot get into his head at all is that it is precisely the spark that is of a *material* nature!

---

a A reference to the ultra-violet rays. Cf. this volume, p. 519.— *Ed.*
b G. W. F. Hegel, *Vorlesungen über die Naturphilosophie...*, § 320, Zusatz.— *Ed.*
c Ibid., § 324, Zusatz; see also this volume, pp. 403-04.— *Ed.*

Already in 1822, Faraday had discovered that the momentary induced current—the first as well as the second, reversed current— "PARTICIPATES MORE OF THE CURRENT PRODUCED BY THE DISCHARGE OF THE LEYDEN JAR THAN THAT PRODUCED BY THE VOLTAIC BATTERY"—herein lay the whole secret (p. 385).

The *spark* has been the subject of all sorts of cock-and-bull stories, which are now known to be special cases or illusions: the spark from a positive body is said to be a "PENCIL OF RAYS, BRUSH, OR CONE", the point of which is the point of discharge; the negative spark, on the other hand, is said to be a "*STAR*" (p. 396). A short spark is said to be always white, a long one usually reddish or purplish. (Wonderful nonsense of Faraday on the spark, p. 400.[a]) The spark drawn from the PRIME CONDUCTOR [of an electric machine] by a metal sphere is said to be white, by the hand—PURPLE, by aqueous moisture—red (p. 405). The spark, i.e., light, is said to be "NOT INHERENT IN ELECTRICITY, BUT MERELY THE RESULT OF THE COMPRESSION OF THE AIR. THAT AIR IS VIOLENTLY AND SUDDENLY COMPRESSED WHEN AN ELECTRIC SPARK PASSES THROUGH IT" is proved by the experiment of Kinnersley in Philadelphia, according to which the spark produces "A SUDDEN RAREFACTION OF THE AIR IN THE TUBE",[b] and drives the water into the tube (p. 407). In Germany, 30 years ago, Winterl and others believed that the spark, or electric light, was "OF THE SAME NATURE WITH *FIRE*" and arises by the union of two electricities. Against which Thomson seriously proves that the place where the two electricities unite is precisely that where the light is least, and that it is two-thirds from the positive and one-third from the negative end! (Pp. 409-10.) That fire is here still something quite *mythical* is obvious.

With the same seriousness Thomson quotes the experiments of Dessaignes, according to which, with a rising barometer and falling temperature, glass, amber, silk, etc., become negatively electrified on being plunged into mercury, but positively electrified if the barometer is falling and the temperature rising, and in summer always become positive in impure, and always negative in pure, mercury; that in summer gold and various other metals become positive on warming and negative on cooling, the reverse being the case in winter; that they are "HIGHLY ELECTRIC" with a high barometer and northerly wind, positive if the temperature is rising, negative if falling, etc. (p. 416).[c]

How matters stood in regard to *heat*: "IN ORDER TO PRODUCE

----

a See this volume, p. 404.— *Ed.*
b Italics by Engels.— *Ed.*
c Cf. this volume, pp. 403-04.— *Ed.*

THERMO-ELECTRIC EFFECTS, IT IS NOT NECESSARY TO APPLY HEAT. ANYTHING *WHICH ALTERS THE TEMPERATURE*[a] IN ONE PART OF THE CHAIN, ... OCCASIONS A VARIATE IN THE DECLINATION OF THE MAGNET." For instance, the cooling of a metal by ice or evaporation of ether! (P. 419.)

The electro-chemical theory (p. 438) is accepted as "AT LEAST VERY INGENIOUS AND PLAUSIBLE".

Fabroni and Wollaston had already long ago, and Faraday recently, asserted that voltaic electricity is the simple consequence of chemical processes, and Faraday had even given the correct explanation of the shifting of atoms taking place in the liquid, and established that the quantity of electricity is to be measured by the quantity of the electrolytic product.

With the help of Faraday, Thomson arrives at the law

"that every atom must be naturally surrounded by the same quantities of electricities, *so that in this respect heat and electricity resemble each other*"![a] [P. 454.]

* * *

Static and dynamic electricity. Static or frictional electricity is the putting into a state of tension of the electricity *already existing* in nature in the *form* of electricity but in an equilibrated, neutral state. Hence the removal of this tension—if and in so far as the electricity during propagation can be conducted—also occurs at one stroke, by a spark, which re-establishes the neutral state.

Dynamic or voltaic electricity, on the other hand, is electricity produced by the conversion of chemical motion into electricity. Under certain definite conditions, it is produced by the solution of zinc, copper, etc. Here the tension is not acute, but chronic. At every moment new + and − electricity is produced from some other form of motion, and not already existing ± electricity separated into + and −. The process is a continuous one, and therefore too its result, electricity, does not take the form of instantaneous tension and discharge, but of a continuous current which can be reconverted at the poles into the chemical motion from which it arose, a process that is termed electrolysis. In this process, as well as in the production of electricity by chemical combination (in which electricity is liberated instead of heat, and in fact as much electricity as under other circumstances heat is set free, Guthrie, p. 210),[296] the current can be traced in the liquid (exchange of atoms in adjacent molecules—this is the current).

---

[a] Italics by Engels.—*Ed.*

This electricity, being of the nature of a current, for that very reason cannot be directly converted into static electricity. By means of induction, however, neutral electricity already existing as such can be de-neutralised. In the nature of things the induced electricity has to follow that which induces it, and therefore must likewise be of a flowing character. On the other hand, this obviously gives the possibility of condensing the current and of converting it into static electricity, or rather into a higher form that combines the property of a current with that of tension. This is solved by Ruhmkorff's machine. It provides an inductional electricity, which achieves this result.

* * *

A pretty example of the dialectics of nature is the way in which according to present-day theory the *repulsion of like* magnetic poles is explained by the *attraction of like* electric currents. (Guthrie, p. 264.)

* * *

Electro-chemistry. In describing the effect of the electric spark in chemical decomposition and synthesis, Wiedemann declares that this is more the concern of chemistry.[a] In the same case the chemists declare that it is rather a matter which concerns physics. Thus at the point of contact of molecular and atomic science, both declare themselves incompetent, while it is precisely *at this point that the greatest results are to be expected.*

* * *

Friction and impact produce an *internal* motion of the bodies concerned, molecular motion, differentiated as warmth, electricity, etc., according to circumstances. *This motion, however, is only temporary: cessante causa cessat effectus.*[b] At a definite stage they all become transformed into a *permanent molecular change, a chemical change.*

---

[a] G. Wiedemann, *Die Lehre vom Galvanismus und Elektromagnetismus,* Bd. II, S. 418.— *Ed.*

[b] Cessation of cause ceases its effect.— *Ed.*

[CHEMISTRY]

* * *

The notion of an actual *chemically uniform matter*—ancient as it is—fully corresponds to the childish view, widely held even up to Lavoisier, that the chemical affinity of two bodies depends on each one containing a common third body. (Kopp, *Entwickelung*, p. 105.)[a]

* * *

How old, convenient methods, adapted to previously customary practice, become transferred to other branches and there are a hindrance: in chemistry, the calculation of the composition of compounds in percentages, which was the most suitable method of all for making it impossible to discover the laws of constant proportion and multiple proportion in combination, and indeed did make them undiscoverable for long enough.

* * *

The new epoch begins in chemistry with atomistics (hence Dalton, not Lavoisier, is the father of modern chemistry[297]), and correspondingly in physics with the molecular theory (in a different form, but essentially representing only the other side of this process, with the discovery of the transformation of the forms of motion). The new atomistics is distinguished from all previous

---

[a] H. Kopp, *Die Entwickelung der Chemie in der neueren Zeit*, Abth. I.— *Ed.*

to it by the fact that it does not maintain (idiots excepted) that matter is *merely* discrete, but that the discrete parts at various stages (ether atoms, chemical atoms, masses, heavenly bodies) are various *nodal points* which determine the various *qualitative* modes of existence of matter in general—right down to weightlessness and repulsion.

* * *

Transformation of quantity into quality: the simplest example *oxygen and ozone,* where $2:3$ produces quite different properties, even in regard to smell. Chemistry likewise explains the other allotropic bodies merely by a difference in the number of atoms in the molecule.

* * *

The significance of *names.* In organic chemistry the significance of a body, hence also its name, is no longer determined merely by its composition, but rather by its position in the *series* to which it belongs. If we find, therefore, that a body belongs to such a series, its old name becomes an obstacle to understanding it and must be replaced by a *series name* (paraffins, etc.).

[BIOLOGY]

* * *

Reaction. Mechanical, physical (ALIAS heat, etc.) reaction is exhausted with each occurrence of reaction. Chemical reaction alters the composition of the reacting body and is only renewed if a further quantity of the latter is added. Only the *organic* body reacts *independently*—of course within its sphere of power (sleep), and assuming the supply of nourishment—but this supply of nourishment is effective only after it has been assimilated, not immediately as at lower stages, so that here the organic body has an *independent* power of reaction, the new reaction must be *mediated* by it.

* * *

Life and death. Already no physiology is held to be scientific if it does not consider death as an essential element of life (note: Hegel, *Encyclopädie*, I, pp. 152-53),[298] the *negation* of life as being essentially contained in life itself, so that life is always thought of in relation to its necessary result, death, which is always contained in it in germ. The dialectical conception of life is nothing more than this. But for anyone who has once understood this, all talk of the immortality of the soul is done away with. Death is either the dissolution of the organic body, leaving nothing behind but the chemical constituents that formed its substance, or it leaves behind a vital principle, more or less the soul, that then survives *all* living organisms, and not only human beings. Here, therefore, by means of dialectics, simply becoming clear about the nature of life and death suffices to abolish an ancient superstition. Living means dying.

* * *

Generatio aequivoca.[a] All investigations hitherto amount to the following: in fluids containing organic matter in decomposition and accessible to the air, lower organisms arise, Protista, Fungi, Infusoria. Where do they come from? Have they arisen by *generatio aequivoca,* or from germs brought in from the atmosphere? Consequently the investigation is limited to a quite narrow field, to the question of plasmogony.[299]

The assumption that new living organisms can arise by the decomposition of others belongs essentially to the epoch of immutable species. At that time men found themselves compelled to assume the origin of all organisms, even the most complicated, by original generation from non-living materials, and if they did not want to resort to the aid of an act of creation, they easily arrived at the view that this process is more readily explicable given a formative material already derived from the organic world; no one any longer believed in the production of a mammal directly from inorganic matter by chemical means.

This assumption, however, directly conflicts with the present state of science. By the analysis of the process of decomposition in dead organic bodies chemistry proves that at each successive step this process necessarily produces products that are more and more dead, that are more and more close to the inorganic world, products that are less and less capable of being used by the organic world, and that this process can be given another direction, such utilisation being able to occur only when these products of decomposition are absorbed early enough in an appropriate, already existing, organism. It is precisely the most essential vehicle of cell-formation, protein, that decomposes first of all, and so far it has never been built up again.

Still more. The organisms whose original generation from organic fluids is the question at issue in these investigations, while being of a comparatively low order, are nevertheless definitely differentiated, bacteria, yeasts, etc., with a life-cycle composed of various phases and in part, as in the case of the Infusoria, equipped with fairly well developed organs. They are all at least unicellular. But ever since we have been acquainted with the structureless Monera,[300] it has become foolish to desire to explain the origin of even a single cell directly from dead matter instead

---

[a] Spontaneous generation.— *Ed.*

of from structureless living protein, to believe it is possible by means of a little stinking water to force nature to accomplish in twenty-four hours what it has cost her thousands of years to bring about.

Pasteur's experiments [301] in this direction are useless; for those who believe in this possibility he will never be able to prove the impossibilty by these experiments alone, but they are important because they furnish much enlightenment on these organisms, their life, their germs, etc.

* * *

MORIZ WAGNER,
NATURWISSENSCHAFTLICHE STREITFRAGEN, I

(Augsburg *Allgemeine Zeitung,* Beilage,
October 6, 7, 8, 1874) [302]

Liebig's statement to Wagner towards the end of his life (1868):

"We may only assume that life is just as old and just as eternal as matter itself, and the whole controversial point about the origin of life seems to me to be disposed of by this simple assumption. In point of fact, why should not organic life be thought of as present from the very beginning just as much as carbon and *its* compounds[a]"(!), "or as the whole of uncreatable and indestructible matter in general, and the forces that are eternally bound up with the motion of matter in universal space?"

Liebig said further (Wagner believes November 1868)

that he, too, regards the hypothesis that organic life has been "imported" on to our planet from universal space as "acceptable".

Helmholtz (Preface to Thomson's *Handbuch der theoretischen Physik,* German edition, part II):

"It appears to me to be a fully correct procedure, *if all our efforts fail to cause the production of organisms from non-living matter,* to raise the question whether life has ever arisen, whether it is not just as old as matter, and whether its germs have not been transported from one heavenly body to another and have developed wherever they have found favourable soil." [P. XI.][b]

---

[a] Here and below italics in quotations are by Engels.— *Ed.*
[b] Engels quotes Preface according to Wagner's article.— *Ed.*

Wagner:

"The fact that matter is indestructible and imperishable, that it ... can by no force be reduced to nothing, *suffices for the chemist to regard it also as 'uncreatable'* .... But, according to the now prevailing view"(?), "life is regarded merely as a 'property' inherent in certain simple elements, of which the lowest organisms consist, and which, as a matter of course, must be as old, i.e., as originally existing, as these basic stuffs and *their compounds*" (!!) "themselves. In this sense one could also speak of vital force, as Liebig does (*Chemische Briefe*, 4th edition), namely as 'a formative principle in and together with the physical forces',[a] hence not acting outside of matter. This vital force as a 'property of matter', however, manifests itself ... only under appropriate conditions which have existed since eternity at innumerable points in infinite universal space, but which in the course of the different periods of time must often enough have changed their place in space." Hence no life is possible on the ancient fluid earth or the present-day sun, but the glowing bodies have enormously expanded atmospheres, consisting, according to recent views, of the same materials that fill all universal space in extremely rarefied form and are attracted by bodies. The rotating nebular mass from which the solar system developed, reaching beyond the orbit of Neptune, contained "also all water" (!) "dissolved in vaporous form in an atmosphere richly impregnated with carbonic *acid*" (!) "up to immeasurable heights, and with that also the basic materials for the existence" (?) "of the lowest organic germs"; in it there prevailed "most varied degrees of temperature in most varied regions, and hence the assumption is *fully justified* that at all times the conditions necessary for organic life were somewhere to be found. According to this the atmospheres of the heavenly bodies, like those of the rotating cosmic nebular masses, would have to be regarded as the permanent repositories of the living form, as the eternal breeding grounds of organic germs."—In the Andes, below the equator, the smallest living Protista with their invisible germs are still present in masses in the atmosphere up to 16,000 feet. Perty says that they are "almost omnipresent". They are only absent where the glowing heat kills them. For them (*Vibrionidae*, etc.) existence is conceivable "also in the vapour belt of *all* heavenly bodies, wherever the appropriate conditions are to be found".[b]

"According to Cohn,[c] bacteria are ... so extremely minute that 633 million can find room in a cubic millimetre, and 636,000 million weigh only a gram. The micrococci are even smaller," and perhaps they are not the smallest. But being very varied in shape, "the *Vibrionidae* ... sometimes globular, sometimes ovoid, sometimes rod-shaped or spiral" (already possess, therefore, a form that is of considerable importance). "Hitherto no valid objection has been raised against the well-founded hypothesis that all the multifarious, more highly organised living beings of both natural kingdoms *could* have developed and *must* have developed in the course of very long periods of time from such, *or similar*, extremely simple" (!!), "neutral, primordial beings, hovering between plants and animals ... on the basis of individual variability and the capacity for hereditary transmission of newly acquired characters to the offspring on alteration of the physical conditions of the heavenly bodies and on spatial separation of the individual varieties produced."

---

[a] G. Liebig, *Chemische Briefe*, Bd. I, S. 349, 372-73.—*Ed.*

[b] M. Perty, *Ueber die Grenzen der sichtbaren Schöpfung, nach den jetzigen Leistungen der Mikroskope und Fernröhre.*—*Ed.*

[c] F. Cohn, *Ueber Bacterien, die kleinsten lebenden Wesen*, S. 6, 8, 10, 11.—*Ed.*

Worth noting is the proof how much of a dilettante Liebig was in biology, although the latter is a science bordering on chemistry.

He read Darwin[a] for the first time in 1861, and only much later the important biological and palaeontological-geological works subsequent to Darwin. Lamarck[b] he had "never read". "Similarly the important palaeontological special researches which appeared even before 1859, of L. v. Buch, d'Orbigny, Münster, Klipstein, Hauer, and Quenstedt on the fossil Cephalodos, that throw such remarkable light on the genetic connection of the various creations, remained completely unknown to him. All the above-mentioned scientists were ... driven by the force of facts, almost against their will, to the Lamarckian hypothesis of descent", and this indeed *before* Darwin's book. "The theory of descent, therefore, had already quietly struck roots in the views of those scientists who had concerned themselves more closely with the comparative study of fossil organisms." As early as 1832, in *Über die Ammoniten und ihre Sonderung in Fomilien,,* and in 1848 in a paper read before the Berlin Academy,[c] L. v. Buch "very definitely introduced in the science of petrifacts" (!) "the Lamarckian idea of the typical relationship of organic forms as a sign of their common descent." In 1848 he based himself on his investigation of the ammonites for the declaration: "that the disappearance of old forms and the appearance of new ones is not a consequence of the total destruction of organic creations, but *that formation of new species out of older forms has most probably only resulted from altered conditions of life*".[d]

Comments. The above hypothesis of "eternal life" and of importation presupposes:

1. The eternal existence of protein.

2. The eternal existence of the original forms from which everything organic can develop. Both are inadmissible.

Ad 1.—Liebig's assertion that carbon compounds are just as eternal as carbon itself, is doubtful, if not false.

(a) Is carbon simple? If not, it is as such not eternal.

(b) The compounds of carbon are eternal in the sense that under the same conditions of mixture, temperature, pressure, electric potential, etc., they are always reproduced. But that, for instance, only the simplest carbon compounds, CO_2 or CH_4, should be eternal in the sense that they exist at all times and more or less in all places, and not rather that they are continually produced anew and pass out of existence again—in fact, out of the elements and into the elements—has hitherto not been

---

[a] Ch. Darwin, *On the Origin of Species....—Ed.*

[b] J.-B.-P.-A. de Monet de Lamarck, *Philosophie zoologique, ou exposition des considérations relatives à l'histoire naturelle des animaux.—Ed.*

[c] L. v. Buch, "Über Ceratiden", *Abhandlungen der Königlichen Akademie der Wissenschaften zu Berlin aus dem Jahre 1848. Physikalische Abhandlungen,* 1850, S. 19.—*Ed.*

[d] Italics by Engels.—*Ed.*

asserted. If living protein is eternal in the same sense as other carbon compounds, then it must not only continually be dissolved into its elements, as is well known to happen, but it must also continually be produced anew from the elements and without the collaboration of previously existing protein—and that is the exact opposite of the result at which Liebig arrives.

(c) Protein is the most unstable carbon compound known to us. It decomposes as soon as it loses the capacity of carrying out the functions peculiar to it, which we call life, and it is inherent in its nature that this incapacity should sooner or later make its appearance. And it is just this compound which is supposed to be eternal and able to endure all the changes of temperature, pressure, lack of nourishment, and air, etc., in universal space, although even its upper temperature limit is so low—less than 100° C! The conditions for the existence of protein are infinitely more complicated than those of any other known carbon compound, because not only physical and chemical functions, but in addition nutritive and respiratory functions, enter, requiring a medium which is narrowly delimited, physically and chemically— and is it this medium that one must suppose has maintained itself from eternity under all possible changes? Liebig "prefers, *ceteris paribus*,[a] the simpler of two hypotheses",[b] but a thing may appear very simple and yet be very complicated.—The assumption of innumerable continuous series of living protein bodies, tracing their descent from one another through all eternity, and which under all circumstances always leave sufficient over for the stock to remain well assorted, is the most complicated assumption possible.—Moreover, the atmospheres of the heavenly bodies, and especially nebular atmospheres, were originally glowing hot and therefore no place for protein bodies; hence in the last resort space must serve as the great reservoir—a reservoir in which there is neither air nor nourishment, and with a temperature at which certainly no protein can function or maintain itself!

Ad. 2.—The vibrios, micrococci, etc., which are referred to here, are beings already considerably differentiated—protein granules that have excreted an outer membrane, but *no nucleus.* The series of protein bodies capable of development, however, forms *a nucleus first of all* and becomes a cell—the cell membrane is then a further advance (*Amoeba sphaerococcus*). Hence the organisms under consideration here belong to a series which, by all previous

---

[a] Under other similar conditions.—*Ed.*
[b] M. Wagner, op. cit., *Allgemeine Zeitung*, No. 279, 1874, S. 4333.—*Ed.*

analogy, proceeds barrenly into a blind alley, and they cannot be numbered among the ancestors of the higher organisms.

What Helmholtz says of the sterility of attempts to produce life artificially is pure childishness. Life is the mode of existence of protein bodies, the essential element of which consists in *continual metabolic interchange with the natural environment outside them*, and which ceases with the cessation of this metabolism, bringing about the decomposition of the protein.* If success is ever attained in preparing protein bodies chemically, they will undoubtedly exhibit the phenomena of life and carry out metabolism, however weak and short-lived they may be.[a] But it is certain that such bodies could *at most* have the form of the very crudest Monera, and probably much lower forms, but by no means the form of organisms that have become differentiated by an evolution lasting thousands of years, and in which the cell membrane has become separated from the contents and a definite inherited form assumed. So long, however, as we know no more of the chemical composition of protein than we do at present, and therefore for probably another hundred years to come cannot think of its artificial preparation, it is ridiculous to complain that all our efforts, etc., "have failed"!

Against the above assertion that metabolism is the characteristic activity of protein bodies may be put the objection of the growth of Traube's "artificial cells".[303] But here there is merely unaltered absorption of a liquid by endosmosis, while metabolism consists in the absorption of substances, the chemical composition of which is altered, which are assimilated by the organism, and the residua of which are excreted together with the decomposition products of the organism itself resulting from the life process. (*N. B.*—Just as we have to speak of invertebrate vertebrates, so also here the unorganised, formless, undifferentiated granule of protein is termed an organism— *dialectically* this is permissible because just as the vertebral column is implicit in the notochord so in the protein granule on its first origin the whole infinite series of higher organisms lies included "*in itself*" as if in embryo.) The significance

---

* Such metabolism can also occur in the case of inorganic bodies and in the long run it occurs everywhere, since chemical reactions take place, even if extremely slowly, everywhere. The difference, however, is that inorganic bodies are destroyed by this metabolism, while in organic bodies it is the necessary condition for their existence.

---

[a] Cf. this volume, pp. 74-77 and 601-02.— *Ed.*

of Traube's "cells" lies in the fact that they show endosmosis and growth as two things which can be produced also in inorganic nature and without any carbon.

The newly arisen protein granule must have had the capacity of nourishing itself from oxygen, carbon dioxide, ammonia, and some of the salts dissolved in the surrounding water. Organic nutritive substances were not present, for the granules surely could not devour one another. This proves how high above them are the present-day Monera, even without nuclei, living on diatoms, etc., and therefore presupposing a whole series of differentiated organisms.

* * *

Dialectics of Nature—REFERENCES.
Nature, No. 294 et seq. Allman on Infusoria.[a] Unicellular character, important. Croll ON ICE PERIODS AND GEOLOGICAL TIME.[b]
Nature, No. 326, Tyndall on *Generatio.* Specific decay and fermentation experiments.[c]

* * *

Protista.[304] Non-cellular, begin with a simple granule of protein which extends and withdraws pseudopodia in one form or another, including the Monera. The Monera of the present day are certainly very different from the original forms, since for the most part they live on organic matter, swallowing diatoms and Infusoria (i.e., bodies higher than themselves and which only arose after them), and, as Haeckel's plate I[d] shows, have a developmental history and pass through the form of non-cellular ciliate swarm-spores.—The tendency towards form which characterises all protein bodies is already evident here. This tendency is more

---

[a] G. J. Allman, "Recent progress in our knowledge of the ciliate infusoria", *Nature,* Vol. XII, No. 294, June 17, 1875, pp. 136-37; No. 295, June 24, pp. 155-57; No. 296, July 1, pp. 175-77.— *Ed.*

[b] J. Croll, *Climate and Time in Their Geological Relations...,* and "Croll's *Climate and Time*" (signed: J. F. B.), *Nature,* Vol. XII, No. 294, June 17, 1875, pp. 121-23; No. 295, June 24, pp. 141-44.— *Ed.*

[c] J. Tyndall, "On Germs. On the optical deportment of the atmosphere in reference to the phenomena of putrefaction and infection", *Nature,* Vol. XIII, No. 326, January 27, 1876, pp. 252-54; No. 327, February 3, pp. 268-70.— *Ed.*

[d] E. Haeckel, *Natürlich Schöpfungsgeschichte,* S. 168-69, 664-65.— *Ed.*

prominent in the non-cellular *Foraminifera,* which excrete highly artistic shells (anticipating colonies? corals, etc.) and anticipate the higher molluscs in form just as the tubular Algae (*Siphoneae*) anticipate the trunk, stem, root, and leaf form of higher plants, although they are merely structureless protein. Hence *Protamoeba* is to be separated from *Amoeba.**

2. On the one hand there arises the distinction of skin (ectosarc) and medullary layer (endosarc) in the sun animalcule *Actinophrys sol* (Nicholson,[305] p. 49). The epidermal layer puts out pseudopodia (in *Protomyxa aurantiaca,* this stage is already a transitional one, see Haeckel, plate I). Along this line of evolution protein does not appear to have got very far.

3. On the other hand, the *nucleus* and *nucleolus* become differentiated in the protein—naked *Amoebae.* From now on the development of form proceeds apace. Similarly, the development of the young cell in the organism, cf. *Wundt* on this (at the beginning).[a] In *Amoeba sphaerococcus,* as in *Protomyxa,* the formation of the cell membrane is only a transitional phase, but even here there is already the beginning of the circulation in the contractile vacuole. [Haeckel, p. 380.] Sometimes we find either a shell of sand grains stuck together (*Difflugia,* Nicholson, p. 47) as in worms and insect larvae, sometimes a genuinely excreted shell. Finally,

4. *The cell with a permanent cell membrane.* According to Haeckel (p. 382), out of this has arisen depending on the hardness of the cell membrane, either plant, or in the case of a soft membrane, animal (? it certainly cannot be conceived so generally). With the cell membrane, definite and at the same time plastic form makes its appearance. Here again a distinction between simple cell membrane and excreted shell. But (in contrast to No. 3) the *putting out of pseudopodia* stops with this cell membrane and this shell. Repetition of earlier forms (ciliate swarm-spores) and diversity of form. The transition is provided by the *Labyrinthuleae* (Haeckel, p. 385), which deposit their pseudopodia outside and creep about in this network with alteration of the normal spindle shape kept within definite limits.—The *Gregarinae* anticipate the mode of life of higher parasites—some are already no longer single cells but *chains* of cells (Haeckel, p. 451), but only

---

* Individualisation small, they divide and also fuse. [Marginal note.]

---

[a] Engels presumably refers to W. Wundt, *Lehrbuch der Physiologie des Menschen,* S. 14.— *Ed.*

containing 2-3 cells—a weak beginning. The highest development
of unicellular organisms is in the Infusoria, in so far as these are
really unicellular. Here a considerable differentiation (see Nicholson). Once again colonies and zoophytes[306] (*Epistylis*). Among
unicellular plants likewise a high development of form (*De-
smidiaceae*, Haeckel, p. 410).*

5. The next advance is the union of several cells into *one* body,
no longer colony. First of all, the *Katallaktae* of Haeckel,
Magosphaera planula (Haeckel, p. 384), where the union of the
cells is only a phase in development. But here also there are
already no pseudopodia (whether there are any as a transitional
phase Haeckel does not state exactly). On the other hand, the
Radiolaria, also undifferentiated masses of cells, have retained
their pseudopodia and have developed to the highest extent the
geometric regularity of the shell, which plays a part even among
the genuinely non-cellular rhizopods. The protein surrounds itself,
so to speak, with its crystalline form.

6. *Magosphaera planula* forms the transition to the true *Planula*
and *Gastrula,* etc. Further details in Haeckel (p. 452 et seq.).[307]

* * *

Bathybius.[308] The stones in its flesh are proof that the original
form of protein, still lacking any differentiation of form, already
bears within it the germ of and capacity for skeletal formation.

* * *

The individual. This concept also has been dissolved into
something purely relative. Cormus, colony, tapeworm—on the
other hand, cell and metamere as individuals in a certain sense
(*Anthropogenie* and *Morphologie*).[309]

* * *

The whole of organic nature is one continuous proof of the
identity or inseparability of form and content. Morphological and
physiological phenomena, form and function, mutually determine

---

* Rudiment of higher differentiation. [Marginal note.]

one another. The differentiation of form (the cell) determines differentiation of substance into muscle, skin, bone, epithelium, etc., and the differentiation of substance in turn determines difference of form.

* * *

Repetition of morphological forms at all stages of evolution: cell forms (the two essential ones already in *Gastrula*)—metamere formation at a certain stage: annelids, arthropods, vertebrates.—In the tadpoles of amphibians the primitive form of ascidian larvae is repeated.—Various forms of marsupials, which recur among placentals (even counting only existing marsupials).

* * *

For the entire evolution of organism the law of acceleration according to the square of the distance in time from the point of departure is to be accepted. Cf. Haeckel, *Schöpfungsgeschichte* and *Anthropogenie,* the organic forms corresponding to the various geological periods. The higher, the more rapid the process.

* * *

The Darwinian theory to be demonstrated as the practical proof of Hegel's account of the inner connection between necessity and chance.[a]

* * *

The struggle for existence. Above all this must be strictly limited to the struggles resulting from plant and animal *over-population,* which do in fact occur at certain stages of plant and lower animal life. But one must keep sharply distinct from it the conditions in which species alter, old ones die out and newly evolved ones take their place, *without* this over-population: e.g., on the migration of animals and plants into new regions where new conditions of

---

[a] Cf. this volume, pp. 498-501.— *Ed.*

climate, soil, etc., bring about the alteration. If *there* the individuals which become adapted survive and develop into a new species by continually increasing adaptation, while the other more stable individuals die away and finally die out, and with them the imperfect intermediate stages, then this can and does proceed *without any Malthusianism*, and if the latter should occur here at all it makes no change to the process, at most it can accelerate it.—Similarly with the gradual alteration of the geographical, climatic, etc., conditions in a given region (drying up of Central Asia for instance). Whether the members of the animal or plant population there exert pressure on one another is a matter of indifference; the process of evolution of the organisms that is determined by this alteration proceeds all the same.—It is the same for sexual selection, in which case, too, Malthusianism is quite unconcerned.—

Hence also Haeckel's "adaptation and heredity" can bring about the whole process of evolution, without need for selection and Malthusianism.

Darwin's mistake lies precisely in lumping together in "NATURAL SELECTION *OR* THE SURVIVAL OF THE FITTEST" [a] two absolutely separate things:

1. Selection by the pressure of over-population, where perhaps the strongest survive in the first place, but can also be the weakest in many respects.

2. Selection by greater capacity of adaptation to altered circumstances, where the survivors are better suited to these *circumstances*, but where this adaptation as a whole can mean regress just as well as progress (for instance adaptation to parasitic life is *always* regress).

The main thing: that each advance in organic evolution is at the same time a regression, fixing *one-sided* evolution and excluding the possibility of evolution in many other directions.

This, however, *a basic law.*

* * *

THE STRUGGLE FOR LIFE.[310] Until Darwin, what was stressed by his present adherents was precisely the harmonious co-operative working of organic nature, how the plant kingdom supplies animals with nourishment and oxygen, and animals supply plants

---

[a] A reference to the title of Chapter IV of Darwin's *On the Origin of Species*....—*Ed.*

with manure, ammonia, and carbonic acid. Hardly was Darwin recognised before these same people saw everywhere nothing but *struggle*. Both views are justified within narrow limits, but both are equally one-sided and prejudiced. The interaction of bodies in non-living nature includes both harmony and collisions, that of living bodies conscious and unconscious co-operation as well as conscious and unconscious struggle. Hence, even in regard to nature, it is not permissible one-sidedly to inscribe only "struggle" on one's banners. But it is absolutely childish to desire to sum up the whole manifold wealth of historical development and complexity in the meagre and one-sided phrase "struggle for existence." That says less than nothing.

The whole Darwinian theory of the struggle for existence is simply the transference from society to organic nature of Hobbes' theory of *bellum omnium contra omnes*[a] and of the economic theory of competition, as well as the Malthusian theory of population. When once this feat has been accomplished (the unconditional justification for which, especially as regards the Malthusian theory, is still very questionable), it is very easy to transfer these theories back again from natural history to the history of society, and altogether too naïve to maintain that thereby these assertions have been proved as eternal natural laws of society.

Let us accept for a moment the phrase "struggle for existence", FOR ARGUMENT'S SAKE. The most that the animal can achieve is to *collect*; man *produces*, he prepares the means of subsistence, in the widest sense of the words, which without him nature would not have produced. This makes impossible any unqualified transference of the laws of life in animal societies to human society. Production soon brings it about that the so-called STRUGGLE FOR EXISTENCE no longer turns on pure means of existence, but on means of enjoyment and development. Here—where the means of development are socially produced—the categories taken from the animal kingdom are already totally inapplicable. Finally, under the capitalist mode of production, production reaches such a high level that society can no longer consume the means of subsistence, enjoyment and development that have been produced, because for the great mass of producers access to these means is artificially and forcibly barred; and therefore every ten years a crisis restores the equilibrium by destroying not only the means of subsistence, enjoyment and development that have been produced, but also a

---

[a] A war of all against all. T. Hobbes, *Elementa philosophica de cive* [Praefatio ad lectores].— *Ed.*

great part of the productive forces themselves. Hence the so-called struggle for existence assumes *the* form: to *protect* the products and productive forces produced by bourgeoîs capitalist society against the destructive, ravaging effect of this capitalist social order, by taking control of social production and distribution out of the hands of the ruling capitalist class, which has become incapable of this function, and transferring it to the producing masses—and that is the socialist revolution.

The conception of history as a series of class struggles is already much richer in content and deeper than merely reducing it to weakly distinguished phases of the struggle for existence.

* * *

Vertebrates. Their essential character: *the grouping of the whole body about the nervous system.* Thereby the development of self-consciousness, etc., becomes possible. In all other animals the nervous system is a secondary affair, here it is the basis of the whole organisation; the nervous system, when developed to a certain extent—by posterior elongation of the head ganglion of the worms—takes possession of the whole body and organises it according to its needs.

* * *

When Hegel makes the transition from life to cognition by means of propagation (reproduction),[a] there is to be found in this the germ of the theory of evolution, that, organic life once given, it must evolve by the development of the generations to a genus of thinking beings.

* * *

What Hegel calls reciprocal action is the *organic body*, which, therefore, also forms the transition to consciousness, i.e., from necessity to freedom, to the idea (see *Logik*, II, conclusion).[b]

---

[a] G. W. F. Hegel, *Wissenschaft der Logik*, Th. 2. Die Subjective Logik, oder: Die Lehre vom Begriff, S. 254.— *Ed.*

[b] Ibid., S. 236-54.— *Ed.*

* * *

Rudiments in nature. Insect states (the ordinary ones do not go beyond purely natural conditions), here even a social rudiment. Ditto productive animals with tools (bees, etc., beavers), but still only subsidiary things and without total effect.—Even earlier: colonies of corals and Hydrozoa, where the individual is at most an intermediate stage and the fleshy COMMUNITY mostly a stage of the full development. See Nicholson.[a]—Similarly, the Infusoria, the highest, and in part very much differentiated, form which a single cell can achieve.

* * *

Work.—The mechanical theory of heat has transferred this category from political economy into physics (for *physiologically* it is still a long way from having been scientifically determined), but in so doing it becomes defined in quite a different way, as seen even from the fact that only a very slight, subordinate part of economic work (lifting of loads, etc.) can be expressed in kilogram-metres. Nevertheless, there is an inclination to re-transfer the thermodynamical definition of work to the sciences from which the category was derived, with a different determination. For instance, without further ado to identify it *brutto*[b] with physiological work, as in Fick and Wislicenus' Faulhorn experiment,[311] in which the lifting of a human body, of *disons*[c] 60 kgs, to a height of *disons* 2,000 metres, i.e., 120,000 kilogram-metres, is supposed to express the *physiological* work done. In the physiological work done, however, it makes an enormous difference *how* this lifting is effected: whether by positive lifting of the load, by mounting vertical ladders, or whether along a road or stair with 45° slope (=militarily impracticable terrain), or along a road with a slope of $^1/_{18}$ hence a length of about 36 kms (but this is questionable, if the same time is allowed in all cases). At any rate, however, in all practicable cases a forward motion also is combined with the lifting, and indeed where the road is quite level this is fairly considerable and as physiological work it cannot be put equal to zero. In some places there even appears to be not a little desire to re-import the thermodynamical category of work back into

---

[a] H. A. Nicholson, *A Manual of Zoology*..., pp. 32 and 102.— *Ed.*

[b] Crudely.— *Ed.*

[c] Say.— *Ed.*

political economy (as with the Darwinists and the struggle for existence), the result of which would be nothing but nonsense. Let someone try to convert any SKILLED LABOUR into kilogram-metres and then to determine wages on this basis! Physiologically considered, the human body contains organs which in their totality, *from one aspect*, can be regarded as a thermodynamical machine, where heat is supplied and converted into motion. But even if one presupposes constant conditions as regards the other bodily organs, it is questionable whether physiological work done, even lifting, can be at once fully expressed in kilogram-metres, since within the body *internal* work is performed at the same time which does not appear in the result. For the body is not a steam-engine, which only undergoes friction and wear and tear. Physiological work is only possible with continued chemical changes in the body itself, depending also on the process of respiration and the work of the heart. Along with every muscular contraction or relaxation, chemical changes occur in the nerves and muscles, and these changes cannot be treated as parallel to those of coal in a steam-engine. One can, of course, compare two instances of physiological work that have taken place under otherwise identical conditions, but one cannot measure the physical work of a man according to the work of a steam-engine, etc.; their external results, yes, but not the processes themselves without considerable reservations.

(All this has to be thoroughly revised.)

[TITLES AND TABLES OF CONTENTS
OF THE FOLDERS[312]]

[FIRST FOLDER]

Dialectics and Natural Science

[SECOND FOLDER]

The Investigation of Nature and Dialectics

1) Notes: a) On the Prototypes of the Mathematical
   Infinite in the Real World
   b) On the "Mechanical" Conception of Nature
   c) On Nageli's Incapacity to Know the Infinite
2) Old Preface to [*Anti*]-*Dühring*. On Dialectics
<3) Natural Science and the Spirit World> [a]
4) The Part Played by Labour in the Transition from Ape to
   Man
<Basic Forms of Motion> [a]
5) Omitted from *Feuerbach*

[THIRD FOLDER]

Dialectics of Nature

1) Basic Forms of Motion
2) Two Measures of Motion
3) Electricity and Magnetism
4) Natural Science and the Spirit World
5) Old Introduction
6) Tidal Friction

[FOURTH FOLDER]

Mathematics and Natural Science. Miscellaneous

---

[a] This heading is crossed out in the manuscript, for Engels decided to transfer
it to the third folder.— *Ed.*

FROM THE PREPARATORY
MATERIALS

FROM ENGELS' PREPARATORY WRITINGS
FOR *ANTI-DÜHRING*[313]

[INTRODUCTION. A ROUGH OUTLINE][314]

Modern socialism, although it arose essentially from the recognition of the class antagonisms existing in the society found at hand between proprietors and non-proprietors, workers and exploiters, appears, however, in its theoretical form at first as a more logical and further extension of the principles laid down by the great French philosophers of the eighteenth century, socialism's first representatives, Morelly and Mably, having also belonged among them. Like every new theory, modern socialism had, at first, to connect itself with the intellectual stock-in-trade, ready to its hand, however deeply its roots lay in material facts.

The great men, who in France prepared men's minds for the coming revolution, were themselves extreme revolutionists. None of the existing authorities had validity for them. Everything, including religion, natural science, political institutions, and society, was subjected to the most unsparing criticism. Everything must justify its existence before the supreme court of reason, or give up existence. Reason was put forward as the sole measure. It was the time when, as Hegel says, the world stood upon its *head*; first in the sense that man's head and the principles arrived at by means of thought wished to be recognised as the basis of all human views, action and association, and then later, in the sense that, as reality was found to contradict these principles completely, things were, in fact, turned upside down. Every form of society and government then existing, every old traditional view was denounced as being irrational and was thrown out; the world had hitherto allowed itself to be led by absurd prejudices; now, for the first time, the light of day dawned, reason reigned and the whole past deserved only pity and contempt.

We know today that this kingdom of reason was nothing more than the idealised kingdom of the bourgeoisie, that this eternal Right then proclaimed found its corresponding realisation in bourgeois justice; that the government of reason, the Contrat Social of Rousseau, came into being, and only could come into being, as a democratic bourgeois republic. The great thinkers of the eighteenth century could, no more than those of former ages, go beyond the limits imposed upon them by their epoch.

But, side by side with the antagonism between the nobility, monarchy and the burghers, was the general antagonism of exploiters and exploited, of poor workers and rich idlers, and it was precisely this circumstance that made it possible for the representatives of the bourgeoisie to put themselves forward as representing suffering humanity; there also existed, though as yet undeveloped and not in the foreground, the contradiction between workers and capitalists. This prompted individual minds to go further in their criticism, to demand equality not only of political rights, but also of social standing, and to demand the abolition of class differences. Both directions were interwoven with Saint-Simon; the latter predominated with the French ascetic communists; while Owen systematically, in the country with the most developed capitalist production and the contradictions created by it, developed it in direct relation to French materialism.

Right from its beginnings, bourgeois development possessed this inherent contradiction. Thomas Münzer, the Levellers.[315] Thomas More's *Utopia*, and so on.

The new transformation of society was again supposed to be based on the eternal laws of reason and justice, but these are as different from those of the bourgeois French philosophers as heaven from hell. A world constructed by these philosophers and according to their principles is quite as irrational and unjust, so it was disposed of just as readily as all the earlier forms of society and government. And if pure reason and justice have not, hitherto, ruled the world, this has been the result of the as yet incorrect understanding of them. What was wanted was the individual man of genius, who has now arisen and understands the truth; the fact that he has arisen is not an inevitable event, a necessary link in the chain of human development, but a mere happy incident. He might just as well have been born 500 years earlier, and might then have spared humanity 500 years of suffering and error.

This mode of outlook is essentially that of all English, French and of the first German socialists, including Weitling. Socialism is the expression of absolute truth, reason and justice and has only to be discovered to conquer all the world; but when precisely it is discovered is a matter of pure chance. And in this process absolute reason, truth, and justice are different with the founder of each individual school—compare Owen, Fourier, the Saint-Simonists, Louis Blanc, Proudhon, Pierre Leroux, and Weitling; and since the criterion of truth and justice for each of them is his own subjective understanding, the subjective measure of his knowledge and his intellectual training, the only possible outcome is that they mutually erode one another. To make science of socialism, it had to be placed upon a real basis and be provided with firm, unshakable foundation. And this was done by Marx.

Meanwhile, alongside and after French eighteenth-century philosophy, the new German philosophy which culminated in Hegel had arisen. Its greatest merit was the taking up again of dialectics as the highest form of reasoning. The old Greek philosophers were all born natural dialecticians, and Aristotle, the Hegel of the Ancient World, had already analysed the most essential forms of dialectic thought. The newer philosophy, on the other hand, although it also had brilliant exponents of the dialectic (Descartes and Spinoza, for example), was, especially through English influence, become rigidly fixed in the metaphysical mode of reasoning, which also dominated the French of the eighteenth century. Metaphysical reasoning considers things and their mental reflexes, ideas, as isolated, one after the other and apart from each other, as objects of investigation fixed, rigid, given once for all. A thing either is or is not; a thing cannot be, at one and the same time, both itself, and something else. This mode of thought, luminous at first sight, was the metaphysical one. Dialectics, on the other hand, is not satisfied with this; it interprets things and concepts in their interdependence, in their interrelations, in their interaction and their consequent changes, in their emergence, development and demise. Since things do not, however, exist on their own in the world, but affect and influence one another, change, appear and disappear, it is easy to understand that metaphysical thought, although correct in certain very broad, but, at the same time, restricted areas, the scale of which is determined by the nature of the given circumstances, sooner or later reaches, in every area, a limit beyond which it becomes one-sided, limited, *abstract*, and falls into irresolvable contradictions, out of which only dialectics can help it. For everyday purposes, we know, e.g., whether an animal is alive or not; closer inquiry cannot establish absolutely when it began to exist. The jurists know this; they have vainly tried to determine a limit beyond which the killing of a human embryo is murder (and it is just as impossible to determine absolutely the moment of physiological death, which is a protracted process with many stages, as can be read in any physiology textbook). In the same way, every organic being is every moment the same and not the same; every moment some cells die and others are built anew, so the individual is always the same and, at the same time, something else. An exact representation of the universe, of its evolution, of the development of mankind, and of its reflection in the human mind, can therefore only be obtained through a dialectical approach, with constant regard to the innumerable actions and reactions of the life and death, of progressive or retrogressive changes. And this is how the new German philosophy has worked. Kant turned Newton's stable solar system and its eternal duration, once it had been given the initial impulse, into the result of a historic process of the formation of the sun and all the planets out of an original nebulous mass, a hypothesis that was mathematically substantiated in all its details fifty years later by Laplace and is now accepted by all natural scientists. Hegel completed this philosophy, by creating a system in which the whole world, natural, historical, intellectual, is represented as a *process*, i.e. as in constant motion, change, transformation, development. From this viewpoint the history of mankind no longer appeared as a chaotic jumble of senseless acts of violence, all equally standing condemned before the philosophers' now mature reason, and which are best forgotten as quickly as possible—in comparison with the light of eternal truth that had now dawned—but as the process of evolution of man himself. It was now the task of philosophy to reveal the gradual march of this process through all its devious ways, and to follow the inner law running through all its apparently accidental phenomena.

Whether or not Hegel solved this problem is immaterial here. His merit was that he propounded it. He could not possibly have solved it, however, since he was an idealist, i.e., for him thoughts were not pictures of things, but, conversely, things and their evolution were only the realised pictures of the "Idea", existing somewhere from eternity before the world was. And this, together with the subjective limitations of its creator, is what destroyed the Hegelian system.

The Hegelian system was the last and most consummate form of philosophy, in so far as the latter is represented as a special science superior to every other. All philosophy collapsed with this system. But there has remained the dialectic method of thinking and the conception that the natural, historical and intellectual world moves and transforms itself endlessly in a constant process of becoming and passing away. Not only philosophy but *all* sciences were now required to discover the laws of motion of this constant process of transformation, each in its particular domain. And this was the legacy which Hegelian philosophy bequeathed to its successors.

Meanwhile, the development of capitalist production had advanced with giant strides, especially in its first homeland— England. The antagonism between the bourgeois and the proletarians was becoming more and more acute; in 1842 the Chartist movement reached its peak, and facts more and more strenuously gave the lie to the teachings of bourgeois economy. In France, the Lyons insurrection of 1834[316] had likewise proclaimed the struggle of the proletariat against the bourgeoisie. The English and French socialist theories acquired historic importance and were bound to have their repercussions and criticism in Germany as well, although industry there was only just beginning to climb out of the stage of small-scale production. The theoretical socialism that now took shape, rather among Germans than in Germany, had therefore to import all its material in fact to [...][a]

Written by Engels in autumn 1876

First published in: *Marx/Engels Gesamtausgabe.* F. Engels, *Herrn Eugen Dührings Umwälzung der Wissenschaft/Dialektik der Natur.* Sonderausgabe. Moscow-Leningrad, 1935

Printed according to the manuscript

Published in English for the first time

---

[a] Here the manuscript breaks off.— *Ed.*

596

PART ONE

To Part I[a]

Ch. III

[Ideas—Reflections of Reality]

All ideas are taken from experience, are reflections—true or distorted—of reality.

Ch. III, pp. 33-34

[Material World and Laws of Thought]

Two kinds of experience—external, material, and internal—laws of thought and forms of thought. Forms of thought also partly inherited by development (self-evidence, for instance, of mathematical axioms for Europeans, certainly not for Bushmen and Australian Negroes).

If our premises are correct and we apply the laws of thought correctly to them, the result must tally with reality, just as a calculation in analytical geometry must tally with the geometrical construction, although the two are entirely different methods. Unfortunately, however, this is almost never the case, and if so, only in very simple operations.

The external world, in its turn, is either nature or society.

Ch. III, pp. 33-34; Ch. IV, pp. 39-42; and Ch. X, pp. 88-89

[Relation of Thinking and Being]

The sole content of thinking is the world and the laws of thought.

---

[a] The part and chapter references, and also the page references for the corresponding excerpts from this volume, have been provided by the Institute of Marxism-Leninism of the CC CPSU.— *Ed.*

The general results of the investigation of the world are obtained at the end of this investigation, hence are not *principles,* points of departure, but *results,* conclusions. To construct the latter in one's head, take them as the basis from which to start, and then reconstruct the world from them in one's head is *ideology,* an ideology which tainted every species of materialism hitherto existing; because while in *nature* the relation of thinking to being was certainly to some extent clear to materialism, in history it was not, nor did materialism realise the dependence of all thought upon the historical material conditions obtaining at the particular time.—As Dühring proceeds from "principles" instead of facts he is an ideologist, and can screen his being one only by formulating his propositions in such general and vacuous terms that they appear *axiomatic, flat.* Moreover, nothing can be concluded from them; one can only read something *into* them. Thus, for instance, the principle of *sole being.* The unity of the world and the nonsense of a hereafter are a result of the whole investigation of the world but are here to be proved *a priori,* proceeding from an *axiom of thought.* Hence bosh.—But without this turning around *a philosophy apart is impossible.*

Ch. III, pp. 35-36

[The World as a Coherent Whole. Knowledge of the World]

Systematics[a] impossible after Hegel. The world clearly constitutes a single system, i.e., a coherent whole, but the knowledge of this system presupposes a knowledge of *all* nature and history, which man will *never* attain. Hence he who makes systems must fill in the countless gaps with *figments of his own imagination,* i.e., engage in *irrational* fancies, ideologise.

Rational fantasy—*alias* combination!

Ch. III, pp. 36-39

[Mathematical Operations and Purely Logical Operations]

Calculative reason—*calculating machine!*—Curious confusion of mathematical operations, which are capable of material demonstra-

---

[a] Here in the sense of building up an absolutely completed system.—*Ed.*

tion, of proof because they are based on direct, even if abstract, material contemplation, with *purely* logical ones, which are capable only of proof by deduction, hence are incapable of the positive certainty possessed by mathematical operations—and how many of them wrong! Machine for *integration*; cf. Andrews' speech, *Nature*, Sept. 7, 76.[317]

Scheme=stereotype.

Ch. III, pp. 36-38; Ch. IV, pp. 39-41

[Reality and Abstraction]

It is just as impossible for Dühring to prove the exclusive *materiality* of all being with the aid of the proposition of the oneness of all-embracing being, which the Pope and the Sheikh-ul-Islam[318] can subscribe to without detracting from their infallibility and religion, as it is impossible for him to construct a triangle or a sphere or derive the Pythagorean theorem from any mathematical axiom. Both require real preconditions and it is only upon an investigation of these that the above results are arrived at. The certainty that no spiritual world exists separately, besides the material world, is the result of a long and wearisome investigation of the real world, *y compris*[a] of the products and processes of the human brain. The results of geometry are nothing but the natural properties of the various lines, planes and solids or their combinations, which for the most part occurred in nature long before man existed (Radiolaria, insects, crystals, etc.).

Ch. VI, p. 55 et seqq.

[Motion as the Mode of Existence of Matter]

Motion is the mode of existence of matter, hence more than a mere property of it. There is no matter without motion, nor could there ever have been. Motion in cosmic space, mechanical motion of smaller masses on a single celestial body, the vibration of molecules as heat, electric tension, magnetic polarisation, chemical decomposition and combination, organic life up to its highest product, thought—at each given moment each individual atom of matter is in one or other of these forms of motion. All equilibrium is either only relative rest or even motion in equilibrium, like that

---

[a] Inclusive.— *Ed.*

of the planets. Absolute rest is only conceivable in the absence of matter. Neither motion as such nor any of its forms, such as mechanical force, can therefore be separated from matter nor opposed to it as something apart or alien, without leading to an absurdity.

Ch. VII, pp. 65-67

[Natural Selection]

Dühring ought to rejoice over NATURAL SELECTION, as it furnishes the best illustration of his theory of conscious end and means.— Whereas Darwin inquires into the *form,* natural selection, in which a slow alteration takes place, Dühring demands that Darwin should also name the *cause* of the alteration, of which Herr Dühring likewise knows nothing. No matter what progress science has made, Herr Dühring will always declare that something is still lacking and so will have ample grounds for grumbling.

Ch. VII

[On Darwin]

How great is the stature of the thoroughly modest Darwin, who not only collects, arranges and elaborates thousands of facts from the whole of biology but takes delight in quoting any predecessor, however insignificant, even to the diminution of his own glory, in comparison with that braggadocio Dühring, who while contributing nothing of value himself is over-exacting of others, and who....

Ch. VII, pp. 66-67; Ch. VIII, p. 74

Dühringiana. Darwinism, p. 115.[a]

Adaptation of plants is a combination of physical forces or chemical agents; hence, no adaptation. If, "in growing, a plant takes the path along which it will receive most light", it does so in various ways and by various means, which differ according to its species and peculiarities. The physical forces and chemical agents, however, act differently here in each plant and help the plant,

---

[a] The pages given refer to Dühring's *Cursus der Philosophie als streng wissenschaftlicher Weltanschauung und Lebensgestaltung.—Ed.*

which after all is something other than these "chemical and physical, etc.", to get the light it needs in the way that has become peculiar to it by lengthy precedent evolution. Indeed, this light acts as a stimulus on the plant cells and sets in motion within them, as a response, precisely those forces and agents.* Since this process goes on in an organic cellular structure and assumes the form of stimulation and response, which occurs here just as it does in transmission by nerves in the human brain, the identical expression, adaptation, fits in both cases. And if adaptation is to be accomplished absolutely through the medium of consciousness, where do consciousness and adaptation begin and where do they end? With the moneron, with the insect-eating plant, with the sponge, with the coral, with the first nerve? Dühring would do a very great favour to natural scientists of the old stripe if he should draw this boundary line. Protoplasm stimulation and protoplasm response are to be found wherever there is living protoplasm. And since the influence of slowly changing stimuli calls forth change in the protoplasm too, otherwise it would perish, the same expression, adaptation, *must* be applied to all organic bodies.

Ch. VII, p. 66 et seqq.

[Adaptation and Heredity]

With regard to the evolution of the species, Haeckel perceives adaptation as negative, or altering; heredity as positive, or preserving factor. Dühring on the contrary states (p. 122) that heredity also has negative results, produces *alterations.* (Besides, nice trash about preformation.[319]) Now nothing is easier than to turn such opposites, like all other opposites of this kind, around and prove that adaptation, precisely by altering the *form*, preserves the essence, the *organ itself,* while heredity, by the fact alone of the mixture of two individuals different each time, constantly brings about changes the accumulation of which does not exclude a change in species. As a matter of fact, the results of adaptation are also inherited! But this does not get us one step further. We must take the *facts of the case* as they are and investigate them, and then we shall of course find that Haeckel is quite right in considering heredity essentially the conservative, positive side of the process and adaptation, its revolutionising, negative side. Domestication

---

* And among animals, too, spontaneous adaptation is most important. [Marginal note.]

and breeding as well as spontaneous adaptation speak louder here than all of Dühring's "subtle conceptions".

Ch. VIII, pp. 75-77

Dühring, p. 141.

Life. That exchange of matter is the most important phenomenon of life has been asserted innumerable times during the last twenty years by physiological chemists and chemical physiologists and is here repeatedly extolled as the definition of life. But neither an exact nor an exhaustive one. Exchange of matter is encountered also in the *absence* of life, e.g., in simple chemical processes which, given an adequate supply of raw material, constantly reproduce their own conditions, a definite body being the carrier of the process (for example, see Roscoe, 102, manufacture of sulphuric acid[a]), in endosmose and exosmose (through dead organic and even inorganic membranes?), in Traube's artificial cells[320] and their medium. Exchange of matter, supposed to constitute life, itself requires more exact defining. Thus, despite all deeper foundations, subtle conceptions and closer investigations, we have not yet got to the bottom of this thing and still ask what life is.

To science definitions are worthless because always inadequate. The only real definition is the development of the thing itself, but this is no longer a definition. To know and show what life is we must examine all forms of life and present them in their interconnection. On the other hand, for *ordinary purposes,* a brief exposition of the commonest and at the same time most significant features of a so-called definition is often useful and even necessary, and can do no harm if no more is expected of it than it can convey. Let us therefore attempt to give such a definition of life, an attempt in which so many people have racked their brains in vain (see Nicholson[b]).

Life is the mode of existence of albuminous bodies and this mode of existence essentially consists in the constant renewal of their chemical constituents by nutrition and excretion...

---

[a] H. E. Roscoe, *Kurzes Lehrbuch der Chemie nach den neuesten Ansichten der Wissenschaft*, p. 102.— *Ed.*

[b] See H. A. Nicholson, *A Manual of Zoology,* General Introduction, Section 4: Nature and Conditions of Life, where the author gives various definitions of life.— *Ed.*

Then, from the organic exchange of matter as the essential function of albumen and from its peculiar plasticity, are derived all the other most simple functions of life—irritability, which is already included in the mutual interaction between nutrition and albumen; contractibility in the consumption of food; possibility of growth, which at the lowest stage (moneron) includes propagation by fission; internal movement, without which neither swallowing nor assimilation of food is possible. But how the advance from simple plastic albumen to the cell and thus to the organism is accomplished must first be learnt from observation, yet such an inquiry is no part of a simple practical definition of life. (On p. 141 Dühring mentions besides a whole intermediate world, inasmuch as there is no real life without a system of circulation canals and a "germ scheme". A superb passage.)

Ch. X, pp. 89-95

Dühring—Political Economy.—The Two Men

As long as morality is the point at issue Dühring can set them down as equal, but as soon as political economy comes under discussion that ceases to be so. If, for example, the two men are a yankee BROKEN INTO ALL TRADES and a Berlin student who brings along nothing but his graduation certificate and the philosophy of reality, and in addition arms that on principle have never been strengthened by fencing, where does equality come in? The yankee produces everything, the student only helps here and there, but distribution takes place according to the contribution of each; soon the yankee will have the means capitalistically to exploit any eventual increase in the population of the colony (births or immigration). The whole modern order, capitalist production and all that, can therefore be brought into being by the two men without either of them needing a sabre.

Ch. X, pp. 95-99

Dühringiana.

Equality—Justice.—The idea that equality is the expression of justice, the principle of consummated political and social regulation, arose quite historically. It did not exist in primitive communities, or only very limitedly so, for full members of individual communities, and was saddled with slavery. Ditto in the democracy of antiquity. Equality of all people—Greeks, Romans and barbarians, freemen and slaves, subjects and aliens, citizens and peregrines, etc.—was not only insane but criminal to the mind of the ancients, and in Christendom its first beginnings naturally were persecuted.—In Christianity there was first the *negative equality of all human beings before God as sinners,* and, more narrowly construed, the equality of all children of God redeemed by the grace and the blood of Christ. Both versions are grounded in the role of Christianity as the religion of the slaves, the banished, the dispossessed, the persecuted, the oppressed. With the victory of Christianity this circumstance was relegated to the rear and prime importance attached next to the antithesis between believers and pagans, orthodox and heretics.—With the rise of the cities and thereby of the more or less developed elements of the bourgeoisie, as well as of the proletariat, the demand for equality as a condition of bourgeois existence was bound gradually to resurge, interlinked with the proletariat's drawing of the conclusion to proceed from political to social equality. This naturally assumed a religious form, sharply expressed for the first time in the Peasant War.[321]—The bourgeois side was first formulated by Rousseau, in trenchant terms but still on behalf of all humanity. As was the case with all demands of the bourgeoisie, so here too the proletariat cast a fateful shadow beside it and drew its own conclusions (Babeuf). This connection between bourgeois equality and the proletariat's drawing of conclusions should be developed in greater detail.

So it took almost all of past history to elaborate the principle of equality=justice, and this success was achieved only when a bourgeoisie and a proletariat had come into existence. The principle of equality signifies, however, that there must be no *privileges,* hence is essentially *negative,* pronounces all past history wretched. Because of its lack of positive content and its offhand rejection of the entire past it is just as suitable for proclamation by a great revolution, 1789-1796, as for the later blockheads engaged in manufacturing systems. But to represent equality=justice as the highest principle and ultimate truth is absurd. Equality exists only in opposition to inequality, justice—in opposition to injustice; hence they are still saddled with the opposition to old, past history, and hence to old society itself.*

This suffices to bar them from constituting *eternal* justice and truth. A few generations of social development under a communist regime and increased resources must bring mankind to a stage

* The idea of equality [follows] from the equality of general human labour in commodity production. *Das Kapital*, p. 36. [Marginal note.][322]

where this boasting about equality and right appears as ridiculous as boasting of privileges of nobility and birth appears today, where the opposition to the old inequality and to the old positive law and even to the new, transitional law, disappears from practical life, where anyone who pedantically insists on being given his equal and just share of the products is laughed to scorn by being given twice as much. Even Dühring will find this to be "foreseeable", and where else will there be room then for equality and justice if not in the lumber-room of historical reminiscences? The fact that such phrases make excellent propaganda material today will not turn them into an eternal truth by a long shot.

(The *content* of equality must be elucidated.—Restriction to rights, etc.)

Moreover, an abstract equality theory is still an absurdity today and will remain such for a considerable length of time. It would never occur to a socialist proletarian or theoretician to recognise the abstract equality between himself and a Bushman or Tierra del Fuegan, or even a *peasant* or semi-feudal agricultural day-labourer; and as soon as this has been overcome, even if only in Europe, the standpoint of abstract equality will also be overcome. With the introduction of rational equality that equality loses all meaning. If equality is now demanded, this is so in anticipation of the intellectual and moral *equalisation* which thus *under present historical conditions* follows of itself. *Eternal* morality must have been possible at all times and must *everywhere* be possible. But even Dühring does not maintain this in regard to equality; on the contrary, he allows for a provisional period of repression, hence admits that equality is not an eternal truth but a historical product and attribute of definite historical conditions.

The equality of the bourgeoisie (abolition of class *privileges*) is very different from that of the proletariat (abolition of the classes themselves). If driven further than the latter, i.e., if conceived abstractly, equality becomes an absurdity. And so Herr Dühring is finally compelled to reintroduce, by a back-door, both armed as well as administrative, judicial and police force.

Thus the *idea of equality* is *itself a historical product* and its elaboration required the whole of preceding history; hence it did not exist from all eternity as a truth. The fact that now most people take it for granted—*en principe*[a]—is not due to its being axiomatic but to the *spread of the ideas of the eighteenth century*. And, therefore, if the two famous men today take their stand on the

---

[a] In principle.— *Ed.*

principle of equality, that is to be explained by their being presented as "eddicated" people of the nineteenth century and its being *"natural"* with them. How *real* people behave and did behave depends and always did depend on the historical conditions under which they lived.

Ch. IX, pp. 86-87; Ch. X, pp. 95-99

[Dependence of Ideas on Social Relations]

The notion that *the ideas and conceptions of people create their conditions of life* and not the other way round is contradicted by all past history, in which results constantly differed from what had been desired and in the further course of events were in most cases even the opposite. Only in the more or less distant future can this notion become a reality in so far as men will understand in advance the necessity of changing the social system [*Verfassung*] (*sit venia verbo*[a]), on account of changing conditions, and will desire the change before it forces itself upon them without their being conscious of it or desiring it.—The same is true of the conceptions of *law*, hence of politics (AS FAR AS THAT GOES, this point is to be dealt with under "Philosophy", while "force" is reserved for political economy).

Ch. XI, pp. 105-06 (cf. also Part III, Ch. V, pp. 300-02)

Even the correct reflection of *nature* is extremely difficult, the product of a long history of experience. To primitive man the forces of nature were something alien, mysterious, superior. At a certain stage, through which *all* civilised peoples passed, he assimilates them by means of personification. It was this urge to personify that created gods everywhere, and the *consensus gentium*,[b] as regards proof of the existence of God, proves after all only the universality of this urge to personify as a necessary transition stage, and consequently the universality of religion too. Only real knowledge of the forces of nature ejects the gods or God from one position after another (Secchi and his solar system).[c] This

---

[a] If one may be permitted to use this word.— *Ed.*
[b] Consensus of the peoples.— *Ed.*
[c] See this volume, p. 480.— *Ed.*

process has now advanced so far that theoretically it may be considered concluded.

In the sphere of *social* phenomena reflection is still more difficult. Society is determined by economic relations, production and exchange, and besides by historical preconditions.

Ch. XII, pp. 110-12 (see also Introduction, pp. 22-24)

Antithesis—if a thing is saddled with its antithesis it is in *contradiction* with itself, and so is its expression in thought. For example, there is a *contradiction* in a thing remaining the same and yet constantly changing, being possessed of the antithesis of "inertness" and "change".

Ch. XIII

[Negation of the Negation]

All Indo-Germanic peoples began with *common* property. Among almost all of them it was abolished, *negated,* in the course of social development, extruded by other forms—private property, feudal property, etc. To negate this negation, to restore common property on a higher plane of development, is the task of the social revolution. Or: the philosophy of antiquity was originally spontaneous materialism. The latter gave rise to idealism, spiritualism, negation of materialism, first in the shape of the antithesis of soul and body, then in the doctrine of immortality and in monotheism. This spiritualism was universally disseminated through the medium of Christianity. The negation of this negation is the reproduction of the old on a higher plane, modern materialism, which, in contrast with the past, finds its theoretical conclusion in scientific socialism....

It goes without saying that these natural and historical processes have their reflection in the thinking brain and reproduce themselves in it, as is seen in the above examples: $-a \times -a$, etc.; and it is just the paramount dialectical problems that are solved by this method alone.

But there is also a bad, barren negation.—True, natural, historical and dialectical negation (taken formally) is precisely what constitutes the driving principle of all development—the splitting into antitheses, their struggle and resolution. At the same time, on the basis of the experience gained, the original point of departure is again arrived at (in history partly, in thought wholly), but on a higher plane.—A barren negation is a purely subjective, individual one. Not being a stage of development of the thing itself, it is an *opinion* introduced from without. And as nothing can result from it, the negator must be at loggerheads with the world, sullenly finding fault with everything that exists or ever happened, with the whole historical development. True, the Greeks of antiquity accomplished a few things, but they knew nothing of spectral analysis, chemistry, differential calculus, steam-engines, *chaussées,* the electric telegraph or the railway. Why dwell at length on the products of people of such minor importance? Everything is bad—so far this sort of negator is a pessimist—save our own exalted selves, who are perfect, and thus our pessimism resolves itself into optimism. And thus we ourselves have perpetrated a negation of the negation!

Even Rousseau's way of looking at history—original equality, deterioration through inequality, restoration of equality on a higher plane—is a negation of the negation.

Dühring constantly preaches idealism—*ideal* conception, etc. If we draw conclusions about the future from existing relations, if we perceive and investigate the *positive* side of the *negative* elements operative in the course of history—and even the most narrow-minded progressist, the idealist Lasker, does that, in his own way—Dühring calls it "idealism" and deduces from it the right to design a plan for the future that provides even the curricula for schools, a plan that, however, is fantastic because based on ignorance. And he overlooks the fact that in doing so he, too, *is committing a negation of the negation.*

Ch. XIII, pp. 127-28

Negation of the Negation and Contradiction.

The "nothing" of a positive is a definite nothing, says Hegel.[a]

"Differentials can be considered and treated as *real zeros,*[b] which stand in a relation to one another that is determined by the state of the question under discussion." Bossut continues that mathematically this is *not nonsense.*[323]

---

[a] G. W. F. Hegel, *Wissenschaft der Logik.* In: *Werke,* Bd. 3, p. 74.—*Ed.*
[b] Here and below italics by Engels.—*Ed.*

$\frac{0}{0}$ may represent a very definite value if obtained by the simultaneous disappearance of the numerator and the denominator. Ditto $0:0 = A:B$, where $\frac{0}{0} = \frac{A}{B}$, consequently changes with a change in the value of A or B (p. 95, examples). And is it not a "contradiction" that zeros form ratios, i.e., can have not only value in general but even various values which are expressible in figures? $1:2 = 1:2$; $1-1:2-2 = 1:2$; $0:0 = 1:2$.

Dühring himself says that those summations of infinitely small magnitudes are the highest, etc., of mathematics, in plain words, integral calculus. And how is this done? I have two, three or more variable quantities, i.e., such as maintain a definite relation among themselves when changing—say, two quantities, x and y, and am to solve a definite problem which is not solvable by ordinary mathematics and in which x and y function. I differentiate x and y, i.e., I take x and y as so infinitely small that in comparison with any real quantity, however small, they disappear—that nothing is left of x and y but *their reciprocal relation*, without any material basis; consequently $\frac{dx}{dy} = \frac{0}{0}$, but $\frac{0}{0}$ expressed in the ratio $\frac{x}{y}$. That this ratio between two quantities which have disappeared, the fixed moment of their disappearance, is a contradiction cannot disturb us. And now, what have I done but *negate* x and y, though not in such a way that I need not bother about them any more, but in the way that corresponds with the facts of the case? In place of x and y I have their negation, dx and dy, in the formulas or equations before me. I operate then with these formulas as usual, treating dx and dy as if they were real quantities, and at a certain point I negate the negation, i.e., I integrate the differential formula, and in place of dx and dy put the real quantities x and y, and am then not where I was at the beginning, but by using this method I have solved the problem on which ordinary geometry and algebra break their jaws in vain.

To part II

Ch. II

Wherever *slavery*[324] is the main form of production it turns labour into servile activity, consequently makes it dishonourable for freemen. Thus the way out of such a mode of production is barred, while on the other hand slavery is an impediment to more developed production, which urgently requires its removal. This contradiction spells the doom of all production based on slavery and of all communities based on it. A solution comes about in most cases through the forcible subjection of the deteriorating communities by other, stronger ones (Greece by Macedonia and later Rome). As long as these themselves have slavery as their foundation there is merely a shifting of the centre and a repetition of the process on a higher plane until (Rome) finally a people conquers that replaces slavery by another form of production. Or slavery is abolished by compulsion or voluntarily, whereupon *the former mode of production perishes* and large-scale cultivation is displaced by small-peasant squatters, as in America. For that matter Greece too perished on account of slavery, Aristotle having already said that intercourse with slaves was demoralising the citizens, not to mention the fact that slavery makes work impossible for the latter. (Domestic slavery, such as exists in the Orient, is another matter. Here it forms the basis of production not directly but indirectly, as a constituent part of the family, and passes imperceptibly into the family (female harem slaves).)

Ch. III

In Dühring's reprehensible history *force* holds sway. In the real, progressive historical movement, however, what dominates are the *material gains* which are *retained.*

Ch. III

How is force, the army, maintained? By *money*, hence again dependent on production. Cf. Athens' fleet and policy of 380-340. The force exercised against the allies came to nought for lack of the material means to wage long and energetic wars. The English subsidies, granted by the new industry, modern industry, defeated Napoleon.

Ch. III

[The Party and Military Training]

In considering the struggle for existence and Dühring's declamations against struggle and arms it should be emphasised that a revolutionary party must know also how to struggle. It will have to make the revolution, possibly some day in the near future, but not against the present military-bureaucratic state. Politically that would be as insane as Babeuf's attempt to jump from the

Directorate immediately into communism; even more insane, for the Directorate was after all a bourgeois and peasant government.[325] But in order to safeguard the laws issued by the bourgeoisie itself the Party may be compelled to take revolutionary measures against the bourgeois state which will supersede the present state. Hence the universal conscription is in our interest and should be taken advantage of by all to learn how to fight, but particularly by those whose education entitles them to acquire the training of an officer in one year's voluntary service.

Ch. IV

On "Force"

It is recognised that force also operates with revolutionary effect, namely, in all "critical" epochs of decisive importance, such as the transition to sociality, but even then only in self-defence against reactionary enemies abroad. However the upheaval in England in the sixteenth century depicted by Marx[326] also had its revolutionary side. It was a basic condition of the conversion of feudal landed property into bourgeois landed property and of the development of the bourgeoisie. The French Revolution of 1789 likewise applied force to a considerable extent; August 4 merely sanctioned the peasants' deeds of violence and was supplemented by the confiscation of the estates of the nobility and church.[327] The forcible conquest by the ancient Germans, the foundation, on conquered territory, of states in which the country, and not the town, dominated, as in antiquity, was accompanied—precisely for the latter reason—by the transformation of slavery into the milder serfdom, or feudal dependence (in antiquity the transformation of tilled land into pastures was a concomitant feature of the latifundia).

Ch. IV

[Force, Community Property, Economics and Politics]

When the Indo-Germans migrated to Europe they ejected the aboriginal inhabitants by *force* and tilled the land, which was owned by the community. Among the Celts, Germans and Slavs community ownership can still be traced historically and among the Slavs, Germans and also the Celts (RUNDALE) it still exists even in the form of direct (Russia) or indirect (Ireland) feudal bondage. Force ceased as soon as the Lapps and Basques had been driven off. In internal affairs equality or voluntarily conceded privilege prevailed. Where private ownership of land by individual peasants arose out of common ownership, this division up to the sixteenth century took place purely spontaneously among the members of the community. It occurred in most cases quite gradually and remnants of common possession could be encountered very frequently. There was no idea of using *force*; it was applied only against these remnants (England in the eighteenth and nineteenth centuries, Germany mainly in the nineteenth century). Ireland is a special case. This common ownership quietly persisted in India and Russia under the most diverse forcible conquests and despotisms, and formed their basis. Russia is proof of how the production relations determine the political relations of force. Up to the end of the seventeenth century the Russian peasant suffered little oppression, enjoyed the right of movement and was hardly a bondsman. The first Romanov attached the peasants to the soil. With Peter began the foreign trade of Russia, which had only agricultural products to export. *This* brought on the oppression of the peasants. It grew in the same measure as *exports, for the sake of which it had been introduced,* until Catherine made the oppression complete and completed legislation on the subject. This legislation, however, permitted the landed proprietors to grind down the peasants more and more, so that their yoke became ever harder to bear.

Ch. IV

If force is the cause of social and political conditions, what is the cause of force? The appropriation of *products* of the labour of others and of labour-*power* of others. Force was able to change the consumption of products but not the mode of production itself; it could not transform bond labour into wage-labour unless the requisite conditions existed and bond labour had become a fetter on production.

Ch. IV

Hitherto force—from now on sociality. Purely a pious wish, a demand of "justice". Thomas More set up this demand already 350 years ago,[a] but it has not yet been met. Why should it be fulfilled now? Dühring is at a loss for an answer. In reality, modern industry

---

[a] See Th. More, *Utopia.—Ed.*

sets up this demand not as a demand of justice but as a necessity of production, and that changes everything.

TO PART III

Ch. I

Fourier (Nouveau Monde industriel et sociétaire).[328]

Element of *inequality*: "man, being by instinct an enemy of equality", [p.] 59. "This swindling mechanism, which is called civilisation", [p.] 81.

"One should avoid relegating them" (women), "as we are wont to do, to thankless tasks, to the menial roles assigned to them by the philosophy which claims that women were made only to wash pots and patch old trousers", [p.] 141.

"God has endowed manufacturing labour with a doze of attractiveness which corresponds to only *one quarter* of the time which social man can give to work." The rest is to be devoted to agriculture, cattle raising, the kitchen, the industrial armies, [p.] 152.

"Tender morality, the kind and pure friend of trade", [p.] 161. "Critique of Morality", [p.] 162 *et seqq.*

In present-day society, "in the civilised mechanism", "duplicity of action, contradiction between individual and collective interests" dominate; it is "a universal war of the individuals against the masses. And our political sciences dare to speak of unity of action!" [p.] 172.

"The moderns failed everywhere in the study of nature because they did not know the theory of exceptions or transitions, the theory of *hybrids*." (Examples of "hybrids": "the quince, nectarine, eel, bat, etc.") [p.] 191.

PART TWO

[The second part of the MS of the preparatory writings for *Anti-Dühring* consists of excerpts from Dühring's *Cursus der National- und Socialökonomie.* We give here only some of Engels' marginal notes and briefly explain to which of Dühring's statements they refer.]

[On Dühring's assertion "that the volitional activity by means of which the various forms of human association are created is itself subject to natural laws" [1], Engels remarked:]

And so, no mention of *historical* development. Mere eternal law of nature. Everything is psychology and the latter unfortunately is much more "backward" than politics.

[In connection with Dühring's disquisition on slavery, wage bondage and property based on force as "social-economic *constitutional forms of a purely political nature*" [5], Engels wrote:]

Always the belief that political economy has only eternal laws of nature and that all change and distortion are brought about by wicked politics.

Hence this much is correct in the whole theory of force that hitherto all forms of society needed *force* to maintain themselves and to some extent or other were even established by force. This force, in its organised form, is called *state*. So we have here the banal idea that as soon as man rose above the wildest conditions states existed everywhere and the world did not wait for Dühring to learn this.—But state and force are precisely what all hitherto existing forms of society have had *in common*, and if I should try to explain, for instance, the Oriental despotisms, the republics of antiquity, the Macedonian monarchies, the Roman Empire and the feudalism of the Middle Ages by stating that they were all based on *force*, I have explained nothing as yet. The various social and political forms must therefore be explained not as due to force, which after all is always the same, but as due to that *to which the force is applied*, as due to that *which* is being robbed—the products and productive forces of the epoch in question and their distribution, resulting from them themselves. It would then appear that Oriental despotism was founded on common property, the antique republics on the cities engaged in agriculture, the Roman Empire on the latifundia, feudalism on the domination of the country over the town, which had its material causes, etc.

[Engels quoted the following from Dühring: "The natural laws of economy can be revealed in all their strictness only by mentally obliterating the effects of the state and social institutions" (!) "particularly those of property based on force and connected with wage bondage, and by being careful not to regard the latter as necessary consequences of man's abiding nature (!)..." [5]. Engels made the following comment on this descourse of Dühring's:]

So then the natural laws of economy are discovered only when one *abstracts one's mind from all hitherto existing economy*; until now they have never manifested themselves undistortedly!—*Abiding* nature of man—from ape to Goethe!

Dühring is supposed to explain by this theory of "force" how it happens that everywhere from time immemorial the majority has consisted of those subjected to force and the minority of those applying force. This alone is proof that the relation of force is based on the economic conditions, which it is not so simple to upset by political means.

In Dühring rent, profit, interest and wages are not explained; it is merely stated that they have been instituted by *force*. Whence force? *Non est.*[a]

---

[a] There is none, namely, no reply.— *Ed.*

Force gives rise to possession and possession to economic power. Hence force=power.

Marx has shown in *Capital* (Accumulation) how at a certain stage of development the laws of commodity production necessarily engender capitalist production with all its chicanery and that *no force whatever is needed* for that purpose.[a]

When Dühring considers political action to be the ultimate decisive power of history and would have you believe it was something new, he merely repeats what was said by all former historians who also held the view that social forms are determined solely by political forms and not by production.

C'est trop bon![b] The whole Free Trade school, beginning with Adam Smith, indeed, all pre-Marxian political economy regards the economic laws, in so far as it understands them, as "natural laws" and maintains that their action is being distorted by the state, by the "action of the state and social institutions"!

Anyhow, this entire theory is merely an attempt to let Carey substantiate socialism: economics by itself is harmonious, the state by its interference spoils everything.

Eternal justice is a complement of force; it will appear on p. 282.

[Dühring's views, developed in his criticism of Smith, Ricardo and Carey, were characterised as follows by Engels: "In its most abstract form production may be studied quite well by taking Robinson as an example; distribution, by taking two people alone on an island and imagining all stages intermediate between complete equality and complete opposition between master and slave..." Engels quotes the following sentence from Dühring: "The point of view which in the last analysis is really decisive for the theory of distribution can be arrived at only by *serious social*"(!) "meditation" [10]. To which Engels remarked:]

So one first abstracts from real history the various legal relations and separates them from the historical basis on which they arose and on which alone they make sense and transfers them to two individuals, Robinson and Friday, where they naturally appear wholly arbitrary. After they have thus been reduced to pure force they are transferred back to real history, and thus one proves that here too everything is based on sheer force. That force must be applied to a material substratum and that the point is precisely to establish where this came from, leaves Dühring unaffected.

[Engels quoted the following passage from Dühring's *Cursus der National- und Socialökonomie:* "The traditional view shared by all systems of political economy

---

[a] See K. Marx, *Das Kapital,* pp. 607-08. See present edition, Vol. 35, Part VII, Chapter XXIV, Section 1. See this volume, pp. 150-51.—*Ed.*

[b] That is too good!—*Ed.*

considers distribution only what may be called a transient process which is concerned with a mass of products created by production and considered as finished joint output; ... a *deeper* foundation must rather scrutinise a distribution which is concerned with the economic or economically operating *laws* themselves and not only with the transient and accumulative consequences of these laws" [10-11]. Engels commented on this as follows:]

Thus it is not enough to investigate the distribution of current production.

Land rent presupposes landed property, profit—capital, wages—propertyless workers, possessors of labour-power only. Inquiry should therefore be made where this comes from. In so far as this was his concern, Marx did this in Volume I with regard to capital and propertyless labour-power; investigation of the origin of modern landed property belongs to land rent, and is therefore part of his Volume II.[329]—Dühring's investigation and historical foundation is confined to the single word: *force*! Here there is direct *mala fides*.[a] For Dühring's *explanation* of big landed property see *Wealth* and *Value*; these had better be dealt with here.

And so it is force that creates the economic, political, etc., conditions of life of an epoch, a people, etc. But who creates force? Organised force is primarily the *army*. And nothing depends more on economic conditions than precisely the composition, organisation, armament, strategy and tactics of an army. Armament is the foundation, and it in turn is directly dependent on the level of production. Arms of stone, bronze and iron, armour, cavalry, gunpowder, and then that tremendous revolution which modern industry had brought about in warfare by means of the rifled breech-loader and artillery—products which only modern industry with its rhythmically working machines that turn out almost absolutely identical products could manufacture. Composition and organisation, strategy and tactics, in their turn, depend on armament. Tactics also on the means of communication—the disposition of the troops and successes achieved in the battle of Jena[330] would be impossible with the present *chaussées*—and lastly the railways! Hence it is precisely force that is dominated more than anything else by the existing conditions of production, something even Captain Jähns has realised. (*Kölnische Zeitung*—Machiavelli, etc.)[b]

---

[a] (Acting, done) in bad faith.— *Ed.*
[b] M. Jähns, *Macchiavelli und der Gedanke der allgemeinen Wehrpflicht.— Ed.*

Particular stress is to be laid on modern methods of warfare, from the rifle and bayonet to breech-loader, where the issue is decided not by the man with the sabre but by the weapon; the line, or the column when the troops are bad, but it must be covered by riflemen (Jena contra Wellington),[a] and finally the general dispersion into skirmishers and the change from the slow march to the double.

[According to Dühring, "a skilled hand and a clever head must be regarded as a means of production belonging to society, as a *machine* whose output belongs to *society*" [D. C. 260]. To which Engels remarked:]

But while a machine *does not add value, a skilled hand does*! The economic law of value, *quant à cela*,[b] is therefore being prohibited and yet it is to remain in force.

[On Dühring's conception of the "*politico-juridical foundation* of the whole of sociality" [D. C. 320-21] Engels had the following comment to make:]

Thus at once the idealist measuring stick is applied. Not production itself, but *law*.

[Concerning Dühring's "economic commune" [322] and the system of division of labour, distribution, exchange and money system obtaining in it, Engels remarked:]

Hence also *payment of wages* [324] to the individual worker by society.

Hence also hoarding, usury, credit and all consequences up to and including money crises and money scarcity. Money explodes the economic commune as inevitably as at the present moment it is about to explode the Russian commune, and the family commune as well, once exchange between the individual members is brought about by the agency of money.

[Engels quoted the following sentence from Dühring, giving his comment in parentheses: "Real work in any form therefore constitutes the social law of nature governing healthy organisations [15] (from which it follows that all prior ones were unhealthy)... This occasioned Engels to observe:]

Labour is here conceived either as economic, materially productive labour, in which case the sentence is nonsense and is at variance with all past history. Or labour is conceived in a more general form, so as to comprise every kind of activity necessary or

---

[a] See this volume, p. 627.— *Ed.*
[b] As far as that goes.— *Ed.*

useful in a period, such as governance, administration of justice and military exercises, in which case it is an enormously inflated platitude and has nothing to do with political economy. But to try to impress the socialists with this old trash by styling it "natural law" is A TRIFLE IMPUDENT.

[On Dühring's discussion of the connection between wealth and loot [see D. C. 17] Engels remarked:]

Here we have his whole method. Every economic relation is first conceived from the point of view of *production* apart from all historical determination. Hence only the most general of all generalities can be said, and if Dühring wants to go beyond that he must take into account the definite historical relations of the epoch in question, i.e., must tumble out of abstract production and create chaos. Then the same economic relation is conceived from the angle of *distribution,* i.e., the historical process that has gone on hitherto is reduced to the word *force,* after which indignation is voiced at the evil consequences of force. When we get to natural laws we shall see where this will bring us to.

[On Dühring's assertion that it takes slavery or feudal dependence to manage a large-scale enterprise [see D. C. 18] Engels commented as follows:]

Therefore, firstly, the history of the world begins with large landed property! The cultivation of large tracts of land is identical with cultivation by large landed proprietors! Italy's soil, which was turned into pasturage by the latifundists, had lain untilled before! The United States of America owes its vast expansion not to free farmers but to slaves, serfs, etc.!

Again a *mauvais calembour*[a]: "Cultivation in tracts of considerable size" *is to be* equivalent to clearing them, but is immediately interpreted as cultivation on a large scale, is made equal to large landed property! And in this sense what an enormous new discovery that if some one possesses more land than he and his family can till he cannot farm it all without the labour of others! Moreover, *cultivation by serfs* is not cultivation of considerable tracts, but of *small holdings* and the cultivation always antedates the serfdom (Russia, the Flemish, Dutch, and Frisian colonies in the Slavic mark, see Langethal[b]), the originally free peasants are *made* serfs, here and there voluntarily *on the face of it.*

---

[a] Bad pun.—*Ed.*
[b] Ch. E. Langethal, *Geschichte der teutschen Landwirtschaft.—Ed.*

[Dühring's statement that the magnitude of value is determined by the magnitude of the resistance which the process of satisfying wants encounters and which "necessitates a greater or lesser expenditure of economic energy" (!) [19-20], evoked this comment by Engels:]

Overcoming resistance—a category borrowed from mathematical mechanics and rendered absurd in political economy. Instead of: "I successively spin, weave, bleach and print cotton", one must now say: "I overcome the resistance of the cotton to being spun, of the yarn to being woven, of the cloth to being bleached and printed." "I am making a steam-engine" means "I am overcoming the resistance of the iron to being transformed into a steam-engine." I am expressing the matter in high-sounding circumlocutions, which add nothing but distortion. But in this way I can bring in the *distribution value* where, too, there is supposed to be resistance that has to be overcome. That's why!

[Dühring claims that "distribution value exists in pure and exclusive form only where the power to dispose of unproduced things, or" (!), "to use a commoner expression, where these" (unproduced!) "things themselves are exchanged for services or things of real production value" [27], to which Engels remarked:]

What is an unproduced thing? Land *cultivated the modern way*? or are things meant which the owner did not produce himself? But then there is the antithesis of "real production value". The following sentence shows that we have here again a *mauvais calembour*. Objects found in nature, which were not produced, are thrown on one pile with "component parts of value which are appropriated without counter-service" [27].

[Dühring's claim that all human institutions are strictly determined but that, "unlike the play of external forces in nature", they are not at all "practically unalterable in their main features" [60] was criticised by Engels as follows:]

Consequently it is and remains natural law.

That hitherto the laws of economy in all unplanned and unorganised production confront men as objective laws, against which they are powerless, hence *in the form of natural laws*—of that not a word.

[Dühring formulated the "basic law [66] of all political economy" as follows: "The productivity of economic means—natural *resources and human energy—is enhanced by inventions and discoveries* and this takes place quite irrespective of distribution, which as such may nevertheless be subject to or cause considerable change, but does not determine the *imprint*" (!) "of the principal result" [65]. Engels' comment:]

The concluding part of the sentence: "and this takes place", etc., adds nothing new to the law, for if the law is true, distribution can change nothing in it and it is superfluous to say that it is correct for every form of distribution, otherwise it would not be a natural law. It is added, however, simply because Dühring was too ashamed to dish up this inane and utterly meaningless law in all its platitude. Besides it is self-contradictory, because, if distribution *may*, nevertheless, cause considerable change, one cannot say "quite irrespective" of it. We therefore delete the concluding part and then obtain the law pure and simple—the *fundamental law of all political economy.*

But this is not shallow enough. We are further instructed:

[Engels quotes further extracts from Dühring's *Cursus der National- und Socialökonomie.*]

[Dühring asserts that economic progress does not depend on the total of means of production "*but only on knowledge and the general technical methods of procedure*" and this, in Dühring's opinion, "appears at once, if capital is understood in its *natural* meaning, as an instrument of production" [70]. On this Engels remarked:]

The steam ploughs of the Khedive[331] lying in the Nile and the threshing machines, etc., of the Russian nobility standing idle in their sheds are proof of this. Steam, etc., too has its historical preconditions which, while comparatively easy to establish, must nevertheless be established. But Dühring is quite proud of having thereby deteriorated that thesis, the sense of which is wholly different, to such an extent that this "idea coincides with our law of overriding importance", p. 71. The economists still thought this law contained something substantial. Dühring has reduced it to the merest commonplace.

[Dühring's formulation of the natural law of the division of labour states: "The cleaving of trades and the dissection of activities raises the productivity of labour" [73]. On this Engels observed:]

This formulation is wrong, as it is right only for bourgeois production and the division into specialities here too is already becoming restrictive of production because it cripples and ossifies the individual and in the future will cease altogether. We can see already here that this division into specialities in the manner of *today* is to Dühring's mind something permanent, valid also for the *sociality.*

Written by Engels in 1876-1877

Printed according to the manuscript

First published in full in: *Marx/Engels Gesamtausgabe.* F. Engels, *Herrn Eugen Dührings Umwälzung der Wissenschaft/ Dialektik der Natur.* Sonderausgabe. Moscow-Leningrad, 1935

APPENDICES

INFANTRY TACTICS,
DERIVED FROM MATERIAL CAUSES [332]
1700-1870

In the fourteenth century gunpowder and fire-arms became known in Western and Central Europe and every schoolchild knows that these purely technical advances wholly revolutionised methods of warfare. But this revolution proceeded at a very slow pace. The first fire-arms were very crude, particularly the arquebus. And although a great number of separate improvements were invented at an early date—the rifled barrel, the breech-loader, the wheel-lock, etc.—still it took over three hundred years before, at the end of the seventeenth century, a musket was constructed suitable for equipping the entire body of infantry.

In the sixteenth and seventeenth centuries the foot-soldiery consisted partly of pikemen and partly of arquebusiers. Originally the pike carriers' task was to effect a decision by charging the enemy, while the arquebus fire served the purposes of defence. The pikemen therefore fought in compact masses many ranks deep, like in the ancient Greek phalanx; the arquebusiers stood in formations eight to ten ranks in depth, because that many could fire in succession before one could load. Anyone whose weapon was loaded jumped in front, fired and withdrew to the last rank in order to load again.

The gradual perfection of fire-arms changed this relation. The matchlock musket could finally be loaded so rapidly that only five men, i.e., troops only five men deep, were required to maintain continuous fire. Thus the same number of musketeers could now hold a front almost twice as long as before. Because of the much more devastating effect of gun-fire on mass formations many men deep the pikemen too were now drawn up in only six to eight ranks, so that the battle order gradually approximated the line formation, in which musket fire decided the issue and the pikemen were no longer kept for the attack but only as cover for the sharpshooters against mounted troops. At the end of this period we find a battle array consisting of two combat detachments and a reserve, each detachment drawn up in line, mostly six men deep, guns and horsemen partly in the intervals between battalions, partly at the wings; each infantry battalion consisted at the most of one-third pikemen and at least of two-thirds musketeers.

At the end of the seventeenth century the flint-lock musket with a bayonet and ready-made cartridges was at last produced. With this the pike disappeared once and for all from infantry service. Loading took less and less time, the more rapid fire was itself a protection and the bayonet replaced the pike in case of necessity. Thus the depth of the line could be reduced from six to four, later to three and finally here and there to two ranks. Hence the line lengthened steadily with the same number of men, and ever more muskets were in use simultaneously. But these long, thin lines became thereby also more and more unwieldy and could move in formation only on level, unobstructed ground, and even then only very slowly, 70-75 paces a minute; and it was just in a plain that the line, in particular its flanks, offered the enemy cavalry prospects of successful attack. Partly to protect these flanks and partly to strengthen the fighting line, which decided the day, the cavalry was totally massed on the wings so that the battle line proper consisted solely of footmen and their light battalion guns. The extremely unwieldy heavy guns were mounted in front of the wings and changed position at the most only once during a battle. The foot-soldiers were drawn up in two detachments whose flanks were covered by infantry drawn up at an angle, the whole array forming a single very long hollow rectangle. This cumbrous mass, when it was not to move as a whole, could only be divided into three parts, the centre and the two wings. This shifting of parts was confined to moving up the wing numerically superior to the enemy's in order to outflank him, while the other wing was held back as a menace, to prevent him from re-arranging his front accordingly. A complete change in the dislocation of troops during a battle consumed so much time and exposed so many weak spots to the enemy that the attempt almost always ended in defeat. The original array therefore governed throughout the battle and as soon as the footmen joined battle one crushing blow decided the day. This entire method of warfare, developed to the highest pitch by Frederick II, was the inevitable result of two jointly operating material factors: first, the human material of that time, the mercenary armies of princes, rigorously drilled but quite unreliable and only held together by the rod, many of them hostile prisoners of war who had been pressed into service; and second, the armament—the cumbersome heavy guns and the smoothbore rapid but badly firing flint-lock muskets with bayonets.

This method of combat prevailed as long as both adversaries remained on the same level with regard to manpower and armament and it suited both to adhere to the prescribed rules. But when the American War of Independence[333] broke out the well-drilled mercenary troops were unexpectedly met by hordes of rebels who, while not knowing how to exercise, were splendid shots who for the most part carried accurate rifles and fought in their own cause, hence did not desert. These rebels did not do the English troops the favour of dancing with them the well-known battle minuet, stepping slowly across open plain, observing all the traditional rules of military etiquette. They drew their opponent into dense forests, where his long columns in marching order were, without the possibility of defence, exposed to the fire of scattered invisible skirmishers. Operating in loose order they took advantage of every bit of cover the terrain afforded to harass the enemy, maintaining at the same time great mobility that could never be matched by the cumbersome mass of the enemy troops. The combat fire of scattered skirmishers, which had been of importance as early as the introduction of the portable fire-arm, proved therefore superior here, in certain cases, particularly in small encounters, to the linear formation.

The soldiers that composed the mercenary troops of Europe were not suitable for fighting in loose order; their armament was still less so. True, the musket was no longer pressed against the chest on firing, as had been necessary with the old matchlocks; the musket was brought up to the shoulder, as now. But there could still be no question of aiming, since with a perfectly straight stock continuing the line of the barrel the eye could not freely run down the latter. It was only in 1777 that in France the slanting of the butt characteristic of the hunting rifle was also adopted for the infantry rifle and effective *tirailleur* fire made possible. A second improvement to be mentioned was the lighter but still solid gun-carriage constructed in the middle of the eighteenth century by Gribeauval, which alone made possible the greater mobility later demanded of artillery.

It was reserved to the French Revolution [334] to utilise these two technical improvements on the field of battle. When allied Europe attacked it it placed at the disposal of the government all the members of the nation capable of bearing arms. But this nation had no time to practise the intricate manoeuvres of linear tactics sufficiently to be able to oppose the veteran Prussian and Austrian infantry in similar formation. On the other hand, France lacked not only the primeval forests of America but also its virtually boundless territory for retreat. What was needed was to defeat the enemy between the frontier and Paris, that is, to defend a definite area, and that in the long run could be done only in open mass battle. Consequently it became necessary to find, in addition to the skirmish chains, still another form in which the badly drilled French masses could face Europe's standing armies with some prospect of success. This form was found in the close column, which was already being used in certain cases, but mostly on parade grounds. The column was easier to keep in order than the line. Even when thrown somewhat into disarray its compact mass nevertheless continued to offer at least passive resistance. The column was easier to handle, was more under the direct control of the commander and could move faster. Its speed rose to 100 paces and more a minute. But the most important result consisted in the following: the use of the column as the exclusive mass battle formation made it possible to divide up the cumbrous uniform whole of the old linear order of battle into separate parts, each granted a certain degree of independence, each adapting its general instructions to the circumstances confronted, and each composed, if so desired, of all three arms of the service. The column was plastic enough to permit of every possible combination of troop employment; it allowed the use of villages and farm-houses, which Frederick II had still strictly forbidden; henceforth they became the main points of support in every battle. The column could be employed in any terrain; and finally it could counter linear tactics—where all was staked on one card—with combat tactics in which the line was fatigued and so worn down by skirmish chains and the gradual use of troops to protract the engagement that it could not withstand the thrust of the fresh fighters that had been kept in reserve to the very end. Whereas the linear formation was equally strong at all points, an adversary fighting in close column formation could keep part of the line engaged by feint attacks of small bodies of troops and concentrate his main force for the assault on the key position.—Loose bodies of skirmishers now did most of the firing while the columns attacked with the bayonet. This restored the similar relation that had existed between the skirmish chains and the mass of pikemen at the beginning of the sixteenth century, with the exception, however, that the modern columns could at any time disperse to form skirmish chains and the latter again mass to form columns.

This new method of combat, the use of which Napoleon developed to the acme of perfection, was so superior to the old that the latter hopelessly collapsed when faced by it, the last time being at Jena,[335] where the cumbersome, slow moving Prussian lines, largely useless for skirmishing, virtually melted away when the French *tirailleurs* poured in their fire, to which they could reply only with platoon fire. But even if the linear battle order succumbed, this was by no means true of the line as combat formation. A few years after the Prussians had made out so badly with their lines at Jena, Wellington led his English troops in line formation against the French columns and as a rule beat them. But Wellington, to be sure, had adopted the whole of French tactics, with the exception that he had his close-formation infantry fight in line, and not in column formation. He thus secured the advantage of bringing into simultaneous action, when firing, all his rifles, and when attacking, all his bayonets. In this battle array the English fought up to a few years ago and got the best of the bargain both in attack (Albuera) and defence (Inkerman)[336] even when considerably outnumbered. Until his death, Bugeaud, who had faced those English lines, preferred them to the column.

Moreover, the infantry fire-arm was extremely bad, so bad that at a hundred paces it could hit a person standing alone only seldom and at three hundred paces a whole battalion just as seldom. Thus, when the French came to Algiers they suffered heavy losses from the Bedouins' long firelock muskets fired at distances at which their own muskets scored no hits. Here only the rifled musket could be of any use. But it was precisely in France that the rifle, even as an emergency weapon, had always been objected to, because it took so long to load and clogged so quickly. But now when the need for an easily loaded musket made itself felt it was met at once. The preparatory work of Delvigne was followed by Thouvenin's tige-rifle and Minié's expansive bullets, the latter having placed the rifled and the smoothbore musket on an absolute par with regard to loading time, so that now the entire infantry could be equipped with accurate long-range rifles. But before the rifled muzzle-loader could establish the tactics suitable to its use it was supplanted by the most up-to-date weapon, the rifled breech-loader, while at the same time rifled ordnance developed ever increasing efficiency.

The arming of the entire nation, which the revolution had ushered in, soon experienced considerable restriction. Only part of the young people liable to military service were called up, by lot, into the standing army and a greater or smaller part of the rest of the citizens were, at most, formed into an untrained National Guard. Or, in those countries where universal conscription was really strictly enforced, as in Switzerland, at most a militia was formed which was drilled under the colours for no more than a few weeks. Financial considerations made necessary the choice between conscription and militia. Only one country in Europe, and at that one of the poorest, attempted to combine universal conscription and standing army. That was Prussia. And even though the universal obligation to serve in the standing army was enforced only approximately, also necessitated by financial considerations, the Prussian *Landwehr*[337] system nevertheless placed at the disposal of the government such a considerable number of trained people organised in ready cadres that Prussia was decidedly superior to any other country of equal population.

In the Franco-German War of 1870 the French conscription system succumbed to the Prussian *Landwehr* system. In this war, however, both sides were for the first time equipped with breech-loading rifles, while the regulations for moving and fighting remained essentially the same as at the time of the old flint-locks. At most the *tirailleur* chains were somewhat more compact. As for the rest, the French still fought in the old battalion column formation, at times also in line formation, while on the German side at least an attempt was made, in the introduction of the company column formation, to find a form of fighting which was better adapted to the new type of arms. Thus one managed in the first few battles. But when, in the storming of St. Privat (August 18), three brigades of the Prussian Guard tried to apply the company column formation seriously, the devastating power of the breech-loaders became apparent. Of the five chiefly engaged regiments (15,000 men) almost all officers (176) and 5,114 men, that is, upwards of one-third, fell. The Guard Infantry alone, whose strength had been 28,160 men when it joined the fray, lost 8,230 men including 307 officers that day.[338] From that time on the company column as a battle formation was condemned no less than the battalion mass formation or the line. All idea of further exposing troops in any kind of close formation to enemy rifle fire was abandoned; on the German side all subsequent fighting was conducted only in those compact chains of *tirailleurs* into which the columns had so far regularly dispersed of themselves under a deadly hail of bullets, although this had been opposed by the higher commands on the ground that it was contrary to good battle formation. Once again the soldier had been shrewder than the officer; it was *he* who instinctively found the only way of fighting which has proved of service up to now under the fire of breech-loading rifles, and in spite of opposition from his officers he carried it through successfully. Likewise *the double* was the only step now used within the range of the frightful rifle fire.

Written by Engels in the first half of 1877

Printed according to the manuscript

First published in: *Marx/Engels Gesamtausgabe.* F. Engels, *Herrn Eugen Dührings Umwälzung der Wissenschaft/Dialektik der Natur.* Sonderausgabe. Moscow-Leningrad, 1935

ADDITIONS TO THE TEXT OF *ANTI-DÜHRING*
MADE BY ENGELS

IN THE PAMPHLET *SOCIALISM
UTOPIAN AND SCIENTIFIC*[339]

Introduction. Ch. I[a]

p. 16

[In *Socialism Utopian and Scientific* the sentence: "Like every new theory, modern socialism had, at first, to connect itself with the intellectual stock-in-trade ready to its hand, however deeply its roots lay in economic facts" reads as follows:]

Like every new theory, modern Socialism had, at first, to connect itself with the intellectual stock-in-trade ready to its hand, however deeply its roots lay in material economic facts.

p. 16

[The following note is supplied to the sentence: "It was the time when, as Hegel says, the world stood upon its head".]

This is the passage on the French Revolution: "Thought, the concept of law, all at once made itself felt, and against this the old scaffolding of wrong could make no stand. In this conception of law, therefore, a constitution has now been established, and henceforth everything must be based upon this. Since the sun had been in the firmament, and the planets circled round him, the sight had never been seen of man standing upon his head—*i.e.*, on the Idea—and building reality after this image. Anaxagoras first said that the Nous, reason, rules the world; but now, for the first time, had man come to recognise that the Idea must rule the

---

[a] The part and chapter references, the page references for the corresponding excerpts from this volume, and the explanations given in brackets, have been provided by the Institute of Marxism-Leninism of the CC CPSU.—*Ed.*

mental reality. And this was a magnificent sunrise. All thinking Beings have participated in celebrating this holy day. A sublime emotion swayed men at that time, an enthusiasm of reason pervaded the world, as if now had come the reconciliation of the Divine Principle with the world" (Hegel, *Philosophy of History,* 1840, p. 535). Is it not high time to set the anti-Socialist law [340] in action against such teachings, subversive and to the common danger, by the late Professor Hegel?

p. 19

[The sentence: "Now, for the first time, appeared the light of day, henceforth superstition, injustice, privilege, oppression, were to be superseded by eternal truth, eternal Right, equality based on nature and the inalienable rights of man"—reads as follows:]

Now, for the first time, appeared the light of day, the kingdom of reason; henceforth superstition, injustice, privilege, oppression, were to be superseded by eternal truth, eternal Right, equality based on Nature and the inalienable rights of man.

p. 19

[The sentence: "But, side by side with the antagonism of the feudal nobility and the burghers, was the general antagonism of exploiters and exploited, of rich idlers and poor workers"—reads as follows:]

But, side by side with the antagonism of the feudal nobility and the burghers, who claimed to represent all the rest of society, was the general antagonism of exploiters and exploited, of rich idlers and poor workers.

p. 19

[The sentence: "For example, at the time of the German Reformation and the Peasant War, Thomas Münzer; in the great English Revolution, the Levellers; in the great French Revolution, Babeuf"—reads as follows:]

For example, at the time of the German Reformation and the Peasants' War, the Anabaptists [341] and Thomas Münzer; in the great English Revolution, the Levellers; in the great French Revolution, Babeuf.

632   Appendices

pp. 19-20

[The sentence: "A communism, ascetic, Spartan, was the first form of the new teaching"—reads as follows:]

A Communism, ascetic, denouncing all the pleasures of life, Spartan, was the first form of the new teaching.

p. 20

[The sentence: "Like the French philosophers, they do not claim to emancipate a particular class, but all humanity"—reads as follows:]

Like the French philosophers, they do not claim to emancipate a particular class to begin with, but all humanity at once.

p. 20

[Instead of the sentence: "This mode of outlook is essentially that of all English and French and of the first German socialists, including Weitling"—the following is added:]

The Utopians' mode of thought has for a long time governed the socialist ideas of the nineteenth century, and still governs some of them. Until very recently all French and English Socialists did homage to it. The earlier German Communism, including that of Weitling, was of the same school.

p. 21

[The sentence: "When we consider and reflect upon nature at large or the history of mankind or our own intellectual activity, at first we see the picture of an endless entanglement of relations and reactions in which nothing remains what, where and as it was, but everything moves, changes, comes into being and passes away"—reads as follows:]

When we consider and reflect upon Nature at large, or the history of mankind, or our own intellectual activity, at first we see the picture of an endless entanglement of relations and reactions, permutations and combinations, in which nothing remains what, where, and as it was, but everything moves, changes, comes into being and passes away. We see, therefore, at first the picture as a whole, with its individual parts still more or less kept in the background; we observe the movements, transitions, connections, rather than the things that move, combine, and are connected.

p. 22

[After the sentence: "This is, primarily, the task of natural science and historical research: branches of science which the Greeks of classical times, on very good grounds, relegated to a subordinate position, because they had first of all to collect the material"—the following was made:]

A certain amount of natural and historical material must be collected before there can be any critical analysis, comparison, and arrangement in classes, orders, and species.

pp. 23-24

[The sentence: "Nature is the proof of dialectics, and it must be said for modern science that it has furnished this proof with very rich materials increasing daily, and thus has shown that, in the last resort, nature works dialectically and not metaphysically"—reads as follows:]

Nature is the proof of dialectics, and it must be said for modern science that it has furnished this proof with very rich materials increasing daily, and thus has shown that, in the last resort, Nature works dialectically and not metaphysically; that she does not move in the eternal oneness of a perpetually recurring circle, but goes through a real historical evolution. In this connection Darwin must be named before all others. He dealt the metaphysical conception of Nature the heaviest blow by his proof that all organic beings, plants, animals, and man himself, are the products of a process of evolution going on through millions of years.

pp. 24-25

[The words: "That Hegel did not solve the problem is here immaterial. His epoch-making merit was that he propounded the problem"—read as follows:]

That the Hegelian system did not solve the problem it propounded is here immaterial. Its epoch-making merit was that it propounded the problem.

pp. 26-27

[The passage: "The new facts made imperative a new examination of all past history. Then it was seen that *all* past history was the history of class struggles; that these warring classes of society are always the products of the modes of production and of exchange—in a word, of the *economic* conditions of their time; that the economic structure of society always furnishes the real basis, starting from which we can alone work out the ultimate explanation of the whole superstructure of juridical and political institutions as well as of the religious, philosophical, and other ideas of a given historical period. But now idealism was driven from its last refuge, the philosophy of history; now a materialistic treatment of history was propounded, and a method found of explaining man's 'knowing' by his 'being', instead of, as heretofore, his 'being' by his 'knowing'.

"But the socialism of earlier days was as incompatible with this materialistic conception as the conception of nature of the French materialists was with dialectics and modern natural science. The socialism of earlier days certainly criticised the existing capitalistic mode of production and its consequences. But it could not explain them, and, therefore, could not get the mastery of them. It could only simply reject them as bad"—reads as follows:]

The new facts made imperative a new examination of all past history. Then it was seen that *all* past history, with the exception of its primitive stages, was the history of class struggles; that these warring classes of society are always the products of the modes of production and of exchange—in a word, of the *economic* conditions of their time; that the economic structure of society always furnishes the real basis, starting from which we can alone work out the ultimate explanation of the whole superstructure of juridical and political institutions as well as of the religious, philosophical, and other ideas of a given historical period. Hegel had freed history from metaphysics—he had made it dialectic; but his conception of history was essentially idealistic. But now idealism was driven from its last refuge, the philosophy of history; now a materialistic treatment of history was propounded, and a method found of explaining man's "knowing" by his "being", instead of, as heretofore, his "being" by his "knowing".

From that time forward Socialism was no longer an accidental discovery of this or that ingenious brain, but the necessary outcome of the struggle between two historically developed classes—the proletariat and the bourgeoisie. Its task was no longer to manufacture a system of society as perfect as possible, but to examine the historico-economic succession of events from which these classes and their antagonism had of necessity sprung, and to discover in the economic conditions thus created the means of ending the conflict. But the Socialism of earlier days was as incompatible with this materialistic conception as the conception of Nature of the French materialists was with dialectics and modern natural science. The Socialism of earlier days certainly criticised the existing capitalistic mode of production and its consequences. But it could not explain them, and, therefore, could not get the mastery of them. It could only simply reject them as bad. The more strongly this earlier Socialism denounced the exploitation of the working-class, inevitable under Capitalism, the less able was it clearly to show in what this exploitation consisted and how it arose.

Part III. Ch. I

p. 244

[The passage: "The antagonism between rich and poor, instead of dissolving into general prosperity, had become intensified by the removal of the guild and other privileges, which had to some extent bridged it over, and by the removal of the charitable institutions of the Church. The development of industry upon a capitalistic basis made poverty and misery of the working masses conditions of existence of society"—reads as follows:]

The antagonism between rich and poor, instead of dissolving into general prosperity, had become intensified by the removal of the guild and other privileges, which had to some extent bridged it over, and by the removal of the charitable institutions of the Church. The "freedom of property" from feudal fetters, now veritably accomplished, turned out to be, for the small capitalists and small proprietors, the freedom to sell their small property, crushed under the overmastering competition of the large capitalists and landlords, to these great lords, and thus, as far as the small capitalists and peasant proprietors were concerned, became "freedom *from* property". The development of industry upon a capitalistic basis made poverty and misery of the working masses conditions of existence of society. Cash payment became more and more, in Carlyle's phrase, the sole nexus between man and man.[a]

p. 245

[The passage: "But modern industry develops, on the one hand, the conflicts which make absolutely necessary a revolution in the mode of production, conflicts not only between the classes begotten of it, but also between the very productive forces and the forms of exchange created by it. And, on the other hand, it develops, in these very gigantic productive forces, the means of ending these conflicts"—reads as follows:]

But Modern Industry develops, on the one hand, the conflicts which make absolutely necessary a revolution in the mode of

---

[a] See Th. Carlyle, *Past and Present*, p. 198.—*Ed.*

production, and the doing away with its capitalistic character—
conflicts not only between the classes begotten of it, but also between
the very productive forces and the forms of exchange created by it.
And, on the other hand, it develops, in these very gigantic
productive forces, the means of ending these conflicts.

p. 245

[The text: "The propertyless masses of Paris, during the Reign of Terror,
were able for a moment to gain the mastery. But, in doing so, they only proved
how impossible it was for their domination to last under the conditions then
obtaining"—reads as follows:]

The "have-nothing" masses of Paris, during the Reign of
Terror, were able for a moment to gain the mastery, and thus to
lead the bourgeois revolution to victory in spite of the bourgeoisie
themselves. But, in doing so, they only proved how impossible it
was for their domination to last under the conditions then
obtaining.

p. 246

[Before the sentence: "Already in his Geneva letters, Saint-Simon lays down the
proposition that 'all men ought to work'"—two paragraphs were added:]

Saint Simon was a son of the great French Revolution, at the
outbreak of which he was not yet thirty. The Revolution was the
victory of the third estate, *i.e.*, of the great masses of the nation,
working in production and in trade, over the privileged *idle*
classes, the nobles and the priests. But the victory of the third
estate soon revealed itself as exclusively the victory of a small part
of this "estate", as the conquest of political power by the socially
privileged section of it, *i.e.*, the propertied bourgeoisie. And the
bourgeoisie had certainly developed rapidly during the Revolution, partly by speculation in the lands of the nobility and of the
Church, confiscated and afterwards put up for sale, and partly by
frauds upon the nation by means of army contracts. It was the
domination of these swindlers that, under the Directorate, brought
France to the verge of ruin, and thus gave Napoleon the pretext
for his *coup d'état.*[342]
Hence, to Saint Simon the antagonism between the third estate
and the privileged classes took the form of an antagonism between
"workers" and "idlers". The idlers were not merely the old
privileged classes, but also all who, without taking any part in

production or distribution, lived on their incomes. And the workers were not only the wage-workers, but also the manufacturers, the merchants, the bankers. That the idlers had lost the capacity for intellectual leadership and political supremacy had been proved, and was by the Revolution finally settled. That the non-possessing classes had not this capacity seemed to Saint Simon proved by the experiences of the Reign of Terror. Then, who was to lead and command? According to Saint Simon, science and industry, both united by a new religious bond, destined to restore that unity of religious ideas which had been lost since the time of the Reformation—a necessarily mystic and rigidly hierarchic "new Christianity". But science, that was the scholars; and industry, that was, in the first place, the working bourgeois, manufacturers, merchants, bankers. These bourgeois were, certainly, intended by Saint Simon to transform themselves into a kind of public officials, of social trustees; but they were still to hold, *vis-à-vis* of the workers, a commanding and economically privileged position. The bankers especially were to be called upon to direct the whole of social production by the regulation of credit. This conception was in exact keeping with a time in which Modern Industry in France and, with it, the chasm between bourgeoisie, and proletariat was only just coming into existence. But what Saint Simon especially lays stress upon is this: what interests him first, and above all other things, is the lot of the class that is the most numerous and the most poor (*"la classe la plus nombreuse et la plus pauvre"*).[343]

p. 246

[The sentence: "But to recognise the French Revolution as a class war between nobility, bourgeoisie, and the non-possessors, was, in the year 1802, a most pregnant discovery"—reads as follows:]

But to recognise the French Revolution as a class war, and not simply one between nobility and bourgeoisie, but between nobility, bourgeoisie, and the non-possessors, was, in the year 1802, a most pregnant discovery.

p. 248

[The sentence: "He divides its whole course, thus far, into four stages of evolution—savagery, the patriarchate, barbarism, civilisation. This last is identical with the so-called bourgeois society of today"—reads as follows:]

He divides its whole course, thus far, into four stages of

evolution—savagery, barbarism, the patriarchate, civilisation.[a] This last is identical with the so-called civil, or bourgeois, society of to-day—i.e., with the social order that came in with the sixteenth century.

p. 249

[The sentence: "Nevertheless, even then it was producing crying social abuses—the herding together of a homeless population in the worst quarters of the large towns; the loosening of all traditional moral bonds, of patriarchal subordination, of family relations; overwork, especially of women and children, to a frightful extent; complete demoralisation of the working class, suddenly flung into altogether new conditions"—reads as follows:]

Nevertheless, even then it was producing crying social abuses— the herding together of a homeless population in the worst quarters of the large towns; the loosening of all traditional moral bonds, of patriarchal subordination, of family relations; overwork, especially of women and children, to a frightful extent; complete demoralisation of the working-class, suddenly flung into altogether new conditions, from the country into the town, from agriculture into modern industry, from stable conditions of existence into insecure ones that changed from day to day.

p. 250

[The following reference is given for the last quotation from Owen's book:]

From *The Revolution in Mind and Practice*, p. 21, a memorial addressed to all the "red Republicans, Communists and Socialists of Europe", and sent to the provisional government of France, 1848, and also "to Queen Victoria and her responsible advisers".

Part III. Ch. II

p. 256

[The sentence: "But where, in a given society, the fundamental form of production is that spontaneous division of labour, there the products take on the form of *commodities* whose mutual exchange, buying and selling, enable the individual producers to satisfy their manifold wants"—reads as follows:]

---

[a] The German editions of *Die Entwicklung des Sozialismus von der Utopie zur Wissenschaft* have "...savagery, the patriarchate, barbarism, civilisation".— *Ed.*

But where, in a given society, the fundamental form of production is that spontaneous division of labour which creeps in gradually and not upon any preconceived plan, there the products take on the form of *commodities,* whose mutual exchange, buying and selling, enable the individual producers to satisfy their manifold wants.

p. 260

[The following note is given for the word "mark" in the sentence that runs: "Hence, exchange was restricted, the market narrow, the methods of production stable; there was local exclusiveness without, local unity within; the mark in the country; in the town, the guild"—a note is given:]

See *Appendix.* [Here Engels refers to his work *The Mark.* See present edition, Vol. 24.]

p. 265

[The sentence: "At a further stage of evolution this form also becomes insufficient: the official representative of capitalist society—the state—will ultimately have to undertake the direction of production"—is replaced by the following passage:]

At a further stage of evolution this form also becomes insufficient. The producers on a large scale in a particular branch of industry in a particular country unite in a "Trust", a union for the purpose of regulating production. They determine the total amount to be produced, parcel it out among themselves, and thus enforce the selling price fixed beforehand. But trusts of this kind, as soon as business becomes bad, are generally liable to break up, and, on this very account, compel a yet greater concentration of association. The whole of the particular industry is turned into one gigantic joint-stock company; internal competition gives place to the internal monopoly of this one company. This has happened in 1890 with the English *alkali* production, which is now, after the fusion of 48 large works, in the hands of one company, conducted upon a single plan, and with a capital of £6,000,000.

In the trusts, freedom of competition changes into its very opposite—into monopoly; and the production without any definite plan of capitalistic society capitulates to the production upon a definite plan of the invading socialistic society. Certainly this is so far still to the benefit and advantage of the capitalists. But in this case the exploitation is so palpable that it must break down. No nation will put up with production conducted by trusts, with so barefaced an exploitation of the community by a small band of dividend-mongers.

In any case, with trusts or without, the official representative of capitalist society—the State—will ultimately have to undertake the direction of production.

p. 265

[The sentence: "Otherwise, the Royal Maritime Company, the Royal porcelain manufacture, and even the regimental tailor of the army would also be socialistic institutions"—reads as follows:]

Otherwise, the Royal Maritime Company,[344] the Royal porcelain manufacture, and even the regimental tailor of the army would also be socialistic institutions, or even, as was seriously proposed by a sly dog in Frederick William III's reign, the taking over by the State of the brothels.

pp. 265-66

[In three cases the words "and trusts" are added after "joint-stock companies".]

pp. 268-69

[The sentence: "It does not prevent the ruling class, once having the upper hand, from consolidating its power at the expense of the working class, from turning its social leadership into an exploitation of the masses"—reads as follows:]

It does not prevent the ruling class, once having the upper hand, from consolidating its power at the expense of the working-class, from turning their social leadership into an intensified exploitation of the masses.

p. 270

[Before the chapter's last paragraph the following résumé was added:]

Let us briefly sum up our sketch of historical evolution.

I. *Mediaeval Society.*—Individual production on a small scale. Means of production adapted for individual use; hence primitive, ungainly, petty, dwarfed in action. Production for immediate consumption, either of the producer himself or of his feudal lord. Only where an excess of production over this consumption occurs is such excess offered for sale, enters into exchange. Production of commodities, therefore, only in its infancy. But already it contains within itself, in embryo, *anarchy in the production of society at large.*

II. *Capitalist Revolution.*—Transformation of industry, at first by means of simple co-operation and manufacture. Concentration of the means of production, hitherto scattered, into great workshops. As a consequence, their transformation from individual to social means of production—a transformation which does not, on the whole, affect the form of exchange. The old forms of appropriation remain in force. The capitalist appears. In his capacity as owner of the means of production, he also appropriates the products and turns them into commodities. Production has become a *social* act. Exchange and appropriation continue to be *individual* acts, the acts of individuals. *The social product is appropriated by the individual capitalist.* Fundamental contradiction, whence arise all the contradictions in which our present day society moves, and which modern industry brings to light.

A. Severance of the producer from the means of production. Condemnation of the worker to wage-labour for life. *Antagonism between the proletariat and the bourgeoisie.*

B. Growing predominance and increasing effectiveness of the laws governing the production of commodities. Unbridled competition. *Contradiction between socialised organisation in the individual factory and social anarchy in production as a whole.*

C. On the one hand, perfecting of machinery, made by competition compulsory for each individual manufacturer, and complemented by a constantly growing displacement of labourers. *Industrial reserve-army.* On the other hand, unlimited extension of production, also compulsory under competition, for every manufacturer. On both sides, unheard of development of productive forces, excess of supply over demand, over-production, glutting of the markets, crises every ten years, the vicious circle: excess here, of means of production and products—excess there, of labourers, without employment and without means of existence. But these two levers of production and of social well-being are unable to work together, because the capitalist form of production prevents the productive forces from working and the products from circulating, unless they are first turned into capital—which their very superabundance prevents. The contradiction has grown into an absurdity. *The mode of production rises in rebellion against the form of exchange.* The bourgeoisie are convicted of incapacity further to manage their own social productive forces.

D. Partial recognition of the social character of the productive forces forced upon the capitalists themselves. Taking over of the great institutions for production and communication, first by joint-stock companies, later on by trusts, then by the State. The bourgeoisie demonstrated to be a superfluous class. All its social functions are now performed by salaried employees.

III. *Proletarian Revolution.*—Solution of the contradictions. The proletariat seizes the public power, and by means of this transforms the socialised means of production, slipping from the hands of the bourgeoisie, into public property. By this act, the proletariat frees the means of production from the character of capital they have thus far borne, and gives their socialised character complete freedom to work itself out. Socialised production upon a predetermined plan becomes henceforth possible. The development of production makes the existence of different classes of society thenceforth an anachronism. In proportion as anarchy in social production vanishes, the political authority of the State dies out. Man, at last the master of his own form of social organisation, becomes at the same time the lord over Nature, his own master—free.

NOTES
AND
INDEXES

NOTES

1 *Anti-Dühring* is the title under which Engels' classical work *Herr Eugen Dühring's Revolution in Science* is widely known.

The attention of Marx and Engels was first drawn to Dühring when his review of Volume One of *Capital* was published in *Ergänzungsblätter*, Vol. III, issue No. 3, in December 1867. They expressed a critical attitude towards him in a number of letters of January to March 1868.

In the mid-1870s, Dühring exerted quite a significant influence on German Social-Democrats. The second edition of *Kritische Geschichte der Nationalökonomie und des Sozialismus* (November 1875) and the publication of *Cursus der Philosophie als streng wissenschaftlicher Weltanschauung und Lebensgestaltung* (the last issue appeared in February 1875) made his views more popular. His most active followers were Johann Most, Friedrich Wilhelm Fritzsche and Eduard Bernstein. Even August Bebel came under the influence of Dühring's views for a short time. In March 1874, two of Bebel's articles about Dühring published anonymously under the title "Ein neuer 'Communist'" in the *Volksstaat*, the central organ of the Social-Democratic Workers' Party (Eisenachers), aroused sharp protest on the part of Marx and Engels.

The spread of Dühring's views made Liebknecht, on February 1 and April 21, 1875, propose to Engels that they be criticised in the *Volksstaat*.

Engels criticised Dühring for the first time in February 1876, in an article "Prussian Vodka in the German Reichstag", published in *Volksstaat* (see present edition, Vol. 24). Later, in his letter to Marx of May 24, 1876, he writes of the need to initiate a campaign against the spread of Dühring's views in Germany. Replying on May 25, Marx supported Engels' idea and suggested that, first of all, Dühring himself be sharply criticised (see present edition, Vol. 45). Engels broke off his work on *Dialectics of Nature*, and by May 28 informed Marx of the general plan and character of the proposed work.

Engels worked on *Anti-Dühring* for two years—from late May 1876 to early July 1878. Part I of the book was written mainly between September 1876 and January 1877. It was published as a series of articles entitled *Herrn Eugen Dühring's Umwälzung der Philosophie* in *Vorwärts* in January-May 1877 (Nos. 1-7, 10 and 11, January 3, 5, 7, 10, 12, 14, 17, 24 and 26; Nos. 17, 24 and 25, February 9, 25 and 28; Nos. 36 and 37, March 25 and 28; Nos. 44, 45, 49 and 50, April 15, 18, 27 and 29; Nos. 55 and 56, May 11 and 13). Later, beginning in 1878, with the first separate edition, the first two chapters of this part were made into an independent general introduction to all three parts.

Part II of the book was written mainly between June and August 1877. The last, X chapter of this part was written by Marx (see this volume, pp. 9, 15). In addition, in his letters to Engels of March 7 and August 8, 1877, Marx explained a number of economic problems, especially those connected with Quesnay's *Tableau économique,* which was difficult to understand (see this volume, p. 239). Engels also read the whole manuscript of *Anti-Dühring* to Marx before sending it to the printers (see this volume, p. 9).

Part II was published under the title *Herrn Eugen Dühring's Umwälzung der politischen Oekonomie* in *Wissenschaftliche Beilage* and in the supplement to *Vorwärts* from July to December 1877 (No. 87, July 27; Nos. 93 and 96, August 10 and 17; Nos. 105 and 108, September 7 and 14; No. 127, October 28; Nos. 130 and 139, November 4 and 28; No. 152, December 30).

Part III of the book was written mainly between August 1877 and April 1878. It was published as *Herrn Eugen Dühring's Umwälzung des Sozialismus* in the supplement to *Vorwärts* in May to July 1878 (Nos. 52 and 61, May 5 and 26; Nos. 64 and 75, June 2 and 28; No. 79, July 7).

The publication of *Anti-Dühring* in *Vorwärts* aroused strong resistance on the part of Dühring's followers. At the next congress of the Socialist Workers' Party of Germany, in Gotha from May 27 to 29, 1877, they attempted to ban the publication of this work in the Party's central organ. It was due to them that *Anti-Dühring* was being printed at lengthy intervals.

In July 1877, Part I of Engels' work was published in Leipzig as a separate pamphlet: *Herrn Eugen Dühring's Umwälzung der Wissenschaft. I. Philosophie.* In July 1878, Parts II and III were also published as a separate pamphlet: *Herrn Eugen Dühring's Umwälzung der Wissenschaft. II. Politische Oekonomie. Sozialismus.*

The entire work was first published in book form in Leipzig on about July 8, 1878, with a preface by Engels: F. Engels, *Herrn Eugen Dühring's Umwälzung der Wissenschaft. Philosophie. Politische Oekonomie. Sozialismus.* Its title is an ironical paraphrase of the title of Dühring's work *Carey's Umwälzung der Volkswirtschaftslehre und Socialwissenschaft.* At the end of October 1878, after the Anti-Socialist Law had been put into force in Germany, *Anti-Dühring* was banned along with Engels' other works. Its second edition appeared in Zurich, in 1886. The third, revised and supplemented edition was published in Stuttgart, in 1894, i.e., after the Anti-Socialist Law was repealed (1890). This was the last edition during Engels' lifetime. The second and third editions bore the same title, but the subtitle *Philosophie. Politische Oekonomie. Sozialismus* was omitted.

In 1880, at Paul Lafargue's request, Engels used three chapters of *Anti-Dühring* (Chapter I of the Introduction and chapters I and II of Part III) to provide a separate popular pamphlet, first published under the title *Socialism Utopian and Scientific,* and later as *The Development of Socialism from Utopia to Science* (see present edition, Vol. 24).

Anti-Dühring was published in English for the first time in 1907, in Chicago as F. Engels, *Landmarks of Scientific Socialism. Anti-Duering.* Translated and edited by Austin Lewis. This work has been repeatedly reprinted.

p. 1

² At the congress held in Gotha from May 22 to 27, 1875, the two trends in the German working-class movement—the Social-Democratic Workers' Party (Eisenachers), headed by August Bebel and Wilhelm Liebknecht, and the

Lassallean General Association of German Workers—united into the Socialist Workers' Party of Germany.   p. 5

³ The reference is in particular to August Bebel's article "Ein neuer 'Communist'", printed anonymously in the *Volksstaat* on March 13 and 20, 1874 with a favourable review of Dühring's book *Cursus der National- und Sozialökonomie, einschließlich der Hauptpunkte der Finanzpolitik* and describing Dühring as a supporter of scientific socialism.   p. 5

⁴ The reference is to lectures given to the Berlin workers on the solution of social problems, in July 1876 by Most, who popularised Dühring's views. These lectures came out as a separate pamphlet in 1876 in Berlin: J. Most, *Die Lösung der socialen Frage*. Dühring's views were also actively disseminated by the Social-Democratic newspaper *Berliner Freie Presse*.   p. 5

⁵ This refers to the protest lodged by Most with the editors of the *Volksstaat*, who did not print his article praising Dühring and Fritzsche's speech at the regular congress of the Socialist Workers' Party of Germany in August 1876, demanding that the Party's central organ *Volksstaat* disseminate Dühring's ideas.
                                                                    p. 5

⁶ The Sixth World Industrial Fair opened in Philadelphia on May 10, 1876 in connection with the centenary of the founding of the USA (July 4, 1776). Reuleaux, director of the Berlin Industrial Academy appointed by the German Government as chairman of the German panel of judges, had to admit that German-made goods were far inferior to those of other countries and that German industry's guiding principle was "cheap and nasty". This statement evoked wide comment in the press. From July to September, the *Volksstaat*, for instance, published a series of articles on this scandalous fact.
                                                                    p. 7

⁷ The phrase "really never learnt a word", which gained wide currency, is to be found in a letter by the French Admiral de Panat. It is sometimes ascribed to Talleyrand. It was made with reference to the royalists, who proved incapable of drawing any lessons from the French Revolution of the late 18th century.
                                                                    p. 7

⁸ The *Anti-Socialist Law* was passed by the German Reichstag on October 21, 1878, to counter the socialist and working-class movement. Extended in 1881, 1884, 1886, 1888, it banned all party organisations, mass workers' organisations and the socialist and labour press; Social-Democrats were subjected to reprisals. The Social-Democratic Party, with the help of Marx and Engels, managed, however, to overcome the opportunist (Höchberg, Bernstein and others) and "ultra-Left" (Most and others) tendencies in its ranks and, while the law was in force, correctly combined legal and illegal work to strengthen and extend its influence considerably among the masses. The law was abrogated on October 1, 1890. Engels assesses it in the article "Bismarck and the German Working Men's Party" (present edition, Vol. 24).   p. 8

⁹ The *Holy Alliance*—an association of European monarchs, founded in 1815 by Tsarist Russia, Austria and Prussia, to suppress revolutionary movements and preserve feudal monarchies in European countries.   p. 8

¹⁰ This manuscript, to which Marx himself gave the title *Randnoten zu Dührings Kritische Geschichte der Nationalökonomie*, was written before March 5, 1877 and then sent to Engels. (The facsimile of the first page of the manuscript is to be found in this volume, p. 213). It was first published by the Institute of

Marxism-Leninism, CC CPSU in: *Marx/Engels Gesamtausgabe*, F. Engels, *Herrn Eugen Dühring's Umwälzung der Wissenschaft/Dialektik der Natur*. Sonderausgabe, Moscow-Leningrad, 1935, pp. 341-71.   p. 9

[11] Dühring attempted to refute some of Engels' criticisms in the book: Dühring, *Kritische Geschichte der Nationalökonomie und des Sozialismus*, Dritte, theilweise umgearbeitete Auflage, Leipzig, 1879, pp. 566-67.   p. 9

[12] In July 1877, Dühring was deprived of the right to lecture at Berlin University for his sharp criticism of university practices. His dismissal sparked off a vociferous protest campaign by his supporters and was condemned by broad democratic circles.   p. 10

[13] Initially, the French translation was made by Lafargue, and published under the title *Socialisme utopique et socialisme scientifique* in the journal *Revue socialiste*, Nos. 3-5, March-May 1880.   p. 10

[14] The Russian translation was first published, as Научный социализм (Scientific Socialism), in the illegal journal Студенчество (Students), No. 1, of December 1882; a separate pamphlet Развитие научного социализма (The Development of Scientific Socialism) was put out by the Emancipation of Labour group in Geneva, in 1884.   p. 10

[15] Engels left his Manchester business on July 1, 1869 and moved to London on September 20, 1870.   p. 11

[16] In the introduction to his fundamental work on agrochemistry, Justus Liebig speaks of the evolution of his scientific views and notes: "Chemistry is moving forward at an incredible speed, and the chemists wishing to keep up with it are in a state of constant moulting. One sheds one's old feathers, no longer suitable for flight, but new ones grow in their stead and one flies all the better." See J. Liebig, *Die Chemie in ihrer Anwendung auf Agricultur und Physiologie*, 7. Aufl., Braunschweig, 1862, Th. I, p. 26.   p. 11

[17] This refers to the letter written by the German Social-Democrat Heinrich Wilhelm Fabian to Marx on November 6, 1880 (Engels described Fabian in his letters to Kautsky of April 11, 1884, to Bernstein of September 13, 1884, and to Sorge of June 3, 1885. See present edition, Vol. 47).   p. 11

[18] Marx's 1,000-odd sheets of mathematical manuscripts were written mainly in the 1860s, 1870s and early 1880s. The most complete texts of these manuscripts and the abstracts and excerpts of Marx's own notes were first published by the Institute of Marxism-Leninism in the language of the original and translated into Russian in К. Маркс, Математические рукописи (Mathematical Manuscripts), Moscow, 1968.   p. 13

[19] A reference to the works of the Irish physicist Thomas Andrews (1869), the French physicist Louis Paul Cailletet and the Swiss physicist Raoul Pierre Pictet (1877).   p. 13

[20] According to the theory expounded by Rudolf Virchow in *Die Cellularpathologie*, first published in 1858, the individual animal breaks up into tissue, the tissue into cell-states, and the cell-states into cells, so that, in the final analysis, the individual animal is a mechanical sum of separate cells.

Speaking of the "progressive" nature of this theory, Engels alludes to Virchow's membership of the German bourgeois Party of Progress, organised in June 1861.   p. 14

[21] This refers to Rousseau's theory of equality (see this volume, p. 129) expounded in his *Discours sur l'origine et les fondemens de l'inégalité parmi les hommes*, Amsterdam, 1755, and *Du contrat social; ou, Principes du droit politique*, Amsterdam, 1762.   p. 19

[22] The *Reformation* (16th century)—a broad socio-political and ideological movement of a complex social content and composition. It assumed a religious form of struggle against the Catholic doctrine and Church and was basically anti-feudal in character; it spread over most of Western and Central Europe.

The *Peasant War of 1524-26*—the biggest insurrection of German peasants (supported by townspeople) against the feudal yoke in South-western and Middle Germany.

The *Levellers*—the "true Levellers" or "Diggers"—representatives of the ultra-Left trend during the English bourgeois revolution of the mid-17th century, consisting of the poorest sections of the population, suffering from feudal and capitalist exploitation in town and countryside.   p. 19

[23] Engels has in mind, first of all, the works of Thomas More (*Utopia*, published in 1516) and Tommaso Campanella (*City of the Sun*, published in 1623).
    p. 19

[24] Denis Diderot's discourse *Le neveu de Rameau* was written in about 1762 and subsequently revised twice by the author. It was first published, in Goethe's German translation, in Leipzig in 1805; in French in *Oeuvres inédites de Diderot*, Paris, 1821, put out, in fact, in 1823.   p. 21

[25] The *Alexandrian period* (the Alexandrian culture, the Alexandrian age) derives its name from the Egyptian city of Alexandria, which was a major centre of Hellenic culture. Alexandria, to which city thousands of Greeks moved in the 3rd century B.C., witnessed a rapid advance of mathematics, mechanics (Euclid, Archimedes), geography, astronomy, physiology and other sciences.   p. 22

[26] Laplace's hypothesis of the origin of the solar system was first expounded in the last chapter of his treatise *Exposition du systême du monde*, T. I-II, Paris, 4th year of the French Republic [1796]. In the last, sixth edition of this book, prepared during Laplace's lifetime and published posthumously, in 1835, the hypothesis is expounded in the last, seventh note.

The existence of incandescent masses of gas was proved in 1864 by the English astronomer William Huggins, who made widespread use of the method of spectral analysis (evolved in 1859 by Gustav Kirchhoff and Robert Bunsen) in astronomy. Here Engels used A. Secchi's *Die Sonne*, Braunschweig, 1872, pp. 787, 789-90.   p. 24

[27] In the first German edition of *Die Entwicklung des Sozialismus von der Utopie zur Wissenschaft* (1882), Engels introduced fundamental specification, which was repeated in the authorised English edition (1892). He formulated the given proposition in the following words: "...*all* past history, with the exception of its primitive stages, was the history of class struggles...".   p. 26

[28] Dühring's works, quoted by Engels, are referred to in brackets in abbreviated form in the following way:

> D.Ph. stands for: Dühring, *Cursus der Philosophie*, Leipzig, 1875;
> D.K.G.   "   "   Dühring, *Kritische Geschichte der Nationalökonomie und des Sozialismus*, 2. Aufl., Berlin, 1875;
> D.C.   "   "   Dühring, *Cursus der National- und Socialökonomie*, 2. Aufl., Leipzig, 1876,

and the relevant pages.   p. 28

29 *Phalansteries*—the buildings in which, according to the French utopian socialist Charles Fourier, the members of phalanges, ideal harmonious communities, would live and work. p. 31

30 G. W. F. Hegel's *Encyclopädie der philosophischen Wissenschaften im Grundrisse,* Heidelberg, 1817 consists of three parts: 1) logic, 2) philosophy of nature, 3) philosophy of the mind.

In his work on *Anti-Dühring* and *Dialectics of Nature,* Engels used Hegel's writings primarily published after Hegel's death by his pupils in: G. W. F. Hegel, *Werke. Vollständige Ausgabe durch einen Verein von Freunden des Verewigten: Ph. Marheineke, J. Schulze, Ed. Gans, Lp. v. Henning, H. Hotho, C. Michelet, F. Förster,* Bd. I-XVIII, Berlin, 1832-1845. p. 34

31 Engels is presumably alluding to *Die Epiphanie der ewigen Persönlichkeit des Geistes* (published in separate installments in 1844, 1847 and 1852), the work of the Hegelian philosopher K. L. Michelet, who published the works of his teacher. p. 34

32 Engels made a note here, which he subsequently included in *Dialectics of Nature* (see this volume, pp. 544-49). p. 34

33 In the original, here and elsewhere, the term "Ideologie" is used, as a rule, as a synonym for "idealism". p. 35

34 This is an allusion to the servile submissiveness of the Prussians, who accepted the Constitution granted by King Frederick William IV on December 5, 1848, when the Prussian Constituent Assembly was dissolved. The Constitution drawn up with the participation of the Minister of the Interior, Baron Manteuffel, was finally approved by Frederick William IV on January 31, 1850, after numerous amendments had been introduced. p. 38

35 In Part I of *Anti-Dühring,* all page references made by Engels are to Dühring's *Cursus der Philosophie.* p. 39

36 Engels enumerates a number of major battles in European wars of the nineteenth century.

The *battle of Austerlitz* (now Slavkov in Czechoslovakia), December 2, 1805, in which Napoleon I defeated a combined Russo-Austrian army.

The *battle of Jena,* October 14, 1806, in which Napoleon I crushed the Prussian army.

The *battle of Königgrätz* (now Hradec Králové), or of Sadowa, July 3, 1866, in Bohemia, in which Prussian forces defeated the army of Austria and Saxony, thereby securing Prussia's victory over Austria in the war of 1866.

The *battle of Sedan,* September 1-2, 1870, in which Prussian forces defeated the French army under MacMahon and compelled it to surrender. This was the decisive battle in the Franco-Prussian war of 1870-71. p. 40

37 A reference to the research carried out by the German mathematician Karl Friedrich Gauss into non-Euclidean geometry. p. 47

38 In 1886, in his *Ludwig Feuerbach and the End of Classical German Philosophy,* Engels wrote the following on the Copernican system: "For three hundred years the Copernican solar system was a hypothesis with a hundred, a thousand or ten thousand chances to one in its favour, but still always a hypothesis. But when Leverrier, by means of the data provided by this system, not only deduced the necessity of the existence of an unknown planet, but also calculated the position in the heavens which this planet must necessarily occupy,

and when Galle really found this planet, the Copernican system was proved"
(see present edition, Vol. 26). The planet mentioned in the quotation is
Neptune, which was discovered in 1846 by Johann Galle of the Berlin
Observatory. p. 53

[39] Engels made a note here, which he subsequently included in *Dialectics of Nature*
(see this volume, pp. 530-34). p. 62

[40] *Protista* (from the Greek *protistos*—meaning first) are, according to Haeckel's
classification, a vast group of simple, both unicellular and non-cellular,
organisms.

Monera (from the Greek *moneres*—meaning single) are, according to
Haeckel, structureless masses of albumen, devoid of a nucleus but performing
all the essential vital functions: eating, locomotion, reaction to irritation,
multiplication.

The terms *protista* and *monera* were introduced by Haeckel in 1866 in his
book *Generelle Morphologie der Organismen*. p. 68

[41] The reference is to the Sumerian epic of Gilgamesh and the Accadian version
of the Deluge story discovered in 1872 by George Smith, the English Assyriologist
and archaeologist. p. 68

[42] *Ring of the Nibelung*—Richard Wagner's monumental tetralogy: *Rheingold,
Valkyrie, Siegfried* and *Götterdämmerung*.

Here Engels jokingly calls Dühring the "composer of the future", referring
to the term "composition" proposed by Dühring. Wagner's adversaries had
ironically called his music the "music of the future", the occasion being
Wagner's book *Das Kunstwerk der Zukunft*, Leipzig, 1850. p. 70

[43] *Zoophytes*—a name which, from the sixteenth century onwards, designated a
group of invertebrates (mainly sponges and coelenterata). From the mid-
nineteenth century, the term *zoophytes* was used as a synonym for coelenterata;
it has now dropped out of use. p. 73

[44] This classification was given in Huxley's *Lectures on the Elements of Comparative
Anatomy*, London, 1864, Lecture V. It provided the basis for H. A. Nicholson's
Manual of Zoology (first published in 1870), which Engels used in his work on
Anti-Dühring and *Dialectics of Nature*. p. 73

[45] *Traube's artificial cells*—inorganic formations representing a model of living
cells; they were created by the German chemist and physiologist Moritz Traube
by mixing colloidal solutions. He read a paper on his experiments to the 47th
Congress of German Naturalists and Physicians in Breslau, on September 23,
1874. Marx and Engels thought highly of Traube's discovery (see Marx's letter
to Pyotr Lavrov of June 18, 1875, and to Wilhelm Alexander Freund of
January 21, 1877, present edition, Vol. 45). p. 76

[46] Here Engels relates a report in the journal *Nature* of November 16, 1876
dealing with the paper read by Dmitry Mendeleyev on September 3, 1876 at
the 5th Congress of Russian Naturalists and Physicians in Warsaw. Mendeleyev
reported on the results of his experiments, conducted jointly with Józef Jerzy
Boguski in 1875-76, to verify the Boyle-Mariotte law.

Engels evidently wrote this note when checking the proofs of this chapter
of *Anti-Dühring*, which was printed in *Vorwärts* on February 28, 1877. Engels
added the end of the note, given in parentheses, in 1885, when he was
preparing the second edition of *Anti-Dühring*. p. 85

47 Rousseau's *Discours sur l'origine et les fondemens de l'inégalité parmi les hommes* was written in 1754 and published in 1755.   p. 90

48 The *Thirty Years' War* (1618-48)—an all-European war caused by the struggle between Protestants and Catholics. Germany became the main arena of this war, and consequently the object of military pillage and the predatory claims of the belligerents.   p. 92

49 This refers to Stirner's *Der Einzige und sein Eigenthum,* Leipzig, 1845; for criticism of it see *The German Ideology* by Marx and Engels (present edition, Vol. 5, pp. 117-450).   p. 92

50 Engels' main source of data on these events was, evidently, the American diplomat Eugene Schuyler's *Turkistan. Notes of a Journey in Russian Turkistan, Khokand, Bukhara, and Kuldja,* in two volumes, Vol. II, London, 1876, pp. 356-59.   p. 94

51 The *American Constitution of 1787,* officially proclaiming the USA a federal republic, was the most progressive bourgeois constitution of its time. Yet it virtually legalised slavery. Marx wrote on this: "The Constitution ... recognises slaves as property and obliges the Union government to protect this property" (see present edition, Vol. 19, p. 36).   p. 98

52 Karl Marx, *Das Kapital,* Bd. I, 2. Aufl., Hamburg, 1872, p. 36 (see present edition, Vol. 35, Part I, Chapter I, Section 3, A, 3: The Equivalent Form of Value).

In *Anti-Dühring,* Engels quotes from the 2nd German edition of Vol. I of *Capital.* He used the 3rd German edition of *Capital,* Vol. I only when he revised Part II, Chapter X for the 3rd edition of *Anti-Dühring.*   p. 99

53 Lassalle was arrested in February 1848 on a charge of inciting to steal a cash-box with documents to be used in the divorce case of Countess Sophie Hatzfeldt, whose lawyer he was from 1846 to 1854. Lassalle's trial took place from August 5 to 11, 1848; he was acquitted by a jury.   p. 100

54 *Code pénal*—the French Penal Code, adopted in 1810, which came into force in France and French-conquered regions of Western and South-western Germany in 1811; along with the Civil Code, it remained in force in the Rhine Province after it had been annexed by Prussia in 1815.   p. 101

55 *Code Napoléon*—the French Civil Code was adopted in 1804. Engels called it "a classical legal code of bourgeois society" in his *Ludwig Feuerbach and the End of Classical German Philosophy* (see present edition, Vol. 26).

Here Engels is speaking of it in the broad sense, having in mind the five codes adopted under Napoleon from 1804 to 1810: civil, civil-procedure, trade, criminal and criminal-procedure.   p. 101

56 In *Ethica ordine geometrico demonstrata et in quinque partes distincta* (first published in Amsterdam in 1677), Part I, Addendum, Spinoza said that ignorance is no argument, in opposition to the clerical-teleological view that everything is determined by "divine Providence" as the final cause and that the only means of argumentation is the plea of ignorance of other causes.   p. 102

57 *Corpus juris civilis*—code of civil laws regulating property relations in Roman slave-owning society; it was drawn up from 528 to 534 under the Byzantine Emperor Justinian. In *Ludwig Feuerbach and the End of Classical German Philosophy,* Engels described it as the "first world law of a commodity-producing society" (see present edition, Vol. 26).   p. 102

58 The law on the compulsory civil registration of births, marriages and deaths was passed in Prussia on October 1, 1874 and a similar one for the whole German Empire on February 6, 1875. The law deprived the Church of the right to such registration, thereby considerably curtailing its influence and income. It was directed primarily against the Catholic Church.   p. 103

59 The reference is to the provinces of Brandenburg, East Prussia, West Prussia, Posen, Pomerania and Silesia, which were part of the Kingdom of Prussia until the Vienna Congress of 1815.   p. 104

60 *Personal equation*—a correction made for variation in astronomical observation due to a person's individual peculiarities.   p. 105

61 Dühring drew these data on the structure of Marx's *Capital* from the Preface to the first German edition (see present edition, Vol. 35). From 1867 onwards, when Vol. I of *Capital* was published, Marx's plan was to have the entire work brought out in three volumes in four books, the 2nd and the 3rd of which were to comprise Vol. II. After Marx's death, Engels published the 2nd and 3rd books as vols. II and III. The last, fourth book, *Theories of Surplus-Value*, was published after Engels' death.   p. 113

62 Chapter XXIV of Vol. I of *Capital*—"The So-called Primitive Accumulation"— takes up pp. 742-93 of the 1872 German edition. The last, seventh paragraph of this chapter—"Historical Tendency of Capitalist Accumulation"—begins on p. 791 of that edition.   p. 123

63 The reference is to Rousseau's *Discours sur l'origine et les fondemens de l'inégalité parmi les hommes*, written in 1754 (see Note 47). Below, Engels quotes the second part of this work (1755 edition, pp. 116, 118, 146, 175-76 and 176-77).   p. 129

64 The expression *determinatio est negatio* is to be found in Spinoza's letter to Jarigh Jelles of June 2, 1674 (see B. Spinoza, *Epistolae doctorum quorundam virorum ad B. de Spinoza et auctoris responsiones ...*, Letter 50), where it is used in the sense of "determination is a negation". The expression *omnis determinatio est negatio* and its interpretation as "every determination is a negation" are to be found in Hegel's works, from which they have become widely known (see G. W. F. Hegel, *Encyclopädie der philosophischen Wissenschaften*, Erster Teil, § 91, Zusatz; *Die Wissenschaft der Logik*, Erstes Buch, Erster Abschnitt, Zweites Kapitel: "b. Qualität"; *Vorlesungen über die Geschichte der Philosophie*, Erster Teil, Erster Abschnitt, Erstes Kapitel, Paragraph über Parmenides).   p. 131

65 Engels has in mind, above all, Marx's works *The Poverty of Philosophy* (1847), *A Contribution to the Critique of Political Economy* (1859) and Vol. I of *Capital* (1867). Marx carried out a thorough study of precapitalist forms of production in his *Economic Manuscripts of 1857-58* (first version of *Capital*). (See present edition, vols. 6, 28, 30, 35).   p. 139

66 In Part II, except Chapter X, of *Anti-Dühring*, Engels quotes from the second (1876) edition of Dühring's *Cursus der National- und Socialökonomie*.   p. 140

67 *Reptiles*—a nickname widespread in Germany in the 1870s for journalists subsidised by the government. This expression, but in a different sense, was used by Bismarck on January 30, 1869, in the Prussian Chamber of Deputies, this time with reference to the government's adversaries.   p. 142

68 Engels is referring to the *July Revolution of 1830* in France, which brought big bankers and industrialists to power; from this time on, as a result of the final

victory of the bourgeoisie over the nobility, the struggle between the proletariat and the bourgeoisie came to the fore.   p. 145

[69] The *Restoration*—the second rule of the Bourbon dynasty in France (1814-15, 1815-30), overthrown by the Revolution at the end of the 18th century. It was brought to an end by the *July Revolution of 1830* (see Note 68).   p. 147

[70] Engels took these facts from W. Wachsmuth's *Hellenische Alterthumskunde aus dem Gesichtspunkte des Staates*, Th. II, Abth. I, Halle, 1829, p. 44.

The source for the number of slaves in Corinth and Aegina during the Greco-Persian wars (5th cent. B.C.), is *Banquet of Sophists*, Book VI, by the ancient Greek writer Athenaeus.   p. 149

[71] This refers to absolute monarchy (absolutism)—a form of state in the last period of the existence of feudalism.   p. 152

[72] The reference is to the guns produced by Krupps, the biggest German steel firm, and rifles designed and produced by the German engineers and entrepreneurs, the Mauser brothers.   p. 153

[73] Engels means the protracted economic crisis of 1873-79 in German industry, in spite of the seizure of Alsace and East Lorraine and the 5,000 million francs of war indemnities that France paid to Germany under the terms of the Frankfurt peace treaty (1871), after her defeat in the Franco-Prussian war of 1870-71.   p. 154

[74] The War of Independence in North America (1775-83) was the first bourgeois revolution on the American continent.   p. 156

[75] A reference to the bourgeois-democratic revolution in France at the end of the 18th century.   p. 156

[76] The *Prussian Landwehr system* provided for the formation of army units from among people of the older age groups who were liable to military service and had served in the regular army and been in the reserve for the established period. The *Landwehr* first appeared in Prussia in 1813-14 as a people's militia to combat Napoleon.   p. 157

[77] The reference is to the Austro-Prussian war of 1866.   p. 157

[78] In the *battle of Saint-Privat*, or of *Gravelotte*, August 18, 1870, the German troops defeated the French Rhenish army at the cost of enormous losses.

On the source from which the data on the losses sustained by the Prussian Guard were taken see Note 338.   p. 157

[79] The *Crimean war* (1853-56) between Russia and a coalition of Britain, France, Turkey and Sardinia, broke out as a result of a clash of their economic and political interests in the Middle East.   p. 160

[80] See Note 72.   p. 161

[81] The phrase in parentheses was added by Engels in the third edition of *Anti-Dühring*.   p. 161

[82] Dühring called his "dialectics" "natural dialectics" to distinguish it from Hegel's "unnatural" dialectics. See E. Dühring, *Natürliche Dialektik. Neue logische Grundlegungen der Wissenschaft und Philosophie*, Berlin, 1865, p. 13.   p. 163

[83] Dealing with a common subject, the works of Georg Ludwig Maurer (12 volumes) study the agrarian, urban and state system of mediaeval Germany. These works are: *Einleitung zur Geschichte der Mark-, Hof-, Dorf- und Stadt-*

Verfassung und der öffentlichen Gewalt, München, 1854; *Geschichte der Markenverfassung in Deutschland,* Erlangen, 1856; *Geschichte der Fronhöfe, der Bauernhöfe und der Hofverfassung in Deutschland,* Bd. I-IV, Erlangen, 1862-63; *Geschichte der Dorfverfassung in Deutschland,* Bd. I-II, Erlangen, 1865-66; *Geschichte der Städteverfassung in Deutschland,* Bd. I-IV, Erlangen, 1869-71. The first, second and fourth of these works are devoted to a study of the German mark system.
p. 163

84 Engels ironically changes the title of Heinrich LXXII—one of the two influential Reuss princes of the Younger branch (Reuss-Lobenstein-Ebersdorf). Greiz—capital of the Reuss principality (Elder branch, Reuss-Greiz). Schleiz—a domain of the Reuss princes (Younger branch, Reuss-Schleiz)—was not a possession of Heinrich LXXII.
p. 164

85 This is an expression from Frederick William IV's New Year message (January 1, 1849) to the Prussian Army. For a critical assessment of this message see Marx's article "A New-Year Greeting" (present edition, Vol. 8, pp. 222-26).
p. 170

86 The reference is to the laws on maximum prices adopted by the revolutionary government during the War of Independence in North America (see Note 74) and the National Convention during the French Revolution (see Note 75).
p. 177

87 A detailed criticism of the Lassallean slogan of "full" or unlimited "proceeds of labour" is given in Section 1 of Marx's *Critique of the Gotha Programme* (see present edition, Vol. 24).
p. 187

88 Marx intended to include the third book in Vol. II of *Capital* (see Note 61).
p. 199

89 According to a Biblical story, when Jericho was besieged by the Israelites under Joshua, its impregnable walls came tumbling down at the sound of holy trumpets and the shouts of the besiegers (Joshua 6 : 1-4, 9, 19).
p. 200

90 This is an allusion to King Frederick Wilhelm IV's speech from the throne at the opening of the United Diet in Prussia on April 11, 1847, in which he stated that he would never allow "the natural relations between the monarch and the people" to be turned into "conventional, constitutional ones" and "the used up sheet of paper" take the place of "primordial holy loyalty".
p. 200

91 See Note 36.
p. 200

92 This chapter, based on Marx's manuscript of 1877 (see this volume, p. 15 and notes 1 and 10) was evidently edited by Engels in the second half of May 1894, while he was preparing the third German edition of *Anti-Dühring.* That is why this chapter contains a reference to the third German edition of Marx's *Capital* (1883). Engels restored Marx's original text as fully as possible. The main object of Marx's criticism here was the second edition of Dühring's *Kritische Geschichte der Nationalökonomie und des Sozialismus,* in which the author attempted to describe the history of political economy and in which Marx's teaching was the object of his libellous attacks.
p. 211

93 *Mercantilism*—a school of bourgeois political economy, that emerged in the last third of the fifteenth century; it expressed the interests of the merchant bourgeoisie in the age of the primitive accumulation of capital, identified the wealth of the country with the accumulation of money and attached primary importance in this to the state. Marx called the early period of mercantilism the monetary system (see present edition, Vol. 36).
p. 216

[94] William Petty's *Quantulumcunque concerning Money* was written in 1682 in the form of an address to Lord Halifax and published in London in 1695. Marx used the 1760 edition.

Petty's *The Political anatomy of Ireland* was written in 1672 and published in London in 1691.   p. 219

[95] The reference here is to the French chemist A. L. Lavoisier's "De la richesse territoriale du royaume de France" and "Essai sur la population de la ville de Paris, sur la richesse et ses consommations", as well as the joint work "Essai d'arithmétique politique", written by Lavoisier and the French mathematician Lagrange published in *Mélanges d'économie politique. Précédés de notices historiques sur chaque auteur, et accompagnés de commentaires et de notes explicatives, par MM. E. Daire et G. de Molinari*, Vol. 1, Paris, 1847, pp. 575-620.
                                                                             p. 220

[96] Engels is referring here to the attempt by John Law, a Scottish economist, to put paper money into circulation in France, where his idea received support in court quarters. In 1716 he founded a private bank, the Banque générale, which, in 1718, was reorganised into the state Banque royale. The unlimited issue of bank-notes by Law's bank was accompanied by the withdrawal of coins from circulation. As a result, Stock Exchange speculation reached an unprecedented scale and culminated, in 1720, in the bankruptcy of the bank and of the Law system itself.   p. 221

[97] An inaccuracy in the text: the first edition of Richard Cantillon's *Essai sur la nature du commerce en général* appeared not in 1752, but in 1755, as Marx himself pointed out in *Capital*, Vol. I (see present edition, Vol. 35, Part VI, Chapter XXI). Adam Smith mentions Cantillon's work in Volume I of his *An Inquiry into the Nature and Causes of the Wealth of Nations*, Chapter VIII, Of the Wages of Labour.   p. 227

[98] In 1866, acting through his adviser Hermann Wagener, Bismarck requested Dühring to draw up a memorandum for the Prussian government on the labour question. Dühring, who advocated harmony between capital and labour, complied with this request. His work was published, however, without his knowledge, first anonymously, and later under the signature of Wagener. This gave Dühring grounds for initiating proceedings against Wagener on a charge of breaking copyright laws. In 1868, Dühring won his case. At the height of this scandalous trial, Dühring published *Die Schicksale meiner socialen Denkschrift für das Preussische Staatsministerium* (see this volume, p. 144).   p. 228

[99] *Livre tournois*—a French coin named after the town of Tour; from 1740 onwards it was equal to one franc; in 1799, it was replaced by the franc.
                                                                             p. 233

[100] Engels is referring to the beginning of Chapter I of the "Introduction" (see this volume, pp. 16, 19). He wrote this footnote when *Anti-Dühring* was published in the newspaper. It remained unchanged in all editions of the book published during Engels' lifetime (see Note 1). In all subsequent separate editions, the first two chapters were joined together under the heading "Introduction". The numbers of the other chapters were not changed, so "Philosophy" now begins with Chapter III (see this volume, p. 33).   p. 244

[101] The *Reign of Terror*—the period of Jacobin revolutionary-democratic dictatorship (June 1793-July 1794), which relied on the revolutionary bloc of the urban petty and middle bourgeoisie, the majority of the peasants and plebeians.

The *Directorate*—the organ of executive power in France (from November 1795), formed under the 1795 Constitution. Existing until the Napoleon's *coup d'état* of November 9 (18 Brumaire), 1799 it upheld the interests of big bourgeoisie and brutally suppressed the revolutionary actions of the popular masses.

In 1804, Bonaparte, who actually became the head of the state under the Consulate after 18 Brumaire, was proclaimed Emperor of the French.

p. 244

102 A reference to the slogan "Liberty, Equality, Fraternity" current during the French Revolution.   p. 245

103 Saint-Simon's first work, *Lettres d'un habitant de Genève à ses contemporains* was written in Geneva in 1802 and published anonymously in Paris in 1803, without the place and date of publication being indicated. When working on *Anti-Dühring*, Engels made use of: G. Hubbard, *Saint-Simon. Sa vie et ses travaux. Suivi de fragments des plus célèbres écrits de Saint-Simon*, Paris, 1857. This edition contains inaccuracies regarding the publication dates of various works by Saint-Simon.

The first most important work of Charles Fourier was *Théorie des quatre mouvements et des destinées générales*, written in the early nineteenth century and published anonymously in Lyons in 1808 (the title page gives Leipzig as the place of publication).   p. 245

104 The allied armies of the sixth anti-French coalition (Russia, Austria, Britain, Prussia and other countries) entered Paris on March 31, 1814. Napoleon's empire fell and Napoleon himself, after abdicating, was banished to the Island of Elba. The Bourbon monarchy was restored in France for the first time (1814-15).   p. 247

105 The *Hundred Days*—the period of brief restoration of the Napoleonic Empire—from the day of Napoleon's return from exile on Elba to Paris on March 20, 1815, until his second abdication on June 22 of the same year, after his army's defeat at Waterloo on June 18, 1815 by Anglo-Dutch forces under Wellington and by the Prussian army under Blücher.   p. 247

106 After Dühring had been deprived of the right to lecture at Berlin University for criticising university practices and attacking such prominent scientists as Helmholtz, Virchow and others (see this volume, pp. 9-10), a just campaign, in the columns of the Social-Democratic press included, grew into an unrestrained apologia for Dühring, owing to the efforts of his supporters. This is what Engels is hinting at. Dühring's attacks on the German Social-Democrats in reactionary newspapers, in the autumn of the same year led, however, to a fall in his authority and influence not only among socialists, but also among people of progressive views in general.   p. 247

107 This idea had been enunciated in Charles Fourier's first book—*Théorie des quatre mouvements*—which contains the following general thesis: "Social progress and changes of a period are accompanied by the progress of women towards freedom, while the decay of the social system brings with it a reduction of the freedoms enjoyed by women." Fourier concludes: "Extension of the rights of women is the basic principle of all social progress" (Fourier, *Oeuvres complètes*, t. I, Paris, 1841, pp. 195-96).   p. 248

108 In a note to the relevant passage in *Socialism Utopian and Scientific* (see this volume, p. 10), Engels gives the source of the last three quotations: R. Owen, *The Revolution in the Mind and Practice of the Human Race; or, the Coming Change*

from Irrationality to Rationality, London, 1849, pp. 21, 22. The facts from Owen's biography mentioned above are from the same source.   p. 250

109 The Bill moved on Owen's initiative in June 1815, was passed by Parliament only in July 1819, having been greatly curtailed. The Act regulating labour in cotton mills banned the employment of children under the age of nine, limited the working day to 12 hours for young people under 18 and established for all workers two breaks, one for breakfast and the other for lunch, with a total duration of one and a half hours.   p. 251

110 A Congress of Co-operative Societies and Trades Unions, presided over by Owen, was held in London in October 1833. This Congress formally founded the Grand National Consolidated Trades Union, the Charter of which was adopted in February 1834. It was Owen's intention that this Union would take over the management of production and remake society peacefully. This utopian plan collapsed very soon. In the face of strong opposition from employers and the state, the Union ceased to exist in 1834.   p. 251

111 *Equitable Labour Exchange Bazaars* were founded by workers' co-operatives in various towns of England; the first of these bazaars was founded by Owen in London in September 1832 and existed until mid-1834.   p. 251

112 The reference is to Proudhon's idea of organising an exchange bank, first put forward in his pamphlet *Organisation du Crédit et de la Circulation et Solution du problème sociale,* which was published in early April 1848. This idea was developed in detail in his other works. Proudhon's main idea was to replace gold and silver as a means of circulation, with bank-notes, which were, in fact, impersonal bills. These bank-notes of the exchange bank were secured by products of labour and, in this, according to Proudhon, lay their principal difference from other paper money issued by banks and secured by precious metals, landed property, etc.

To put this idea into practice, the Banque du peuple was founded in Paris on January 31, 1849. It went bankrupt, however, and closed in early April 1849.   p. 251

113 *Harmony Hall*—the name of the communist community founded by English utopian socialists, led by Owen, at the close of 1839 in Queenwood, Hampshire, England. It existed until 1845.   p. 253

114 In *Socialism Utopian and Scientific,* Engels gives a note referring to his work *The Mark* (see present edition, Vol. 24).   p. 260

115 This refers to the wars between the major European powers in the seventeenth and eighteenth centuries for control of trade with India and America and for seizure of colonial markets. The principal rivals were initially England and Holland, later England and France. England won these wars and, towards the close of the eighteenth century, almost all world trade was concentrated in her hands.   p. 260

116 The reference is to the Prussian Royal Maritime Company, which was founded as a commercial and banking company in 1772 and granted a number of important privileges by the state. It advanced big loans to the government and, in fact, became its banker and broker.   p. 265

117 The slogan *"a free people's state"*—is criticised in section IV of Marx's *Critique of the Gotha Programme,* Engels' letter to August Bebel of March 18-28, 1875 (see present edition, vols. 24 and 45), and Lenin's *The State and Revolution,*

Chapter I, Paragraph 4, and Chapter IV, Paragraph 3 (*Collected Works*, Vol. 25, pp. 395-401 and 439-42). p. 268

[118] These figures are from Robert Giffen's paper "Recent Accumulations of Capital in the United Kingdom", read at the Statistical Society on January 15, 1878 and printed in the London *Journal of the Statistical Society* in March 1878.

p. 270

[119] Speaking about the "German Empire of the Prussian nation", Engels underlines, on the one hand, that the country's unification under Prussian supremacy was completed by Bismarck on a militaristic basis and, on the other, alludes to the name "the Holy Roman Empire of the German nation" which, from the end of the fifteenth century until its formal liquidation in 1806, was part of the archaic state formation, the mediaeval feudal empire, founded in 962 by the German king Otto I and embracing the territory of Germany and several other Central European states. The empire was a precarious unity of feudal principalities and free towns recognising the supreme power of an emperor. p. 283

[120] Engels had in mind a speech delivered by Bismarck in the Lower Chamber of the Prussian Landtag on March 20, 1852, stating that, if there were another upsurge of the revolutionary movement, large towns, as centres of the revolutionary movement, ought to be wiped out from the face of the earth.

p. 283

[121] The ledger (*Kommerzbuch*) is described by Wilhelm Weitling in *Garantien der Harmonie und Freiheit*, Section II, Ch. 10, Vivis, 1842. According to Weitling's utopian plan, in the future society, every able-bodied person would have to work a certain number of hours a day and, in return, would receive the necessary means of subsistence. Every person would have the right to work several "commercial hours" over and above this time and, in return, to receive luxury items, different entertainments, theatre and concert tickets, etc. These additional working hours and the products received for them would be recorded in a ledger. p. 288

[122] *Non olet* (it [money] does not stink): these words were spoken by the Roman Emperor Vespasian (69-79 A.D.) in reply to his son, who reproached him for introducing a tax on lavatories. p. 289

[123] See Note 111. p. 291

[124] See Note 87. p. 297

[125] In the original *"Zarucker"*—from the German *zurück* (*zaruck*—in Berlin dialect), meaning "retrograde person", "reactionary" ("Rückschrittler", "Reaktionär"). See A. Glaßbrenner, *Herr Buffey in der Zaruck-Gesellschaft* in: *Berlin wie es ist und—trinkt*, Leipzig, 1848, pp. 14-15. p. 299

[126] An expression from the resolution written by Prussian King Frederick II on July 22, 1740 in reply to an inquiry from Minister von Brand and President of the Consistory Reichenbach as to whether Catholic schools might be permitted in a Protestant Prussian state. p. 300

[127] *May laws*—four laws on creed adopted on Bismarck's initiative in May 1873. These laws established rigid state control over the Catholic Church and were the culmination of Bismarck's so-called drive for culture from 1872 to 1875, which was directed against the Catholic clergy as the mainstay of the "Centre" party, representing the interests of the separatists in South and South-western

Germany. Police persecution met with desperate resistance by Catholics and brought them the halo of martyrdom. From the late 1870s, in order to unite all the reactionary forces against the working-class movement, Bismarck's government was compelled first to relax and then to repeal almost all the anti-Catholic laws.   p. 302

128 The *Magic Flute*—a Mozart opera with a libretto by Emanuel Schikaneder. Composed and performed in 1791, it mirrored Masonic ideas; both the author of the libretto and Mozart himself having been Masons.   p. 308

129 *Referendary*—in Germany a junior official, chiefly a lawyer trained at court or in a state office.   p. 309

130 *Dialectics of Nature* is one of Frederick Engels' major works. It gives a dialectical materialist generalisation of the principal natural scientific achievements of the mid-nineteenth century, develops materialist dialectics, and criticises metaphysical and idealist conceptions in the natural sciences.

Dialectics of Nature was the culmination of profound scientific studies carried out by Engels over many years. Originally, in about January 1873 (see this volume, pp. 482-87), he planned to summarise the results of his research in the form of a polemical work criticising Ludwig Büchner, a vulgar materialist. Later, he decided to set himself a more comprehensive task; by May 30, 1873, he had completed the plan for this work and set it out in a letter to Marx (see present edition, Vol. 44). Marx showed the letter to Carl Schorlemmer, a prominent chemist. The original of that letter bears comments by Schorlemmer, who approved of the main points of Engels' plan.

Engels wrote the items included in *Dialectics of Nature* between 1873 and 1882, during which time he studied a vast amount of source material on major problems of the natural sciences and more or less completed 10 articles and chapters and many notes and fragments; all in all, almost 200 sketches.

Engels' work on *Dialectics of Nature* may be divided into two major periods: early 1873 to January 1878 and summer 1878 to summer 1882. During the former, Engels was engaged mostly in collecting data, and wrote most of the fragments and the "Introduction". During the latter period, he drew up a specific plan for the future work (see this volume, pp. 313-14, 317) and wrote the other fragments and almost all the chapters and articles. When Marx died, the job of completing the publication of *Capital* and of leading the international working-class movement became a full-time occupation for Engels, so he virtually had to discontinue his work on *Dialectics of Nature*, which remained unfinished.

Dialectics of Nature has come down to us in the form of four folders in which Engels grouped all the articles and notes relating to this work. He gave the folders the following headings: (1) "Dialectics and Natural Science", (2) "The Investigation of Nature and Dialectics", (3) "Dialectics of Nature", and (4) "Mathematics and Natural Science. Miscellaneous". Only two of the folders—the second and the third—have tables of contents compiled by the author, indicating the arrangement of the material in the folders (see this volume, p. 591). As for the first and fourth folders, we cannot be certain that the sheets are arranged exactly as Engels would have wished.

The first folder ("Dialectics and Natural Science") consists of two parts: (1) Notes written on 11 double sheets, numbered by the author, each sheet entitled "Dialectics of Nature". These notes, which are separated from one another by dividing lines (in the present volume by asterisks), were written in the chronological order in which they were arranged on the numbered sheets of the manuscript. (2) Twenty unnumbered sheets, each containing one longer note or several shorter ones are separated by dividing lines. Many of these notes contain information enabling us to put date to them.

The second folder ("The Investigation of Nature and Dialectics") consists of three large notes: "On the Prototypes of the Mathematical Infinite in the Real World", "On the 'Mechanical' Conception of Nature", "On Nägeli's Incapacity to Know the Infinite"; "Old Preface to [Anti-]Dühring. On Dialectics", the article "The Part Played by Labour in the Transition from Ape to Man" and a large fragment entitled "Omitted from Feuerbach". The table of contents, drawn up by Engels for this folder, indicates that it originally included two more articles: "Basic Forms of Motion" and "Natural Science in the Spirit World". Subsequently, Engels crossed out these headings from the table of contents of the second folder and transferred them to the third, in which he incorporated the more complete components of his unfinished work.

The third folder ("Dialectics of Nature") contains the six most complete articles: "Basic Forms of Motion", "The Measure of Motion.—Work", "Electricity", "Natural Science in the Spirit World", "Introduction" and "Tidal Friction" (see notes 170, 175, 187, 157, 138 and 183).

The fourth folder ("Mathematics and Natural Science. Miscellaneous") consists of two unfinished chapters: "Dialectics" and "Heat"; 18 unnumbered sheets, each containing one longer note or several shorter ones, separated by dividing lines, and several sheets with mathematical calculations. The notes in the fourth folder include two plan outlines for Dialectics of Nature (see notes 131 and 137).

The detailed index of contents of the folders and the chronological list of chapters and fragments of Dialectics of Nature compiled by the editors may be found at the end of this volume (pp. 686-95).

There are some manuscripts among the material for Dialectics of Nature that were not originally intended for it: the "Old Preface to [Anti-]Dühring. On Dialectics", two "Notes to Anti-Dühring" ("On the Prototypes of the Mathematical Infinite in the Real World" and "On the 'Mechanical' Conception of Nature"), "Omitted from Feuerbach", "The Part Played by Labour in the Transition from Ape to Man" and "Natural Science in the Spirit World" (see notes 154, 280, 271, 217, 199, 157).

The present edition of Dialectics of Nature includes everything contained in Engels' four folders, except for a few pages with fragmentary mathematical calculations not accompanied by any explanatory text, and the following notes, which are obviously unconnected with Dialectics of Nature: 1) the original outline of the "Introduction" to Anti-Dühring (see this volume, pp. 591-95); 2) a fragment on slavery (see this volume, pp. 608-09); 3) extracts from Charles Fourier's Le Nouveau Monde industriel et sociétaire (see this volume, p. 612) (these three notes are part of the preparatory material for Anti-Dühring) and 4) a small note with a comment by Engels on the negative view held by Philip Pauli, the German chemist, of the labour theory of value.

The material is here arranged by subject matter, in keeping with the basic lines of the two plan outlines (see this volume, pp. 313-15, 317). Despite some differences, the basic contents of the manuscript are quite in keeping with the main lines of the plan of Dialectics of Nature. The distinction drawn between more or less complete articles and chapters, on the one hand, and preparatory notes, on the other, as indicated by Engels himself in grouping the materials by folders, is retained. Thus, the work is divided into two parts: 1) articles and chapters, and 2) notes and fragments, in each of which the material is arranged according to the main lines of Engels' plan.

These basic lines indicate the following sequence of parts: a) historical introduction, b) general questions of materialist dialectics, c) classification of the sciences, d) considerations concerning the dialectical content of individual sciences, e) examination of some important methodological problems of natural science, f) transition to social sciences, the penultimate part being almost unelaborated.

The basic lines of the plan account for the following sequence of articles and chapters of *Dialectics of Nature,* constituting the first part of the book:

(1) Introduction;
(2) Old Preface to [*Anti-*]*Dühring*. On Dialectics;
(3) Natural Science in the Spirit World;
(4) Dialectics;
(5) Basic Forms of Motion;
(6) The Measure of Motion.—Work;
(7) Tidal Friction;
(8) Heat;
(9) Electricity;
(10) The Part Played by Labour in the Transition from Ape to Man.

As for all these articles and chapters, the order according to subject matter coincides in the main with the chronological order, except for the article "The Part Played by Labour ...", which in its subject belongs to the last part of the plan, but was written before most of the articles and chapters (see Note 199). The article "Natural Science in the Spirit World" appears in third place among the articles and chapters because, like the two preceding it, it is of general methodological significance and is fairly closely connected with the "Old Preface to [*Anti-*]*Dühring*" as far as its basic ideas are concerned (the need for theoretical thought in empirical natural science).

As for the rough drafts, notes and fragments forming the second part of the work, they are arranged in keeping with Engels' plan outlines as follows:

(1) From the History of Science;
(2) Natural Science and Philosophy;
(3) Dialectics;
(4) Forms of Motion of Matter. Classification of the Sciences;
(5) Mathematics;
(6) Mechanics and Astronomy;
(7) Physics;
(8) Chemistry;
(9) Biology.

The arrangement of the fragments, almost entirely corresponds to that of the articles and chapters of *Dialectics of Nature.* The first section of the fragments corresponds to the first article of *Dialectics of Nature*; the second section to the second and third articles; the third section to the fourth article; the fourth section to the fifth article; the sixth section to the sixth and seventh articles; and the seventh section to the eighth and ninth articles. The tenth article has no counterpart among the fragments.

Within the sections, the fragments are again arranged by subject matter. First come fragments dealing with more general questions, then ones devoted to more specific issues. The fragments in the section "From the History of Science", are arranged in historical sequence: from the rise of the sciences among the ancient peoples to Engels' contemporaries. In the section "Dialectics", first come notes on the general issues and basic laws of dialectics, then those on so called subjective dialectics. As far as possible, each section ends with fragments that serve as a transition to the next section.

The material for *Dialectics of Nature* was never published in Engels' lifetime. Only two of the articles came out after his death: "The Part Played by Labour in the Transition from Ape to Man", published in *Die Neue Zeit* in 1896, and "Natural Science in the Spirit World", published in the yearbook *Illustrirter Neue Welt-Kalender* in 1898 (see notes 199, 157). The full text of *Dialectics of Nature* was first published in the Soviet Union in 1925, the German text appearing alongside a Russian translation (*Marx-Engels Archiv*, Book II). It was subsequently reprinted more than once, corrections being introduced on each occasion into the reading of the manuscript and improvements being made in the arrangement of the material. The most important of the subsequent editions were the original-language version (*Marx/Engels Gesamtausgabe*, F. Engels, *Herrn Eugen Dühring's Umwälzung der Wissenschaft/Dialektik der Natur*. Sonderausgabe, Moscow-Leningrad, 1935) and the Russian-language edition of 1941, on which numerous editions in other countries were patterned.

In this volume, the material of *Dialectics of Nature* is arranged on the pattern of Volume 20 of Marx and Engels, Second Russian Edition, Moscow, 1961, which also served as the basis for Marx/Engels, *Werke*, Bd. 20, Berlin, 1962. Besides, compared with previous editions, more precise dates are given here for the writing of the whole work and of its individual parts, owing to the work done in preparing *Dialectics of Nature* for publication in Vol. 26 of the first section of *MEGA* (Berlin, 1985). p. 311

131 The general plan for *Dialectics of Nature* drawn up by Engels in late August or early September 1878 outlines the structure of this work. Indications of the date are provided by: reference in "Old Preface to [*Anti-*]*Dühring*" (see Note 154), Haeckel's pamphlet *Freie Wissenschaft und freie Lehre*, published in July 1878, and Engels' letter to Lavrov of August 10, 1878 (see present edition, Vol. 45). p. 313

132 *Plastidules* was the name Haeckel gave to the smallest particles of live plasma, each of which, according to his theory, is a protein molecule of highly complex structure and possesses a kind of elementary "soul" (see E. Haeckel, *Die Perigenesis der Plastidule*, Berlin, 1876).

The problem of the "soul of the plastidule", the existence of embryonic consciousness in elementary live organisms, and the relationship between consciousness and its material substratum were discussed by Haeckel, Nägeli and Virchow at the 50th Congress of German Natural Scientists and Physicians, held in Munich in September 1877. Haeckel devoted a special chapter in his *Freie Wissenschaft und freie Lehre* (Stuttgart, 1878) to defending his views against Virchow's attacks. As Engels' letter to Lavrov of August 10, 1878, shows, he had already obtained the pamphlet by that time (see present edition, Vol. 45). p. 314

133 Engels has in mind a discussion held by Ernst Haeckel and Rudolf Virchow at the 50th Congress of German Natural Scientists and Physicians in 1877 on the teaching of Darwinism in schools. The discussion developed into an argument about the freedom of science teaching in general. Virchow, who saw a direct link between the spread of Darwinism and the socialist movement, took a negative stand in this discussion (see R. Virchow, *Die Freiheit der Wissenschaft im modernen Staat*, Berlin, 1877, p. 12). p. 314

664 Notes

134 On Virchow's concept of an individual animal as a federation of cell-states see Note 20. p. 314

135 Engels was prompted to criticise inconsistent Darwinists (particularly, Haeckel and Schmidt) by the discussion at the 50th Congress of German Natural Scientists and Physicians in September 1877 (see Note 133), by Oskar Schmidt's intention to read a paper "Darwinismus und Socialdemocratie" at the forthcoming 51st Congress in September 1878 (Engels learned about this from the journal *Nature* of July 18, 1878, Vol. XVIII, No. 455, p. 316) and by the publication of Haeckel's pamphlet *Freie Wissenschaft und freie Lehre*, which Engels obtained in early August 1878. See, on this, Engels' letters to Oskar Schmidt of July 19 and to Pyotr Lavrov of August 10, 1878 (present edition, Vol. 45). p. 314

136 H. Helmholtz, *Populäre wissenschaftliche Vorträge*, Zweites Heft, Braunschweig, 1871. Helmholtz is speaking of the physical concept of "work" chiefly in his lecture "Ueber die Erhaltung der Kraft" of 1862 on pp. 137-79 of the book mentioned. Engels examines the category of "work" in the chapter "The Measure of Motion.—Work" (see this volume, pp. 378-91). p. 314

137 This outline was written in the latter half of February 1880 once Engels had thought out in detail point 5 of the outline of the general plan (see this volume, pp. 313-14, 317) and was used to a considerable extent in the writing of the chapter "Basic Forms of Motion" (see this volume, pp. 362-77). On the other hand, there is a whole group of chapters—interconnected by subject matter and period—that correspond to it, namely, "The Measure of Motion.—Work", "Tidal Friction", "Heat" and "Electricity" (see this volume, pp. 378-91, 392-96, 397-401, 402-51). p. 317

138 In Engels' table of contents to the third folder of material for *Dialectics of Nature*, this "Introduction" is called the "Old Introduction" (see this volume, p. 588). Its text contains two passages making it possible to determine the approximate date when it was written. Thus Engels says that the cell "is a discovery not yet forty years old" (see this volume, p. 328) and, in a letter to Marx dated July 14, 1858 he mentions 1836 as the approximate date of this discovery (see present edition, Vol. 40, p. 326). Elsewhere, Engels writes that "it is only about ten years ago that the fact became known that completely structureless protein exercises all the essential functions of life" (see p. 329), probably with reference to Ernst Haeckel's monera, first described in his *Generelle Morphologie der Organismen*, in 1866. Engels wrote the original outline of this "Introduction" at the end of 1874 (see this volume, pp. 473-76). We may thus conclude that this "Introduction" was written between November 1875 and May 1876.

In the margins Engels made some notes, the main ones supplementing the text are given in footnotes. p. 318

139 Luther's most important contribution to the development of German language and literature was his translation of the Bible, thanks to which the standards of the German national language were fixed. Its first complete edition, in Luther's translation, came off the presses in Wittenberg in 1534. p. 319

140 Engels is referring to Luther's choral "Ein feste Burg ist unser Gott" ("God is our firm stronghold"), which Heine, in his *Zur Geschichte der Religion und Philosophie in Deutschland*, called the "Marseillaise of Reformation" ("Der Salon", Bd. 2, Hamburg, 1835, p. 80). Engels repeats Heine's words in his letter to Schlüter of May 15, 1885 (see present edition, Vol. 47). p. 319

141 In December 1520, in the courtyard of Wittenberg University, Luther publicly burned the Papal Bull on his excommunication.   p. 320

142 It was on the day of his death, May 24 (Old Style), 1543, that Copernicus received a copy of his book, *De revolutionibus orbium coelestium*, setting out the heliocentric system of the world, which had just come off the presses in Nuremberg.   p. 320

143 The first logarithmic tables were published in 1614 in Edinburgh in *Mirifici logarithmorum Canonis discriptio...* by John Napier, a Scottish mathematician.
                                                                          p. 321

144 See Note 26.   p. 323

145 Engels has in mind the idea Newton expressed in the conclusion to the second edition of his main work *Philosophiae naturalis principia mathematica*, Vol. II, Book III, "General Scholium". "Hitherto," wrote Newton, "we have explained the phaenomena of the heavens and of our sea by the power of gravity, but have not yet assigned the cause of this power...." After listing some properties of gravity, Newton continued: "But hitherto I have not been able to discover the cause of those properties of gravity from phaenomena, and I frame no hypotheses; for whatever is not deduced from the phaenomena is to be called an *hypothesis*; and hypotheses, whether metaphysical or physical, whether of occult qualities or mechanical, have no place in experimental philosophy. In this philosophy particular propositions are inferred from the phaenomena, and afterwards rendered general by induction."
    With reference to Newton's statement, Hegel said, in his *Encyklopädie der philosophischen Wissenschaften*, § 98, Zusatz 1: "Newton ... gave physics an express warning to beware of metaphysics...".   p. 323

146 *Nebular hypothesis*—a cosmogonic theory that considers the solar system and other celestial bodies to have been formed out of a rarefied nebula. p. 324

147 Grove's book *The Correlation of Physical Forces*, first published in London in 1846, was based on a lecture Grove read at the London Institution in January 1842, which was published shortly afterwards. Engels used the 3rd edition of the book, published in London in 1855.   p. 325

148 *Amphioxus* (the lancet fish)—a small fish-like animal (about 8 centimetres in length), which is a transitional form between invertebrates and vertebrates.
    Lepidosiren (an Amazon mudfish) belongs to the order of lung fishes, or Dipnoi, which have both lungs and gills.   p. 326

149 *Ceratodus* (the barramunda)—a fish with both lungs and gills, found in Australia.
    Archaeopteryx—an extinct bird possessing certain reptilian features.
    Working on *Dialectics of Nature* Engels used one of the early (not later than 1874) editions of A. Nicholson's popular *Manual of zoology* (1870; numerous reprints).   p. 326

150 Engels is referring to Wolff's thesis "Theoria generationis" (published in 1759) which refuted the theory of preformation and proved the theory of epigenesis scientifically.
    Preformation theory implies that the organism is preformed in the germ cell. According to this theory, development of the organism involves the purely

quantitative growth of existing organs, while no development in the proper sense of the term, that is, new formation, or epigenesis, takes place at all.

p. 327

[151] See Note 40. p. 327

[152] Here Engels used his extracts from J. H. Mädler, *Der Wunderbau des Weltalls, oder Populäre Astronomie* and A. Secchi, *Die Sonne*, that he presumably made in January and February 1876 (see this volume, pp. 552-55). p. 328

[153] *Eozoon canadense*—a fossil, found in Canada, which was regarded as the remains of ancient primitive organisms. In 1878 the German zoologist Möbius refuted the view of the organic origin of this fossil. p. 329

[154] This is the heading given to this article in the table of contents of the second folder, where Engels placed it when grouping the material for *Dialectics of Nature* (see this volume, p. 588). The manuscript proper has only a "Preface" as a heading, and a note "Dühring, Revolution in Science" at the top of the first page. The article was written in May or early June 1878 as a preface to the first edition of *Anti-Dühring*, but Engels decided to replace this long preface with a shorter one (see this volume, pp. 5-8) in which he used the first five paragraphs of the "Old Preface". p. 336

[155] See Note 6. p. 337

[156] According to the *phlogistic theory*, developed about 1700 by G. Er. Stahl, combustion is attributed to the presence of a particular substance phlogiston (Gr. "Phlox"—fire) in combustible bodies. In the eighteenth century this theory became the basis for the development of chemistry. It was proved untenable by Lavoisier only in the late eighteenth century, when he gave an explanation of the process of combustion as the combination of a burning substance with oxygen. Engels deals with the phlogistic theory also in the preface to Volume II of *Capital* (see present edition, Vol. 36). p. 344

[157] This heading is on the first page of the manuscript. In the table of contents of the third folder where Engels placed it, it reads: "Natural Science and the Spirit World" (see this volume, p. 588). The article was written not before January 1878, as may be concluded from the fact that Engels speaks in it about "recent triumphant reports" on the experiments (see this volume, p. 352) carried out by Zöllner in Leipzig on December 17, 1877.

Engels' article was first published in the Social-Democratic yearbook *Illustrirter Neue Welt-Kalender für das Jahr 1898*, Hamburg, 1898, pp. 56-59.

p. 345

[158] This refers to Francis Bacon's *Historia naturalis et experimentalis ad condendam philosophiam* (London, 1622), containing material that was to go into the third part of *Instauratio magna*, an encyclopaedic work Bacon planned, but never wrote. p. 345

[159] The reference is to Isaac Newton's *Observations upon the Prophecies of Daniel and the Apocalypse of St. John*, published in London in 1733, 6 years after his death.

p. 345

[160] *Mesmerism*—an unscientific system of "animal magnetism", widespread in the late eighteenth century and named after Franz Mesmer (1734-1815), the Austrian physician. p. 346

161 *Phrenology*—a theory, advanced by Franz Joseph Gall, an Austrian physician and anatomist, widespread in the first half of the nineteenth century; it maintains that each of Man's mental faculties is the responsibility of a specific section of the cerebrum, which can supposedly be located by feeling the shape of the skull.   p. 346

162 *Barataria* (Spanish *barato*—"cheap"), the name of a non-existent island in Cervantes' *Don Quixote*, to which Sancho Panza was appointed governor.
                                                            p. 346

163 *Thallium* was discovered by William Crookes in 1861.
The *radiometer*, invented by Crookes in 1873-74, is an instrument for detecting and measuring the intensity of radiation.   p. 350

164 This refers to the Commission for the Investigation of Spiritualist Phenomena, set up by the Physical Society at St. Petersburg University on May 6, 1875; it completed its work on March 21, 1876. The Commission included Dmitry Mendeleyev and other prominent scientists. It proposed to the persons disseminating spiritualism in Russia—A. N. Aksakov, A. M. Butlerov and N. P. Wagner—that they provide information on "genuine" spiritualist phenomena. It came to the conclusion that "spiritualist phenomena arise from unconscious movements or deliberate deception", and that "the spiritualist doctrine is superstition"; its conclusions were published in the newspaper *Голосъ* (Voice) on March 25, 1876. Mendeleyev published the material of the Commission in book form: *Матеріалы для сужденія о спиритизмѣ* (Materials for a Judgment about Spiritualism) (St. Petersburg, 1876).   p. 352

165 Engels is hinting at the proposal made by the German scientist Rudolf Virchow, previously a Darwinist, at a congress of natural scientists in Munich in 1877 that the teaching of Darwinism be banned. He asserted that Darwinism was closely connected with the socialist movement and, therefore, constituted a danger to the existing social order (see R. Virchow, *Die Freiheit der Wissenschaft im modernen Staat,* Berlin, 1877, p. 12). Attacks against Darwinism intensified in Germany particularly after the Paris Commune of 1871 (see also notes 133 and 135).   p. 353

166 On July 18, 1870, the Dogma of Papal Infallibility was proclaimed in the Vatican. The German Catholic theologian Ignaz von Döllinger refused to accept it.   p. 354

167 These words are from the letter written on January 29, 1869 by the biologist Thomas Huxley to the London Dialectical Society, which had invited him to take part in the work of the committee to study spiritualist phenomena. Huxley declined the invitation, making a number of ironical remarks about spiritualism. Huxley's letter is quoted on page 389 of Davies' *Mystic London* (1875).
                                                            p. 355

168 This is the title of the article on the first page of the manuscript. The fifth and ninth pages (the top of the second and third sheets) of the manuscript bear the words "Dialectical Laws" on the top margins. The article written in 1879, not before September, remained unfinished. The article can be dated from the fact that it quotes the second part of the second volume of Schorlemmer's *Ausführliches Lehrbuch der Chemie,* published in early September 1879 (see this volume, p. 361), but there is no mention of the discovery of scandium (1879), which Engels could not have failed to mention in connection with the discovery of gallium, if he had written the article after 1879.   p. 356

[169] The periodic law was discovered by Dmitry Mendeleyev in 1869. In 1870-71, Mendeleyev gave a detailed description of the several missing elements of the periodic system. Gallium, the first element Mendeleyev predicted, was discovered in 1875, followed by scandium (1879) and germanium (1886).

p. 361

[170] The heading "Basic Forms of Motion" appears in the table of contents of the third folder of *Dialectics of Nature* (see this volume, p. 588). This chapter was probably written in 1880 or 1881.

p. 362

[171] This refers to the general amount of motion, of motion in its quantitative determination in general. "Quantity of motion" in the special sense of mv is indicated in German by the word *Bewegungsgrösse*. Here and in the text that follows, however, Engels uses the expression *Bewegungsmenge*, which we give in brackets to avoid confusion with the magnitude mv. Instead of the expression "Bewegungsmenge", Engels sometimes uses "die Masse der Bewegung", also in the sense of the general amount of every kind of motion.

p. 364

[172] Engels took these data from Helmholtz's lecture *Über die Wechselwirkung der Naturkräfte und die darauf bezüglichen neuesten Ermittelungen der Physik*, which he delivered on February 7, 1854 in Königsberg. The lecture was included in the book: H. Helmholtz, *Populäre wissenschaftliche Vorträge* (H. 2, Braunschweig, 1871, pp. 134-36). The copy of this book from Engels' library, with his numerous notes, is extant.

p. 366

[173] Engels has in mind Mayer's works *Bemerkungen über die Kräfte der unbelebten Natur* (1842) and *Die organische Bewegung in ihrem Zusammenhang mit dem Stoffwechsel* (1845), which were included in the book, J. R. Mayer, *Die Mechanik der Wärme in gesammelten Schriften*, 2. Aufl., Stuttgart, 1874. Engels used this edition when working on *Dialectics of Nature*.

p. 370

[174] Engels probably intended to quote Hegel's note to the paragraph "Der formelle Grund" in Chapter 3, Section 1, Volume 2 of the *Wissenschaft der Logik*. In this note Hegel ridicules the formal method of explanation by tautological grounds. "This method of explanation," he writes, "recommends itself by its great clarity and comprehensibility; for nothing is clearer and more readily comprehensible than, for instance, the statement that a plant has its ground in a vegetative, i.e. plant-producing, power." "If in answer to the question why somebody goes to town, the ground is presented that there is an attractive power in town which draws him there", this sort of answer is no more senseless than explanations of the "vegetative power" kind. Moreover, Hegel remarks, "the sciences, and especially physical science, are full of tautologies of this kind, which constitute, as it were, a prerogative of science".

p. 372

[175] The heading "The Measure of Motion.—Work" is on the title page of this chapter and the first page of the manuscript. In the table of contents of the third folder, this chapter is entitled "Two Measures of Motion" (see this volume, p. 588). It was apparently written in 1880 or 1881.

p. 378

[176] [G. W. v. Leibniz] Godofredi Guilielmi Leibnitii, *De causa gravitatis, et defensio sententiae suae de veris naturae legibus contra Cartesianos* in: *Acta Eruditorum*, Lipsiae, 1690, pp. 228-39. Probably, Engels gives these data according to Kant's *Gedanken von der wahren Schätzung der lebendigen Kräfte...*, § 92 (I. Kant, *Sämmtliche Werke*, Bd. I, Leipzig, 1867, pp. 98-99).

p. 379

[177] The title page of the first edition of this work by Kant, published in Königsberg, gives 1746 as the year of publication. It is obvious, however,—in

particular from the dedication, which is dated April 22, 1747—that the book did not come out until the next year.   p. 379

[178] The reference is to the polemics on Descartes' measure of motion (mv) between Leibniz and the French physicist, abbé Catelan in 1686 and 1687 in the scientific journal *Nouvelles de la République des Lettres* (published in Amsterdam from 1684 to 1687). Catelan had two articles published in the journal: *Courte remarque de M. l'Abbé D. C. où l'on montre à Mr. G. G. Leibnits le paralogisme contenu dans l'objection précédente* and *Remarque de M. l'Abbé D. C. sur la réplique de M. L. touchant le principe mécanique de M. Descartes, contenu dans l'article III de ces Nouvelles, mois de Février 1687* (September 1686, pp. 999-1005 and June 1687, pp. 577-90).   p. 382

[179] A reference to an anecdote about an uneducated Prussian non-commissioned officer, who could never understand when to use the dative case *"mir"* and when the accusative case *"mich"* (Berliners often confuse these two forms). In order not to have to worry about this question, he decided always to use *"mir"* when on duty and always *"mich"* when off duty.   p. 382

[180] In nineteenth-century British scientific literature, the term "natural philosophy" was used to mean "theoretical natural science", "theoretical physics".   p. 382

[181] This refers to a battle during the Danish war of 1864, in which Denmark was opposed by Prussia and Austria.

Rolf Krake—the Danish battleship that, on the night of June 28, 1864, lay off the coast of Alsen Island, its assignment being to prevent Prussian troops from crossing to the island.   p. 386

[182] Engels is referring to the lecture "Force", delivered by Peter Guthrie Tait at the 46th Congress of the British Association for the Advancement of Science in Glasgow on September 8, 1876. The lecture was published in *Nature*, Vol. 14, No. 360, on September 21, 1876, pp. 459-63.   p. 388

[183] The heading "Tidal Friction. Kant and Thomson-Tait" figures on the title page preceding this chapter; the rest of the heading is on the first page of the chapter itself. In the table of contents of the third folder this chapter is entitled "Tidal Friction" (see this volume, p. 588). The chapter was written apparently in 1880 or 1881.   p. 392

[184] Previously Thomson and Tait had spoken of the direct resistances to the motion of bodies, such as that which air offers to the flight of a rifle bullet.
                                                                        p. 392

[185] The chapter written not earlier than the end of April 1881 and not later than mid-November 1882, is unfinished. The first date is suggested by the fact that Engels quotes from *Leibnizens und Huygen's Briefwechsel mit Papin*, published in Berlin in April 1881 (see this volume, p. 400). The second date is deduced from a comparison of the end of the first part of the chapter (see this volume, p. 398) with Engels' letter to Marx, dated November 23, 1882 (see note 186).
                                                                        p. 397

[186] In a letter to Marx dated November 23, 1882 (see present edition, Vol. 46), Engels introduced an important correction into the question of the measure of such a form of motion as electricity. He proceeded from the solution of the problem of the two-fold measure of mechanical motion, as he gave it in the chapter "The Measure of Motion.—Work", and from Wilhelm Siemens' speech

made at the 52nd Congress of the British Association for the Advancement of
Science in Southampton on August 23, and published in *Nature*, Vol. 26,
No. 669, August 24, 1882. Siemens proposed introducing the watt, a new unit
of electricity expressing the true power of an electric current. This is why, in
the above-mentioned letter, Engels defined the distinction between the volt and
the watt, two units of electricity, as that between the measure of the quantity of
electric motion in cases when it does not turn into other forms of motion and
the same measure in cases when it does.   p. 398

[187] Engels is quoting from a review of the book by Mascart and Joubert, *Leçons sur
l'électricité et la magnetisme*, Vol. 1, Paris, 1882. The review, entitled "Mascart
and Joubert's *Electricity and Magnetism*" and signed G. C., appeared in *Nature*,
Vol. 26, No. 659, June 15, 1882.

The reference to this issue of *Nature* shows that Engels wrote this chapter
mainly after June 15, 1882. In Engels' table of contents to the third folder, this
chapter is headed "Electricity and Magnetism" (see this volume, p. 588).
                                                                   p. 402

[188] Thomson gives this quotation from Faraday on page 400 of *An Outline of the
Sciences of Heat and Electricity*, 2nd ed., London, 1840. It is taken from Faraday's
work *Experimental Researches in Electricity*, 12th Series, published in the journal
Philosophical Transactions of the Royal Society of London for the year 1838, p. 105.
Thomson does not quote the passage accurately: He gives "as if a metallic particle
had been put into the place of the discharging particle" instead of "as if a metallic
wire had been put into the place of the discharging particle".   p. 404

[189] Here and below, Engels cites the results of thermochemical measurements by
Julius Thomsen from Alexander Naumann, *Handbuch der allgemeinen und
physikalischen Chemie*, Heidelberg, 1877, pp. 639-46.   p. 418

[190] In a number of places Wiedemann speaks of "atoms of hydrochloric acid",
meaning molecules of this acid.   p. 420

[191] On tendencies and representatives of Bible criticism in Germany, see F. Engels,
Ludwig Feuerbach and the End of Classical German Philosophy, Ch. I (see present
edition, Vol. 26) and "On the History of Early Christianity" (see present
edition, Vol. 27). Among the most important works on this question Engels
mentions: D. F. Strauß, *Das Leben Jesu*, Bd. 1-2, Tübingen, 1835-36; B. Bauer,
Kritik der evangelischen Geschichte des Johannes, Bremen, 1840; *Kritik der
evangelischen Geschichte der Synoptiker*, Bd. 1-2, Leipzig, 1841; *Kritik der
evangelischen Geschichte der Synoptiker und des Johannes*, Braunschweig, 1842.
                                                                   p. 423

[192] From the mid-1860s, chemists no longer used old chemical equivalent values.
                                                                   p. 427

[193] A reference to an anecdote about an old Major in the army who, having heard
from one of the "one-year" conscripts that he was a Doctor of Philosophy, and
not wanting to trouble himself with distinguishing between a doctor of
philosophy and a doctor of medicine, declared: "It is all the same to me,
saw-bones is saw-bones".   p. 430

[194] Here and below, Engels cites the results of Poggendorff's experiments from
Wiedemann's *Die Lehre vom Galvanismus und Elektromagnetismus...*, Vol. I
pp. 369-73.   p. 433

¹⁹⁵ A reference to a galvanic cell invented by John Frederick Daniell in 1836.

p. 433

¹⁹⁶ This result of Berthelot's thermochemical measurements is cited by Engels from Alexander Naumann's *Handbuch der allgemeinen und physikalischen Chemie*, Heidelberg, 1877, p. 652.

p. 436

¹⁹⁷ This refers to the difference between the internal diameter of the barrel and the diameter of the bullet.

p. 438

¹⁹⁸ *Experimentum crucis*—literally "experiment of the cross"; a decisive experiment; the expression derives from Fr. Bacon, *Novum Organum*, Book II, Aphorism XXXVI, coming from the habit of putting crosses to show the way at crossroads.

p. 442

¹⁹⁹ The article was originally planned by Engels as the introduction to a more extensive work entitled *Die drei Grundformen der Knechtschaft*. Later Engels altered this title to *Die Knechtung des Arbeits. Einleitung*. The work remained unfinished, and finally Engels gave its introductory portion the heading "The Part Played by Labour in the Transition from Ape to Man", which conforms to the content of the main part of the manuscript.

This was the heading Engels gave to the article in the table of contents of the second folder of materials for *Dialectics of Nature* (see this volume, p. 588). In the "Outline of the General Plan", Engels placed this material in point 11 (see this volume, pp. 313-14, 317). The article was apparently written in May and June 1876, as is evidenced by the letter of Wilhelm Liebknecht to Engels, dated June 10, 1876 (see present edition, Vol. 45), in which Liebknecht writes that he is impatiently awaiting Engels' work *Über die drei Grundformen der Knechtschaft*, which he had promised for the newspaper *Volksstaat*. The article was first published in 1896 in the magazine *Die Neue Zeit* (Jahrgang XIV, Bd. 2, 1895-1896, Nr. 44, pp. 545-54).

p. 452

²⁰⁰ The hypothesis concerning the existence in the Indian Ocean of a continent "Lemuria" spreading from Madagascar to India and Sumatra, which later sank, was advanced in the 1870s by Philip Lutley Sclater, a British zoogeographer.

p. 452

²⁰¹ Engels is referring to the testimony of Labeo Notker, a German monk (c. 952-1022), quoted in Jakob Grimm's *Deutsche Rechtsalterthümer*, Göttingen, 1828, p. 488. Engels quotes Notker in his unfinished work *The History of Ireland* (see present edition, Vol. 21, p. 175).

p. 458

²⁰² With regard to the effect of Man's activity on plant life and the climate, Engels used C. Fraas, *Klima und Pflanzenwelt in der Zeit*, Landshut, 1847 und M. J. Schleiden, *Die Pflanze und ihr Leben*, Leipzig, 1848. In a letter dated March 25, 1868 (see present edition, Vol. 42), Marx called Engels' attention to Fraas' book. Engels mentions Schleiden in his letter to Jenny and Laura Marx of May 11, 1858 (see present edition, Vol. 40, p. 314).

p. 460

²⁰³ Engels is referring to the world economic crisis of 1873, which overtook Germany in May of that year, when the period of rapid expansion following the Franco-Prussian war ended in a disastrous crash (see also Note 73).

p. 464

²⁰⁴ Engels wrote this fragment in November 1875. It is preparatory material for the "Introduction" (see this volume, pp. 318-35). He used the following

sources: E. Haeckel, *Natürliche Schöpfungsgeschichte...*; W. Whewell, *History of the Inductive sciences, from the earliest to the present times...*; J. W. Draper, *History of the intellectual development of Europe...*   p. 465

205 See Note 25.   p. 465

206 This fragment was probably written by Engels in September-October 1874. It consists of extracts from G. W. F. Hegel's *Vorlesungen über die Geschichte der Philosophie* and Engels' own notes on it. Extracts from the works of authors of antiquity are given according to Hegel's above-mentioned work.   p. 467

207 *De placitis philosophorum* belongs not to Plutarch, as Hegel writes, but to the so-called Pseudo-Plutarch. It derives from Aetius, who lived in about the year 100 A. D.   p. 468

208 Excerpts from Leucippus and Democritus are in Marx's hand and consist of quotations (from Tauchnitz editions) in Greek from Aristotle's *Metaphysica* and from the compilatory work of Diogenes Laertius, *De vitis philosophorum*. The note probably dates from September-October 1874, though a later date is also quite possible. All italics in the quotations are Marx's.   p. 470

209 It is not possible to give the exact date when this fragment was written, but it was obviously written no later than the end of May 1876 and constitutes preparatory material or an addition to the "Introduction" (see this volume, pp. 318-35).

In May 1453, the Turks captured Constantinople, capital of the Byzantine Empire.   p. 471

210 The first universities in mediaeval Europe appeared in the eleventh century in Italy (as higher secular schools), at the end of the twelfth and in the thirteenth centuries in France, England, Spain, and Portugal, in the fourteenth century in Central Europe—Bohemia, Poland, Germany.   p. 472

211 In 395 A. D., Constantinople became the capital of the Eastern Roman (later Byzantine) Empire, which survived until 1453.

In 476 A. D., Odoacr dethroned Romulus Augustulus, the last emperor of the Western Roman Empire, which is considered to have come to an end at this date.   p. 472

212 As in the case of the previous fragment (see Note 209), no exact date can be given for when this draft was written. It, too, was probably preparatory material for the "Introduction" and written no later than the end of May 1876.
                                                                                  p. 472

213 This fragment constitutes the original draft of the "Introduction" (see this volume, pp. 318-35), presumably written before November 1875.   p. 473

214 The *Declaration of Independence*, adopted on July 4, 1776, at the Second Continental Congress in Philadelphia by delegates from thirteen English colonies in North America, proclaimed the secession of these colonies from England and the establishment of an independent republic, the United States of America.   p. 474

215 See Note 141.   p. 474

216 See Note 142.   p. 474

217 This is the heading of the fragment given in the table of contents of the second folder of materials for *Dialectics of Nature* (see this volume, p. 588). The fragment takes up four pages of the original manuscript of *Ludwig Feuerbach*

and the End of Classical German Philosophy, numbered 16, 17, 18 and 19. At the top of page 16 there is a note in Engels' hand: "Aus *Ludwig Feuerbach*". This fragment was part of Chapter II of *Ludwig Feuerbach* and was intended to follow immediately after the description of the three principal "limitations" of the eighteenth-century French materialists (see present edition, Vol. 26). When he finally revised the manuscript of *Ludwig Feuerbach,* Engels removed these four pages and replaced them with another text, but the basic contents of the fragment (on the three great discoveries made in natural science in the nineteenth century) were reproduced in an abbreviated form in Chapter IV of *Ludwig Feuerbach.* Since Engels' *Ludwig Feuerbach* was originally printed in the April and May issues of the magazine *Die Neue Zeit* for 1886, it may be assumed that this fragment dates from late 1885-early 1886. The text of the fragment begins in mid-sentence. The beginning of the sentence, restored according to the text printed in *Die Neue Zeit,* is given in square brackets. p. 476

218 After vain attempts to find work as a professor in Berlin, Jena, Marburg and Freiburg, in 1836 Feuerbach settled in the village of Bruckberg, near the town of Ansbach. p. 479

219 *"Sire, je n'avais pas besoin de cette hypothèse"*—Laplace's reply to Napoleon's question as to why he had not mentioned God in his work *Mécanique céleste.* Engels is presumably quoting from G. W. F. Hegel, *Vorlesungen über die Geschichte der Philosophie,* Bd. 3, Berlin, 1836, p. 552. p. 480

220 The reference is to the battle of Jena and Auerstädt on October 14, 1806, between the Prusso-Saxon and Napoleon I's armies. The Prussians were crushed and Prussia capitulated. p. 480

221 See Note 56. p. 481

222 Engels is referring to J. Tyndall's *Inaugural Address* at the 44th annual meeting of the British Association for the Advancement of Science, held in Belfast, on August 19, 1874 (published in *Nature,* Vol. X, No. 251, August 20, 1874). In a letter to Marx dated September 21, 1874 (see present edition, Vol. 45), Engels gives a more detailed account of this speech. p. 481

223 The fragment headed "Büchner" was written before the other parts of *Dialectics of Nature.* It is the opening note of the manuscript's first folder. The fragment is apparently a synopsis of a work Engels planned to write against Büchner, as an exponent of vulgar materialism and social Darwinism (see Note 130). Judging by the contents of the fragment and by Engels' marginal notes in his copy of Büchner's book *Der Mensch und seine Stellung in der Natur...,* a second edition of which appeared in 1872, this was the work by Büchner that Engels intended to criticise primarily. The laconical comment in Wilhelm Liebknecht's letter to Engels, dated February 8, 1873—"As for Büchner, go ahead!"—seems to suggest that this fragment was written in February and no later than May 30, 1873, because it is immediately followed, on the same sheet of the manuscript, by the fragment "Dialectics of Natural Science" (see this volume, p. 527). p. 482

224 Between 1850 and 1860 3 works characteristic of this tendency and of its representatives appeared: J. Moleschott, *Der Kreislauf des Lebens,* Mainz, 1852; L. Büchner, *Kraft und Stoff,* Frankfurt am Main, 1855; K. Vogt, *Köhlerglaube und Wissenschaft,* Giessen, 1855. Speaking of "mutual assurance", Engels hints at these authors' attempts to prove their point of view by referring to the works

of their colleagues. This is felt most strongly in L. Büchner's *Kraft und Stoff*, in which the author constantly refers to the natural scientific and philosophical views of Vogt and Moleschott, using quotations from Moleschott's work as epigraphs to the chapters of his own book.   p. 482

225 Engels probably has in mind particularly L. Büchner's *Der Mensch und seine Stellung in der Natur...*, in which he attempts to transfer Darwin's theory of evolution to the sphere of social relations and to reduce the latter to the struggle for existence, and *Kraft und Stoff* (8. Aufl., Leipzig, 1864), also dealing with the importance of Darwin's theory, and Büchner's lectures delivered in a number of German cities in 1866 and 1868, and published in 1868 in Leipzig under the title: *Sechs Vorlesungen über die Darwin'sche Theorie von der Verwandlung der Arten und die erste Entstehung der Organismenwelt...* These lectures are mentioned in Marx's letters to Engels of November 14 and 18, 1868 and to Kugelmann of December 5, 1868 (see present edition, Vol. 43).   p. 482

226 Engels is referring to the following passage from the Preface to the second edition of Hegel's *Encyclopädie der philosophischen Wissenschaften im Grundrisse*, Th. 1. Die Logik: "Lessing said, in his time, that people treated Spinoza like a dead dog". Hegel's source was F. H. Jacobi, "Über die Lehre des Spinoza, in Briefen an Herrn Moses Mendelssohn", *Werke*, Bd. IV, Abt. I, Leipzig, 1819, p. 68.   p. 482

227 The reference is to L. Büchner, *Der Mensch und seine Stellung in der Natur in Vergangenheit, Gegenwart und Zukunft*, 2. Aufl., Leipzig, 1872. On pp. 170-71 of his book, Büchner says that, as mankind gradually develops, a moment arrives when Nature becomes aware of itself in Man and when Man stops submitting passively to the blind laws of nature and becomes master of them, that is, when quantity becomes quality, to use Hegel's phrase. In his copy of Büchner's book, Engels marked this passage with a stroke and commented: "Umschlag!" ("A turning point!").   p. 485

228 Newton discovered the differential and integral calculus independently of and earlier than Leibniz, but the latter, who also made this discovery independently, gave it a better form. When giving his opinion of Leibniz and Newton, Engels is presumably taking into account here Hegel's description of them (see G. W. F. Hegel, *Vorlesungen über die Geschichte der Philosophie*, Bd. 3, Berlin, 1836, pp. 447, 451). Two years after writing this fragment, Engels arrived at somewhat different conclusions concerning the elaboration of the differential and integral calculus by Newton and Leibniz (see this volume, p. 537).   p. 486

229 Lorenz Oken substantiated his ideas concerning the development of the organic world primarily in *Abriß der Naturphilosophie*, Göttingen, 1805; *Lehrbuch der Naturphilosophie*, Jena, 1809; *Lehrbuch der Naturgeschichte*, Leipzig, 1813-23; *Allgemeine Naturgeschichte für alle Stände*, Stuttgart, 1841.   p. 486

230 Engels has in mind the following passage from Hegel's *Encyclopädie der philosophischen Wissenschaften*, § 5, Anmerkung: "Everybody allows that, to know any other science, one must first have studied it and that one can only claim the right to express a judgment upon it in virtue of such knowledge. Everybody allows that, to make a shoe, one must have learnt and practised the craft of the shoemaker... For philosophy alone, are such study, application and effort not supposed to be requisite."   p. 486

231 Hegel, *Encyclopädie der philosophischen Wissenschaften*, § 6, Anmerkung: "To divorce reality from the idea is, especially, the favourite procedure of the mind that looks upon its dream-like abstractions as something true and real, and prides itself on the imperative 'ought', which it takes especial pleasure in prescribing in the political sphere. As if the world had waited for it, in order to learn how it ought to be, and was not. If the world were as it ought to be, where would be the old Man's wisdom of that mind's imperative ought?" p. 486

232 The reference is to Hegel's argument on the transition from a naively unsophisticated state to a state of reflection, both in the history of society and in the development of the individual: "In fact, however, ... the awakening of consciousness occurs in Man himself: and this is history repeating itself in every human being" (*Encyclopädie der philosophischen Wissenschaften*, § 24, Zusatz). p. 487

233 A "mathematical poem" is a term applied in the book by W. Thomson and P. G. Tait *A Treatise on Natural Philosophy*, Vol. I, Oxford, 1867, p. 713 to the book by the French mathematician Jean Baptiste Joseph Fourier *Théorie analytique de la chaleur*, Paris, 1822. In Engels' synopsis of this book by Thomson and Tait this passage is copied out and underlined. p. 487

234 E. Haeckel, *Natürliche Schöpfungsgeschichte*, 4. Aufl., Berlin, 1873, pp. 58-59, where Haeckel refers to L. Agassiz, *An Essay on Classification. Contributions to the Natural History of the United States*, Vol. 1, London, 1859.

Engels obviously received this edition of Haeckel's book no later than early 1874. p. 488

235 This note is written by Engels about A. W. Hofmann, *Ein Jahrhundert chemischer Forschung unter dem Schirme der Hohenzollern*, Berlin, 1881.

On page 26 of his book, Hofmann gives the following quotation from K. Rosenkranz's *System der Wissenschaft*, Königsberg, 1850, § 475, p. 301: "...Platinum is ... basically only a paradox of silver, wishing to occupy the highest stage of metallicity, which properly belongs to gold alone...".

On pages 5-6 of his book, Hofmann speaks of the "services" of the Prussian King Frederick William III in organising the sugar-beet industry. p. 488

236 The *Cassinis*—French astronomers: the Italian-born Giovanni Domenico Cassini (1625-1712), his son Jacques Cassini (1677-1756), his grandson César François Cassini de Thury (1714-1784) and his great-grandson Jacques Dominique comte de Cassini (1748-1845). All four consecutively held the office of director of the Paris Observatory from 1669 to 1793. The first three maintained incorrect, anti-Newtonian notions of the shape of the earth; only the last was compelled, by more accurate measurements of its volume and shape, to admit that Newton had been correct concerning the oblateness of the globe along the axis of its rotation. p. 488

237 Haeckel (*Natürliche Schöpfungsgeschichte*, 4. Aufl., Berlin, 1873, pp. 89-94) stresses the contradiction in Kant's *Kritik der teleologischen Urteilskraft* (the second part of Kant's *Kritik der Urteilskraft*) between the "mechanical methods of explanation" and teleology, depicting the latter, in opposition to Kant, as the doctrine of external aims, of external expediency. Examining the same §§ 64, 66 and 76 of Kant's *Kritik der Urteilskraft* (3. Aufl., Berlin, 1799) in his *Vorlesungen über die Geschichte der Philosophie*, Bd. III (*Werke*, Bd. XV, Berlin, 1836, p. 603), Hegel brought Kant's conception of "inner expediency" to the fore; according to this, in organic beings "everything is purpose and, reciprocally, also means" (quotation from Kant given by Hegel). p. 489

238 Engels wrote this fragment immediately after the article "Polarity" (see this volume, p. 497); which is why it begins with the words "another example of polarity". p. 489

239 See Note 145. p. 491

240 In November 1848, the counter-revolutionary government of Count Branden-burg came to power in Prussia. Manteuffel was appointed to the post of Minister of the Interior. The activities of this government (the dissolution of the Constituent Assembly, the bringing of troops to Berlin, etc.) constituted a signal for the counter-revolutionary offensive all over Germany. The only response of the liberal-bourgeois majority of the Constituent Assembly was an appeal to passive resistance. p. 493

241 The reference is to the coup d'état of December 2, 1851, which led to the fall of the Second Republic in France and to the dictatorship of President Louis Bonaparte, who, under the name of Napoleon III, was proclaimed Emperor of the French on December 2, 1852. p. 493

242 Compsognathus longipes—an extinct animal of the dinosaur order, belonging to the class of reptiles, but closely related to birds in the structure of its pelvis and hind extremities (see H. A. Nicholson, A Manual of zoology, 5th ed., Edinburgh and London, 1878, p. 545).
On Archaeopteryx lithographica see Note 149. p. 493

243 Engels is referring to multiplication by budding or division among coelente-rata. p. 493

244 G. W. F. Hegel, Encyclopädie der philosophischen Wissenschaften, § 135, Zusatz: "The limbs and organs of a live body should not be regarded as mere parts of it: only in their unity are they what they are, and they are certainly not indifferent towards that unity. These limbs and organs become mere parts only in the hands of the anatomist, and his occupation is thus no longer with live bodies, but with corpses." p. 494

245 G. W. F. Hegel, Encyclopädie der philosophischen Wissenschaften, §§ 115, 230-31. Here Hegel says that the very form of judgment speaks of the distinction between the subject and the predicate. p. 495

246 See J. Grimm, Geschichte der deutschen Sprache, 2. Aufl., Bd. 1, Leipzig, 1853, p. 580. In all probability, Engels used this, the second edition of the work. He speaks of the Frankish dialect in greater detail in his work The Frankish Dialect, written in 1881-82 (see present edition, Vol. 24). This note must have been written in October 1877. p. 498

247 Kismet—destiny, fate; the word came into Turkish from Arabic, after the adoption of Islam. p. 499

248 A quotation from Heine's Romanzero, 3. Buch: Hebräische Melodien. Disputation, which depicts a dispute between a Franciscan monk and a learned Rabbi, allegedly held at the Court of King Pedro the Cruel of Castile (1350-69). In the course of the dispute, the Rabbi referred to Tausves-Jontof (more correct Tossafot-Jomtowb), but the monk refused to accept this as valid.
Tossafot (literally: addition)—critical comments on the Talmud. Heine had in mind Tossafot by Abraham Jomtowb Ischbili, who lived in Seville in the first half of the fourteenth century. p. 501

249 A reference to the following passage from Hegel's Phänomenologie des Geistes:

"The bud disappears when the blossom bursts open, and it might be said that the former is refuted by the latter; in the same way, the blossom is declared by the fruit to be a false existence of the plant, and the fruit supersedes the blossom as the truth of the plant". Engels is quoting from G. W. F. Hegel, *Werke*, Bd. II, 2. Aufl., Berlin, 1841. p. 502

250 *Dido*—Engels' dog, which he mentioned in his letters to Marx of April 16, 1865, and August 10, 1866 (see present edition, Vol. 42). p. 503

251 Hegel explains the correspondence between the division of logic into three parts (the logic of being, of essence, and of notion) and the four-part classification of judgments as follows: "the different kinds of judgment are determined by the universal forms of the logical idea itself. Accordingly, initially we have three main kinds of judgment, corresponding to the stages of Being, Essence and Notion. The second of these main kinds is, in accordance with the character of Essence, as the stage of differentiation, duplicated further within itself" (Hegel, *Encyclopädie der philosophischen Wissenschaften*, § 171, Zusatz). p. 504

252 On pages 75-77 of the fourth edition of his *Natürliche Schöpfungsgeschichte* (Berlin, 1873), Haeckel relates how Goethe discovered the existence of the intermaxillary bone in Man. "The empirical knowledge then available," he writes, "suggested the induction that all mammals possessed the intermaxillary bone. *Goethe* deduced from this that Man, who, in all other features of his organisation, did not differ fundamentally from mammals, must also possess that bone; and, on closer investigation it was, in fact, discovered. The deduction was confirmed and verified by subsequent experience." (Goethe discovered the intermaxillary bone in the human embryo and, in occasional atavistic cases, in adults). Engels says that the induction of which Haeckel speaks is incorrect because it was contradicted by the proposition, considered correct, that the mammal "Man" has no intermaxillary bone. p. 507

253 Here Engels is referring to Linnaeus' classification of animals and plants and the changes Haeckel later introduced into it. See E. Haeckel, *Natürliche Schöpfungsgeschichte*, pp. 435-39. p. 507

254 Engels is obviously referring to Whewell's two main works: *History of the inductive sciences*, London, 1837 and *The Philosophy of the inductive sciences*, London, 1840.
Engels describes inductive sciences as "comprising" the purely mathematical sciences, presumably in the sense that Whewell places them around "deductive sciences" which, according to him, include primarily geometry and algebra, as well as logic and metaphysics. According to Whewell, deductive sciences investigate the conditions for the construction of any theory and, in this sense, hold the central position in the system of sciences. In the *History of the Inductive Sciences* (Vol. I, Introduction) Whewell contrasts "deductive sciences" with "inductive" ones, among which he includes mechanics, astronomy, physics, chemistry, mineralogy, botanics, zoology, physiology and geology. p. 507

255 In the formula U-I-P, U denotes the Universal, I—the Individual, and P—the Particular. Hegel uses this formula in analysing the logical essence of inductive conclusions. See Hegel, *Wissenschaft der Logik*, Th. 2. Die subjective Logik, oder: Die Lehre vom Begriff, pp. 148-50. Hegel's proposition—mentioned by Engels further on—that inductive conclusion is, in effect, problematic appears in the same place. p. 507

256 See Note 148.   p. 508

257 G. W. F. Hegel, *Encyclopädie der philosophischen Wissenschaften*, § 39: "Mere experience does afford perceptions of changes succeeding *one another* ... but it presents no *necessary* connection".   p. 509

258 This heading is given in the table of contents drawn up by Engels for the second folder of materials for *Dialectics of Nature* (see this volume, p. 588). The note, written in October-November 1877, was a critical analysis of the basic theses put forward by the botanist Nägeli in his lecture "Die Schranken der naturwissenschaftlichen Erkenntnis". Engels quotes it according to the *Tageblatt der 50. Versammlung deutscher Naturforscher und Aerzte in München 1877*, Supplement, September 1877. He probably received this edition from Carl Schorlemmer, who attended the congress.   p. 512

259 Engels is referring to the discovery of oxygen in 1774 by Joseph Priestley, who had no idea that his discovery would cause a revolution in chemistry. Engels speaks in more detail about this discovery in his preface to Volume II of Marx's *Capital* (see present edition, Vol. 36).   p. 514

260 This is a quotation, slightly modified by Engels, from the treatise *Della moneta* (t. II) by the Italian economist Galiani. This same quotation was used by Marx in Volume I of *Capital* (see present edition, Vol. 35, Part 2, Ch. IV). Marx and Engels used the Custodi edition *Scrittori classici italiani di economia politica*. Parte moderna, Tomo III, Milano, 1803, p. 156.   p. 517

261 Engels is referring to the section on quantity in Hegel's *Wissenschaft der Logik*, Th. 1. Die objective Logik, Abth. 1. Die Lehre vom Seyn, which says that astronomy is worth admiration not because of the bad infinity of immeasurable distances, time and the immeasurable multitude of stars, with which this science deals, but "rather because of those *relations of measure* and those *laws* which reason recognises in these objects, and which are the rational infinite in contrast to that irrational infinity".   p. 517

262 The words "So also $\frac{1}{r^2}$" were added by Engels later. Apparently, this refers to the law according to which the force of interaction between bodies and electrically charged particles is in inverse proportion to the square of the distance between them.   p. 517

263 G. W. F. Hegel, *Vorlesungen über die Naturphilosophie*, § 280, Zusatz: "The sun serves the planet, just as, in general, sun, moon, comets, and stars are merely conditions of the Earth".   p. 518

264 Engels is referring to G. J. Romanes' review "Ants, Bees and Wasps" of J. Lubbock's *Ants, Bees, and Wasps; a Record of Observations on the Social Hymenoptera*, London, 1882. The review was published in the journal *Nature*, No. 658, June 8, 1882, pp. 121-23.   p. 519

265 This item was probably written by Engels in connection with the 44th meeting of the British Association for the Advancement of Science held in Belfast in August 1844. Engels might have become acquainted with the material of this meeting from the journal *Nature*, Nos. 251 and 253, August 20 and September 3, 1874. Engels expressed his opinion of the speeches made at this meeting by J. Tyndall and Th. Huxley in his letter to Marx of September 21, 1874 (see present edition, Vol. 45).   p. 520

266 Engels is referring to a peculiar philosophical argument in verse between

Goethe and Haller. In 1730, Haller asserted in his poem "Falschheit der menschlichen Tugenden": "No mortal man can Nature's inner secrets tell, too happy if he knows but Nature's outer shell". Goethe, in his verses "Allerdings" (1820) and "Ultimatum" (1821), asserted that Nature was a single unity that cannot be divided, as Haller did, into an unknowable inner core and an outer shell accessible to man. Hegel twice mentions this argument between Goethe and Haller, in his *Encyclopädie der philosophischen Wissenschaften,* § 140 and *Vorlesungen über die Naturphilosophie,* § 246, Zusatz. p. 520

267 This note was written on the same sheet as "Outline of the Part Plan" (see this volume, p. 317) and is a conspectus of the ideas Engels developed in the chapter "Basic Forms of Motion" (see ibid., pp. 317 and 362-77). p. 526

268 See Note 147.

By "affections of matter" Grove means "heat, light, electricity, magnetism, chemical affinity, and motion" (op. cit., p. 15) and by "motion" he means mechanical motion or transplantation. p. 527

269 This note was written on the back of the first sheet of the first folder of the material for *Dialectics of Nature.* In its contents, it coincides with Engels' letter to Marx dated May 30, 1873 (see present edition, Vol. 44), which begins with the words: "This morning the following dialectical ideas about natural science occurred to me in bed". These ideas were expressed more definitely in the letter than in the present note. So it may be inferred that the note was written before the letter, on the same day, May 30, 1873. p. 527

270 Originally, in *Wissenschaft der Logik* (Th. 2. Die subjective Logik, oder: Die Lehre vom Begriff, pp. 167-228), Hegel divided sciences into "Mechanismus", "Chemismus" and "Teleologie". In his *Vorlesungen über die Naturphilosophie,* he denoted three main divisions of natural science by the terms "mechanics", "physics" and "organics". p. 529

271 This note is one of the three longer ones (*Noten*) that Engels included in the second folder of material for *Dialectics of Nature* (see this volume, p. 588 and Note 130). This note, as well as the fragment "On the Prototypes of the Mathematical Infinite in the Real World" (see this volume, pp. 544-49) are Notes or Addenda to *Anti-Dühring,* in which Engels elaborates some very important ideas that were only outlined or briefly stated in various parts of *Anti-Dühring.* The third note, "Nägeli's Inability to Cognise the Infinite" (see ibid., pp. 512-16) has nothing to do with *Anti-Dühring.* The first two were, in all probability, written in December 1877 or January 1878. They were originally intended for the first edition of *Anti-Dühring,* which appeared in Leipzig in July 1878. Engels gives page references to his *Herrn Eugen Dühring's Umwälzung der Wissenschaft.* 1: Philosophie (see this volume, pp. 33-134), which was published as a pamphlet in Leipzig, in July 1877. The pagination in the pamphlet and in the first edition of the book coincide.

Engels gave the heading "On the 'Mechanical' Conception of Nature" in his table of contents to the second folder of material for *Dialectics of Nature.* The sub-heading "Note 2 to p. 46": "The various forms of motion and the sciences dealing with them" occurs at the beginning of this notice. p. 530

272 Engels has in mind Chapter VII of *Anti-Dühring* (see this volume, pp. 61-70), first published as an article in *Vorwärts,* No. 17, February 9, 1877 (see also Note 1). p. 530

273 This refers to an item "On entering upon ..." in *Nature*, No. 420, November 15, 1877, p. 55, summarising August Kekulé's speech on October 18, 1877, when he assumed the post of rector of Bonn University. In 1878, the speech was published in pamphlet form, under the title *Die wissenschaftlichen Ziele und Leistungen der Chemie*.   p. 530

274 The *Lothar Meyer curve* shows the relationship between the atomic weights and atomic volumes of the elements. It was drawn up by the German chemist Meyer, who included it in his article "Die Natur der chemischen Elemente als Funktion ihrer Atomgewichte", published in *Annalen der Chemie und Pharmacie*, Leipzig, Bd. 7, 1870, pp. 354-64.

The discovery of the correlation between the atomic weights of the elements and their physical and chemical properties was made by the Russian scientist Dmitry Mendeleyev, who was the first to formulate the periodic law of the chemical elements, in his article "The Correlation of the Properties of the Elements and Their Atomic Weights", published in March 1869 in the *Журнал Русского химического общества* (Journal of the Russian Chemical Society). Meyer, too, was close to establishing the periodic law when he learned about Mendeleyev's discovery. His curve graphically illustrated the law discovered by Mendeleyev, except that it gave it an external and, unlike Mendeleyev's, one-sided expression.

Mendeleyev's conclusions went much further than Meyer's. On the basis of the periodic law he had discovered, Mendeleyev predicted the existence and specific properties of chemical elements that were as yet unknown.   p. 531

275 This fragment was written on a separate sheet, marked *Noten*, and is an original outline of the Second Note to *Anti-Dühring* headed "On the 'Mechanical' Conception of Nature" (see this volume, pp. 530-34). It was presumably written in the latter half of November 1877 (see Note 271).

                                                                              p. 534

276 In the former case, Engels has in mind Hegel's remark that, in arithmetic, thinking is engaged in "an activity that is, at one and the same time the extreme externalisation of itself, in the forced activity of *moving* in *thoughtlessness* and linking that which is not capable of any necessity". (*Wissenschaft der Logik*. Th. 1. Die objective Logik. Abth. 1. Die Lehre vom Seyn). In the latter case, Hegel's statement that "already the natural numerical system exemplifies a *nodal line* of qualitative moments, which manifest themselves in the merely external progression", etc. (ibid., pp. 432-33).   p. 538

277 This expression occurs in Ch. Bossut's *Traités de Calcul différentiel et de Calcul intégral*, T. I, Paris, an VI [1797-98], p. 38, to which Engels refers in the fragment "Straight and Curved" (see this volume, pp. 543-44). In the chapter on "Integral Calculation with Finite Differences", Bossut first examines the following problem: "To integrate or sum the whole number steps of a variable magnitude x". Bossut assumes the difference Δx to be constant, denoting it by the Greek letter ω. Since the sum of Δx or of ω is equal to x, the sum of $\omega \times 1$ or of $\omega x°$ is also equal to x. Bossut writes this equation in the form $\Sigma \omega x°=x$. He then takes out the constant ω, putting it before the summation sign, to obtain the expression $\omega \Sigma x°=x$, and hence the equation $\Sigma x°=\frac{x}{\omega}$. This last equation is then used to find the magnitudes Σx, Σx^2, Σx^3, etc., for solving other problems.   p. 541

278 This is what Bossut calls the curves considered in the system of polar co-ordinates.   p. 543

279 Engels has in mind Fig. 17 and the explanation given of it on pp. 148-51 of Bossut's *Traités*. This figure has the following form: *BMK* is the curve. *MT* is its tangent. *P* is the pole or origin of the co-ordinates. *PZ* is the polar axis. *PM* is the ordinate of the point *M* (Engels calls it "real abscissa"; nowadays it is called the radius-vector). *Pm* is the ordinate of point *m* lying infinitely close to *M* (Engels calls this radius-vector the "differential imaginary abscissa"). *MH*, perpendicular to the tangent *MT*. *TPH*, perpendicular to the ordinate *PM*. *Mr*, the curve described by the radius *PM*. As *MPm* is an infinitesimal angle, *PM* and *Pm* are considered parallel. The triangles *Mrm* and *TPM*, as also the triangles *Mrm* and *MPH*, are regarded as similar. p. 543

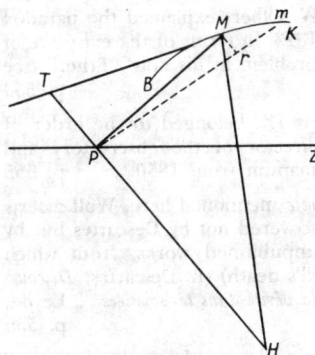

280 On the writing of this note, see Note 271, Engels gave the heading "On the Prototypes of the Mathematical Infinite in the Real World" in the table of contents of the second folder of material for the *Dialectics of Nature*. The sub-heading "Re pp. 17-18, Concordance of Thought and Being.—The Infinite in Mathematics" stands at the beginning of the note. p. 544

281 *Nihil est in intellectu, quod non fuerit in sensu* (nothing is in the mind that has not been in the senses) is the basic tenet of sensualism, which goes back to Aristotle (see his *Posterior Analytics*, Book I, Ch. 18 and *De anima*, Book III, Ch. 8). p. 545

282 Reuss of the Younger branch (or Reuss-Gera-Schleiz)—one of the dwarf German states in Thüringia (territory 826 square kilometres), forming part of the German Empire since 1871. p. 548

283 Here Engels probably had in mind Haeckel's psychophysical monism and his views on the structure of matter. In *Die Perigenesis der Plastidule* (Berlin, 1876), Haeckel affirms, for example, that the elementary "soul" is inherent not only in "plastidules" (see Note 132), but also in atoms, and that all atoms are "animate" and possess "sensation" and "volition". In the same book, Haeckel describes atoms as being absolutely discrete, absolutely indivisible and absolutely unalterable, while alongside the discrete atoms, he recognises the existence of ether as something absolutely continuous (op. cit., pp. 38-40). p. 549

284 Engels is referring to Clausius' lecture "Über den zweiten Hauptsatz der mechanischen Wärmetheorie", delivered in Frankfurt am Main, on September 23, 1867, at the 41st Congress of German Natural Scientists and Physicians, and published in pamphlet form in Brunswick the same year. p. 551

285 This and the two following notes consist of extracts from the following books: J. H. Mädler, *Der Wunderbau des Weltalls, oder Populäre Astronomie*, Abschn. 9. *Die Fixsterne* and Abschn. 10. *Die Nebelflecke und die ihnen ähnlichen Bildungen* and A. Secchi, *Die Sonne*, Th. 3. *Die Sonne oder die Fixsterne*. These extracts were presumably made in late 1875 or early 1876. Engels used them in the second part of the "Introduction" to *Dialectics of Nature* (see this volume, pp. 327-35). p. 552

[286] The question of existence in interstellar space of a material habitat absorbing light had been discussed by astrophysicists since the beginning of the nineteenth century. German astronomer H. W. Olbers explained the paradox of the dark night sky, which he described in 1823, in terms of the existence of interstellar substance. Engels returns to this problem in his note "Ether" (see this volume, p. 565).   p. 554

[287] P. A. Secchi, who had close contacts with Pius IX, belonged to the order of Jesuits from 1833 onwards and was also director of the observatory and professor of astronomy at the Collegium Romanum from 1850.   p. 555

[288] In the passage from his *Geschichte der Astronomie* mentioned here, Wolf asserts that the law of the refraction of light was discovered not by Descartes but by Snell in 1618, who formulated it in his unpublished works, from which Descartes subsequently borrowed it (after Snell's death) (R. Descartes, *Discours de la méthode bien conduire sa raison et chercher la vérité dans les sciences ...*, Leyde, 1637).   p. 556

[289] Cf. the following proposition by Hegel concerning force: "In terms of content, it expresses nothing other than what the phenomenon, namely the relation of these bodies to one another, contains in its motion, only this is expressed in the form of determination reflected in itself, of force", the result being an "empty tautology". (Hegel, *Wissenschaft der Logik*. T. 1, Die objective Logik, Abth. 2. Die Lehre vom Wesen, p. 90.)   p. 560

[290] Engels is referring to Lavrov's book Опыт истории мысли (Attempt at a History of Thought), Vol. 1, published anonymously in St. Petersburg in 1875, which he received from the author in the summer of that year. On page 109 of this book, in the chapter entitled "The Cosmic Basis of the History of Thought", Lavrov writes: "Extinct suns with their dead systems of planets and satellites continue their motion in space as long as they do not fall into a new nebula in the process of being formed. Then the remains of the extinct world become material for accelerating the process of the formation of the new world." In a footnote, Lavrov quotes Zöllner's opinion that the state of torpor of extinct heavenly bodies "can be ended only by external influences, e.g., by heat generated on collision with some other body".   p. 561

[291] This note is evidently a remark on R. Clausius' pamphlet (see Note 284). On p. 16, Clausius mentions the ether as existing outside the heavenly bodies; and on p. 6 he assumes that the ether also fills the interstices between the particles of the bodies.   p. 564

[292] *Horror vacui*, abhorrence of a vacuum. The view, dating from Aristotle (*Physika*, IV, 6-9), that "nature abhors vacuum", that is, does not allow one to form, prevailed in natural science till the mid-seventeenth century. In 1644, Torricelli discovered atmospheric pressure and thereby refuted the Aristotelian notion of the impossibility of a vacuum.   p. 564

[293] Engels, who wrote Lavrov's name in Russian characters, meant his book Опыт истории мысли (see Note 290). On pp. 103-04, in the chapter "The Cosmic Basis of the History of Thought", Lavrov mentions the views of various scientists (Heinrich Wilhelm Olbers, Wilhelm von Struve) on the extinction of light in interstellar space.   p. 565

[294] Engels is referring to the diagram on page 632 of Secchi's book, *Die Sonne*, showing the relationship between the length of the wave and the intensity of

the thermal, luminar and chemical actions of solar rays, the main portion of which is reproduced below:

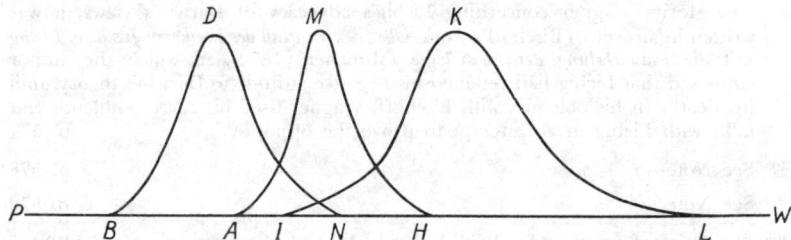

The curve *BDN* represents the intensity of heat radiation from the longest wave heat-rays (at point *B*) to the shortest wave rays (at point *N*). The curve *AMH* represents the intensity of light radiation, from the longest wave rays (at point *A*) to the shortest wave rays (at point *H*). The curve *IKL* represents the intensity of chemical rays, from the longest wave rays (at point *I*) to the shortest wave rays (at point *L*). In all three cases, the intensity of the rays is shown by the distance of the point on the curve from the line *PW*. p. 565

[295] Here and below Engels is quoting from Th. Thomson's book, *An Outline of the Sciences of Heat and Electricity*, 2nd edition, London, 1840. He used these quotations in the chapter "Electricity" (see this volume, pp. 402-51). p. 566

[296] Here and in the following note Engels is referring to Frederick Guthrie's *Magnetism and Electricity*, London and Glasgow, 1876. On page 210 Guthrie writes: "The strength of the current is proportional to the amount of zinc dissolved in the battery that is oxidized, and is proportional to the heat which the oxidation of that zinc would liberate." p. 568

[297] When speaking of John Dalton as "the father of modern chemistry", Engels had in mind his work *A New System of Chemical Philosophy*, vols. 1-2, Manchester, 1808-1827. p. 570

[298] G. W. F. Hegel, *Encyclopädie der philosophischen Wissenschaften*, § 81, Zusatz 1: "The true conception, however, is this: that life as such bears, in itself, the germ of death and that, in general, the finite contradicts itself in itself and thereby transcends itself". p. 572

[299] *Plasmogony* was the term Haeckel used to denote the hypothetical origin of an organism when it arises within some organic liquid, in contrast to *autogeny*, i.e., the direct origin of living protoplasm from inorganic matter (E. Haeckel, *Natürliche Schöpfungsgeschichte*, p. 302). p. 573

[300] See Note 40. p. 573

[301] Engels is referring to the experiments carried out by Louis Pasteur in 1860, by which he proved that microorganisms (bacteria, yeasts, infusoria) in any nutritive (organic) medium develop only from germs already present in the medium or that reach it from outside. Pasteur concluded that the spontaneous generation of now live microorganisms, and spontaneous generation in general, were not possible. Marx also took an interest in Pasteur's experiments, as can be seen from his letter to Engels of June 9, 1866 (see present edition, Vol. 42). p. 574

302 The excerpts from Moritz Wagner's article are taken from Augsburg *Allgemeine Zeitung*, pp. 4333-4335, 4351-4352, 4370-4372, Nos. 279-281, 1874. The article was an episode in the polemics between Theodor Ludwig Wilhelm von Bischoff and Moritz Wagner concerning Liebig's advocacy of Darwin's views; it was written in answer to Bischoff's work *Über den Einfluß des Freiherrn Justus v. Liebig auf die Entwickelung der Physiologie* (München, 1874), in which the author supposed that Liebig had retained his negative attitude to Darwin's theory until his death. In his polemics with Bischoff, Wagner used his correspondence and talks with Liebig in an attempt to prove the opposite.   p. 574

303 See Note 45.   p. 578

304 See Note 40.   p. 579

305 Engels is referring to H. A. Nicholson's *Manual of zoology* (see Note 149).
                                                                                  p. 580

306 See Note 43.   p. 581

307 In the fourth edition of his book *Natürliche Schöpfungsgeschichte*, Haeckel enumerates the following first five stages in the development of the embryo in multi-cellular animals: *Monerula, Ovulum, Morula, Planula* and *Gastrula*, which, he claimed, corresponded to the five initial stages in the development of animal life in general. In the later editions of the book, Haeckel altered this scheme substantially, but his basic idea, to which Engels gave a positive appraisal, that of the parallelism between the individual development of an organism (ontogenesis) and the historical development of a particular organic form (phylogenesis) has become firmly established in science.   p. 581

308 The word *bathybius* means "living in the depths". In 1868, Huxley described a sticky slime, dredged from the bottom of the ocean, which he regarded as primitive, structureless living matter—protoplasm. In honour of Haeckel, he named this—as he thought—simplest living organism *Bathybius Haeckelii*. Haeckel considered the bathybius a species of modern, still living Monera (see Note 40). Haeckel speaks of bathybius and the small calcareous modules enclosed in it on pp. 165-66, 306, 379 of the fourth edition of his *Natürliche Schöpfungsgeschichte*, Berlin, 1873.   p. 581

309 In the first volume of his *Generelle Morphologie der Organismen*, Berlin, 1866, Haeckel devotes four lengthy chapters (VIII-XI) to the concept of the organic individual and the morphological and physiological individuality of organisms. He also considers the notion of the individual in a number of passages of *Anthropogenie oder Entwickelungsgeschichte des Menschen*, Leipzig, 1874. He divides organic individuals into six classes or orders: plastids, organs, antimeres, metameres, individuals, and cormuses. Those of the first order are pre-cellular organic forms of the Monera (cytode) type and cells; they are "elementary organisms". The individuals of each order, from the second onwards, consist of individuals of the preceding order. The individuals of the fifth order are, in the case of superior animals, "individuals" in the narrow sense of the term.

Cormus—a morphological individual of the sixth order, constituting a colony of individuals of the fifth order. The series of marine lucifers may serve as an example.

Metamere—a morphological individual of the fourth order, a recurrent limb of an individual of the fifth order. The segments of the tapeworm provide an example.   p. 581

310 This note coincides almost word for word with Engels' letter to Lavrov of November 12-17, 1875 (see present edition, Vol. 45). p. 583

311 The experiment carried out by the German physiologist Adolf Fick and German chemist Johannes Wislicenus in August 1865, refuted Liebig's view that protein was the sole source of energy for muscular activity and proved the efficacy of the law of preservation of energy during muscular contractions.

Faulhorn—peak of the Bernese Oberland, in the canton of Bern, Switzerland. p. 586

312 The titles Engels gave to the four folders and the tables of contents of the second and third folders of material for *Dialectics of Nature* were not written before 1886, for the list of contents of the second folder includes the fragment "Omitted from *Feuerbach*", which was written in early 1886. p. 588

313 Engels' preparatory writings for *Anti-Dühring* consist of two parts. The first is made up of separate sheets of various format (altogether—35 manuscript pages), containing extracts from Dühring's books and Engels' notes, those that were used in *Anti-Dühring* being crossed out. The second part consists of large sheets (altogether 17 manuscript pages) divided into two columns: the left-hand column contains mainly extracts from the 2nd edition of Dühring's *Cursus der National- und Socialökonomie*, while the right-hand column contains critical notes by Engels; some of the entries, the ones used in *Anti-Dühring*, are crossed out vertically.

In addition, the preparatory writings for *Anti-Dühring* include: a note on slavery, extracts from Fourier's *Le nouveau monde industriel et sociétaire* (see this volume, pp. 608-09, 612) and the rough draft of the "Introduction" to *Anti-Dühring* (see Note 314). These three notes are in the first folder of material for *Dialectics of Nature* (see Note 130).

The present edition contains preparatory writings that essentially supplement the basic text of *Anti-Dühring*. The notes of the first part of the preparatory writings are arranged in accordance with the text of *Anti-Dühring* to which they refer. Fragments of the second part are given in the sequence they occur in Engels' manuscript. The extracts from Dühring's book, to which the critical notes refer, are given in abridged form and enclosed in square brackets.

The notes comprising the first part of the preparatory writings for *Anti-Dühring* were evidently written in 1876, and those of the second part in 1877. These preparatory writings were first published, partially, by the Institute of Marxism-Leninism of the CC CPSU in 1927 (in *Marx-Engels Archiv*, Bd. II, Frankfurt am Main, 1927), and most fully in 1935 (in *Marx/Engels Gesamtausgabe*, F. Engels, *Herrn Eugen Dührings Umwälzung der Wissenschaft/ Dialektik der Natur*. Sonderausgabe, Moscow-Leningrad, 1935). p. 591

314 The given text, which is published in English for the first time, is the original version of "Introduction", or more precisely, of Chapter I of Part I of *Anti-Dühring* (see Note 1). The text of the rough outline of "Introduction" is preserved in the first folder of material for *Dialectics of Nature* under the title "Modern Socialism" (see Note 130 and p. 688 of this volume). p. 591

315 See Note 22. p. 592

316 Here Engels is referring to the second uprising of the Lyons workers, in April 1834; in the final version of "Introduction", he wrote that "in 1831, the first working-class rising took place in Lyons" (see this volume, p. 26). p. 595

317 Engels is referring to the introductory speech of Th. Andrews at the 46th Congress of the British Association for the Advancement of Science, convened in Glasgow on September 6, 1876. The speech was published in the journal *Nature*, No. 358, September 7, 1876, p. 393.   p. 598

318 *Sheikh-ul-Islam*—title of the head of the Moslem priesthood in the Ottoman Empire.   p. 598

319 *Preformation*—see Note 150.   p. 600

320 See Note 45.   p. 601

321 See Note 22.   p. 603

322 Engels is quoting from the second German edition: K. Marx, *Das Kapital*, Bd. I, Hamburg, 1872, pp. 35-36; see present edition, Vol. 35, Part I, Chapter I, Part 3. A. 3. The Equivalent Form of Value.   p. 603

323 On pp. 95-96 of Bossut's *Traités de calcul différentiel et de calcul intégral*, the thesis on the relation between zeros is explained as follows. Let us add, says Bossut, that there is nothing absurd or unacceptable in the surmise that a relationship exists between two zeros. Let there be the following proportion $A:B = C:D$; from which it follows that $(A - C):(B - D) = A:B$; if $C = A$ and, consequently, $D = B$, then $0:0 = A:B$; this relationship changes depending on the value of A and B. Engels illustrates this argument of Bossut's, giving in his own example the values: $A = C = 1$ and $B = D = 2$.   p. 607

324 The fragment on slavery is preserved in the first folder of material for *Dialectics of Nature* (see Note 130 and p. 688 of this volume).   p. 608

325 See Note 101.   p. 610

326 The reference is to Marx's *Capital*, Vol. I, Part VIII: The So-called Primitive Accumulation, Chapter XXVII: Expropriation of the Agricultural Population from the Land (see present edition, Vol. 35).   p. 610

327 On August 4, 1789, under pressure from the growing peasant movement, the French Constituent Assembly proclaimed the abrogation of a number of feudal duties that had, in effect, been abolished by the insurgent peasants. However, the laws promulgated immediately afterwards repealed only personal duties without redemption. Only under the Jacobin dictatorship, by a law of July 17, 1793, were all feudal duties repealed without redemption.

The decree on the confiscation of Church property was passed by the Constituent Assembly on November 2, 1789, and that on the confiscation of the property of nobles in exile was passed by the Legislative Assembly on February 9, 1792.   p. 610

328 The extracts from Fourier's *Nouveau monde industriel et sociétaire*, which Engels made according to the edition: Ch. Fourier, *Oeuvres complètes*, t. VI, Paris, 1845, are preserved in the first folder of material for *Dialectics of Nature* (see Note 130 and p. 688 of this volume).   p. 612

329 On the structure of *Capital* see Note 61.   p. 615

330 See Note 36.   p. 615

331 The *Khedive*—the title of the hereditary rulers of Egypt during the period of Turkish domination (from 1867 till 1914).   p. 619

332 This article was initially a fragment of the manuscript of Part II of *Anti-Dühring* (MS: end of p. 20, and pp. 21-24 and a large part of p. 25). It was included in Chapter III of Part II. Subsequently, Engels replaced this with a shorter text (see this volume, pp. 153-58) and gave the former text the title *Infantry Tactics, Derived from Material Causes, 1700-1870*. The fragment in question was written in the first half of 1877, during work on Part II of *Anti-Dühring* (see Note 1). This article was first published in 1935 in *Marx/Engels Gesamtausgabe*, F. Engels, *Herrn Eugen Dühring's Umwälzung der Wissenschaft/Dialektik der Natur*. Sonderausgabe, Moscow-Leningrad, 1935.
p. 623

333 See Note 74. p. 625

334 See Note 75. p. 626

335 On the *battle of Jena* see Note 36. p. 627

336 In the *battle of Albuera* (Spain), May 16, 1811, the British army under Viscount Beresford, besieging the fortress of Badajos, defeated the French troops under Marshal Soult moving to help the French garrison occupying the fortress. Engels describes the battle in the article "Albuera" (see present edition, Vol. 18, pp. 10-11).

The *battle of Inkerman*, November 5, 1854, was fought by the Russian Army and Anglo-French forces during the Crimean war (1853-1856). The Russian forces were defeated, but their active operations and the heavy losses suffered by the Allies, particularly the British, forced the Allies to abandon their plan for an assault on Sebastopol and to go over to a protracted siege of the fortress. Engels describes this battle in detail in the article "The Battle of Inkerman" (see present edition, Vol. 13, pp. 528-35). p. 627

337 See Note 76. p. 628

338 Engels evidently obtained all the information on the strength and losses of the Prussian Army in the *battle of Saint-Privat* (see Note 78) from studying material on the official history of Franco-Prussian war of 1870-1871, as compiled by the military-historical department of the Prussian general staff (see *Der Deutsch-französische Krieg 1870-71*, Th. I, Bd. 2, Berlin, 1875, p. 669 ff., 197*-99*, 233*). p. 628

339 While adapting the three chapters of *Anti-Dühring* into the pamphlet *Socialism Utopian and Scientific* (see Note 1), Engels made some additions and changes. Some of these additions Engels included in the text of the second edition of *Anti-Dühring* (see this volume, p. 10). Below are the additions made by Engels while preparing the first (1882) and the supplemented fourth (1891) German editions of *Socialism Utopian and Scientific* (see present edition, Vol. 24), but not included in the text of *Anti-Dühring* published in his lifetime.
p. 630

340 See Note 8. p. 631

341 *Anabaptists*—members of a Christian sect that reject infant baptism and practises baptism of adults. In the sixteenth century—participants in the religious and political movement that constituted one of the most democratic trends of the *Reformation* (see Note 22) and soon became a form of the revolutionary movement of the peasant and plebeian masses. p. 631

688

342 On the *Directorate* and *coup d'état* of Napoleon I see Note 101. p. 636

343 Saint-Simon's idea that society's aim must be improvement of the life of the most numerous and the poorest class is expressed most clearly in his last work (*Nouveau Christianisme*), which first appeared anonymously in Paris in 1825.

p. 637

344 See Note 116. p. 640

INDEX OF CONTENTS OF THE FOLDERS*
IN
DIALECTICS OF NATURE

[First Folder]
Dialectics and Natural Science

---

* Notes and fragments from one and the same sheet of the manuscript are bracketed together. The numbers on the left indicate the pagination of Engels' manuscript. Asterisks refer to the notes made in preparation for the writing of *Anti-Dühring*. The relevant pages in this volume are given in brackets on the right.

[Second Folder]

The Investigation of Nature and Dialectics

[Third Folder]

Dialectics of Nature

[Fourth Folder]
Mathematics and Natural Science. Miscellaneous

1) Dialectics (pp. 356-61)
2) Heat (pp. 397-401)
3) Hegel, *Logik*, Bd. I (pp. 501-02)
   [Mathematical calculations—5 pages]
4) Hegel, *Enzyklopädie*, I (p. 487)
5) *Gravity as the most general determination of materiality* is commonly accepted (pp. 522-23)
6) Impact and friction (p. 557)
7) *Descartes* discovered that the ebb and flow of the tides are caused by the attraction of the moon (p. 556)
8) *Theory and empiricism* (pp. 488-89)
9) *Aristarchus of Samos* (p. 471)
10) A pretty example of the dialectics of nature is... (p. 569)
11) The contempt of the empiricists for the Greeks receives a peculiar illustration... (p. 489)
12) Attraction and gravitation (pp. 523-24)
13) The first, naïve outlook is as a rule more correct than the later, metaphysical one (pp. 557-58)
14) The *geocentric* standpoint in astronomy is prejudiced and has rightly been abolished (pp. 518-19)
15) How little Comte can have been the author of his encyclopaedic arrangement of the natural sciences... (p. 529)
16) Physiography (p. 530)
17) The new epoch begins in chemistry with atomistics (pp. 570-71)
18) Hegel constructs the theory of light and colour out of pure thought (p. 566)
19) *Zero*, because it is the negation of any definite quantity, is not therefore devoid of content (pp. 539-41)
20) *One* (pp. 538-39)
21) *Static and dynamic electricity* (pp. 568-69)
22) When Coulomb says... (pp. 566-68)
23) *Electricity* (pp. 565-67)
24) Hegel's division (the original one) into mechanics, chemics, and organics (pp. 529-30)
25) *Electro-chemistry* (p. 569)
26) How old ... methods become transferred to other branches (p. 570)
27) [Outline of the Part Plan] (p. 317)
28) Conclusion for Thomson, Clausius, Loschmidt (p. 563)
29) *Molecule and differential* (p. 544)
30) *Force and conservation of force* (p. 558)
31) *Trigonometry* (pp. 543-44)
32) *The consumption of kinetic energy* (p. 557)
33) In the motion of gases ... the motion of masses passes directly into molecular motion (p. 563)
   [Mathematical calculations]
34) The Darwinian theory to be demonstrated as ... (p. 582)
35) What Hegel calls reciprocal action is the *organic body* (p. 585)
36) *Transformation of quantity into quality* (p. 571)

CHRONOLOGICAL LIST
OF CHAPTERS AND FRAGMENTS* IN
DIALECTICS OF NATURE

1873

1) Büchner (pp. 482-87)
2) Dialectics of natural science (pp. 527-28)
3) Divisibility (p. 524)
4) Cohesion (p. 563)
5) States of aggregation (p. 563)
6) Secchi and the Pope (p. 555)
7) Newtonian attraction and centrifugal force (p. 551)
8) Laplace's theory (p. 552)

1874

9) Friction and impact produce an *internal* motion (p. 569)
10) *Causa finalis*—matter and its inherent motion (p. 522)
11) The form of development of natural science, in so far as it thinks, is the *hypothesis* (pp. 520-21)
12) The transformation of attraction into repulsion and vice versa (p. 523)
13) The character of mutual opposites belonging to the thought determinations of reason (p. 494)
14) For one who denies causality every natural law is a hypothesis (p. 512)
15) *The thing-in-itself* (p. 521)
16) The true nature of the determinations of "essence" is expressed by Hegel himself (p. 494)
17) The so-called axioms of mathematics (p. 536)
18) Part and whole, for instance... (p. 494)
19) Abstract identity (pp. 495-96)
20) *Positive and negative* (p. 497)
21) *Life and death* (p. 572)
22) *Bad infinity* (pp. 516-17)
23) Simple and compound (pp. 494-95)
24) *Primordial matter* (p. 522)

---

* The figures in brackets indicate the corresponding pages of this volume.

68) *Mathematics* (pp. 536-37)
69) *Asymptotes* (p. 542)
70) *Zero powers* (p. 541)
71) *Straight and curved* (pp. 542-43)
72) Ether (p. 565)
73) *Vertebrates* (p. 585)
74) *Radiation of heat into universal space* (pp. 561-62)
75) *Newton's parallelogram of forces* (p. 552)
76) *Bathybius* (p. 581)
77) *Understanding and reason* (p. 503)
78) *To the Pan-Inductionists* (pp. 508-09)
79) *The kinetic theory* (p. 564)
80) Clausius—if correct—proves... (pp. 562-63)
81) The notion of an actual *chemically uniform matter* (p. 570)
82) *Hard and fast lines* (pp. 493-94)
83) Dialectics, so called, *objective* dialectics, prevails throughout nature (pp. 492-93)
84) *The struggle for life* (pp. 583-85)
85) *Light and darkness* (pp. 565-67)
86) *Work* (pp. 586-87)
87) *Induction and analysis* (p. 509)
88) *The successive development* of the separate branches of natural science should be studied (pp. 465-66)
89) *Clausius' second law...* however it may be formulated (p. 563)
90) Difference between the situation at the end of the ancient world and at the end of the Middle Ages (pp. 471-72)
91) Historical material.—Inventions (pp. 472-73)
92) *Mädler, The Fixed Stars* (pp. 552-54)
93) *Nebulae* (pp. 554-55)
94) Secchi: *Sirius* (p. 555)

1875-1876

95) Introduction (pp. 318-35)

1876

96) *Dialectics of Nature*—references (p. 579)
97) The Part Played by Labour in the Transition from Ape to Man (pp. 452-64)
98) *The eternal laws of nature* (pp. 517-18)
99) Hegel, *Logik*, Bd. I (p. 502)

1877

100) Haeckel's nonsense: induction against deduction (p. 507)
101) By induction it was discovered 100 years ago... (p. 507)
102) *Polarisation* (p. 497)
103) *Polarity* (pp. 497-98)
104) Another example of polarity in Haeckel... (pp. 489-90)
105) Valuable self-criticism of the Kantian *thing-in-itself*... (p. 521)
106) When Hegel makes the transition from life to cognition... (p. 585)
107) According to Hegel, infinite progress is a barren waste (p. 517)

108) Quantity and quality (pp. 537-38)
109) *Number* (p. 538)
110) *Mathematics* (p. 542)
111) *Conservation of energy* (p. 558)
112) At absolute 0° no gas is possible (p. 564)
113) *One* (pp. 538-39)
114) √‾ 1.—The negative magnitudes of algebra (p. 541)
115) Application of mathematics (p. 550)
116) The differential calculus... (p. 550)
117) That positive and negative are equivalent... (p. 497)
118) The contempt of the empiricists for the Greeks receives a peculiar illustration... (p. 489)
119) Abstraction and gravitation (p. 523)
120) The first, naïve outlook is as a rule more correct than the later, metaphysical one (pp. 557-58)
121) The *geocentric* standpoint in astronomy is prejudiced and has rightly been abolished (pp. 518-19)
122) How little Comte can have been the author of his encyclopaedic arrangement of the natural sciences (p. 529)
123) Physiography (p. 530)
124) The new epoch begins in chemistry with atomistics (pp. 570-71)
125) Hegel constructs the theory of light and colour out of pure thought (p. 566)
126) When Coulomb says... (pp. 566-67)
127) *Electricity* (p. 566)
128) Hegel's division (the original one) into mechanics, chemics, and organics (pp. 529-30)
129) *Electro-chemistry* (p. 569)
130) How old ... methods become transferred to other branches (p. 570)
131) *Static and dynamic electricity* (pp. 568-69)
132) *The struggle for existence* (pp. 582-83)
133) *Force* (see above) (p. 561)
134) *Motion and equilibrium* (pp. 525-26)
135) *Causality* (pp. 510-12)
136) *Newtonian gravitation* (pp. 551-52)
137) *Force* (p. 561)
138) On Nägeli's Incapacity to Know the Infinite (pp. 512-16)
139) Chance and Necessity (pp. 498-501)
140) The Darwinian theory to be demonstrated as... (p. 582)
141) What Hegel calls reciprocal action is the *organic body* (p. 585)
142) *Transformation of quantity into quality* (p. 571)
143) If Hegel regards nature as a manifestation of the eternal "idea" in its alienation... (p. 487)
144) The empiricism of observation alone can never adequately prove necessity (pp. 509-10)
145) *Ad vocem* Nägeli (p. 516)
146) Hegel, *Enzyklopädie*, I (p. 487)
147) *Gravity as the most general determination of materiality* is commonly accepted (pp. 522-23)
148) Impact and friction (p. 557)
149) *Descartes* discovered that the ebb and flow of the tides are caused by the attraction of the moon (p. 556)
150) *Theory and empiricism* (pp. 488-89)
151) *Aristarchus of Samos* (p. 471)

NAME INDEX

Peninsular war (1808-14) commanded a unit of the French army.—627

Butlerov, Alexander Mikhailovich (1828-1886)—Russian chemist, founder of the theory of the structure of organic compounds.—352

C

Calvin, John (real name—Jean Chauvin) (1509-1564)—Swiss theologian, Protestant reformer.—320, 499

Camphausen, Ludolf (1803-1890)—German banker; a leader of the Rhenish liberal bourgeoisie; Prussian Prime Minister (March-June 1848).—100

Cantillon, Richard (1680-1734)—British economist, forerunner of the physiocrats.—227

Carey, Henry Charles (1793-1879)—American vulgar economist, protectionist; advocated harmony of class interests in capitalist society.—179, 208, 241, 614

Carlyle, Thomas (1795-1881)—British writer, historian, philosopher, Tory; preached views bordering on feudal socialism up to 1848.—635

Carnot, Nicolas Léonhard Sadi (1796-1832)—French physicist and engineer, a founder of thermodynamics and the author of Réflexions sur la puissance motrice du feu et les machines propres à développer cette puissance (1824).—344, 400, 509

Carolingians—royal and imperial dynasty of the Franks; replaced the Merovingians in 751 and ruled France (till 987), Germany (till 911) and Italy (till 887).—498

Cassini, Giovanni (Jean) Domenico (1625-1712)—French astronomer of Italian descent, the first director of the Paris Observatory (from 1669). He organised and led numerous geodetic surveys of France.—488

Cassini, Jacques (1677-1756)—French astronomer and geodesist, the second director of the Paris Observatory; son of Giovanni Domenico Cassini.—488

Cassini de Thury, César François (1714-1784)—French astronomer and geodesist, the third director of the Paris Observatory; son of Jacques Cassini.—488

Cassini, Jacques Dominique, comte de (1748-1845)—French astronomer and geodesist, the fourth director of the Paris Observatory; son of César François Cassini de Thury.—488

Catelan, François (died after 1719)—French abbot and physicist, follower of Descartes.—382

Catherine II (1729-1796)—Empress of Russia (1762-96).—611

Cervantes Saavedra, Miguel de (1547-1616)—Spanish novelist.—58, 298

Charles the Great (Charlemagne) (c. 742-814)—King of the Franks (768-800) and Holy Roman Emperor (800-814).—472

Child, Sir Josiah (1630-1699)—English economist, mercantilist; banker and merchant.—226

Cicero (Marcus Tullius Cicero) (106-43 B. C.)—Roman statesman, orator and philosopher.—467, 468

Clapeyron, Benoît Paul Emile (1799-1864)—French physicist and engineer, author of several works on thermodynamics.—400

Clausius, Rudolf (1822-1888)—German physicist, known for his works on the fundamentals of thermodynamics and on the kinetic theory of gases; the first to formulate the second law of thermodynamics (1850); introduced the concept of entropy (1865).—313, 386, 390, 391, 397, 398, 400, 497, 524, 551, 558, 562-64

Cobbett, William (1763-1835)—English radical politician and writer.—228

Cohn, Ferdinand Julius (1828-1898)—German botanist and micro-biologist.—575

Colding, Ludwig August (1815-1888)—Danish physicist and engineer, determined the mechanical equivalent of heat independently of Mayer and Joule.—370, 387, 477, 505

Columbus, Christopher (1451-1506)—Genoese-born navigator, discoverer of America.—462

Comte, Auguste (1798-1857)—French philosopher, founder of positivism.—313, 529

Confucius (K'ung Fu-tse) (c. 551-479 B. C.)—Chinese philosopher.—242

Copernicus, Nicolaus (Mikolaj Kopernik) (1473-1543)—Polish astronomer, founder of the heliocentric theory.—53, 320, 322, 474

Coulomb, Charles Augustin (1736-1806)—French physicist and engineer; discovered the law of electrostatic and magnetic interaction.—566

Croll, James (1821-1890)—Scottish geologist.—579

Crookes, William (1832-1919)—British chemist and physicist, adherent of spiritualism.—350, 351, 353, 354

Cuvier, Georges Léopold Chrétien Frédéric Dagobert, baron de (1769-1832)—French naturalist, author of works on comparative anatomy, palaeontology and the classification of animals.—324, 466, 475

D

D'Alembert, Jean Baptiste le Rond (1717-1783)—French philosopher and mathematician, Encyclopaedist and leading figure of the French Enlightenment.—379-81, 388

Dalton, John (1766-1844)—English chemist and physicist, set forth the atomic theory of chemical composition.—326, 339, 402, 403, 570

Daniell, John Frederic (1790-1845)—English physicist, chemist and meteorologist.—433, 441, 444, 447

Darwin, Charles Robert (1809-1882)—English naturalist, founder of the theory of natural selection of species.—30, 63-69, 75, 117, 133, 260, 327, 331, 345, 452, 454, 459, 475, 477, 501, 534, 576, 583, 584, 599, 633

Davies, Charles Maurice (1828-1910)—British clergyman, author of books on religion.—351

Davy, Sir Humphry (1778-1829)—English chemist and physicist.—489

Defoe, Daniel (c. 1660-1731)—English writer and publicist, author of Robinson Crusoe.—143-44, 147-48, 153-54, 614

Delvigne, Henri Gustave (1799-1876)—French army officer and military inventor.—627

Democritus (c. 460-c. 370 B. C.)—Greek philosopher, one of the founders of the atomistic theory.—339, 470, 471

Descartes, René (in Latin: Renatus Cartesius) (1596-1650)—French philosopher, mathematician and scientist.—21, 50, 56, 113, 321, 325, 339, 363, 370, 378, 379, 407, 525, 537, 556, 558, 593

Dessaignes, Victor (1800-1885)—French chemist.—403, 404, 567

Diderot, Denis (1713-1784)—French philosopher of the Enlightenment, atheist, leader of the Encyclopaedists.—21

Diez, Christian Friedrich (1794-1876)—German philologist, author of the Grammatik der romanischen Sprachen, founder of the comparative study of the Romance languages.—305

Diogenes Laertius (3rd cent.)—Greek historian of philosophy; compiled a large work on the ancient philosophers.—339, 340, 468-71

Hume, David (1711-1776)—Scottish philosopher, historian and economist.—15, 115, 223-29, 241, 313, 560

Huxley, Thomas Henry (1825-1895)—English naturalist and biologist, a friend and follower of Charles Darwin, an active populariser of his theory.—73, 355

Huygens (or *Huyghens*), *Christian* (1629-1695)—Dutch physicist, astronomer and mathematician; author of the wave theory of light.—378

I

Iamblichus (Jamblichus) (c. 250-c. 330)—Greek philosopher, the chief representative of Syrian Neoplatonism.—348

J

Jähns, Max (1837-1900)—Prussian army officer, military writer; served on the General Staff and taught the history of military art at a military academy.—159, 615

Joule, James Prescott (1818-1889)—English physicist, experimentally substantiated the law of conservation of energy.—325, 370, 387, 407, 412, 441, 479, 505

Juvenalis, Decimus Junius (b. in the 60s-d. after 127)—Roman satirical poet.—138, 441

K

Kant, Immanuel (1724-1804)—German philosopher.—12, 24, 30, 46-47, 53-54, 58, 61, 229, 248, 314, 323, 324, 326, 327, 340, 342, 364, 366, 378-79, 392, 394-95, 475, 486, 489, 506, 519, 521, 556, 594

Kaufmann, Konstantin Petrovich (1818-1882)—Russian general and statesman; from 1867, commander of the Turkestan military district and gover-nor-general of Turkestan Province.—94

Kekulé von Stradonitz, Friedrich August (1829-1896)—German chemist; developed organic and theoretical chemistry.—339, 451, 530, 534

Kepler, Johannes (1571-1630)—German astronomer.—12, 321, 474

Ketteler, Wilhelm Emmanuel, Baron von (1811-1877)—German ecclesiastic, Roman Catholic bishop of Mainz (from 1850).—354

Kinnersley, Ebenezer (1711-1778)—American experimental physicist.—567

Kirchhoff, Gustav Robert (1824-1887)—German materialist scientist, physicist; studied electrodynamics and mechanics; in 1859, in collaboration with Robert Bunsen (1811-1899), laid the foundations for spectral analysis.—12, 383, 388, 390

Klipstein, Philipp Engel (1747-1808)—German geologist and palaeontologist.—576

Kohlrausch, Friedrich Wilhelm Georg (1840-1910)—German physicist known for his works on electrical and magnetic measurements, electrolysis and thermoelectricity; son of Rudolf Hermann Arndt Kohlrausch.—422, 423, 442, 451

Kohlrausch, Rudolf Hermann Arndt (1809-1858)—German physicist; studied galvanic current.—443

Kopp, Hermann (1817-1892)—German chemist and historian of chemistry.—570

L

Lafargue, Paul (1842-1911)—prominent figure in the French and international working-class movement, zealous propagandist of Marxism, member of the General Council of the First International, a founder of the Workers' Party of France

O

Ohm, Georg Simon (1787-1854)—German physicist; in 1826, discovered the basic law of the electric circuit, which defines the relationship between the resistance, electromotive and current force.—412

Oken, Lorenz (1779-1851)—German naturalist and natural philosopher.—12, 327, 486, 488

Olbers, Heinrich Wilhelm Matthias (1758-1840)—German astronomer.—554

Orbigny, Alcide Dessalines d' (1802-1857)—French palaeontologist and traveller.—576

Owen, Sir Richard (1804-1892)—English zoologist, anatomist and palaeontologist; advanced the idealist concept of an "archetype" as the structural plan of vertebrates; in 1863, described the archaeopteryx of the Jurassic period.—487

Owen, Robert (1771-1858)—English utopian socialist.—20, 31, 137, 186, 245, 249-53, 278, 279, 288, 290-91, 306, 592, 593, 638

P

Paganini, Niccolo (1782-1840)—Italian violinist and composer.—454

Papin, Denis (1647-1712, according to some sources, 1714)—French physicist, an inventor of the steam-engine.—400

Pasteur, Louis (1822-1895)—French microbiologist and chemist, founder of modern microbiology and immunology.—574

Perty, Joseph Anton Maximilian (1804-1884)—German naturalist.—575

Peter I (the Great) (1672-1725)—Russian Tsar (1682-1721), Emperor of Russia (1721-25).—611

Petty, Sir William (1623-1687)—English economist and statistician, founder of classical bourgeois political economy in England.—15, 214, 217-23, 226, 227, 228

Phidias (c. 500-c. 430 B.C.)—Greek sculptor.—308

Plato (c. 427-347 B.C.)—Greek philosopher.—207, 215

Pliny (Gaius Plinius Secundus) (A.D. 23-79)—Roman naturalist, author of the 37-volume Historia naturalis.—164, 489

Plutarch (c. 46-c. 125)—Greek moralist writer and philosopher.—468

Poggendorff, Johann Christian (1796-1877)—German physicist, known for his studies of electricity and magnetism; founded and published the journal Annalen der Physik und Chemie.—433, 446, 447

Polo, Marco (1254-1324)—Venetian traveller; made a trip to China and lived there from 1275 to 1292.—472

Prévost, d'Exiles, Antoine François (1697-1763)—French novelist.—481

Priestley, Joseph (1733-1804)—English chemist and materialist philosopher, public figure.—344, 514

Proudhon, Pierre Joseph (1809-1865)—French journalist, economist and sociologist, ideologist of the petty bourgeoisie, one of the founders of anarchism.—173, 242, 251, 297, 298, 593

Ptolemy (Claudius Ptolemaeus) (2nd cent.)—Greek mathematician, astronomer and geographer.—320

Pythagoras (c. 571-497 B.C.)—Greek mathematician and philosopher.—468-70, 534, 598

Q

Quenstedt, Friedrich August (1809-1889)—German mineralogist, geologist and palaeontologist, professor at Tübingen University.—576

INDEX OF LITERARY AND MYTHOLOGICAL NAMES

INDEX OF QUOTED
AND MENTIONED LITERATURE

WORKS BY KARL MARX AND FREDERICK ENGELS

Marx, Karl. *Capital. A Critique of Political Economy. Volume I. Book One. The Process of Production of Capital* (present edition, Vol. 35)

— *Das Kapital.* Kritik der politischen Oekonomie. Erster Band. Buch I: Der Produktionsprocess des Kapitals. Hamburg, 1867.—9, 100, 295, 614

— Zweite verbesserte Auflage. Hamburg, 1872.—100, 112-24, 130, 143, 150-51, 183-85, 187-91, 193, 196-99, 202-03, 211, 215, 223, 224, 256, 261-62, 278, 280-81, 288, 303, 307, 343, 603, 614

— Dritte vermehrte Auflage. Hamburg, 1883.—212, 216

— *The Poverty of Philosophy. Answer to the "Philosophy of Poverty" by M. Proudhon* (present edition, Vol. 6)

— Misère de la philosophie. Réponse à la Philosophie de la misère de M. Proudhon. Paris-Bruxelles, 1847.—9

— *A Contribution to the Critique of Political Economy* (present edition, Vol. 29)

— Zur Kritik der politischen Oekonomie. Erstes Heft. Berlin, 1859.—225, 299

Engels, Frederick. *Socialism Utopian and Scientific* (present edition, Vol. 24)

— Socialisme utopique et socialisme scientifique. Traduction française par P. Lafargue. Paris, 1880.—10

— Il socialismo utopico e il socialismo scientifico. Benevento, 1883.—10

— Socyjalizm utopijny a naukowy. Genève, 1882.—10

— Die Entwicklung des Sozialismus von der Utopie zur Wissenschaft. Hottingen-Zürich, 1882.—10

— Zweite unveränderte Auflage. Hottingen-Zürich, 1883.—10

— Dritte unveränderte Auflage. Hottingen-Zürich, 1883.—10

— Развитие научного социализма. Женева, 1884.—10

— Socialismens Udvikling fra Utopi til Videnskab. Kjöbenhavn, 1885.—10

— *Anti-Dühring. Herr Eugen Dühring's Revolution in Science* (this volume)

— Herrn Eugen Dühring's Umwälzung der Philosophie. Herrn Eugen Dühring's Umwälzung der politischen Oekonomie. Herrn Eugen Dühring's Umwälzung des Sozialismus. In: *Vorwärts,* 3. Januar 1877-7. Juli 1878.—6, 336, 530

— Herrn Eugen Dühring's Umwälzung der Wissenschaft. Philosophie. Politische Oekonomie. Sozialismus. Leipzig, 1878.—6, 8, 530, 545

— Herrn Eugen Dühring's Umwälzung der Wissenschaft. Zweite Auflage. Zürich, 1886.—8-10, 15

— Dritte, durchgesehene und vermehrte Auflage. Stuttgart, 1894.—15

— *The Condition of the Working-Class in England. From Personal Observation and Authentic Sources* (present edition, Vol. 4)

— Die Lage der arbeitenden Klasse in England. Nach eigner Anschauung und authentischen Quellen. Leipzig, 1845.—261

— *Schelling and Revelation. Critique of the Latest Attempt of Reaction Against the Free Philosophy* (present edition, Vol. 2)

— Schelling und die Offenbarung. Kritik des neuesten Reaktionsversuchs gegen die freie Philosophie. Leipzig, 1842.—48

— *Outlines of a Critique of Political Economy* (present edition, Vol. 3)

— Umrisse zu einer Kritik der Nationaloekonomie. In: *Deutsch-Französische Jahrbücher,* hrsg. von Arnold Ruge und Karl Marx. 1-ste und 2-te Lieferung. Paris, 1844.—295

— *The Origin of the Family, Private Property and the State. In the Light of the Researches of Lewis H. Morgan* (present edition, Vol. 26)

— Der Ursprung der Familie, des Privateigenthums und des Staats. Im Anschluss an Lewis H. Morgan's Forschungen. Hottingen-Zürich, 1884.—10

Marx, Karl and Engels, Frederick. *Manifesto of the Communist Party* (present edition, Vol. 6)

— Manifest der Kommunistischen Partei. London, 1848.—9, 166

WORKS BY DIFFERENT AUTHORS

Allman, G. J. *Recent progress in our knowledge of the ciliate infusoria. Anniversary address to the Linnean Society,* May 24, 1875. In: *Nature,* Vol. XII, Nos. 294-296, June 17 and 24, and July 1, 1875.—579

Andrews, Th. *Inaugural address* [*delivered at the forty-sixth annual meeting of the British Association for the Advancement of Science in Glasgow*]. In: *Nature,* Vol. XIV, No. 358, September 7, 1876.—598

Aristoteles. *De coelo.*—470

— *De republica.* In: *Aristotelis opera* ex recensione I, Bekkeri, Tomus X, Oxonii, 1837.—215, 216

— *Ethica Nicomachea.* In: *Aristotelis opera* ex recensione I, Bekkeri, Tomus IX, Oxonii, 1837.—216

— *Metaphysica.* Ad optimorum librorum fidem accurate edita. Editio stereotypa C. Tauchnitii. In: *Aristotelis opera omnia,* Vol. II, Lipsiae, 1832.—467-71

Bacon, F. *Historia naturalis et experimentalis ad condendam philosophiam.* Londini, 1622.—345

— *Novum Organum.* Londini, 1620.—442, 557

Baudeau, l'abbé. *Explication du Tableau économique* (1767). In: *Physiocrates. Avec une introduction sur la doctrine des physiocrates, des commentaires et des notices historiques,* par E. Daire, Deuxième partie, Paris, 1846.—231

Bauer, B. *Kritik der evangelischen Geschichte des Johannes.* Bremen, 1840.—423

— *Kritik der evangelischen Geschichte der Synoptiker,* Bd. 1-2. Leipzig, 1841.—423

— *Kritik der evangelischen Geschichte der Synoptiker und des Johannes.* Braunschweig, 1842.—423

Bible

The Old Testament
Deuteronomy.—87
Exodus.—87
Genesis.—87, 143, 469
Joshua.—399

The New Testament
John.—565
Matthew.—22, 104, 286
The Revelation of St. John.—345

Boisguillebert, P. *Dissertation sur la nature des richesses, de l'argent et des tributs.* In: *Economistes financiers du XVIII-e siècle. Précédés de notices historiques sur chaque auteur, et accompagnés de commentaires et de notes explicatives,* par E. Daire, Paris, 1843.—220

Bossut, Ch. *Traités de calcul différentiel et de calcul intégral,* Tome I, Paris, an VI [1797-98].—541-44, 607-08

Buch, L. von *Über Ceratiden.* In: *Abhandlungen der Königlichen Akademie der Wissenschaften zu Berlin aus dem Jahre 1848. Physikalische Abhandlungen,* 1850.—576

Büchner, L. *Kraft und Stoff,* 8 Aufl., Leipzig 1864.—482

— *Der Mensch und seine Stellung in der Natur in Vergangenheit, Gegenwart und Zukunft. Oder: Woher kommen wir? Wer sind wir? Wohin gehen wir?* Zweite, vermehrte Auflage, Leipzig, 1872.—482, 486

[Cantillon, R.] *Essai sur la nature du commerce en général.* Londres, 1755.—227

Carey, H. C. *The Past, the present, and the future,* Philadelphia, 1848.—241

Carlyle, Th. *Past and Present.* London, 1843.—635-36

Carnot, S. *Réflexions sur la puissance motrice du feu et sur les machines propres à développer cette puissance.* Paris, 1824.—344, 400, 509

[Catelan, F.] *Courte remarque de M. l'Abbé D. C. où l'on montre à Mr. G. G. Leibnits le paralogisme contenu dans l'objection précédente.* In: *Nouvelles de la République des Lettres.* Amsterdam, 1686.—382

— *Remarque de M. l'Abbé D. C. sur la réplique de M. L. touchant le principe mécanique de M. Descartes, contenu dans l'article III de ces Nouvelles, mois de*

Février 1687. In: *Nouvelles de la République des Lettres.* Amsterdam, 1687.—382

Cervantes de Saavedra, M. *El ingenioso hidalgo Don Quijote de la Mancha.*—58, 298, 346

Cicero. *De Natura Deorum.*—467, 468

Clausius, R. *Die mechanische Wärmetheorie.* Zweite umgearbeitete und vervollständigte Auflage des unter dem Titel "Abhandlungen über die mechanische Wärmetheorie" erschienenen Buches. Band. I, Entwickelung der Theorie, soweit sie sich aus den beiden Hauptsätzen ableiten lässt, nebst Anwendungen. Braunschweig, 1876.—386, 390-91, 398

— *Über den zweiten Hauptsatz der mechanischen Wärmetheorie.* Ein Vortrag, gehalten in einer allgemeinen Sitzung der 41. Versammlung deutscher Naturforscher und Aerzte zu Frankfurt a. M. am 23. September 1867. Braunschweig, 1867.—391, 551, 562-64

Cobbett, W. *A History of the protestant "reformation", in England and Ireland; showing how that event has impoverished and degraded the main body of the people in those countries.* In a series of letters, addressed to all sensible and just Englishmen. London, 1824.—228-29

Cohn, F. *Ueber Bacterien, die kleinsten lebenden Wesen.* Berlin, 1872.—575

Comte, A. *Cours de philosophie positive,* Tome I. Paris, 1830.—529

Copernicus, N. *De revolutionibus orbium coelestium.* Norimbergae, 1543.—474

Croll, J. *Climate and time in their geological relations; a Theory of secular changes of the earth's climate.* London, 1875.—579

Crookes, W. *The Last of "Katie King". The photographing of "Katie King" by the aid of the electric light.* In: *The Spiritualist Newspaper,* Vol. IV, No. 23, June 5, 1874.—350, 351

D'Alembert. *Traité de dynamique, dans lequel less loix de l'équilibre et du mouvement des corps sont réduites au plus petit nombre possible, et démontrées d'une manière nouvelle, et où l'on donne un principe général pour trouver le mouvement de plusieurs corps qui agissent les uns sur les autres, d'une manière quelconque.* Paris, 1743.—379-81

Dalton, J. *A new System of chemical philosophie,* Vols. 1-3, Manchester, 1808-1827.—600

Darwin, Ch. *The Descent of man, and selection in relation to sex.* In two volumes. London, 1871.—452

— *On the origin of species by means of natural selection, or the Preservation of favoured races in the struggle for life.* London, 1859.—327, 454, 501, 576, 583

— *The Origin of species by means of natural selection, or the Preservation of favoured races in the struggle for life,* Sixth edition, with additions and corrections. London, 1872.—67, 69

Davies, Ch. M. *Mystic London: or, Phases of occult life in the metropolis.* London, 1875.—351, 355

Defoe, D. *The Life and strange surprising adventures of Robinson Crusoe.*—143-44, 147-48, 154, 614

Der deutsch-französische Krieg 1870-71, Theil I, Band II, Berlin, 1875.—157, 628

Descartes, R. *Discours de la méthode bien conduire sa raison et chercher la vérité dans les sciences.* Leyde, 1637.—556

— *Principia Philosophiae.* Amstelodami, 1644.—50, 525

Diderot, D. *Le neveu de Rameau.* In: *Oeuvres inédites de Diderot,* Paris, 1821.—21

Diogenes Laertius. *De vitis philosophorum libri X. Cum indice rerum.* Ad optimorum librorum fidem accurate editi. Editio stereotypa. C. Tauchnitii. Tomus II. Lipsiae, 1833.—339, 340, 467-70

Draper, J. W. *History of the intellectual development of Europe.* In two volumes. London, 1864.—334, 511

Du Bois-Reymond, E. *Über die Grenzen des Naturerkennens. Ein Vortrag in der zweiten öffentlichen Sitzung der 45. Versammlung Deutscher Naturforscher und Ärzte zu Leipzig am 14. August 1872.* Leipzig, 1872.—314

Dühring, E. *Carey's Umwälzung der Volkswirtschaftslehre und Socialwissenschaft,* Zwölf Briefe. München, 1865.—1

— *Cursus der National- und Socialökonomie einschliesslich der Hauptpunkte der Finanzpolitik,* Zweite, theilweise umgearbeitete Auflage. Leipzig, 1876.—28-309, 612-19

— *Cursus der Philosophie als streng wissenschaftlicher Weltanschauung und Lebensgestaltung.* Leipzig, 1875.—28-309, 596-608

— *Kritische Geschichte der Nationalökonomie und des Socialismus.* Berlin, 1871.—121-22

— Zweite, theilweise umgearbeitete Auflage. Berlin, 1875.—28-309

— *Kritische Grundlegung der Volkswirthschaftslehre.* Berlin, 1866.—207

— *Marx, Das Kapital, Kritik der politischen Oekonomie, 1. Band, Hamburg 1867.* In: *Ergänzungsblätter zur Kenntniß der Gegenwart,* Band III, Heft 3. Hildburghausen, 1867.—114, 121-22

— *Natürliche Dialektik. Neue logische Grundlegungen der Wissenschaft und Philosophie.* Berlin, 1865.—163

— *Neue Grundgesetze zur rationellen Physik und Chemie,* Erste Folge, Leipzig, 1878.—7, 8

— *Die Schicksale meiner socialen Denkschrift für das Preussische Staatsministerium.* Berlin, 1868.—144

Enß, A. *Engels Attentat auf den gesunden Menschenverstand oder Der wissenschaftliche Bankerott im Marxistischen Sozialismus. Ein offener Brief an meine Freunde in Berlin,* Grand-Saconnex (Schweiz), 1877.—298

Euclides. *Elementa.*—173

Feuerbach, L. *Nachgelassene Aphorismen.* In: K. Grün. *Ludwig Feuerbach in seinem Briefwechsel und Nachlass sowie in seiner philosophischen Charakterentwicklung,* Band II. Leipzig und Heidelberg, 1874.—476, 480

— *Die Unsterblichkeitsfrage vom Standpunkt der Anthropologie.* In: *Ludwig Feuerbach's sämmtliche Werke.* Band III. Leipzig, 1847.—479

Fick, A. *Die Naturkraefte in ihrer Wechselbeziehung. Populaere Vortraege.* Würzburg, 1869.—565

Flamsteed, J. *Historia coelestris Britannica complectens stellar...*, Vols. 1-3. London, 1725.—552

Fourier, Ch. *Le Nouveau Monde industriel et sociétaire, ou Invention du procédé d'industrie attrayante et naturelle distribuée en séries passionnées.* In: *Oeuvres complètes de Ch. Fourier, T.* 6, Paris, 1845.—248, 261, 263, 264, 279

— *Théorie de l'unité universelle.* Premier volume. In: *Oeuvres complètes de Ch. Fourier, T.* 2, Paris, 1843.—248

— *Théorie de l'unité universelle.* Quatrième volume. In: *Oeuvres complètes de Ch. Fourier, T.* 5, Paris, 1841.—248

— *Théorie des quatre mouvements et des destinées générales.* In: *Oeuvres complètes de Ch. Fourier, T.* 1, Paris, 1841.—245, 247, 248, 263

Fourier, J. B. J. *Théorie analytique de la chaleur.* Paris, 1822.—344, 487

Fraas, C. *Klima und Pflanzenwelt in der Zeit.* Landshut, 1847.—460

Galiani, F. *Della moneta* (1750). Libro II. In: *Scrittori classici italiani di economia politica. Parte moderna.* Tomo III. Milano, 1803.—517

Giffen, R. *Recent accumulations of capital in the United Kingdom.* In: *Journal of the Statistical Society,* Vol. XLI, Part I, London, 1878.—270

Goethe, J. W. von. *Allerdings.*—520

— *Faust.* Der Tragödie, Erster Theil.—86, 88, 134, 254, 298, 331

— *Ultimatum.*—520

Grimm, J. *Deutsche Rechtsalterthümer.* Göttingen, 1828.—458

— *Geschichte der deutschen Sprache.* Zweite Auflage, Bd. 1, Leipzig, 1853.—498

Grove, W. R. *The Correlation of physical forces.* Third edition. London, 1855.—325, 326, 512, 525

Grün, K. *Ludwig Feuerbach in seinem Briefwechsel und Nachlass sowie in seiner Philosophischen Charakterentwicklung,* Bd. 2, Leipzig, 1874.—476, 480

Guthrie, F. *Magnetism and electricity.* London and Glasgow, 1876.—568

Haeckel, E. *Anthropogenie oder Entwickelungsgeschichte des Menschen. Gemeinverständliche wissenschaftliche Vorträge über die Grundzüge der menschlichen Keimes- und Stammesgeschichte.* Leipzig, 1874.—489, 581, 582

— *Freie Wissenschaft und freie Lehre. Eine Entgegnung auf Rudolf Virchow's Münchener Rede über "Die Freiheit der Wissenschaft im modernen Staat".* Stuttgart, 1878.—314

— *Generelle Morphologie der Organismen. Allgemeine Grundzüge der organischen Formen- Wissenschaft, mechanisch begründet durch die von Charles Darwin reformirte Descendenz-Theorie.* Band I: *Allgemeine Anatomie der Organismen.* Berlin, 1866.—573, 581

— *Natürliche Schöpfungsgeschichte. Gemeinverständliche wissenschaftliche Vorträge über die Entwickelungslehre im Allgemeinen und diejenige von Darwin, Goethe und Lamarck im Besonderen,* Vierte verbesserte Auflage, Berlin, 1873.—12, 66, 129, 489, 507, 534, 573, 579-82

— *Die Perigenesis der Plastidule oder die Wellenzeugung der Lebenstheilchen. Ein*

Kohlrausch, F. *Das elektrische Leitungsvermögen der wässerigen Lösungen von den Hydraten und Salzen der leichten Metalle, sowie von Kupfervitriol, Zinkvitriol und Silbersalpeter.* In: *Annalen der Physik und Chemie,* herausgegeben von G. Wiedemann. Neue Folge, Band VI, No. 1. Leipzig, 1879.—422

Kopernik—see Copernicus

Kopp, H. *Die Entwickelung der Chemie in der neueren Zeit.* Abt. I: Die Entwickelung der Chemie vor und durch Lavoisier. München, 1871.—570

Lamarck, J.-B.-P.-A. de Monet. *Philosophie zoologique, ou exposition des considérations relatives à l'histoire naturelle des animaux.* Paris, 1809.—576

Langethal, Ch. E. *Geschichte der teutschen Landwirtschaft,* Bücher I-IV, Jena, 1847-1856.—6

Laplace, P. S. *Exposition du système du monde,* Tome II, Paris, l'an IV de la République Française [1796].—24, 323, 324, 328, 522, 594

[Лавров, П. Л.] *Опыт истории мысли.* Том I. С. Петербург, 1875.—561, 565

Law, J. *Considérations sur le numéraire et le commerce.* In: *Économistes financiers du XVIII-e siècle. Précédés de notices historiques sur chaque auteur, et accompagnés de commentaires et de notes explicatives,* par E. Daire, Paris, 1843.—221

[Leibniz, G. W. von] Leibnitii, G. G. *De causa gravitatis, et defensio sententiae suae de veris naturae legibus contra Cartesianos.* In: *Acta Eruditorum,* Lipsiae, 1690.—379

Leibnizens und Huygens' Briefwechsel mit Papin, nebst der Biographie Papin's und einigen zugehörigen Briefen und Actenstücken. Bearbeitet und herausgegeben von E. Gerland. Berlin, 1881.—400

Liebig, J. *Die Chemie in ihrer Anwendung auf Agricultur und Physiologie.* In zwei Theilen, Siebente Auflage, Theil I: Der chemische Process der Ernährung der Vegetabilien. Braunschweig, 1862.—11

— *Chemische Briefe.* Vierte umgearbeitete und vermehrte Auflage. Band I, Leipzig und Heidelberg, 1859.—575

List, F. *Das nationale System der politischen Oekonomie.* Band I: Der Internationale Handel, die Handelspolitik und der deutsche Zollverein. Stuttgart und Tübingen, 1841.—217

Locke, J. *Some considerations of the consequences of the lowering of interest, and raising the value of money.* London, 1691.—221-23

Lubbock, J. *Ants, Bees, and Wasps: a Record of Observations on the Social Hymenoptera.* London, 1882.—519

Luther, M. *Ein feste Burg ist unser Gott.*—319

Lyell, Ch. *Principles of geology, being an attempt to explain the former changes of the earth's surface, by reference to causes now in operation.* Vols. 1-3. London, 1830-1833.—325

Mädler, J. H. *Der Wunderbau des Weltalls, oder Populäre Astronomie.* Fünfte, gänzlich neu bearbeitete Auflage. Berlin, 1861.—323, 328, 333, 471, 552-56, 565

Maskelyne, J. N. *Modern Spiritualism. A short account of its rise and progress, with some exposures of so-called spirit media.* London, 1876.—349-51

Massie, J. *An Essay on the governing causes of the natural rate of interest; wherein the sentiments of Sir William Petty and Mr. Locke, on that head, are considered.* London, 1750.—226

Maurer, G. L. *Einleitung zur Geschichte der Mark-, Hof-, Dorf- und Stadt-Verfassung und der öffentlichen Gewalt.* München, 1854.—163

— *Geschichte der Dorfverfassung in Deutschland.* Bd. I-II, Erlangen, 1865-1866.—163

— *Geschichte der Fronhöfe, der Bauernhöfe und der Hofverfassung in Deutschland.* Bd. I-IV, Erlangen, 1862-1863.—163, 165

— *Geschichte der Markenverfassung in Deutschland.* Erlangen, 1856.—163

— *Geschichte der Städteverfassung in Deutschland.* Bd. I-IV, Erlangen, 1869-1871.—163

Maxwell, J. C. *Theory of heat.* Fourth edition, London, 1875.—390, 466, 565

Mayer, J. R. *Bemerkungen über die Kräfte der unbelebten Natur.* In: *Annalen der Chemie und Pharmacie.* Bd. 42. Leipzig, 1842.—325

— *Die organische Bewegung in ihrem Zusammenhang mit dem Stoffwechsel. Ein Beitrag zur Naturkunde.* Heilbronn, 1845.—370

— *Die Mechanik der Wärme in gesammelten Schriften.* Zweite umgearbeitete und vermehrte Auflage. Stuttgart, 1874.—370, 505, 556, 558

Mélanges d'économie politique. Précédés de notices historiques sur chaque auteur, et accompagnés de commentaires et de notes explicatives, par E. Daire et G. de Molinari. Vol. I, Paris, 1847.—220

Meyer, L. *Die Natur der chemischen Elemente als Funktion ihrer Atomgewichte.* In: *Annalen der Chemie und Pharmacie.* Supplementband 7. Leipzig, 1870.—531

Moleschott, J. *Der Kreislauf des Lebens.* Mainz, 1852.—482

Molière, J. B. *Le Bourgeois gentilhomme.*—132, 206, 361

[Montesquieu, Ch.] *De l'esprit des loix.* Genève, 1748.—224

Morgan, L. H. *Ancient society or Researches in the lines of human progress from savagery, through barbarism to civilization.* London, 1877.—10

Morus, Th. *Utopia.*—592, 611

Mozart. W. A. *The Magic Flute.*—353

M[un], T. *A Discourse of trade, from England into the East-Indies: answering to diverse objections which are usually made against the same.* London, 1609.—217, 218

— *England's treasure by forraign trade. Or, the Ballance of our forraign trade is the rule of our treasure.* Written by Thomas Mun of Lond., merchant, and now published for the common good by his son John Mun. London, 1664.—217, 218

Nägeli, C. *Die Schranken der naturwissenschaftlichen Erkenntniss.* Vortrag, gehalten in der zweiten allgemeinen Sitzung. In: *Tageblatt der 50. Versammlung deutscher Naturforscher und Aerzte in München 1877.* Beilage.—314, 337, 512-16

Napier, J. *Mirifici logarithmorum canonis descriptio; ejusque usus, in utraque, trigonometria, ut etiam in omni logistica mathematica...* Edinburgh, 1614.—321

Napoléon. *Dix-sept notes sur l'ouvrage intitulé, Considérations sur l'art de la guerre, imprimé à Paris, en 1816.* In: *Mémoires pour servir à l'histoire de France, sous*

Napoléon, écrits à Sainte-Hélène, par les généraux qui ont partagé sa captivité, et publiés sur les manuscrits entièrement corrigés de la main de Napoléon. Tome I, écrit par le général comte de Montholon. Paris, 1823.—119

Naumann, A. *Handbuch der allgemeinen und physikalischen Chemie.* Heidelberg, 1877.—390, 414, 418, 428, 436, 442

Newton, I. *Observations upon the Prophecies of Daniel and the Apocalypse of St. John.* London, 1733.—345

— *Philosophiae naturalis principia mathematica.* Editio secunda. Cantabrigiae, 1713.—323, 491

Nicholson, H. A. *A Manual of zoology.* 5th ed. Edinburgh and London, 1870.—73, 326, 493, 507, 580, 581, 586, 601

[North, D.] *Discourses upon trade; principally directed to the cases of the interest, coynage, clipping, increase of money.* London, 1691.—221-22

Oken, L. *Abriß der Naturphilosophie.* Göttingen, 1805.—486

— *Allgemeine Naturgeschichte für alle Stände.* Stuttgart, 1841.—486

— *Lehrbuch der Naturgeschichte.* Leipzig, 1813-1823.—486

— *Lehrbuch der Naturphilosophie.* Jena, 1809.—486

Owen, Richard. *On the nature of limbs.* A discourse delivered on Friday, February 9, at an evening meeting of the Royal Institution of Great Britain. London, 1849.—487

Owen, Robert. *The book of the new moral world.* Parts I-VII, London, 1836-1844.—253

— *Report of the proceedings at the several public meetings, held in Dublin, By Robert Owen Esq.* On the 18th March, 12th April, 19th April and 3rd May; preceded by an Introductory Statement of his Opinions and Arrangements, at New Lanark; extracted from his "Essays on the Formation of Human Character". Dublin, 1823.—251

— *The Revolution in the mind and practice of the human race; or, the coming change from irrationality to rationality.* London, 1849.—249, 250, 639

Perty, M. *Über die Grenzen der sichtbaren Schöpfung, nach den jetzigen Leistungen der Mikroskope und Fernröhre.* Berlin, 1874.—575

Petty, W. *The Political anatomy of Ireland, 1672.* To which is added Verbum sapienti. London, 1691.—218

— *Quantulumcunque concerning Money.* 1682. To the Lord Marquess of Halyfax. London, 1695.—219, 220, 222

— *A Treatise of taxes and contributions.* London, 1662.—218, 219, 222

Plato. *Res publica.* In: *Platonis opera omnia.* Recognoverunt I. G. Baiterus, I. C. Orellius, A. G. Winckelmannus, Vol. XIII, Turici, 1840.—215

Plinius. *Naturalis historiae.* Liber XVIII.—164

Plutarchos. *Quaestiones convivales.*—468

Prévost, A. F. *Histoire du chevalier des Grieux et de Manon Lescaut.*—481

Proudhon, P. J. *Qu'est-ce que la propriété? ou Recherches sur le principe du droit et du gouvernement.* Premier mémoire. Paris, 1840.—173

[Pseudo-Plutarch]. *De placitis philosophorum.*—468

Quesnay, F. *Analyse du Tableau économique* (1766). In: *Physiocrates. Avec une introduction sur la doctrine des physiocrates, des commentaires et des notices historiques,* par E. Daire, Première partie, Paris, 1846.—15, 229-38, 252

Raff, G. *Naturgeschichte für Kinder, zum Gebrauch in Stadt- und Landschulen.* Göttingen, 1778.—304

Ricardo, D. *On the principles of political economy, and taxation.* Third edition, London, 1821.—182

Rochow, F. E. *Der Kinderfreund. Ein Lesebuch zum Gebrauch in Landschulen.* Brandenburg und Leipzig, 1776.—172

Rodbertus, J. K. *Sociale Briefe an von Kirchmann. Zweiter Brief: Kirchmann's sociale Theorie und die meinige.* Berlin, 1850.—204

Romanes, G. J. "Ants, Bees, and Wasps." In: *Nature,* Vol. XXVI, No. 658, June 8, 1882.—518

Roscher, W. *System der Volkswirthschaft. Band I: Die Grundlagen der Nationalökonomie.* Dritte, vermehrte und verbesserte Auflage. Stuttgart und Augsburg, 1858.—215

Roscoe, H. E. *Kurzes Lehrbuch der Chemie nach den neuesten Ansichten der Wissenschaft.* Deutsche Ausgabe, under Mitwirkung des Verfassers bearbeitet von Carl Schorlemmer. Braunschweig, 1867.—601

Roscoe, H. E. und Schorlemmer, C. *Ausführliches Lehrbuch der Chemie.* Band II: *Die Metalle und Spectralanalyse.* Braunschweig, 1879.—361

Rosenkranz, K. *System der Wissenschaft. Ein philosophisches Encheiridion.* Königsberg, 1850.—488

Rousseau, J. J. *Discours sur l'origine et les fondemens de l'inégalité parmi les hommes.* Amsterdam, 1755.—21, 90, 91, 129, 130

— *Du Contract social; ou, Principes du droit politique.* Amsterdam, 1762.—19, 244

Saint-Simon, H. *Lettres à un américain.* In: H. Saint-Simon, *L'Industrie, ou Discussions politiques, morales et philosophiques, dans l'intérêt et tous les hommes livrés à des travaux utiles et indépendans.* Tome 2. Paris, 1817.—246

— *Lettres d'un habitant de Genève à ses contemporains.* Paris [1803].—247, 248

— *Nouveau Christianisme, dialogues entre un novateur et un conservateur.* In: *Oeuvres de Saint-Simon.* Paris, 1841.—636-37

Saint-Simon, H. et Thierry, A. *De la réorganisation de la société européenne, ou De la nécessité et des moyens de rassembler les peuples de l'Europe en un seul corps politique, en conservant à chacun son indépendance nationale.* Paris, 1814.—247

— *Opinion sur les mesures à prendre contre la coalition de 1815.* Paris, 1815.—247

Sargant, W. L. *Robert Owen, and his social phylosophy.* London, 1860.—252, 253

Schiller, F. *Die Bürgschaft.*—447

— *Don Carlos.*—5, 143

Schleiden, M. J. *Die Pflanze und ihr Leben.* Leipzig, 1848.—460

Schlosser, F. C. *Weltgeschichte für das deutsche Volk.* Band XVII. *Neuere Geschichte.* Neunter Theil. *(Geschichte des achtzehnten Jahrhunderts.)* Frankfurt a. M., 1855.—228

Schmidt, O. *Darwinismus und Socialdemocratie.* Ein Vortrag gehalten bei der 51. Versammlung deutscher Naturforscher und Aerzte in Cassel. Bonn, 1878.—314

Secchi, A. *Die Sonne. Die wichtigeren neuen Entdeckungen über ihren Bau, ihre Strahlungen, ihre Stellung im Weltall und ihr Verhältniss zu den übrigen Himmelskörpern.* Autorisirte deutsche Ausgabe. Braunschweig, 1872.—24, 328, 332, 333, 480, 553-55, 565, 605

Serra, A. *Breve trattato delle cause che possono far abbondare li regni d'oro e d'argento dove non sono miniere* (1613). In: *Scrittori classici italiani di economia politica.* Parte antica. Tomo 1. Milano, 1803.—217

Shakespeare, W. *King Henry IV.*—147

Sismondi, J. C. L. Simonde de. *Études sur l'économie politique.* Tome 2. Bruxelles, 1838.—273

Smith, A. *An Inquiry into the nature and causes of the wealth of nations.* In two volumes. Vol. 1. London, 1776.—210, 227

Spinoza, B. *Epistolae doctorum quorundam virorum ad B. de Spinoza et auctoris responsiones; ad aliorum ejus operum elucidationem non parum facientes.* In: *Opera posthuma* [Amsterdam], 1677.—131

— *Ethica ordine geometrico demonstrata et in quinque partes distincta.* In: *Opera posthuma* [Amsterdam], 1677.—102, 481, 511

Starcke, C. N. *Ludwig Feuerbach.* Stuttgart, 1885.—479-81

Steuart, J. *An Inquiry into the principles of political economy.* In two volumes. London, 1767.—241

Stirner, M. *Der Einzige und sein Eigenthum.* Leipzig, 1845.—92, 214

Strauß, D. F. *Das Leben Jesu.* Bd. 1-2. Tübingen, 1835-1836.—423

Suter, H. *Geschichte der mathematischen Wissenschaften.* Th. II: Vom Anfange des XVII. bis gegen das Ende des XVIII. Jahrhunderts. Zürich, 1875.—379-82, 384

Tait, P. G. *Force. Evening lecture at the Glasgow meeting of the British Association, Sept. 8.* In: *Nature,* Vol. XIV, No. 360, September 21, 1876.—388

Terentius, P. *Adelphoe.*—193

Thomson, Th. *An Outline. of the sciences of heat and electricity.* Second edition, remodelled and much enlarged. London, 1840.—400, 403, 404, 489, 566-68

Thomson, W. *Review of evidence regarding physical condition of the earth.* In: *Nature,* Vol. XIV, No. 359, September 14, 1876.—456

— *The size of atoms.* In: *Nature,* Vol I, No. 22, March 31, 1870.—546

Thomson, W. and Tait, P. G. *Handbuch der theoretischen Physik.* Autorisirte deutsche Übersetzung. Band I, Theil II, Braunschweig, 1874.—574

Thomson, W. and Tait, P. G. *Treatise on natural philosophy*, Vol. I, Oxford, 1867.—382, 390, 392-96, 488

Tyndall, J. *Inaugural address [delivered at the forty-fourth annual meeting of the British Association for the Advancement of Science in Belfast]*. In: *Nature*, Vol. X, No. 251, August 20, 1874.—481

— *On Germs. On the optical deportment of the atmosphere in reference to the phenomena of putrefaction and infection*. Abstract of a paper read before the Royal Society, January 13th. In: *Nature*, Vol. XIII, No. 326-327, January 27, and February 3, 1876.—579

Vanderlint, J. *Money answers all things: or, an Essay to make money sufficiently plentiful amongst all ranks of people*. London, 1734.—223, 227

Virchow, R. *Die Cellularpathologie in ihrer Begründung auf physiologische und pathologische Gewebelehre*. Vierte, neu bearbeitete und stark vermehrte Auflage. Berlin, 1871.—14, 486

— *Die Freiheit der Wissenschaft im modernen Staat. Rede, gehalten in der dritten allgemeinen Sitzung der fünfzigsten Versammlung deutscher Naturforscher und Aerzte zu München am 22. September 1877*. Berlin, 1877.—7, 316, 337, 338, 353

Vogt, K. *Köhlerglaube und Wissenschaft*. Giessen, 1855.—482

Wagner, M. *Naturwissenschaftliche Streitfragen*. 1. Justus v. Liebigs Ansichten über den Lebensursprung und die Descendenztheorie. In: Beilage zur *Allgemeinen Zeitung*, Nr. 279-281, 6.-8. Oktober 1874.—574-77

Wallace, A. R. *On miracles and modern spiritualism*. Three essays. London, 1875.—345-51, 353, 355

Weitling, W. *Garantien der Harmonie und Freiheit*. Vivis, 1842.—288

Whewell, W. *History of the inductive sciences, from the earliest to the present times*. In three volumes. London, 1837.—507

— *The Philosophy of the inductive sciences, founded upon their history*. In two volumes. London, 1840.—507

Wiedemann, G. *Die Lehre vom Galvanismus und Elektromagnetismus*. Zweite neu bearbeitete und vermehrte Auflage. Braunschweig, 1872-1874. Band I: Die Lehre vom Galvanismus. Band II: Die Lehre von den Wirkungen des galvanischen Stromes in die Ferne. Abt. 1: Elektrodynamik, Elektromagnetismus und Diamagnetismus. Abt. 2: Induction und Schlusscapitel.—402-51, 544, 569

Wolff, C. F. *Theoria generationis*. Halae [1759].—327

Wolf, R. *Geschichte der Astronomie*. München, 1877.—471, 556

Wundt, W. *Lehrbuch der Physiologie des Menschen*. Dritte völlig umgearbeitete Auflage. Erlangen, 1873.—580

Xenophontis. *Cyropaedia*.—215

DOCUMENTS

Code Napoléon.—101

Code pénal.—101

Corpus juris civilis.—102

The Declaration of Independence (1776).—474

ANONYMOUS ARTICLES AND REPORTS
PUBLISHED IN PERIODIC EDITIONS

Nature. Vol. XII, Nos. 294-295, June 17 and 24, 1875 (signed: J.F.B.). Croll's *"Climate and time".*—579

— Vol. XV, No. 368. November 16, 1876: *Notes* [*On the report of Prof. Mendeléeff, maid at the Warsaw meeting of Russian naturalists, on the results of researches, pursued by him during 1875 and 1876 for the verification of Mariotte's law*].[a]—85

— Vol. XVII, No. 420, November 15, 1877: *University and educational intelligence: Bonn* [*On the address on the scientific position of chemistry, and the fundamental principles of this science, delivered by Prof. Kekulé on entering upon the duties of rector of the University*].[a]—530

— Vol. XXVI, No. 659, June 15, 1882: C., G. Mascart and Joubert's *Electricity and magnetism.*—402

---

[a] In the original the titles of articles are given in square brackets.— *Ed.*

INDEX OF PERIODICALS

SUBJECT INDEX

— as abstraction—37, 130-31, 356, 503
— concreteness of—503
— cognition, study of laws of nature, society and thinking—11, 24, 70-71, 105-06, 132, 259, 266, 321, 326, 328, 330, 339, 344, 361, 372-73, 461, 497, 505, 514, 520, 545, 595
Law of conservation and transformation of energy—13, 50, 315, 339, 363, 364, 370, 405-06, 411-12, 421-22, 424, 429, 430-31, 432-33, 439, 443, 450-51, 477, 499-500, 503-06, 518-19, 558, 562-63, 570
Law of negation of the negation—120-32, 315, 356, 472, 502, 606-08
Law of transformation of quantity into quality—42-43, 61, 115-19, 122, 315, 356-61, 494, 513, 530, 531-32, 538, 564, 570-71
Law of unity and struggle of opposites—23, 47, 54, 110-13, 315, 354, 356, 374, 433-34, 463-64, 492-502, 539, 606-07
Law of value—97-98, 199, 297-98, 615
Life—74-77, 578, 601-02
— as a form of motion of matter—55, 61-62, 112, 332, 357-58, 362, 506, 511, 525-28, 599
— origin and development of—61-62, 68, 70, 73-74, 112, 328-30, 334-35, 474-75, 477-80, 495, 525, 530, 573-85, 602
— and metabolism—23-24, 74-77, 112, 495, 578-79, 601-02
— and death—23-24, 112, 495, 572-73, 594
— other-worldly—490, 574-77
Light—62, 325, 332, 372-74, 398, 401, 405, 407, 477, 508, 510, 511, 528, 534, 548, 552-54, 556, 565-66
Linguistics—305, 497-98
Literature—319, 471
Logic
— as science of thinking—26, 84, 338-39, 491, 520
— historical character of—84, 338-39, 356, 503-04, 520
— and formal—26, 125, 339, 491, 503-04, 520
See also *Dialectics*—and logic; *Hegel, Hegelianism*—logic

M

Machines (machinery)—145, 175, 255-56, 261-62, 278
Malthusianism—63-64, 70, 583, 584
Manufacture—97, 117, 152, 211, 248, 255-57, 260, 278, 319, 641
Market—27, 180, 188-89, 215, 256, 258-60, 262-63, 272, 295
Marxism (general characteristics)—145, 168-69, 254-55, 271, 630, 634-35
— theoretical sources of—12, 16, 26, 591, 630
— component parts of—8-10, 26-28, 33, 135, 138-39, 244
— emergence and development of—9, 26-28
— as theoretical basis for the proletarian movement—255, 271, 634-35
— dissemination of its ideas—9, 15, 145
See also *Communism, scientific*; *Marxist philosophy*; *Marxist political economy*
Marxist philosophy
— essence of—10, 14, 24-26, 35-36, 128, 131, 356, 491, 545, 593, 604
— its place in the history of philosophy—8-15, 25-27, 128, 606
— and scientific communism—26-27, 606
See also *Dialectical materialism*; *Dialectics*; *Historical materialism, materialist conception of history*
Marxist political economy—135-40, 211-15, 291-92, 616-18
— and materialist conception of history—26-28
— and scientific communism—26-28, 189, 190
Materialism
— materialist outlook—128, 469-70, 479, 489
— and idealism, their opposition—10, 25-27, 34, 35, 128, 459, 476-77, 479, 480, 521, 544-45, 597, 606, 612-13
— and natural science—10-11, 25-26, 41, 128, 322, 340, 342-43, 346, 353-54, 459, 467-70, 476-82, 488, 499, 501, 521, 528, 533, 634